THE PROVINCE OF ADMINIST

The Province of Administrative Law

Edited by
MICHAEL TAGGART

·HART·
PUBLISHING

OXFORD
1997

Hart Publishing
Oxford
UK

© Michael Taggart and the Contributors severally, 1997

Hart Publishing is a specialist legal publisher based in Oxford, England. To order further copies of this book or to request a list of other publications please write to:

Hart Publishing, 19 Whitehouse Road, Oxford, OX1 4PA
Telephone: +44 (0)1865 434459 or Fax: (0)1865 794882
e-mail: hartpub@janep.demon.co.uk

Payment may be made by cheque payable to 'Hart Publishing' or by credit card.

British Library Cataloguing in Publication Data
Data Available
ISBN 1–901362–01–9 (cloth)
ISBN 1–901362–02–7 (paperback)

Typeset in 10pt Sabon
by SetAll, Abingdon
Printed in Great Britain on acid-free paper
by Biddles Ltd., Guilford and Kings Lynn

To
JOHN WILLIS

Pioneering Administrative Lawyer

Foreword

One result of the worldwide export of the ideology of economic liberalism has been a remarkable parallelism in the shrinkage of state apparatuses and the introduction of commercial enterprise into the performance of functions historically regarded as the state's. This in turn has provided a novel focal point for specialist lawyers in the common law world, so that from being essentially exercises in the comparison of discrete legal systems, their exchanges have begun to be multifaceted approaches to a unitary phenomenon.

A further consequence, as the second millennium gives way to third, is that the sculptural image of law enthroned is having to give way to a somewhat more cinematic one of people in gowns running up a downward-moving escalator. It was during the 1980s, while practitioners, judges and academics were congratulating themselves on the approach of a comprehensive system of public law, that politics throughout the common law world set about dismantling the very structures of which public law had assumed the continued existence. With the systematic dispersal of the sites of power beyond the confines of what we had learned to recognise as the state, the old certainties of public law are no longer there.

Even so, for many of the retained core functions of the state, as with the lager, less means more: more invigilation of the undeserving, more surveillance of the unrespectable, more suspicion of the uninvited. Here the materiality of public law's insistence on due process in decision-making is proportionately great. For those functions which are dispersed, law also continues to have claims – but claims which it is no longer easy to allocate to a distinctly public sphere. Hence the carefully chosen title of this volume. We are looking now not merely at grand constitutional schemes embracing the entirety of public power but at what lawyers, in the heyday of executive supremacy in the United Kingdom half a century and more ago, were willing to recognise as a legal culture indigenous to the agencies by which functions of public regulation are performed – the province of administrative law.

The assumption, which I think is common to these essays, that this phenomenon should at some level continue to form part of law's empire is one which can be readily defended; but it is one which now has powerful legal and political opponents. Their standpoint is that the market affords not only a different and better version of rationality but forms of fairness and models of law which make those of political statism and its incubus, judicial review, redundant except perhaps as a final safety net. At its extreme, where logic parts company with reason, it proposes a free market in hard drugs; but at its centre it has come to represent the common sense and the efficient ideology of the common law world. The contributors to this volume, being lawyers rather than politicians or economists, all seek in different ways to come to terms with it, not by quarrelling with its premises but by grappling with its consequences.

It is this coherence of subject matter, variegated by political history and legal culture, which seems to me to give the present collection of essays its special value. Coming as they do from Australia, Canada, New Zealand, the United Kingdom and the United States, they have a set of concerns which recent political history has made common to them all. Moreover, as essays they dovetail in ways which reflect the interactive character of the conference which was the birthplace of the volume. It is thus more than an assembly of papers: it is a kaleidoscopic attempt by some of the brightest scholars in the common law world to think through, not defensively but creatively, the challenges to the rule of law posed by the changes in our polities. It is encouraging too to see that, while the ghost of Albert Venn Dicey unavoidably stalks their pages, these are contributors who in general pass unafraid through his clammy spectre.

Any enterprise like the present one is going to be tantalisingly incomplete. Beyond each peak climbed another one arises. Does the market need the rule of law or is it itself a novel form of law? Are the atheoreticism of the common law and its want of a principled concept of the state handicaps or a positive advantage in confronting such an issue? Is the logical end of public law's rediscovery of private law virtues the judicial invigilation of the legality, rationality and fairness of the doings of that most statutory of creatures, the limited liability company? What does interpretative deference have to say when it finds itself deferring to inconsistent decisions? What is so stimulating about these essays is that they throw up such radical questions, and that they do so with elegance, intellectual rigour and legal profundity. For those who, like me, missed the Saskatchewan conference in October 1996, reading this volume is handsome compensation.

April 1997
Stephen Sedley
Royal Courts of Justice
London

Contents

Foreword vii
    Sir Stephen Sedley
Preface xi
List of Contributors xiii
Table of Cases xv

1 The Province of Administrative Law Determined?   1
    Michael Taggart

2 Constitutionalism and the Contractualisation of Government   21
    Murray Hunt

3 A Public Lawyer's Responses to Privatisation and Outsourcing   40
    Mark Aronson

4 Theoretical and Institutional Underpinnings of a Separate Administrative Law   71
    John W.F. Allison

5 Administrative Law for a New Century   90
    Alfred C. Aman, Jr.

6 Public Service Law and the New Public Management   118
    H. Wade MacLauchlan

7 Administrative Law at the Margins   134
    David Mullan

8 Intermediate Associations and the State   160
    Janet McLean

9 The Reach of Administrative Law in the United States   171
    Jack M. Beermann

10 Public Law and Control Over Private Power   196
    Paul Craig

11 The Underlying Values of Public and Private Law   217
    Dawn Oliver

12 Criminal Justice from the Bottom-Up: Some Thoughts on Police Rulemaking Processes   243
    Hudson Janisch and *Ron Levi*

13 The Politics of Deference: Judicial Review and Democracy   279
    David Dyzenhaus

14 The "Ebb" and "Flow" of Administrative Law on the "General   308

Question of Law"
   Madame Justice Claire L'Heureux-Dubé
15 Feminism, Pluralism and Administrative Law   331
   Alison Harvison Young

Bibliography   357
Index   375

Preface

The papers in this collection were presented at a conference held in Saskatoon, Canada, on 17–19 October 1996 under the auspices of the College of Law, University of Saskatchewan. There are many people and several institutions to thank for making that conference, and this collection of essays, possible.

The organisation of the conference was one of the pleasurable duties I undertook in 1996 as the Law Foundation of Saskatchewan Visiting Professor at the College of Law, University of Saskatchewan. This Chair was established in 1989 under an agreement between the Law Foundation of Saskatchewan and the University of Saskatchewan, and supports the appointment of a Visiting Professor at the College of Law. I am most grateful to the Law Foundation and the College of Law for the opportunity to work in such a congenial and stimulating environment. My "home" university, The University of Auckland, generously gave me leave to take up the position.

In putting on the conference I drew on the expertise and goodwill of many friends and colleagues, too many to name individually, and I thank them all. Two people, however, deserve special mention: Professor Peter MacKinnon, Dean of the College of Law, supported fully the conference and assuredly raised the funding necessary to make it a reality; and Mandy Hill, who not only assisted with the organisation of the conference, but also prepared under considerable time pressure the edited typescript for publisher.

From the beginning I have had the willing support and co-operation of the contributors. Some came long distances to speak at the conference, and they all met a short deadline for revisions to their papers. I thank them, and also Sir Stephen Sedley for agreeing to write the foreword.

It has been a pleasure to work with Richard Hart and his team at Hart Publishing, who expertly guided this book through the production process with audacious speed.

This book is dedicated, without permission, to John Willis, a legendary figure in Canadian administrative law.

Michael Taggart

Contributors

John W.F. Allison is University Lecturer and Fellow of Queens' College, University of Cambridge.

Alfred C. Aman, Jr. is Dean and Professor of Law at the Indiana University School of Law, Bloomington.

Mark Aronson is Professor of Law at the University of New South Wales.

Jack M. Beermann is Professor of Law at Boston University.

Paul Craig is Professor of Law and Fellow of Worcester College, University of Oxford.

David Dyzenhaus is Professor of Law and Philosophy at the University of Toronto.

Alison Harvison Young is Professor of Law at McGill University.

Murray Hunt is a Barrister whose chambers are in 4–5 Gray's Inn Square, London.

Ron Levi is a doctoral candidate in the Faculty of Law, University of Toronto.

The Hon. Madame Justice Claire L'Heureux-Dubé is a Justice of the Supreme Court of Canada.

Hudson Janisch is Associate Dean of Graduate Studies and Professor of Law at the University of Toronto.

H. Wade MacLauchlan is Professor of Law at the University of New Brunswick.

Janet McLean is Senior Lecturer in Law at The University of Auckland.

David Mullan is Professor of Law at Queen's University, Ontario.

Dawn Oliver is Dean and Professor of Constitutional Law at University College London.

Michael Taggart is Professor of Law at The University of Auckland.

xxvi *Table of Cases*

S. in Re [1992] 3 WLR 806...236
Samuell *v.* New York Racing Assoc. 58 NY 2d 231, 447 NE 2d 706 (1983),
  amended by 69 NY 2d 805 (1984) 189, 191
San Francisco Arts & Athletics Inc. *v.* US Olympic Committee 483 US 522
  (1987)..179
Sanjuan *v.* American Board of Psychology and Neurology Inc.
  40 F 3d 247 (1994), cert. denied 116 S.Ct. 1044
  (1996) 187, 188, 191
Save Richmond Farmland Society *v.* Richmond [1990] 3 SCR 1213..........345
Selvarajan *v.* Race Relations Board [1976] 1 All ER 12..............................333
Semchuk *v.* Board of Education of Regina (1986) 26 Admin LR 88,
  affd. (1987) 37 DLR (4th) 738...140
Service Employees' International Union, Local No. 333 *v.* Nipawin District
  Staff Nurses Assoc. [1975] 1 SCR 382..312
Shapiro *v.* Butterfield 921 SW 2d 649 (Mo.Ct.App.1996).........................188
Shearson Lehmann Hutton Inc. *v.* Maclaine Watson & Co. Ltd. [1989] 2
  Lloyd's Rep. 570..213
Sheet Metal Workers Local No. 218 *v.* Massie 255 Ill.App. 3d 697, 627 NE
  2d 1154 (1993) 189
Sim v Stretch (1936) 52 TLR 669...238
Simpson-Sears case *see* Ontario Human Rights Commission and O'Malley
  v. Simpson-Sears Ltd.
Smith *v.* Van Gorkom 488 A 2d 858 (1985)..182
Soucie *v.* David 448 F 2d 1067 (1971)...173
Stevenage Borough Football Club Ltd. *v.* Football League Ltd. *The Times* 1
  Aug 1996 (Ch.D) 152
Stewart-Brady, *ex parte, The Times* 22 Nov. 1996 153
Syndicat des employés *v.* Canada Labour Relations Board [1984]
  2 SCR 412 ....289, 291, 293
Syndicat des employés de production du Quebec et de l'Acadie *v.* Canada
  (Human Rights Commission) [1989] 2 SCR 879 333

Telecom Corp. of New Zealand Ltd. *v.* Clear Communications Ltd.
  [1995] 1 NZLR 385..49, 50
Texas Rural Legal Aid Inc. *v.* Legal Services Corp. 940 F 2d 685,
  (1991) 104
Thames Valley Electric Power Board *v.* NZFP Pulp and Paper Ltd.
  [1994] 2 NZLR 641 20
Thomas C.Assaly Corp. Ltd. *v.* Canada (1990) 44 Admin. LR 145
Town Investments *v.* Department of the Environment [1978]
  AC 359...77, 78
Tremblay *v.* Quebec [1992] 1 SCR 952 288
Trident General Insurance Co. Ltd. *v.* McNiece Pty. Ltd. (1988)
  165 CLR 107 64

R. v. Secretary of State for Employment *ex parte* Equal Opportunities
Commission [1993] 1 All ER 1022 241
R. v. Secretary of State for Foreign & Commonwealth Affairs *ex parte*
World Development Movement [1995] 1 All ER 611, [1995]
1 WLR 386 .... 26, 241
R. v. Secretary of State for the Home Department *ex parte*
Bentley [1994] 2 WLR 101 28
R. v. Secretary of State for the Home Department *ex parte* Fire Brigades
Union [1995] 2 WLR 464 241
R. v. Secretary of State for the Home Department *ex parte*
Mohammed Al Fayed, *The Times* 18 Nov.1996 140
R. v. Secretary of State for the Home Department *ex parte* Northumbria
Police Authority [1989] QB 35 250
R. v. Secretary of State for the Home Office *ex parte* Doody [1994]
AC 531 221
R. v. Somerset County Council *ex parte* Fewings [1995]
1 All ER 513 .... 5, 228
R. v. Tottenham & District Rent Tribunal *ex parte* Northfield (Highgate)
Ltd. [1957] 1 QB 103 311
R. v. Universities Funding Council *ex parte* Institute of Dental Surgery
[1994] 1 WLR 242 221
R. v. Visitors to the Inns of Court *ex parte* Calder [1993] 2 All ER 876,
[1994] QB 1 .... 46, 201
R. v. Waltham Forest London Borough Council *ex parte* Baxter [1987]
3 All ER 671 229
R. v. Wear Valley District Council *ex parte* Binks [1985]
2 Alkl ER 699 230
Racal Communications Ltd., *Re* [1981] AC 374 .... 213, 291
RDS v. The Queen (1995) 145 NSR (2d) 284 345
Rees v. United Assoc.of Journeymen & Apprentices (1974) 46 DLR
(3d) 518 146
Reference *Re* Constitutional Questions Act (Ontario) [1957]
7 DLR (2d) 222 250
Reilly v. Steelcase Canada Ltd. (1979) 26 OR (2d) 725 142
Rendell-Baker v. Kohn 457 US 830 (1982) 99
Ridge v. Baldwin [1964] AC 40 .... 87, 137, 138, 140, 147, 287
Rigby v. Connol (1880) 14 Ch.D 482 138
Riggs v. Palmer 115 NY 506, 22 NE 188 (1889) 224
Roberts v. United States Jaycees 468 US 609 (1984) 354
Rogers v. Clarence Hotel Co. Ltd. [1940] 3 DLR 583 .... 12, 13, 14, 15
Ross v. New Brunswick School District No. 15 [1996]
1 SCR 825 .... 309, 314, 317, 325, 333
Rushworth v. Council of Economic Advisors 762 F 2d 1038
(1985) 176S. 236

R. v. Inspectorate of Pollution *ex parte* Greenpeace Ltd. (No. 2) [1994]
4 All ER 329 ....26, 241
R. v. Jockey Club, *ex parte* Massingberd-Mundy [1993]
2 All ER 207 ....88, 203
R. v. Jockey Club *ex parte* RAM Racecourses [1993]
2 All ER 225...88, 202, 203
R. v. Labour Party *ex parte* Hughes, Unreported, QBD, June 1990 46
R. v. Lavalée [1990] 1 SCR 852...334, 350
R. v. Legal Aid Board, *ex parte* Donn & Co. (a firm) (1996) 3 All ER 1..143
R. v. Lewisham London Borough Council *ex parte* Shell UK Ltd.
[1988] 1 All ER 938...229, 231
R. v. Lloyds of London *ex parte* Briggs [1993] 1 Lloyd's Rep. 176,
COD 66...203
R. v. London Borough of Ealing *ex parte* Times Newspapers
(1987) 85 LGR 316..229, 231
R. v. Lord Chancellor *ex parte* Hibbit & Saunders [1993] COD 326,
The Times, 12 March 1993 ....34, 35, 228
R. v. Lord President of the Privy Council *ex parte* Page [1993]
AC 682...213, 283
R v. Minister for the Civil Service, *ex parte* Council of Civil
Service Unions [1985] AC 374...............................218, 221, 223, 226, 232
R. v. Morgentaler [1988] 1 SCR.30 350
R. v. Morin (1995) 37 CR (4th) 395 244
R. v. Panel on Take-overs and Mergers *ex parte* Datafin plc [1987]
1 QB 815 ....28, 29, 30, 31, 33, 36, 45, 46, 47, 70, 135, 147,
152, 154, 198, 199, 200, 201, 202, 231, 233
R. v. Panel on Take-overs and Mergers *ex parte* Guiness plc [1990]
1 QB 146..47, 201
R. v. Ponting [1985] Crim LR 318..75
R. v. Portsmouth City Council *ex parte* Coles *The Times* 13 Nov.
1996..143
R. v. Power [1994] 1 SCR 601...252, 253
R. v. R. [1991] 4 All ER 481...234, 239
R. v. R.D.S. (1995) unreported, 2 December 1994..............................345, 346
R. v. Ron Engineering & Construction (Eastern) Ltd. [1981]
1 SCR 111..144
R. v. Royal Life Saving Society *ex parte* Howe, Unreported,
CA, May 1990..46
R. v. Schacht (1973) 30 DLR (3d) 641 251
R. v. Scott [1990] 3 SCR 979 ....252, 253
R. v. Seaboyer [1991] 2 SCR 577..350
R. v. Simpson (1993) 12 OR (3d) 182..276
R. v. Social Services Secretary *ex parte* Child Poverty Action Group
[1990] 1 QB 540..241

R. v. Civil Service Appeal Board *ex parte* Bruce [1988] ICR 649,
[1989] ICR 171 201
R. v. Civil Service Appeal Board *ex parte* Cunningham [1991]
4 All ER 310 221
R. v. Code of Practice Committee of the Assoc. of British
Pharmaceutical Industry *ex parte* Professional Counselling
Aids Ltd. (1990) 10 BMLR 21 (QBD), [1991] COD 228 .... 48, 201
46R. v. Commissioners of Inland Revenue *ex parte* Unilever plc
[1996] STC 681 .... 221, 231
R. v. Criminal Injuries Compensation Board *ex parte* Lain [1967]
2 QB 864 .... 27, 28
R. v. Derbyshire County Council *ex parte* Noble [1990]
ICR 808 .... 141, 142
R. v. Disciplinary Committee of the Jockey Club *ex parte* Aga Khan
[1993] 2 All ER 853 .... 33, 46, 87, 152, 153, 154, 200, 202, 204, 231
R. v. Disciplinary Committee of the Jockey Club *ex parte* Massingberd-
Mundy [1993]2 All ER 207 202
R. v. East Berkshire Health Authority *ex parte* Walsh [1985] QB 152 199
R. v. Fernhill Manor School *ex parte* Brown (1993) 5 Admin LR 159,
[1992] COD] 446 .... 36, 201
R. v. Fernhill Manor School *ex parte* A [1993] 1 FLR 620 46
R. v. Financial Intermediaries Managers and Brokers Regulatory Assoc.
ex parte Cochrane [1990] COD 33 201
R. v. Football Assoc. Ltd. *ex parte* Football League Ltd. [1993]
2 All ER 833 .... 32, 46, 153, 203, 204, 205
R. v. Football Assoc. of Wales, *ex parte* Flint Town United Football
Club [1991] COD 44 203
R. v. General Council of the Bar, *ex parte* Percival [1991] 1 QB 212 46
R. v. Governors of Haberdasker's Aske's Hatchem College Trust
ex parte Tyrell [1995] COD 399; *The Times* 19 Oct. 1994 .... 35, 37
R. v. Gwent Training and Enterprise Council *ex parte* Ghafoor,
Unreported decision of Brooke J., QB 22 Feb. 1995 37
R. v. Higher Education Funding Council *ex parte* Institute of Dental
Surgery [1994] 1 WLR 242 304
R. v. Imam of Bury Park James Masjid Luton *ex parte* Sulaiman
Ali [1992] COD 132 .... 32, 205
R. v. Inland Revenue Commissioners, *ex parte* Matrix Securities Ltd.
[1994] 1 WLR 334 231
R. v. Inland Revenue Commissioners *ex parte* MFK Underwriting
Services Ltd. [1990] 1 All ER 91 221
R. v. Inland Revenue Commissioners *ex parte* National Federation of
Self-Employed & Small Businesses [1982] AC 617 241
R. v. Inland Revenue Commissioners *ex parte* Preston [1985]
AC 835 221

xxii   *Table of Cases*

Operation Dismantle *v.* The Queen [1985] 1 SCR 441 135
O'Reilly *v.* Mackman [1983] 2 AC 237 .... 85, 199
Original Lawrence County Farm Organization Inc. *v.* Tennese Farm
   Bureau Federation 907 SW 2d 419 (1995) 186, 188
O'Rourke *v.* Schacht (1976) 000
Osborn *v.* Bank of United States 22 US 738 (1824) 103
Osborne *v.* Amalgamated Society of Railway Servants [1910] AC 107 161

Paccar case *see* CAIMAW *v.* Paccar of Canada Ltd.
Padfield *v.* Minister of Agriculture [1968] AC 997 .... 223, 229
Page case *see* R. *v.* Lord President of the Privy Council, *ex parte* Page
Paine *v.* University of Toronto (1981) 34 OR (2d) 770 149
Pearlman *v.* Keepers and Governors of Harrow School [1979] QB 56 291
Pembroke (City) Police Services Board *v.* Kidder (1995) 123 DLR
   (4th) 596 (Ont.Gen.Div.) 250
Perry *v.* Sindermann 408 US 593 (1972) 185
Peter Kiewit Sons Ltd. *v.* Richmond (City) (1992) 7 Admin LR (2d)
   124 143
Peterboro Lock Mfg. Co., *Re* (1954) 4 LAC 1499 300
Pezim *v.* British Columbia (Superintendent of Brokers) [1994]
   2 SCR 557 .... 295, 317
Pharmaceutical Society of Great Britain *v.* Dickson [1970] AC 403 233
Phillips *v.* Nova Scotia (Commission of Inquiry into the Westray Mine
   Tragedy) [1995] 2 SCR 97 333
Plessy *v.* Ferguson 163 US 537 (1896) 340
Pollock *v.* Saunders (1897) 15 NZLR 581 .... 9, 10
Port Arthur Shipbuilding *v.* Arthurs [1969] SCR 85 309
Prince Rupert Grain Ltd. *v.* ILWU (20 June 1996), No 24428 322
Proclamations' Case (1611) 12 Co. Rep 74 222
Prohibitions Del Roy (1607) 12 Co. Rep 63 222

Quirola *v.* Xerox Canada Inc. (1996) 16 CCEL (2d) 235 142

R. *v.* Advertising Standards Authority *ex parte* The Insurance Service plc
   [1990] 2 Admin LR 77, [1990] COD 42 .... 30, 46, 154, 201
R. *v.* Beare [1988] 2 SCR 387 251
R. *v.* Brent London Borough Council *ex parte* Assegai (1987) 151 L G
   Review 891 229
R. *v.* British Pharmaceutical Industry Association Code of Practice
   Committee, *ex parte* Professional Counselling Aids Ltd. [1991]
   COD 228 31
R. *v.* Brydges [1990] 1 SCR 190 252
R. *v.* Chief Rabbi of the United Hebrew Congregations *ex parte* Wachmann
   [1993] 2 All ER 249 .... 31, 46, 153, 205

Metropolitan Life Insurance Co. v. IUDE [1970] SCR 425........309, 310, 311
Meyer v. Bush 981 F 2d 1288 (1993)..176
Minister of Justice for the Dominion of Canada v. City of Levis
  [1919] AC 505 7
Mohr v. Vancouver New Westminster & Fraser Valley District
  Council of Carpenters (1988) 33 Admin LR 154..................................147
Morris and Morris, Re (1973) 42 DLR (3d) 550 rev'g.
  (1973) 35 DLR (3d) 447 149
Morris v. C W Martin & Sons Ltd. [1966] 1 QB 716..............................19
Mossop case see Canada (Attorney General) v. Mossop
Motor Vehicles Manufacturers Assoc. v. State Farm Mutual
  Automobile Insurance Co.463 US 29 (1983)..181
Munn v. Illinois 94 US 77 (1876) 7

NAACP v. Golding 342 Md. 663, 679 A 2d 554 (1996).................186, 189
Nagle v. Feilden [1966] 2 QB 633..138, 139, 233
National Assoc. of Sporting Goods Wholesalers Inc. v. F.T.L.
  Marketing Corp. 779 F 2d 1281 (1985)...187, 188
National College Athletic Assoc. v. Tarkanian 488 US 179 (1988)....189, 190
National Corngrowers Assoc. v. Canada (Import Tribunal) [1990]
  2 SCR 1324 ....296, 297, 308, 310, 311, 333
National Fuel Gas Corp. v. FERC 811 F 2d 1563 (1987).......................320
National Labour Relations Board v. United Food & Commercial
  Workers Union, Local 23 484 US 112 (1988) 320
National Railroad Passenger Corp. v. Boston & Maine Corp. 503 US
  407 (1992) 320
Network Project v. Corporation for Public Broadcasting 4 Media
  L.Rep. 2399 (1979)..104
New South Wales (Attorney General) v. Perpetual Trustee Co. [1955]
  AC 457 251
New Zealand Maori Council v. Attorney General of New Zealand
  [1994] 1 AC 466 26
Newfoundland Telephone Co. v. Newfoundland (Board of
  Commissioners) of Public Utilities [1992] 1 SCR 62...................345, 349
Nicolson v. Haldimand-Norfolk Regional Board of Commissioners of
  Police [1979] 1 SCR 311..287, 288, 289, 301
Nipawin case see Service Employees' International Union, Local
  No.333 v. Nipawin District Staff Nurses Assocn
Noble case see R. v. Derbyshire County Council, ex parte Noble
Oklahoma Natural Gas Co. v. FERC 28 F 3d 1281 (1994).....................321
Old St. Boniface Residents Assocn Inc v. Winnipeg [1990] 3 SCR 1170-...345
Ontario Human Rights Commission and O'Malley v. Simpson-Sears Ltd.
  [1985] 2 SCR 536..353
286880 Ontario Ltd. v. Parke (1974) 52 DLR (3d) 535 251

Law v. National Greyhound Racing Club Ltd. [1983] 1 WLR 1302 202
Lebron v. National Railroad Passengers Assoc. 115 S Ct. 961
 (1995) 18, 103, 104, 174, 177, 178
Lee v. Showmen's Guild of Great Britain [1952] 2 QB 329...............139, 149
Lester (W.W.) (1978) Ltd. v. United Assoc. of Journeymen and
 Apprentices [1990] 3 SCR 644..294, 300
Lewis v. United States 680 F 2d 1239 (1982)...179
Liberty Mortgage Corp. Ltd. v. Federal Home Loan Mortgage
 Corp. 822 F Supp. 956 (1993) 178
Lindenburger v. United Church of Canada (1985) 17 CCEL 143;
 aff'd. (1987) 17 CCEL 172 156
Lloyds Bank plc v. Rosset [1991] 1 AC 107..237
Loew's Montreal Theatres Ltd. v. Reynolds (1921) 30 RJQ 459 12
Londoner v. Denver 210 US 373 (1908) 183
Longive v. Intercontinental Hotels [1993] 4 LRC 221..................................8
Lugar v. Edmondson Oil Company Inc. 457 US 922 (1982) 99
Lujan v. Defenders of Wildlife 504 US 555 (1992) 110

M, *In Re* [1994] 1 AC 377...135
M. v. Home Office [1993] 3 WLR 433 78
Majorie Webster Junior College Inc. v. Middle States Assoc.
 of Colleges 432 F 2d 650 (DC Cir.1970), cert. denied 400 US 965
 (1970)..188
Malloch v. Aberdeen Corpn [1971] 2 All ER 1278 141
Malone v. Metropolitan Police Commissioner [1979] Ch 344 ....227, 228
Marlborough Harbour Board v. Goulden [1985] 2 NZLR 378......................5
Marrone v. Washington Jockey Club of the District of Columbia
 227 US 633 (1912) 9
Marshall v. Southhampton Area Authority (Teaching) (C-152-84) [1986]
 ECR 1651; [1986] QB 401...74
Masters v. Ontario (1993) 110 DLR (4th) 407; aff'd. (1994) 18 OR
 (3d) 551 147
Mathews v. Eldridge 424 US 319 (1976)...186, 215
Matthews v. Bay Head Improvement Assoc. 95 NJ 306, 471 A 2d
 355 cert.denied 469 US 821 (1984) 190
Mayor, Alderman and Burgesses of the Borough of Bradford v. Pickles
 [1895] AC 587 16
McCaw v. United Church of Canada (1991) 37 CCEL 214..............138, 149, 150
McCrea v. Marsh 78 Mass. 211 (1858)...9
McCulloch v. Maryland 17 US 316 (1819)..103
McKinney v. University of Guelph [1993] 3 SCR 718......................352, 354
McKnight v. Rees 88 F 3d 417 (1996) 99
Mercury Energy Ltd. v. Electricity Corp. of New Zealand Ltd. [1994]
 2 NZLR 385; [1994] 1 WLR 521 ....18, 37, 49, 158

Health Care Developers Inc. *v.* Newfoundland (1996) 141 Nfl'd and
    PEIR 34 ....143, 144, 145
Heatley *v.* Tasmanian Racing and Gambling Commission (1976–7)
    137 CLR 487 10
Herring *v.* Templeman [1973] 3 All ER 569 233
Hibbit & Saunders case *see* R. *v.* Lord Chancellor, *ex parte* Hibbit &
    Saunders (a firm)
Hill *v.* Church of Scientology [1995] 2 SCR 1130 150
Hofer case *see* Lakeside Colony of Hutterite Bretheren *v.* Hofer
Hofer *v.* Hofer [1970] SCR 958 167
Holmberg *v.* Sault Ste. Marie Public Utilities Commission (1966)
    58 DLR (2d) 125 14
Houle *v.* National Bank of Canada [1990] 3 SCR 122 16
Hunter *v.* Canary Wharf Ltd. [1996] 2 WLR 348 238
Hurst *v.* Picture Theatres Ltd. [1915] 1 KB 1 9

Immigration and Naturalization Service *v.* Cardoza-Fonseca
    480 US 421 (1987) 319, 320
International Woodworkers of America Local 2-69 *v.* Consolidated
    Bathurst Packaging Ltd. [1990] 1 SCR 282 ....287, 333

Jackson *v.* Culinary School of Washington 788 F Supp. 1233
    (1992) 104
Jackson *v.* Metropolitan Edison Co. 419 US 345 (1974) 179
Jacmain *v.* Attorney General of Canada [1978] 2 SCR 15 291
Jacobson *v.* New York Racing Assoc. 33 NY 2d 144,
    305 NE 2d 765 (1973) 188, 190
John *v.* Rees [1969] 2 All ER 274 139
Johnson *v.* Educational Testing Service 754 F 2d 20 (1st Cir.1985),
    cert.denied 472 US 1029 (1985) 191
Johnson *v.* Sparrow (1899) 15 CS 104 ....12, 13
Johnston *v.* Chief Constable of the Royal Ulster Constabulary
    (C-222/84) [1986] ECR 1651; [1987] QB 129 74

Kaye *v.* Robertson [1991] FSR 92 238
Khorasandjian *v.* Bush [1993] QB 727 238
Knight *v.* Indian Head School Division No. 19 [1990]
    1 SCR 653 ....140, 141, 145, 301, 302

Lakeside Colony of Hutterian Brethren *v.* Hofer [1992]
    3 SCR 165 ....138, 148, 149, 150, 152, 154, 166,
                                                                            167, 168, 233
Lapointe *v.* L'Association de Bienfaisance [1906] AC 535 233
Lavallée case *see* R. *v.* Lavallée

Dorf Industries Pty Ltd. *v.* Toose (1994) 127 ALR 654 46
Doughty *v.* Rolls-Royce plc [1992] 1 CMLR 1045; [1992] IRLR 126..........74
Drummond Wren, *Re* [1945] 4 DLR 674 14

Edmonson *v.* Leesville Concrete Co. 500 US 614 (1991)............................99
Edwards *v.* SOGAT [1971] Ch. 354..138, 233
Energy Research Foundation *v.* Defense Nuclear Facilities
 Safety Board 917 F 2d 581 (1990) 176
Entick *v.* Carrington (1765) 19 St Tr 1030 227
Faccini Dori *v.* Recreb Srl (C-91/92) [1995] All ER (EC) 1 74
Falcone *v.* Middlesex County Medical Society 34 NJ 582,
 170 A 2d 791 (1961)...188
Faramus *v.* Film Artistes Assoc. [1964] AC 925..139
Feurtry, TC 29 Feb. 1908 ....73, 78
Fisher *v.* Keane (1878) 11 Ch.D 353 138
Football Association case *see* R. *v.* Football Association, *ex parte*
 Football League Ltd.
Forbes *v.* Eden (1867) 48 LR 1 HL 568 138
Forbes *v.* New South Wales Trotting Club Ltd. (1978–9) 143 CLR 242 10
Foster *v.* British Gas plc (C-188/89) [1990] ECR 1-3313 ....74, 86, 208
Franklin *v.* Evans (1924) 55 OLR 349 12
Franklin *v.* Massachusetts 112 S.Ct. 2797 (1992)..............................173, 175
Free Church of Scotland *v.* Overtoun [1904] AC 515........................148, 162

Gale *v.* Miracle Food Mart (1993) 12 Admin LR 267.........346, 347, 348, 349
Gallant *v.* Trono (1989) 36 Admin LR 261..275
Garcia *v.* San Antonio Metropolitan Transit Authority 469 US 528
 (1985)..178
GCHQ case *see* Council for Civil Service Unions *v.* Minister for the
 Civil Service and R. *v.* Minister for the Civil Service *ex parte*
 Council of Civil Service Unions
Gillick *v.* West Norfolk Health Authority [1986] AC 112....................88, 234
Glynn *v.* Keele University [1971] 1 WLR 487 233
Gough *v.* Canada (National Parole Board) (1990) 45 Admin.
 LR 304 ....275, 276
Gould *v.* Yukon Order of Pioneers [1996] 1 SCR 571 ....5, 150, 151, 152,
                                                       154, 225, 297, 309, 314, 318, 325,
                                                       331, 351, 352, 353, 354, 355, 356
Greisman *v.* Newcomb Hospital 40 NJ 389, 192 A 2d 817 (1963) 190
Groenvelt *v.* Burwell 1 Ld Raym 454 (1700)..198

Hamilton City Council *v.* Waikato Electricity Commission [1994] 1
 NZLR 741..3, 20
Harris *v.* Dackwood (1810) 3 Taunt. 264 232

Cardoza case *see* Immigration and Naturalization Service *v* Cardoza-Fonseca
Chandler *v*. Director of Public Prosecutions [1964] AC 763......................75
Chapmans Ltd. *v*. Australian Stock Exchange Ltd. (1994)
  123 ALR 215 46
Charles O. Finley *v*. Kuhn 569 F 2d 527 (1978),
  cert. denied 439 US 876 (1978) 187, 188
Chastain *v*. British Columbia Hydro & Power Authority (1972)
  32 DLR (3d) 443 (BC SC)...17
Chevron USA Ltd. *v*. NRDC 467 US 837 (1984) 319, 320, 321
Christie *v*. The York Corporation [1940] 1 DLR 81 ....12, 13
Citizens to Preserve Overton Park *v*. Volpe 401 US 402 (1971) 215
Cleveland Board of Education *v*. Loudermill 470 US 532 (1985)......................
  185Committee for Justice and Liberty *v*. National Energy Board
  [1978] 1 SCR 369...347
Constantine *v*. Imperial Hotels Ltd. [1944] 1 KB 693 ....14, 146
Corngrowers case *see* National Corn Growers Assoc. *v*. Canada
  (Import Tribunal)
Costello-Roberts *v*. UK, Series A, No. 247-C...................................39
Council of Civil Service Unions *v*. Minister for the Civil Service
  [1985] AC 374 ....28, 134, 135
Cowell *v*. Rosehill Racecourse Co. Ltd. (1936-7) 56 CLR 605.................9, 11
Crevier *v*. Attorney General of Quebec [1981] 2 SCR 220.......................291
Crowell *v*. Benson 285 US 22 (1932) 93
Crown Milling Co. Ltd. *v*. R. [1927] AC 394...................................49
CUPE case *see* Canadian Union of Public Employees Local 963 *v*. New
  Brunswick Liquor Corporation

Dagenais *v*. Canadian Broadcasting Corp. [1994] 3 SCR 835 150
Dalton *v*. Specter 511 US 462 (1994) 175
Datafin case *see* R. *v*. Panel on Take-overs and Mergers, *ex parte*
  Datafin plc
Davis *v*. United Church of Canada (1991) 8 OR (3d) 75.........................146
Davy *v*. Spelthorne Borough Council [1984] AC 262 19
Dawkins *v*. Antrobus (1879) 17 Ch.D 615 138
Dayco (Canada) Ltd. *v*. CAW-Canada [1993] 2 SCR 230 ....296, 341
Derbyshire County Council *v*. Times Newspapers Ltd. [1993]
  AC 534 230
Dickason *v*. Edwards (1913) 10 CLR 243 139
Dickason *v*. University of Alberta [1992] 2 SCR 1103 ....309, 352
Dickson *v*. Pharmaceutical Guild [1967] 2 WLR 718................................139
Dolan *v*. City of Tigard 114 S.Ct. 1624 (1995) 110
Dole *v*. United Steelmates of America 494 US 26 (1990)..................321
Domtar Inc. *v*. Quebec [1993] 2 SCR 756.................................298, 299

Beresford-Hope v. Lady Sandhurst (1889) 23 QB 79 235
Berg case see University of British Columbia v. Berg
Bhadauria v. Board of Governors of Seneca College of Applied Arts and
    Technology (1979) 105 DLR (3d) 707........................14, 15, 17, 313
Bi-Metallic Investment Co. v. State Board of Equalization 293 US 441
    (1915)...184
Bibeault case see UES Local 298 v. Bibeault
Blanco, TC, 8 Feb.1873 ....72, 73
Board of Pardons v. Allen 482 US 369 (1987).............................185
Board of Governors of Seneca College of Applied Arts and
    Technology v. Bhadauria [1981] 2 SCR 181 ....14, 313
    see also Bhadauria v. Board of Governors of the Seneca College of
    Applied Arts and Technology
Board of Regents v. Roth 408 US 564 (1972)..............................184
Bolt v. Stennett (1800) 8 TR 606' 101 ER 1572............................88
Bradco case see United Brotherhood of Carrpenters and Joiners of
    America v. Bradco Construction Ltd.
Breen v. Amalgamated Engineering Union [1971] 2 QB 175 ....87, 233
British Coal v. National Union of Mineworkers *The Times*
    13 Aug.1996..230
British Columbia Telephone Co. v. Shaw Cable Systems (B.C.) Ltd.
    [1995] 2 SCR 738 ....298, 299, 300, 302
British Oxygen Ltd. v. Board of Trade [1971] AC 610............................223
Brown v. Waterloo Regional Board of Commissioners of Police (1983)
    150 DLR (3d) 729...142, 147
Brownlow v. Cox and Michil (1615) 3 Bulst 32 222
Burton v. Scherpf 83 Mass. 133 (1861) 9

CAIMA v. Paccar of Canada Ltd. [1989] 2 SCR 983................288, 292, 293,
    294, 295, 297, 300, 302, 306, 322
Canada (Attorney General) v. Mossop [1993] 1 SCR 554 ....297, 309,
    314, 315, 316, 317, 318, 322, 324, 325,
    326, 327, 328, 334, 341, 342, 350
Canada (Attorney General) v. Public Service Alliance of Canada
    [1991] 1 SCR 614 ....301, 322
Canada (Attorney General) v. Saskatchewan Water Corp. (1993)
    18 Admin LR (2d) 91...135
Canadian National Railway Co. v. Canada (Canadian Human Rights
    Commission) [1987] 1 SCR 1114 ....313, 334, 353
Canadian Pacific Ltd. v. Matsqui Indian Band [1995] 1 SCR 3..................333
Canadian Union of Public Employees Local 963 (CUPE) v.
    New Brunswick Liquor Corp. [1979] 2 SCR 227 ....19, 282, 287,
    288, 289, 290, 291, 292, 293, 294, 295, 296, 297, 298,
    301, 302, 308, 309, 312, 319, 321, 322 324, 341, 344

Table of Cases

ABM case *see* American Bankers Mortgage Corpn *v.* Federal Home Loan Mortgage Corpn
Action Travail des Femmes case *see* Canadian National Railway Co. *v.* Canada (Canadian Human Rights Commission)
Aga Khan case *see* R. *v.* Disciplinary Committee of the Jockey Club, *ex parte* Aga Khan
Ainsley Financial Corp. *v.* Ontario Securities Commission (1994) 121 DLR (4th) 79...................254
Airline Pilots Assoc. *v.* FAA 3 F 3d 449 (1993)...................320
Allen *v.* Flood [1898] AC 1...................16
Allnutt *v.* Inglis (1810) 12 East 527, 104 ER 206...................88
American Bankers Mortgage Corp. *v.* Federal Home Loan Mortgage Corp. 75 F 3d 1401 (9th Cir.1996), cert. denied 117 S Ct. 58 (1996)...................178, 179
American Federation of Technical Engineers *v.* La Jeunesse 63 Ill. 2d 263, 347 NE 2d 712 (1976)...................187
Anisminic Ltd. *v.* Foreign Compensation Commission [1969] 2 AC 147...................213, 282, 291, 310
Arnett *v.* Kennedy 416 US 134 (1974)...................185
Associated Provincial Picture Houses Ltd. *v.* Wednesbury Corp. [1948] 1 KB 223...................228

Babbitt *v.* Sweet Home Chapter of Communities for a Great Oregon 115 S Ct. 2407 (1995)...................321
Baltimore Gas & Elec. Co. *v.* NRDC 462 US 87 (1983)...................181
Bank of Scotland *v.* Investment Management Regulatory Organization Ltd. [1989] SLT 432...................201
Barclays Bank *v.* O'Brien [1994] AC 180...................236
Barnswell *v.* National Amusement Co. (1915) 23 DLR 615...................9, 12
BC Tel *see* British Columbia Telephone Co. *v.* Shaw Cable Systems (BC) Ltd.
Bell *v.* Ontario Human Rights Commission [1971] SCR 756.....309, 310, 311, 312
Bell Canada *v.* Canada (Canadian Radio-Television and Telecommunications Commission) [1989] 1 SCR 1722...................295
Bennet & Fisher Ltd. *v.* Electricity Trust of South Australia (1962) 106 CLR 492...................48
Dr. Bentley's Case (1723) 1 Str 557; 93 ER 698...................138, 139
Bentley case *see* R. *v.* Secretary of State for the Home Department, *ex parte* Bentley

Triester *v.* American Academy of Orthopaedic Surgeons 78 Ill. App. 3d 746, 396 NE 2d 1225 (1979) 187
Tse *v.* Trow Consulting Engineering Ltd. (1995) 14 CCEL (2d) 132 142
Tully *v.* Farrell (1876) 23 Grant 40..138
Typing Centre of New South Wales *v.* Toose, Unreported NSW Sup.Ct. 15 Dec.1988 46
Tyrell case *see* R. *v.* Haberdashers' Aske's Hatcham College Trust, *ex parte* Tyrell

U.E.S., Local 298 *v.* Bibeault [1988] 2 SCR 1048 ....289, 291, 296, 315, 322, 323, 324, 328, 333
Ukrainian Greek Orthodox Church *v.* Ukrainian Greek Orthodox Cathedral of St. Mary [1940] SCR 586 138
United Brotherhood of Carpenters and Joiners of America, Local 579 *v.* Bradco Construction Ltd. [1993] 2 SCR 316 ....296, 316, 341
United States *v.* Lopez 115 S.Ct. 1624 (1995) 110
University of British Columbia *v.* Berg [1993] 2 SCR 353 ....309, 314, 316, 324, 325, 327, 341, 354
Unocal Corp. *v.* Mesa Petroleum Co. 493 A 2d 946 (1985) 183
USA Group Loan Services Inc. *v.* Riley 82 F 3d 708 (1996) 95, 107
Uston *v.* Resorts International Hotel Ltd. 445 A 2d 370 (1982) 11, 12

Van Gorkom case *see* Smith *v.* Van Gorkom
Vermont Yankee Nuclear Power Corp. *v.* Natural Resources Defense Council Inc. 435 US 519 (1978) 174
Vestey *v.* Inland Revenue Commissioners (No. 2) [1980] AC 1148..........223
Volker Stevin NWT (1992) Ltd. *v.* Northwest Territories (Commissioner) (1994) 113 DLR (4th) 639 143

W. (A Minor), *In re* [1992] 3 WLR 758..236
Wachmann case *see* R. *v.* Chief Rabbi of the United Hebrew Congregations of Great Britain and the Commonwealth, *ex parte* Wachmann
Walford *v.* Miles [1992] 2 AC 128 145
Warren *v.* Government National Mortgage Assoc. 611 F 2d 1229 (1980), cert. denied 449 US 847 (1980) 104
West *v.* Atkins 487 US 42 (1988) 193
West *v.* Secretary of State for Scotland 1992 SLT 636...............................232
West Glamorgan County Council *v.* Rafferty [1987] 1 All ER 1005.........229
Wheeler *v.* Leicester City Council [1985] AC 1054.........................229, 231
Wood *v.* Leadbitter (1845) 13 M & W 838; 153 ER 351..........................8, 9

Yarmirr *v.* Australian Telecommunications Corp. (1990) 96 ALR 739.......67
Young *v.* Young [1994] 4 SCR 3 150

Zapata Corp. *v*. Maldonado 430 A 2d 779 (1981) 182
Zurich Insurance Co. *v*. Ontario (Human Rights Commission)
  [1992] 2 SCR 321..309, 315, 316, 323, 325

1

The Province of Administrative Law Determined?

MICHAEL TAGGART*

This is not the kind of editor's introduction to a published set of conference papers which gives nutshell accounts of the papers to follow. The papers speak for themselves and even if I could put each into a nutshell the authors would not allow them to remain there for long. My purpose in this paper is to make a contribution to some of the themes running through the collection and to indicate some linkages between the papers.

First of all, a word of explanation is necessitated by the ubiquity of the term "public law". The reference in the title of this book to administrative law, rather than to public law, is deliberate. In this I follow the late Professor S.A. de Smith, who, in his inaugural lecture at the London School of Economics and Political Science, said: "I regard constitutional law and administrative law as occupying distinct provinces, but also a substantial area of common ground".[1] Moreover, to pass muster under truth-in-advertising laws a book title using "Public Law" would have required more sustained treatment in the Canadian context of the Charter of Rights and Freedoms and of the public/private divide in other countries with "capital c" Constitutions and/or Bills of Rights. The province of administrative law, in the sense of a branch of learning, is not coextensive with that of constitutional or public law.[2] Nevertheless, the terms are commonly used interchangeably without causing any confusion; as they are in many of the papers in this volume.

---

* This paper was written after the conference but, in essence, reflects my comments during the conference and in my closing remarks.

[1] S.A. de Smith, *The Lawyers and the Constitution* (G. Bell & Sons Ltd., London, 1960), 16.

[2] See also P. Cane, "Mapping the Frontiers", in P. Birks (ed.), *The Frontiers of Liability* (Oxford University Press, Oxford, 1994), vol. 1, 137.

ADMINISTRATIVE LAW AS SYMBOL IN AN AGE OF PRIVATISATION

Pointing out that institutional writers ignored administrative law for decades after it had become part of the working system of the British Constitution, Felix Frankfurter observed half a century ago that:[3]

> "[people] seldom realise at the time how deeply dynamic changes are cutting. Old pictures of a political and legal scene remain current long after it has been drastically altered."

This remains true today. The profound changes brought about by deregulation, commercialisation, corporatisation, public sector downsising, privatisation and globalisation have fundamentally altered the political and social landscapes in countries around the world. As a group lawyers were rather slow to appreciate the impact of these changes on legal systems and societies, but early on some administrative lawyers saw the threat to their subject posed by "the contracting state".[4] Many papers in this volume deal with these phenomena from various perspectives; particularly those by Murray Hunt, Mark Aronson, Wade MacLauchlan, David Mullan, Paul Craig and Alfred Aman.

The growth of these phenomena in the United Kingdom in the early 1980s coincided with an upsurge in theoretical interest in and writing about administrative law[5] and a period of judicial activism there. The substantial body of case-law in the United Kingdom since then, mostly concerning judicial review of self-regulatory bodies and contracting out—far greater in quantity than in any other Commonwealth country—is considered in detail in the papers by Murray Hunt, Mark Aronson and Paul Craig. It is fair to say that the courts have failed so far to adopt a consistent and principled approach to these issues.[6]

Some light is shed on the strains in this case-law, and more generally between public law and private law, by appreciating the symbolic importance of administrative law.

A long time ago, in a once influential but now largely forgotten book called *The Symbols of Government*, Thurman Arnold wrote about law (as well as economics) as symbolic thinking which conditions the behaviour of people

---

[3] F. Frankfurter, "The Final Report of the Attorney-General's Committee on Administrative Procedure" (1941) 41 *Col LR* 585.

[4] See M. Taggart, Book review (1993) 4 *PLR* 271, 271–2. The brilliant double entendre is taken from the title of Ian Harden's well known book, *The Contracting State* (Open University Press, Buckingham, 1992).

[5] For surveys of the literature see D. Galligan, *Administrative Law* (Dartmouth, Aldershot, 1992), xi–xxi and M. Loughlin, "The Pathways of Public Law Scholarship", in G.P. Wilson (ed.), *Frontiers of Legal Scholarship: Twenty-five years of Warwick Law School* (John Wiley & Sons, Chichester, 1995), 163.

[6] This case-law has been said recently to reflect "the growing crisis in judicial review" in the United Kingdom: M. Loughlin, "Courts and Governance", in Birks, above at n. 2, 91, 98–107 and 110–11.

and groups.⁷ Arnold wrote in the aftermath of the Great Depression and in the midst of the New Deal, a time when many reform ideas were in the air. The trouble with the schemes of idealistic reformers, observed Arnold—no matter how unanswerable the case for reform:⁸

> "is that they violate currently important symbolism. Therefore even if the reform is accomplished it is apt to find itself twisted and warped by the contradictory ideas which are still in the background in spite of the reform."

Today's "idealistic reformers" are largely economists, who glorify economic efficiency and give priority to the private sector and the "level playing field" of the market place. The influence of these ideas has been profound, transcending both national and ideological borders. The far-reaching structural adjustments brought about by these phenomena rival those wrought by the Depression.

The relevance of Arnold's insight to "the shiny new world of the late twentieth century"⁹ is two-fold. First of all, it seems to me to explain what can only be described as the haphazard experience of judicial review of corporatised entities, self-regulatory bodies and of contracting out initiatives. Second, the response of many lawyers to these "reforms" has been to distil the essence of administrative law for transporting to the newly deregulated and privatised areas. It is no coincidence, in my view, that the self-conscious identification of "public law values" dates back to the early 1980s in Britain and was a response to deregulation, privatisation and the underlying theoretical attacks on the "public-regarding" starting point of administrative law.¹⁰

The list of public law values includes openness, fairness, participation, impartiality, accountability, honesty and rationality, and while they were distilled primarily from administrative law there is much common ground here with constitutional law.

One tension between some of the papers in this volume is over the question whether the courts should extend these public law values into the newly deregulated and privatised environment. The perennial critiques of judicial review, reiterated regularly throughout the Commonwealth,¹¹ are given new impetus with the temptation to judges to fill the accountability vacuum left by the retreating state. This genre is represented in this volume by Mark

---

⁷ T.W. Arnold, *The Symbols of Government* (Yale University Press, New Haven, 1935), iv. On Thurman Arnold generally, see N. Duxbury, "Some Radicalism about Realism? Thurman Arnold and the Politics of Modern Jurisprudence" (1990) 10 *OxJLS* 11.

⁸ Ibid, 9–10.

⁹ *Hamilton City Council v. Waikato Electricity Commission* [1994] 1 NZLR 741, 759, per Hammond J. (H.C.).

¹⁰ See especially P. McAuslan, "Administrative Law, Collective Consumption and Judicial Policy" (1983) 46 *MLR* 1 and P. McAuslan, "Public Choice and Public Law" (1988) 51 *MLR* 687.

¹¹ See, e.g., R. Cranston, "Reviewing Judicial Review", in G. Richardson and H. Genn (eds), *Administrative Law and Government Action: The Courts and Alternative Mechanisms of Review* (Clarendon Press, Oxford, 1994), 45; G.D.S. Taylor, "The Limits of Judicial Review" (1986) 12 *NZULR* 178; W.H. Angus, "Judicial Review: Do We Need It?" (1974) 26 *Admin LR* 301.

Aronson, who prefers to see public law values insinuated into legislation and administrative schemes. In contrast, Murray Hunt's paper indicates greater willingness in the United Kingdom to view judicial review as one, but only one, accountability mechanism in this new environment. It appears that the degree to which judicial activism in this sense causes a stir in a particular society turns to some extent on the degree of satisfaction with the courts, legislature, executive and administration in that society.

This top down, court-centred approach prevalent in the United Kingdom[12] contrasts with bottom-up approaches, such as that advocated by Hudson Janisch and Ron Levi in their paper on police rulemaking in this volume. The vital role government lawyers play in inculcating and preserving public law values in the reconfigured administrative landscape is emphasised in Wade MacLauchlan's paper.

The recent emphasis on public law values allows the influence of administrative law doctrine and values to transcend the limited and uncertain contours of judicial review, and to cast a long shadow over the recently levelled terrain of what was once called public administration. Administrative lawyers armed only with public law values have to fight it out in the ideological trenches with those with competing views and values.[13]

Of central importance in this skirmishing is the public/private divide, which has its roots in liberalism.[14] Although the distinction is much criticised, its rumoured decline is greatly exaggerated.[15] It is well known that demarcating the public and private spheres of life is a complex, indeed tricky, business. It is done for many different purposes in many contexts. Although as a shorthand expression we refer to the public/private distinction, there is not one distinction but many. Almost all of them have in common that at some level or other the words "public" and "private" say something about the legitimacy or otherwise of state action, and the freedom or otherwise of the individual to pursue her own ends in her own way.

One useful way to view the distinction between public law and private law is in terms of Arnold's reference to "conflicting symbolism".[16] The difference can be seen as one of starting point. The starting point of private law, put

---

[12] See R. Rawlings, "Courts and Interests", in I. Loveland (ed.), *A Special Relationship? American Influences on Public Law in the UK* (Clarendon Press, Oxford, 1995), 99.

[13] Cf. M. Horwitz, "Law and Economics: Science or Politics?" (1980) 8 *Hofstra LR* 905, 912.

[14] See generally P. Cane, "Public Law and Private Law: A Study of the Analysis and Use of a Legal Concept", in J. Eekelaar and J. Bell (eds), *Oxford Essays in Jurisprudence, third series* (Clarendon Press, Oxford, 1987), 57. It should be noted, in light of Alison Harvison Young's paper in this volume, that feminism arguably also has its roots in liberalism. See C. Pateman, "Feminist Critiques of the Public/Private Divide", in S.I. Benn and G.F. Gaus (eds), *Public and Private in Social Life* (Croom Helm, London, 1983), ch. 12.

[15] Cf. D. Kennedy, "The Stages of the Decline of the Public/Private Distinction" (1982) 130 *UPaLR* 1349. The earlier attack on the public/private distinction by the Legal Realists was at best only partially successful. See W.W. Fisher III, M.J. Horwitz and T.A. Reed (eds), *American Legal Realism* (Oxford University Press, New York, 1993), 100.

[16] Above at n. 7, 17.

crudely, is the primacy of self-regarding behaviour. Whereas the point of departure for administrative law is the primacy of public-regarding (or other-regarding) behaviour. This distinction is brought out clearly by Laws J. in *R. v. Somerset County Council, ex parte Fewings*,[17] quoted in Dawn Oliver's paper.

Of course, there are many doctrines in the common law (quite a few of which have an equitable origin) which place limits on the private law's instinctive privileging of self-regarding behaviour, and legislative interventions are even more numerous and invasive. So much so that in particular instances the results derived from private law analysis may well approximate those derived from administrative law analysis. Starting points leading in different directions do not necessarily lead to different end points. At a reasonably high level of abstraction public law and private law share several underlying values, as Dawn Oliver demonstrates in her paper.

There is a good deal of interaction between the two bodies of law, and there is increasing evidence of cross-fertilisation.[18] As David Mullan points out in his paper, employment law is one area where the influence of public law values can be seen.[19] The implication of terms favouring the employee into the employment contract has been described recently as "a privatised form of judicial review".[20] But the trade is not all one way. For example, the law of trusts and fiduciary law has been called to aid in the recognition of a public trust doctrine, imposing a trustee obligation on politicians and public servants owed to the public they serve.[21] The poverty of public law in this area was illustrated by "fire sale" privatisations where publicly owned assets were sold by politicians sometimes at gross undervalues without any direct accountability.[22]

What we are witnessing in some areas at least is a synthesis or blending of public and private law principles.[23] The artificial separation of common law and statute law, and the common law's innate superiority complex, has blinded us to this blending in many areas. While the distinction between, and the symbolic functions of, private law and public law are unlikely to fall

---

[17] [1995] 1 All ER 513, 524.

[18] See C. Sampford, "Law, Institutions and the Public/Private Divide" (1991) 20 *Fed LR* 185, 210–14.

[19] See also *Marlborough Harbour Board* v. *Goulden* [1985] 2 NZLR 378, 385, per Cooke J.; G. England, "Recent Developments in the Law of the Employment Contract: Continuing Tension Between the Rights Paradigm and the Efficiency Paradigm" (1995) 20 *Queen's LJ* 557, esp. 573; C.J. Peck, "Some Kind of Hearing for Persons Discharged from Private Employment" (1979) 16 *San Diego LR* 313.

[20] R. Rideout, "Implied Terms in the Employment Contract", in R. Halson (ed.), *Exploring the Boundaries of Contract* (Dartmouth, Aldershot, 1996) 119, 120.

[21] See P. Finn, "Public Trust and Public Accountability" (1994) 3 *Griffith LR* 224. On the doctrine generally, see R.A. Epstein, "The Public Trust Doctrine" (1987) 7 *Cato Journal* 411.

[22] See generally C. Graham and T. Prosser, *Privatising Public Enterprises: Constitutions, The State and Regulation in Comparative Perspective* (Clarendon Press, Oxford, 1991).

[23] For an early exhortation along these lines, see W.G. Friedmann, "Public and Private Law Thinking: The Need for Synthesis" (1959) 5 *Wayne LR* 291.

away, the tension between them is being mediated in ways that look interestingly familiar to both public and private lawyers.

OF PUBLIC UTILITIES, RACECOURSES, CASINOS AND RESTAURANTS

The public/private law divide was not always firm. Madame Justice Claire L'Heureux-Dubé in her paper essays the judges' treatment of determinations by human rights commissions, but the stance of the common law towards discrimination is a tale worth telling in this context.[24] It illustrates how the law shifts over time (but almost always with some lag) in line with economic and political trends. But earlier, displaced ideas are never lost sight of entirely, and lie in the common law as resources to be rediscovered or utilised in legal and political argument. If nothing else they have symbolic importance. The story of the common law anti-discrimination principle,[25] or equality principle as it has sometimes been called,[26] also underscores the power (and arbitrariness) of legal classification. Furthermore, the interplay of statutory regulation and the development of the common law brings out issues of institutional competence and the respective law-making spheres of the judiciary and the legislature. In short, many of the issues explored in this volume can be seen at work in this area.

There are three inter-related but distinct doctrines which make up the common law anti-discrimination principle.[27] The first is the law relating to common callings. In the medieval period the common law defined and regulated the obligations of persons who followed callings in which labour or services were made available to the public. These callings were described as "common callings" because the goods or services were held out to the general public. There were dozens of common callings in the medieval period but by the turn of the 18th century the number had dwindled to the three that survive to this day—the innkeeper, the ferryman and the common carrier. The common law regulated these common callings by obliging them to serve all comers without discrimination and to charge only reasonable prices for their goods or services. Failure to do so would render the person or corporation liable under both civil and criminal law.

The second and closely related doctrine comes from the writings of Sir Matthew Hale in the seventeenth century, and is known as the principle of

---

[24] See also the paper by David Mullan in this volume.
[25] Note, "The Anti-discrimination Principle in the Common Law" (1989) 102 *Harv LR* 1193.
[26] C.M. Haar and D.W. Fessler, *The Wrong Side of the Tracks: A Revolutionary Rediscovery of the Common Law Tradition of Fairness in the Struggle Against Inequality* (Simon and Schuster, New York, 1986).
[27] Here I draw on earlier work and refer the interested reader to that work for elaboration and references to the literature. See M. Taggart, "Corporatisation, Privatisation and Public Law" (1991) 2 *PLR* 77 and M. Taggart, "Public Utilities and Public Law", in P.A. Joseph (ed.), *Essays on the Constitution* (Brooker's, Wellington, 1995), 214.

"business affected with a public interest". Here the common law extended a similar control over persons or corporations enjoying a *de jure* or *de facto* monopoly in the provision of services to the general public. The courts regulated these monopolies "in the public interest" and, required them also to serve the public at reasonable prices and without discrimination. This doctrine is especially well known in the United States where for nearly sixty years after the Supreme Court decision in *Munn* v. *Illinois*[28] the doctrine justified State legislation regulating prices and thereby deflected constitutional challenges to the validity of such legislation.

The third manifestation of these ideas is the so-called "prime necessity" doctrine, prevalent in Commonwealth law. This doctrine, which stems from the Privy Council decision in *Minister of Justice for the Dominion of Canada* v. *City of Levis*,[29] holds the suppliers of "prime necessities" with a practical monopoly under an implied duty to supply those necessities to all those requiring them and who are prepared to pay a fair and reasonable price.

The last two doctrines relate to what are commonly called "public utilities"; that is, companies providing the public (or a section of it) with gas, water, telephone, telegraph, transportation, telecommunications or electricity. Early on in America a coherent body of law developed under this rubric of public utilities. The defining characteristic of American public utilities law being the imposition at common law of duties to provide service to all, without discrimination, and at a reasonable price. In the 19th century the American courts accepted the analogy with the "common carrier" (especially the railroad) and extended the duty to serve without discrimination to gas, telegram/telephone, electricity, water companies and the like. To be sure, other factors were at work here—presence of a franchise, delegated powers of eminent domain, monopoly, and statutory immunity from suit—but it seems to me that the common calling analogy was very important in this regard, if not decisive. So here we have in 19th century America, important (in both social and economic terms) *extensions* of common calling status for the purpose of *common law* regulation of utilities. Puzzlingly, the British courts refused to so extend the "common callings" to the newly developing public utilities, and that regulatory role fell to the legislature. This ensured the fragmentation and marginalisation of these bodies of law, and retarded the development of a unified public utilities law in Britain for more than a century. It is only with the move to utility privatisation in the early 1980s that a body of public utility law worthy of the name has emerged there.

At the same time American courts were extending the common callings doctrine by analogy to public utilities of various sorts, those courts refused to extend the categories of common callings from inns or hotels to taverns, restaurants and places of entertainment to combat racial discrimination. In a recent interesting article, Joseph Singer has exhaustively documented the

[28] 94 U.S. 77 (1876).
[29] [1919] AC 505.

American courts failure to apply the common law anti-discrimination principle to theatres, restaurants and the like.[30] Singer argues that this was both a conscious judicial curtailment of common calling status and was racially motivated. This does not explain, however, why the same stunted legal development occurred even earlier in Britain, where race issues did not assume the same importance. This suggests to me that the rising tide of liberalism left the extant common callings of innkeeper, ferryman and common carrier high and dry as isolated islands of status-like obligation amid a sea of *laissez-faire* thinking in both countries (although I concede this leaves unexplained the cross-cutting extension of common calling liability in the utility sphere in the United States).

I want to move from public utilities to look at the common law's treatment of ejection from racecourses, casinos and then return to restaurants, taverns and theatres.[31]

Wood v. *Leadbitter*[32] is the all-but-forgotten case which established that a purchased ticket of admission to privately owned land (in this case, a racecourse) constituted only a revocable licence at common law, with the consequence that an owner can remove the patron at any time with or without cause. The ejected patron may have a common law action for damages, but likely this would only cover the cost of the ticket.[33] Moreover, and most importantly, the ticket did not create a proprietary interest in the land which the courts would enforce to prevent ejection.

This doctrine has had a somewhat chequered career. It was said in a 1915 English case to lead to "startling results" and not to have survived the merger

---

[30] J.W. Singer, "No Right to Exclude: Public Accommodations and Private Property" (1996) 90 *NwULR* 1283.

[31] In jurisdictions with Constitutions and/or Bills of Rights arguments that decisions by utilities to disconnect or by restaurants and places of entertainment not to admit or to eject patrons are "state action", and thus subject to constitutional scrutiny, have largely failed. For a recent survey of "state action" doctrine, see D. Barak-Erez, "A State Action Doctrine for An Age of Privatization" (1994–5) 45 *Syracuse L.R.* 1169.

A few Constitutions, however, have "horizontal" as well as "vertical" effect (for a discussion in a different context see Paul Craig's paper in this volume), so that discrimination by private individuals, companies or associations may infringe constitutional guarantees owed to other private individuals.

A good example is *Longive* v. *Intercontinental Hotels* [1993] 4 LRC 221, where the Zambia High Court held that the Hotel's policy of excluding women unaccompanied by men from entering the bar to be unconstitutional gender discrimination. Note that counsel for the successful petitioner argued, in the alternative, that the hotel was a public place, as regulated and licensed by the State, and reliance was placed on the innkeeper's common calling obligation (ibid., 223–4). The Court did not need to address this argument having found the Constitution to apply to both the State and the citizenry.

For a critique of the public/private divide in a comparative constitutional law perspective see A.S. Butler, "Constitutional Rights in Private Litigation: A Critique and Comparative Analysis" (1993) 22 *Anglo-Am LR* 1. See also A. Clapham, *Human Rights in the Private Sphere* (Clarendon Press, Oxford, 1993), ch. 6.

[32] (1845) 13 M & W 838; 153 ER 351.

[33] This was a later development. In *Wood's* case the jury direction upheld by the Court said that the ejected patron was not entitled to his guinea admission fee back.

of equity and common law,³⁴ but it was followed by Holmes J. speaking for the United States Supreme Court in *Marrone* v. *Washington Jockey Club of the District of Columbia*³⁵ and later by the High Court of Australia in *Cowell* v. *Rosehill Racecourse Co. Ltd.*³⁶

Leaving to one side the intricacies of proprietary interests in land and the merger of common law and equity, the revocable licence analysis originating in *Wood* v. *Leadbitter* conceived of ejection in private law property and contractual terms. The land owner having the unfettered discretion to revoke the licence at any time, for good, bad or no reason, without being under any duty to explain why or to hear the patron; whose only remedy would be to sue for damages for breach of contract, which would likely be nominal even if the action succeeded. This completely one-sided analysis flowed from the private law rights of property owners and contractual analysis. It should be noted that the ejection in *Wood* v. *Leadbitter* was not racially inspired,³⁷ which may explain why neither counsel nor the Court referred to any of the sources of the common law anti-discrimination principle.

Sixty years later, and half the world away, more resourceful counsel was no more successful. In *Pollock* v. *Saunders*,³⁸ a professional bookmaker who had been ejected from a racecourse, sued the club on the ground that as it operated a state-licensed totalisator machine on the course the racecourse was "affected with a public interest" and hence the public had the right to enter and bet on the totalisator. This ingenious argument, relying on a thin line of English and American authority, was rejected by the New Zealand Court of

---

³⁴ *Hurst* v. *Picture Theatres Ltd.* [1915] 1 KB 1, 5, per Buckley L.J. The ground of ejection from the movie theatre in *Hurst's* case was the management's mistaken belief that the patron had not paid for admission. *Hurst's* case was followed by a majority of the British Columbia Court of Appeal in *Barnswell* v. *National Amusement Co.* (1915) 23 DLR 615. There a Black man was turned away from a theatre on the basis of an internal theatre policy not to admit coloured people. He successfully sued for breach of contract, and was awarded $50 in damages for humiliation, which award was affirmed on appeal. The report in the most accessible series of reports does not disclose the plaintiff's race or anything else suggesting that the case involved racial discrimination. I have relied here on the historical research of Constance Backhouse, "Racial Segregation in Canadian Legal History: Viola Desmond's Challenge, Nova Scotia, 1946" (1994) 17 *Dal LJ* 299, 337 and 343 n. 131.

³⁵ 227 U.S. 633 (1912). This was a racecourse case, and did not involve racially motivated ejection, but one of the cases cited with approval by Holmes J. did. See *McCrea* v. *Marsh*, 78 Mass. 211 (1858). This may be explained as a combination of what A.V. Dicey described as Holmes's "religious reverence for the dicta of Westminster Hall" (Dicey's review of O.W. Holmes, *The Common Law*, reprinted as App. II to Touster, "Holmes A Hundred Years Ago: *The Common Law* and Legal Theory" (1982) 10 *Hofstra LR* 673, 713) and Holmes' less than tender attitude to civil liberties (see Y. Rogat, "Mr Justice Holmes: A Dissenting Opinion" (1962-3) 15 *Stan LR* 3, 254 (2 pts)). Others have explained Holmes's position in *Marrone's* case as stemming from his profound distrust of the jury, and jurors' speculations as to motive. See A.F. Conard, "The Privilege of Forcibly Ejecting An Amusement Patron" (1942) 90 *UPaLR* 809, 819-20.

³⁶ (1936-7) 56 CLR 605. In that case Dixon J. referred specifically to *Burton* v. *Scherpf*, 83 Mass. 133 (1861), where, following *Wood* v. *Leadbitter*, the Supreme Court of Massachusetts permitted the ejection of an African-American from a public concert: ibid., 638–9.

³⁷ The ejection was on the ground of "some alleged malpractices . . . on a former occasion, connected with the turf": above at n. 32, 838; 352.

³⁸ (1897) 15 NZLR 581.

Appeal, which inferred from the "extreme paucity" of case-law that "the interference with and restriction of the rights of private property, if allowed at all, must be allowed with great care, and only in cases where the necessities of the case require it",[39] and this was not such a case.

What Sir Stephen Sedley has described as "the long sleep" of English administrative law[40] has been credited with contributing to the absence of an anti-discrimination principle in modern English common law.[41] However, in recent times in Australia a partial administrative law solution has emerged to the problem of ejection and exclusion from racecourses. In these cases the High Court of Australia has relied on many of the factors which in earlier times justified common law regulation of common callings and businesses affected with a public interest. Emphasis has been given to the detailed statutory scheme regulating racing and betting; the multi-faceted roles and monopolistic position of the Racing and Gaming Commission, and its authorisation of race meetings held by registered clubs; the "holding out" of race meetings to the public, and the consequent legitimate expectation that upon payment of a fee members of the public will be admitted. As Aickin J. noted in the first case, *Heatley v. Tasmanian Racing and Gaming Commission*,[42] racecourses "are in a practical sense 'open to the public' " giving rise to an expectation that members of the public will be freely admitted on payment of a fee.

These factors, plus the detriment suffered by the patron by unilateral exclusion from a racecourse, persuaded the majority in *Heatley's* case to temper the statutory power to exclude individuals from racecourses with procedural fairness. By the very nature of procedural protection this requires the racecourse authorities to provide the gist of their reasons for proposing exclusion, something that the revocable licence analysis did not. While it is possible in theory to cleave procedure and substance, in practice this proves much more difficult, and in many instances is impossible.

In a subsequent case, *Forbes v. New South Wales Trotting Club Ltd.*,[43] again a majority of the High Court of Australia read a rule of the New South Wales Trotting Club authorising the exclusion of any person from any course as subject to procedural fairness. The Club sought to justify its action as an exercise of its proprietary right as owner to exclude or eject whomever it liked (which was argued to be independent of its power of exclusion under the Club's rules). The majority rejected this justification on several grounds. Of particular interest for my purpose is the widest ground, staked out by Murphy J.:[44]

---

[39] (1897) 15 NZLR 581, 589, per Denniston J.
[40] "The Sound of Silence: Constitutional Law Without a Constitution" (1994) 110 *LQR* 270, 282.
[41] C. McCrudden, "Racial Discrimination", in C. McCrudden and G. Chambers (eds), *Individual Rights and the Law in Britain* (Clarendon Press, Oxford, 1994), 409, 411.
[42] (1976–7) 137 CLR 487, 507.
[43] (1978–9) 143 CLR 242.
[44] Ibid., 274–6.

"the respondent exercises power which significantly affects members of the public, tens of thousands of whom go to watch the spectacles, many to bet as a hobby, and some, like the appellant, to try to make a living by betting. . . . The functions of the respondent in relation to the conduct of race meetings on its land are qualitatively different from that of the ordinary householder exercising his private property rights. . . . A householder exercising his property rights of exclusion is not in the same position as persons with licences to conduct public halls, restaurants, theatres or racecourses. From early times, the common law has declined to regard those who conduct public utilities, such as inns, as entitled to exclude persons arbitrarily. However, in *Cowell* v. *Rosehill Racecourse Co. Ltd.*, the Court, in my opinion wrongly, dealt with exclusion from a racecourse as if the case were concerned with private rights only. . . .

When rights are so aggregated that their exercise affects members of the public to a significant degree, they may often be described as public rights and their exercise as that of public power. . . . There is a difference between public and private power but, of course, one may shade into the other. . . .

When one departs from the purely domestic area of householder and from contracts affecting only individuals, into the sphere where there is an accumulation of rights the exercise of which affects the public to a significant degree, then increasingly, requirements of due process are imposed and arbitrary and unreasonable conduct is not permitted. . . . The stage has been reached where the exercise of power to exclude a person indefinitely from a public racecourse should be treated as public power subject to due process."

Although the Trotting Club refused to give Forbes reasons for his purported exclusion from the racecourses (which the High Court held to be invalid, for procedural unfairness) it appears his only sin was that he was too successful at on-course betting due to his astute observation of the horses' condition at the track.

This aspect of the decision, as well as the broader reasoning of Murphy J., resonates with the most liberal United States authority involving the exclusion of successful gamblers from casinos. Casinos, like horse racing, are a heavily regulated activity and in both cases the State benefits significantly by way of taxation.[45] The plaintiff in *Uston* v. *Resorts International Hotel Ltd.*[46] was a professional and highly successful "card counter", who had been given notice of exclusion from this Hotel's gambling tables. The Supreme Court of New Jersey held that the Casino Control Act reposed the power to exclude in the Casino Control Commission, not the individual Casino, but went on to carefully consider the Casino's claim that it had the right at common law to exclude anyone for any reason. The Court held the right of an amusement place owner to exclude unwanted patrons had to be balanced against the

---

[45] Note, "Arbitrary Exclusion of 'Undesirable' Racetrack and Casino Patrons: The Courts' Illusory Perception of Common Law Public/Private Distinctions" (1983) 32 *Buffalo LR* 699, 702–3.

[46] 445 A. 2d 370 (1982).

patron's competing right of reasonable access to such facilities.[47] Pashman J. said for the Court:[48]

> "when property owners open their premises to the general public in the pursuit of their own property interests, they have no right to exclude people unreasonably. On the contrary, they have a duty not to act in an arbitrary or discriminatory manner towards persons who come on their premises. That duty applies not only to common carriers . . . , innkeepers . . . , owners of gasoline service stations . . . or to private hospitals . . . , but to all property owners who open their premises to the public. Property owners have no legitimate interest in unreasonably excluding particular members of the public when they open their premises for public use."

The Court held that in the absence of a valid Commission regulation excluding card counters, Uston was free to employ his card-counting strategy at the Hotel's blackjack tables.[49]

These cases involving racecourses and casinos concern ejection or exclusion for reasons other than race. There is considerable evidence, however, that in the sphere of theatres, restaurants, taverns and places of entertainment the facially neutral doctrine of revocable licence was applied in a racially discriminatory fashion both in the United States[50] and Canada.[51] I will focus here on the Canadian experience.[52]

In two early cases courts in Quebec and British Columbia awarded damages for racially motivated ejection from theatres.[53] Thereafter there is an unbroken string of cases (which largely ignore the earlier ones to the contrary) in which Canadian courts applied freedom of contract doctrine and revocable licence analysis to deny relief to Blacks refused service in taverns, restaurants, theatres, etc.[54] Typically the majority judges in these cases saw no relevance in the state licensing and regulatory underpinning of these enterprises, and they consistently refused to extend the common calling obligations of innkeepers and hoteliers to persons operating taverns, restaurants and theatres.

These cases are punctuated by dissenting judgments,[55] often in resounding terms, which reach back into the past, extracting the essence of common call-

---

[47] 445 A. 370, 373 (1982).
[48] Ibid., 375 (citations omitted).
[49] The Court noted that the Commission currently had no regulation governing card counters, and expressly declined to decide whether the Commission had power under the Casino Control Act to exclude card counters from New Jersey's casinos.
[50] See generally Singer, above at n. 30.
[51] See generally Backhouse, above at n. 34.
[52] See Backhouse, ibid., 321-34 and H. Molot, "The Duty of Business to Serve the Public: Analogy to the Innkeeper's Obligation" (1968) 46 *Can BR* 612.
[53] *Johnson v. Sparrow* (1899) 15 C.S. 104 (Quebec S.C.) and *Barnswell v. National Amusement Co.*, above at n. 34.
[54] See *Loew's Montreal Theatres Ltd.* v. *Reynolds* (1921) 30 R.J.Q. 459 (Quebec K.B.); *Franklin v. Evans* (1924) 55 OLR 349 (Ont. H.C.); *Christie v. The York Corporation* [1940] 1 DLR 81 (S.C.C.); *Rogers v. Clarence Hotel Co. Ltd.* [1940] 3 DLR 583 (B.C.C.A.).
[55] See, e.g., *Loew's Montreal Ltd.* v. *Reynolds*, ibid. (dissent by Carroll J.); *Christie v. The York Corporation*, ibid. (dissent by Davis J.); *Rogers v. Clarence Hotel Co. Ltd.*, ibid. (dissent by O'Halloran J.). For a complete list, see Backhouse, above at n. 34, 321–34.

ings law and business "affected with a public interest" doctrine to apply in new social circumstances.[56] Of particular note, in light of David Dyzenhaus's paper in this volume, is the emphasis on equality. In the early case of *Johnson* v. *Sparrow* Archibald J. stressed the democratic character of the Canadian constitution which did not admit of distinctions of races or classes: "All men are equal before the law and each has equal rights as a member of the community".[57] Similarly, in dissent in *Rogers* v. *Clarence Hotel Co. Ltd.* O'Halloran J.A. said:[58]

> "refusal to serve the respondent solely because of his colour and race is contrary to the common law, [which] is founded upon the equality of all British citizens before the law. . . . All British subjects have the same rights and privileges under the common law—it makes no difference whether white or coloured; or of what class, race or religion."

Ideas have their seed-time and their fruit-time,[59] and it was not long after *Rogers* case that the "gap" in the common law exposed by this line of cases began to be filled by federal and provincial anti-discrimination legislation.[60] The first Canadian statute to prohibit racial discrimination in "hotels, victualling houses, theatres or other places to which the public is customarily admitted" was the Saskatchewan Bill of Rights Act 1947.[61]

The noted Canadian jurist Bora Laskin thought this was quite the right way round. Laskin saw rights of equality as matters to be addressed primarily by the legislature, as the positive state intervention required could only come through legislation, not through adjudication.[62] The lessons learnt at Harvard in the 1930s and afterwards taught Laskin that an active role for the judiciary in relation to social and economic issues was likely to cut against the interests of those who most needed help. As Sharpe observed of Laskin's thought on this issue, "[a]n active judicial role was something to be feared rather than encouraged".[63]

Something of Laskin's unease with such a judicial role can be sensed in his case note on *Christie* v. *The York Corporation*,[64] the 1940 case in which a

---

[56] The outstanding example is O'Halloran J.'s dissent in *Rogers* v. *Clarence Hotel Co. Ltd.*, ibid., which draws copiously on the various doctrines that make up the common law anti-discrimination principle. For a sympathetic but critical comment on what we might call today judicial "overkill", see C.A. Wright, "Discrimination—Licensed Beer Parlour Refusing To Serve Negro" (1946) 18 *Can BR* 730.
[57] Above at n. 53, 107 (translated by Backhouse, above at n. 34, 344).
[58] Above at n. 54, 588.
[59] F. Frankfurther, "Introduction" to "A Symposium on Administrative Law Based Upon Legal Writings 1931–33" (1933) 18 *Iowa LR* 129.
[60] W.D.K. Kernaghan, "Civil Liberties in the Canadian Community", in C. Beck (ed.), *Law and Justice: Essays in Honor of Robert S. Rankin* (Duke University Press, Durham, 1970), 323, 342.
[61] Backhouse, above at n. 34, 332.
[62] See generally R.J. Sharpe, "Bora Laskin and Civil Liberties" (1985) 35 *UTLJ* 632 and esp. 633 and 637.
[63] Ibid., 638.
[64] Above at n. 54.

majority of the Supreme Court of Canada (Davis J. dissenting) held that freedom of commerce is a general principle of law in Quebec which entitled the licensed tavern keeper to refuse to serve beer to coloured people. In observing that no question of innkeepers' common calling liability arose in the case of a tavern, he said in a disapproving tone: "whatever may be said nowadays as to the desirability of perpetuating old 'innkeeper's law' when the conditions which prompted its development have long since disappeared".[65] Although critical of the majority decision and preferring, "especially on grounds of policy", the dissenting view of Davis J., Laskin clearly favoured an administrative regulatory solution to discriminatory practices (which he described in a footnote as a "public utility" approach to the issue).[66]

Forty years later, long after Canada had embraced the Human Rights Codes and administrative enforcement machinery hoped for by Laskin,[67] the competing views of relative institutional competence were played out in the fascinating case of *Board of Governors of Seneca College of Applied Arts and Technology v. Bhadauria*.[68]

Dr. Bhadauria alleged that she was refused employment because of her ethnic origin and, instead of filing a complaint under the Ontario Human Rights Code, she came directly to court claiming damages for discrimination. The College sought to have the claim struck out as disclosing no reasonable cause of action, but in a wide-ranging judgment, Bertha Wilson J.A, speaking for the Ontario Court of Appeal, recognised a new tort of discrimination.[69] Against the background of authorities such as *Constantine v. Imperial London Hotels Ltd.*,[70] O'Halloran J.A.'s dissent in the *Rogers* case and *Re Drummond Wren*,[71] Wilson J.A. saw the preamble to the Ontario Human Rights Code as evidencing "the public policy of [the] Province [of Ontario] respecting fundamental human rights" and thought it appropriate that the declared rights of equality and freedom from discrimination "receive the full protection of the common law".[72] Wilson J.A. did not regard the presence of the Code "as at all impeding the appropriate development of the common law in this important area", as the fundamental human rights were recognised in the Code but

---

[65] B. Laskin, "Tavern Refusing to Serve Negro—Discrimination" (1940) 18 *Can BR* 314. See also *Holmberg v. Sault Ste. Marie Public Utilities Commission* (1966) 58 DLR (2d) 125, 132, per Laskin J.A. (Ont. C.A.): "I do not think that the ancient law governing such 'public callings' as carriers and innkeepers can be applied to the statutory authority vested in municipal corporations and public utility commissions under the *Public Utilities Act*".

[66] Ibid., 316.

[67] For an overview, see B. Vizkelety, "Discrimination, the Right to Seek Redress and the Common Law: A Century-Old Debate" (1992) 15 *Dal LJ* 304.

[68] [1981] 2 SCR 181.

[69] *Bhadauria v. Board of Governors of Seneca College of Applied Arts and Technology* (1979) 105 DLR (3d) 707.

[70] [1944] 1 KB 693, discussed in David Mullan's paper in this volume.

[71] [1945] 4 DLR 674.

[72] Above at n. 69, 715.

not created by it.⁷³ Nor did she see in the Code any legislative intention to exclude the common law remedy.⁷⁴

On further appeal to the Supreme Court of Canada, Chief Justice Bora Laskin, coming to the end of a long and distinguished judicial career, had the opportunity to display his constancy of view. He could not have agreed less with the approach of the court below. Laskin C.J. recited the substantive and enforcement provisions of the Code, proclaiming its obvious "comprehensiveness".⁷⁵ The Chief Justice acknowledged the "possibility of a breakdown in enforcement" due to the exercise of Ministerial discretion at various points in the process, but this was viewed as simply "an element in the scheme" and not as justifying a civil suit to fill the potential gap.⁷⁶ Presumably any misperformance of such duties was a matter for political and legislative, but not judicial, concern.

Laskin C.J. assailed the "new" tort as an "economic" tort created by "judicial fiat", the subject matter of which had no analogue in tort law, and nor was it supported by the background cases referred to by Wilson J.A.⁷⁷ The force of the dissenting judgment of O'Halloran J.A. in *Roger's* case, relied on by Wilson J.A., was said to be weakened somewhat by reliance on an innkeeper case; which law, Laskin C.J. said, had developed historically along different lines from that respecting restaurants and taverns.⁷⁸

This "bold" attempt by the Ontario Court of Appeal "to advance the common law", Laskin C.J. concluded, was "foreclosed by the legislative initiative which overtook the existing common law in Ontario and established a different regime which does not exclude the Courts but rather makes them part of the enforcement machinery under the Code".⁷⁹

Hudson Janisch has rightly said that the *Bhadauria* case exemplifies Laskin's belief in the efficacy of the administrative process,⁸⁰ a belief unshaken at the time by criticism of the operation of the Ontario human rights machinery.⁸¹ Since then the political winds have not been kind to human rights commissions across Canada: the list of woes include budget-cutting, staff reductions, heavy and increasing case loads, long delays in processing complaints, increasingly formalised procedures, under-enforcement, patronage

---

⁷³ Idem.
⁷⁴ Idem.
⁷⁵ Above at n. 68, 188.
⁷⁶ Idem.
⁷⁷ Ibid., 189–91.
⁷⁸ Ibid., 191. *Accord*, La Forest J. in *Yukon Order of Pioneers* v. *Gould* [1996] 1 SCR 571, 620, where membership in the Order was said to contrast sharply with services such as restaurants, bar and public utilities. The *Gould* case is discussed in the papers by Madame Justice Claire L'Heureux-Dubé, David Mullan and Alison Harvison Young.
⁷⁹ Ibid., 194-5.
⁸⁰ H. Janisch, "Bora Laskin and Administrative Law: An Unfinished Journey" (1985) 35 *UTLJ* 557, 562.
⁸¹ See, e.g., I.A. Hunter, "Civil actions for discrimination" (1977) 55 *Can BR* 106 and I.B. McKenna, "A Common Law Action for Discrimination in Job Applications" (1982) 60 *Can BR* 122, 135–6.

appointments, and what has been found to be their generally poor reputations among community organisations.[82] The attitude of the Courts in reviewing human rights commissions' determinations, written about by Madame Justice L'Heureux-Dubé in this volume, is yet another cross the commissions must bear, and may itself reflect in part the perceived malaise of human rights administration.

What lessons relevant to the papers in this volume are to be drawn from this brief account of the common law anti-discrimination principle?

Perhaps the first lesson is the surprise some readers will experience in seeing this topic treated in a volume concerning administrative law. This illustrates the importance and power of legal classification; a point seen in Jack Beermann's paper. "Legal categories are not simply housekeeping devices", as Gregory Alexander reminds us, ". . . [t]hey inhabit our imagination of what is acceptable, indeed, of what is possible".[83] There is no better illustration of that than the hardening of the arteries of common calling law. Nevertheless, as Alexander urges, we need to remind ourselves constantly that we created the categories and hence are capable of remaking them,[84] thereby liberating the legal imagination. This also can be seen in the case-law surveyed above.

The marked difference in public law and private law approaches revealed in the case-law is underpinned by the absence of an abuse of rights doctrine in the common law. This French-inspired doctrine is widely accepted in civil law countries and the Canadian civil law Province of Quebec, and basically prevents a right-holder abusing the right by exercising it for the sole purpose of harming another or for a purpose other than that for which it was granted or in an unreasonably disproportionate fashion. [85] The common law turned its face against such a doctrine at the end of the 19th century,[86] refusing to investigate the motives or reasons for the exercise of lawful powers by private individuals or corporations, no matter how discriminatory or harmful to the public interest. Nothing could be more at odds with the starting point of administrative law, and the absence of such a doctrine—unless and until this position is re-examined[87]—will hinder to some extent at least the blending or synthesis of public and private law, alluded to earlier.

---

[82] See generally R.B. Howe and M.J. Andrade, "The Reputations of Human Rights Commissions in Canada" (1994-5) 9 (2) *Canadian Journal of Law and Society* 1 and K. Norman, "Problems in Human Rights Legislation and Administration", in S.L. Martin and K.E. Mahoney (eds), *Equality and Judicial Neutrality* (Carswell, Toronto, 1987), 398.

[83] G.S. Alexander, "The Transformation of Trusts as a Legal Category, 1800–1914" (1987) 5 *Law and History Review* 303.

[84] Idem.

[85] The English-language literature on the doctrine is collected in J.M. Perillo, "Abuse of Rights: A Pervasive Legal Concept" (1995) 27 *Pacific LR* 37, 39 n. 2. The summarised version of the abuse of rights doctrine in the text is drawn from the new Civil Code of the Netherlands, quoted in Perillo, ibid., 40. For the law of Quebec, see *Houle* v. *National Bank of Canada* [1990] 3 SCR 122.

[86] *The Mayor, Alderman and Burgesses of the Borough of Bradford* v. *Pickles* [1895] AC 587 (H.L.) and *Allen* v. *Flood* [1898] AC 1 (H.L.).

[87] Perillo has drawn on the following developments to demonstrate that American law now recognises a doctrine of abuse of rights: abusive discharge of at-will employees, non-employment

The case-law also has a lesson for those, like David Dyzenhaus in his paper in this volume, who desire to reorient judicial review on a more democratic and hence legitimate basis, by taking equality as a starting point. The common law's protection of equality here (as elsewhere) was decidedly mixed. For those, like Mark Aronson in his paper and Bora Laskin, who might see the reference back to the "old learning" as unhelpful antiquarianism, the danger of placing one's faith solely in legislative and administrative processes may be illustrated by the treatment of human rights commissions in Canada. While the primary focus should and must be on those avenues, is it right to deny the courts any role? If I was arguing before a parliamentary select committee for the type of finely calibrated disconnection policies in relation to the poor advocated by Aronson, it would help to be able to refer to case-law invalidating discriminatory utility policies relating to the poor.[88]

The *Bhadauria* case also provides a somewhat different vantage point to observe the playing out of functionalism and pluralism, discussed in Alison Harvison Young's paper. Bertha Wilson J. was the first woman appointed to the Supreme Court of Canada (in 1982) and her record in relation to review for error of law (discussed by Alison Harvison Young and David Dyzenhaus in their papers) supported strongly a deferential posture to administrative agencies and their law-making. The continuities with Bora Laskin's thought and judicial posture in administrative law are obvious,[89] but *Bhadauria* illustrates real differences in approach and methodology. It is not obvious to me which way "contextualisation" cuts in a case like *Bhadauria*. Nor can it be assumed in administrative law more generally that "contextualisation" will always lead in one direction only (usually assumed to be the most liberal, progressive or whatever).[90]

BORROWINGS AND TRANSPLANTS

There is a tendency in Commonwealth countries to venerate United States public law, without fully understanding its operation in context.[91] This is especially so in relation to Constitutional law, to which administrative law in

---

cases of retaliation, threat to exercise a right as duress, bad faith in the performance of a contract, abusive refusal to consent to the assignment of a lease or franchise, abusive terminations of contracts, bad faith in enforcement of the contract, abuse of rights as a crime and a miscellany of abuse of rights cases: Perillo, above at n. 85.

[88] See, e.g., *Chastain v. British Columbia Hydro & Power Authority* (1972) 32 DLR (3d) 443 (B.C.S.C.).
[89] See Janisch, above at n. 80.
[90] This point is made in the somewhat different context of criminal law by N. Lacey, "Feminist Legal Theory Beyond Neutrality" [1995] *Current Legal Problems* 1, 18–19.
[91] For the identification of this tendency in the context of "public interest" litigation, see C. Harlow and R. Rawlings, *Pressure Through Law* (Routledge, London, 1992), 124–6 and 290–3.

the United States plays second fiddle.⁹² In contrast to the popularity of Constitution-watching from afar, American administrative law is a closed book to most Commonwealth administrative lawyers. This is due in large part to the domination of the subject by the federal and state Administrative Procedure Acts, whose concepts require a significant amount of "decoding" to be useful for comparative purposes.

Jack Beermann's paper in this volume is a welcome introduction to federal United States administrative law and its constitutional aspects. It allows administrative lawyers outside the United States to draw informed comparisons between the reach of procedural fairness in Commonwealth jurisdictions and that of "due process" in the United States. As to the applicability of judicial review (in the administrative law sense), one has to be struck by the similarity between the Supreme Court decision in *Lebron* v. *National Railroad Passenger Corporation*⁹³ and the Privy Council decision in *Mercury Energy Ltd.* v. *Electricity Corporation of New Zealand.*⁹⁴

United States administrative law is a rich source of case-law, theory and ideas—as Alfred Aman's paper on the impact of globalisation on administrative law shows—often dealing with cutting-edge issues first. While it must constantly be borne in mind that the constitutional and administrative laws of a particular country are uniquely products of that society's history and culture, inevitably as judges and jurists learn about the public laws of other countries "borrowings" take place.⁹⁵

Increasingly North American doctrine and practice in relation to scope of review is being looked to with interest and sometimes envy from outside.⁹⁶ Scope of review is the American term for judicial review of statutory interpretation by administrative agencies, which in the Commonwealth is variously described as jurisdictional error or review for error of law. The American case-law and the literature on this topic is large and sophisticated, and has clearly influenced Canadian law.⁹⁷ This should not be a surprise as Canada is a "natural meeting ground" of the British and American administrative law traditions.⁹⁸

To an outside observer the most distinctive and striking feature of Canadian administrative law is the commitment to judicial restraint or deference.⁹⁹ This is symbolised by the oviferous decision of the Supreme Court of

---

⁹² Note, e.g., the attempt to find non-constitutional public law space for administrative law in J. Vining, *Legal Identity: The Coming of Age of Public Law* (Yale University Press, New Haven, 1978).

⁹³ 115 S. Ct. 961 (1995), discussed by Jack Beermann and Alfred Aman in their papers.

⁹⁴ [1994] 2 NZLR 385, discussed in David Mullan's paper.

⁹⁵ See D. Feldman, "Courts, Constitutions and Commentators: Interpreting the Invisible" (1993-4) 16 *Holdsworth LR* 37.

⁹⁶ See, e.g., P. Bayne, "The Court, the Parliament and the Government—Reflections on the Scope of Judicial Review" (1991) 20 *Fed LR* 1, 32–40 and P.P. Craig, *Administrative Law* (Sweet and Maxwell, London, 3rd ed. 1994), ch. 10.

⁹⁷ M. Taggart, "Outside Canadian Administrative Law" (1996) 46 *UTLJ* 649, 650.

⁹⁸ H.N. Janisch, Review essay (1977-8) 4 *Dal LJ* 824, 830.

⁹⁹ Above at n. 97.

Canada in *Canadian Union of Public Employees Local 963* v. *New Brunswick Liquor Corporation*.[100] This case, and the vast case-law and commentary it has spawned, are discussed in this volume by Madame Justice L'Heureux-Dubé, Alison Harvison Young, David Mullan and David Dyzenhaus. The contrast with the prevailing view in the United Kingdom and elsewhere is stark, and underscores once again the different judicial temper in the various jurisdictions represented in this volume.

Looking further afield, John Allison in his paper sketches the importance of the State tradition in civil law systems and laments its absence in the common law. The theoretical and practical advantages of the common law accepting the significance of the "State" are then explored.

The pervasive influence of European law and institutions on the law of the United Kingdom is manifest. It may be expected, as Martin Loughlin remarked, that the "formalism and rationalism of continental jurisprudence . . . must have a profound impact on British public law".[101] But the common law, which Lord Diplock (as he became) once described as a maze rather than a motorway,[102] will not go down without a fight. For there is a "persistent Anglo-American attitude that our relatively unprincipled law of public situations has produced better practical results than those produced by the more highly organised and principled public law systems of the Roman-inspired world".[103]

This attitude is exemplified by Lord Wilberforce. In *Davy v. Spelthorne Borough Council*[104] he cautioned against applying the civil law distinction between public and private law, saying "typically English law fastens, not upon principles but upon remedies", and in another place said:[105]

> "[t]o extract certain concepts from French administrative law without the French procedures or remedies, and in relation to a vastly different legislative and administrative apparatus, may amount to a transplant that will not take."

By way of reply Roger Errera of the *Conseil d'Etat* noted that Lord Wilberforce also said that "something resembling a system of public law" was developing in England, [106] and asked "will not such a system have to 'fasten' on principles? If so, which ones?".[107] One thing is certain, however, the British "cannot develop a state tradition overnight".[108]

---

[100] [1979] 2 SCR 227.
[101] M. Loughlin, "Sitting on a fence at Carter Bar: In praise of J.D.B. Mitchell" [1991] *Juridical Review* 135, 150.
[102] *Morris v. C.W. Martin & Sons Ltd.* [1966] 1 QB 716, 730. For A.V. Dicey's description of "the province of 'so-called' constitutional law" as "a sort of maze", see his *Introduction to the Study of the Law of the Constitution* (Macmillan, London, 10th ed. 1959), 7.
[103] H. Levinson, "Towards Principles of Public law" [1970] *Journal of Public Law* 326, 344.
[104] [1984] AC 262, 272.
[105] Lord Wilberforce, "Foreword" to M. Taggart (ed.), *Judicial Review of Administrative Action in the 1980s: Problems and Prospects* (Oxford University Press, Auckland, 1986), ix.
[106] *Davy v. Spelthorne Borough Council*, above at n. 104, 272.
[107] R. Errera, "Changes in Judicial Review: An Outsider's Reflections" (1986) 64 *Public Administration* 189, 190.
[108] Loughlin, above at n. 101, 151.

CONCLUSION

Some will recognise this chapter's title as a borrowing from John Austin's book, *The Province of Jurisprudence Determined*. Given Austin's influence on A.V. Dicey[109] and the extent to which Dicey's "ghost" still haunts administrative law, as evidenced by the echo of his clanging chains in several papers in this volume,[110] that may be appropriate. But the question mark is new. Can the province of administrative law ever be determined?

The literature of administrative law abounds with references to the drawing of boundaries, and the expansion and contraction of these boundaries over time. Madame Justice L'Heureux-Dubé, following Cardozo, spoke in her paper of the ebb and flow of judicial review,[111] while others prefer the metaphor of a pendulum.[112] In a recent New Zealand case, Cooke P. openly acknowledged the variability of review over time:[113]

> "Like other branches of common law, administrative law develops and changes according to current perceptions of what is required of the Courts in their distinctive judicial function. . . . At times it becomes necessary to give especial weight to human and civil rights, including class or group rights . . . and of course in New Zealand race rights. At times the emphasis will be more on non-interference with the legitimate exercise of governmental or other administrative discretion."

Those that expected the province of administrative law to shrink in parallel with the contracting state thus far must be disappointed. The symbolic importance of administrative law and the liberation of its values from the confines of judicial review have played their part. It is a distinctive feature of administrative law in the common law system (leaving to one side the United States with its federal codification) that the reach of administrative law is whatever the judges say it is,[114] unless and until reversed by Parliament.

---

[109] See generally R.A. Cosgrove, *The Rule of Law: Albert Venn Dicey, Victorian Jurist* (Macmillan, London, 1980). Cf. D. Sugarman, "The Legal Boundaries of Liberty: Dicey, Liberalism and Legal Science" (1983) 46 *MLR* 102, 105–6.

[110] See the papers by Murray Hunt, David Dyzenhaus, Janet McLean and John Allison.

[111] The "tidal metaphor" is criticised in *Hamilton City Council* v. *Waikato Electricity Commission*, above at n. 9.

[112] See Wilberforce, above at n. 105, ix.

[113] *Thames Valley Electric Power Board* v. *NZFP Pulp & Paper Ltd.* [1994] 2 NZLR 641, 653.

[114] See also Sedley, above at n. 40, 277, where this point is made in relation to constitutional law.

2

Constitutionalism and the Contractualisation of Government in the United Kingdom

MURRAY HUNT

In the United Kingdom, as in other liberal democracies, the last decade has been a period of quiet revolution in public administration. Successive governments elected on political platforms promising to "roll back the state" have presided over changes in the mode of governance which have transformed the relation between public and private. In the United Kingdom the changes began in the most obvious way in the 1980s with the relatively straightforward transfer of public corporations to the private sector. Virtually all of the main utilities (telecommunications, water, electricity, gas, rail transport) are now in private ownership, subject in each case to a specific statutory regime of regulation.

In addition to privatisation in this most obvious sense, the reinvention of government has taken a variety of other forms. Activities previously subject to close administrative controls have been deregulated, and other activities formerly carried out directly by public bodies have been "contracted out" to the private sector. Perhaps most dramatically of all, however, the techniques of public administration have been refashioned in the mould of the private commercial sector. Many of the responsibilities of central government departments have been transferred to executive agencies, whose relationship with its parent department is regulated by a Framework Document. "Internal markets" have been introduced into the provision of the most fundamental of public services such as health and education, organised around a central separation between "purchasers" and "providers" of such services. Contract has replaced command and control as the paradigm of regulation.

As public lawyers we must not shrink from recognising the significance of what has happened. In short, the state has been reconceived on the model of market ordering. Such a development obviously has the most profound implications for public law. I propose to concentrate in particular on its implications for the notion of "constitutionalism". I deliberately use the term loosely throughout this paper to embrace the various ways in which it is possible to be committed to the notion that in any democratic system there are certain transcendent values which enjoy a "constitutional" status, in the sense that they embody fundamental ideals or aspirations which democracy itself presupposes and which therefore cut across the political programmes of particular governments. Although I use the term loosely, I will suggest that the bare minimum that is required of a commitment to constitutionalism is a rejection of the instrumentalist conception of law, which sees it as a mere tool to be used by governments in order to achieve their political goals, and a corresponding acceptance of the legitimacy of a judicial role in the protection and enforcement of constitutional values.

It is against this background that I turn briefly to consider some of the academic responses to the paradigm shift in public administration. Inevitably, the reception by public lawyers has been mixed. Harden, in an early and influential contribution, saw much of value in the shift to the contract paradigm of regulation, including great potential for the promotion of constitutional values such as individual rights, participation and accountability.[1] He sought to ensure that contractual discourse was not appropriated by the ideological enemies of public services, and explored the possibility that contract could provide the constitutional framework for the delivery of public services that had for so long been lacking in the United Kingdom. Norman Lewis, who in 1986, with Harden, famously lamented the lack of substance to the rule of law in Britain,[2] has recently gone even further than Harden in his embrace of the contract paradigm.[3] In an imaginative piece of legal futurology, he sees in the contract revolution the seeds of an exciting reconceptualisation of the United Kingdom's legal order in which the conditions for personal choice are constitutionalised and our choosing natures liberated.

I propose to focus in this paper, however, on a less optimistic strand of academic response to the contractualisation of government in the United Kingdom, exemplified by Prosser and Freedland. Tony Prosser, reflecting on his extensive comparative experience of the privatisation of public enterprises under different constitutional conditions,[4] is concerned at the lack of a constitutional dimension to the privatisation and contractualisation process in the United Kingdom.[5] He blames the Diceyan tradition of parliamentary sovereignty, and its associated emphasis on political rather than legal controls on government, for the lack of a developed concept of the state as something

---

[1] I. Harden, *The Contracting State* (Open University Press, Buckingham, 1992).

[2] I. Harden and N. Lewis, *The Noble Lie: The British Constitution and the Rule of Law* (Hutchinson, London, 1986).

[3] N. Lewis, *Choice and the Legal Order: Rising Above Politics* (Butterworths, London, 1996).

[4] See, e.g., C. Graham and T. Prosser, *Privatizing Public Enterprises: Constitutions, the State and Regulation in Comparative Perspective* (Clarendon Press, Oxford, 1991); M. Moran and T. Prosser (eds), *Privatization and Regulatory Change in Europe* (Open University Press, Milton Keynes, 1994).

[5] T. Prosser, "Bringing Constitutional Principles Back In", in R. Bellamy, V. Bufacchi and D. Castiglione (eds), *Democracy and Constitutional Culture in the Union of Europe* (Lothian Foundation Press, London, 1995).

wider than the government of the day.⁶ That lack of a constitutional concept of the state in the United Kingdom, together with a predominantly instrumental conception of law, are in turn related to the relative weakness of public law's autonomous response to the privatisation and contractualisation process. I shall have more to say below on the relationship between the Diceyan tradition and the judicial response to contractualisation, but for now it is enough to note that, for Prosser, the challenge posed to English public lawyers by the reconceiving of the administrative state is how to "bring constitutional principles back in".⁷

In similar vein, Mark Freedland has suggested that there are major concerns about the capacity of the English system of public law to respond adequately to the new challenges posed by the process of contractualisation.⁸ His article draws attention to some fundamental problems about the way in which English public law approaches the contractualisation of government, and suggests that there is a fundamental tension between the new patterns of public administration and English public law, which exposes serious deficiencies in public law's conceptual apparatus. In his view, probably the most significant of all the difficulties faced by English public law in responding to the challenge of government by contract is the public/private divide, and the restriction of judicial review to matters or decisions containing a public law element.⁹ Since this question, of who is amenable to the supervisory control of the High Court and in respect of what decisions and activities, goes to the heart of what the proper province of public law should be, I propose to take it as the focus for my study of whether English public law has the conceptual apparatus to assert constitutionalism in the face of concerted contractualisation. First, however, it is necessary to establish the theoretical framework in which this study will be carried out.

TWO VERSIONS OF "CONSTITUTIONALISM"

Underlying both Prosser's and Freedland's concerns appears to be an assumption that, due to Dicey's influence, there is no tradition of constitutionalism in the United Kingdom on which the courts can draw in order to assert some judicial supervision over formerly "state" functions where those functions manifest themselves in private form. The implication is that English public law, being founded on the Diceyan doctrine of the absolute and continuing sovereignty of Parliament, has no room for a notion of constitutionalism in which courts have a legitimate role in the protection of constitutional values.

---

⁶ Ibid., 38.
⁷ Borrowing J. Dearlove's phrase, "Bringing the Constitution Back In: Political Science and the State" (1989) 37 *Political Studies* 521.
⁸ M. Freedland, "Government by Contract and Public Law" [1994] *PL* 86.
⁹ Ibid., 100.

Indeed, in most accounts of Dicey's influence on English public law, it appears to be assumed that, in his famous "description" of the English constitution in his *Introduction to the Study of the Law of the Constitution*,[10] he identified the English system with a pure parliamentary sovereignty model, and rejected a constitutional rights model as being alien to English traditions. Indeed, for many writers, the "Diceyan model" and the sovereignty model are synonymous.

This paper proceeds on an interpretation of Dicey which differs from those accounts in emphasis only but in a way which has significant implications when it comes to assessing the capacity of English courts to respond adequately to the contractualisation of government. In essence the difference is that what Dicey both identified and helped to legitimate was not a pure sovereignty model of public law, but a thinly concealed compromise of a parliamentary sovereignty and a constitutional rights model, in which the courts do in fact exercise a jurisdiction of a constitutional nature in the shape of their protection of common law rights, but do so in a way which ostensibly accepts Parliament's absolute sovereignty. The sustainability of this interpretation rests on the significance to be accorded to Dicey's account of the "rule of law" ideal which he also identified as a distinguishing characteristic of the English constitution alongside the constitutional principle of parliamentary supremacy.

It is clear from his elaboration of the meaning of that ideal that, for Dicey, the rule of law was nothing short of the encapsulation of his particular Whig conception of societal ordering, according to which the individual's private rights, of property, personal liberty and freedom of discussion and association, ought to be sacrosanct from interference by the state.[11] The combined effect of Dicey's "kindred conceptions" of the rule of law, identifying the supremacy of the ordinary law of the land, administered by the ordinary courts, as one of the distinguishing characteristics of the country's constitution, was to make a claim for the supremacy of the rights protected at common law as fundamental rights. To claim that the general principles of the constitution were the result of judicial decisions determining the rights of private persons, that for example "the right to individual liberty is part of the constitution, because it is secured by the decisions of the courts",[12] was to claim that individual private rights recognised and protected at common law were, quite literally, "constitutive". His account of the rule of law, in short, does nothing less than constitutionalise private law rights and with them the private law model of adjudication by which they are determined. While claim-

---

[10] A.V. Dicey, *Lectures Introductory to the Study of the Law of the Constitution* (Macmillan, London, 1st ed. 1885).
[11] For a valuable recent demonstration of the political and historical contingency of Dicey's formulation of the rule of law, see B.J. Hibbitts, "The Politics of Principle: Albert Venn Dicey and the Rule of Law" (1994) 23 *Anglo-Am LR* 1.
[12] Dicey, above at n. 10, 197.

ing to identify and endorse the sovereignty model and unequivocally reject the idea of constitutional rights, Dicey in fact helped to legitimate a covert compromise between the two in which the courts professed unbending allegiance to the absolute sovereignty of Parliament while at the same time contriving to protect, mainly through statutory interpretation, selected values recognised and prioritised by the common law. The Diceyan model, in other words, was a particular version of constitutionalism.

Dicey's constitutionalisation of the private law paradigm manifested itself in the growth of administrative law in the face of the growing administrative state during most of the 20th century. Notwithstanding the courts' ostensible commitment to the sovereignty of Parliament, judges contrived to impede the achievement of the goals of the administrative state by, for example, interpreting wide discretionary powers strictly against background common law presumptions so as to minimise their impact on pre-existing private rights, and imposing onerous procedural requirements on decision-makers whose decisions affected such rights. This was an exercise in Diceyan constitutionalism: the judicial protection of certain property and liberty interests against the assault made upon them by the administrative state in the name of redressing inequality.[13]

It is only relatively recently that English public law has begun to mature into a more modern version of constitutionalism capable of co-existing with the modern administrative state. In the more modern version, courts are more explicit about the constitutional nature and legitimacy of the common law, but, instead of being a mere repository of "the old notions", as Willis would have described it, the common law is acknowledged to have the capacity to develop to reflect the principles underpinning rights-in-legislation. In recent years English courts have gradually moved beyond the ostensibly sovereignty-based approach of the Diceyan model, which effectively reduces them to the status of inferior bodies exercising a derivative or subordinate jurisdiction whenever a statute falls to be interpreted, towards the articulation of an independent basis for their review jurisdiction. They have also begun to formulate more general principles and standards of administrative law which it is the courts' function to police, in place of the more traditional catalogue of property, liberty, freedom of contract and other economic rights which were privileged in the Diceyan version.

What has been emerging is a more modern version of constitutionalism, which has an explicitly normative foundation, in the sense that it accepts the legitimacy of a judicial role in the protection of constitutional values, but which seeks also to accommodate the democratic concerns of the sovereignty

---

[13] John Willis famously described these presumptions of legislative intent as "a sort of common law 'Bill of Rights'": "Statutory Interpretation in a Nutshell" (1938) 16 *Can Bar Rev* 1, 17. Willis noted, "English and Canadian judges have no power to declare Acts unconstitutional merely because they depart from the good old ways of thought; they can, however, use the presumptions to mould legislative innovation into some accord with the old notions".

model without forfeiting a meaningful claim to "constitutionalism". This more modern constitutionalism rejects the Diceyan conceptions of the rule of law and the common law tradition, which privilege the private values of classical liberalism over the public interests advanced by regulatory legislation, but instead of jettisoning those concepts altogether it seeks to reconceive them in the light of our institutions' ostensible commitment to equality before the law and the equal freedom of all citizens. At the same time it rejects the instrumentalist conception of law as a mere vehicle for political will, but uses the democratic concerns which are said to justify the sovereignty of Parliament to inform the courts' conception of the limits of their role.

The doctrinal manifestations of this paradigm shift, from Diceyan to a more modern constitutionalism, are many and span the entire range of substantive public law. Judicial recognition of new administrative law principles and concepts such as legitimate expectation, public interest standing and (implicitly at least) proportionality, a more context-sensitive approach to procedural fairness, recognition of the presumptive importance of fundamental human rights, and the first faltering steps towards a more worked out doctrine of deference through the notion of justiciability are just a few examples of the transformation taking place. Recently both the courts[14] and the Law Commission[15] have explicitly recognised the concept of a "public interest challenge", which many would see as a defining moment in the shift from a private law to a public law paradigm of adjudication.[16] The transition, however, is far from complete, and English courts continue to veer unpredictably between confident assertions of modern constitutionalism and relapses into the Diceyan version.

The contractualisation of government presents a real threat to the completion of that transition, because it threatens to reinstate the private law paradigm at the constitutional level before enough judges have forsaken their old attachment to Diceyan constitutionalism. The great irony is that, just as English courts are on the verge of articulating for themselves a version of constitutionalism which gives them a legitimate role in the protection of constitutional values in the administrative state, that state, as it has traditionally been conceived, is starting to disappear, as the political branches promote the private over the public. Courts which remain wedded to Diceyan constitutionalism are unlikely to countenance judicial supervision of the expanding private sphere performing formerly "public" functions. This is partly because a Diceyan court considers its public law jurisdiction to depend on there being

[14] See, e.g., *R. v. Inspectorate of Pollution, ex parte Greenpeace Ltd. (No. 2)* [1994] 4 All ER 329; *R. v. Secretary of State for Foreign and Commonwealth Affairs, ex parte World Development Movement Ltd.* [1995] 1 WLR 386 (public interest standing); *New Zealand Maori Council v. Attorney General of New Zealand* [1994] 1 AC 466 (no order for costs against unsuccessful applicant in public interest challenge).

[15] *Administrative Law: Judicial Review and Statutory Appeals* (Law Commission No. 226, 1994), paras 2.5, 5.19 to 5.22, and 10.5 to 10.6.

[16] See A. Chayes, "The Role of the Judge in Public Law Litigation" (1976) 89 *Harv LR* 1281.

an exercise of derivative power to review, which there is not where a power is exercised pursuant to contract, and partly because the purpose of Diceyan constitutionalism in any event was to ensure the priority of the private over the public, a task which it is no longer necessary for courts to perform when such priority is already afforded by the political branches. The advent of the contractualisation of government has therefore made it all the more urgent that courts complete the transition from Diceyan to modern constitutionalism, because otherwise the province of public law will inevitably shrink as the private sphere expands.

It is against this background of English public law being in a state of transition from Diceyan to modern constitutionalism that I turn to consider the present English law on amenability to review, to demonstrate both the partial nature of the transition that has so far taken place, and the consequent urgent need for English courts to articulate the legitimate basis for their public law jurisdiction if they are to respond adequately to the contractualisation of government.

THE PROVINCE OF PUBLIC LAW DETERMINED: ENGLISH APPROACHES TO AMENABILITY TO REVIEW

For most of this century the approach of English courts to delimiting the province of public law faithfully reflected the premises on which Diceyan constitutionalism was founded. Whether a particular decision or activity was subject to the High Court's supervisory jurisdiction depended entirely on the source of the power being exercised. If it was statutory, judicial review was available, but if its source lay in private law, such as contract, administrative law remedies were excluded by the availability of private law remedies.[17] This position reflected the fact that in the Diceyan model the constitutional basis for the judicial review jurisdiction was the sovereignty of Parliament and the associated doctrine of *ultra vires*, while Dicey's particular conception of the rule of law ensured the priority of private law remedies over public. So long as English courts applied a pure "source of the power" test for determining the limits of public law, it was clear that the Diceyan model of constitutionalism was alive and well.

In a series of cases since the 1960s, however, English courts have gradually extended the scope of their supervisory jurisdiction so as to cover bodies exercising powers which have a considerable public impact but whose source is not to be found in any statute. This expansion of the coverage of judicial review was presaged in the now famous cases in which powers having their

---

[17] As Parker C.J. put it in *R. v. Criminal Injuries Compensation Board, ex parte Lain* [1967] 2 QB 864, 882: "Private or domestic tribunals have always been outside the scope of certiorari since their authority is derived solely from contract, that is, from the agreement of the parties concerned".

source in the prerogative were held to be reviewable. The trend began with the decision in *R v. Criminal Injuries Compensation Board, ex parte Lain*,[18] in which it was held that decisions of a body set up pursuant to prerogative powers were reviewable. As Sedley has observed,[19] the full significance of the decision in *Lain* went largely unnoticed for nearly two decades until the House of Lords in the *GCHQ* case[20] established beyond doubt the reviewability of prerogative powers notwithstanding their non-statutory source. The question left open in *GCHQ*, whether direct exercises of the royal prerogative are reviewable, has been answered in the affirmative in *Bentley*.[21]

This assumption of a review jurisdiction over non-statutory powers exercised by the executive marked an important shift away from Diceyan constitutionalism, in which the province of administrative law was dependent on the statutory source of the power, towards a more modern conception of constitutionalism. In the emerging new paradigm, the province of public law depended less on the source of the power being exercised and more on the consequences of its exercise for constitutional values which enjoy the presumptive protection of the High Court's public law jurisdiction.

However, this extension of the province of public law to the exercise of non-statutory powers only began to include the powers of what were formerly considered to be purely private or domestic bodies and tribunals with the decision of the Court of Appeal in *R. v. Panel on Take-overs and Mergers, ex parte Datafin plc*.[22] In that case, the Take-over Panel, which carries out an important financial regulatory function, but does so as part of a self-regulatory framework and "without any visible means of legal support",[23] was held by the English Court of Appeal to be judicially reviewable. Since the Panel "has no statutory, prerogative or common law powers and is not in contractual relationship with the financial market or with those who deal in that market",[24] the decision that it is nevertheless amenable to judicial review raises fundamental theoretical questions as to the constitutional basis of the courts' public law jurisdiction.

The significance of the *Datafin* decision is that it marked an important shift away from a source of the power approach to the province of public law towards an approach based on the nature of the function being exercised. Sir John Donaldson M.R. observed that it was possible to find in the law reports enumerations of factors giving rise to the courts' public law jurisdiction, but

[18] Idem.
[19] Sir Stephen Sedley, "Governments, Constitutions, and Judges", in G. Richardson and H. Genn (eds), *Administrative Law and Government Action: The Courts and Alternative Mechanisms of Review* (Clarendon Press, Oxford, 1994), 35, 39.
[20] *Council for Civil Service Unions v. Minister for the Civil Service* [1985] AC 374 (hereafter referred to as *GCHQ*).
[21] *R. v. Secretary of State for the Home Department, ex parte Bentley* [1994] QB 349.
[22] [1987] QB 815 (hereafter referred to as *Datafin*).
[23] Ibid., 824, per Sir John Donaldson M.R.
[24] Ibid., 825.

described it as "a fatal error" to regard the presence of all those factors as essential or as being exclusive of other factors:[25]

> "Possibly the only essential elements are what can be described as a public element, which can take many different forms, and the exclusion from the jurisdiction of bodies whose sole source of power is consensual submission to its jurisdiction."

The other two members of the Court of Appeal also rejected the source of the power as being the sole test for whether a body is subject to judicial review. Between the two ends of the spectrum at which the source of the power is determinative—that is, where the power is derived from either statute or contract—it would be "helpful" to look at the nature of the power as well to see whether the body is "exercising public law functions, or if the exercise of its functions have public law consequences", or if it is "under some public duty".[26]

It was clear from the reasoning in *Datafin* that the thrust of the decision was to move from a "source of the power" test for reviewability to a "nature of the function" test. This led some commentators to greet the *Datafin* decision as the welcome advent of a broad, functional approach to the question of what decisions of which bodies are within the province of public law, an approach which rested entirely on the consequences of the exercise of the power and the nature of the interests affected by it, rather than the purely formal consideration of the source from which the power emanated.[27] However, that shift was not complete, because the Court of Appeal retained the source of the power as one of the many different factors to be taken into account in determining the nature of the function. In determining whether a power is "public" in nature so as to attract the courts' supervisory jurisdiction, a court is to have regard to both the source of that power and the consequences of its exercise. The Court of Appeal in *Datafin* therefore achieved a hybrid of the two tests, by making reviewability turn on the "nature" of the functions of the body, to be determined by reference to both the source and effect of the exercise of its powers. Former Treasury Devil and now High Court Judge John Laws was therefore premature when in 1989 he said:[28]

> "The court will extend judicial review to bodies whose decisions have substantial consequences for members of the public or groups in circumstances distinct from the mere distribution of rights and obligations under private arrangements."

---

[25] Ibid., 838.
[26] Ibid., 847, per Lloyd L.J. See to the same effect Nicholls L.J., ibid., 850.
[27] See, e.g., C. Forsyth, "The Scope of Judicial Review: 'Public Duty' not 'Source of Power'" [1987] *PL* 356; M. Beloff, "Pitch, Pool, Rink . . . Court? Judicial Review in the Sporting World" [1989] *PL* 95, 108; D. Pannick, "Who is Subject to Judicial Review and in Respect of What?" [1992] *PL* 1; M. Sinclair, "Judicial Review of the Exercise of Public Power" [1993] *Denning LJ* 193; S.A. de Smith, Lord Woolf and J. Jowell, *Judicial Review of Administrative Action* (Sweet and Maxwell, London, 5th ed. 1995), para. 3–050.
[28] J. Laws, "The Ghost in the Machine: Principle in Public Law" [1989] *PL* 27, 29.

That formulation underplays the fact that, even after *Datafin*, the definition of "publicness" for the purposes of reviewability still required courts to look to the source of the power as one indication of its appropriate characterisation as "public" or "private".[29]

The *Datafin* decision therefore exemplifies the recent trend in English public law whereby courts have begun to make the transition away from the Diceyan paradigm towards a more modern constitutionalism, but have stopped short of articulating a sufficiently distinct basis for that more modern approach which is free of Dicey's influence. In this instance, the evidence of Dicey's continuing influence is the retention of the source of a body's power as one of the factors relevant to determining whether a particular decision has the requisite "public element". As a result, English courts have been unable to escape completely from the Diceyan model when determining the reach of public law. Although since *Datafin* courts have professed to apply the new approach based on the nature of the function, the judicial development of the test for "public element" or "public duty" demonstrates the continued vitality of Diceyan thinking in two respects.

First, courts have shown a marked reluctance to abandon reliance on "source" to justify the assumption of jurisdiction over the exercise of non-statutory powers, even resorting to fictions about parliamentary intention to justify the assumption of a public law jurisdiction over powers which are clearly not derived from such a source. Second, courts have continued to rely on the fact that a particular power has its "source" in contract, or some other consensual submission, in order to justify *not* assuming a public law jurisdiction over such powers. Each of these will now be considered in turn before returning to consider the extent to which this unsatisfactory half-way house is likely to impede a proper judicial response to the contractualisation of government.[30]

In a significant number of cases, whether the necessary public element or public duty is present has been said to depend on whether, if the body being reviewed did not exist, Parliament would have created such a body to carry out its functions. In R. v. *Advertising Standards Authority, ex parte The Insurance Service plc*,[31] for example, the advertising industry's self-regulatory authority was held to be reviewable notwithstanding that "it has no powers granted to it by statute or at common law, nor . . . any contractual relationship with the advertisers whom it controls",[32] because it was "clearly exer-

---

[29] See *Datafin*, above at n. 22, 838 (per Sir John Donaldson M.R.) and 838 (per Nicholls L.J.).

[30] Cf. the critique in Mark Aronson's paper in this volume of "the *Datafin* project" as deserving to fail because of its attempt to force the reality of mixed administration into the straightjacket of the legal paradigm. I do not share Aronson's scepticism of the *Datafin* response to the restructuring of the state, partly because I consider the "liberal legal paradigm" to be undergoing a significant reorientation around a quite different public law model of litigation, and partly because I consider judicial review to be merely one of a number of necessary tools for delivering accountability and legitimacy.

[31] (1990) 2 Admin LR 77.

[32] Ibid., 86, per Glidewell L.J. for the Divisional Court.

cising a public law function which, if the Authority did not exist, would no doubt be exercised by the Director General of Fair Trading".[33]

Similarly in *R. v. British Pharmaceutical Industry Association Code of Practice Committee, ex parte Professional Counselling Aids Ltd.*,[34] a voluntary self-regulating body which was part and parcel of a regulatory system controlling the advertisement of medicinal products in the public interest was held to be within the *Datafin* test for a "public element" and therefore reviewable. The Minister intended to regulate partly by means of regulations issued pursuant to a statutory power, and partly by supporting the voluntary controls of the self-regulatory organisation, and this was held to be sufficient to give the Committee the requisite "public aspect" to bring it within the scope of the High Court's supervisory jurisdiction.

In *R. v. Chief Rabbi of the United Hebrew Congregations of Great Britain and the Commonwealth, ex parte Wachmann*[35] Simon Brown J. summarised the approach which had been taken since *Datafin* and observed that it was a feature of all the cases in which non-governmental bodies had been held reviewable that, "were there no self-regulatory body in existence, Parliament would almost inevitably intervene to control the activity in question".[36] He said:[37]

> "[t]o say of decisions of a given body that they are public law decisions with public law consequences means something more than that they are decisions which may be of great interest or concern to the public or . . . which may have consequences for the public."

and later added:[38]

> "whether or not a decision has public law consequences must be determined otherwise than by reference to the seriousness of its impact upon those affected."

There must be "not merely a public but potentially a governmental interest in the decision-making power in question" for it to be reviewable. Such governmental interest was usually indicated by some support to the self-regulatory scheme in the form of statutory powers or penalties.[39]

In the case itself, the functions of the Chief Rabbi which were being challenged could not be said to be "public" because he was not regulating a field of public life which, but for his offices, the government would step in to regulate statutorily. Rather he was exercising intimate, spiritual and religious functions "which the government could not and would not seek to discharge in his place were he to abdicate his regulatory responsibility".[40] In *R. v. Imam*

[33] Idem.
[34] [1991] COD 228.
[35] [1993] 2 All ER 249.
[36] Ibid., 254.
[37] Idem.
[38] Ibid., 255.
[39] Ibid., 254.
[40] Idem.

of *Bury Park James Masjid Luton, ex parte Sulaiman Ali*, a challenge to a decision of the Imam as to who was eligible to vote in mosque elections was rejected on the ground that there was not a sufficient "public element", because there was no statutory underpinning and Parliament would not have intervened if the Imam did not exist.[41] Similarly in *R. v. Football Association Ltd., ex parte Football League Ltd*.[42] the same test of supposed parliamentary intent was applied, with the result that the Football Association was held not to be amenable to review, because there was no sign of any underpinning by the organs of the state, nor any indication that if the organisation did not exist the state would intervene to create such a body.

This is a highly artificial approach to the question of which bodies should be amenable to the High Court's supervisory jurisdiction. As Pannick has asked, "why should the jurisdiction of the court depend on a hypothesis as to what Parliament would do but for the existence of the body in question?".[43] The answer lies in the persistence of the judicial perception that, to be legitimate, everything the courts do in public law must be justifiable by reference to parliamentary intent. Such reference to the underlying purpose of the particular body is a way of analysing the control of non-statutory powers in terms of *vires* or jurisdiction, so bringing it within the traditional justification of the review power. Just as the extension of judicial review to prerogative powers is justified by some judges on the basis of a fictitious imputation of parliamentary intention that prerogatives which still exist only do so with Parliament's implied consent, so the extension of review to other non-statutory bodies which do not even derive their power from the prerogative is justified by reference to a wholly hypothetical parliamentary intention. Before the exercise of power can legitimately be subjected to the courts' review jurisdiction, it must be derivative, traceable ultimately to a parliamentary source. In this way all exercises of the judicial review power can be brought within the conceptual basis of *ultra vires* from which it derives its legitimacy.

The test for whether a body is "public", and therefore whether administrative law principles presumptively apply to its decision-making, should not depend on the fictional attribution of derivative status to the body's powers. The relevant factors should include the nature of the interests affected by the body's decisions, the seriousness of the impact of those decisions on those interests, whether the affected interests have any real choice but to submit to the body's jurisdiction, and the nature of the context in which the body operates. Parliament's non-involvement or would-be involvement, or whether the body is woven into a network of regulation with state underpinning, ought not to be relevant to answering these questions. The very existence of institutional power capable of affecting rights and interests should itself be a

---

[41] [1992] COD 132.
[42] [1993] 2 All ER 833.
[43] Pannick, above at n. 27, 5–6.

sufficient reason for subjecting exercises of that power to the supervisory jurisdiction of the High Court, regardless of its actual or would-be source.

Where a power is derived from contract, English courts have also demonstrated the persistent influence of Diceyan ideas on their approach to reviewability. In *R. v. Disciplinary Committee of the Jockey Club, ex parte Aga Khan*,[44] for example, many of the criteria which might have been thought to satisfy the *Datafin* test for "public element" were present. The Jockey Club was acknowledged to effectively regulate an important national activity, exercising powers which affected the public and were exercised in the public interest. It had been granted a royal charter. Those who wanted to race horses had no alternative but to be bound by the Jockey Club's rules. Most significantly, "if the Jockey Club did not regulate this activity, the government would probably be driven to create a public body to do so", and any statutory code administered by such a body would probably approximate to the Jockey Club's own Rules of Racing.

Notwithstanding the presence of all these factors, the Court of Appeal held that the decision of the Disciplinary Committee was not susceptible to judicial review because the sole source of its authority was the agreement between the parties. Although the Club's powers might be described as public, they were in no sense governmental and the Club was therefore not performing a public governmental function such as to attract the courts' supervisory jurisdiction. The applicant was therefore confined to his rights in contract against the Club.

This decision amounts to more than a narrowing of the *Datafin* "public element" test. It amounts to a reassertion of an approach in which the only relevant factor is the source of the power. The nature of the function, admitted to be "public" here, is irrelevant, because the lack of any statutory or other "governmental" source is determinative. The impact of the exercise of the power on those affected is equally irrelevant, because it is enough that they supposedly submitted to the Club's jurisdiction by agreement. Any taking account of the genuineness of that consent is precluded by the narrow concentration on the source of the power. The opportunity for such a return to what amounts to a wholly source-based test was made possible by the retention of the source of the power as an element in the so-called "functional" test for reviewability in *Datafin*. Until the true basis of the courts' jurisdiction over non-statutory powers is admitted, doctrinal relapses such as the recent decision in *Aga Khan* will be inevitable.

CONTRACTUALISATION AND AMENABILITY TO REVIEW

The retention of the source of the power as a factor in determining amenability to judicial review, and in particular the tendency evident in *Aga Khan* to

[44] [1993] 2 All ER 853 (hereafter referred to as *Aga Khan*). See N. Bamforth, "The Scope of Judicial Review: Still Uncertain" [1993] PL 239.

assert that a decision-maker deriving power from contract cannot be amenable to the supervisory jurisdiction, has given rise to concern about the ability of public law to respond to the contractualisation of government. For if government chooses to constitute the delivery of a particular service by way of contractual arrangements with private bodies, there must be a very real danger that courts will treat such activity as being beyond the reach of public law, and regulated by the private law of contract only. As Freedland puts it, the fear is of a total transfer of public activity into the private sphere and thereby into the realm of private rather than public law.[45]

So far there has been very little litigation in the United Kingdom arising out of the contractualisation of governmental activity to test whether such concerns are well-founded. In some cases the indications have been that the courts may indeed adopt a position on reviewability which, as Freedland observes, would enable the government to "privatise" its activities by placing their administration in the private sector, because it is thereby placing such activities beyond the reach of public law. In *R. v. Lord Chancellor, ex parte Hibbit & Saunders (A firm)*,[46] for example, it was held that the decision of the Lord Chancellor to award the contract for shorthand reporting services to a particular firm was not susceptible to judicial review at the instance of the firm which had held the contract for over 80 years. Moreover, that decision was reached notwithstanding that the court had already considered the applicant firm's public law challenge to the decision and found that the applicant firm had been treated unfairly in the tendering process, because the Lord Chancellor had acted in breach of its legitimate expectation by departing from the criteria contained in the instructions for tendering by giving an opportunity to submit lower tenders to certain bidders.

The Divisional Court took the view that the Lord Chancellor was only susceptible to judicial review in respect of those of his decisions which are either in some way statutorily underpinned or involve some other sufficient public law element, as to which, the Court observed, there was no universal test. Since the Lord Chancellor was exercising on behalf of the Crown what was described as a "common law right to contract", it was held that the decision to award the contract was entirely in the private sphere of commercial contracting and as such lacked the public law element necessary to make it susceptible to judicial review. The court was not prepared to accept the analogy between tendering conditions laid down pursuant to a common law right to contract and statements of policy or practice in the fields of immigration and revenue, which, it is well established, are capable of giving rise to a legitimate expectation.

---

[45] Freedland, above at n. 8, 102.
[46] The Times, 12 Mar. 1993. See D. Oliver, "Judicial Review and the Shorthand Writers" [1993] *PL* 214; S. Arrowsmith, "Protecting the Interests of Bidders for Public Contracts: The Role of the Common Law" [1994] *CLJ* 104, 104–13.

The decision in *Hibbit & Saunders* provides some support for the pessimistic view of Freedland and others that the entire conceptual framework of English public law is fundamentally unsuited to ensuring that constitutional values continue to be observed even as government and administration are increasingly contracted out to the politically unaccountable private sector. That decision, however, was concerned with the reviewability of the process of contracting out itself, at the suit of a rival tenderer disappointed by failing to obtain the contract. This does not necessarily provide much guidance as to the reviewability of the performance of the contract by the contractor delivering the services, at the suit of the third party (public) beneficiary of the contract. On the few occasions when that question has so far arisen in English courts, there is some indication that courts may be prepared to assert their jurisdiction over the delivery of contracted out services, and thereby ensure that constitutionalism survives contractualisation.

In *R. v. Governors of Haberdashers' Aske's Hatcham College Trust, ex parte Tyrell*,[47] for example, a disappointed applicant for admission to Haberdashers' Aske's College, a City Technology College (CTC), applied for judicial review of the College's refusal to admit him. City Technology Colleges were set up pursuant to section 105(1) of the Education Reform Act 1988, which provides that the Secretary of State may enter into an agreement with any person whereby that person undertakes to establish and maintain an independent school to be known as a City Technology College, and in return the Secretary of State agrees to make payments. By section 105(2) of the Act, the characteristics of City Technology Colleges are that they are situated in an urban area providing education for pupils of different abilities drawn wholly or mainly from the areas in which the schools are situated, whose curriculum is broad but with an emphasis on science and technology. Detailed regulation of the provision of education by such colleges is contained, not in regulations made by statutory instruments or other delegated legislation, but in the agreements made between the Secretary of State and the particular college. Under that agreement, payments by the Secretary of State are dependent on the fulfilment by the CTC of various conditions, imposed for purposes such as to ensure that the schools are non fee-paying. Haberdasher's Aske's College, which was formerly a school maintained by the Inner London Education Authority, entered into an agreement with the Secretary of State pursuant to section 105 of the Education Reform Act. The College was a charitable company limited by guarantee, with a Memorandum and Articles of Association.

The applicant, a disappointed applicant for admission to the College, sought judicial review of the decision refusing him a place on the ground that the criteria actually adopted in the admissions process departed substantially from those set out in the College's prospectus. On the preliminary

---

[47] [1995] COD 399; The Times, 19 Oct. 1994.

jurisdictional question of whether the CTC's decision was amenable to judicial review at all, it was common ground that admissions decisions of public sector schools were amenable to judicial review, but that such decisions made by private schools were not. The applicant argued that CTCs were to be treated as public sector schools for this purpose, because they owed their existence to section 105 of the Act, since no CTC could be established unless the Secretary of State entered into the agreement there envisaged, and they were wholly or partly publicly funded. They were amenable to judicial review, it was argued, because both their existence and their essential characteristics derived from the exercise by government of a statutory power. The City Technology College argued that such colleges were to be treated the same as private schools for the purpose of deciding whether or not their admissions decisions were reviewable. It had already been established, in R. v. *Fernhill Manor School, ex parte Brown*,[48] that the relationship between a private school and its pupils was founded on private contract and not underpinned by statute, and the College sought to argue by analogy that relations between a CTC and its pupils and their parents were consensual, and not regulated by statute. A CTC's constitution, powers and duties were not to be found in any statutory provisions but were contained in the company's Articles of Association and Scheme of Government.

Dyson J.'s view of *Datafin* was that it recognised that it was not a necessary condition of amenability to review that the source of the power was statutory or the prerogative, and thereby extended judicial review to a body whose birth and constitution owed nothing to any exercise of governmental power but which had been woven into the fabric of public regulation. Not surprisingly, on this approach, he held that the admissions decision of the CTC was amenable to judicial review. Significantly, in explaining why the position of City Technology Colleges was materially different from that of private schools, Dyson J. placed some reliance on the source of the power pursuant to which CTCs came into being. Their existence was said to derive from section 105 of the 1988 Act and the exercise by the Secretary of State of his powers under that section. Although section 105 did not literally establish CTCs, Parliament had provided in that section the means by which free education with an emphasis on science and technology in urban areas was to be funded, and by entering into the agreement with the College the Secretary of State had chosen to exercise that power. Certain fundamental characteristics of CTCs were imposed by section 105 itself, and the Secretary of State could through the terms of the agreement control aspects of the running of the school, including its admissions policies. None of these features was present in the case of private schools, which, although they operated within a statutory framework of control, did not owe their existence to governmental power.

[48] (1993) 5 Admin LR 159.

Thus far, Dyson J.'s conclusion that CTCs were amenable to review was dependent on distinguishing the source of their power from the wholly private source of a private school's power. However, he added a further consideration which he said reinforced that conclusion and which is of great potential significance in establishing the amenability to review of many of the bodies now providing services to the public under contractual arrangements with the government. If CTCs were not susceptible to judicial review, he held, pupils and parents would be left without a remedy if they were the victims of a wrong, because there was no contractual relationship between parents and CTCs.[49] It will, of course, often be the case that, while there is a contract between the purchaser of public services such as education, health or other social services and the provider, there is no contractual relationship between the provider and the public recipient of such services. If the mere existence of a contractual relationship between purchaser and provider had been treated by courts as sufficient to displace the supervisory jurisdiction, contractualisation would have deprived administrative law of a very substantial part of the area it currently occupies. The approach adopted by Dyson J. in *Tyrell* should help to ensure that such an eventuality does not come to pass.

A similar question as to the reviewability of ostensibly "private" bodies regulated by agreement arose in R. v. *Gwent Training and Enterprise Council, ex parte Ghafoor*.[50] Training and Enterprise Councils (TECs), are, like City Technology Colleges, limited companies whose relationship with the Secretary of State is governed by an Operating Agreement. Although not literally established by statute, TECs owe their existence to the exercise by government of a statutory power, namely section 2 of the Employment and Training Act 1973, as substituted by section 25(1) of the Employment Act 1988, empowering the Secretary of State to "make such arrangements as he considers appropriate for the purpose of assisting persons to select, train for, obtain and retain employment suitable for their ages and capacities or of assisting persons to obtain suitable employees". The terms of the operating agreement set out the respective responsibilities of the TEC and the Secretary of State for the funding, provision and support of training, enterprise and other activities. TECs are almost exclusively publicly funded, and through funding and the terms of the Operating Agreement the Secretary of State could exert control over the running of the TECs.

The applicant, who was disabled, sought to challenge the TEC's refusal to fully fund his place on a postgraduate course, arguing that, on the proper interpretation of the operating agreement between the TEC and the Secretary

---

[49] On the significance of the absence of any other remedy, see Sir Harry Woolf, "Public Law-Private Law: Why the Divide? A Personal View" [1986] *PL* 220, 224–5 and *Mercury Energy Ltd.* v. *Electricity Corporation of New Zealand Ltd.* [1994] 1 WLR 521, 526, per Lord Templeman ("Decisions made in the public interest by the corporation, a body established by statute, may adversely affect the rights and liberties of private individuals without affording them any redress").

[50] Unreported decision of Brooke J., Queen's Bench, 22 Feb. 1995.

of State, he was entitled to be funded. There was no contractual relationship between the applicant and the TEC, and if the TEC was not susceptible to judicial review he would have been left without a remedy in respect of any decision taken affecting him. The case therefore again raised the question of the extent to which the third party beneficiary is entitled to enforce by way of judicial review the terms of an agreement to which he is not a party.[51] Leave was refused on other grounds, but Brooke J. was willing to hold that it was arguable that TECs are amenable to judicial review notwithstanding that they are largely regulated by agreement.

AN OPPORTUNITY TO EXPAND THE PROVINCE OF PUBLIC LAW?

What is revealed by this brief survey of English approaches to amenability to review is that the contractualisation of government only presents a threat to the province of public law so long as English courts remain in thrall to the Diceyan version of constitutionalism. To the extent that English judges continue to adhere to an essentially Diceyan conception of their role and function, Freedland and Prosser are right to be concerned about the capacity of English public law to respond appropriately to contractualisation by ensuring that constitutional values are observed by private actors performing public functions. However, given the extent to which English public law has already moved away from the Diceyan paradigm, and reconceptualised itself in terms of a more modern constitutionalism, their assessment seems overly pessimistic. In the case-law on amenability to review, this move has manifested itself in the emergence of an approach based on the nature of the function being exercised. In this, as in all other areas of public law doctrine, two steps forward have been followed by one step back as the deep-rooted Diceyan premises reassert themselves, but the overall trend remains in the direction of the recognition of a modern version of constitutionalism. Provided that transition is properly articulated and conceptualised, it is arguable that the contractualisation of government in fact brings new opportunities for English public law to expand its province into what was formerly considered to be the exclusively private sphere. As contractualisation proceeds, the public/private distinction becomes less pronounced and a corresponding opportunity arises for courts to assert their general public law principles over all exercises of power, regardless of the source of that power.

Such an extension of the reach of public law to apply to private bodies has long been advocated in the United Kingdom by a number of commentators. In 1986 Sir Harry Woolf (now Lord Woolf M.R.) tentatively raised the question whether public law principles ought not to be equally applicable to

---

[51] Such cases reveal particularly starkly the overlap between the public law rules of standing and the private law doctrine of privity: see M. Taggart, "Corporatisation, Privatisation and Public Law" (1991) 2 *PLR* 77, 99.

powerful bodies whose actions were capable of affecting the public interest, regardless of the source of their power.[52] In 1987 Dawn Oliver, in an influential article questioning the theoretical justification for the supervisory jurisdiction, argued that bodies whose power affects the public interest or the rights or vital interests of individuals or organisations ought to be subject to judicial supervision as to how that power is exercised.[53] In 1989 Sir Gordon Borrie similarly argued for the regulation of private as well as public power by public law principles, suggesting that all those who wield power should be accountable and subject to general principles of good administration.[54] More recently, Andrew Clapham has provided a sustained and persuasive argument for the recognition and protection of human rights in the private sphere,[55] and both the United Nations Human Rights Committee and the European Court of Human Rights have recently fired some warning shots that states cannot evade their human rights responsibilities by contracting out state functions to the commercial sector.[56]

CONCLUSION

This paper has attempted to respond to the gloomy assessment of English public law's capacity to assert a notion of constitutionalism in the face of contractualisation. It has argued that the Diceyan tradition itself legitimated judicial control of reforming governments, when, in the days of the ever-advancing administrative state, it was the courts and the common law which ensured the priority of the private in the face of what were perceived as raids upon it in the name of the public by the legislature and the executive. Now that those values enjoy the political ascendancy, as Parliament legislates to prioritise the private sphere, and the executive acts to privatise administrative functions, the constitutional role acquired by the courts needs updating not discarding. If English courts continue to forsake the Diceyan model of constitutionalism as the basis for their jurisdiction, as many have been doing in recent years, and continue to make progress towards articulating the nature of that jurisdiction in terms of the enforcement of constitutional values in the face of exercises of power, the disappearance of any rigid public/private distinction may provide the long-awaited opportunity for public law to extend its fiefdom to the formerly "private" sphere of what at present still remains the largely unaccountable power of corporate interests.

---

[52] Above at n. 49, 238.
[53] "Is the *Ultra Vires* Rule the Basis of Judicial Review?" [1987] *PL* 543.
[54] "The Regulation of Public and Private Power" [1989] *PL* 552.
[55] *Human Rights in the Private Sphere* (Clarendon Press, Oxford, 1993); "The Privatisation of Human Rights" [1996] *EHRLR* 20.
[56] See, e.g., comments of the United Nations Human Rights Committee on the United Kingdom's Compliance Report (1995), para. 16; *Costello-Roberts* v. *UK*, Series A, No. 247-C.

3

A Public Lawyer's Responses to Privatisation and Outsourcing

MARK ARONSON*

THE PASSING OF THE OLD REGIME

It seems an eternity since Charles Reich's classic lament in 1964:[1]

> "Ahead there stretches—to the farthest horizon—the joyless landscape of the public interest state. The life it promises will be comfortable and comforting. It will be well planned—with suitable areas for work and play. But there will be no precincts sacred to the spirit of man."

Reich was protesting against the overweening discretionary power ceded to the state when dispensing welfare, pensions, contracts, or other forms of what he argued was wrongly called largesse. His protest was not against the welfare state as such, but against the debilitating effects upon the spirit of individualism of any pervasive state which predicates its action upon the "public interest". His concerns were at least consistent with those of mainstream administrative law scholarship of the time. Discretionary power was in those days seen as *the* great problem of administrative law. If it was to be legitimated, it had to be confined, structured and checked, according to the American scholar, Professor K.C. Davis. Writing in 1969, Davis devoted considerable attention to the processes of turning unnecessary discretions into rules, and into making those wielding necessary discretions more accountable.[2] On the other side of the Atlantic, Professor Wade wrote in 1961 that the state's expansion presented the threat of arbitrary power, whose great counterpoise was not rules but judicial power.[3] Each writer maintained his point of view for the next 30 years,[4] reflecting, no doubt, the different polit-

---

* The author gratefully acknowledges the funding provided by the Australian Research Council, the research assistance and comments provided by Naomi Sharp, and the comments and assistance provided by Jill Anderson, Annie Cossins, Denis Harley, Holly Raiche and Mike Taggart.

[1] C.A. Reich, "The New Property" (1964) 73 *Yale LJ* 733, 778.

[2] K.C. Davis, *Discretionary Justice: A Preliminary Inquiry* (University of Chicago Press, Urbana, 1969).

[3] H.W.R. Wade *Administrative Law* (Clarendon Press, Oxford, 1st ed. 1961), 1.

[4] K.C. Davis and R.J. Pierce Jr, *Administrative Law Treatise* (Little Brown & Co, Boston, 3rd ed. 1994), vol. 1, 260–66 and 365–70 and H.W.R. Wade and C.F. Forsyth, *Administrative Law* (Clarendon Press, Oxford, 7th ed. 1994), 4–7.

ical and institutional cultures of their countries. And yet, how the administrative landscape has changed in each country.

The landscape in each country may still be joyless, but it can hardly be described as the public interest state. Nor can it in Australia. Such promises as remain of a comfortable and comforting life are now suspect from the perspective of the dominant ideology, which focuses increasingly on limiting state action to the correction of market failures. What has happened has been nothing less than a loss of faith in the state. Governments everywhere are revising the way they see themselves. Spurred on by Peter Drucker's theory that the state can formulate and mobilise policy, but cannot effectively or efficiently implement it,[5] governments have self-consciously sought to reconfigure themselves.

A number of methods has been used. They have sought, for example, to bring commercial disciplines into their public services, which they have increasingly fractured into two principal components—service delivery, and policy formation. The increased commercial focus has often been thought to be achievable by changing the structure or legal form of the government service provider. Whilst there have always been government corporations, these have proliferated over the last 15 years or so, in the belief that a change of substance will follow this change of form.[6] Deregulation and responsive regulation have also been embraced. This paper, however, will confine itself to only two restructuring methods, namely, privatisation and outsourcing. Neither method has a universally accepted definition. I will be using privatisation to refer to government asset sales, particularly of utilities. I will take outsourcing to refer to the agency process of securing another to provide goods or services directly to the public. Neither definition is watertight, but they will suffice for present purposes.

It is evident that privatisation and outsourcing became pervasive instruments of so-called "restructuring"[7] in an enormously disparate range of

---

[5] P.F. Drucker, *The Age of Discontinuity: Guidelines to our Changing Society* (Heinemann, London, 1969), ch. 10. It is worth noting that the notion of privatisation (he called it "reprivatisation") made its debut in this book. It is, however, a somewhat less demanding notion than its current versions, because it is said to be relatively indifferent to the legal question of who owns a productive unit, and more concerned with the incentive structures and behavioural characteristics associated with a unit. Drucker's principal arguments against a state ever being able to engage as effectively as business in the production of goods and services were that only the business producer could maintain the profit motive, fear bankruptcy, and stop production on economic grounds without concern for social or political concerns.

[6] R. Wettenhall, "Corporations and Corporatisation: An Administrative History Perspective" (1995) 6 *PLR* 7. In contrast to some other countries, Australian efforts to commercialise their service provision agencies were preceded by efforts to restructure their policy-making departments so as to make them more responsive to the portfolio Ministers. The political Executive's assault on the mandarins' policy-making monopolies started in the 1970s in Australia, whilst the explicit adoption of managerialism within its public services was a phenomenon of the 1980s. See J. Halligan, "Political and Managerial Reform in a Small State: The Relevance of the 1980s", in A. Farazmand (ed.) *Handbook of Bureaucracy* (Marcel Dekker, New York, 1994), 561, 569–71.

[7] A term of great imprecision: see B. Probert, "Globalisation, Economic Restructuring and the State", in S. Bell and B. Head (eds), *State, Economy and Public Policy in Australia* (Oxford University Press, Melbourne, 1994), 98, 99.

countries, from the former socialist states of Eastern Europe to Thatcherite England, social-democratic France, and Australia and New Zealand, no matter which political party was in power. There have been various reasons for this. For third world countries, the main reason has been external pressure from the banks to implement structural adjustment programmes.[8] Elsewhere, the reasons have included a blind ideological belief[9] that governments can *never* provide goods and services as well as the private market.[10]

Australia has no shortage of ideologues of the latter variety, but they tended until recently to be on the fringes of those providing serious commentary.[11] They now, however, appear to constitute the national government's official voice. The National Commission of Audit's *Report to the Commonwealth Government*[12] said that the only reasons for the existence of government business enterprises (GBEs) were either historical (in the sense that the private sector was originally incapable of providing the relevant service), or born of one or both of the views that some natural monopolies more appropriately belonged to the public sector, and that public ownership was the best way to ensure the delivery of community service obligations (CSOs). The report suggested that these reasons were all obsolete, because the private sector was now more mature, regulation usually provided a better alternative to ownership of natural monopolies, and CSOs were more appropriately delivered "through a tendering process and explicit budget funding rather than through hidden cross subsidies".[13]

---

[8] Brendan Martin's *In the Public Interest: Privatization and Public Sector Reform* (Zed Books and Public Services International, London, 1993) blames a combination of blind ideology, the aggrandisement of power and opportunistic greed in the "privatisation advisory industry" and financial institutions (particularly the World Bank and the International Monetary Fund) for the rush to third world privatisation despite its catastrophic results.

[9] That might be a tautology. In any event, its most obvious recent example comes from the Republican Party's belief that terminating welfare payments to the poor will strengthen their family values and individual virtue.

[10] It would be wrong to place J. Farrar and B. McCabe, "Corporatisation, Corporate Governance and the Deregulation of the Public Sector Economy" (1995) 6 *PLR* 24 into the "blind ideology" camp. But the authors do express puzzlement at Australia's failure to embrace privatisation more enthusiastically because, they argue, a corporation's agency costs will almost always be higher when government owns it.

[11] See Industry Commission (Commonwealth of Australia), *Improving the Efficiency of GBEs: Information Paper* (May 1994), 25-6, where it is conceded that the economic case for privatising GBEs (Government Business Enterprises) is strong, but not always compelling. Now called the Productivity Commission, the Commission has consistently been to the right of economic debate in the community of official policy makers. As a matter of emphasis, it is interesting to compare the Commission's 1994 publication with D. Osborne and T. Gaebler, *Reinventing Government: How the Entrepreneurial Spirit is Transforming the Public Sector* (Penguin, New York, 1993). This highly influential book states that government cannot be run as a business (p. 21), but argues forcefully that privatisation is "is not *the* solution. Those who advocate it on ideological grounds—because they believe that business is always superior to government—are selling the American people snake oil" (p. 45).

[12] (Australian Government Printing Service, June 1996), 24. The authors were R. Officer (chairperson), E. Alexander, J. Fraser and M. Newman.

[13] Idem.

The economist's natural aversion to cross subsidies is evident, as is the implicit reductionism in seeing CSOs (or cross subsidies) as the only non-economic function of a government business enterprise. With a frame of reference so tightly restricted to an economic paradigm, it is little wonder that the report was able to conclude:[14]

> "Broadly, government commercial activities or services that operate in a competitive market where customers have freedom of choice, and which return a dividend to government after paying full costs, should be retained in public ownership *only* where it is in the public interest that they be retained. 'Public interest' largely implies that there is some market failure, for example, in areas such as quarantine and air safety. In general, if the private sector is adequately providing, or can provide, the service, there is unlikely to be a public interest reason for government to deliver the service."

This, of course, is anathema to most Australian public lawyers, whose conceptions of the public interest are wider than the correction of market failure or the delivery of cross subsidies. Indeed, whilst their advocacy of state intervention and regulation acknowledges the need to protect the poor, they have a much broader agenda than the correction of market failure. Their lists of guiding values include openness, fairness, participation, accountability, consistency, rationality, legality, impartiality, and accessibility of judicial and administrative individual grievance procedures.[15] Perhaps these could all be subsumed under the label of legitimacy. Certainly, administrative law was long regarded as one way of providing legitimacy to the exercise of state power, particularly discretionary power.

However, just as the state is self-consciously redefining itself, so, also, are administrative law scholars questioning their own values and goals. Mainstream administrative law scholarship once sought to tackle its concerns about the legitimacy of discretionary state power with programmes for greater openness and participation. There is now a discernible trend towards embracing processes which cut directly against those programmes. Professor Davis' grand goal is questioned, with rules being attacked as a hangover of the command and control mentality. More and more administrative law scholars (particularly in the United States) are joining the economists' pilgrimage to the new Jerusalem, which beckons with responsive regulation, regulatory negotiation and regulation by performance outcome and through economic incentives. The new rules are qualitatively and operationally different, with a heavy emphasis on regulatory flexibility. In many regulatory areas in which business interests prevail, the great project of turning discretions into rules has been turned on its head.

---

[14] Ibid, 26.
[15] See M. Aronson and B. Dyer, *Judicial Review of Administrative Action* (Law Book Co., Sydney, 1996), 1–7.

It is my belief that the ascendancy of the economic paradigm has been principally responsible for this shift. I also believe that as an administrative lawyer, there is little that I can do by way of providing an effective[16] challenge to the economic arguments. I am not equipped to undertake that task. In any event, I believe that there is much which can be done *within* the dominant economic paradigm's own terms and goals to make the system work fairly and accountably.[17]

Whilst economic beliefs are the driving force behind the recent changes, there have also been other factors closer to home. Many administrative lawyers have shown an increasing disenchantment with judicial review. It is not so long ago that some influential administrative law scholars were writing of judicial review in class terms. It was, they argued, the conservatives' covert weapon against the good intentions of the collectivist and redistributivist state.[18] Others argued that judicial review in particular, and administrative lawyers in general, tended to assume too easily that the best regulatory and accountability techniques were those modelled at least loosely on the judicial method. According to Nicola Lacey,[19] the problem with Davis' approach of getting lawyers interested in administrative discretions was that they tended to see *any* "public" discretion as a problem, a challenge to a liberal legal paradigm in which public power must be exercised according to rules knowable in advance and in accordance with due process. They should rather, according to Lacey, temper their jurisprudential predispositions with empirical and sociological work on the nature and function of each particular discretion. If this were done, they would not automatically see the managerial discretion as the antithesis of the rule of law,[20] and they would not necessarily confine their attention to *public* discretionary power.

Lacey's analysis is particularly important as we try to rethink the roles of

---

[16] The economic paradigm is too dominant. In addition, the practical reality is that privatisation is irreversible. Whilst some countries have historical experiences of renationalisation, that is highly unlikely nowadays. The USSR's collapse signalled not only the political defeat of command economies, but also of a mainstream, serious western belief in the moral and technical virtues of state ownership. Globalisation has also decreased the capacity of individual states to renationalise. Further, the English experience is that the Labour Party seriously damaged itself within its own constituencies by threatening renationalisation; see P. Saunders and C. Harris, *Privatization and Popular Capitalism* (Open University Press, Buckingham, 1994), 129–37.

[17] See, e.g., N. Lewis, *Choice and the Legal Order: Rising Above Politics* (Butterworths, London, 1996), esp. 175–7.

[18] See P. McAuslan, "Administrative Law, Collective Consumption and Judicial Policy" (1983) 46 *MLR* 1 and C. Harlow and R. Rawlings, *Law and Administration* (Weidenfeld & Nicolson, London, 1984), chs 1 and 2.

[19] N. Lacey, "The Jurisprudence of Discretion: Escaping the Legal Paradigm", in K. Hawkins (ed.), *The Uses of Discretion* (Clarendon Press, Oxford, 1992), 360.

[20] Ibid., 369, where Lacey characterises the traditional administrative lawyers' approach thus: "Managerial discretion fails to live up to the rule-of-law ideal in that only the legal method aspires to operate by way of clear, promulgated, prospective, stable, general rules which are consistently applied and possible to comply with. Managerial discretion, by contrast, is seen as unconstrained by any such norms, and tends to be associated with the arbitrary and even capricious exercise of power".

administrative law in the context of a state which wants to redefine its own roles. In what follows, I shall be assuming that there are, indeed, many non-economic aspects of the public interest which still call for non-economic regulation, and even some market failures which still call for regulatory responses. I shall be confining my attention to the regulatory options which policy makers should consider when designing privatisation or outsourcing programmes or projects. Whilst I yield to no-one in advocating the fundamental importance of having a sound, constitutional basis for the new arrangements, I shall be questioning the extent to which the judicial model of rules and dispute resolution provides the answer.

THE LIMITS OF JUDICIAL REVIEW

I examine judicial review first for a number of reasons. It tends still to be thought of as an indispensable accountability device, and that idea needs to be questioned at the outset. Further, it is instructive to examine why it fits so poorly with the problems raised by privatisation and outsourcing, and by the shift away from the "command and control" model of regulation.

The most overt resort to what Lacey calls the legal paradigm has occurred in the English law of judicial review. For the sake of convenience, I shall call it the *Datafin* project, after a case of the same name[21] which seems to represent its highest point. Paul Craig's contribution to this book exonerates me from the need to discuss the details. Suffice it to say here that the English Court of Appeal decided that it could exercise judicial review over the decisions of a body which was exercising regulatory powers in the capital markets, in a deregulated environment in which the body was "without visible means of legal support".[22] Lord Donaldson's reference to its lack of "legal support" was a reference to the fact that no charter, warrant, Act or Statutory Instrument underpinned the body's existence or functions. Indeed, it was a precursor of a range of regulatory bodies of the new style, in that its legitimacy came ultimately from two factors. Its appointments came from government and the capital markets sectors, and its decisions were not authorised by statute, but carried consequences recognised by statute. Whilst the court said that the body was in truth exercising governmental or executive power, it might have been more accurate to say that it was *sharing* its non-governmental power with the government. It was a partnership between industry and government which operated without accountability to Parliament.[23] Furthermore, the rules which

---

[21] R. v. *Panel on Take-overs and Mergers, ex parte Datafin plc* [1987] 1 QB 815 (hereafter referred to as *Datafin*).

[22] Ibid., 835, per Lord Donaldson M.R.

[23] Indeed, it was a partnership in which the government played the senior role, and in which that role was regulatory. These factors may explain the relative lack of success in attempts to push *Datafin* much further than its own regulatory context. See Aronson and Dyer, above at n. 15, 134.

the body administered did not bind it, because the body could change them without seeking the concurrence of any other political or legal institution.

Most attempts to push *Datafin* further into the realm of privately sourced power which affects the public generally have failed, with the courts denying judicial review jurisdiction over the decisions of sporting bodies such as the Jockey Club,[24] the Royal Life Saving Society[25] and the Football Association,[26] as well as other bodies, such as the Chief Rabbi,[27] the British Labour Party[28] and a private school.[29] There have admittedly been some instances of *Datafin*'s application beyond its own regulatory context,[30] but despite the enthusiasm of its proponents, the *Datafin* project has not made much of an inroad into the realms of self-regulatory bodies, no matter how powerful they might be.[31]

Datafin has failed to dent the common law's refusal to treat contractual power as public power, with the result that contractual power is usually not amenable to the common law of judicial review.[32] Cases interpreting Australia's statutory restatement[33] of the law of judicial review are largely consistent in this respect with the common law.[34] The view that contracting belongs entirely to the private sector is a regrettable, but predictable, result of a binary approach which insists on seeing power as being either public or private.

Whilst there are elements of the *Datafin* project which are attractive, its failure is ultimately deserved because in its present form, at least, it is unviable. It presents too many problems for too little reward. Its rigid dichotomy of public and private power undercuts what was obviously the fact in that case,

---

[24] *R. v. Disciplinary Committee of the Jockey Club, ex parte Aga Khan* [1993] 2 All ER 853 (hereafter referred to as *Aga Khan*).

[25] *R. v. Royal Life Saving Society, ex parte Howe* (unreported, CA, May 1990).

[26] *R. v. Football Association Ltd., ex parte Football League Ltd.* [1993] 2 All ER 833.

[27] *R. v. Chief Rabbi of the United Hebrew Congregations of Great Britain and the Commonwealth, ex parte Wachmann* [1993] 2 All ER 249.

[28] *R. v. Labour Party, ex parte Hughes* (unreported, QBD, June 1990).

[29] *R. v. Fernhill Manor School, ex parte A* [1993] 1 FLR 620.

[30] See e.g., *R. v. General Council of the Bar, ex parte Percival* [1991] 1 QB 212 (a professional conduct committee of the Bar Council); *R. v. Visitors to the Inns of Court, ex parte Calder* [1994] QB 1; *R. v. Code of Practice Committee of the Association of the British Pharmaceutical Industry, ex parte Professional Counselling Aids Ltd.* (1990) 10 BMLR 21 (QBD); and *R. v. Advertising Standards Authority Ltd., ex parte The Insurance Service plc* (1989) 2 Admin LR 77. These and other cases are discussed in Aronson and Dyer, above at n. 15, 134–8.

[31] Australia has no real analogues to *Datafin*, which was noted in *Chapmans Ltd. v. Australian Stock Exchange Ltd.* (1994) 123 ALR 215, 223–4. Two cases seemed to accept with only minimal argument that the Advertising Standards Council (a purely self-regulatory industry body) is amenable to judicial review: *Typing Centre of New South Wales v. Toose* (unreported, New South Wales Sup. Ct, Mathews J., 15 December 1988) and *Dorf Industries Pty Ltd. v. Toose* (1994) 127 ALR 654, 666–7.

[32] *Aga Khan*, above at n. 24. This case, however, could be read down in two ways. The contractual power in question was that of a non-governmental body, and the applicant could have sought contractual remedies.

[33] Administrative Decisions (Judicial Review) Act 1977 (Commonwealth of Australia).

[34] Aronson and Dyer, above at n. 15, 78–9, 81–3 and 177–83.

namely, that the regulatory body in question was exercising a *mix* of governmental and industrial power. This makes it difficult to choose sensibly within a dichotomous legal structure which is not reflected in political reality. It therefore becomes difficult to predict which sorts of power will be adjudged public, and which private.

Even if the power is classified as public, the level of review which *Datafin* provides is minimal, for two reasons. First, aside from review for breach of natural justice, the court said that its remedies would be only declaratory, and only prospective.[35] Secondly, whilst it offered the theoretical prospect of review where the regulatory body has misinterpreted its own rules, it particularly emphasised the unlikelihood of this ever occurring, given the court's deference to the body's expertise. Lord Donaldson subsequently emphasised this vagueness about the principles of administration which *Datafin* is meant to enforce, by saying that the court should perhaps fashion an "innominate" ground of review for this sort of regulatory body, replacing "formal categorisation" with review which would be "more in the round than might otherwise be the case".[36] Indeed, what else could he say? The regulatory scheme and method at stake in *Datafin* did not conform to Lacey's legal paradigm. What is the point in supervising the way a body interprets rules which it can change without legal formality? The further a regulatory regime travels from the legal paradigm, the less relevant is judicial review as an accountability device.

In addition to the problems flowing from *Datafin*'s own language, it is not much of an answer to the issues raised by privatisation and outsourcing. Judicial review of a regulator (where there is one) will quell very few of the non-economic (or social justice) anxieties posed by privatisation and outsourcing, particularly where (as in *Datafin*) the regulator is free to rewrite its rules. Judicial review of the service provider (where that is different from the regulator) is subject to all of the usual defects of judicial review generally, together with some peculiar to that area. The usual defects are familiar. Judicial review can occasionally remedy individual grievances, but rarely provides systemic relief. The decisions to litigate and to maintain the litigation can be happenstantial. Judicial review proceedings often pose no real threat to the respondent, which is usually free, on its redetermination of the substantive issue, to come to the same result but in a way which is impervious to judicial criticism. And however manipulable the demarcation line may be between a decision's merits and its legality, it is a line which judicial review continues to draw, with the result that the judge's role is substantially limited. Review in the wake of privatisation and outsourcing carries the additional problem that the complainant is typically conceived as a consumer with a consumer complaint, which is not the business of judicial review.

Judicial review's professed indifference to the substantive merits of the impugned decision is not always convincing, and not ultimately reconciliable

---

[35] [1987] 1 QB 815, 842.
[36] R. v. *Panel on Take-overs and Mergers, ex parte Guinness plc* [1990] 1 QB 146, 159–60.

with some of the grounds of review.[37] But even though the difference between judicial review and a merits appeal may at places be only one of degree, it is important to maintain that difference. Judicial deference to the views and actions of the primary decision maker is in one sense the essence of judicial review's technique. That deference is underpinned by a political sense of the court's secondary role in relation to the primary decision maker, and by the practical sense of the latter's institutional competence in the substantive issues relative to that of the court.

Professor Taggart believes, with some foundation, that there is still a chance that the New Zealand judiciary might rediscover their common law powers regarding the old common callings.[38] He carefully confines his argument to New Zealand,[39] which must have the most deregulated utility environment in the western world, and which also has a body of case-law recognising the applicability of common law duties lying upon monopolists affected with a public interest in their supply of prime necessities. But his argument raises an issue of principle which is worth considering in any common law country. In essence, he wants the judges to reassert their old regulatory powers over essential utilities in three respects. In the absence of a statutory regime which either provides to the contrary or covers the same field, the utilities should be under a common law duty to supply their services to all without discrimination and at a reasonable price. I have no argument with his first and second duties, but I challenge his advocacy of a common law power to set a reasonable price.

Taggart's argument is specifically directed to resurrecting the common law of common callings, and is advanced as being applicable to any utility supplying prime necessities, whether the utility be publicly or privately owned. This has the advantage of avoiding judicial review's central dichotomy of public/private,[40] but it cannot avoid the judiciary's reasons for avoiding this type of exercise like the plague, whether or not it be conducted in a supervisory capacity. Taggart noted with dismay the Privy Council's expression of disbe-

---

[37] Review for "unreasonableness", e.g., clearly involves an examination of the impugned decision's merits, albeit from a perspective of a large degree of deference.

[38] M. Taggart, "Public Utilities and Public Law", in P.A. Joseph (ed.), *Essays on the Constitution* (Brooker's, Wellington, 1995), 214. Taggart pointed out elsewhere that there used to be dozens of occupations classified as common callings, but that they were whittled down to three; namely, carriers, innkeepers and ferrymen. Those engaged in a common calling had special privileges, but also special obligations (such as strict liability in contract and tort): M. Taggart, "Corporatisation, Privatisation and Public Law" (1991) 2 *PLR* 77, 105–6.

[39] Ibid., 264. He also discusses the Australian High Court's rejection in *Bennett and Fisher Ltd.* v. *Electricity Trust of South Australia* (1962) 106 CLR 492 of an appeal to American public utility law, which was in its turn based on older English law long since forgotten in its country of origin. The High Court, he said, took "a wrong turning" (Taggart, "Public Utilities and Public Law", ibid., 250).

[40] Cf. N. Dixon, "Should Government Business Enterprises be Subject to Judicial Review?" (1996) 4 *Aust J of Admin Law* 198, where public ownership is advanced as a sufficient ground for subjecting all Government Business Enterprises (GBEs) to judicial review.

lief in the *Mercury* case[41] that judges could really engage in the task of setting reasonable prices for prime necessities. I agree with his criticisms of the Privy Council's failure[42] to engage with the arguments and issues in that case, which had been conducted throughout[43] on the basis that if the electricity utility in that case were to be found free of any relevant statutory or contractual obligations, then the court itself would have to set a reasonable price for the utility's services.[44] But however uneducated, uncalled for and intuitive the Privy Council's reaction may have been, I would suggest that their intuition was ultimately correct.[45]

I do not accept Taggart's argument that judicial price setting is "no more difficult" than price setting by regulators, and that it is basically the same exercise as the courts perform in *quantum meruit* and such like contexts.[46] Nor do the courts accept it. It is instructive to refer to the Australasian experience of judicial supervision of laws regulating anti-competitive conduct.

There is economic evidence that current competition laws requiring monopolist suppliers of essential commodities to deal with firms downstream in the production chain where the monopolist is also a downstream competitor are likely to be either ineffective or even counter-productive. The evidence is that the requirement to deal with a downstream firm will work only where the upstream price is set by a regulatory body. And yet the evidence points to the conclusion that the Australian, New Zealand and United States courts have consistently tried to avoid performing that regulatory function,[47] even where such avoidance might completely neutralise a regulatory scheme.

Thus the central issue in *Clear Communications*[48] was the reach of a provision prohibiting anti-competitive conduct between firms operating in a market which needed a critical component available only from an upstream monopolist which happened also to be competing in the downstream market. The Privy Council rejected the notion that the section empowered the court to set a reasonable price for the critical component, and pointed to all sorts

---

[41] *Mercury Energy Ltd. v. Electricity Corporation of New Zealand Ltd.* [1994] 1 WLR 521, 525.

[42] There is a parallel with the Privy Council's controversial rebuff to the New Zealand courts in *Crown Milling Co. Ltd. v. R.* [1927] AC 394, 402: "It is not for this tribunal, nor for any tribunal, to adjudicate as between conflicting theories of political economy. Strong views may be entertained on the one side or the other . . ." Commentators were quick to point out that their Lordship's belief that they were not taking sides in an economic debate was an illusion.

[43] Before the Privy Council, and in the courts below.

[44] See M. Taggart, "State-Owned Enterprises and Social Responsibility: A Contradiction in Terms?" [1993] *NZ Recent Law Review* 343 and "Corporatisation, Contracting and the Courts" [1994] *PL* 351.

[45] I hasten to add that I also reject being placed in Taggart's category of lawyers prepared to advance this line for "long-pursed public utility companies": Taggart, "Public Utilities and Public Law", above at n. 38, 260.

[46] Ibid., 249.

[47] G.A. Hay and K. McMahon, "The 'Duty to Deal' Under Section 46: Panacea or Pandora's Box?" (1994) 17 *UNSWLJ* 54 and G.A. Hay, "Reflections on *Clear*" (1996) 3 *Comp & Consumer LJ* 231 (commenting on the Privy Council's decision in *Telecom Corporation of New Zealand Ltd. v. Clear Communications Ltd.* [1995] 1 NZLR 385).

[48] *Telecom Corporation of New Zealand Ltd. v. Clear Communications Ltd.*, ibid.

of technical and policy investigations and issues involved in calculating such a price: "[a]s the experts agreed, and as the High Court found, such investigations are the function of regulatory bodies who can make decisive value judgments. They are the daily diet of a regulatory body".[49]

There is also an abundance of regulatory and economic literature poring over the many difficult issues implicit in price regulation of utilities.[50] These include the normal accounting issues which arise when a utility is privatised, including the vexed issues as to how to value assets which may well have been under-priced at the time of privatisation. They also include the social issues of determining both a reasonable return on capital, and the requisite level of reinvestment in infrastructure. Litigation must be the least effective method, and the worst place imaginable,[51] for determining these issues. Furthermore, no matter who sets a reasonable price, there are social issues at stake which are better handled by a regulatory agency. One of the big fears, for example, about the privatisation of utilities whose services are regarded as socially essential is that the poor will increasingly find themselves disconnected and thereby reduced to living in totally unacceptable conditions.[52] I shall argue below that price regulation is not enough to cope with that issue; there must in addition be rules regarding debt management and disconnection for debt.

Some of the English commentators have argued that there are some Acts of Parliament which are so contrary to the rule of law that the judges must disobey them. They are woolly on the detail,[53] but I doubt that their spectre of judicial disobedience is intended to cover economic legislation. If I am correct in that, then the possibility of common law regulation of the price of a monopolist's provision of prime necessities would be doomed politically, because the odds of legislative reversal to abolish this vestigial common law power would be high indeed. Judicial price setting would not be a politically attractive option.

My final reason for doubting the appropriateness of resort to judicial review or judicial price fixing to counteract the anti-social effects of privatisation and outsourcing is more complex. It proceeds upon the assumption that any such judicial role would in fact be performed with extreme caution. Using administrative law language, the judges could be expected to show great deference

---

[49] [1995] 1 NZLR, 385, 408.

[50] See, e.g., M. Beesley (ed.), *Regulating Utilities: The Way Forward* (Institute of Economic Affairs, London, 1994) and J. Ernst, *Whose Utility? The Social Impact of Public Utility Privatization and Regulation in Britain* (Open University Press, Buckingham, 1994).

[51] There is a clear separation of powers dimension to this issue.

[52] See Martin, above at n. 8, 119–20 for a graphic account of what happens in the stair wells of apartment blocks when one of the tenants is disconnected from their sewerage utility for debt.

[53] See T.R.S. Allan, "Pragmatism and Theory in Public Law" (1988) 104 *LQR* 422; Lord Browne-Wilkinson, "The Infiltration of a Bill of Rights" [1992] *PL* 397; Sir John Laws, "Is the High Court the Guardian of Fundamental Constitutional Rights?" [1993] *PL* 59; A.W. Bradley, "The Sovereignty of Parliament—In Perpetuity?", in J. Jowell and D. Oliver (eds), *The Changing Constitution* (Clarendon Press, Oxford, 3rd ed. 1994), ch. 4; Lord Woolf, "Droit Public—English Style" [1995] *PL* 57, 67–9; and Sir John Laws, "Law and Democracy" [1995] *PL* 72.

to the primary decision makers whose acts or omissions they were called upon to review or alter. That means that the judges would be paying deference not only to the primary decision makers' expertise and strategic advantages. They would also be deferring to some extent to the primary decision makers' *values*. In that way, those values would be co-opted, to some extent, by the court itself. And what are those values? In Australia, at least, the empirical evidence[54] is that the senior echelons of the public service are overwhelmingly and vehemently economic rationalists. They share with their senior counterparts in the private sector a profound mistrust of many of the state's non-economic or social missions. Indeed, far from attributing their values to a mere reflection of those of their Ministers, there is some evidence for the theory that they have been instrumental in pushing the politicians further and further to the right of the economic spectrum.[55] My point is that the specifically judicial or legal values of the administrative lawyer would be infiltrated by the economic and managerial values of the primary decision makers. Judicial review's values have, over time, the chameleon quality of reflecting their subjects' values. There might occasionally be a defiant judge who tries to subvert the dominant paradigm, but this is sporadic, and usually covert.

SOME TROUBLESOME DICHOTOMIES AND MIXED ADMINISTRATIONS

It often assists analysis to set up opposing models as ideal types, even if we know that their differences may be only a matter of degree, and that not everything fits comfortably within the construct. The real difficulties occur when too little fits within the construct, or when it starts to limit one's vision. It will be noticed that this paper occasionally refers to "public law", "public power" and "public lawyers" as if they and their "private" antitheses were unproblematic. I fully recognise, however, the limited utility of these concepts, and also some of the darker roles they may sometimes perform. I want in particular to examine three dichotomies. They are the distinctions between public and private, between public law and private law, and between policy making and its execution. My aim is ultimately to question whether only a public law response is appropriate for an issue involving public power, and whether only a private law response is appropriate for an exercise of government power which uses the quintessential private law device of contract law.

---

[54] M. Pusey, *Economic Rationalism in Canberra: A Nation-Building State Changes its Mind* (Cambridge University Press, Melbourne, 1991).
[55] Ibid., 75. See also E. McCoy and C.A. McCoy, "Privatisation and State Activity: The 'Privatisation' of Public Service Culture and the Privatisation of Tradeable Enterprise as Contradictory Elements within an Analysis of New State Reform" [1990] *Policy, Organisation and Society* 32.

1. Public/private

The divisions between public and private have never been more under challenge than nowadays. For some time, those challenges came from social and political theorists on the grounds of the interpenetrations of state and civil society. More recently, feminist critiques have added to the challenge. These have questioned the normative dualism often associated with the public/private dichotomy,[56] and have in consequence challenged the often implicit assumption that abuse of power is always more intolerable if it is state power in question.[57] I readily acknowledge that the public/private dichotomies so pervasive in administrative law can be deployed to hide "private" abuses of power, and that the distinction itself can be collapsed. It can still be useful, without making the challenged assumptions, and a working distinction between public and private power, however malleable and dependent on perspective and context, seems inevitable if we are to make anything of the transformations currently occurring in the way the state sees itself. If one looks at the administrative law consequences of privatisation and outsourcing, however, it seems to me that it might be more useful to deploy a trichotomy.

Economists have long described our economies as "mixed", in the sense that government and private capital play shared productive roles. If we are comfortable in talking of mixed economies, we should become equally comfortable in talking of mixed administrations, being administrations in which government and private actors play shared regulatory roles. As with the mixed economy, we have long had the mixed administration, but we have perhaps failed to give it sufficient acknowledgment until relatively recently. Corporatism as a mode of government is no longer recent, but its acknowledgment by administrative lawyers was sparse and belated.[58] Similarly, governments have long relied on not-for-profit organisations to provide state funded social welfare services. Once again, however, that did not attract much administrative law scholarship (at least in Australia) until recently.[59] The

---

[56] For example, R. Dworkin *Law's Empire* (Belknap Press, Boston, 1986), 296: "Most of us believe, as I said, that we have no general duty to treat all other members of our community with equal care and concern in everything we do. But we believe our government, the community personified, *does* have this duty, and we might hope to find in this pervasive public responsibility some explanation why we as individuals sometimes have that duty as well". See also R. Dworkin, *Taking Rights Seriously* (Duckworth, London, 1977), 272–3.

[57] See S. Berns, P. Baron and M. Neave, *Gender and Citizenship: Materials for Australian Law Schools* (Department of Employment, Education and Training, Canberra, 1996), 143–245.

[58] See R. Stewart, "The Reformation of American Administrative Law" (1975) 88 *Harv LR* 1667, 1796 (where note 579 refers to unfavourable comparisons made in England and the United States between fascism and formal interest group representation on government bodies) and P. Birkinshaw, I. Harden and N. Lewis, *Government by Moonlight: The Hybrid Parts of the State* (Unwin, London, 1990).

[59] Administrative Review Council, *Administrative Review and Funding Programs: A Case Study of Community Services Programs* (Report No. 37, Australian Government Printing Service, Canberra, 1994).

academic study of government business enterprises (GBEs) does go back a long way, but what is perhaps surprising for Australia, which has such a long history of government investment leading private capital in many areas of the economy, is that it has only recently become a mainstream concern of Australian administrative lawyers.

Australia seems to have been a relative latecomer to the intensified use of privatisation and outsourcing as a tool of economic restructuring, and that may explain why its administrative law scholarship has only recently started to focus on the issues raised by the phenomenon of the mixed administration. It may also explain the strength of the views that public and private law are different, and that administrative law should be viewed as a single and indivisible package.

2. Public law/private law

The perception that administrative law is a single and indivisible package may well be a peculiarly Australian phenomenon. It is most evident in the writings of those who confine their attention to so-called Commonwealth administrative law. They are assisted in this regard by the Commonwealth Parliament, which has actually defined "Commonwealth administrative laws" for the purposes of its corporations laws.[60] It can indeed be convenient to talk sometimes of administrative law as consisting of a single package, but it is not always appropriate. The exact contents of the package will vary between contexts and commentators, leading to arid definitional disputes.[61] More importantly, a package concept is not always appropriate. The concept of the mixed administration entails a recognition that there are contexts in which it is inappropriate to ask only whether the whole package should be applied *or* disapplied. One might, for example, want to apply some aspects of Freedom of Information law to the operations of a privatised utility, whilst at the same, not retain judicial review. Or one might want to replace the government ombudsman with an industry ombudsman.

Whilst the "single package" conception of administrative law might be peculiarly Australian, it bears a striking resemblance to a concept which is not. We are all familiar with the notion of some writers that administrative law should strive to make itself "distinctive", and with the related notion of

---

[60] The Corporations Act 1989 (Commonwealth of Australia), s. 4(1) states that "Commonwealth administrative laws" means 5 Acts and the regulations thereunder. The Acts concerned relate to the Administrative Appeals Tribunal, judicial review of administrative decisions under Commonwealth enactments, Freedom of Information, the Ombudsman, privacy, and the Administrative Review Council.

[61] For example, one might regard the Commonwealth's legislative definition as deficient, in failing to mention legal issues relating to public archives, corruption, whistle blowers, and consultative processes applicable to the making of rules with statutory force. Of course, one reason for this deficiency might be the gaping holes in the Commonwealth statute book in this regard!

the English courts that judicial review is sufficiently distinctive to require that it be governed exclusively by a separate procedural regime.[62] The "distinctiveness" project has always had problems, because it cuts against a fundamental political aspiration of removing from government as many privileges as possible.[63] It is an even more difficult project nowadays, as privatisation and outsourcing have combined with other restructuring tools to reduce the size of government dramatically as measured by public service staffing levels, but not quite so drastically as measured by expenditures.[64] In other words, it is difficult wholly to exclude from the administrative lawyer's consideration anything not done solely by the public service. It should suffice to give two Australian examples of the single package conception of administrative law, and of the related view that administrative law should be kept distinct. In the context of its discussion of outsourcing, the Commonwealth Ombudsman's office has on a number of occasions[65] recounted a pensioner's difficulties in making a complaint about damage to his letter box. Apparently, the letter box had been damaged by the negligence of a contractor delivering the mail for Australia Post. The contractor's insurance had an excess greater than the amount of the damage, and so the contractor was not prepared to compensate the pensioner in full. Australia Post thought it was none of their business because they were not vicariously liable, and the pensioner was too poor to sue. So the Ombudsman successfully pursued the matter against Australia Post.

The Ombudsman concluded that the agency and the contractor should have had a clearer regime in their contractual arrangements for determining their division of responsibilities for complaints handling, and that the agency should not be able to off-load the risks to the general public. I agree that the poor pensioner in that case was given a hard time, when each party had said that the complaint should be taken up with the other. But it appears that as between the agency and its contractor, the contractual arrangements as to the allocation of responsibility were indeed clear, although arguably unfair to the pensioner. They put all of the responsibility on the contractor. The Ombudsman said that it was never fair to have an arrangement which allowed

[62] See Aronson and Dyer, above at n. 15, 211–12.

[63] See C. Harlow, "Changing the Mindset: The Place of Theory in English Administrative Law" (1994) 14 *OxJLS* 419, 432–3.

[64] See C. Hood, "Rolling Back the State or Moving to a Contract and Subsidiarity State", in O.P. Coaldrake and J.R. Nethercote (eds), *What Should Government Do?* (Hale and Iremonger, Sydney, 1989), ch. 3.

[65] See, e.g., P. Smith, "Client Service: Perceptions and Reality", address to the Commonwealth Public Service Commission Seminar (Feb. 1995); J. Mullins, "Handling Complaints Related to Government Services Delivered by Contractors", in K. Cole (ed), *Administrative Law and Public Administration: Form vs Substance* (Australian Institute of Administrative Law (AIAL), Canberra, 1996), 218–37; P. Smith, "How Micro-economic Reform Impinges on Administrative Law", paper delivered at the 1996 Administrative Law Forum (Sydney) of the AIAL (12 Apr. 1996); Industry Commission, *Competitive Tendering and Contracting by Public Sector Agencies* (Report No. 48, Australian Government Printing Service, Canberra, 1996), 88 and Commonwealth Ombudsman, *Annual Report 1995–96* (Australian Government Printing Service, Canberra, 1996), 10–11.

an agency to privatise this sort of risk. That must always be a relevant issue when designing the outsourcing regime in question, but I would suggest that its resolution should not always be the same. If one were to add another ingredient to the Ombudsman's case, one might ask why the agency should have assumed liability if it was operating in a contestable market in which none of its competitors assumed that extra liability. Even without that extra ingredient, one could question whether the real issue was not a possible weakness in tort law's vicarious liability principles, which allow a principal so easily to avoid responsibility for some of the costs of their activities.[66] If the case is viewed as indicating a need to reform vicarious liability principles, then one could well conclude that it would be unwise to effect that reform by way of contract, rather than legislation, and that it would be unfair to reform those principles only so far as they apply to public sector agencies.

The case of the damaged letter box involved an assumption too readily drawn that a public law remedy should provide the answer to a problem, simply because it involved a government agency. My second example involves the logical corollary of that assumption. The New South Wales government is currently considering the imposition upon utilities of a range of consumer protection and social justice principles, but it seems that the utility must be government owned.[67] There seems to have been an assumption that the principles might be radically different, or even unnecessary, if the utility's ownership should pass from the public to the private sector.

The frailty of the public law/private law distinction is particularly important in the case of outsourcing. Ian Harden has demonstrated that contractual regimes for the delivery of goods and services to the public have a rhetorical appeal.[68] Contracts are a classic instance of the legal paradigm. They involve autonomous parties freely negotiating their own set of rules, which the courts will enforce regardless of any status difference as between the parties. But behind the private law form lies a pure exercise of government power, because

---

[66] One could also ask why it should necessarily be assumed that the Ombudsman should have jurisdiction.

[67] Department of Fair Trading, *Consumer Protection and Competition Policy in New South Wales: A Green Paper for Consultation* (Sydney, June 1996). Admittedly, the document is not entirely consistent. It asks whether a government or an industry ombudsman (or neither) would be appropriate where a government utility operates in a contestable market, and whether "different public accountability mechanisms [should] be applied to private sector businesses": p. 24. In introducing the Gas Supply Bill 1996, the New South Wales government intended that legislation relating to consumer protection for domestic consumers of electricity and gas would also draw the same distinction between businesses which are publicly and privately owned. Direct legislative protection was already provided in the case of electricity, whilst the government proposed that the gas utilities would have to draw up codes, perhaps after consumer and public consultations. The Treasurer justified this difference *solely* on the ground that the electricity utilities were publicly owned, whilst the gas companies were not: (1996) *Parl. Deb.* (New South Wales) 3136–37 and 3141 (19 June 1996). He was defeated, however, by an Independent MP's amendment which inserted cl. 83(3) into the Bill, requiring that regulations be made providing for standard form contracts, the form and content of bills, debt collection procedures, service standards, and the constitution and procedures of advisory customer councils.

[68] I. Harden, *The Contracting State* (Open University Press, Buckingham, 1992).

it is in the nature of outsourcing that the consumer has no more say in the formation or terms of the contract than in the pre-outsourcing days when government provided the service direct. Harden has also shown that the law has always had difficulty with the notion that there is a contractual relationship between utilities and their domestic customers, whether the utility be privately or publicly owned. The trend to deeming the relationship to be contractual has not altered the difficulties in that regard, where price and other terms are standardised and stipulated by authoritative decision. Harden contends for a greater use of public law's "notice and comment" procedures in the setting of terms and standards.

3. Policy making/service delivery

The troublesome distinction between policy and administration was with us for some time, but the intensified drive towards privatisation and outsourcing has brought it back in a somewhat different guise. The viability of the policy/administration dichotomy has never been so critical. The distinction used to be deployed to explain the demarcation of responsibilities as between Ministers and their departments and agencies. The distinction was useful for those wishing to believe in the political neutrality of the public service, or in the efficacy of the Westminster doctrine of Ministerial responsibility. It has been a long time, however, since anyone took seriously the claim that Ministers made policy and the bureaucracy merely implemented it. And yet a new version of the policy/administration distinction has emerged.

It has become an article of faith in public administration circles to accept a distinction between policy making on the one hand, and either its administration or service delivery on the other. The fiction that only Ministers make policy has been replaced with the fiction that only the central agencies or departments make it. This fiction underpins the English division between departments and Next Step agencies.[69] The same fiction is used to help justify outsourcing.[70] It is said to be important to distinguish between government as the purchaser of services, and government as the service provider. The theory is that government should do as little providing as possible, because the combination of roles diminishes the effectiveness of each. Specifically, the

---

[69] New South Wales uses it to explain the differing Ministerial roles as regards State Owned Corporations (SOCs). SOCs have two shareholders, the Treasurer and one other Minister, whose job it is to consider the "broader" economic and management issues. The portfolio Minister is responsible for the corporation's *administration* of its functions, but does not hold shares. See State Owned Corporations Act 1989 (New South Wales).

[70] It will be interesting, however, to see what happens to this fiction in the context of English outsourcing since the passage of that country's Deregulation and Contracting Out Act 1994. Subject to certain exceptions, s. 69 allows Ministers to authorise contractors to exercise functions conferred on Ministers by statute. Such authorisations can be granted where statute or the common law (that is, the *Carltona* doctrine) would allow the relevant function to be performed by a person holding office under the Minister.

purchaser/provider split is advocated as a powerful mechanism for enhancing cost-effectiveness. That might often be right,[71] but the problems which then arise are the extent to which policy making has been or should be privatised along with service delivery, and the extent to which government's policy making capacity has diminished.

The argument was presented to Australia's Industry Commission as a concern that "truly responsive services and appropriate forward planning" can suffer, when the "'coal face' service providers" are separated from the "decision makers".[72] It is interesting that the submission accepted the fundamental distinction between decision making and service provision. That made the Commission's task of rejecting it easier, because it was able to respond that the decision makers could preserve the quality of their decisions by ensuring an appropriate flow of information to them.[73]

The Commission's response assumes that the service provider's values and experience are either irrelevant or easily communicated, *and* that when it comes to a clash of values, those of the service provider should not prevail.[74] At first sight, it also seems to assume that policy is better made comprehensively, rather than incrementally. Incremental policy making and large scale outsourcing find it difficult to co-exist, because effective outsourcing requires great precision and foresight on the part of those designing the contract specifications. The contractor must know in advance exactly what is required, in terms of service and performance standards. This makes it difficult to be flexible when novel cases with policy implications arise.[75] The concept of bounded rationality[76] can be useful here, in indicating a practical limit to the government's contractual capacities.

To be fair, the Industry Commission did refer broadly to the difficulty in making adequate contractual provision for policy and other non-economic

---

[71] The international literature on government contracting for service delivery to the public (both contracts "out" and "in") is reviewed by G. Hodge, *Contracting Out Government Services: A Review of International Evidence* (Monash University Graduate School of Government, Melbourne, 1996). Hodge notes the dramatic improvements in the areas of maintenance, cleaning and refuse collection. But he concludes that the figures from those areas should not be extrapolated to other areas. Even in the three nominated areas, he questions whether contracting out produces significant differences to contracting in.

[72] Submission of the Victorian Council of Social Services, quoted in Industry Commission, above at n. 65, 118.

[73] Ibid., 118–9.

[74] Pusey, above at n. 54, makes the point in ch. 3 that the ascendancy of the central agencies (Prime Minister and Cabinet, Treasury and Finance) over the "market-oriented departments" under-scored the ascendancy of the "hard-nosed" values of the central agencies over the "captured" or "soft" values of the other departments.

[75] See C.S. Diver, "Policymaking Paradigms in Administrative Law" (1981) 95 *Harv LR* 393, for the classic account of the distinction between two models of policy making, namely, the incrementalist model and the comprehensive rationality model. See also Aronson and Dyer, above at n. 15, 189–92.

[76] Wherein the behaviour of a person or firm may be as nearly optimal with regard to their goals as their physical, cognitive and informational resources will allow.

factors. One of its indicative criteria for agencies not using competitive tendering and contracting (CTC) was:[77]

> "Are there any accountability, privacy, security, consumer protection, access and equity or other policy considerations that cannot be addressed satisfactorily through contract specification and contract management and performance monitoring? The less difficult these considerations are, the greater is the case for CTC."

The Commission leaves its readers with an overwhelming sense, however, of the relative rarity of occasions in which these policy issues might tell against the use of outsourcing. Further, even this limited acknowledgment of the policy component of service delivery assumes that policy is better made before and separately from the delivery of services. There is little sense here that policy making might occasionally be better made incrementally, and from the bottom up, by the service providers rather than the financial controllers. Further, there seems to be no awareness that policy might in fact be made that way, even if the financial controllers are unaware of it.

It is trite to observe that the successful implementation of outsourcing regimes, as well as the socially responsible regulation of privatised utilities, are dependent on an adequate supply of information to the government parties. Where policy is largely a reflection of a service provider's accumulated wisdom and decision making, then the information needs of government and the public are even more critical, if policy making is to be accountable and capable of being changed at higher levels.

THE PIVOTAL ROLE OF INFORMATION

Economically rational people, the economists tell us, need lots of information. However, it is remarkable how wedded to confidentiality free marketeers can be when they come to assess the information needs of government and the public as regards privatisation, the operation of privatised utilities, and outsourcing. Asset valuation details are secret at the time of most privatisations, and remain secret thereafter. Regulatory control over privatised utilities encounters difficulties at the most basic level when, as in the early years of British Telecom's private sector existence, the regulator is reduced to cajoling the utility to compile vital information about compliance with performance standards.[78] In the area of outsourcing, basic contractual details such as performance standards and price are frequently kept secret, for fear of prejudicing the contractor's competitive position.

Documents marked "commercial, in confidence" are currently entitled to a range of privileges in Australia's Freedom of Information (FOI) Acts. The

---

[77] Industry Commission, above at n. 65, 259.

[78] C. Graham and T. Prosser, *Privatizing Public Enterprises: Constitutions, the State, and Regulation in Comparative Perspective* (Clarendon Press, Oxford, 1991), 217–9.

most relevant provisions here are those incorporating the equity of confidentiality into the FOI regimes,[79] and those protecting trade secrets or other information having a commercial value, or even just business information whose release could reasonably be expected to have an adverse impact on the business of a person, firm or agency.[80] There are also provisions exempting documents from FOI accessibility where their disclosure would reveal material generated by an agency as part of its deliberative processes.[81] Provisions of the latter sort are admittedly hedged about with their own exceptions, including an overriding requirement that disclosure be contrary to the public interest. In addition, however, to these document-specific exemptions from Australia's FOI regimes, the Acts typically name a range of agencies, and create for their documents a blanket exemption to the extent that the documents relate to the agency's commercial activities.[82] Similarly, corporatised GBEs are in Australia[83] typically exempted from FOI, under the theory that their playing fields should be level with those of their private sector competitors.[84]

Indeed, the level playing field is a powerful rhetorical device in this area. By itself, however, it does not indicate whether the level which is to be set should be that generally applying to the government sector or to the private sector. That function is performed by the natural assumption of anyone adhering to the public/private, public law/private law dichotomies, that any firm (government or private) conducting a commercial operation in a contestable market should be free of requirements to disclose information. There are several reasons for questioning this conclusion.

The effectiveness of outsourcing often requires greater transparency than currently stipulated. Agencies need information to enable them to bargain effectively. Information sharing between agencies, and between governments within a federal system, can therefore help them get better value for the taxpayers' dollar. It should be added that it is not just agencies who can be assisted in this regard. In an environment of truly competitive tendering, the losing bidders should be able to have a broad idea of how they must lift their game, if they are to be successful in any further or comparable tendering. The danger is otherwise that they might repeat the same mistakes, or eventually give up hope, thereby leaving the field that much less competitive.

The regulatory body's need for information requires no argument here, but it is worth noting how extensive that need can be. A telecommunications

---

[79] See, e.g., Freedom of Information Act 1982 (Commonwealth of Australia), s. 45.
[80] Ibid., s. 43.
[81] Ibid., s. 36.
[82] Ibid., Sch. 2, Pts II and III.
[83] For New Zealand, see Taggart, "Corporatisation, Privatisation and Public Law", above at n. 38, 88–9, relating a Select Committee's rejection of a generalised claim for FOI exemption for State-Owned Enterprises. Indeed, the Consumer Affairs Ministry submitted to the Committee that there might be a case for requiring similar openness from private firms.
[84] M. Allars, "Private Law but Public Power: Removing Administrative Law Review from Government Business Enterprises" (1995) 6 *PLR* 44, 47–52.

regulator, for example, must be able to do more than simply access existing documentation in the hands of its subject firms.[85] It should also be empowered to require the generation and analysis of information. Further, if its tariff regulation is to be truly effective, it will have to dig deeper than historical pricing formulas, to ensure that technology savings are passed on to the consumer.

Informational needs are not confined to regulators, agencies and potential contractors. One of the goals of privatisation and outsourcing is to turn citizens into consumers, and to treat the consumer as sovereign. There are a number of problems with that, not the least of which is that consumer influence is in proportion to their access to information. In addition to the traditional consumer remedy of buying elsewhere, a remedy which is not always available, the literature is replete with devices for enhancing the consumer voice. These devices include consumer councils, and systems for registering consumer views with a view to acting on them either under the contract, or when it comes up for renewal. In some contexts, it would also be appropriate to have a consumer input into the process of articulating some of the contract specifications or regulatory goals. These, and indeed, any other regulatory mechanisms are dependent upon good quality information flows. Information is not an end in itself,[86] but it is a precondition to the effectiveness and legitimacy of virtually any other regulatory and participatory device.

These arguments for greater access to information are all instrumental, being based upon enhancing competition. My other arguments are normative, and might be more readily recognisable in an administrative law context. Those advocating a split between purchaser and provider have argued with some force that it enhances the focus of each actor, if their sole role is either to purchase or provide. This enhanced focus promotes accountability in the government context, where there is always potential for a clash between the interests of government to rein in spending, and its political interests in denying the fact of overspending, and culpability for it. The fact is, however, that there will always be a political incentive to cover up a poor return for government expenditure. Government is not simply another purchaser. It is an agency of a wider public, spending other peoples' money. As with any agency, there is a potential for a conflict of interests; hence the existence of auditors general and parliamentary public accounts committees.

Recent Australian experience, however, has shown that these mechanisms need reinforcement. The Victorian government has legislated to curtail their auditor's powers.[87] In New South Wales, the State Treasurer preferred a day's

---

[85] This is essentially the limit of Australian FOI regimes, which grant access to existing documents, rather than to information.

[86] There must be a defined need for it, which means that those designing the regulatory scheme must have in mind what they might want to do with the information.

[87] The Audit Act 1994 (Victoria) omits to guarantee the Auditor General's independence. It also creates an "independent auditor", who is appointed by a parliamentary committee, and whose job it is to audit the Auditor General. The latter is prohibited from questioning

suspension from Parliament for contempt of the Legislative Council, to disclosing documentation relating to an apparently extremely unwise contract with Rupert Murdoch's Fox studios.[88] It is worth noting that the Treasurer's explicit defence was that the documents he was refusing to hand over were "commercial in-confidence". They related to a massive government subsidy to Mr Murdoch. On this logic, government accountability via information disclosure diminishes in exact proportion as government operations become more "commercial". Government's "commercial" operations are thus treated as being its "private" concern.

In the case of the New South Wales Treasurer, the matter was referred to the standing anti-corruption body.[89] Most States, however, have no such body; nor does the Commonwealth government. Although the Treasurer was cleared of any corruption in this particular instance,[90] the important point to note is that his very secrecy created suspicions, which had to be exaggerated to the level of a suspicion of corruption to enable an independent body to have access to the relevant documentation. One suspects that there would have been no corruption allegations if there had been a broader disclosure regime.

Where there are government contracts, licences and privileges, there are opportunities for corruption, and where there are opportunities, corruption will occasionally happen. Its likely frequency must surely be significantly increased when one adds government secrecy to these risk factors. The independence and powers of Auditors General should be strengthened, not reduced, and the commitment to open government should transcend the private sector's commitment to secrecy.[91]

One might argue that proposals for more publicly accessible information are essentially political arguments about the accountability and legitimacy of

government policy objectives, which are defined to include Ministerial "policy directions", policy statements in the Budget Papers, the objectives stipulated in the corporate plans of corporatised GBEs where these have been approved Ministerially, and "any other document evidencing a policy decision of the Government or a Minister": s. 16(9). The Financial Management and Audit Acts (Amendment) Act 1995 (Victoria) further weakened the Auditor General's powers, and increased the government's ability to reduce substantially the amount of information contained in agencies' annual financial statements. The 1995 Act also produced the astonishing result that Regulations made under the Audit Act are no longer disallowable under the normal procedures of the Subordinate Legislation Act 1962 (Victoria).

[88] The debate on the contempt motion is recorded at (1995) *Parl. Deb.* (New South Wales), 2988–3008 (13 Nov. 1995).

[89] The Independent Commission Against Corruption.

[90] Because he was cleared, the documents remained confidential.

[91] There is a curious contrary argument in Industry Commission, above at n. 65, 276–82. The Commission decided against making any recommendations aimed specifically against collusive tendering, because it had found no substantive evidence of it, and because it thought that the existing commercial and criminal laws were sufficient. At the same time, it noted the importance of transparency in counteracting both collusion and conscious or unconscious bias in the tender evaluation process. As to the latter process, it also noted (once again, without making any recommendations) the presence of an independent expert (usually, it seems, an accountant) on the tender evaluation committees of some agencies. In that regard, it noted the possibility that "where appropriate", the independent person could be drawn from a community organisation.

democratic government. But accountability and legitimacy are also two of the central goals of administrative lawyers, and my purpose is to point out a seeming paradox in the way these goals must be met. The official rhetoric is that government must remain accountable, no matter whether it delivers goods and services itself, or purchases their delivery from the private sector. According to the Industry Commission:[92]

> "While there were differences of view about many aspects of the impact of contracting on accountability, there was general agreement across all levels of government and among other inquiry participants that, while responsibility to do certain things can be transferred, accountability cannot."

Perhaps inevitably, "accountability" became a slippery term in the Commission's hands. It was defined as meaning responsibility for service delivery, transparency as to the performance of the agency and its contractors, and an opportunity for redress where performance is substandard. The transparency component, however, had in the Commission's eyes to be traded off against commercial confidentiality:[93]

> "Recognising the balance between commercial confidentiality and accountability, governments should make public as much information as possible to enable interested people to assess contracting decisions made by agencies. Of particular importance is information on the specifications of the service, the criteria for tender evaluation, the criteria for measurement of performance and how well the service provider has performed against those criteria."

The Commission excluded from its transparency requirement all matters whose disclosure could "pose a commercial disadvantage to the contracting firm".[94] The Commission noted debate about whether there should be disclosure of contractual terms and the overall price, but declined to offer its own opinion. In other words, the Commission's only sure criteria for disclosure related to the information needed to assess whether the contractor was living up to its side of the bargain, but no detail as to why this contractor beat the other tenderers, and no detail as to how much it was all costing. In the Commission's assumed paradigm of a free market which disciplines poor performers, that might indeed be all the information needed. If one accepts, however, the instrumental and normative arguments made above for greater information needs in the case of government funded goods and services, then the private sector's concept of "commercial, in confidence" needs at least as much adjustment as the public sector's concepts of accountability and legitimacy.

This results in the paradox that there will be contexts in which the mechanisms for delivering governmental transparency should be expanded, rather than contracted, as government adopts privatisation and outsourcing. The

---
[92] Industry Commission, above at n. 65, 86.
[93] Ibid., 95.
[94] Idem.

precise nature of the adjustment will vary according to context. Even the Industry Commission's limited list of topics on which there should always be transparency would require adjustments to be made to the FOI Acts, so as to narrow those Acts' privileges for "commercial, in confidence". One might well imagine compromises being made on other topics. For example, certain contractual terms (including the overall price) might have to be revealed within a year or two of the contract's making, but could in the meantime be kept secret. This sort of compromise could prove particularly useful in the context of privatisations, where questions are often raised, and rarely satisfactorily answered, as to the appropriate selling price.[95] There is clearly some need for secrecy in the stages leading up to the valuation and sale of the government asset, but the thought that the secrecy would not last forever might[96] act as a disincentive to deliberate undervaluations for sectional or corrupt reasons.[97]

None of this should be taken as implying that the special information needs generated by privatisation and outsourcing can be met by rethinking the scope of the FOI Acts. Indeed, the public scrutiny functions performed by those Acts usually constitute a safety net, in the event that more specific monitoring systems have not worked. The case for expanding FOI, however, needs to be made to counteract the view that it should yield to the private sector's notion of commercial confidentiality.

STAKEHOLDERS' TRIBUNAL AND JUDICIAL REMEDIES

Privatisation and outsourcing have forced administrative lawyers to think again about the appropriateness of a range of tribunal and judicial remedies. Judicial review used to occupy administrative law's centre stage, but I have already argued that there is not much scope for it under the new arrangements.

In Australia, the generalist Administrative Appeals Tribunal (AAT) has arguably displaced judicial review's pre-eminence for some time, but its appropriateness to some of the issues raised by outsourcing has also been questioned. It presently has no scope at all where the governmental decision in question was made under a contract, rather than an Act. That prompted the Administrative Review Council to look at possible extensions in the case of government funded community service programmes.[98] Its recommendations distinguished sharply between the rights of contracted service providers and

---

[95] Other pre-sale issues sometimes questioned relate to debt write-offs and capital injections.

[96] Although not necessarily. The British government was remarkably impervious to *ex post facto* criticism of underpricing, a criticism repeatedly made by the relevant Parliamentary committee; see Graham and Prosser, above at n. 78, 94–5.

[97] The valuation is performed by an independent commission in France, and is susceptible to judicial review; see ibid., 97–104. The French system is not entirely transparent, however, because the commission's valuation need not be accompanied by reasons.

[98] Administrative Review Council, above at n. 59.

those of "consumers". It was recommended that service providers be given full access to the AAT, where disputes arise between themselves and their funding agency. The biggest limitation to that proposal was that it should apply only to decisions relating to recurrent funding; the initial decision to contract with a service provider should be immune from AAT review. Consumers, however, were to be given no access to the AAT. Instead, the Council recommended the creation of in-house and external complaints monitoring and mediation mechanisms, whose substantive criteria would be stipulated in charters of consumers' rights, and in which the ombudsman would have a role. However, none of these mechanisms would involve the power of redecision. If attempts at mediation failed, the biggest stick which the Council proposed was that the ombudsman (or some other appropriate body) should act as a monitoring agency of the service provider's performance. Information thus gathered would be passed on to the funding agency so that it might be better informed when considering contract renewal.

This distinction between contracted service providers and their clients is interesting. It is difficult to justify a scheme which values the provider's business interests more highly than those of its clients whom it is paid to serve. Whilst one could not advocate consumer access to the AAT in respect of all of the finer details of a working relationship between a provider and their client,[99] some of the more important aspects of that relationship might well be appropriately subjected to a merits appeal in the AAT. For example, a government funded nursing home's decision to evict one of its clients could well be amenable to AAT scrutiny if the criteria for eviction were allegedly breached. The AAT, however, might not be the only possible adjudicative avenue.

The Australian High Court decision in the *Trident Insurance* case[100] suggests an alternative approach. The *Trident* plaintiff was a company intended to be benefitted by an insurance policy purchased by an unrelated company. Whilst the majority's reasons exhibited significant differences, *Trident's* overall outcome was to compel the insurer to treat the plaintiff as if the latter had been the purchaser.[101] It is not clear how much of a dent the decision has made into contract law's requirements that there be privity of contract, and that consideration move from the promisee. But the case did point to legislative and common law reforms in some jurisdictions, and therefore shows that similar reform is possible where the government contracts with the private sector for the provision of goods and services to defined members of the public.

[99] Just as one could not advocate the service provider's access to the AAT over all of the finer details of the contract's management.
[100] *Trident General Insurance Co. Ltd.* v. *McNiece Bros Pty Ltd.* (1988) 165 CLR 107.
[101] This was subject to three conditions. The plaintiff's ability to enforce the contract was subordinate to the contracting parties' rights to terminate or vary. The insurer was to have the same defences against the plaintiff as it could have raised against the purchaser. It also had to be clear that the contracting parties had intended that the third party be able to sue directly.

I return to the case of the patient who is about to be evicted from the service provider's government funded nursing home, allegedly in breach of the terms of the contract between the home's operator and the funding agency. A simple legislative reform could ensure the patient's access to the courts (including a consumer claims tribunal if the amount at stake is small enough) to enforce the contract, or to sue for its breach. It might be thought appropriate to reserve for the agency the right to intervene in the patient's case, but once again, this would be a simple legislative reform.

Granting the patient contractual rights[102] makes more sense, in fact, than looking to the agency to sue on the contract as if it were the wounded party. Quantification of the agency's loss, if any, might produce a very different outcome from an assessment of the patient's loss.

Harden points to other problems in relying solely on the funding agency to press for compensation from the service provider.[103] The agency may not be guaranteed independence from its Minister, and it may be too disposed to waive insistence on the strict letter of the contract. Third party enforcement by affected individuals reduces these dangers of discretionary governmental powers.

Third party enforcement is not the only option. Sometimes, indeed, it could be ineffective. It might in some situations be more appropriate to have a regulator, agency, or public interest group take enforcement action on behalf of individuals. Utility regulators in England, for example, can order customer rebates where the utility's service standards have been breached.

A variation on the approach of extending private law's contractual remedies to those for whose benefit the contract is made could also be used as part of the response to the worrying problem of privatised utilities disconnecting bad debtors, even though the service which the utility provides is essential. In the cases of water, waste disposal, sewerage, electricity and gas, it is astonishing to contemplate a government policy which would allow disconnection for debt, at least for any length of time. Disconnection will typically punish others, as well as the debtor. Even in those cases where only the debtor is involved, disconnection is too uncivilised an option for mere debt. There are ways, of course, in which the utilities concerned can ameliorate the problems. Much work has been done in England on the possibilities of using pre-paid meters, and on developing alternative reminder and persuasion strategies to disconnection.[104] But at the end of the day, there will always be the customer who cannot or will not pay. It is submitted that in the case of essential services, either the government or the utility should foot the bill, in return for a right of recovery[105] against the debtor. If it were the government footing the

---

[102] Which would no doubt have to be subordinate to the contracting parties' rights to terminate or vary.

[103] Harden, above at n. 68, ch. 5.

[104] Ernst, above at n. 50, 136–54.

[105] For what it is worth. Government currently has legislative assistance in recovering money, enabling it not only to sue as for a debt, but also to deduct amounts from welfare payments, and to collect a debtor's money through the taxation system.

bill, then the economists would probably describe the operation as an instance of a community service obligation (CSO).

INFORMAL REGULATION

I have already noted the way in which the economists' aversion to the notion of a cross subsidy has combined with their reduced vision of government to produce the view that the "social" obligations of government service providers are best reduced to the economic concept of the community service obligation (CSO). It can be particularly difficult to identify and quantify CSOs, which no doubt adds to the administrative lawyer's suspicion that their social worth is being marginalised. It is also doubtful whether the concept is capable of universal application. Just as it is sometimes impossible in practical terms to quantify a firm's economic externalities, so also is it sometimes impractical to assess the "spillover" or beneficial effects generated for the whole community by some activities of government. A healthy and well educated populace, for example, benefits us all. There are limits, therefore, to the practicality of using the CSO notion as a method of regulation. Whilst it is simply one of a number of regulatory devices open to government, it has risen to prominence in the wake of corporatisation, privatisation and outsourcing, and therefore deserves special mention here.

Leaving aside the issues relating to their practicality and to the wisdom of using them, the CSO is still a fairly strange creature for the administrative lawyer. They are often legislatively defined to mean any social or community obligation whose fulfilment would not be commercially justified in the eyes of the relevant firm. In such cases, the firm is obliged to meet the obligation only when directed. The direction is usually given by the Minister, who is usually under a vaguely[106] worded obligation to compensate the firm for compliance. Such a scheme is deliberately cumbersome, and is designed to minimise any distractions from the firm's principal focus, which is commercial. This form of CSO, therefore, does not come into being until the Minister so directs; it is an entirely discretionary power to impose a social obligation.[107]

Another variant of the CSO involves the non-commercial obligations being spelled out in the Act itself. Legislation which corporatises government trading enterprises, for example, typically lists the firm's objectives. The usual objects clause requires the firm to be a successful business, operating at least as efficiently as any comparable business. It also requires the firm to "exhibit a sense of social responsibility". Since 1995, those two objectives (amongst others) have ranked equally in New South Wales, although in other places,

---

[106] In the case of GBEs.
[107] See generally M. Aronson, "Ministerial Directions: The Battle of the Prerogatives" (1995) 6 PLR 77, 84–6.

the firm's social commitments need usually be met only when it is practicable or feasible to do so.

Neither of these forms of the CSO offers much comfort to the administrative lawyer, because they are so easily postponed or avoided. The New Zealand experience of trying to enforce them through public interest litigation has been dismal, because the courts are understandably reluctant to involve themselves in supervising issues with such broad policy ramifications.[108] Australia's telecommunications legislation imposes elaborate CSOs on the biggest telephone company, with a view to ensuring nation-wide, universal access to the standard telephone system on an equitable basis. In this case, an independent regulator is in charge of ensuring that the CSOs are performed,[109] and the Federal Court has declared its extreme reluctance to supervise the regulator's performance in that regard, let alone to make its own judgment on whether the company is in breach.[110] The court stressed that the relevant CSO was better regarded as an aspirational ideal, than a legally enforceable obligation.[111]

Whilst the regulatory device of the CSO has been prompted by the economists' project of making cross subsidies transparent, the way in which it works is far from transparent. It would be impracticable, of course, to expect Parliament to make detailed provision for their application. That must necessarily be the task of the Minister, or, preferably, an independent regulator. Further, one can well understand the court's reluctance to get involved, either in setting policy or reviewing it. In the case of the telecommunications CSOs, the independent regulator has published its guidelines.[112] Regrettably, that level of transparency is highly unusual in Australia. Similarly, whilst the mere publication of the guidelines could probably be counted as some measure of accountability, their relative informality is reasonably typical of the way that much of the "social" regulation of government is now conducted.

It appears to be a feature of Australian legislative schemes governing the community or social obligations of utilities, whether they be publicly or privately owned, that usually, those obligations are found neither in the Acts nor in disallowable instruments formally made pursuant to those Acts. Typically,

---

[108] See Aronson and Dyer, above at n. 15, 141–2.

[109] And in supervising the elaborate system for calculating the contributions which must be made by the other carriers.

[110] *Yarmirr v. Australian Telecommunications Corporation* (1990) 96 ALR 739.

[111] Ibid., 749–50. Section 3 of the Gas Supply Act 1966 (New South Wales) lays out in very broad terms the general goals of industry, the regulators and the Minister. Its final sub-section then states that nothing in that section creates a civil cause of action; nor shall it be "taken into account" in any civil cause of action. An Independent MP's amendment to delete this was lost, because the principal political parties were agreed that judicial review could enforce compliance with the section, and that this was sufficient to give the section teeth: (1996) *Parl. Deb.* (New South Wales) 3138 (19 June 1996). It would be interesting to know whether that attitude would have been adopted had the parties been aware of how reluctant the courts are to supervise such provisions.

[112] See M. Armstrong (ed.), *Communications Law and Policy in Australia* (Butterworths, Sydney, loose-leaf service), para. 45,470.

they are to be found in operating licences, or in approvals of mission statements or of annual corporate plans.

The point has already been made that when it comes to outsourcing, the obligations are largely confined to the contract documentation between the funding agency and its service providers. This is not to suggest that we should revert to the traditional legal paradigm identified by Lacey, where the only valid forms of regulation are relatively inflexible instruments having the status of legislation or delegated legislation. The need for regulatory reform has recognised for some time the advantages of using less formal regulatory devices in many contexts.[113] But it is possible to achieve the regulatory reform objectives of flexibility, responsiveness, minimum compliance costs and expertise whilst still adhering to the goals of transparency and accountability. The case for transparency has already been argued. Perhaps paradoxically for those attuned to the Westminster myth that Ministerial powers represent the constitutional paradigm of accountability, there is a strong case for moving such social regulation devices as the imposition of CSOs, licensing, and the approvals of corporate plans out of the Minister's office and into the realm of the independent regulator. It seems to be easier to impose duties of openness and public consultation upon regulators than upon governments.[114] Ministers should be left only with those powers for which they are truly prepared to be accountable.[115]

Comparative studies of regulatory design and implementation are always dangerous, because they can so easily overlook critical social, economic, cultural or political differences between the countries studied. But it is interesting to note that most comparisons between England's style of regulating their utilities and that of the United States have remarked on how much the English style operates behind closed doors, and on how much it depends upon the personal style of each regulator (as opposed to the culture of an institutional regulator).[116] It is probably too early to tell as regards Australia, but the portents are that we tend to follow the American transparent tribunal model in the field of economic regulation relating to the utilities, but we tend to be more British as regards social (including consumer protection) regulation. Australian tariff and third party access regulation occurs reasonably transparently in a tribunal context, with full rights of appeal and review for the

---

[113] For Australia, it might suffice to refer to Industry Commission, *Regulation and its Review: 1994–1995* (Office of Regulation Review, Canberra, 1995) and New South Wales Government, *Regulatory Innovation: Regulation for Results (Discussion Paper)* (Sydney, 1995).

[114] See the interesting taxonomy of primary, secondary and tertiary rules in Britain in R. Baldwin, *Rules and Government* (Clarendon Press, Oxford, 1995), 306–7.

[115] The case for reducing Ministerial power in favour of regulators' power is made in Aronson, above at n. 107, 94–5.

[116] See Graham and Prosser, above at n. 78, ch. 7; Ernst, above at n. 50, 53–68; and T. Prosser, "Regulation, Markets and Legitimacy", in J. Jowell and D. Oliver (eds), *The Changing Constitution* (Clarendon Press, Oxford, 3rd ed. 1994), 236, 254–8.

major commercial players, if not for individuals or public interest groups. Such regulation is governed directly by legislation.[117]

Indeed, all Australian governments are committed[118] to the introduction of broadly similar legislative schemes in this regard. There is no such inter-governmental commitment as regards social regulation. CSOs, consumer protection via licence conditions and the like, and environmental issues, tend to be regulated by Ministers. To be fair, consultative processes are commonplace, and are sometimes required by legislation. But that seems to be as far as the public's involvement gets with regard to the development of social regulation.[119]

CONCLUSION

Administrative law has travelled a long way since Reich's protest against the public interest state. The public interest in those days was about patriotism, morals, social welfare and conformity. The economic paradigm is dominant nowadays, and it is bent upon transforming the public interest into something not far removed from commercial interests. The state's shift from a sense of public interest mission to a more focused concern with the economy has been accompanied by other shifts. Economic theories of government intervention to correct market failure have been supplemented with theories of intractable failure by government itself. The liberal division between the public and private realms has long been challenged, particularly by economic and political theorists who prefer to talk of the mixed economy, in recognition of the inter-penetrations of state and private sector power.

Administrative law has only more recently recognised that alongside the mixed economy, our governmental methods are themselves mixed. Mixed governmental methods fracture the old dichotomy between public and private power, into a trichotomy which recognises the sharing of governmental functions between organs of the state and organisations sourced in the private sector. A new variant of the old, theoretically challenged dichotomy between administration and policy making has been introduced. It is the distinction between policy making and service delivery. Because that distinction is questionable, and also because the efficiency and effectiveness goals behind the

---

[117] For example, Trade Practices Act 1974 (Commonwealth of Australia) Pt IIIA and Gas Supply Act 1996 (New South Wales) Pt 2.

[118] By virtue of the Competition Principles Agreement reached by the Council of Australian Governments (COAG) on 25 Feb. 1994. The Agreement has been legislatively recognised by all Australian legislatures.

[119] These observations are offered with some diffidence (although less so with regard to New South Wales), because it is currently based largely on first impressions. There has been an enormous amount of relevant legislative and administrative activity in recent times, and the issue remains to be studied in depth. For New South Wales, the debate on the passage of the Gas Supply Act 1996 seems to be fairly representative; see (1996) *Parl. Deb.* (New South Wales), 2553–57, 2877–83 and 3124–41 (19 June 1996).

strategy of separating government purchaser from service provider are critically dependent upon sustaining good information flows, the province of Freedom of Information laws might have to be expanded. FOI's present boundary line at the barrier marked "commercial, in confidence" needs adjustment where the information is of both commercial and governmental relevance.

Judicial review was once regarded as one of administrative law's central devices for ensuring accountability. The *Datafin* project represented a hesitant and flawed attempt to apply judicial review to a situation of mixed power, shared by government and the private sector. It necessarily failed because it sought accountability to a model of legal regulation (Lacey's legal paradigm), in a context of a regulatory reform movement which seeks increasingly to use other regulatory models. Its failure could also be attributed to an understandable lack of will on the part of the judiciary to involve itself too closely in economic or social regulation.

More generally, administrative law's goals of accountability and participation are still important, but the way in which the state has restructured both itself and its delivery of goods and services, requires that the tools for achieving those goals might also have to be adapted. On occasions, it will even raise questions as to whether the best way of handling an issue might not be an adaptation of private law doctrines, such as tort or contract law. Australia's economic regulation of utilities has largely embraced the now familiar administrative law tools of regulatory bodies operating at arms length from government, in a more or less open fashion and with a limited degree of public access and accountability. Its devices for regulating on social, environmental and consumer issues, however, are lagging behind. Social regulation is often exercised in the Minister's office. Official recognition of the failure of the doctrine of Ministerial accountability was one of the driving forces behind the expansion of Australian administrative law. That recognition should prompt a further expansion of administrative law, once again at the Minister's expense.

It is not too late to recognise the need for bringing social regulation into the more public arena of the independent regulatory body, where community and consumer organisations, lobby groups and individuals can engage more directly in the policy making processes. If we fail to do that, then the prospect is of the economy stretching forward to the farthest horizon, offering a joyless landscape of merely commercial interests. It would promise a life of allocative and productive efficiency, with no precincts sacred to the spirit of community.

4
Theoretical and Institutional Underpinnings of a Separate Administrative Law

JOHN W. F. ALLISON

An important issue in contemporary English debates on the distinction between public and private law is the relevance of abstract analysis and, in particular, an account of the state. In his leading article, Peter Cane considers the distinction in the light of various theories—what he calls "developmental individualism", "Diceyan integrationism", and "passive individualism"—but doubts the significance of his abstract analysis.[1] He concludes as follows:[2]

> "I have suggested that different attitudes to the public-private distinction can be related, at a very abstract level, to different accounts of the role of the individual in political life and hence to different accounts of the nature of democracy and the state. But, at a more concrete level, attitudes to the distinction are more complex than the abstract analysis can capture."

In contrast, Professor Carol Harlow opposes the distinction directly by reference to the "structure of the modern state" in which no "activity is typically governmental in character nor wholly without parallels in private law".[3] Then, Lord Woolf's and Professor Jeffrey Jowell's analysis of the distinction in the fifth edition of De Smith's *Judicial Review of Administrative Action* again raises the issue of the relationship between the distinction and a concept of the state. Woolf and Jowell use "public function" as the principal criterion for determining the province of public law but stress that "[p]ublic functions need not be the exclusive domain of the state".[4]

---

[1] "Public Law and Private Law: A Study of the Analysis and Use of a Legal Concept", in J. Eekelaar and J. Bell (eds), *Oxford Essays in Jurisprudence*, third series (Clarendon Press, Oxford, 1987), 57.
[2] Ibid., 78. See also P. Cane, *An Introduction to Administrative Law* (Clarendon Press, Oxford, 3rd ed. 1996), 18 (hereafter referred to as *Introduction*).
[3] C. Harlow, " 'Public' and 'Private' Law: Definition without Distinction" (1980) 43 *MLR* 241, 257.
[4] S.A. de Smith, Lord Woolf and J. Jowell, *Judicial Review of Administrative Action* (Sweet and Maxwell, London, 5th ed. 1995) (hereafter referred to as Woolf and Jowell).

The relationship between the "state" and an English distinction between public and private law is the subject of this paper. From a comparative and historical perspective, I will first describe how the concept of the state and, so, related concepts like the "executive", the "government" or the "state administration", have played little role in the English common law tradition. I will then suggest that, when they did begin to receive attention in this century, the state was becoming increasingly indistinct. Finally, I will consider implications for identifying the province of English public or administrative law. Elsewhere, I have considered a certain systematic approach to law, separation of powers, and procedural model as other underpinnings for the distinction between public and private law.[5] Here, I will focus only on the "state" and stress its significance to the distinction in the sense of a division generally affecting the procedural, institutional, and substantive legal consequences of disputes.[6]

THE STATE IN THE CIVIL LAW

On the Continent, the concept of the state has enjoyed a far greater prominence in public law doctrine than it has in the common law tradition. In England, Dicey's "rule of law" expressed a principle of legality applicable to private individuals and public officials alike.[7] His analysis emphasised, not the state, but the "ordinary law" applied by the "ordinary law courts" to all persons whatever be their rank or station.[8] In Germany, however, the equivalent principle is expressed with the notion of the *Rechtsstaat* centred on the concept of the state and which may literally be described as "law-based state" or "state under law".[9]

In France, the distinction between public and private law was formally drawn and given significance with explicit reference to the state. For example, in the famous case of *Blanco*, the *Tribunal des Conflits* established that state liability for injuries arising out of the activities of a *service public* fell under the jurisdiction of the *Conseil d'Etat*.[10] It stressed that the state itself would be held liable according to rules different from those of private law. In *Feutry*

---

[5] J.W.F. Allison, *A Continental Distinction in the Common Law: A Historical and Comparative Perspective on English Public Law* (Clarendon Press, Oxford, 1996), chs 3 and 6–10.

[6] See generally ibid., chs 4 and 5. Cf. Craig's inquiry into the structural considerations relevant to the public-private divide, in his paper in this volume.

[7] A.V. Dicey, *An Introduction to the Study of the Law of the Constitution* (Macmillan and Co. Ltd., London, 10th ed. 1959), ch. 4.

[8] Ibid., 202–3.

[9] R.C. van Caenegem, *An Historical Introduction to Western Constitutional Law* (Cambridge University Press, Cambridge, 1995), 16. See generally R.C. van Caenegem, "The 'Rechtsstaat' in Historical Perspective" in *Legal History: A European Perspective* (The Hambledon Press, London, 1991), ch. 8. Note Van Caenegem's assumption in *Historical Introduction*, ibid., 5: "public law is the law of the state".

[10] TC, 8 Feb. 1873.

the *Tribunal* confirmed that the *Conseil d'Etat*'s jurisdiction extended over the activities of a *département*. The *Commissaire du Gouvernement* concluded as follows:[11]

> "Il semble *a priori* qu'on ne puisse même pas concevoir la possibilité d'une différence entre la situation des départements ou des communes et celle de l'État. *La puissance publique est une*, le caractère de ses actes ou de ses opérations ne change pas suivant l'importance territoriale de l'administration qui agit. Les actes accomplis par les représentants ou les agents de l'administration ont la même nature, quelle que soit l'étendue de la circonscription où exercent ces agents."

In short, he justified the extension of the *Conseil d'Etat*'s jurisdiction by equating the activities of *départements* and *communes* with those of the state.

The concepts of the state and administration have not merely played a formal role in the demarcation of the *Conseil d'Etat*'s jurisdiction. As elaborated by theorists such as Constant and Duguit, they have generally oriented French public law.[12] They have also been intrinsic to the justification for the French distinction between public and private law with its institutional, procedural, and substantive legal consequences. The retention of separate administrative courts has typically been defended because, to use the words of Duguit, of their cognisance "of the conditions under which it is necessary to operate the state".[13] Similarly, in the field of procedure, the special investigative role of the administrative judge has been justified as a corrective to the fundamental inequality between the individual and the state administration, particularly, the inequality of access to the evidence necessary to prove administrative illegality.[14] And, in *Blanco*, the *Tribunal des Conflits* declared that state liability "has its own special rules which vary according to the needs of the service and the necessity to reconcile the rights of the state with private rights".[15] The *Tribunal* explicitly justified the application of special substantive rules of law by referring to the "rights of the state".

The centrality of the state in the civil law tradition is reflected in a certain distinction between public and private in modern European law. According to

---

[11] TC, 29 Feb. 1908: "[i]t seems *a priori* that one cannot even conceive of the possibility of a difference between the position of *départements* and *communes* and that of the State itself. *The Public power is one*—the nature of its acts or its tasks does not change according to the territorial importance of the administration that performs them. Acts done by representatives or agents of the administration are of the same kind, whatever the extent of the territorial competence exercised by such agents" (emphasis added). See also *Terrier*, CE, 6 Feb. 1903.

[12] Allison, above at n. 5, ch. 4, esp. 50 ff.

[13] L. Duguit, *Law in the Modern State* (F. and H. Laski (trs.)) (Howard Fertig, New York, 1970), 159. See also, e.g., L. Rolland, *Précis de droit administratif* (Librairie Dalloz, Paris, 9th ed. 1947), para. 314; R. Odent, *Cours de contentieux administratif* (Les Cours de Droit, Paris, 1977–81), 746–7.

[14] See, e.g., J-P. Colson, *L'Office du juge et la preuve dans le contentieux administratif* (LGDJ, Paris, 1970); C. Debbasch, *Procedure administrative contentieuse et procedure civile* (LGDJ, Paris, 1962), 442.

[15] Above at n. 10. Translation by L.N. Brown and J.S. Bell, *French Administrative Law* (Clarendon Press, Oxford, 4th ed. 1993), 174.

article 189 of the European Community Treaty, a "directive shall be binding, as to the result to be achieved, upon each Member State to which it is addressed". The European Court of Justice (ECJ) has therefore attributed to directives capable of having direct effect vertical, not horizontal, direct effect. In other words, it has recognised that a directive with direct effect may be relied upon against an organ of the state but "may not of itself impose obligations on an individual" or "be relied upon as such against such a person".[16] In *Marshall*, the ECJ was concerned "to prevent the state from taking advantage of its own failure to comply with community law".[17] It therefore held that a person "is able to rely on a directive as against the state . . . regardless of the capacity in which the latter is acting".[18] In *Foster* the ECJ suggested criteria for determining the kind of body against which a directive may be relied upon. It held that the Equal Treatment Directive 76/207 may be relied upon against a body "whatever its legal form, which has been made responsible, pursuant to a measure adopted by the State, for providing a public service under the control of the State and has for that purpose special powers".[19] The concept of the state is central to these criteria and the ECJ's continuing denial of horizontal direct effect to directives.[20]

THE STATE IN THE COMMON LAW TRADITION

The pioneering systematic works on the common law of the eighteenth and nineteenth centuries reveal a very different approach from that which developed on the Continent. In his *An Analysis of the Civil Part of the Law*, Sir Matthew Hale dealt with what we would classify as public law, under the "rights of persons", and, more particularly, "the political rights of persons" (section 2), such as, "rights as relate to the King's person" (section 3), "rights concerning the Prerogatives of the King" (section 4), "rights concerning the King's Rights of Dominium, or Power of Empire" (section 5), etc.[21] Blackstone and Austin adopted a similar classification. In his *Commentaries on the Laws of England*, William Blackstone distinguished between "public relations" (between governors and governed) and "private relations" (between master and servant, husband and wife, parent and child, and guardian and ward), but discussed public relations in his Book 1 entitled *Of the Rights of Persons*.[22] Austin defined public law (exclusive of criminal law) as "that

[16] *Marshall v. Southampton and South West Hampshire Area Health Authority (Teaching)* (C-152-84) [1986] ECR 723, [1986] QB 401, para. [48]. See also *Johnston v. Chief Constable of the Royal Ulster Constabulary* (C-222/84) [1986] ECR 1651, [1987] QB 129.
[17] Ibid., para. [49].
[18] Idem.
[19] *Foster v. British Gas plc* (C-188/89) [1990] ECR 1–3313 at 1–3349. See also *Doughty v. Rolls-Royce plc* [1992] 1 CMLR 1045, [1992] IRLR 126.
[20] *Faccini Dori v. Recreb Srl* (C–91/92) [1995] All ER (EC) 1.
[21] T. Cadell, London, 4th ed. 1779.
[22] Facsimile of 1st ed. of 1765–9, The University of Chicago Press, Chicago, 1979.

portion of law which is concerned with political *conditions*: that is to say, with the powers rights duties capacities and incapacities, which are peculiar to political superiors, supreme and subordinate".[23] He inserted public law in this sense in the law of persons: "[t]here can be no more reason for opposing public law to the rest of the legal system, than for opposing any department of the Law of Persons to the bulk of the *corpus juris*".[24] Austin's classification of public law under the law of persons later provoked Paton's criticism: "[t]o consider the powers of the State in connection with the status of married women, infants, and lunatics seems to suggest a lack of proportion".[25] Indeed, it suggests a general neglect of the state and its administration in the common law tradition.

Dicey's analysis of the rule of law perpetuated that tradition. In each of the three meanings he attributed to the rule of law, he stressed the individual role of officials. First, he described "the exercise by persons in authority of wide, arbitrary, or discretionary powers of constraint" as contrary to the rule of law.[26] Secondly, he equated individuals and officials by requiring that "every man" be "subject to the ordinary law of the realm".[27] Thirdly, he omitted any reference to the state or its administration where he asserted that "the general principles of the constitution . . . are with us the result of judicial decisions determining the rights of *private persons* in particular cases brought before the courts".[28] Dicey refers to the state only in passing, where he mentions that "officials" includes "all persons employed in the service of the state".[29]

Doctrinal neglect of the state is matched by its rare use in legislation or case law. "[S]afety or interests of the state" is used in section one of the Official Secrets Act 1911 but proved peculiarly problematic for the House of Lords. In *Chandler v. Director of Public Prosecutions*, Lord Reid recognised the conceptual difficulty and uncertainty:[30]

> " 'State' is not an easy word. It does not mean the Government or the Executive. 'L'Etat c'est moi' was a shrewd remark, but can hardly have been intended as a definition even in the France of the time. And I do not think that it means, as counsel argued, the individuals who inhabit these islands. The statute cannot be referring to the interests of all those individuals because they may differ and the interests of the

---

[23] J. Austin, *Lectures on Jurisprudence, or, The Philosophy of Positive Law* (John Murray, London, 5th ed. 1885), 744.
[24] Ibid., 750.
[25] G. Paton, *A Textbook of Jurisprudence* (Clarendon Press, Oxford, 4th ed. 1972), 328 n. 2.
[26] Dicey, above at n. 7, 188.
[27] Ibid., 193.
[28] Ibid., 195 (emphasis added). See C. Harlow and R. Rawlings, *Law and Administration* (Weidenfeld and Nicolson, London, 1984), 14–7.
[29] Idem. Where Dicey elaborates on parliamentary sovereignty and the role of the ordinary courts, his recognition of the state is only partial and implicit. He did not alter the later editions of *Law of the Constitution* (above at n. 7) to reflect his belated recognition of administrative authorities in his revisionist article "The Development of Administrative Law in England" (1915) 31 *LQR* 148. See generally Hunt's analysis of Dicey's private law paradigm in this volume.
[30] [1964] AC 763, 790. Cf. ibid., 807–8, 813. See *R. v. Ponting* [1985] *Crim LR* 318.

majority are not necessarily the same as the interests of the State. Again we have seen only too clearly in some other countries what can happen if you personify and almost deify the State. Perhaps the country or the realm are as good synonyms as one can find and I would be prepared to accept the organised community as coming as near to a definition as one can get."

Lord Reid's unfamiliarity with the "state" is evident in the foreign references and many suggested synonyms.

Neglect of the state in the common law tradition requires explanation, particularly because, already in the seventeenth century, Hobbes had been preoccupied with "that great Leviathan called a common-wealth, or state".[31] Traditional neglect is related to two features of the English context—the comparative lateness and limited extent of administrative centralisation and the theoretical insularity of the English legal profession.

First, the seventeenth century revolutionary settlement between Parliament and the English Crown, unlike the French revolution and its aftermath,[32] did not secure a powerful centralised administration. It did not express a theory of popular sovereignty conducive to administrative centralisation and comparable to the Rousseauist theory of the general will.[33] Rather, by enshrining the sovereignty of Parliament and the supremacy of the common law courts, it reinforced legislative and judicial centralisation.[34] Later, Dicey described as a fundamental feature of the English Constitution "the omnipotence or undisputed supremacy throughout the whole country of the central government", but by that supremacy he meant the sovereignty of Parliament that had replaced the supremacy of the Crown.[35]

In contrast to the pre-Revolutionary beginnings of administrative centralisation in France,[36] only through the course of the nineteenth century did central government in England similarly begin to extend its administrative controls by replacing boards and commissions with ministries and by providing for government inspectors in legislation on factories, public health, and relief for the poor. About the turn of the century, when countervailing calls for decentralisation were being heard in France, the English administrative system was still in the process of becoming more centralised.[37] The adminis-

[31] T. Hobbes, *Leviathan* (R. Tuck (ed.)) (Cambridge University Press, Cambridge, 1991), 9. See Q. Skinner, "The State", in T. Ball, J. Farr, and R.L. Hanson (eds), *Political Innovation and Conceptual Change* (Cambridge University Press, Cambridge, 1989), 90, 121.

[32] See Allison, above at n. 5, 50–5.

[33] See K.H.F. Dyson, *The State Tradition in Western Europe: A Study of an Idea and Institution* (Martin Robertson, Oxford, 1980), 40–1.

[34] See generally R.C. van Caenegem, *The Birth of the English Common Law* (Cambridge University Press, Cambridge, 2nd ed. 1988); R.C. van Caenegem, *Judges, Legislators and Professors: Chapters in European Legal History* (Cambridge University Press, Cambridge, 1987), 93–6.

[35] Above at n. 7, 183.

[36] See Allison, above at n. 5, 44 ff.

[37] M. Hill, *The State, Administration and the Individual* (Martin Robertson in association with Fontana/Collins, London, 1976), 17–52; Harlow and Rawlings, above at n. 28, 6–10. See generally R. Barker, *Political Ideas in Modern Britain* (Methuen and Co. Ltd., London, 1978), 7–49 and

trative centralisation that did occur remained limited by the role of local authorities which continued to provide numerous services albeit subject to the supervision of central government.[38]

English administrative centralisation, later and more limited than that in France, did not command the same attention. It did not bring the state to the forefront of academic debate. Hobbes "left an abiding impact" in France, not England.[39] In the eighteenth and nineteenth centuries, his concept of the state did not become the theoretical cornerstone of the English political system. The administrative role of central government did increase in the nineteenth century but was neglected by the prescriptive *laissez-faire* theory of the time.[40] And understandings of the state in England were left theoretically unelaborated by a philosophical tradition that was to become predominantly linguistic and analytic and by an historiography and a political science that were inclined to be empirical and mistrustful of abstractions.[41]

Secondly, the English legal profession was generally insulated from whatever significance the state had acquired in political thought.[42] Historically linked to the Inns of Court and traditionally concerned with its independence, the profession has long been preoccupied with remedies, the practice of law, and the law as posited, to the exclusion of political theory with a normative emphasis on the state. The early doctrinal writers, such as Hale, Blackstone, Austin, and Dicey, inherited that preoccupation.

Whereas, on the Continent, the concept of the state was developed to describe the governmental apparatus, in England, academic and practising lawyers used other concepts to deal with government. In particular, they used two concepts—the abstract concept of the crown and the familiar concept of the person or individual official.

The concept of the crown has evolved from a medieval symbol suggesting dynastic continuity[43] into a contemporary "synonym" for powers formerly exercised by the monarch[44] or the bodies and persons which now exercise those powers.[45] In various ways, it has not approximated to a developed

---

126–8; P.P. Craig, *Administrative Law* (Sweet and Maxwell, London, 3rd ed. 1994), 41–59 and 67–9.

[38] S. Flogaïtis, *Administrative Law et droit administratif* (LGDJ, Paris, 1986), 59–65.

[39] Q. Skinner, "Thomas Hobbes and his Disciples in France and England" (1966) 8 *Comparative Studies in Soc. & Hist.* 153, esp. 154.

[40] A.J. Taylor, *Laissez-faire and State Intervention in Nineteenth-Century Britain* (Macmillan, London, 1972), 18–26, 39–49, 53–4; Hill, above at n. 37, 25–9. See generally the debate amongst historians: Taylor, ibid., Craig, above n. 37, 50–2.

[41] Dyson, above at n. 33, 196–201; A. Vincent, *Theories of the State* (Blackwell, Oxford, 1987), 1–2. See generally Dyson, ibid., 36–44 and 186–96.

[42] Dyson, ibid., 41–3.

[43] See F. Pollock and F.W. Maitland, *The History of English Law before the Time of Edward I* (Cambridge University Press, Cambridge, 2nd ed. 1898), vol. 1, 511–26, esp. 524–6; E.H. Kantorowicz, *The King's Two Bodies: A Study in Medieval Political Theology* (Princeton University Press, Princeton, 1957), 336 ff.

[44] Woolf and Jowell, above at n. 4, 204.

[45] See *Town Investments v. Department of the Environment* [1978] AC 359.

concept of the state or its administration with the passing of time. First, to the extent that the concept is clear, it seems to refer only to the institutions and powers of central government—ministers, their departments, and, generally, bodies under their direct control.[46] Secondly, the concept of the crown, with its monarchical connotations, has carried with it the historical baggage of crown immunity[47] and is still obscured by a certain "mystical historical haze".[48]

Thirdly, the crown has remained conceptually confused. In the Tudor period, the crown was, for the first time, conceived as a corporation sole, a corporation of one, not unlike a parson in church property law.[49] At the turn of the twentieth century, Maitland famously ridiculed this conception as metaphysical or, rather, "metaphysiological",[50] even, metapsychological, fiction: "the personality of the corporate body is concentrated in and absorbed by the personality of its monarchical head".[51] To the conception of the Crown as corporation sole, Maitland preferred the conception of a "corporation aggregate of many", like other corporations, but "complex and highly organised", headed by the Monarch and called the Commonwealth.[52] Wade and Forsyth, in the latest edition of their textbook, nevertheless define the crown in its corporate capacity as a "corporation sole" with all its conceptual shortcomings.[53] By defining the crown as a corporation of one, they seek to remain true to the rule of law, according to which the crown's prerogatives and immunities should not extend to its officers.[54] Woolf and Jowell are less sure. They associate the crown with both the "state" and the "government"[55] and do not decide whether it be a corporation sole or corporation aggregate.[56]

Apart from the enduring and confused concept of the crown, English jurists have traditionally referred to individual officials when dealing with government or the governmental apparatus. Austin, for example, in his discussion of the distinction between public and private law, emphasised the role of "public or political persons", of "political superiors, supreme and subordinate".[57]

---

[46] See *Town Investments* v. *Department of the Environment* [1978] AC 359; Woolf and Jowell, above at n. 4, 204–10; Cane, *Introduction*, above at n. 2, 236–7. Cf. *Feutry*, above at n. 11.

[47] See, e.g., *M* v. *Home Office* [1993] 3 WLR 433, 451 and 453.

[48] Woolf and Jowell, above at n. 4, 205. See, e.g., *M* v. *Home Office*, ibid., 448. Cf. generally P. Allott, "The Theory of the British Constitution", in H. Gross and R. Harrison (eds), *Jurisprudence: Cambridge Essays* (Clarendon Press, Oxford, 1992), 173, esp. 186–7, 191–2 and 198–9.

[49] F.W. Maitland, "The Crown as Corporation" (1901) 17 *LQR* 131. See generally F.W. Maitland, "The Corporation Sole" (1900) 16 *LQR* 335.

[50] Maitland, "The Crown as Corporation", ibid., 134.

[51] Ibid., 133.

[52] Ibid., 140.

[53] H.W.R. Wade and C.F. Forsyth, *Administrative Law* (Clarendon Press, Oxford, 7th ed. 1994), 819–20.

[54] Ibid., 53–4. See also H.W.R. Wade, "The Crown—Old Platitudes and New Heresies" (1992) 142 *NLJ* 1275, 1315 (2 pts); Allison, above at n. 5, 104–7.

[55] Above at n. 4, 204–6.

[56] Ibid., n. 15. See also *M.* v. *Home Office*, above at n. 47, 465.

[57] Above at n. 23, 749 and 744.

And he recognised "the difficulty of drawing the line of demarcation, by which the conditions of private persons are severed from the conditions of political subordinates".[58] For that reason, he, like Hale and Blackstone, preferred to classify what we might call public law issues under the law of persons. Dicey's analysis of the rule of law shared that focus to the exclusion of an elaboration of the state and its administration.

TAKING ACCOUNT OF A MODERN STATE

Gradually English academic lawyers did respond to the centralisation that had occurred through the course of the nineteenth century by taking account of the state. Holland for one defined public law and administrative law by reference to the state but did not break completely with the past preoccupation with persons. He defined the state as "a great juristic person" with rights and duties resembling those of individuals.[59] For Holland, the state was itself a person, a juristic person.

Around 1900, a few other academics began to draw attention to governmental expansion and the conception of the state. Maitland observed:[60]

> "We are becoming a much governed nation, governed by all manner of councils and boards and officers, central and local, high and low, exercising the powers which have been committed to them by modern statutes. . . . The governmental powers, the subordinate legislative powers of the great officers, the Secretaries of State, the Treasury, the Board of Trade, the Local Government Board, and again of the Justices in Quarter Sessions, the Municipal Corporations, the Guardians of the Poor, School Boards, Boards of Health and so forth; these have become of the greatest importance, and to leave them out of the picture is to make the picture a partial one-sided obsolete sketch."

Salmond also emphasised the extension of government and analysed the state with care: "[b]ut the modern state does many things, and different things at different times and places. It is a common carrier of letters and parcels, it builds ships, it owns and manages railways, it conducts savings-banks, it teaches children, and feeds the poor".[61]

The state that began to receive attention, however, was changing. In France, Duguit was describing an increasingly decentralised system with

---

[58] Ibid., 747.

[59] T.E. Holland, *The Elements of Jurisprudence* (Clarendon Press, Oxford, 13th ed. 1924), 127–8, 374–5 and 387–8, esp. at 387. See also F. Pollock, *A First Book of Jurisprudence for Students of the Common Law* (Macmillan & Co. Ltd., London, 6th ed. 1929), 95–6 and 121; F.W. Maitland, "Introduction", in O. Gierke, *Political Theories of the Middle Ages* (Cambridge University Press, Cambridge, 1900), esp. xi and xxxvii.

[60] F.W. Maitland, *The Constitutional History of England: A Course of Lectures* (Cambridge University Press, Cambridge, 1908), 501 and 506.

[61] J.W. Salmond, *Jurisprudence, or, The Theory of Law* (Stevens and Haynes, London, 1902), 184–5.

public services not only provided by central government but also by regional representatives, industrialised departments, "autonomous group[s] of officials", "technical experts" within a department and "private citizen[s] acting under government control".[62] Laski at the London School of Economics, initially[63] much influenced by Duguit, summarised his contribution with approval:[64]

> "He [Duguit] saw that the government of a State is simply a body of men issuing orders, and that these, in themselves, have no colour of any kind. Orders of government do not embody the will of the nation, for the simple reason that the nation, as such, has no will. The State, so to say, is a parallelogram of forces in which now one element, now another, prevails."

In this century, legal academics began to consider a conception of the state that was changing as its capacities were enhanced by advances in technology and communications and as social problems were aggravated by industrialisation and urbanisation. Changes affecting the distinctness of the state administration were evident in three general areas—liberal theory, institutional forms, and governmental processes.

First, liberal theory shifted between poles that may be described either by reference to conceptions of individual freedom or the role of the state. It shifted from what Berlin famously called a negative freedom, requiring a certain freedom from governmental interference, towards a positive freedom, allowing or requiring government to facilitate individual development and fulfilment by providing services and enabling meaningful political participation.[65] Changes in the conception of the state roughly corresponded to changes in the conception of individual freedom. Hill describes the change from the state as "controller" to the state as "provider".[66] The night-watchman state with relatively discrete law-and-order functions was replaced by the welfare state with an indeterminate range of functions relating *inter alia* to health, housing, and social security.

Consequently, in his *Jurisprudence*, Salmond struggled to identify "the modern state".[67] Salmond still regarded the state's old night-watchman functions—"*war* and the *administration of justice*"—as "primary and essential" but recognised an open-ended category of secondary functions:[68]

> "The secondary functions of the state may be divided into two classes. The first consists of those which serve to secure the efficient fulfilment of the primary functions,

---

[62] Above at n. 13, 20–2 and 52–4. See generally Allison, above at n. 5, 61–6.

[63] See H.A. Deane, *The Political Ideas of Harold J. Laski* (Columbia University Press, New York, 1955); Barker, above at n. 37, 97–8, 129–31 and 165–71.

[64] H.J. Laski, "Duguit's Conception of the State", in W.I. Jennings *et al.*, *Modern Theories of Law* (Oxford University Press, London, 1933), 52, 65.

[65] See I. Berlin, "Two Concepts of Liberty", in A. Quinton (ed.), *Political Philosophy* (Oxford University Press, London, 1967), 141.

[66] Hill, above at n. 37, 44. See generally Craig, above at n. 37, 58–60.

[67] Above at n. 61.

[68] Ibid., 185 and 190–1 (emphasis added).

and the chief of these are two in number, namely legislation and taxation. . . . *The remaining class of secondary functions comprises all other forms of activity which are for any reason deemed especially fit to be undertaken by the state.* . . . Considerations such as these have, especially in modern times, induced the state to assume a great number of secondary and unessential functions, which in a peaceful and law-abiding community *tend even to overshadow and conceal from view those primary functions in which the essential nature of the state is to be found.*"

By implication, Salmond recognised that the secondary functions assumed by the state had rendered it less distinct.

Secondly, hybrid institutional forms—institutions variously related to central government—increased in importance in England,[69] as they did in France.[70] Public corporations, resulting from the nationalisation of industries, such as the Port of London Authority (1908) and the Central Electricity Board (1926), proliferated, as did QUANGOs (quasi-autonomous non-governmental organisations),[71] such as the Independent Television Authority (1954) and National Economic Development Council (1962). Especially after the Second World War, the number of public corporations increased as a result of various nationalising statutes, such as the Coal Industry Nationalisation Act 1946, the Gas Act 1948, and the Iron and Steel Act 1949. In 1965, Mitchell recognised the problem posed by hybrid institutions for the conceptualisation of the state administration: "[t]he 'administration' does not exist. Instead the law contemplates two things: 'the crown'—which is very broadly the central government, and other public authorities—largely local authorities with *public corporations existing in an uncanny half-world*".[72] Also defying classification in that "uncanny half-world" were QUANGOs, trade unions, mixed enterprises, pressure groups, professional associations, and, arguably, certain of the huge industrial corporations that developed through the course of this century.[73]

Thirdly, central governmental processes adapted to the increasing importance of corporations and to the enhanced potential of greater governmental wealth. From about the 1930s onwards and especially in the 1960s and 1970s,

---

[69] W. Friedmann, "The Public Corporation in Great Britain", in W. Friedmann (ed.), *The Public Corporation: A Comparative Symposium* (Stevens and Sons, London, 1954), 162; W. Friedmann and J.F. Garner (eds), *Government Enterprise: A Comparative Study* (Stevens and Sons, London, 1970); A. Barker (ed.), *Quangos in Britain: Government and the Networks of Public Policy-Making* (The Macmillan Press Ltd., London, 1982); I. Harden and N. Lewis, *The Noble Lie: The British Constitution and the Rule of Law* (Hutchinson, London, 1986), 56–62 and 153–87; P. Birkinshaw, I. Harden and N. Lewis, *Government by Moonlight: The Hybrid Parts of the State* (Unwin Hyman, London, 1990).

[70] See Allison, above at n. 5, 63–5.

[71] See, e.g., A. Shonfield, *Modern Capitalism: The Changing Balance of Public and Private Power* (Oxford University Press, London, 1965), 151–75.

[72] J.D.B. Mitchell, "The Causes and Effects of the Absence of a System of Public Law in the United Kingdom" [1965] *PL* 95, 113 (emphasis added).

[73] See W. Friedmann, *Law in a Changing Society* (Stevens and Sons, London, 2nd ed. 1972), 119–60, 312–22 and 329–30; H. Collins, *Justice in Dismissal: The Law of Termination of Employment* (Clarendon Press, Oxford, 1992), esp. 271–2; J.K. Galbraith, *The New Industrial State* (Andre Deutsch, London, 1972).

central government used its bargaining and contractual powers to achieve extraneous policy objectives, for example, to enforce a pay policy in the fight against inflation and a "Buy British" policy in the exploitation of North-Sea Oil.[74] Daintith identifies a general shift from governmental use of *imperium*, the power to pass prohibitive and authorising statutes, to the use of its *dominium* or wealth to secure its policy objectives.[75] Because of the increasing use of contractual powers, in Turpin's first edition of *Government Contracts* (1972), he described the "New Partnership", "a much closer relationship of mutual dependence" involving continuing consultation and co-operation in planning and research between central government and big industry to secure the most efficient and productive use of resources.[76] Although Turpin denied a blurring of public and private sectors comparable to that in the United States, his description of the public functions devolved to corporations and their public importance, together with his adoption of the concept of partnership,[77] suggest the increasing indistinctness of the state administration. By implication, the partners were equal in important respects. By implication, the state administration had become less distinct.

Identifying the state and its administration has not been facilitated by the privatisation schemes of the last two decades. Consider their effect on each of the three general changes described above—the state's extension, the proliferation of hybrid institutions, and governmental contracting with industry.

First, statutes, such as the British Aerospace Act 1980 and the Telecommunications Act 1984, sought to roll back the frontiers of the state, but the state's former role, together with its continuing role chiefly through regulation,[78] contributes to the vague sense that a public function is still being performed by the privatised industry. A commentator in *The Economist* observed: "[m]any of the once-nationalised companies do retain much of the feel of state behemoths".[79] The contraction of the state administration, like its earlier extension, obscures its distinctness.

Secondly, after initially attempting to reduce the number of hybrid institutions, central government increased expenditure on them, created new agencies (e.g. OFTEL and OFGAS) to regulate the privatised industries, and hived

---

[74] C. Turpin, *Government Contracts* (Penguin Books, Harmondsworth, 1972), 244–65.

[75] T.C. Daintith, "The Techniques of Government", in J. Jowell and D. Oliver (eds), *The Changing Constitution* (Clarendon Press, Oxford, 3rd ed. 1994), 209. See generally P.P. Craig, *Public Law and Democracy in the United Kingdom and the United States of America* (Clarendon Press, Oxford, 1990), 187 ff.

[76] Turpin, above at n. 74, 260–5, esp. 260–1. Cf. C. Turpin, *Government Procurement and Contracts* (Longman, Harlow, 2nd ed. 1989), 257–67.

[77] Turpin, *Government Contracts*, above at n. 74, 263–5.

[78] See generally C. Graham and T. Prosser, *Privatizing Public Enterprises: Constitutions, the State, and Regulation in Comparative Perspective* (Clarendon Press, Oxford, 1991); C.D. Foster, *Privatization, Public Ownership and the Regulation of Natural Monopoly* (Blackwell, Oxford, 1992); T. Prosser, "Regulation, Markets, and Legitimacy", in Jowell and Oliver, above at n. 75, 237.

[79] 27 July 1991, 16.

off more executive functions to quasi-governmental agencies (e.g., the Housing Action Trusts) and to the many new semi-autonomous departmental agencies envisaged by the Next Steps Programme.[80]

Thirdly, although central government has preferred regulation as the formal corrective to privatisation, it has nevertheless continued, in fact, to bargain with the privatised industries[81] and has also effectively promoted the "contracting-out" of numerous service functions.[82] In the second edition of his book on government contracts, Turpin describes how the new emphasis on *"value for money, competition* and *arm's length bargaining"* did not end the close relationship between government and industry:[83]

> "Despite the radical changes which have taken place in the aims and procedures of government contracting since 1979, there still exists a 'procurement community' of purchasing departments and their major suppliers, and in some important sectors of government procurement this is a restricted community whose members are locked together in a relationship of interdependence and shared interests. Features of this relationship are a continuous exchange of information, migration of personnel, hard bargaining and search for common ground. The Government concerns itself with the health of supplying industries, with their capacity to deliver what is wanted and to innovate so as to meet future governmental requirements. Industry looks to government for a flow of orders, seeks to resist foreign intrusion, and keeps up the pressure on government for improved levels of profit and more favourable contractual conditions."

The state administration remains at least as indistinct within the procurement community as it was within the old relationship between government and industry. Every so often, politicians on both sides of the British political divide lay claim to a "New Partnership", or, rather, a renewed partnership, still, by implication, a relationship between partners, who are equal in important respects.

In short, privatisation has not resulted in a clearly-defined core of government[84] or minimal state administration. Woolf and Jowell rightly conclude that the:[85]

> "legal relationships that arise out of . . . new forms of service provision (e.g. through contracting out and the 'hiving off' of central departmental responsibilities to new agencies) are neither wholly 'public' nor 'private'."

---

[80] R. Baldwin and C. McCrudden (eds), *Regulation and Public Law* (Weidenfeld and Nicolson, London, 1987), 28–30; Birkinshaw, Harden and Lewis, above at n. 69; G. Drewry, "Revolution in Whitehall: The Next Steps and Beyond", in Jowell and Oliver, above at n. 75, 155.
[81] Graham and Prosser, above at n. 78, 164 ff.
[82] See generally I. Harden, *The Contracting State* (Open University Press, Buckingham, 1992) and Mark Aronson's paper in this volume.
[83] Turpin, *Government Procurement and Contracts*, above at n. 76, 259 and 263.
[84] See Drewry, above at n. 80.
[85] Above at n. 4, 165. See also Mark Aronson's paper in this volume.

DISTINGUISHING WHILE DISPENSING WITH THE "STATE"

The traditional neglect of the state in the common law and the more recent blurring of the public-private divide have provoked various responses. One is to doubt their significance or decisive impact for the reason that an English distinction between public and private law, unlike the French, is not dependent upon or closely related to an abstract concept of the state. This response takes different forms.

Developing distinguishing criteria

Consider the approach in the fifth edition of De Smith's *Judicial Review of Administrative Action*. Lord Woolf and Professor Jowell recognise the blurring of the public-private divide but use it to reinforce the need for clear criteria with which nevertheless to distinguish public law from private law:[86]

> "The role of the state expanded enormously over the twentieth century. Recently attempts have been made to halt the expansion and even to roll back the boundaries of government. . . . These changes make it all the more desirable to have clear criteria for identifying the kinds of official decision that are subject to public law and a clear division in a modern state as to what constitutes the 'public' and the 'private' realm. . . . As the exercise of distinguishing between the public and private exercise of power becomes more complex, in order to avoid the danger of technical procedural barriers creating unnecessary obstacles to the redress of legitimate complaints by those aggrieved by unlawful, unfair or unreasonable decisions, it becomes increasingly important that the activities governed by public law should be clearly defined."

To demarcate the province of public law as applied in judicial review, Woolf and Jowell accept public function as the principal distinguishing criterion. They define "public function" by reference to legitimate authority: "[a] body is performing a "public function" when it seeks to achieve some collective benefit for the public or a section of the public and is accepted by the public or that section of the public as having authority to do so".[87] They add: "[c]harities, self-regulatory organisations and other nominally private institutions (such as universities, the Stock Exchange, Lloyd's of London, churches) may in reality also perform some types of public function. As Sir John Donaldson M.R. urged, it is important for the courts to 'recognise the realities of executive power' ".[88] They stress that "[p]ublic functions need not be the exclusive domain of the state".[89]

---

[86] Woolf and Jowell, above at n. 4, 163 and 167.
[87] Ibid., 167.
[88] Ibid., 168.
[89] Idem.

This approach of Woolf and Jowell is problematic for several reasons. First, they define public function by reference to the vague notions of authority, acceptance of authority, and benefit for a section of the public, all of uncertain application to hybrid institutions such as charities and pressure groups. They do refer to the supplementary criteria used by the English courts, such as governmental underpinning of a body's work or consensual submission to its authority, but accept considerable uncertainty:[90]

> "Undue reliance upon any one of the above criteria—while perhaps helpful in promoting certainty in this area of the law—should be avoided. The test of public function should be overriding and the qualities enumerated in the criteria should be weighed and balanced in the context of each specific case."

Such uncertainty has provoked continuing and fruitless litigation in the years since *O'Reilly* v. *Mackman*[91] and the English attempt to establish an exclusive public law procedure.

Secondly, the analysis of Woolf and Jowell seems to include an implicit and unanalysed functional notion of the state and its government or administration. They refer to the judicial supplementary criterion of governmental underpinning and the "but for" test ("whether, but for the existence of a non-statutory body, the government would itself almost inevitably have intervened to regulate the activity in question").[92] Both the criterion and the test refer to government. Woolf's and Jowell's definition of public function uses concepts—the public, collective benefit, and legitimate[93] authority—that would be at home in a theory of the state. And they call the ECJ's jurisprudence on whether a body should be regarded as exercising state powers "instructive".[94] Their approach endorses uncertainty and seems to return us to the concept of the state.

Thirdly, their concept of public function formally detached from, and unexplained by reference to, state powers or responsibilities provides little general direction for judicial review. They leave the courts armed with a concept in a theoretical twilight zone.

Regard for context

Cane provides another response to the blurring of the public-private divide. He recognises the difficulty of distinguishing public from private but questions therefore the usefulness of a classification of institutions or functions

---

[90] Ibid., 172. Cf. generally the reservations of Janet McLean in her paper in this volume.
[91] [1983] 2 AC 237. See generally Allison, above at n. 5, 90–5.
[92] Above at n. 4, 170.
[93] The concept of legitimacy is explicitly used to describe the necessary acceptance of authority: ibid., 167 n. 60.
[94] Ibid., 174. Cf. Woolf and Jowell, above at n. 4, 173 n. 94 and 191 n. 72.

"according to their intrinsic nature"[95] and doubts the significance of an abstract account of the state.[96] He rejects the "descriptive attack" on the distinction, the argument, such as Harlow's, that the distinction has become incongruous in contemporary society:[97]

> "The descriptive attack is, however, flawed in a fundamental way. The terms 'public' and 'private' are, in a very important sense, not descriptive terms. To say of some body or activity that it is 'public' or 'private' is not to say that it possesses some 'brute' characteristics but rather that, according to some norm or set of norms, the term 'public' or 'private' is appropriately applied to that body."

He argues that "there are various reasons for distinguishing between public and private law" and suggests that the distinction be drawn with regard to the specific reason in a specific context.[98]

Cane's contextual normative approach deserves careful attention. Although the terms public and private are not simply descriptive, they are also not simply normative. Benn and Gaus, cited by Cane as the authority for his argument that the terms are normative, stress that they are also descriptive:[99]

> "[I]t does not follow from a concept's being normative in the sense specified that it cannot also function descriptively. On the contrary: precisely because 'private' relates to social norms, to describe an object as private implies that it satisfies some, at least, of a bounded set of conditions specified in the norms, without which the normative implications would not hold."

Precisely because of the indistinctness of modern government, the term public in the relevant norms cannot reliably fulfil a descriptive function when applied to some institution or function. Cane refers us to relevant reasons for drawing a distinction in a particular context—whether they relate to the extent of government power, access to government information, the separation of powers, or procedural protections for public authorities.[100] The reasons listed, however, refer us back to concepts like government, governmental functions, or public authorities. We are repeatedly returned to the old issue of the state and its administration, the issue of what institution or function is sufficiently different to warrant the application of some rule, principle, or procedure of public law.

---

[95] *Introduction*, above at n. 2, 18.
[96] "Public Law and Private Law", above at n. 1, 78.
[97] Ibid., 65.
[98] *Introduction*, above at n. 2, 18.
[99] S.I. Benn and G.F. Gaus, "The Public and the Private: Concepts and Action", in S.I. Benn and G.F. Gaus (eds), *Public and Private in Social Life* (Croom Helm, London, 1983), 3, 12. See Cane, *Introduction*, above at n. 2, 16.
[100] Cane, *Introduction*, above at n. 2, 12–18; Cane, "Public law and Private Law", above at n. 1, 64–5 and 71–8. See also the opinion of Van Gerven AG in *Foster*, above at n. 19, paras. [11] & [21].

A theory of power

Another response to the blurring of the public-private divide is to use the increasingly-invoked[101] concept of power in place of the "state". But to use such a concept together with a distinction between public and private law, lawyers would still need to distinguish public from private power. In her article on the *ultra vires* rule, Professor Oliver mentioned a few differences:[102]

> "Supervisory jurisdiction has to take account of some important differences between public and private power. Where purely private power is concerned, three factors argue against extensive judicial supervision. Respect for the individual liberty of the parties, certainty in the law, and the needs of the market, would indicate that the courts ought not, in the name of good administration, to impose too many restraints on personal liberty, or introduce a general duty to subordinate private interests to the public interest unless a statute so requires."

Oliver's references to public and private power, however, are conclusory. They do not indicate when individual liberty, legal certainty, and the needs of the market should take precedence. Later in the same article, Oliver recognises the "absence of workable concepts and of a framework of theory about the nature of power, whether public or private, upon which to build the supervisory jurisdictions of the courts".[103] Oliver therefore suggests that "[p]olitical theorists and philosophers can assist lawyers in their understanding of the nature and incidence of power".[104]

By changing a conception of the state for one of power, however, English lawyers and legal academics would be moving from the unknown to the more unknown, from one area of difficult political theory to another, even more difficult.[105] They long struggled with the related concept of *vires*[106] and, before *Ridge* v. *Baldwin*, failed successfully to distinguish judicial, quasi-judicial, and

---

[101] See, e.g., *Breen* v. *Amalgamated Engineering Union* [1971] 2 QB 175, 190; G. Samuel, "Public Law and Private Law: A Private Lawyer's Response" (1983) 46 *MLR* 558, 575; Sir Harry Woolf, "Public Law-Private law: Why the Divide? A Personal View" [1986] *PL* 220, 224–5; Sir Harry Woolf, *Protection of the Public—A New Challenge* (Stevens and Sons, London, 1990), 26; D. Oliver, "Is the *Ultra Vires* Rule the Basis of Judicial Review?" [1987] *PL* 543, 565–9; Sir Gordon Borrie, "The Regulation of Public and Private Power" [1989] *PL* 552; Collins, above at n. 73, 192 and 270–4. But see Hoffmann L.J.'s disregard for the mere fact of power in *R.* v. *Disciplinary Committee of the Jockey Club, ex parte Aga Khan* [1993] 2 All ER 853, 874.

[102] Above at n. 101, 566.
[103] Ibid., 568.
[104] Idem.
[105] Cf., e.g., J.K. Galbraith, *The Anatomy of Power* (Hamish Hamilton, London, 1984) (see Oliver, above at n. 101, 568–9); M. Foucault, *Power/Knowledge: Selected Interviews and Other Writings 1972–1977* (C. Gordon (ed.)) (The Harvester Press, Brighton, 1980); M. Foucault, "Governmentality" (1979) 6 *Ideology & Consciousness* 5. See N. Rose, "Beyond the Public/Private Division: Law, Power and the Family" (1987) 14 *J of Law & Soc.* 61.
[106] See E.G. Henderson, *Foundations of English Administrative Law: Certiorari and Mandamus in the Seventeenth Century* (Harvard University Press, Cambridge, 1963), esp. 6–7.

purely administrative powers.[107] Now, they would need to elaborate a "genealogy of powers"[108] or an "anatomy of power" with concepts like "condign power", "compensatory power", and "conditioned power".[109] They might even be required to read the work of Foucault and his description of the ubiquity of power. Somehow Hercules would have to determine the boundaries of judicial review. He would have to determine, for example, whether someone like Mrs. Gillick, who challenged the legality of departmental guidance on contraceptive advice to young people, should be required to proceed by way of judicial review because parental power or the power of the doctor or expert is in issue.[110] Distinguishing criteria would be elusive.

In recent years, the concept of monopolistic power has been used in the context of judicial review.[111] If adopted as a criterion, it could bring within the province of public law monopolistic service provision and the state generally if defined as a monopoly of the use of force. It might prove useful in dealing with privatised corporations and national sporting associations. It is likely, however, to be too narrow and too broad as a criterion for determining the province of public law: too narrow, because, with its etymological connotations of exclusivity and the marketplace, it does not suit the many situations in which complementary or opposing authorities perform a variety of tasks; too broad, because it also covers private activities controlled through legislation on fair trading. It is probably therefore yet to be adopted, or reinstated[112] and elaborated, to enable the distinction between public and private law to be applied satisfactorily without a concept of the state.

ACCEPTING THE SIGNIFICANCE OF THE "STATE"

If academic and practising lawyers in the English common law cannot escape the issue of the state, whether by developing specific distinguishing criteria, adopting a contextual approach, elaborating a theory of power, or by some

---

[107] [1964] AC 40. See generally E.C.S. Wade and A.W. Bradley, *Constitutional and Administrative Law* (Longman, London, 10th ed. 1985), 604–7.

[108] Foucault, *Power/Knowledge*, above at n. 105.

[109] Galbraith, above at n. 105, esp. 4–6.

[110] See *Gillick* v. *West Norfolk and Wisbech Area Health Authority* [1986] AC 112.

[111] See, e.g., *R.* v. *Jockey Club, ex parte Massingberd-Mundy* [1993] 2 All ER 207, 222; *R.* v. *Jockey Club, ex parte RAM Racecourses* [1993] 2 All ER 225, 247; Woolf and Jowell, above at n. 4, 170–1, 182–3 and 185. But cf. H.W.R. Wade, "Beyond the Law: A British Innovation in Judicial Review" (1991) 43 *Admin LR* 559.

[112] See the old common law authorities for imposing a requirement of reasonableness on the exercise of monopolistic powers: Sir Matthew Hale, "De Portibus Maris", in F. Hargrave (ed.), *Collection of Tracts Relative to the Laws of England* (Dublin, 1787), 45, 77–8; *Bolt* v. *Stennett* (1800) 8 TR 606, 101 ER 1572; *Allnutt* v. *Inglis* (1810) 12 East 527, 104 ER 206. See generally P.P. Craig, "Constitution, Property and Regulation" [1991] *PL* 538; M. Taggart, "Public Utilities and Public Law", in P.A. Joseph (ed.), *Essays on the Constitution* (Brooker's, Wellington, 1995), 214.

other method, they need to accept its significance.[113] They need to accept that the distinction in the common law, like that in the civil law, is closely related to the "state".

Accepting the state's significance would have explanatory value. The traditional neglect of the state and the indistinctness of the modern state administration could then be expected to have serious implications for identifying the province of public law. That neglect could well explain the rejection of the distinction between public and private law by Dicey and others in the common law tradition. And that indistinctness could well explain many of the difficulties, the uncertainties, the continuing litigation, and the judicial retreat following the attempt in the last fifteen years to secure special procedures for public law cases in England.[114]

Accepting the state's significance should affect the understanding of the problem facing the English common law and the way in which it is addressed. If the state is closely related to the distinction, uncertainty about the state can be expected to produce general uncertainty about the province of public law, about the legal consequences of administrative disputes generally, whether those consequences involve special procedures, special courts, or special principles of accountability. The uncertainty is not confined to the procedural minefield produced by the English procedures developed for public law cases. And to address that uncertainty in the English common law, further analysis of the state is required—analysis of the distinctness of its administration and of those attributes that justify the use of special legal principles, institutions, and procedures.

The attempt to demarcate the province of English public law regardless of the "state"—whether through an unrelated criterion of public function, regard for context, or a theory of power—will be extremely difficult and is anyway likely to return us to the old issue, in the words of Durkheim: "[w]hat, moreover, is the State? Where does it begin and where does it end?"[115] To which we might add, "what are the peculiar functions or powers of its administration?" and, once those have been identified and characterised, "what are their implications for the role of the courts?" If those questions are unanswerable or have become too difficult, a separate administrative law will continue to lack theoretical justification.

---

[113] See, e.g., T.R.S. Allan, *Law, Liberty, and Justice: The Legal Foundations of British Constitutionalism* (Clarendon Press, Oxford, 1993), 157–62; N.E. Simmonds, *The Decline of Juridical Reason: Doctrine and Theory in the Legal Order* (Manchester University Press, Manchester, 1984), ch. 9.

[114] See Allison, above at n. 5, 80–1, 90–100 and 237–9.

[115] E. Durkheim, *The Division of Labour in Society*, (G. Simpson (tr.)) (The Free Press, New York, 1964), 68.

5

Administrative Law for a New Century

ALFRED C. AMAN, JR.*

INTRODUCTION

Deregulation, cost-benefit analysis, market-oriented regulatory approaches, declining regulatory budgets, devolution and the delegation of public tasks to the private sector are but some of the hallmarks of what I have called the global era of administrative law.[1] These regulatory trends are not limited to the United States. In various degrees, they typify new approaches to public law in various countries around the world.[2] Almost all of these reforms are market-oriented; that is, they either substitute markets and the private sector for regulatory regimes or have public agencies use market approaches, structures and incentives to achieve their regulatory goals.

The changes occurring in public law have parallels in the private sector. In both sectors, downsizing,[3] decentralising regulatory (or deregulatory) responsibilities,[4] and increasing efficiency are among the parallel trends that conceptually transform citizens into consumers.[5] Corporate "downsizing", "outsourcing", "off-shore production" and "re-engineering"[6] are indicative of private sector attempts to maximise efficiency and profits in a manner that takes full advantage of new global technologies[7] and newly emerging, worldwide markets.[8] Corporate structures, both for manufacturing and distribution

---

* I wish to thank Professors Carol Greenhouse, Jost Delbrück and Lauren Robel for their very helpful comments on this paper, as well as Ursula Doyle, for her excellent research assistance.

[1] A.C. Aman, *Administrative Law In A Global Era* (Cornell University Press, Ithaca, 1992).

[2] See, "Symposium, Project: Privatization: The Global Scale-Back of Government Involvement in National Economies" (1996) 48 *Admin LR* 435. See also J. Kelsey, *Economic Fundamentalism* (Pluto Press, London, 1995) and the papers by Mark Aronson and Murray Hunt in this volume.

[3] Executive Order No. 12875, 3 CFR, reprinted in 5 U.S.C. § 601 (1993). In this order, President Clinton provides state, local, and tribal governments with "more flexibility to design solutions to the problems faced by citizens in this country without excessive micro-management and unnecessary regulation from the federal government".

[4] See generally Gore Commission, *National Performance Review* (1995).

[5] Idem.

[6] Peter Dicken, *Global Shift: The Internationalization of Economic Activity* (Guilford Press, New York, 2nd ed. 1992), 169.

[7] Ibid., 47.

[8] Ibid., 24–7.

purposes, are changing, with corporate webs—regional and often global in their reach—and smaller, decentralised units of production increasingly typifying the more flexible ways in which businesses organise themselves and operate.[9] In this paper, I will argue that globalisation is having a similar effect on the organisation of the regulatory state.

The parallel changes in the public law and private sectors are occurring within a global context whose most significant feature is an unprecedented degree of interconnectedness among national economies.[10] A second characteristic feature of globalisation is intense competition among national economies and many of the corporate entities that operate within them.[11] Given today's computer and information technologies, global economic processes also challenge traditional analytical concepts such as core and periphery,[12] or comparative advantage. They involve new patterns of trade and corporate finance.[13] More importantly, the essence of globalisation today is that these processes occur without direct agency of the state.[14] Thus, they not only are changing the shape of and the ways in which the private sector does business, but these processes also challenge fundamental ideas of what the state is, what its relationship to the private sector should be, and what actions the state can realistically take to deal effectively with perceived social, economic and political problems.

It is within this context of globalisation that this paper addresses a basic question: what role can the state effectively play as a regulator, given the collapse of the distinction between domestic and global, as well as that between public and private? Since globalisation processes are so varied, globalisation is a term with many meanings, some of which have long been a part of our economic and political landscapes. I shall argue, however, that the impact of today's globalisation processes on United States administrative law is transforming it in new ways. Indeed, there are changing roles for the state to play based largely on new ways of incorporating market regulatory approaches (and the private sector generally) to public interest ends. Four broad regulatory innovations signal the beginning of a new transformation of administrative law: (1) the delegation of public functions to the private sector; (2) the increasingly common recourse to market regulatory approaches as a

---

[9] Ibid., 207–23.
[10] Ibid., 14.
[11] Ibid., 44.
[12] Ibid., 11–14.
[13] Idem. For an excellent analysis of the fundamental changes brought about by globalisation on various industries, especially the information technology industries, see S. Sassen, *The Global City: New York, London, Tokyo* (Princeton University Press, Princeton, 1991). See also S. Sassen, *Cities in a World Economy* (Pine Forge Press, Thousand Oaks, 1994).
[14] See J. Delbrück, "Globalization of Law, Politics, and Markets—Implications for Domestic Law—A European Perspective" (1993) 1 *Ind J Global Legal Stud* 9. See also A.C. Aman, "The Earth as Eggshell Victim: A Global Perspective on Domestic Regulation" (1993) 102 *Yale LJ* 2107 and S. Sassen, "Towards A Feminist Analytics of the Global Economy" (1997) 4 *Ind J Global Legal Stud* 55.

substitute for command-control rules; (3) application of market organisational models such as federal corporations and (4) procedural processes such as negotiated rulemaking. The effect of such a transformation shifts the role of the legal system primarily from legitimating new extensions of public power and increased state intervention, to legitimating new mixes of public and private power, new uses of private power and increased reliance on market approaches to further public interest goals. This transformation is the major theme of this paper.

To set the story for this basic shift in administrative law focus, Part I of this paper will first examine the role administrative law has played in two different regulatory eras—the *laissez-faire* era of the 19th and early 20th century and the regulatory era of the New Deal and beyond. Part II will then set forth some examples of current regulatory reform approaches involving new mixes of state and private power. Part III will then provide various perspectives on these developments, arguing that though we are in the midst of an important transformation in administrative law, policy makers, courts and the public can interpret these changes in various ways. This paper concludes by arguing that it is necessary to see these changes in a way that can create the legal structures and doctrines necessary to facilitate new governmental approaches to problems and the new public/private relationships necessary to carry them out. This is necessary if the state is to play a meaningful regulatory role and provide an opportunity for a broad public interest discourse on the many policy questions that will confront our increasingly interconnected, global societies.

ADMINISTRATIVE LAW AND THE STATE—PAST APPROACHES

The Role of Administrative Law—Past Regimes

Administrative law is directly linked to the dominant theory of the state in vogue at any given point in time. For most of the nineteenth century, at least until the rise of the Industrial Revolution, it was assumed that the state would play a limited and essentially negative role.[15] The administrative law that developed in this time was also limited. So-called "red light" theories of administrative law predominated,[16] as the guiding theory of administrative procedure was to maximise protections of citizens from governmental action. This occurred quite naturally, as a function of administrative law's confine-

---

[15] See C. Harlow and R. Rawlings, *Law and Administration* (Weidenfeld and Nicolson, London, 1984), 9–10. As Harlow and Rawlings have noted: "its role was to act as a 'policeman', providing the framework in which citizens could go about their business. According to Locke, the state's functions are limited to the presentation of the rights of its members against infringement by others. . . . It is this and nothing more; a state exceeds its legitimate function if it endeavors to go beyond these limits": idem.

[16] Ibid., chs 1 and 2.

ment to the courts, thus ensuring that an adversary model of justice would apply, as would basic common law doctrines.[17]

As modern government grew, especially with the creation of various New Deal programmes in the 1930s and beyond, a new theory of administrative law—one that articulated the rationales of a more interventionist state—was necessary. Procedure came to be viewed more functionally, as a means of carrying out the politically legitimate commands of the state. The consistent application of such a theory by the courts and even the legislature developed slowly, however, in part because procedural issues were often thought of as separate and distinct from the substantive issues involved. A judicial, adversary model of procedure was usually synonymous with what constituted fairness to the litigants. Prior to the Administrative Procedure Act (APA), there was no generally accepted alternative procedural model to the adversary model provided by the courts, even when policy issues were predominant. Procedures, of course, have substantive effects, as well. The more adversarial the procedures, the fairer the process might appear, particularly to those who objected to the substance of the regulation to be implemented in the first place, but the more difficult and costly it was to carry out the governmental programmes involved. The use of procedure to achieve substantive ends, contrary to the substantive goals of a particular governmental programme, has a long history in the United States.[18] It was, thus, a major step simply to be able, constitutionally speaking, to move adjudicatory proceedings from the courts to administrative agencies, to which the Supreme Court gave its constitutional blessing in *Crowell* v. *Benson* in 1932.[19]

But simply moving proceedings from courts to agencies did not automatically mean more efficient procedures. It was often politically difficult to apply other than adversarial procedural approaches to regulatory issues, no matter where the case was litigated—court or agency. Indeed, the APA, ultimately passed in 1946, had elements of both the traditional, adversarial procedural

---

[17] See P. Verkuil, "The Emerging Concept of Administrative Procedure" (1978) 78 *Col LR* 258. As Professor Verkuil has noted with respect to early United States administrative law, "[t]he substantive values of the nineteenth-century liberal, non-interventionist state and the procedural values of the common law, adversary model of decisionmaking have a common core and are mutually supportive. Both sets of values reflected a common philosophical premise that the correct result would be achieved by the free clash of competing forces in the marketplace, or in the courtroom. As Jerome Frank noted, the 'fight [or adversary] theory of justice is a sort of *laissez-faire*' ": Verkuil, ibid., 264, quoting from J. Frank, *Courts on Trial: Myth and Reality in American Justice* (Princeton University Press, Princeton, 1949), 92.

[18] For a case study of the uses and misuses of procedures, see A.C. Aman, "Institutionalizing The Energy Crisis: Some Structural and Procedural Lessons" (1980) 65 *Cornell LR* 491.

[19] *Crowell* v. *Benson*, 285 U.S. 22 (1932). This was a watershed case and a major victory for the administrative process. As Professor Verkuil has noted: "The lawyers of the time fought hard . . . to keep decision-making in the courts for two reasons. First, the adversary system with its opportunity for jury trials and other procedural protections meant less control by the decision-maker over the process. Second, the judiciary's antipathy to government programs provided a favorable environment for decision. Thus, the adversary system held its place as an important value of classical liberalism even as the definition of liberalism was changing": above at n. 17, 265.

approach to regulation and a more functional approach.[20] The Act provided for the full panoply of adversarial procedures[21] and they often were applied with regularity, even when policy making issues predominated.[22]

Of course, the APA also represented an important procedural breakthrough. Commenting on the Attorney-General's Report of 1941 that was to become an important basis for the APA, Professor Verkuil highlighted some of the newer aspects of this legislation:[23]

> "Procedures were seen as means to the end of fair implementation of government programs and their efficacy was to be measured by their contribution to that end. This functional view of procedure argued for flexibility and informality along with a recognition of adversary hearings. . . . Automatic and unexamined reliance upon the judicial model would never again satisfactorily resolve debate."

Though alternative procedural models in an administrative setting were now possible, the judicial model continued to hold its own, particularly because some economic regulation from the 1940s to the 1960s was, in one form or another, viewed as a kind of ratemaking.[24] More often than not, adjudicatory procedures were used, even in administrative agency settings where the disputes clearly had important policy implications. The choice of procedures—rulemaking or adjudication—was largely left to the agency,[25] and most agencies regularly opted for adjudicatory procedures.[26]

Quite apart from the procedures used to implement agency programmes, the fundamental question of agency legitimacy loomed large, especially as the scope of regulation increased. The courts were largely responsible for providing the legal framework that transformed administrative law from the traditional common law model of public law to one more appropriately suited to an interventionist state.[27] Courts did this, in large part, by expanding the

---

[20] The functional approach was best represented by the broad category of agency actions that the APA considered to be informal and beyond formal procedural protection. See M. Shapiro, "APA: Past, Present, Future" (1986) 72 *Va LR* 447.

[21] See 5 U.S.C. § 554, 556, 557 (1946) (APA adjudicatory procedures).

[22] See generally B. Boyer, "Alternatives to Administrative Trial-Type Hearings for Resolving Complex Scientific, Economic and Social Issues" (1972) 71 *Mich LR* 111.

[23] Verkuil, above at n. 17, 275.

[24] Certainly, utility price-setting fits this form, but many other forms of utility regulation such as the allocation priorities for gas suppliers among interstate competitors also were set by adjudicatory procedures. In addition, the National Labour Relations Board (NLRB) was notorious for its use of adjudication, even when rulemaking was appropriate.

[25] Boyer, above at n. 22, 115–6.

[26] Ibid., 112–3. The relatively lean and efficient rulemaking procedures of the APA were seldom used, but with the advent of health, environmental and safety regulation in the 1960s and 1970s, rulemaking became far more important. It also became increasingly judicialised. See W.F. Pedersen, "The Decline of Separation of Functions in Regulatory Agencies" (1978) 64 *Va LR* 991.

[27] R.B. Stewart, "The Reformation of American Administrative Law" (1975) 88 *Harv LR* 1667. As Stewart noted (ibid., 1669–70):

> "The traditional model of administrative law, developed out of judicial decisions and legislative enactments during the first six decades of this century, has sought to reconcile the competing claims of governmental authority and private autonomy by prohibiting official

opportunities for interested parties to participate in agency and judicial proceedings, thereby making the administrative process a surrogate political process. In his influential article, "The Reformation of American Administrative Law",[28] Professor Stewart summed up this transition in this way:[29]

> "In the space of a few years, the Supreme Court has largely eliminated the doctrine of standing as a barrier to challenging agency action in court, and judges have accorded a wide variety of affected interests the right not only to participate in, but to force the initiation of, formal proceedings before the agency. Indeed, this process has gone beyond the mere extension of participation and standing rights, working a fundamental transformation of the traditional model. Increasingly, the function of administrative law is not the protection of private autonomy but the provision of a surrogate political process to ensure the fair representation of a wide range of affected interests in the process of administrative decisions."

In the global era, administrative law now appears to be moving from its role as legitimating new extensions of public power, to legitimating new blends of public and private power and/or private power used for public interest ends. The new administrative law of market approaches and structures is largely the creation of the legislative and executive branches of government.[30] It is unclear just what the role of courts will be, and it may well be that the Supreme Court's interest in reviving the 10th Amendment as well as the Takings Clause of the Constitution could undercut the legislative flexibility necessary to create new regulatory models involving federal, state and local regulation.[31]

The move towards greater political participation and ultimately greater transparency of agency decision-making processes that typified modern administrative law in the 1960s and 1970s was the crucial aspect of the transformation of administrative law that Professor Stewart documents and it is precisely this aspect of the process that is most in jeopardy from some of the processes of globalisation. In a global economy, many significant economic

---

intrusions on private liberty or property unless authorised by legislative directives. . . . Two fundamental criticisms have been levied against the traditional model. First . . . the limitation of the traditional model's protections to recognised liberty and property interests is no longer appropriate in view of the seemingly inexorable expansion of government power over private welfare. Second . . . agencies have failed to discharge their respective mandates to protect the interests of the public in given fields of administration, and that the traditional model has been unable to remedy such failure. In responses to these criticisms, judges have greatly expanded the machinery of the traditional model to protect new classes of interests."

[28] Idem.
[29] Ibid., 1670.
[30] It appears that, once gain, courts may be in the "red light" position, but this situation is not the same red light—this is a different junction with different traffic. See A.C. Aman, "Fragmentation, Federalism and the Global Economy" (work in progress).
[31] See text accompanying nn. 70–75 below. Courts may also react negatively to corporatist procedural approaches. See, e.g., *USA Group Loan Services, Inc.* v. *Riley*, 82 F. 3d 708 (7th Cir. 1996) (discussed below at nn. 64–70). See P.J. Harter, "First judicial review of Reg Neg a disappointment" (1996) 22 *Admin & Reg L News* 1.

issues are decided before they can even become matters of public concern or involvement.[32] Capital markets function independently of any one nation's concerns but they can place enormous pressure on states to conform to the dictates of the market.[33] The public/private distinction, so long a part of United States public law, shields much of this economic decision-making activity from public law, but financial decisions of this sort are so influential that they can structure the terms in which the public sector will act.

This kind of financial pressure can undercut significantly the ability of a state to engage in traditional forms of economic regulation. Moreover, in a global economy, investments in plant and labour know no boundaries. If costs in the form of taxes and regulatory burdens are too high, such investment can easily flow to locations where its return is greater.[34] Corporations that do business in various parts of the world may, thus, choose to expand or move their operations to more favourable jurisdictions. Even if such "locational threats" never materialise, they have the capacity to affect seriously the politics and political decisions at federal, state and local levels. Indeed, rather than appear weak, the state may try to be proactive by adopting a "pro-growth" economic policy that affirmatively emphasises lower taxes and less regulation. Such an approach enables the state to "do something", even though the substance of its actions is to minimise its overall role in the economy.

Approaching regulatory reforms, however, as if they are either in the public sphere or the private sphere gives more meaning and significance to the public/private distinction than it should have. In some instances, privatising a particular policy area may not be accomplished necessarily to eliminate government and public participation, but rather to apply the discipline of the market to the implementation of the public policies involved. In other areas, it may be that the decisions to be made are wholly private and best left to the market—such as the price of gas or oil at the wellhead. The use of private or market discourses to further collective public ends should be seen as separate from the uses of private power intended to be wholly separate from any kind of public, collective decision-making processes.

ADMINISTRATIVE LAW AND THE STATE—SOME CURRENT APPROACHES

Recent regulatory reforms at the federal level include some clear examples of privatisation—that is, the complete withdrawal of the government and the

---

[32] See generally S. Strange, *Casino Capitalism* (Blackwell, Oxford, 1986).
[33] Ibid., 3.
[34] D.M. Andrews, "Capital Mobility and State Autonomy: Toward a Structural Theory of International Monetary Relations" (1994) 38 *International Studies Quarterly* 193. For an analysis of capital mobility and its relationship to labour mobility, see S. Sassen, *The Mobility of Labour and Capital* (Cambridge University Press, Cambridge, 1988).

return of various decisions wholly to the private market. Certain aspects of airlines were deregulated in the 1970s and the Civil Aeronautics Board was abolished; price controls on oil and gas at the wellhead have been repealed, and most recently the Interstate Commerce Commission has been abolished.[35] With the bulk of regulatory reforms, however, the state remains involved, but it increasingly must incorporate aspects of the market to achieve public interest ends. Indeed, market models, approaches, language and concepts dominate the way the federal government now approaches its regulatory role. This is particularly evident in the language, approach, proposals and tone of the Gore Commission report on reinventing government.

In the first National Performance Review (NPR), published in September 1993, the Gore Commission outlined both the state of the United States government and a plan to "reinvent" the government so that it might better serve its people and continue to lead the world in this new era of globalisation. In this report the Administration stated that its goals were to create a government "that makes sense"; "gets results"; "puts customers first"; and "gets its money's worth". To that end, it directed all agency heads to: "cut obsolete regulations"; "reward results, not red tape"; "get out of Washington and create grassroots partnerships"; and "negotiate, don't dictate". Since issuing the first report, the Administration has published two updates, the latest of which proclaims boldly that "The Era of Big Government is Over".

The application of this new rhetoric in a global context augurs significant changes in United States administrative law that include: (1) new blends of public and private sectors at all levels of government; (2) a redefinition of what is public and what is private, or at least what kinds of functions can be fulfilled in the private sector; (3) greater reliance on bargaining and negotiation models of decision-making when it comes to the exercise of agency discretion; (4) a diminution of public participation stemming from increased reliance on privatisation and the delegation of public functions to private entities; and (5) a market discourse that arguably narrows the role of public interest values, and replaces them with the rhetoric of cost-benefit analysis.

To analyse such changes in regulatory direction, emphasis and language, we shall briefly describe four examples of recent regulatory reforms and their impact on administrative law: (1) the wholesale delegation of public functions to the private sector; (2) the devolution of federal responsibilities to the states and the private sector; (3) the retention of governmental responsibility for implementation purposes, but the privatisation of the procedures and structures used to implement these government programmes; and (4) new procedural approaches designed to produce more consensual and, presumably, enforceable regulations.

---

[35] Interstate Commerce Commission Termination Act of 1995, Pub. L. No. 104–88, 109 Stat 803 (1995).

Delegating Public Responsibilities to the Private Sector

Some might argue with my characterisation of administrative law's new "charge" of blending public and private power by saying that regulation always involves a mix of the public and the private because of the processes used to promulgate them. If a rule is under consideration, comments are requested from the regulated. If adjudication is underway, obviously there is give and take between the private parties and the government during the course of the proceeding. More informal contacts have also been a part of the administrative process, especially if the matters involve future directions the agency might or might not take.

Such contacts, however, usually involve an arm's length set of relationships with the government positioned as a neutral decision-maker and the regulated as interested parties to the proceeding. In rulemaking proceedings, participation is open to all who have an interest and there is a strong bias in favor of having all communications with the agency in the record.

Recent reforms at the state and federal levels, however, seek to involve the private sector in different ways. One approach is to delegate power and functions, usually thought of as public, to the private sectors. Short of a wholesale delegation, a related approach is to subcontract out a significant portion of those functions normally done by the agency to the private sector.[36] Another is to involve not only the private sector in such new partnerships, but to enlist the cooperation and involvement of state and local government as well. Let me briefly explore two such examples: namely private prisons and welfare reform.

Private Prisons

In its 1996 budget proposal, the Justice Department requested $318 million to build three new federal prisons and fund the activation of seven new prisons, of which five will be privatised. "In compliance with reinventing government measures, the request proposes the further utilisation of private companies,

---

[36] The Environmental Protection Agency (EPA) is in the forefront of creating partnerships with the businesses that it regulates. The latest *National Performance Review* reports that "since 1992, EPA has more than tripled membership in its "Partners for the Environment" program, with over 7,100 companies now participating. One of these partnerships was forged . . . with the Gillette Company, which has a good track record of compliance. . . . An independent firm audits Gillette's compliance with environmental regulations, and makes audit reports public. Gillette pays the cost of the audit and gets amnesty to fix non-criminal violations without being fined. EPA makes no further inspections, and Gillette makes no further reports": Gore Commission, *National Performance Review, The Best Kept Secrets in Government* (Washington, D.C., 1996), 14.

EPA has two projects—Project XL and the Common Sense Initiative—designed to further their relationship with business. Project XL is designed to give regulated industries the flexibility to design their own regulatory strategies on the condition that they produce greater environmental benefits: idem. The Common Sense Initiative challenges "companies to take innovative approaches to controlling pollution": ibid., 91.

where most appropriate, to manage federal inmates. This expands the private sector's role in federal corrections by contracting for the management and operation of several federal prisons currently under construction. The majority of future pretrial detention, minimum and low security federal prisons will be privatised".[37]

Privatising prisons differs from deregulating airlines or ending price controls on the price of oil or gas at the wellhead.[38] The airline industry as well as the oil and gas industries are private industries with a substantial number of competitors. Markets can work in setting prices in all of these areas. Prisons, at least in modern times,[39] generally have been thought of as a public function.[40] This does not mean that the "services" associated with running a prison cannot be provided by private companies, but the overall responsibility of providing for prisons has generally been viewed as a governmental responsibility. The implications of privatisation of such a function are different from those involved when an industry such as the gas or oil industry is deregulated. When that occurs, public law procedures no longer apply to how the price is set by market competitors. The antitrust laws usually suffice. In such industries, what once was public and the subject of elaborate ratemaking hearings, is now private. But when responsibility for prisons is delegated to the private sector, important constitutional questions persist: can the government delegate these responsibilities and, if so, what are the constitutional rights of prisoners in a private institution?

Courts have begun to resolve these issues, usually in favor of extending some aspects of the public sphere to what is now the private sector.[41] This is

---

[37] Department of Justice, News Release, "Justice Department Seeks 20 Percent Increase in FY 96 Budget to Reduce Violent Crime and Illegal Immigration" (6 Feb. 1995).

[38] Historically, private prisons, like private fire departments, were prevalent in the 18th and 19th centuries, but they have been, almost exclusively, a state function ever since. See B.B. Evans, "Private Prisons" (1987) 36 *Emory LJ* 253. For a discussion of the constitutionality of the delegation of these functions, see J. Field, "Making Prisons Private: An Improper Delegation of a Governmental Power" (1987) 15 *Hofstra LR* 649.

[39] See J.J. Misrahi, "Factories with Fences: An Analysis of the Prison Industry Enhancement Certification Program in Historical Perspective" (1996) 33 *Am Crim LR* 411.

[40] See above at n. 38.

[41] In *Edmonson* v. *Leesville Concrete Company*, 500 U.S. 614 (1991) the Supreme Court reaffirmed that the appropriate test for determining the presence of "state action" is whether the claimed action resulted from a right or a privilege having its source in state authority and whether the private party charged with the constitutional violation can be described in all fairness as a state actor. The Court further noted that the question of "state action" is determined by the following: the extent to which the actor relies on governmental assistance and benefits; whether the actor is performing a traditional governmental function; and whether the injury caused is aggravated in a unique way by the incidents of governmental authority. See also *Lugar* v. *Edmondson Oil Company Inc.*, 457 U.S. 922, 939–42 (1982).

Such a test seems to militate in favor of a finding of "state action" on the part of any private prison. However, the Court has found that the "acts of private contractors, who build roads, bridges, dams, ships, or submarines for government, do not become acts of government by reason of their significant or even total engagement in performing public contracts": *Rendell-Baker* v. *Kohn*, 457 U.S. 830, 840–41 (1982).

In *McKnight* v. *Rees*, 88 F. 3d 417 (1996) the Sixth Circuit recently held that correctional

accomplished, however, through the application of the state action doctrine, a doctrine that is hardly clear and is highly fact specific.[42] Clearly, this is a doctrine on which much will turn, if there is to be a role for public law in the future. Quite apart from the important legal questions involved, the very nature of this new partnership between the public and private sectors is instructive to us for at least three reasons. First, it suggests that a major source of regulatory reform by means of privatisation is driven by the need to lower the costs of government. Competition among private providers of prison services will enable these services to be provided efficiently. Second, by implication, privatisation of a public function suggests that government is *not* as good or, at least, not as efficient as it needs to be. Third, the equation of market approaches and efficiency with the public interest suggests that even a function such as imprisoning violators of the law is not so different in its mechanics from a traditional market activity as to exclude the private sector. It is important to emphasise, however, that privatising prisons in this way enlists the private sector in a way that does more than arguably save money. It also mixes the private and public sectors in a new way and one that is not isolated, but part of a larger, emerging pattern of governmental attempts to accomplish essentially public responsibilities in cost efficient ways. The question that does arise and which will continue to do so, is the extent to which public law applies to the private side of these partnerships? On a more philosophical level, the question that also arises is whether the kinds of values protected by public law are capable of being translated primarily into an efficiency discourse.[43] Is there anything lost in the translation? Welfare reforms clearly raise such concerns, especially since the prior welfare regime was based on the premise that it was the federal government's duty to provide a safety net for those who could not be accommodated by the market economy.

---

officers in a private prison were not afforded "qualified immunity" as a defense to a prisoner's claim under § 1983 of the Civil Rights Act, 42 U.S.C. The defendants worked for Corrections Corporation of America, a private, for-profit corporation, which had a contract with the state of Tennessee to maintain some of its correctional facilities. The plaintiff McKnight alleged the defendants violated his constitutional rights under the Eighth Amendment by subjecting him to tight restraints during his transport to another prison, ultimately resulting in his hospitalisation. The court recognised that §1983 provides a cause of action against any person who, under color of state law, deprives an individual of any right, privilege, or immunity secured by the Constitution and federal law. It found, however, that "the public policy underpinnings of qualified immunity—which strike a balance between compensation for constitutional injury and the public interest in effective government—do not apply with equal force to actions undertaken by employees of a private, for-profit corporation": ibid., 425. The court refused to grant qualified immunity to the prison officials. The Supreme Court granted a writ of certiorari in this case on 27 Nov. 1996 (Docket No. 96–318).

[42] See R. Krotoszynski, "Back To The Briarpatch: An Argument In Favor Of Constitutional Meta-Analysis In State Action Determinations" (1995) 94 *Mich LR* 302, 303 and generally Jack Beermann's paper in this volume.

[43] See generally Dawn Oliver's paper in this volume.

Welfare Reform

Quite apart from traditional federalism concerns and the role that states are to play in our federal system, devolution of federal responsibilities to the states is also driven by cost considerations and increased competition for foreign investment among individual states. Indeed, many states now have their own trade representatives in various countries around the world and they aggressively seek foreign investment, the jobs that come with this investment as well as new global markets for the products produced in their states. Having a greater chance to control more closely the regulatory and social costs incurred in the state can make efficient states more competitive in the global economy. This is one of many reasons for the drive towards greater state control of welfare assistance programmes.[44] Indeed, the Clinton Administration has issued countless memoranda and orders endorsing the devolution of federal power to the states.[45] Its reason is similar to those given by large corporations that seek to decentralise their operations, and that is, to increase efficiency. According to the federal government, the states "should have more flexibility to design solutions to the problems faced by citizens in this country without excessive micro management and unnecessary regulation from the Federal Government".[46] Welfare reform is one of the most dramatic examples of this kind of governmental decentralisation.

The Welfare Reform Act of 1996, also known as the "Personal Responsibility and Work Opportunity Reconciliation Act of 1996", removes the responsibility of administering welfare to needy families from the federal government and transfers the task to the states through the conferral of "block grants". In so doing, the federal government has given up its traditional safety net function of protecting the poor. The relinquishment of the safety net role is based, in large part, on the belief that individual states can devise their own programmes to deal with the poor and make their own choices as to how best to meet the needs of their poorest citizens. A federal presence, however, remains. A state is eligible to provide welfare under this Act only if it has first submitted a plan to the Secretary of Health and Human Services that meets several requirements, including how the state intends to conduct a programme that: (1) provides assistance to needy families with (or expecting) children and provides parents with job preparation, work and support services to enable

---

[44] See A.C. Aman "A Global Perspective on Current Regulatory Reform: Rejection, Relocation or Reinvention?" (1995) 2 *Ind J Global Legal Stud* 429.

[45] One ground-breaking example of federal-state partnership is the "Oregon Option: A Proposed Model for Results-Driven Intergovernmental Service Delivery". This approach is designed to encourage mutually agreed upon and measurable outcomes for public service delivery. The measure of the success of the Oregon Option will be its 272 human investment "benchmarks". These benchmarks will focus on reduced teen pregnancy, diminished crime and recidivism, lower unemployment, higher per capita income, greater early childhood immunisation, and stronger K-12 student achievement. Several organisations will work together to achieve these goals: state and local governments, civic groups, non-profit corporations, and businesses.

[46] Executive Order No. 12875, above at n. 3, 1.

them to leave the programme and become self-sufficient; and (2) requires a parent or caretaker to engage in work (as defined by the state) once the state determines that the parent or caretaker is ready to engage in work, or once the parent or caretaker has received assistance for 24 months (whether or not consecutive), whichever is earlier. Such loose stipulations imposed on the states by the federal government pay homage to the federal government's oversight authority, but also substantially liberate the states to craft a welfare reform plan suitable to their own needs.[47] Because of the states' new-found freedoms, many of them are interested in employing the private sector in the implementation of their programmes. As the New York Times has noted: "[t]he new law allows states to buy not only welfare services but also gate-keepers to determine eligibility and benefits".[48] It goes on to state:[49]

> "Proponents say turning over welfare to the private sector will prove to be the most cost-effective and humane way for states to face up to the fiscal imperatives of the new law. A profit-making company has the flexibility to reward employees for results . . . and to change the culture of the welfare office from one focused on calculating deprivation and issuing checks to one that quickly helps people into jobs."

Any number of private companies are lining up to take over these functions, including Lockheed and Electronic Data Systems. Whether a conflict of interest between the private sector's need for profit and the public interest values that militate in favour of eligibility develops remains to be seen. Once again, there will be problems of translation when one balances the needs of our poorest individuals with the efficiency concerns of a private firm whose primary task is to determine the eligibility of welfare applicants as efficiently as possible and within the constraints of a relatively small budget. For such a system to work, policy makers, and perhaps courts as well, will have to find ways of blending this kind of public-private partnership and creating the kind of legal discourse necessary to achieve the benefits learned from the discipline of the market, without ignoring important values not fully susceptible to narrow cost-benefit calculations.

---

[47] The Administration recently found Wisconsin and Michigan eligible to run their own welfare programmes and gave each state operation funds which exceed the amount they received under the old welfare law. Despite this finding of eligibility, the Administration voiced concerns over the constitutionality of Wisconsin's 60 day residential requirement before newcomers to the state are eligible for benefits. The Administration considers such a waiting period antagonistic to the Supreme Court's 1969 decision finding such interim periods " 'constitutionally impermissible' because they denied equal protection of the law to new residents and interfered with the 'freedom to travel' ". Moreover, the Administration stated that the Michigan plan might abridge due process requirements because welfare benefits could be reduced or terminated without a "pre-termination hearing". See R. Pear, "States Say Parts of U.S. Welfare Law May Be Unconstitutional", New York Times, 6 Oct. 1996.
[48] Idem.
[49] Idem.

Federal Corporations—Corporatising Government

Another approach to regulatory reform that blends the public and private, if not in new ways, at least in increasingly common ways, is to leave certain public functions in the public sector, but to use a private sector structural model for the supervision and delivery of those services.[50] Federal corporations have long provided a structural framework for such an approach. The federal government's authority to charter corporations is well established and authorised by the Necessary and Proper Clause of the Constitution.[51] The United States Postal Service, the Federal Aviation Administration (FAA), the Federal Railway Administration, and the Overseas Private Investment Corporation (OPIC) are just a few examples of the federal government's use of private models for delivering public services.[52]

These federal corporations take various forms and the state action doctrine looms large in determining the extent to which administrative law or constitutional law will apply to these entities. If the federal government can simply avoid constitutional protections by corporatising governmental agencies, form will clearly have triumphed over substance. This, the court concluded in *Lebron* v. *National Railroad Passenger Corporation*,[53] should not be the case.

---

[50] Some of these constructs take the form of "mixed-ownership government corporations". Examples of such corporations are: Amtrak; the Central Bank for Cooperatives; the Federal Deposit Insurance Corporation; the Federal Home Loan Banks; the Federal Intermediate Credit Banks; the Federal Land Banks; the National Credit Union Administration Central Liquidity Facility; the Regional Banks for Cooperatives; the Rural Telephone Bank when the ownership, control, and operation of the bank are converted under § 410(a) of the Rural Electrification Act of 1936 (7 U.S.C. 950(a)); the United States Railway Association; the Financing Corporation; the Resolution Trust Corporation; and the Resolution Funding Corporation.

[51] In *McCulloch* v. *Maryland*, 17 U.S. 316 (1819) the Court held that the Second Bank of the United States, although largely owned by private persons, was a public agent—and therefore tax exempt—because it was chartered to achieve the public purpose of banking. The Court noted that "the power of establishing a corporation is not a distinct sovereign power or end of government, but only the means of carrying into effect other powers which are sovereign. Whenever it becomes an appropriate means of exercising any of the powers given by the Constitution to the government of the Union, it may be exercised by that government": ibid., 316. See also *Osborn* v. *Bank of the United States*, 22 U.S. 738 (1824). The *Osborn* Court echoed the *McCulloch* Court's reasoning. See also A.M. Froomkin, "Reinventing the Government Corporation" [1995] U Ill LR 543, 551.

[52] Other examples of wholesale government cooptation of private sector models are plentiful. These entities are called "wholly-owned government corporations", 31 U.S.C.A. § 9101(3), and include the following: the Commodity Credit Corporation; the Community Development Financial Institutions Fund; the Export-Import Bank of the United States; the Federal Crop Insurance Corporation; Federal Prison Industries Incorporated; the Corporation for National and Community Service (Americorps); the Government National Mortgage Association; the Pennsylvania Avenue Development Corporation; the Pension Benefit Guaranty Corporation; the Rural Telephone Bank until the ownership, control, and operation of the Bank are converted under § 410(a) of the Rural Electrification Act of 1936 (7 U.S.C. 950(a)); the Saint Lawrence Seaway Development Corporation; the Secretary of Housing and Urban Development when carrying out duties and powers related to the Federal Housing Administration Fund; the Tennessee Valley Authority; the Uranium Enrichment Corporation; the Panama Canal Commission; and the Alternative Agricultural Research and Commercialization Corporation.

[53] 115 S. Ct. 961 (1995) (hereafter referred to as *Lebron*).

In *Lebron* the court held that Congress' decision that Amtrak was a private entity was not determinative for the courts when asked to decide whether the state action doctrine applied.[54] The Supreme Court held that a "corporation is an agency of the government, for purposes of constitutional obligations of the government rather than 'privileges of the government', when the state has specifically created that corporation for the furtherance of a governmental objective and does not merely hold some shares but rather controls the operation of the corporation through its appointees".[55] Recalling its stance as to the status of the Reconstruction Finance Corporation, the Court went on to note that the fact "that . . . Congress chose to call it a corporation does not alter its characteristics so as to make it something other than what it actually is. . . ."[56]

The conclusion that Amtrak is "an agency or instrumentality of the United States for the purpose of individual rights guaranteed against the Government by the Constitution", is founded on the history of government-created and controlled corporations. As the Court noted:[57]

> "a remarkable feature of the heyday of those corporations, in the 1930s and 1940s, was that, even while they were praised for their status 'as agencies separate and distinct, administratively and financially and legally, from the government itself, which has facilitated their adoption of commercial methods of accounting and financing, avoidance of political controls, and utilization of regular procedures of business management', it was fully acknowledged that they were a 'device' of 'government', and constituted 'federal corporate agencies' apart from 'regular government departments'."

Lebron may be the new day, but it is important to note that the courts have not always been so accommodating when it comes to seeing through the "private veil" of the corporate form. Courts have held that the Legal Services Corporation, the Corporation for Public Broadcasting and Communications Satellite Corporation (COMSAT) are all essentially private concerns.[58]

As with privatised prisons, however, both the approach to governing federal corporations and how the courts choose to view them is essential to the development of our understanding of administrative law in the future. Indeed, the use of these various corporate agency forms are increasingly

---

[54] 115 S. Ct. 961, 971 (1995).

[55] Ibid., 974.

[56] Idem.

[57] Idem (quoting from Pritchett, "The Government Corporation Control Act of 1945" (1946) 40 *Am Pol Sci Rev* 495).

[58] See, e.g., *Network Project* v. *Corporation for Public Broadcasting*, 4 Media L. Rep. (BNA) 2399, 2403–8 (D.D.C. 1979); *Texas Rural Legal Aid Inc.* v. *Legal Services Corp.*, 940 F. 2d 685, 699 (D.C. Cir. 1991); *Warren* v. *Government National Mortgage Association*, 611 F. 2d 1229, 1232–5 (8th Cir. 1980), cert. denied, 449 U.S. 847 (1980). See also *Jackson* v. *Culinary School of Washington*, 788 F. Supp. 1233, 1265 (D.D.C. 1992) (holding that the Federal Student Loan Guaranty Association is "not a governmental entity" because Congress designated the corporation "private"). *Lebron*, above at n. 53, itself is not without its own ambiguities. See Krotoszynski, above at n. 42, 301–314.

common.⁵⁹ The government frequently is now expected to look like as well as perform in a manner consistent with private sector models. This is particularly true for the various commercial activities that the government carries out, but the dominance of the market and market models is not so limited. Market discourses have also been used frequently to structure various non-commercial regulatory approaches and incentives, such as the use of market approaches in the amendments to the Clean Air Act.⁶⁰ In addition to the structures of governmental agencies and the market form that regulation now often takes, there also have been some procedural changes that mix the public and the private in new ways. Perhaps the most distinctive and important of these is the increased use of more informal alternative dispute resolution approaches, especially negotiated regulation.

Negotiated Rulemaking

All of the above examples of market structures and market regulatory discourses imply a different relationship between the regulated and government and, more importantly, between government and its citizens. It is possible, however, to view this as simply a change in the means of regulation, but I believe that more is at stake. As the ends of regulation increasingly mimic market results, this inevitably affects not only the regulatory discourse, but the processes by which these results are reached. It simply is not efficient to include large numbers of participants and, in any event, the costs of procedures become as important as the costs imposed by the substantive regulations they produce. Negotiated regulations can offer some relief to litigation costs. They usually invite more market oriented approaches because they give the

---

⁵⁹ See Aman, above at n. 44, 457–8. See also the Federal Railway Administration. Under the Regional Rail Reorganization Act of 1973, Congress mandated the reorganisation of railroads in the Midwest and northeast regions into an "economically viable system capable of providing adequate and efficient rail service to the regions": 45 U.S.C.A. § 701(b)(2). In so doing, Congress established the Consolidated Rail Corporation (Conrail), a for-profit corporation. Congress did not consider Conrail an agency or instrumentality of the Federal Government: 45 U.S.C.A. § 741(b). Conrail was to be governed by a chief executive officer, a chief operating officer, and a board of directors: § 741(d)(1)(2). The federal government operated and controlled Conrail until it was privatised in 1987. See also the Overseas Private Investment Corporation (OPIC). A wholly-owned corporation by the United States government, OPIC was created in 1971 "by Congress to provide support for American business investment in developing countries": S.L. Williams, "Political and Other Risk Insurance: OPIC, MIGA, EXIMBANK and Other Providers" (1993) 5 *Pace Int'l LR* 59, 70–71. Williams describes OPIC as follows (ibid., 72):

"managed by a board of directors, consisting of fifteen members and OPIC's president. The chairman of the board is also the administrator of the Agency for International Development. The vice chairman is the deputy United States trade representative. Eight members of the board appointed directly by the President and confirmed by the Senate are from the private sector. The board also has represenatatives from the Departments of State, Treasury, Commerce and Labour."

⁶⁰ See Clean Air Act Amendments of 1990, Pub. L. No. 101–549 (1990).

regulated more of a chance to shape the rules under consideration. At the same time, successful negotiations require a workable group of participants. This requirement, in turn, can affect the nature of the interest group interactions with government, as well as the numbers of participants in the proceeding.

The Negotiated Rulemaking Act of 1990[61] was designed to involve affected parties in the initial planning stages of the policy-making process, prior to the publication of a notice of proposed rulemaking. The parties themselves, plus a representative from the agency, are expected to generate agreement on a proposed rule and offer it to the agency for acceptance, modification, or rejection. If accepted by the agency, the agreement becomes the basis of a proposed regulation, which is then published for comment.

One important goal of this approach is to encourage the abandonment of the inflexible posturing parties often can get into if, as is usually the case, they anticipate litigation. Negotiated rulemaking provides a forum for accommodation and compromise in order to produce a satisfactory result to the parties and, then, presumably to the agency, without litigation. Rather than having "won" or "lost" at the agency or in court, each party to the negotiations has the opportunity to ensure that the final regulation results from considerations which include important aspects of its own firm or industry.

Of course, this kind of agreement on rules is important to the government as well, especially when its own resources dedicated to enforcement are in decline, and litigation costs adversely affect its budget as well. In short, a more consensual approach to policymaking may not only be more cost-effective for the parties involved, but more realistic for the agencies that enforce the rules that emerge from these processes.

The Act provides that either an interested party or the agency itself may propose that a particular rule be designated for negotiation. It is then up to the agency to appoint a "convener" to assist the agency head in determining whether such an informal negotiation procedure is feasible for the issues under consideration. This is done after considering various factors, including whether all competing interests may be effectively represented on a committee conducting the negotiations.[62] Once the convener considers the issues' suitability for negotiation, she carefully analyses the potential participants' assessments of the value of negotiation. If a party perceives that a better alternative than negotiation exists for resolving the issue, the negotiated rulemaking process will probably fail. Effective negotiation depends upon the participants' understanding that, given the "best alternative to negotiated agreement", negotiation is still more attractive.

If the convener concludes that the negotiated rulemaking is the appropriate vehicle to resolve the issues involved, she recommends the procedure to the

---

[61] Pub. L. No. 101–648. This Act was renewed in 1996. See Pub. L. No. 104–320 (110 Stat. 3870).
[62] 5 U.S.C.A. §583 (b)(1).

agency. If the agency agrees, it appoints a staff member as its representative on the committee. This official cannot bind the agency, but she can voice agency views and make certain the proposals involved do not exceed Congressional limits on agency authority. The government thus plays a proactive role in the negotiation processes. It has, of course, a very important seat at the table as the basic rule takes shape, but so do the affected parties. In the event of a failure to reach consensus, the agency has the background of the proceedings and the established positions of the parties to use in developing its final rule, but if consensus is reached, the negotiating committee transmits a report containing the proposed rule to the agency.[63] The Act itself requires the agency carefully to consider the draft's potential as a text for the proposed rule. The agency then is to solicit comments through a notice of proposed rulemaking. The agency cannot summarily approve the agreement; it must provide its own "reasoned justification for the rule". There undoubtedly are expectations on the part of the parties involved that the consensus version of the rule will, at least, be carefully considered by the agency, if not actually used.

There is certainly more give and take at the earliest stages of rule formulation between the government and the regulated in this process as compared to traditional notice and comment rulemaking proceedings. It occurs early in the process and with a relatively smaller, but representative group of interested parties. It is precisely the value of these negotiations and the bargains struck as well as the role of the agency in this process that sparked the procedural controversy in *USA Group Loan Services, Inc. v. Riley*.[64] In that case, the Department of Education used "negotiated rulemaking" procedures to produce a proposed rule dealing with minimum standards of accountability for student loan servicers. As the court noted, "an official of the Department of Education promised the servicers that the Department would abide by *any consensus* reached by them unless there were compelling reasons to depart".[65] The agency ultimately rejected the consensus rule, apparently without reasons,[66] and the parties claimed the agency had bargained in bad faith. For the court, this claim turned on the propriety of the promise that the parties claimed the agency had made, one which the court concluded "may be questioned":[67]

> "It sounds like an abdication of regulatory authority to the regulated, the full burgeoning of the interest-group state, and the final confirmation of the 'capture' theory of administrative regulation."

The court went on to conclude that though they had very serious doubts about the propriety of this promise, they had "no doubt that the Negotiated

---

[63] 5 U.S.C.A. §586 (d)(2).
[64] Above at n. 31.
[65] Ibid., 714 (emphasis added).
[66] Idem.
[67] Idem.

Rulemaking Act did not make the promise enforceable".[68] To hold otherwise "would extinguish notice and comment rulemaking in all cases in which it was preceded by negotiated rulemaking; the comments would be irrelevant if the agency were already bound by promises that it had made to the industry. There is no textual or other clue that the Act meant to do this".[69]

The court's rejection of the parties' claim was correct in light of the language of the Negotiated Rulemaking Act and the weight the parties placed on the agency's presumed promise to go along with their consensus. Yet, the court did not fully analyse these claims; a reason for the agency's rejection of the consensual rule may have been in order. Nor did the court take seriously how significant a procedural departure this Act was from traditional notice and comment rulemaking.[70] Indeed, to object on the grounds that the agency was being captured or that there was an abdication of regulatory authority suggests the court saw these processes in traditional pluralistic terms. The agency was a judge, not a player in these negotiations. This, however, may be at odds with the overall context within which many of these negotiations now occur, including those in this case. This contest is one in which there are fewer and fewer agency funds and personnel for enforcement purposes and litigation in general, as well as a growing desire on the part of most agencies to create regulatory structures that achieve regulatory goals in cost-effective ways, cost-effective for the industry *and* the agency. The opinion reached the right result and it correctly decried any approach that would, in effect, "give away the store", but it may be that when it comes to such future processes and structures, the legislature will be more explicit in its desire to use procedures that require the government to take any consensus reached by those who must, in fact, implement the rule, far more seriously.

At the same time, this case also shows that multiple perspectives are possible when it comes to analysing new procedural approaches to the creation of new regulations. For this court, there was nothing really new here. In its view, the Negotiated Rulemaking Act did not make explicit enough any major changes in traditional regulatory processes so as to justify treating this case in a new way. But it is by no means clear the court was correct in this perception. The Negotiated Rulemaking Act was intended to change the dynamic between the government and the regulated by involving both more deeply in the bargaining processes that precede a final rule. The changes may not have been as dramatic as the parties perceived them to be, but it was not just business as usual. Because the way courts and policymakers perceive regulatory reforms can trigger different bodies of case-law and administrative law theory, it is useful to consider some of the various perspectives that can apply to the regulatory reforms described in Part II.

---

[68] *USA Group Loan Services, Inc.* v. *Riley*, above at n. 31, 174.
[69] Ibid., 714–5.
[70] The court referred to the Negotiated Rulemaking Act as "a novelty": ibid., 714.

THREE PERSPECTIVES ON REGULATORY REFORM

The market-oriented regulatory reforms that globalisation processes encourage states to pursue can be conceptualised in different ways. Indeed, globalisation itself is a term of art that refers to a variety of complex, dynamic legal and social processes in which states increasingly are "actors" only indirectly. In many instances, these processes significantly undercut a state's autonomy, though the state may not wish to see it that way. For example, a state may wish to implement certain domestic political solutions to ease unemployment caused by increased off-shore production, but regulatory solutions that raise manufacturing costs at home can exacerbate the off-shore problem. If the state imposes higher regulatory costs on domestic industries, these measures can encourage further relocation or expansion off-shore. Thus, a state might make a deregulatory response to this kind of situation. A *laissez-faire* interpretation of this response would stress that markets can and should be allowed to work and that states, by implication, are essentially powerless in the face of such trends. Another interpretation would see the state as initiating a new policy approach, but one that embraces the market. The state can, in effect, appear to mimic the market, adopt its language and to some extent its goals, and in so doing, retain an active role in mediating the impact of global economic, political trends. Whether this is the strategy of a weak or a strong state is hard to discern because many of the market-oriented goals a state may set for itself are sympathetic with, if not the same as, what an unregulated market approach would achieve. By taking "credit" for these results, however, the state may appear to remain a viable actor in processes that it may ultimately be able to influence, but not control.

A state's action or inaction in the face of changing economic forces is thus subject to many interpretations, but it can also trigger different bodies of judicial administrative law precedents and the underlying political theories of the state that these cases represent. Moreover, different interpretations of these changes can fuel various kinds of domestic regulatory politics that suggest very different regulatory visions for the future.

This part of the paper considers three such perspectives on current reforms. In discussing them, it is important that we differentiate the various uses of the market inherent in each of these conceptualisations. This is important because some state action or inaction can appear to be consistent with very different regulatory philosophies and goals. By recognising the various interpretive possibilities that exist, we can help, when necessary, to create, or when possible, to preserve ways of seeing these changes that provide for the kind of legal flexibility or interpretive space necessary for a new administrative law to develop, one appropriate for the new mixtures of public and private power suitable for the regulatory problems in today's global economy.

Back To The Future

One could easily contend that private prisons and state welfare programmes, significant portions of which are privatised, as well as the use of federal corporations—especially those that avoid the state action doctrine—are all steps back to a 19th century, *laissez-faire* conception of the state. Such a theoretical approach to state power resonates deeply with a body of case-law that was developed in the early stages of United States administrative law, emphasising the economic rights of individuals. It also resonates with a constitutional framework that minimises federal power and maximises that of the states.

Moreover, the political regulatory debates that accompany these and similar reforms easily fall on a unidimensional spectrum, with the free market at one end of that spectrum and—in the United States at least, where nationalisation of industries has been rare—some form of extensive command-control regulation at the other. With this spectrum in mind, the regulatory debate appears to be a zero-sum game. One zero-sum view of the overall direction of market-oriented regulatory reforms is that they take us "back to the future"—representing a return to a 19th century *laissez-faire* conception of the proper relationship of the state to the market; that is to say, the state's role is expected to be minimal, especially at the federal level, and most problems are viewed as essentially private and amenable to market solutions or aid provided by institutions thought to be part of "civil society". The administrative law for such a conception of the state would consist largely of the common law doctrines and approaches that dominated the so-called traditional model of administrative law discussed above.[71]

The view that we are, in fact, moving away from an interventionist state to one that relies primarily on free markets coincides with the resurrection of the importance of constitutional provisions and interpretations long thought relatively unimportant to defining the role of the state. These include such provisions as the Takings Clause of the 14th Amendment,[72] the 10th Amendment[73] and a narrowly read Commerce Clause.[74] In addition, recent cutbacks in the doctrine of standing by the Supreme Court also challenge some important assumptions of modern administrative law, by making it more difficult for affected parties to challenge administrative actions in court.[75] If American administrative law was once transformed by the courts, as Professor Stewart has written,[76] no such transformation appears in these

---

[71] See Stewart, above at n. 27; see also Verkuil, above at n. 17, 264.
[72] U.S. Const. amend. XIV. See, e.g., *Dolan v. City of Tigard*, 114 S. Ct. 2309 (1994).
[73] U.S. Const. amend. X. See, e.g., *United States v. Lopez*, 115 S. Ct. 1624 (1995).
[74] Idem.
[75] See *Lujan v. Defenders of Wildlife*, 504 U.S. 555 (1992), in which the Court held that the defendant environmentalists did not show sufficient "imminent injury" to have standing.
[76] Stewart, above at n. 27, 1669–70.

opinions, unless it is the beginnings of a return to the traditional model of administrative law. Though an analysis of these recent Supreme Court cases is beyond the scope of this paper,[77] these opinions all rely heavily on and tend to reinforce bright line distinctions between such categories as public and private, state and federal, as well as party and citizen. Though these opinions too are capable of alternative interpretations, the overall thrust of these cases and the constitutional matrix which they imply may undercut the kind of governmental flexibility that is necessary to react effectively to new global regulatory contexts. Collective approaches to societal problems that blur public/private distinctions may be a source of important, new regulatory reforms that are appropriate for a state that no longer is as autonomous as it once was. Constitutional flexibility when it comes to the respective roles of the federal, state, and local governments as well as the private sector will be necessary for the kind of experimentation that may be necessary.

Quite apart from the potential impact of recent decisions by the Supreme Court, many legislative proposals set forth in the Republican Party's "Contract with America" in the 104th Congress, in fact, provide very specific examples of a back to the future scenario for regulatory reform, one that includes not only attempts to abolish some government agencies and programmes outright, but also one that utilises a *laissez-faire* procedural approach to effectively curtail the power of agencies too popular to abolish.[78] Some supporters of these proposals undoubtedly see procedural reforms as but a way station on the road to a substantive *laissez-faire* approach. Short of abolition of certain agencies, however, procedures advocating elaborate cost-benefit review are the next best approach because they are likely to ensure that any new regulatory action will be unlikely.[79] For legislative proponents of a back to the future view of regulatory reform, the state is like a rubber band that has been stretched too far. At a minimum, a procedural *laissez-faire*

---

[77] See Aman, above at n. 30, 9.

[78] Most of these proposals involved environmental regulation, such as, e.g., those dealing with wetlands or toxic dumps.

[79] For example, the proposed Comprehensive Regulatory Reform Act of 1995 (S 343) restricts agency action to only those issues specifically required by statute; requires peer, congressional, and judicial review of each rule; and mandates a cost-benefit analysis for every rule. Each such analysis should contain: (1) an analysis of the benefit of the proposed rule; (2) an analysis of the costs of the proposed rule; (3) an identification of reasonable alternative approaches (including the alternative of no governmental action); (4) an assessment of the feasibility of establishing a regulatory programme that operates through market-based mechanisms; (5) if scientific assessment is made, a description of actions verifying the quality of such evaluations; (6) an assessment of the effect of the rule on small business; and (7) an analysis of whether the benefits are likely to exceed the costs.

"Takings" legislation can play the same role. Of the several pieces of "takings" legislation that received floor action, the Private Property Protection Act of 1995 (HR 9) was perhaps the most prohibitive. It required that the federal government "compensate an owner of property whose use of any portion of that property has been limited by an agency action, under a specified regulatory law, that diminishes the fair market value of that portion by 20 percent or more. The amount of the compensation shall equal the diminution in value that resulted from the agency action".

approach resists any additional or new role for the state and, over time, the state must be allowed to snap or slip back to a minimalist starting position.

This kind of hard-edged, philosophical view of regulatory reform also drives a certain kind of domestic politics, a politics that sees government as a major contributor to a national problem characterised by declining competitiveness, fewer industrial jobs, high taxes and governmental institutions incapable of offering or implementing any constructive solutions. The public-private dichotomy is often emphasised to the point where almost any governmental attempt to rectify a problem is assumed to be doomed to failure, but the market consistently is seen as a major source of liberation.[80]

Corporatising Government

Closely related to this view of government and the politics it generates is another version of the back to the future thesis, but one which is more optimistic in nature, and one which does not necessarily reject a role for government to play. This approach, which we might call the "economic growth model", posits as free a market economy as possible as the ultimate goal, with the explicit assumption that less regulation and less costly government will increase economic growth in a manner that will benefit everyone. But rather than emphasising a pure philosophical belief in the value of individual freedom from government intrusion, this view places more emphasis on the consequences that can flow from markets and efficient government—namely, economic prosperity for all.[81] Though government will have a role to play, that role should be made to adhere to corporate organisational forms and structures whenever possible and be subject to the discipline and rigours of the market.[82] If it is necessary to enlist the private sector to carry out certain governmental tasks, such as the management of prisons, mental hospitals or public housing, that may be necessary, if it is the most efficient way of proceeding.

Besides reliance on the market, either as a form of bureaucratic organisation or as a substitute for government, another aspect of this perspective on regulatory reform involves some relatively new ways in which interest groups may interact with the government. As noted above, the Negotiated Rulemaking Act can be seen as a step in this direction. Corporatism is a political theory with a great variety of meanings.[83] But there are aspects of the

---

[80] Many of the tax reform proposals fall into this mode of reform, too. Abolishing the IRS and minimising the sources of revenue the federal government has to fund its programmes, of course, would make their passage in the first place less likely.

[81] See generally Peter Passell, "Asia's Path to More Equality and More Money for All", New York Times, 25 Aug. 1996, E5.

[82] See text accompanying nn. 50–59 above.

[83] See, e.g., P.P. Craig, *Public Law and Democracy in the United Kingdom and the United States of America* (Clarendon Press, Oxford, 1990), 148–53 and A. Cawson, *Corporatism and Political Theory* (Blackwell, Oxford, 1986), 22–46.

political theory developed to support corporatism that have resonance with certain trends in United States administrative law, especially those aspects of the theory that assume a bargaining relationship between the government and selected, representative interest groups and an outcome that is really a brokered policy in which the government often plays more of the role of mediator, than judge. These aspects of corporatism thus focus on:[84]

> "the outcome of a bargaining process between state agencies and those organised interests whose power in the political marketplace means that their co-operation is indispensable if agreed policies are to be implemented. The state is not sufficiently powerful for officials to dictate policies and impose them unilaterally, but at the same time it is sufficiently powerful to resist capture by those interests. This notion is clearly implicit in the concept of bargaining: each party must have resources to bargain with; otherwise the relationship is one of subservience or submission."

The need for increased bargaining on the part of the state to achieve goals that are realistically enforceable is indicative of a state that can no longer accomplish its objectives by direct command-control regulations. This is true for a number of reasons. First, as noted above, the processes of globalisation can weaken the state in various ways, not the least of which is that they make it relatively easy for some industries to move production around the globe, avoiding excess costs, but often affecting local employment opportunities as well. There is thus a greater premium on the part of the state to negotiate with potential regulatees, perhaps to convince them of the necessity of the regulation and that what it proposes is as cost-effective as possible. This relates closely to enforcement. As the funding of agencies decreases, effective enforcement of the regulations promulgated increasingly requires the cooperation of the regulated. They need to be given the discretion to reach the desired results in ways that make sense for them. Industries also increasingly need to be part of the planning and regulatory process.

The increasing reliance on markets and market approaches as substitutes for more direct forms of regulation highlights efficiency concerns and it also suggests a regulatory discourse that is much closer to market concerns and modes of operation. This is likely generally to be more in tune with business interests, but a market discourse applies especially easily to companies doing business in multiple countries. They are freer to reject the political costs of doing business in any one jurisdiction if they can move production around the globe relatively easily. Thus, these market approaches and discourses also suggest new roles for the private sector to play when designing new rules or regulatory approaches, and new bureaucratic structures for government to use, structures that seek quite consciously to copy the form and disciplines of corporate structures.[85]

---

[84] Ibid., 35.
[85] Gore Commission, above at n. 4, 1.

Finally, since so many regulatory reforms are driven by cost considerations in both the industries to which they apply and in the agencies that promulgate them, localities in competition for foreign investment also wish to have these functions performed in the most efficient way possible and in a manner that is closest to the level of government actually affected. Thus, devolution of regulatory responsibilities to the states and even to localities within those states is increasingly common, as we have seen with welfare reform, discussed above. But the farther one gets from the national level, the easier it is for forms of interest group-government negotiation to occur that begin to approximate even more directly a kind of corporatism with very selected representatives of key industries and labour unions agreeing on the governmental actions necessary to, for example, attract foreign investment to their particular jurisdiction.[86] The "deals" that ultimately are struck often involve tax breaks that provide added incentives for multinational companies to locate in that area.[87]

Market Cooptation

A third view of regulatory reform begins with the assumption that government regulation can be positive. This view is held by those who philosophically believe in an active government and, more importantly, the ability collectively and legitimately to define something called the public interest. It is not inconsistent, however, for such proponents of regulatory reform also to believe that regulation need not only be the traditional, so-called "command-control" type. New forms of regulation that seek to coopt the market as a regulatory tool can be both effective and efficient. Such reformers thus seek to enlist the private interest for the public good but the public good is not defined by the market alone. The market is a means to an end, not an end in itself.

Using the market in this way represents the public uses of the private interest. Markets are used not just to maximise wealth, however it might be distributed, but to structure incentives in such a way as to achieve public interest goals. The government itself also can function more efficiently and in less expensive ways. In an era of intense global competition and scarce resources, incorporating some of the accountability and the discipline of the market into government activities is, thus, also viewed as an important reform. The more efficient government becomes, the better it can accomplish its public interest goals. Such a view, however, does not see the use of federal corporations or privatised prisons as essentially relieving the state of the responsibility for policy outcomes reached by these privatised structures, but simply as a new, hopefully more effective way of advancing the public interest. If it can be shown, for example, that the cost savings anticipated from privatising prisons

---

[86] See R. Perrucci, *Japanese Auto Transplants In The Heartland* (Aldine De Gruyter, New York, 1994).
[87] Idem.

do not materialise or that important non-economic values were inappropriately excluded from the decision-making processes of federal corporations or privatised welfare programmes, these reformers would be open to different mixes of the public and the private, including a return to older forms of regulation.

It is important to emphasise that, in this perspective, uses of the market and market incentives as a means to further public ends do, indeed, differ significantly from reforms designed to return to the market as an end in itself or from those that seek to have government approximate market structures and outcomes, as ends in themselves. Different conceptions of the roles of the state, the private sector and the public interest are involved in each of the perspectives sketched above and each generates the need for somewhat different legal doctrines or, at least, different conceptual and interpretive approaches to these doctrines. For those who see the market as an end in itself, be they advocates of back to the future or economic growth advocates who see the federal corporate form as an end in itself, a clear distinction between the state and the private sector is necessary. It is, therefore, important that the line between public and private be a bright one. From a constitutional point of view, this means that what falls within the private realm is the domain of the market and private, individual decision-making. The role of law is to assure that such private activity can occur safely beyond the reach of the state. Given the assumption that such a public or governmental role will be relatively small compared to the private sector, there is also a presumption against state intervention in economic matters and in favor of maximum private involvement.

For those who wish to coopt the market for public purposes, the public/private dividing line is problematical. Given that it may be sensible to have a more market-oriented state, the state must still be an independent public interest force. But if the state is to forge new alliances with the private sector to carry out public interest goals, a constitutional structure that too rigorously defines what is private in opposition to what is public can hamper the creativity of these new state/private partnerships or inappropriately shield activities and decisions that have broad public impact from the kinds of procedures that "public" law can provide. Moreover, for those who see the market as a means to achieve public interest ends and believe government agencies can carry out these programmes, the role of the state remains important in setting goals, standards and structuring incentives in new ways that can funnel private interests in public interest directions.

One could argue that with the market cooptation perspective, the interest group model of administrative law remains intact because only the form of regulation has changed. It would be a mistake, however, to assume that even with the more public interest emphasis of the third perspective, the role of the state continues to be the same or, arguably, as powerful or as extensive as in previous eras. Further, the more the market and market approaches are used to reach public interest results, important values that are not easily quantified may, in effect, be omitted entirely from consideration. Costs are usually easier to quantify than benefits. Similarly, while equating citizens with consumers may clarify the role or duties of the state in certain contexts, there is something lost from this translation as well. The concept of citizenship is a deep one that can both include and transcend the role of individuals as mere consumers of state services.

The market metaphor has its limits; its rhetoric can and often does limit the roles the state may play and many of the factors described above as market-oriented can more easily come into play in such contexts. Indeed, as market-oriented regulatory schemes have become common, there also is more need for cooperation between the regulated and the state. As noted above, this is especially true in an era of declining regulatory budgets and the consequent inability of the state effectively to enforce the law. As a result, the bargaining process between the state and the regulated increasingly takes place on more equal footing, with both the state and the regulated concerned about minimising costs.

At the same time, market oriented regulatory schemes that are not steeped in a back to the future mindset raise interesting and important questions concerning, for example, the efficiency of the processes used to formulate and then carry out governmental rules. The interest group model of administrative law errs in the direction of inclusiveness when it comes to who may participate in policy-making processes, whether or not there is some repetition of views. But a model that emphasises efficiency may not. It seeks to minimise overlap and militates in favor of selected interest group representatives. Similarly, an explicit cost-benefit approach to regulation yields a different and arguably more narrow public interest discourse when it comes to, for example, solving value-laden regulatory problems that require some translation of the regulatory issues involved into a cost-benefit calculus. Even greater tensions can arise when the regulation involved has been delegated wholly to the private sector, operating, as it were, as a service provider to the government and, thus concerned primarily with profitability.

The tensions these newer approaches to regulation produce raise important questions involving what is public and what is private and, more importantly, the extent to which the public interest retains any viability as a concept beyond efficiency. Regulatory reforms that rely on the private sector and market incentives do not represent a return to the past or simply more of the same, but the beginnings of a new model of administrative law in which the line between the public and the private is no longer distinct, and the lines between and among levels of government—international, federal, state and local—should not be so sharp as to prevent synergistic interplay among them and the creation of new combinations or partnerships between government and the private sector. Indeed, the future role for administrative law will be to incorporate and justify new mixes of private and public power as well as to try to ensure the opportunity for a broad based public interest discourse, one that resists the idea that narrow, technocratic cost-benefit analyses are always determinative.

CONCLUSION: THE NEW ADMINISTRATIVE LAW

The cumulative effect of various market approaches to regulation, regulatory structures and procedures is to introduce a new mix of private and public power, as well as state and federal power. The overall context of globalisation frames these developments. The emphasis on global competition and economic growth coupled with the general weakness of any single individual state in the face of globalisation processes encourages more negotiation on the part of the state as well as regulatory approaches more sympathetic to the cost-conscious demands of multinational businesses and government as well.

For these approaches to evolve into a new administrative law, however, it is necessary for the courts to provide the doctrinal flexibility to incorporate new mixes of the private and the public without, necessarily, opting for one extreme or the other. Judicial approaches that maximise the differences between public and private power can easily shelter private power used for public interest purposes. At the same time, the automatic judicial imposition of "activist procedures" in situations that call for more nuanced and efficient governmental approaches can be counter-productive. In one instance, essentially public decisions are shielded from procedural protections. In the other, new governmental approaches are made inefficient or unduly burdensome by the imposition of procedural models that fail to take into account the need for efficiency that new global realities dictate. Finally, the new administrative law also will be one that must effectively interact more often and more flexibly with state and municipal law.

If the state is to play a realistic role in the changes brought about by globalisation and a public interest discourse is to remain an important part of policy-making, it is necessary that a new model of administrative law be developed, the outlines of which are already apparent. This new model will need to legitimate new forms of public, private, state and federal partnerships. Unlike the transformations of administrative law in the past, however, the primary source of the new administrative law will be the executive and legislative branches. Given clear signals from those branches, the courts will follow.

6

Public Service Law and the New Public Management

H. WADE MacLAUCHLAN

INTRODUCTION

There is a *prima facie* tension between legal values and the new public management. Public law concerns itself with constitutional and near-constitutional values, with hierarchical order, with due process, with rules and standards, with systemic coherence, and with the manners and sustainability of institutional practices. The new public management is concerned with flexibility, experimentation, responsiveness, cost-effectiveness, cost-cutting and performance. It assumes the state is too large and too costly, and that centralised or rule-oriented solutions are part of the problem.[1]

Where does law fit in the world of new public management? What role do law and lawyers play in the development of new instruments of governance? Is law's concern with precedent and process an impediment to the new public management with its insistence on flexibility? Is it possible for law and lawyers to be responsive in this context without giving up on a long struggle to convince ourselves that there was something unique about public law in the first place? What is the value of public law in a context of downsizing and privatisation? As the public sector shrinks, does public law also "take a cut"?

These are large questions. And the latter two, perhaps the latter three, come at it from the wrong perspective. The issue is not whether public law should "take a cut", but whether public service law can "make the cut". This paper will evoke the image of a discipline of public service law that acquires particular shape and purpose in the context of restrained but creative governance. It will take the view that Anglo-American public law is better suited to be

---

[1] For multi-country reviews of public sector reforms, see *Governance in Transition: Public Management Reforms in OECD Countries* (OECD, Paris, 1995) and B. Guy Peters and Donald J. Savoie (eds), *Governance in a Changing Environment* (McGill-Queen's University Press, Montreal and Kingston, 1994). For a comparative law perspective, see C. Graham and T. Prosser, *Privatizing Public Enterprises: Constitutions, the State and Regulation in Comparative Perspective* (Clarendon Press, Oxford, 1991). For Canada, at the federal level, a bird's eye review can be found in Gene Swimmer (ed.), *How Ottawa Spends 1996–97: Life Under the Knife* (Carleton University Press, Ottawa 1996).

responsive, and to survive, under the new public management than is the continental *droit administratif*.

Anglo-American discourse about public law as a discipline has been cast—with palpable envy—against the continental ideal of a law-infused and law-centered rational bureaucratic edifice. Continental administrative law stood out for its unique institutions and its instrumental role in a highly centralised, rule-driven and autonomous state. The hallmark of *real* public law was the ease with which it could be demarcated from private law.[2]

The issue today is not one of demarcation, but of implication: i.e., relevance. Those interested in law and governance have no choice but to deal with an evolving and permeable conception of the public and the private. A discipline of public service law that builds on Anglo-American legal traditions *and* that is contemporary will be public-spirited but will also recognise the essential and expanding role of private sector players in achieving public service objectives. And it will recognise that an important *devoir* for law—private or public—is to create the climate, the conditions and the values for private sector institutions to lead economic and social development. A public service law in step with the new public management will not insist on a set of remedies and institutions unique from private law; it *will* insist on a public-interested set of values and a public-spirited perspective that respects the rule of law and democratic values.

This paper will evoke a discipline of public service law *en emergence*, and which is already in the process of responding to the challenges of the new public management. A new emphasis on clients produces a more effective integration of law, public policy objectives and practical considerations. The search for more effective means of dispute resolution requires public lawyers to be less derivative, and less subservient to the hierarchies and priorities of a litigation-identified private bar. A rigorous and continuing *remise en cause* of the role of the state, together with the related challenge to develop new instruments of governance, requires an on-going articulation of legal values and, ultimately, of the rule of law. Governance under the new public management is increasingly about the management of values. Public service lawyers are as well suited, and are arguably better suited, for that values-managing climate than are other professional or disciplinary groups in government. In short, the new public management represents a testing ground—at times a caldron—for public service law, offering it an opportunity to find its edges and take on more complete disciplinary shape.

---

[2] See, e.g., K.H.F. Dyson, *The State Tradition in Western Europe: A Study of an Idea and Institution* (Oxford, 1980); S. Flogaïtis, *Administrative Law et droit administratif* (Librarie générale de droit et de jurisprudence, Paris, 1986); and L.N. Brown and J.S. Bell, *French Administrative Law* (Clarendon Press, Oxford, 4th ed. 1993). For a reflection on the impact of new public management in France, see J. Chevallier, "Public Administration in Statist France" (1996) 56 *Pub Admin Rev* 67.

PUBLIC LAW AND GOVERNMENT

It has not been easy for law to find a comfortable "fit" with public administration. It has by times, perhaps typically, been seen as diffident, available to correct or discipline the administration without being fully implicated in the day-to-day activity of making public policy mandates operational. It may even be that law has stood back from being identified with public service. A key feature of law's diffidence has been the centrality of the *ultra vires* principle to public sector legal advice. While jurisdiction-oriented advice has an authoritative or definitive advantage over other disciplinary inputs, law's stand-offishness has left it to play a limited, or even subordinate, role as a technique by which administrators implement policies or as machinery for the redress of grievances.

Academic debates about the scope of public law have for some time sought a more effective integration between law and administration. Woodrow Wilson's 1887 article remains a landmark of this literature. While it was written in the context of the United States in the late 1800s, it has a familiar ring today:[3]

> "The English race, consequently, has long and successfully studied the art of curbing executive power to the constant neglect of the art of perfecting executive methods. It has exercised itself much more in controlling than in energising government. It has been more concerned to render government just and moderate than to make it facile, well-ordered and effective."

Wilson considered it imperative for the study of public law and administration to get beyond what he called the "tinkering of constitutions". He compared the American situation in 1887 unfavourably with that of nineteenth century France and Prussia, where the development of the administrative apparatus of the state and the imposition of liberal principles of governance had been integral, perhaps catalytic, elements of nation-building. His comparative reflection on the American situation has a particularly *piquant* relevance to Canadian public law in the 1990s:[4]

> "Once a nation has embarked on the business of manufacturing constitutions, it finds it exceedingly difficult to close out that business and open for the public a bureau of skilled, economical administration".

A century after Wilson's article, Gavin Drewry looked at the disciplinary connection between law and administration, this time from an English perspective, and arrived at conclusions substantially similar to Wilson's. Drewry lamented the "gulf" and the "paucity of collaboration" between public law

---

[3] "The Study of Administration" (1887) 2 *Pol Sci Q* 197, 206; republished in (1941) 56 *Pol Sci Q* 481, 491.

[4] Idem. Wilson's principal criticism of both public law and administrative study was that "[w]e go on criticising when we ought to be creating": idem.

and public administration.⁵ In his view, the Americans were still preoccupied with constitutional issues. In England the study of administration paid little attention to public law. Drewry makes the following comparison with the situation on the continent and in the United States:⁶

> "The contrast in this respect between Britain and both the continent of Europe and the United States could hardly be sharper. The continental administrator is in general . . . a lawyer, specialising in that branch of law—namely administrative law—which is most concerned with the functions of government. And, across the Atlantic, we find that constitutional issues permeate American law and life to an extent that foreign observers find incredible. Americans have become a people of constitutionalists who substitute litigation for legislation and see constitutional questions lurking in every case."

It is tempting to slide away from the assessments of Wilson and Drewry on the basis that they were primarily concerned with the disciplinary development of public administration. But it is not just public administrators who have been critical of the stand-offishness of law from administration. John Willis was impatient with lawyers' preoccupation with imposing constitutional and near-constitutional limits on the workings of government.⁷ Carol Harlow and Richard Rawlings criticised "red light theories" of administrative law, which they blamed on a Diceyan inheritance.⁸

A number of important attempts have been made to find a middle ground that retains law's role as a supervisory medium but that also pays regard to its contribution as an integral element of administration. Harlow and Rawlings come down between the "green light" and "red light" theories with what they call an "amber" approach.⁹ Denis Galligan advances a "nominalist" theory of administrative law.¹⁰ Some American writers have made courageous efforts to rehabilitate the reputation of judicial review by demonstrating how it is based on principles of good administration and democracy.¹¹ In

---

⁵ "Public Lawyers and Public Administrators: Prospects for an Alliance?" (1986) 64 *Pub Admin* 173.

⁶ Ibid., 174.

⁷ "The McRuer Report: Lawyers' Values and Civil Servants' Values" (1968) 18 *UTLJ* 351.

⁸ C. Harlow and R. Rawlings, *Law and Administration* (Wiedenfeld and Nicolson, London, 1984). In his *Introduction to the Study of the Law of the Constitution*, first published in 1885, A.V. Dicey claimed that *droit administratif* was based upon "ideas foreign to the fundamental assumptions of our English common law, and especially to what we have termed the rule of law": (10th ed. 1959), 329. Dicey was also reported to have said: "In England we know nothing of administrative law, and wish to know nothing about it" (W.A. Robson, "Administrative Law", in M. Ginsberg (ed.), *Law and Opinion in England in the 20th Century* (Stevens and Sons, London, 1959), 193).

For a reflection on the influence of Dicey's views, see P. McAuslan and J.F. McEldowney (eds), *Law, Legitimacy and the Constitution: Essays marking the Centenary of Dicey's Law of the Constitution* (Sweet and Maxwell, London, 1985) and H. Arthurs, "Jonah and the Whale: The Appearance, Disappearance and Reappearance of Administrative Law" (1980) 30 *UTLJ* 225.

⁹ Ibid., 47–59.

¹⁰ "Judicial Review and the Textbook Writers" (1982) 2 *OxJLS* 257.

¹¹ See D.H. Rosenbloom, "The Evolution of the Administrative State and Transformation of Administrative Law", in D.H. Rosenbloom and R.D. Schwartz, *Handbook of Regulation and*

Canada, the most concerted effort to introduce a unique, or at least a self-consciously invigorated, administrative law came in the 1930s, with the writings of academics engaged by the reforms of the New Deal and intrigued by expanded uses of legislative delegation.[12] There has been a subsequent and significant initiative by Quebec writers to develop a body of administrative law doctrine; this work combines a normative interest in the institutions of the state with a full exposé of the doctrine of judicial review and governmental liability.[13]

All of these efforts reflect a struggle to find the right balance between law that stands back from the state and law that accepts its instrumental role in the running of government. In effect, it is an age-old struggle between law and politics. John Willis offered an important insight into the shortcomings of administrative law as a discipline when he criticised academic work in the field for being overly concerned with law, without offering an adequate account of other disciplines, and for being insufficiently empirical:[14]

> "The law-review writing by law teachers on specifically Canadian problems is almost non-existent, for these lie outside the realm of law and in the shadowy and arduous borderland between law, political science and public administration where you have to use your feet as well as your head."

THE ELEMENTS OF A DISCIPLINE OF PUBLIC SERVICE LAW

I am presently involved in a long-term project entitled "Developing a Discipline of Public Service Law". The objectives of the project are: (i) to identify unique or characteristic features of public service lawyering—including

---

Administrative Law (Marcel Dekker, New York, 1994), 3–36; Richard Stewart, "The Transformation of American Administrative Law" (1975) 88 *Harv. LR* 1669.

[12] See W.P.M. Kennedy, "Aspects of Administrative Law in Canada" (1934) 46 *Jur Rev* 203; F.C. Cronkite, "Legal Education—Which Trend?" (1935) 13 *Can Bar Rev* 375; J. Willis, "Three Approaches to Administrative Law: The Judicial, the Conceptual, and the Functional" (1935–6) 1 *UTLJ* 53; J. Willis, "Canadian Administrative Law in Retrospect" (1974) 24 *UTLJ* 225; S. Smith, Book review (1932) 10 *Can Bar Rev* 612; J.A. Corry, "Administrative Law in Canada" (1933) 5 *Proceedings: Canadian Political Science Association* 196; J.A. Corry, "Administrative Law and the Interpretation of Statutes" (1935–6) 1 *UTLJ* 286; J. Finkelman, "Separation of Powers: A Study in Administrative Law" (1935–6) 1 *UTLJ* 313; J. Finkelman, "Government by Civil Servants" (1939) 17 *Can Bar Rev* 166; and E.K. Hopkins, "Administrative Justice in Canada" (1939) 17 *Can Bar Rev* 619.

[13] For an early call to action on this front, see P. Garant, "Les fins du droit public moderne au Québec" (1966–67) 8 *Les Cahiers de Droit* 251. Garant has followed with a series of works on law and administration: *Droit administratif* (Editions Y. Blais, Cowansville, Québec, Montreal, 3rd ed., 1991), 3 vols. In R. Dussault and L. Borgeat, *Administrative Law: A Treatise* (Carswell, Toronto, 2d ed. 1985; trans. by M. Rankin), vol. 1, 12, the authors define administrative law as: "[T]he entire set of rules relating to the organisation, operation and control of the administration. . . . It is for administrative law not only to state but to order and harmonise the rules applicable to the Administration and to those persons who are in contact with it".

[14] J. Willis, "Canadian Administrative Law" (1961) 6 *JSPTL* 53.

underlying values or deontology; and (ii) to articulate, through contact with public service lawyers and non-legally trained public servants, the role and function of law in public administration.

Government lawyers work on a daily basis in Willis's "shadowy and arduous borderland between law, political science and public administration where you have to use your feet as well as your head". The basic skill sets are the obvious ones: litigation, legal advice-giving, legislation and regulation-making, and solicitor's work, notably on contracts and property. There are, of course, variations and combinations of these functions; and there are related corporate legal services.

What is particularly characteristic of all public service law is the policy component; whether as litigators, solicitors, legal advisors, legislation-makers, policy developers or corporate counsel, public service lawyers must appreciate the departmental objectives, policy goals and practical considerations of client ministries or agencies. And they must find a harmonious balance with the broader public interest and general legislative and constitutional considerations. In this process, there can be a multiplicity, sometimes a divergence, of loyalties: to the rule of law, to the public interest, to the client(s).

The question "who is the client?" gets at the paramount challenge, and the essential professionalism, of public service lawyering. In the first instance, the "client" is understood to be the ministry or agency that directly receives, and in some cases pays for, the legal service in question. There is a simultaneous "client" relationship with the government as a whole or with the Crown (most concretely personified as the Cabinet). Public service lawyers—at least those housed in ministries of Justice—also maintain a client-like relationship with the Minister of Justice/Attorney-General, who carries the central-agency function to ensure coherence in government legal positions and respect for the rule of law. Finally, the public service lawyer has a functional and, in some cases, a fiduciary duty to identify and speak up for discrete interests or parties that would not otherwise be represented. Translating this multiplicity of interests and relationships into a coherent and high-quality legal service is the essential challenge of public service lawyering, and it is this feature that most firmly distinguishes public sector from private sector legal services.

The challenge is to find the right balance between a central government and a client-identified orientation. It is to present public interest, or general public service, or rule of law issues in sufficiently compelling terms that the "client" will embrace and identify with those concerns, rather than interpret such advice as a negative trumping of law over policy, or as the ideal overwhelming the practical, or as a failure by legal counsel to appreciate or properly advance departmental or programme priorities. A further and related challenge is to articulate legal advice and other legal services in terms that leave the ultimate choices with the responsible bureaucratic or political decision-makers. Public service lawyers must be effective "advocates" or monitors of the rule of law and careful articulators of the public interest on the one hand, and at the same time resist setting themselves up as ultimate arbiters of public policy and the public interest.[15]

Beyond the juggling of multiple loyalties, there are other important features that characterise public service lawyering. These include the ability to work in teams, and in a multi-disciplinary fashion. Issues are rarely free-standing questions of law. Risk assessment is a common aspect of public service legal judgements. Other disciplines, such as economics, criminology, or environmental science, may have to be weighed in assessing complex factual situations. Communication is another important component of a public service lawyer's *metier*. There are rising expectations of accountability and effective communication from within government and from without. Media interest in legal issues increasingly draws public service lawyers into the limelight. And, because they tend to favour a more demure professional manner and prefer to weigh a broad range of corporate concerns, public sector lawyers do not have the liberty to play on the public stage with the free-wheeling independence displayed by some private sector lawyers who become media favourites.

Public consultation is an increasingly important part of policy-making or administrative initiatives; public service lawyers are expected to be alert to these needs and to have expertise in effective and efficient consultative mechanisms. Public service lawyers should have more developed skills as drafters and interpreters than the general run of lawyers (although that may not be setting the standard very high). Institutional design and organisational understanding are aptitudes that should be found in greater measure in lawyers working in the public service.

The ultimate skill of the public service lawyer is to walk the professional line: to ensure that the rule of law and public service professionalism are fully regarded in government while at the same time being responsive to the political priorities of government and the democratic principles underlying a governing mandate.

So these are the functions and challenges of public service lawyers. They must balance concerns about consistency, fairness and respect for the rule of law with the particular interest and policy objectives of the "client". They must be team players. They must be flexible enough to work in a multi-

---

[15] A Canadian federal Department of Justice publication *In My Opinion: Best Practices of the Department of Justice Lawyers* (Minister of Public Works and Government Services Canada, Ottawa, 1995) enumerates the following qualities of the best lawyers (p.33):

"The best lawyers . . . act with integrity; care about quality; meet deadlines; have a sound knowledge of the law; keep up to date on legal matters and on client matters; know about their client's activities—their objectives, priorities, needs and operational realities; develop a good working relationship with colleagues and clients; consult with others before giving an opinion, when appropriate; work as a team with managers, colleagues and support staff; give useful and timely advice; share information; solve problems by looking for alternatives; distinguish between their legal advice and their views on policy; think strategically, consider the big picture; use plain language when talking or writing about the law; write opinions that assess strengths and weaknesses and clearly state the risks and possible outcomes; take account of the public interests."

disciplinary and an overtly political environment without subordinating their professional contribution as lawyers. They must be effective communicators and ever-ready consulters. They must understand organisations. They must have an aptitude for the written law, and at the same time be responsive to the need to develop new instruments of governance.

DISCIPLINE BUILDING PRACTICES AND PUBLIC SERVICE LAW

As a discipline, public service lawyering is subjected to many strains: to satisfy client needs or expectations, to keep abreast of legal developments, to respond to changes in the external climate, to represent the broader public interest, to deliver quality services in an increasingly tight and demanding fiscal climate, and to inculcate respect for the law and legal values throughout government.

Managing these strains and meeting the challenges of public service lawyering call for a sustained exercise in team-building and professional development. A key element enabling a response to these challenges has been the centralisation of government legal services under a single roof, under the Minister of Justice and the Attorney-General. This degree of centralisation, often referred to as the Justice/Attorney-General "monopoly", carries considerable advantages in terms of career mobility, relative independence of judgment, professional development and team-building. In most parliamentary systems deriving from common law traditions, the tasks of official legal advisor to Cabinet and controller of government litigation will be in differing dimensions shared by the Attorney-General and the Minister of Justice.[16] For example, in the Canadian federal jurisdiction the Minister of Justice has responsibility to: (i) see that the administration of public affairs is in accordance with law; (ii) have the superintendence of all matters connected with the administration of justice (that are not within provincial jurisdiction); (iii) generally advise the Crown on all matters of law referred to the Minister; and, (iv) examine legislation to ascertain whether any provisions are inconsistent with the Canadian Charter of Rights and Freedoms.[17] The Attorney-General retains exclusive responsibility for "regulation and conduct of all litigation for and against the Crown or any Department".[18]

It has not always been the case that Canadian federal government lawyers were primarily based in the Department of Justice. The 1962 Glassco Royal Commission on Government Organisation found that seven-eighths of the lawyers then working for the federal government were employed outside of Justice. Nearly forty per cent of the 330 lawyers employed by the government

---

[16] See J.Ll.J. Edwards, *The Law Officers of the Crown* (Sweet and Maxwell, London, 1964), 141ff, for an account of the rudimentary beginnings of the Attorney-General's office.
[17] See, e.g., Department of Justice Act, R.S.C., c. S-2, ss. 4 (a), (b), (c) and 4.1(1).
[18] Ibid., s. 5(d).

of Canada at the beginning of the 1960s were working for agencies outside the jurisdiction of the Civil Service Commission. And these statistics did not take into account work done by lawyers engaged on a standing or ad hoc basis as "legal agents".[19] The Royal Commission took a dim view of these disparate and ad hoc arrangements and recommended the establishment of an integrated legal service. In the Commission's view, this would improve professional opportunities for lawyers in government, and would enhance the overall quality of service:[20]

> "The value of a lawyer depends on the preservation of his independence from the operating necessities of his department. Secondment from Justice should help to preserve this independence, while opening up opportunities for professional advancement in a legal career service for those solicitors who have, to the present, been locked in isolated departmental compartments."

Today, the federal Department of Justice employs 2,500 people, almost 55% of whom are lawyers.[21] The Department acts as a central agency for the development and delivery of legal services in government, and as a government-wide monitor and propagator of the rule of law in government.[22] In a number of areas, such as legislation and regulation-making, property transactions, contracting out, and constitutional compliance, the Department has developed government-wide guides and standards, for lawyers and non-lawyers. Since 1991 a Departmental assessment of constitutional implications of new policy proposals is a required component of Cabinet submissions.[23] In 1996 the Department adopted a policy on dispute resolution (DR), which aims to include DR clauses in all government contracts, to incorporate DR processes into legislation, and to conduct ongoing DR training for Justice and other government employees.[24] Also in 1996 the Department published a 200 page "question-and-answer" format *Guide to the Making of Federal Acts and Regulations*.[25] Government lawyers have developed a series of *Deskbooks* dealing with substantive questions and best practices in a range of areas, including administrative law, criminal law and civil litigation.

In addition to such discipline-building practices, public service lawyers engage in various educational initiatives. Justice lawyers offer a "Legal Awareness" programme for non-legally trained public servants, and play an important role in delivering a comprehensive "Senior Management Training

---

[19] *Royal Commission on Government Organisation* (Queen's Printer, Ottawa, 1962), vol. 2, 370.
[20] Ibid., 418.
[21] *Department of Justice Employee Demographic Profile*, Dec. 1995, 2.
[22] On the question of central agency status, see B. Doern and R. Phidd, *Canadian Public Policy: Ideas, Structure and Process* (Nelson Canada, Scarborough, 2nd ed. 1992), 59.
[23] "New System for Charter Assessment of Policy Proposals" (Sept. 1991) 12 *Justice Echo* 1; "Enhanced Role for Justice in Cabinet System" (July/Aug. 1991) *Inter Pares*, No. 149; *Justice in the 1990s* (Department of Justice, Ottawa, 1993).
[24] Dispute Resolution Policy, 16 Feb. 1996.
[25] (Public Works and Government Services Canada, Ottawa, 1996).

Programme". These are examples of how government as a whole benefits from the centralisation and continuing development of legal services in a single department. And, there are full programmes of Continuing Legal Education within the Ministry. Perhaps the most pervasive way in which the Justice "monopoly" helps to build a discipline of public service law is through the regular meetings, the hierarchical and committee structures, the internal communications and information systems, and the informal and interpersonal team-building that come with being housed in a single department.

These represent some of the important ways in which a discipline of public service law can be said to be *en emergence*. When we consider the extensive discipline-building practices, the long list of skills and functions characteristic of government lawyering, the strong corporate and personal identifications tied to the Justice "monopoly", and the quality of on-going reflection about the functions and the quality of public service lawyering, it is evident that we are dealing with an identifiable disciplinary group. This is more than an empirical point; the emergence and identification of public service law as a discipline offers a fresh opportunity to think about law and government. This line of analysis has the advantage of being inherently empirical, and of not getting stuck at a preliminary stage on ideological debates about public and private, or about the existence or otherwise of a unique public law. Perhaps most significantly, at a time when new organisational models and new instruments of governance leaning to private sector models are undercutting the reach and efficaciousness of judicial review, an emerging discipline of public service law represents an important and singularly effective vehicle for developing the values of law in government.

THE NEW PUBLIC MANAGEMENT

Anything "new" invites a caricature of the old. Under the old public management, legislatures made laws, primarily in a command-sanction or an interventionist regulatory mode, and delegated their administration to a multitude of agents: prosecutors, line ministries, administrative agencies, the cabinet, government corporations, etc. In addition to being a regulator, government was a service provider, a property owner, an educator, a provider of incentives. Legislatures raised taxes; politicians, with the support of the administration, found ways to spend them, and more. The main dynamic was one of edifice-building, and the rule of law was styled accordingly. In its negative sense, the rule of law enforced the *ultra vires* principle and prevented arbitrary exercises of power, applying the same law to all, including government. In its positive sense, it encouraged systemic coherence, predictability and due process.

Critics of the old public management are concerned primarily about the cost of government (both direct and indirect), and about inflexibility and lack of responsiveness. The positive objectives of the new public management (NPM) are alternatively expressed in terms of value for money, international competitiveness, accountability, and responsiveness to community. NPM seeks to identify a core role for government, to give better and more responsive service, and to develop practices and instruments of governance that achieve policy goals without unduly hampering private sector or citizen initiative.

The OECD has recently completed a multi-volume study of public management reforms dealing with a full range of criticisms, reflections and innovations. The context for the project is succinctly stated by the Secretary-General's introduction to *Governance in Transition*, which includes the following commentary:[26]

> "Although pressures for reform, national cultures, and phases of development differ widely, Member countries have increasingly come to pursue a common reform agenda driven by the need for fiscal consolidation, by the globalisation of the economy, and by the impossibility of meeting an apparently infinite set of demands on public resources."

The OECD's Public Management Committee leads off the Report with a Statement of Conclusions calling for "radical change to the structures and processes for managing public action".[27] While recognising that OECD member countries represent a range of ideological perspectives, and that some countries have set about reducing the size of the public sector while others emphasise the key role of a vigorous public sector, the Public Management Committee identifies a common agenda encompassing efforts to make governments at all levels more efficient and cost-effective, to increase the quality of public services, to enable the public sector to respond more flexibly and more strategically to external changes, and to support and foster national economic performance. The Public Management Committee's assessment of what it calls "traditional public service delivery" reveals an underlying negative view, including a negative view of the role that rules and procedures and institutional inflexibility have played in that traditional public service delivery.

Unchanged governance structures and classic responses of "more of the same" are inappropriate in this intricate policy environment, since:[28]

> (a) maximising economic performance and ensuring social cohesion requires governments to adjust rapidly to changing circumstances, to create and exploit new opportunities and thus to deploy and redeploy resources more rapidly and flexibly;
> (b) highly centralised, rule-bound, and inflexible organisations that emphasise process rather than results impede good performance;

---

[26] Above at n. 1, 3.
[27] Ibid., 7.
[28] Idem.

(c) large government debts and fiscal imbalances exacerbated by recession—and their implications for interest rates, investment and job creation—place limits on the size of the state and require governments to pursue greater cost-effectiveness in the allocation and management of public resources;
(d) extensive and unwieldy government regulations that affect the cost structures and thus the productivity of the private sector restrict the flexibility needed in an increasingly competitive international market place;
(e) demographic changes and economic and social developments are adding to the services that the community expects from governments, while consumers are demanding a greater say in what governments do and how they do it; they expect value for money and are increasingly reluctant to pay higher taxes.

The new public management has been embraced, or at least implanted, in Canada. It has been a centrepiece of successive budget addresses, federal and provincial.[29] It is increasingly prominent in the discourse of public administration.[30] It is being put into practice, through downsizing of service delivery ministries, flattening of public sector hierarchies, outsourcing of traditional public sector services, actively searching for alternatives to traditional regulation, and encouraging initiative and reform-mindedness at all levels of the public service.[31] The question at this stage is how law finds a place in an era of new public management.

PUBLIC SERVICE LAW AND THE NEW PUBLIC MANAGEMENT

This paper opened with the observation that there is a *prima facie* tension between the new public management and traditional views of law in government. New public management targets "highly centralised, rule-bound and inflexible organisations". It encourages autonomy for public service managers. It emphasises performance and results. It rewards entrepreneurial initiative. In important respects, the new public management runs against the grain of law.

---

[29] See, e.g., A. Armit and J. Bourgault, *Hard Choices or No Choices* (The Institute of Public Administration of Canada, Toronto, 1996). For a longer range perspective, see A.W. Johnson, *Reflections on Administrative Reform in the Government of Canada 1962–1991* (Office of the Auditor-General of Canada, Ottawa, 1992).

[30] Although not without debate about its merits, tenor and pace. See S. Borins, "The new public management is here to stay" (1995) 38 *Canadian Public Administration* 122 and D. Savoie, "What is wrong with the new public management?" (1995) 38 *Canadian Public Administration* 112. And the reprise: Savoie, "Just another voice from the pulpit" (1995) 38 *Canadian Public Administration* 133; and Borins, "A last word" (1995) 38 *Canadian Public Administration* 137.

[31] See Swimmer, above at n. 1 and J.I. Gow, *Learning from Others: Administrative Innovations Among Canadian Governments* (Institute of Public Administration Canada, Toronto, 1994).

This brings us to the ultimate question posed by this paper. Are public service law, and public service lawyering, adaptable to the culture of new public management? Or do they require a command-sanction, highly centralised system of governance? Can public service law develop the kind of structures and incentives and performance measures that lie at the heart of the new public management? Perhaps law, instead of being part of the problem—tying up public service in a control model—can contribute to the good manners and efficient process of a public administration oriented to the values of new public management. Perhaps the relationship between law and the new public management is one of healthy tension, rather than opposition. Perhaps public service law has the opportunity, and the serious potential, to give leadership to a reinvigorated and entrepreneurial vocation of public service.

The most immediate way in which government lawyers are challenged to come to terms with the new public management is to hang on to their jobs. Whatever higher ideals may attach to the new public management, a prime objective is to reduce costs of government services—or at least to reduce central budget costs. There is no question that, at least in traditional "core budget" terms, public service law *will* take a cut, along with other government services and functions. In a context of continuing and sometimes radical expenditure reductions, Justice/Attorney-General ministries in Canada have been relatively well treated, presumably out of a recognition that government does not have the choice to drop legal services in the same measure it can drop programmes in such fields as transport or natural resources, or even environment. That said, funding for government legal services has been reduced in real terms, with a corresponding reduction in the number of people capable of being funded from core budgets. In the same time period, government lawyers have had to struggle with a steadily increasing demand for service.[32]

This conjuncture of declining core budgets and increased demand for legal services does not leave many options for public service lawyers. They can increase revenue, decrease demand, or reduce service. In response to strikingly similar circumstances, Canadian and Australian federal government lawyers have developed user-pay programmes known as "Client Driven Services" (CDS) in Canada and "User-Choice" in Australia. In 1996–97, under the Canadian CDS initiative, 38% of Department of Justice legal operations will be funded through contributions from client departments or agencies, although still within the ostensible constraints of the Justice monopoly. The Australian User-Choice initiative is even more fully market-based, with almost two-thirds of the budget of the Commonwealth Legal Practice coming from

---

[32] For a consideration of this increased demand in the Canadian federal context, see the Auditor-General's review of "Department of Justice—Legal Advisory and Litigation Services", in *Report of the Auditor-General of Canada to the House of Commons 1993* (Minister of Supply and Services, Ottawa, 1993), 450–51. For a review of the pressures faced by the Australian Attorney-General's Department, see *Annual Report 1994–95* (Commonwealth of Australia, Canberra, 1995).

fees-generated work.³³ Moreover, a significant portion of the Commonwealth government's legal services was opened up for competition as of July 1995, including competitive bids from the Legal Practice.³⁴

The level of "client" control implied by the Australian or Canadian user-pay developments begs a series of questions about government legal work. Where are the assurances of consistency or independence of judgment? What about the rule of law? Who will look out for the "central agency" or whole government perspective? Who will look out for the interests of unrepresented parties? Who will speak for the general public interest? Ultimately, who will "speak truth to power"?

On the other side, if we insist on maintaining the monopoly, and especially if we insist on funding legal services through appropriations from core budgets, we encounter an even more obvious set of questions. Who is going to do the work? Who is going to pay for it? Is it possible to maintain morale, or standards of professional service, in a context of steadily declining resources and mounting demand for service?

We already know the answers to these latter questions. Within a command culture and on core budgets, government lawyers will be overworked. Some clients will be under-served. There will be limited incentive for clients to control their level of demand for legal services. It will be difficult to obtain reliable information about performance standards, or about client satisfaction, or even about what public service lawyers are doing. It will be difficult to identify or to move in new directions. And it will be increasingly difficult to find the time, or to exercise the authority, to serve the several central agency functions, including as monitor and propagator of the rule of law.

As for the former set of questions, regarding independence, professional motivation and the overall professional integrity of government legal services, there are admittedly downside risks to a client-centered and client-driven system for legal services. But, there are upsides. One is that greater

---

³³ For the Australian situation, see *Review of User Pays System of Provision of Government Legal Services* (1995). For an overview of the situation at the federal level in Canada, see *Department of Justice Outlook on Program Priorities and Expenditures 1995–98* (Minister of Public Works and Government Services, Ottawa, 1995).

³⁴ The following services continue to be funded from the core budget of the Australian Attorney-General's Department, and are provided exclusively by the Legal Practice: legal advice to Cabinet; advice on Cabinet submissions or cabinet memoranda, legislative proposals or draft memoranda; policy advice; public international law and treaties services; drafting of subordinate legislation; and prosecution services on behalf of the Director of Public Prosecutions. The following services are charged to client departments, but they must obtain the service from the Commonwealth Legal Practice: constitutional advice; litigation in courts; legal agreements to be approved by Cabinet; disputes between government agencies; matters having national security implications; government to government work (both domestic and international); and questions of statutory interpretation affecting more than one Commonwealth agency or relating to the expenditure or receipt of public money.

A further Review of the Attorney-General's Legal Practice was commenced in late 1996, with a view to preparing a final report for the Commonwealth government by mid-March 1997. It is considered likely that the Review will commence the opening up of a larger proportion of legal services to competition.

client influence should lead to a more effective professional service, and more discriminating controls on demand. As for the ostensible concern that lawyers will simply cave in to the clients' wishes, we should remember that public servants have a history and a substantial near-constitutional practice of "speaking truth to power". The entire basis of public service professionalism, and of public service lawyering in particular, is to offer objective advice to politically accountable and politically motivated masters. The relationship with a paying public service client should not present any more dramatic tensions, although this point might have to be revisited depending on how client decisions about legal services resources would affect the job security of an individual lawyer. At first blush though, one wants to think of the challenge as one of effective communications about the service being provided to the client, rather than as a question of new conflicts of interest or undermined integrity.

The real challenges, and the opportunities, presented by the combination of public service law and the new public management, are to articulate standards, and an appropriate process, to provide the highest quality legal services *to the immediate client and to government as a whole*. The related challenge is to move from a command to an entrepreneurial culture, while retaining or perhaps even enhancing the central agency perspective of legal services. The opportunity is to move beyond an atmosphere of increasingly grim survivalism to one of team-building and positive professional development.

The check against a descent into an "anything-goes, eat-what-you-kill" entrepreneurialism has to be an emphasis on professional discipline, accompanied by effective communication with clients about the value of independent judgment and the rule of law. Public service lawyers have an opportunity, perhaps even an imperative, to develop even more articulate templates of best practices, legal consciousness and professional quality standards. These templates are even more critically needed in a world of diffuse "public" sector institutions and less command-oriented instruments of governance.

In an important sense, law could become a key site for reinvigorating public service morale, and for animating a discourse of public service values and ethics. This kind of invigoration and animation are desperately needed at a time when spirits are understandably low. Senior managers who are in control of change processes, and who are most likely building careers as "change-agents", will see the new public management from a different perspective than will the line workers whose jobs may very well be threatened, or be perceived to be at risk. At the very least, their workloads have been increased, along with their level of uncertainty.

Perhaps the most fundamental way in which the new public management affects the quality of life and morale of public servants, including lawyers, is through its essential questioning of the command culture. While change is undoubtedly needed, and while the old public service delivery models and command mechanisms were not necessarily edifying or morale-building for bureaucrats, they did have their *raison d'être*: public service, the public interest, the rule of law, organisational legitimacy and order.

These are values that one would hope can be carried over to more invigorated, flexible and service-oriented delivery models. But, if that is to be so, law and public service lawyers have to be central players. Public service lawyers have to think about their own values, professionalism and ethics. They can be important agents in animating a broader discourse in government and beyond.[35] And they have to think about the rule of law as infrastructure, both moral and functional, for good governance.[36]

Beyond a contribution to a discourse about public service ethics, public service lawyers have to be more explicit about their contribution to making the rule of law functional as infrastructure for government. In order to do so most effectively, they have to be more explicit about their own professional contributions, roles and values. In effect, public service lawyers have to recognise that they have a discipline. The failure to so recognise themselves expressly impedes their disciplinary development. Moreover, it can be particularly insidious at a time when there is a strong move to a client-service orientation. If public service lawyers model themselves on the most obvious, perhaps the only available, paradigm—the private sector lawyer on retainer to a particular client—they will miss an opportunity to deliver to *the client(s)* the full service that underpins public service law as a discipline. In fact, unless we are able to think about public service law in stronger disciplinary terms, including the imperatives of how it meshes and must adapt to the new public management, we are not likely to even get the right answer to the question: "who is the client?".

[35] See a the Report of the Study Team on Public Service Values and Ethics, *A Strong Foundation* (Canada, Privy Council, Dec. 1996; available through http://www.ccg.gc.ca), 74 which identifies the following values as underpinning public service: responsibility and accountability, empowerment and trust, loyalty, service, the public interest, citizenship, integrity, the rule of law and leadership, 74 which identifies the following values as underpinning public service: responsibility and accountability, empowerment and trust, loyalty, service, the public interest, citizenship, integrity, the rule of law and leadership. See also K. Kernaghan, *The Ethics Era in Canadian Public Administration* (Canadian Centre for Management Development, Ottawa, 1996) and the Dewar Series, *Values in Public Services* (Canadian Centre for Management Development, Ottawa, 1994).

[36] See the World Bank's *From Plan to Market, World Development Report 1996* (Oxford University Press, Oxford, 1996), which devotes a principal chapter to "Legal Institutions and the Rule of Law", and another to "Property Rights and Enterprise Reform".

The *Report* identifies the rule of law as essential infrastructure for economic development and for the building of market economies, and makes the following comparison between countries where the rule of law is taken for granted and countries where honest institutions of government and general public confidence are badly needed as infrastructure for a market economy (p. 88):

"People in countries with a well-established rule of law rarely stop to wonder where it comes from. But transition economies need to start over, to replace arbitrary rule by powerful individuals and institutions with a rule of law that inspires the public trust and respect that will enable it to endure. . . .

Transition economies struggle with a constant tension between, on the one hand, the need for a strong state to enforce laws and impose order and, on the other, the need for constraints on state power to make room for individual rights. Sorting out where state power is legitimate and where it is not is a constant task of governments everywhere. But whereas established market economies argue these questions at the margin, transition governments are completely refiguring the enforcement functions of public institutions."

7
Administrative Law at the Margins

DAVID MULLAN

INTRODUCTION

The main objective of this paper is to examine the proposition that the substantive and remedial principles of administrative law are having an impact in domains previously considered to be beyond their reach or, at best, at their margins or periphery.

This enterprise assumes, of course, that it is possible to describe a commonly-accepted core set of administrative law principles. Let me therefore start by identifying what for me constitute the key features of the current Canadian regime of judicial review of administrative action. They are the observance of jurisdictional limits (both constitutional and statutory), procedural fairness, and rationality and good faith in the exercise of statutory powers. While this list corresponds in large measure to that provided by Lord Diplock in his important 1985 judgment in *Council of Civil Service Unions* v. *Minister for the Civil Service*,[1] it differs in that it refers to the observance of jurisdictional limits rather than "illegality". I see that difference as justified by the greater preoccupation of Canadian judicial review law with the concept of jurisdiction and the frequent abnegation by Canadian courts of a capacity to review statutory authorities on the basis of mere error of law. However, for current purposes, it is probably of little moment which of the two formulations is accepted.

Within this framework, I intend to argue that, even historically but more so today, these ordering principles are ones that intrude frequently in litigation often conceived of as being beyond the terrain of administrative law. More specifically, I will concentrate on two phenomena: first, the application of administrative law principles to decision-making traditionally regarded as private rather than public, and, secondly, the extension of those same principles to certain State or Crown operations where the courts had previously accorded government a degree of operational autonomy normally associated with the private sector.[2]

---

[1] [1985] AC 374, 410. For a detailed evaluation of this judgment and its influence on English public law, see Dawn Oliver's paper in this volume.

[2] In terms of the State or the Crown, I could also have added those areas where, traditionally, immunities from the general principles of judicial review have prevailed not because of analogies

Indeed, this assimilative tendency has been so forceful that, at times, it has led to the absorption within public or administrative law for both remedial and substantive purposes of activities and organisations previously treated as largely autonomous of the dictates of the State at least in the conduct of their internal affairs. It should, however, be noted right from the outset that my thesis will be developed on a broader canvas than this. In other words, I will not be concerned solely with situations where *both* the remedial and substantive regimes of administrative law have been extended to previously excluded decision-making. As is clear from both Canadian and English jurisprudence described later in this paper, the mere fact that a decision is adjudged not to come within the parameters of the relevant judicial review remedial regime does not necessarily entail a corresponding rejection of the general substantive principles of judicial review. At times, the reasons for the unavailability of judicial review remedies will simply be a consequence of the specific wording of the relevant statutory provisions. However, even where those remedies are not available for more principled reasons, that will not necessarily mean the irrelevance within an otherwise private remedial context of substantive administrative law principles.[3]

It is also a major part of my objective not only to be descriptive but also to account for this phenomenon and, in what is a clear echo of a number of the other papers in this collection,[4] to consider its legitimacy particularly at a time of widespread deregulation, privatisation and corporatisation.

Essentially, my thesis will be twofold. I will first assert that the history of this area of the law provides evidence that here too, as in so many other fields, there is no clear divide between the public and the private, though I will not go as far as some and assert that there is nothing at all to the distinction or that it is necessarily counterproductive to even trade in such concepts. Rather,

---

with the functioning of the private sector but because of considerations peculiar to the State or the Crown. Here too, there have been evolutions. Thus, it is now accepted that the exercise of prerogative powers is amenable to judicial review by reference to the normal principles: *Council of Civil Service Unions* v. *Minister for the Civil Service*, ibid.; *Operation Dismantle* v. *The Queen* [1985] 1 SCR 441. At the remedial level, the whole question of the immunities of the Crown from injunctive relief has been reevaluated: *In re M* [1994] 1 AC 377; *Canada (Attorney General)* v. *Saskatchewan Water Corporation* (1993) 18 Admin LR (2d) 91 (Sask. C.A.).

[3] Conversely, though less frequently, there can be situations where the amenability of a decision-making regime to public law remedies will not necessarily involve the application of the whole panoply of the substantive principles of judicial review. Thus, in *R.* v. *Panel on Take-overs and Mergers, ex parte Datafin plc* [1987] QB 815 (hereafter referred to as *Datafin*) the English Court of Appeal, while holding that the non-statutory panel was subject to review under the relevant English judicial review rules, nonetheless, indicated an unwillingness to apply normal substantive principles of judicial review to the Panel's operations. Only in the case of procedural impropriety would the usual standards apply. In the domains of review for factual inadequacy or legal error, review would be very limited and, in general, be only prospective in operation; i.e., decisions would not be set aside; rather, declarations to guide future actions would be issued: ibid., 840–2, per Donaldson M.R. For further discussion of this case and the related English jurisprudence on the reach of judicial review, see the papers in this volume by Murray Hunt, Mark Aronson and Paul Craig.

[4] Notably those by Dawn Oliver, Murray Hunt, Mark Aronson and Paul Craig.

at one level, I want to argue that some of the relevant jurisprudence has shown an insufficient appreciation of the respective dimensions of public and private ordering within society, leading to too ready an application of the principles of public law in the domain of essentially private, largely autonomous organisations. On the other hand, my second and main point will be that, for the most part, this process of assimilation or the making of relevant connections between the private and public domains is a highly desirable evolution in the law particularly at a time when large segments of national legal regimes are becoming more and more affected by transnational considerations and the imperatives of globalisation.

More generally, I regard the project for the courts as no longer being one where they simply view their role as that of deciding in individual cases whether there are any situation-specific reasons for an interpenetration of the principles of private and public ordering. Under such an approach, administrative law cases at the margins will continue to be viewed as isolated, discrete instances; marginalia, in other words. Rather, what is needed is the development of general principles and criteria for the conducting of such evaluations leading to the eventual emergence of a more coherent set of principles and body of case-law.

Against this background, I also want to suggest that there is no necessary inconsistency or tension between the perpetuation of the tendency to reduce the legal and normative significance of the public/private divide and the desires of many modern states to deregulate, privatise and corporatise. Rather, I will assert that a credible argument can be made for the legitimacy of judicial application of the principles of administrative law in many of the deregulated, privatised and corporatised domains. This argument is one that can be advanced in part by way of analogy to and understanding of the historical pattern and the reasons and justifications for it. It also (at least in some cases) relies on an account of the current political fervour for reducing the ambit of the state and direct state involvement in particular as not necessarily involving a concomitant intention or even logical imperative that judicial review by reference to public values should also disappear. Indeed, under this theory, in the downsized state, judicial scrutiny may be becoming that much more important as a surrogate accountability mechanism in matters of public and state interest for previously existing internal, governmental and parliamentary controls.[5]

---

[5] This should not be read as an attempt to resurrect judicial review as a panacea for the correction of wrongs perpetrated by the State or by those to whom it has delegated state power. Judicial review as an effective, accessible regime for the supervision of government in a systematic, broadly-based way continues to have all of the warts that it has always had. Indeed, one might add that, with the dramatic downsizing of legal aid budgets, it is now even less accessible than it once was. On the other hand, one also has to recognise the situation with other accountability mechanisms that once held hope of greater accessibility and more systematic inquiry such as an Ombudsman office. There is still no general federal Ombudsman in Canada and, in the current economic environment, unlikely ever to be one. Indeed, Newfoundland has in recent years abolished its Ombudsman. As well, in those jurisdictions that have such an office, there seems no

Before commencing the descriptive portion of the paper, let me take one simple example of the final argument: the privatisation of prisons. Just because the state in the name of economic efficiency determines on such a course of action[6] is not necessarily an indicator of a state desire to also reduce the ambit of judicial scrutiny of the treatment of inmates in penitentiaries. To the extent that the detection, prosecution and punishment of those who infringe the criminal law is an archetypical state role in our form of government, the arguments are in fact the other way: the strengthening of judicial scrutiny and safeguards are a matter of clear necessity when the state delegates a part of its important public responsibilities to the private sector.[7] Indeed, in a Canadian context absent the deployment of the section 33(1) legislative override mechanism, the constitutional dictates of section 7 of the Canadian Charter of Rights and Freedoms might well impel that conclusion irrespective of legislative intention.[8]

THE EVOLUTIONARY EVIDENCE

Of the three ordering principles of administrative law identified above, the one where both the historical and contemporary evidence for the breakdown of the public and private divide is at its strongest or, perhaps more accurately, most readily discernible is the requirement of procedural decency or due process. Indeed, to me, one of the most telling features of the famous 1964 decision of the House of Lords in *Ridge* v. *Baldwin*[9] is the extent to which the majority Law Lords, in resurrecting the importance of procedural decencies in the exercise of *public* power, argued by reference to the law covering expulsions from all manner of clubs, trade unions and other non-statutory organisations—private bodies in conventional parlance.[10]

While the dictates of procedural fairness were never, of course, relevant across the spectrum of private power, there were many situations in which

---

disposition to extend its ambit to private sector bodies performing previously public functions and the same is true of the reach of Freedom of Information legislation. More broadly, questions are being raised about the capacity of the press to act as a watchdog in a privatised environment. See Bill Kovach, "When Public Business Goes Private—A threat to the watchdog press", New York Times, 4 Dec. 1996.

[6] Incidentally, I am not hereby assenting to the proposition that there are no constitutional bases for an attack on privatisation of prisons; there may well be.

[7] Indeed, I am led to believe that in the United States, where many examples exist of privatisation of prisons, the jurisprudence is, for the most part, one which subjects privatised prisons to public law due process standards while, at the same time, denying to the privatised prison operators the benefit of various forms of state immunity from suit. See further the papers by Jack Beermann and Alfred Aman in this volume.

[8] For a graphic futuristic vision in a fictional setting of the possibilities of penitentiary privatisation without controls, see Kurt Vonnegut Jr, *Hocus Pocus* (Putnam's, New York, 1990).

[9] [1964] AC 40.

[10] Ibid., 70–1 (per Lord Reid), 118–9 (per Lord Morris of Borth-y-Gest) and 130–32 (per Lord Hodson).

particular forms of private power could not be exercised legally without adherence to those principles. The reasons for that have been variously explained at various times and in various cases.[11] However, what is perhaps most important is that those explanations generally have a component that either parallels one of the justifications for procedural fairness that have influenced the courts in cases involving the exercise of statutory power or an independent public interest perspective other than that of autonomy or, more particularly, freedom of contract.

Thus, just as many of the historical justifications for the requirement of the observance of the rules of natural justice were rooted firmly in the presence of a property interest, so too did much of the law governing clubs, societies, universities and the Church rest on a concept of property. Membership in a club or society was thought to create a property interest in the assets of that club or society generating a claim to procedural fairness in expulsion and suspension proceedings.[12] The holding of an office or a position of power within a university[13] or the Church[14] could also bring with it various forms of property entitlement or the office itself was treated as a species of property right thereby generating claims to procedural decencies. Indeed, it might well be said, at least on the historical evidence recounted in *Ridge* v. *Baldwin,* that deprivation of property rights was the key element that dictated the imposition or implication of procedural fairness requirements with the existence of a state power or presence being merely incidental or supportive at most.

In more recent times, the concept of property for these purposes expanded in both the state and private domains. Thus, in English law in particular (though there were echoes of this in Canadian jurisprudence as well), there was a growing recognition of "property" rights in one's labour and, indeed, in some quarters (with Lord Denning in particular espousing this cause), limited acknowledgment of something in the nature of a common law right to work.[15] Other public values also intruded such as the common law policy

---

[11] For a discussion of Canadian law, see Robert E. Forbes, "Judicial Review of the Private Decision Maker: The Domestic Tribunal" (1976) 15 *University of Western Ontario Law Review* 123.

[12] See, e.g., *Forbes* v. *Eden* (1867) 48 LR 1 HL 568 (mandating the need for the existence of a property interest to entitle the courts to intervene); *Fisher* v. *Keane* (1878) 11 Ch D 353; *Dawkins* v. *Antrobus* (1879), 17 ChD 615 and cf. *Rigby* v. *Connol* (1880) 14 Ch D 482 (holding that a trade unionist had no property interest as against the Union of which he was a member).

[13] *Dr. Bentley's Case* (1723) 1 Str 557; 93 ER 698.

[14] See, e.g., *Tully* v. *Farrell* (1876) 23 Grant 40 (Ont. Ch.), an Ontario case referred to by M.H. Ogilvie in "Ecclesiastical Law—Jurisdiction of Civil Courts—Governing Documents of Religious Organizations—Natural Justice—*Lakeside Colony of Hutterian Brethren* v. *Hofer*" (1993) 72 *Can Bar Rev* 238, 246. See also M.H. Ogilvie, "Ecclesiastical Law—Jurisdiction of Civil Courts—Status of Clergy: *McCaw* v. *United Church of Canada*" (1992) 71 *Can Bar Rev* 597. As well, see *Ukrainian Greek Orthodox Church* v. *Ukrainian Greek Orthodox Cathedral of St. Mary the Protectoress (No. 2)* [1940] SCR 586, 591, where Crocket J. emphasised the need to establish the existence of a property or a civil right before the Canadian courts could intervene in Church affairs.

[15] See, e.g., *Edwards* v. *SOGAT* [1971] Ch 354; *Nagle* v. *Feilden* [1966] 2 QB 633.

against unreasonable restraints of trade.[16] Albeit that these developments were often the product of anti-collectivist tendencies and a clear anti-union animus on the part of the judiciary, they led to a line of jurisprudence that expulsion or suspension from organisations exercising control over access to various forms of employment, be they trade unions or traditional guilds, or non-statutory governing bodies such as a football association or racing club, required adherence to norms of procedural fairness. Indeed, the switch in emphasis from existing property rights to the notion of a common law right to work and an expanding conception of what constituted an unlawful restraint of trade opened up the possibility of not only existing "members" attacking disciplinary actions of various kinds on both procedural and substantive grounds but also applicants being able to challenge at least the substance of rules and decisions respecting membership.[17]

Often, of course, another theory also intruded, one which attempted to reconcile the interventions of the court with the essentially private, autonomous nature of the organisation under attack and the contractual nature of the relationship between member and organisation. This posited that judicial intervention was based on an implied term in the contract between organisation and member. That term imposed an obligation of natural justice on expulsion and suspension decisions even when the constitution or rules were silent.[18] Under such a theory, however, freedom of contract dictated that the parties were at liberty to modify the rules and that courts would have to respect the principle of private autonomy or ordering when there was such an explicit exclusion.[19] Nonetheless, once again, as the terrain for the conduct of at least some of the litigation in this domain shifted to the notion of a right to work or the striking down of unlawful restraints on trade, there also was a recognition by at least some judges and commentators that, in such circumstances, party autonomy to exclude the rules of natural justice had to give way to higher values.[20] This argument was further bolstered by the inevitably "adhesionary" nature of most, if not all, such contracts.

Also lurking in the background of at least some of this jurisprudence was a view of natural justice as, at least in some contexts, having an even greater transcendency than reflected in concepts of a right to work or the evil of restraints of trade. In short, my hunch is that some judges continued to be influenced by the natural law, perhaps even divinely-ordained character of procedural fairness. This may be seen as reflected in the famous statement by Fortescue J. in *Dr. Bentley's Case*[21] in which Bentley was challenging the

---

[16] See, e.g., *Dickson v. Pharmaceutical Guild* [1967] 2 WLR 718.
[17] See, e.g., *Nagle v. Feilden*, above at n. 15; *Faramus v. Film Artistes Association* [1964] AC 925.
[18] See, e.g., *John v. Rees* [1969] 2 All ER 274, 306–7.
[19] See, e.g., *Dickason v. Edwards* (1913) 10 CLR 243, 255.
[20] See, e.g., the *dicta* of Denning L.J. (as he then was) in *Lee v. Showmen's Guild of Great Britain* [1952] 2 QB 329, 342.
[21] Above at n. 13.

revocation of his university degrees and his dismissal from his post as Master of a Cambridge University College: that not even God denied Adam and Eve a hearing before casting them out of the Garden of Eden. At least, where property rights were at stake, the provision of a fair hearing was part of the natural order of things. As such, it could not be excluded in the private domain—freedom of contract and party autonomy had to yield to higher values.[22]

It must, of course, be acknowledged that in *Ridge* v. *Baldwin* itself adherence to the principles of natural justice or procedural fairness did not achieve anywhere near the degree of universal recognition that I have just suggested, even in the domain of employment be it public or private in nature. Notably, Lord Reid in his influential judgment identified two situations where hearing claims could not be made in the context of dismissals from a "job", one in the public arena (removal from an office held at pleasure) and one in the private sector (dismissal from employment at common law).[23] Nonetheless, we know now that *Ridge* v. *Baldwin* was not the end of the story as far as public law is concerned at least in Canada.

In 1990 the Supreme Court of Canada in *Knight* v. *Indian Head School Division No. 19*[24] reevaluated the position of offices held at pleasure and ruled that there was an entitlement to procedural fairness before removal could be effected lawfully. Moreover, what was of considerable significance in that case was that the office held at pleasure was that of a Director of Education employed by a School Board. In many respects, this looks like a statutory form of employment which in earlier judgments has been treated as a category distinct from that of office holder and, in general, akin to employment in the private sector.[25] In fact, this classification seemed reenforced by the seeming acceptance in the majority judgment that the contract[26] governing the relationship could trade away any procedural rights possessed by the plaintiff. It

---

[22] A modern variant on this theory can be found in the at least partial divorce of procedural fairness requirements from legislative intention apparent in the judgment of L'Heureux-Dubé J. in *Knight* v. *Indian Head School Division No. 19* [1990] 1 SCR 653. In talking about the possible existence of "a general right to procedural fairness, autonomous of the operation of any statute", L'Heureux-Dubé J. is presumably appealing to some higher constitutional ordering principle that does not depend for its operation on any presumed parliamentary intent that the particular exercise of power be attended by observance of procedural nicety. There seem to be echoes of this in the very recent decision of the English Court of Appeal in *R.* v. *Secretary of State for the Home Department, ex parte Mohammed Al Fayed*, Nov. 13, 1996 (The Times, Nov. 18 1996) in which Lord Woolf M.R. at points seems to accept the notion of a free-standing right to procedural fairness which is trumped only by explicit legislative exclusion. In their papers in this volume Murray Hunt and David Dyzenhaus argue the case for the liberation of administrative law theory from the shackles of Dicey and his vision of the centrality of the sovereignty of parliament as the dominant constitutional value.

[23] *Ridge* v. *Baldwin*, above at n. 9, 65–6.

[24] Above at n. 22 (hereafter referred to as *Knight*).

[25] *Semchuk* v. *Board of Education of Regina School Division No. 4 of Saskatchewan* (1986) 26 Admin LR 88 (Sask. Q.B.), aff'd (1987) 37 DLR (4th) 738 (Sask. C.A.) (a case involving a graphic artist employed by a school board acting under statutory authority).

[26] *Knight*, above at n. 22, 681.

is also interesting that the case was not one involving judicial review but an action for wrongful dismissal. Nonetheless, L'Heureux-Dubé J. (delivering the majority judgment) was of the view that the position of Director of Education had a sufficient "statutory flavour"[27] to attract categorisation as an office and the concomitant duty to accord procedural fairness. This conclusion she reenforced by reference to a perceived distinction between public and private employment, that being the public interest in the former category "in the proper use of delegated power by administrative bodies".[28] Thus, one of the domains where public authorities previously could act by reference to the same principles as private actors has at the very least been substantially modified by the *Knight* case.

Whether the same outcome would have ensued in the United Kingdom is a matter of speculation. Certainly, it has to be conceded that L'Heureux-Dubé J. relied heavily on the House of Lords' judgment in an appeal from Scotland, *Malloch v. Aberdeen Corporation*.[29] Indeed, the term "statutory flavour" is taken from similar expressions used by Lord Wilberforce in that case.[30] However, in more recent decisions, the English courts seem to be less inclined to move from the statutory nature of employment to the availability of conventional judicial review. Thus in *R. v. Derbyshire County Council, ex parte Noble*,[31] Woolf L.J. (as he then was), after a lengthy examination of the authorities, concluded that a Deputy Police Surgeon appointed under statutory authority could not challenge his dismissal by way of judicial review. There was an insufficient public law element to his position. However, what is interesting is that Woolf L.J. expressly reserved the question of whether Noble could have successfully advanced a procedural unfairness claim in a common law breach of contract action.[32]

Seen in this light, the main reason for the denial of access to judicial review may have been a desire not to make available to such an official any right to reinstatement which would have been the effect of the grant of certiorari-type relief. The claim for procedural fairness was one that should only have been entertained within the framework of private litigation where reinstatement was not a possibility.

If this assessment holds, there is, of course, no necessary inconsistency between *Noble* and the outcome in *Knight* where the Court was in fact adjudicating in the context of a common law wrongful dismissal action. Indeed, what all this suggests is that, at least where it is not precluded by the relevant remedial regime, the mere fact that a position has a sufficient statutory flavour to attract the protection of the public law principles of procedural

---

[27] Ibid., 672.
[28] Ibid., 675.
[29] [1971] 2 All ER 1278.
[30] Ibid., 1293 ("fortified by statute") and 1294 ("support by statute").
[31] [1990] ICR 808 (hereafter referred to as *Noble*).
[32] Ibid., 821.

fairness does not necessarily entail the further proposition that, in situations where procedural fairness is denied, reinstatement by way of certiorari-type or declaratory relief follows automatically. In an appropriately nuanced regime, it should be feasible where appropriate to have a judgment which finds the dismissal wrongful because of procedural unfairness but which denies reinstatement and confines the plaintiff/applicant to damages for wrongful dismissal.[33]

What, however, is also significant in this area of the law is that there are not only examples of withdrawing from public sector actors a previously existing immunity from the public law norms of procedural fairness but also a growing sense that such process values might sometimes deserve recognition in the private employment sector. As an example of the cross-fertilisation that goes on between private law and public law, what is emerging in the common law governing contracts of employment is a judicial sense that there should be an obligation to confront an employee with the relevant allegations in situations where dismissal is being contemplated for cause and to give that employee an opportunity to respond to or meet those allegations.

This is clearly foreseen in the judgment of Woolf L.J. in *Noble*.[34] There is also Canadian lower court authority in favour of this position as well as *dicta* in other judgments expressing sympathy with such an evolution even though feeling constrained by apparently contrary authority not to actually reach such a conclusion.[35] While the consequence of this (save in the case of the unionised sector and those three Canadian jurisdictions[36] that have unfair dismissal statutes) is not reinstatement (at least to this point), what the need to confront an employee with the reasons for dismissal amounts to is in effect the imposition of some form of hearing requirement, the consequences of failure being exposure to liability in damages for wrongful dismissal.

---

[33] This was in effect the ultimate product of the litigation involving Chief Brown of the Waterloo Police Force. While he succeeded in establishing that he had been dismissed from a statutory office contrary to the dictates of procedural fairness, reinstatement by way of a judicial review remedy was not a feasible remedial response given that another Chief had been appointed to replace him some years previously. As a consequence, the only appropriate remedy was a monetary one. See the account of the saga in *Brown v. Waterloo Regional Board of Commissioners of Police* (1983) 150 DLR (3d) 729 (Ont. C.A.) (hereafter referred to as *Brown*).

[34] Note that Noble did not have access to an Industrial Relations Tribunal because his contract was treated as a contract for services as opposed to a contract of service. His only recourse, after the denial of judicial review, was an action at common law: above at n. 31, 812 and 821–2.

[35] The strongest Ontario authority in this domain is in fact not all that recent: *Reilly v. Steelcase Canada Ltd.* (1979) 26 OR (2d) 725 (H.C.). It should also be noted that in *Tse v. Trow Consulting Engineering Ltd.* (1995) 14 CCEL (2d) 132 (O.C.G.D.), Cumming J., while expressing sympathy for the position taken by Keith J. in *Reilly*, thought that, as a first instance judge, he was constrained by the traditional common law position and what he saw as its reaffirmation by the Supreme Court of Canada in *Knight*, above at n. 22. Subsequently, in *Quirola v. Xerox Canada Inc.* (1996) 16 CCEL (2d) 235 (O.C.G.D.), another first instance judge made a strong plea for a change in the law to reflect hearing entitlements in such cases.

[36] Nova Scotia (Labour Standards Act, R.S.N.S. 1989, c. 246, s. 71(1)), Quebec (An Act respecting Labour Standards, R.S.Q., c. N.1.1, s. 124) and federally (Canada Labour Code, R.S.C. 1985, c. L.2 (cases amended by R.S.C. 1985, c. 15 (1st Supp.)), s. 240).

Administrative Law at the Margins 143

What this particular example also suggests is the degree to which the assimilation in common law between the public and private sectors is influenced by legislation. To the extent that the legislature as in both Britain and in varying forms in all Canadian jurisdictions confers on certain private sector employees the benefit of procedural entitlements, it is not unexpected to find the ambit of common law procedural protections achieving much greater status in the contexts of both statutory and non-statutory employment outside the direct protection of the relevant statutory employment regimes but operating in situations where argument by way of analogy makes sense. Indeed, to the extent that such regimes also make provision for reinstatement as a remedy, it would not be at all surprising to also witness the beginnings of a serious reevaluation of the virtual prohibition on reinstatement as a remedy for wrongful dismissal at common law.

Also relevant for an appreciation of both the dimensions of the issue and the way in which the law is changing is the common law regulating government procurement. The jurisprudence in this field is by no means consistent and still comparatively undeveloped outside the United States.[37] Nonetheless, some Canadian judges are now recognising the flaws of traditional law under which the state in this domain was generally equated with the private sector and subject to the general law of contractual tendering. They have conceded that there can be overarching public interest considerations dictating that state actors be constrained in ways that have not normally been relevant in the private sector. Policies on tendering for and the award of state contracts are being subjected to substantive constraints[38] and also have been held to give rise to "legitimate expectations".[39] In addition, there is some, admittedly controversial authority supporting the need to adhere to at least some procedural norms in the conduct of tendering for particular contracts.[40]

Stated in this way, of course, what this suggests is that here too, in certain respects, public contracting is moving away from private contracting in the norms that are applied or the rules that govern with the public sector having in some contexts stronger obligations towards those with whom it deals than a private sector contracting party would in similar circumstances. However,

---

[37] For a description of the relevant Canadian law with extensive reference to other Commonwealth jurisdictions, see S. Arrowsmith, *Government Procurement and Judicial Review* (Carswell, Toronto, 1985). Note also the extent to which English law on tendering for public contracts is now subject to European Community Directives: see S. Arrowsmith, "Protecting the Interests of Bidders for Public Contracts; The Role of the Common Law" [1994] *CLJ* 104 and, e.g., *R. v. Portsmouth City Council, ex parte Coles*, The Times, 13 Nov. 1996 (C.A.).

[38] See, e.g., *Health Care Developers Inc. v. Newfoundland* (1996) 141 Nfl'd and PEIR 34 (Nfl'd C.A.), discussed below at text accompanying nn. 41–6. In an English setting, see *R. v. Legal Aid Board, ex parte Donn & Co. (a firm)* [1996] 3 All ER 1 holding the Legal Aid Board subject to substantive principles of public law in solicitation of tenders for legal aid work.

[39] *Volker Stevin NWT (1992) Ltd. v. Northwest Territories (Commissioner)* (1994) 113 DLR (4th) 639 (N.W.T.C.A.).

[40] See particularly *Assaly (Thomas C.) Corp. Ltd. v. Canada* (1990) 44 Admin LR 89 (F.C., T.D.), though this judgment was specifically rejected in *Peter Kiewit Sons Ltd. v. Richmond (City)* (1992) 7 Admin LR (2d) 124 (B.S.C.S.).

again, what also needs to be recognised is that private sector law is itself showing signs of changing. In particular, the emerging law imposing good faith in the performance of contractual obligations on private sector contracting parties reflects a public law value quite antagonistic to traditional notions of freedom of contract. This can be seen as proceeding from at least some of the same considerations that are leading to the need for greater "rectitude" in government procurement practices.

A recent judgment of the Newfoundland Court of Appeal provides a nice setting for elaborating on some of these matters and, in particular, is another illustration of cross-fertilisation between the public and the private domains. At issue in *Health Care Developers Inc. v. Newfoundland*[41] was a breach of contract action brought against the Government of Newfoundland by two disappointed tenderers for contracts to construct health care facilities. The litigation hinged on whether either of the plaintiffs had been the "preferred" bidder on any of the projects, whether the relevant Department was entitled to depart from the specifications in the call for tenders and to introduce new standards for the award of the contracts, and the conditions (if any) under which the Department or the Cabinet could award the contracts to other than the "preferred" bidders. For present purposes, further detail of what was a complicated factual and legal situation is unnecessary.

What is significant, however, is the extent to which the Court of Appeal (in a judgment delivered by Cameron J.A.) developed in the context of a public defendant the good faith obligations of all (both public and private) who make calls for tenders. Cameron J.A. built on[42] the two contract theory of tendering espoused by Estey J. of the Supreme Court of Canada in *R. v. Ron Engineering & Construction (Eastern) Ltd.*,[43] a theory founded not on notions of freedom of contract but on a perceived need to protect "the integrity of the bidding system".[44] This led to a holding that the Crown owed participants in the process an obligation of good faith which she then proceeded to reduce to more concrete detail.[45]

At one level, this amounts to acceptance that, in an area where the Crown has in general been treated as operating subject to the same laws as the private sector, evolutions in the private law domain have to be taken into account as against the Crown as much as against the private sector. However, when those very evolutions in the private law domain are themselves based on conceptions of the broader public interest in a tendering system which is trusted by the participants, an important regulatory component has been added. It is also significant that the Court of Appeal makes reference to one of the judgments in which, in a public law remedial context, the same kind of

---

[41] Above at n. 38 (hereafter referred to as *Health Care Developers Inc.*).
[42] Ibid., 46.
[43] [1981] 1 SCR 111.
[44] Ibid., 121.
[45] *Health Care Developers Inc.*, above at n. 38, 48–52.

conclusion was reached though by reference to what is a slightly different conception of the public interest.[46] This was the judgment of Strayer J. (as he then was) in *Thomas C. Assaly Corp. Ltd.* v. *Canada*[47] in which he accepts the application of procedural fairness norms and administrative law remedies to government tendering, norms which gave individuals participating in a government tendering process a right to "be aware of the issues which [they] must address to have a chance of succeeding".[48]

None of this is meant to suggest that there is now an exact parallel in tendering law between the private and the public sectors. Thus, on the one hand, it might be asserted that the justifications for imposing good faith and procedural requirements on governments might (in a manner similar to the justification provided by L'Heureux-Dubé J. in *Knight*) also proceed from a norm that probity in such matters is or should be much more of an obligation of government than of private sector solicitors of tenders. Perforce, governments must conduct their commercial affairs in utmost good faith and even-handedly. Conversely, however, either by reference to common law principles or legislation, as in *Health Care Developers Inc.*, there may also be overarching public sector reasons for providing governments with some forms of discretion over the selection of successful bidders that do not have an analogue or apply in the private sector. However, to concede these considerations does not affect the basic arguments: not only is there no clear separation of public and private in this domain but also the common law has played a significant role in bringing broader public policy objectives to a field of commercial activity that, until recently, was characterised in both the private and the public sectors by considerations of freedom of contract, complete discretion in the exercise of contractual power conferred by reference to a literal reading of the language of the written transaction, and, more generally, an entitlement to pursue self-interest at the expense of all other goals. While the market itself might on occasion have imposed discipline for the robust or excessive exercise of or insistence on such rights, the law did not!

Some have criticised the recognition of a "good faith" in performance doctrine in the private law of contracts as being an aberration and an abhorrence, as an altogether inappropriate introduction of yet another element of uncertainty into the scope of contractual entitlements.[49] Indeed, the courts in the United Kingdom have in general rejected such an evolution (or revolution, as it is seen by some).[50] Nevertheless, leaving the detail of the good faith doctrine aside for the moment, this effectuation of broader public regulatory goals through contract law does have an honourable pedigree. Thus, to take just one example, though a highly relevant one in terms of modern legislated

[46] Ibid., 47–8.
[47] (1990) 44 Admin LR 89 (F.C., T.D.).
[48] Ibid., 94.
[49] In the context of an agreement to negotiate, see *Walford* v. *Miles* [1992] 2 AC 128.
[50] See P.S. Atiyah, *An Introduction to the Law of Contract* (Clarendon Press, Oxford, 5th ed. 1995), 212–3.

regulatory law, it was after all the common law that developed the tort of discriminatory denial of access to public utilities. The mandating of contractual access to certain facilities deemed to be public in nature (albeit operated privately and for gain) was in essence an anti-combines law. Those operating inns, ferries, bridges and the like could not take advantage of situational monopolies to extortionate ends. It was in the general public interest and, more specifically, the commercial interests of a rapidly expanding economy that there be equality of treatment in the operation of such facilities. Indeed, somewhat later in the evolution of this area of the law, the courts imposed even broader public policy goals on the operation of public utilities. Thus, in *Constantine* v. *Imperial Hotels*,[51] the tort was "expanded" to embrace the discriminatory denial on racial grounds of accommodation in an hotel even though that hotel was in the City of London and, not in the usual sense, the holder of a situational monopoly: Constantine, the famous Western Indian cricketer, found other comparable accommodation on the night in question.[52]

At this point, however, I want to move to what is a somewhat more problematic aspect of the assimilation of the public and the private domains and, more particularly, of the assimilation of administrative law norms within the private domain. Both British Columbia[53] and Ontario[54] have Judicial Review Procedure Acts, the primary purpose of which was to simplify the traditional remedies of judicial review and, in essence, to combine them into a single application for judicial review embracing the entire or combined reach of the assimilated modes of relief. In both statutes, the language by which this transition was achieved was the same: applications for relief "in the nature of" the various prerogative writs and proceedings for declaratory and injunctive relief in relation to the exercise of statutory power were, subject to limited exceptions, to be commenced by way of an application for judicial review.

On the basis that the term "statutory power" qualified only declaratory and injunctive relief and that relief given in proceedings against clubs, unions and churches was "in the nature of" the old prerogative remedies or writs (i.e. like in effect to), a number of judges in Ontario have felt no compunction in extending the reach of the Judicial Review Procedure Act to such bodies or organisations.[55] In contrast, in what as a matter of statutory interpretation is

[51] [1944] 1 KB 693.

[52] For an argument in favour of the reemergence of this aspect of public utilities law in an era of deregulation, privatisation and corporatisation, see M. Taggart, "Public Utilities and Public Law", in P.A. Joseph (ed.), *Essays on the Constitution* (Brooker's, Wellington, 1995), 214. See also Henry Molot, "The Duty of Business to Serve the Public: Analogy to the Innkeeper's Obligation" (1968) 46 *Can Bar Rev* 612.

[53] Judicial Review Procedure Act RSBC 1979, c. 209.

[54] Judicial Review Procedure Act RSO 1990, c. J.1.

[55] See, in particular, *Rees* v. *United Association of Journeymen & Apprentices of the Plumbing & Pipefitting Industry of the United States and Canada, Local 527* (1974) 46 DLR (3d) 518 (Ont. H.C., Div. Ct.) (allowing application for judicial review against a trade union over the fining and suspension of a member). See also *Lindenburger* v. *United Church of Canada* (1985) 17 CCEL 143 (Ont. H.C., Div. Ct.), aff'd (1987) 17 CCEL 172 (Ont. C.A.), and *Davis* v. *United Church of Canada* (1991) 8 OR (3d) 75 (Ont. H.C., Div. Ct.), basing intervention by way of judicial review

probably a better view, the British Columbia courts have been unanimous in holding that their Act does not reach such entities; this was public law remedial reform and the reference to "in the nature of" the prerogative writs could be explained readily on the basis that the writs themselves had not existed for a considerable time and it was customary to designate their equivalents or successors in the relevant Rules of Court as relief in the *nature of the prerogative writs*. One made application for relief in the nature of certiorari.[56]

For present purposes, however, it does not really matter which view one takes of the statutory interpretation dilemma. Indeed, nor does it matter much at the level of orders that are obtainable by reference to the Judicial Review Procedure Act; quashing of invalid decisions, restraining proceedings and action by way of prohibitory or injunctive orders, declaring the rights of the parties, and even commanding the performance of duties are all "weapons" that one would expect to be in the armoury of the courts in litigation involving challenges to the authority and actions of clubs, unions and churches.

What does concern me, however, is the extent to which, whether under a Judicial Review Procedure Act or perhaps even in the context of an expansive notion of the reach of the traditional modes of relief, the use of such remedies against clubs, unions and particularly churches implies the automatic or unthinking application of the substantive standards of administrative law/judicial review in those contexts. Similarly, in the remedial domain, where rights to an office or position are in question, there are serious questions as to whether it is appropriate in certain of these domains to declare the relevant decision a nullity thereby effectively reinstating the affected person to his or her position.[57]

Once again, this is not meant to suggest that any degree of assimilation is undesirable. Indeed, as indicated earlier, a case can be made that it has always existed to a degree that has not been sufficiently articulated or even acknowledged. However, the availability of the same remedies or modes of relief does not necessitate a complete parallel in the standards or grounds by reference to which those remedies are awarded in particular contexts. Care should always

---

on the United Church's incorporation by *federal* statute. Also of note in the Ontario jurisprudence is the application of *Datafin*, above at n. 3, in *Masters* v. *Ontario* (1993) 110 DLR (4th) 407 (O.C., Gen. Div.), aff'd (1994) 18 OR (3d) 551 (Div. Ct.), to allow judicial review of an investigative report leading to the dismissal of a civil servant appointed under prerogative power notwithstanding the fact that the relevant investigatory powers were not founded on any statute but depended on an internal policy directive dealing with workplace discrimination and harassment.

[56] See particularly *Mohr* v. *Vancouver, New Westminster and Fraser Valley District Council of Carpenters* (1988) 33 Admin LR 154 (B.C.C.A.).

[57] It must, of course, be noted that, even in the domain of statutory offices, it is by no means clear that reinstatement necessarily follows from a quashing of a removal or a declaration of nullity. Indeed, in *Ridge* v. *Baldwin*, above at n. 9, itself, the exact consequences for Ridge of a declaration of nullity were left undetermined: see the judgment of Lord Reid where the matter was remitted back with no direction as to the exact relief to be awarded although Lord Reid noted that the Ridge was not seeking reinstatement: ibid., 81. See also *Brown*, above at n. 33.

be taken in the delineation of the competing arguments in the assimilation debate and, more particularly, in the assessment of claims to autonomy and privacy against an undifferentiated application of public or administrative law standards or grounds of review. Indeed, this may sometimes be so just as much in the domain of procedural norms as with respect to substantive interventions.

The dimensions of this issue are well-illustrated by the judgment of the Supreme Court of Canada in *Lakeside Colony of Hutterian Brethren* v. *Hofer*.[58] At issue here was whether Hofer and members of his family were denied natural justice when they were expelled from the Hutterite Colony of which they were members or aspiring members. The Court held by a majority of six to one that there had not been adequate procedural safeguards. However, in delivering the judgment of the majority, Gonthier J., by reference to an influential article by Chafee,[59] conceded the grave difficulties encountered by lay courts in trying to tailor the demands of a flexible common law concept such as natural justice to the customs and traditions of an institution of which the courts had little real understanding.[60] Indeed, in her dissenting judgment, McLachlin J. makes a strong case for the majority having really failed to appreciate the values and practices of Hutterite colonies where sanctioning of conduct of members and their families was concerned.[61]

What does have to be acknowledged is that the members of the Colony were the plaintiffs in these proceedings in that they were seeking the assistance of the courts in the eviction of the Hofers from the Colony. As a consequence, it might be argued that, having voluntarily submitted themselves to the jurisdiction of the civil courts, the Hutterites were in fact signing on to the values of the common law. Indeed, the Colony even conceded in argument that it must fail if the Court were to find that it had breached the standards of natural justice.[62] In addition, the Colony had sought the assistance of the civil law for the purposes of establishing a legal framework for the effective operation of the colony—the Colony was an incorporated body.

However, it is questionable whether those indicators are enough especially when it is a case of disturbing a process that appeared to be the accepted one in such cases. Absent expert or other compelling testimony that this manner of proceeding was outside the norm for Hutterite communities, I doubt the wisdom of the Court's intervention. Seeking the assistance of the courts for the eviction of alleged trespassers rather than exercising rights of self-help should not be seen as involving the Colony in also acceding to the other norms

---

[58] [1992] 3 SCR 165.

[59] Z. Chafee, "The Internal Affairs of Associations Not For Profit" (1930) 43 *Harv LR* 993. For an example of where judicial intervention in the affairs of a Church required legislative rectification, see *Free Church of Scotland* v. *Overtoun* [1904] AC 515. The rectifying legislation was the Churches (Scotland) Act 1905.

[60] Above at n. 58, 190–91.

[61] Ibid., 228–33.

[62] Ibid., 175–6.

of the civil law system and its public law face at that. As for incorporation, the mere fact of incorporation under statute has seldom brought with it subjection to the norms of public or administrative law. Indeed, it is interesting that, while the Canadian courts have been prepared to accord deference to the procedural norms of bodies such as universities which have a hybrid public/private character,[63] the procedures adopted here in a case involving the lifestyle of a religiously-based, communally living group did not attract any express level of deference from the Supreme Court. The Court apparently reviewed the procedures adopted by reference to a correctness standard.[64]

It is also interesting to note that McLachlin J. (who dissented) was troubled by the property aspects of the expulsion. Expulsion brought with it the loss of any entitlement to a share of the communal property. This was described by both the Manitoba Court of Appeal[65] and McLachlin J.[66] as an "apparent inequity". While this statement and the accompanying discussion are clearly *dicta* and while McLauchlin J. does not state definitively that she would have interfered in the normal functioning of the community's property regime, what does seem to be suggested is that, in a claim by Hofer for some share in the communal assets when he left the Colony, the Colony would at the very least be placed on the defensive in the sense of having the onus of demonstrating the justice of the need to enforce its property norms. In a sense, this form of substantive intrusion would be even more problematic for concepts of autonomy and religious freedom than the procedural intervention that actually occurred.

As mentioned already, I do not mean to suggest that cases such as this bring into question much of the growing body of jurisprudence in which public values have trumped private rights of privacy and autonomy. Nor am I intending to cast into doubt all cases in which there has been interference in the affairs of a church or religiously-based community. Where a Church has not lived up to its own procedural norms, as in *McCaw* v. *United Church of Canada*[67] and there is no indication that such norms are matters of internal

---

[63] See, e.g., *Paine* v. *University of Toronto* (1981) 34 OR (2d) 770 (Ont. C.A.).

[64] The only point at which deference intruded was on the question of whether the Court should take jurisdiction over the dispute: "The courts are slow to exercise jurisdiction over the question of membership in a voluntary association, especially a religious one": above at n. 58, 173–4. Interestingly, on this point, the Court then (by reference to *Lee v. Showmen's Guild of Great Britain*, above at n. 20) adopted a quite flexible approach; jurisdiction to intervene did not depend so much on whether it could be said in strict theory that a property or contractual right was at stake but rather depended more on whether the matter was "of sufficient importance to deserve the intervention of the court and whether the remedy sought is susceptible of enforcement by the court": ibid., 175. Arguably, the extent of discretion and flexibility obviously present in this standard is itself at odds with a posture of reluctant intervention! For a much more favourable view of the holding of the majority in *Hofer*, see Ogilvie, above at n. 14.

[65] (1991) 77 DLR (4th) 202, 235, per Huband J.A.

[66] Above at n. 58, 233.

[67] (1991) 37 CCEL 214 (Ont. C.A.) (hereafter referred to as *McCaw*). However, worth contrasting with both *Hofer* and *McCaw* is *Re Morris and Morris* (1973) 42 DLR (3d) 550 (Man. C.A.), rev'g (1973) 36 DLR (3d) 447 (Man. Q.B.), in which the Manitoba Court of Appeal reversed a judgment of the Court of Queen's Bench awarding an order in the nature of mandamus

recognition only in the sense of being correctable solely through grievance mechanisms established by the church itself, there is a strong basis for intervention.

What the discussion is, however, meant to advance and exemplify is that there is a danger in the universalisation of standards of procedural and substantive intervention; that the range of permissible arrangements within our society is extensive and that there remain pockets at least (particularly in the religious domain) where the principles of autonomy and the private nature of the arrangements have a greater claim to recognition. Furthermore, as *McCaw* exemplifies, the remedies awarded for procedural and substantive failure in such situations may also be reflective of the generally autonomous or private nature of the institution under review. *McCaw*, though clearly treated in breach of the Church's rules, did not achieve, or even ask for, reinstatement to his previous "parish"; only general reinstatement to the Roll of ordained ministers and damages for loss of employment. To in effect reinstate in the circumstances of the case, according to the Court, may have been too great an intrusion in the internal affairs of the Church.[68] Indeed, now that the Supreme Court is beginning to concede the relevance of the Charter to the evolution and development of the common law,[69] it seems inevitable that *Hofer* itself and McLachlin J.'s loss of property rights hypothetical would today almost certainly be litigated in the shadow of the Charter and its protection in section 2(a) of "freedom of conscience and religion".

What also emerges from *Hofer* particularly when it is contrasted with *Gould* v. *Yukon Order of Pioneers*, a more recent decision of the Court,[70] is that the Supreme Court of Canada has yet to come to terms with the dimensions of the phenomenon of the intersection between the public and private domains. It has still to develop coherent and consistent principles for dealing with the various manifestations of this problem.

In *Gould* the Supreme Court confronted an issue common to most Canadian human rights/anti-discrimination legislation, the proscribing of discrimination in "offering or providing services, goods, or facilities to the public".[71] It was alleged that this provision was broken by a service club, the

---

compelling Morris to institute religious proceedings necessary to achieve recognition of a civil divorce within the Jewish faith. Irrespective of whether a duty existed within the relevant religious community for Morris to take this step, it was not the province of the civil courts to enforce such an obligation.

[68] *McCaw*, above at n. 67, 222–4.

[69] See H. Lessard, B. Ryder, D. Schneiderman and M. Young, "Developments in Constitutional Law: The 1994–95 Term" (1996) 7 *Supreme Court LR (2d)* 81, 144–54, discussing the impact of *Dagenais* v. *Canadian Broadcasting Corporation* [1994] 3 SCR 835; *Hill* v. *The Church of Scientology* [1995] 2 SCR 1130; and, incidentally, *Young* v. *Young* [1994] 4 SCR 3.

[70] [1996] 1 SCR 571 (hereafter referred to as *Gould*). This case is dealt with from different perspectives in the papers by Alison Harvison Young and Madame Justice Claire L'Heureux-Dubé in this volume.

[71] Human Rights Act, R.S.Y. 1986 (Supp.), c. 11, s. 8(1).

Yukon Order of Pioneers which restricted membership to males. For the majority of the Supreme Court of Canada, the issue was dealt with quite simply. In so far as the Order served the public of the Yukon by collecting and providing historical material, it did not discriminate since that material was available to all without any form of discrimination.[72] As for the allegation that membership was also a service offered to the public, the majority reasoned that this was not covered by the Act's proscription because membership discrimination was dealt with specifically in a separate subsection and it proscribed membership discrimination only in the case of a "trade union, trade association , occupational association, or professional association".[73] While this did not necessarily mean that the "public services" provision could never apply to membership discrimination, to apply it on the facts of this case would be to "deprive section 8(3) of all meaning".[74]

None of the other members of the Court, La Forest J. (concurring) or L'Heureux-Dubé and McLachlin JJ. (dissenting) was prepared to adopt the position that the explicit membership discrimination provision controlled the meaning of service offered to the public and prevented its application to discrimination in membership rules with respect to other organisations not controlling or affecting employment opportunities. In other words, they were prepared to hold that membership itself could be a "service" and, in the case of the two dissenting judges, was in fact a service in this case, a finding which had also been made by the initial Board of Adjudication. For current purposes, what is particularly significant is the extended analysis that McLachlin J. provides in reaching this conclusion. After noting that the Order provided a number of public functions such as the collecting and preservation of the history of the Yukon,[75] she goes on to describe the special status in the community provided by membership:[76]

"The Order has assumed an important role in defining the pioneers of the Yukon, and that recognition as a member of the Order and recognition of a person as a Yukon pioneer are largely synonymous in the mind of the public. This is evidenced by the role that the Order of Pioneers has in the public life of the Yukon, representing pioneers in general. The Order of Pioneers has reserved burial sites for pioneers in the public cemetery. The Order of Pioneers participates in annual public parades in Whitehorse and Dawson City as the only delegation of pioneers. The Order of Pioneers' Lodge in Dawson City is a tourist attraction because of its historical roots for pioneers. The Order of Pioneers' annual day of celebration, 'Discovery Day' was proclaimed a statutory holiday by the Territory."

---

[72] *Gould*, above at n. 70, 589, per Iacobucci J. (delivering a judgment in which Lamer C.J., Sopinka, Gonthier, Cory and Major JJ. concurred).
[73] Section 8(3).
[74] *Gould*, above at n. 70, 588.
[75] Ibid., 656.
[76] Ibid., 657.

In short, the Order had brought itself within the ambit of the relevant provision by "arrogat[ing] to itself important public functions" and by "conferr[ing] important public status on its members".[77]

There are two things that are striking about this analysis. First, to the extent that *Hofer* and *Gould* are both concerned with drawing lines between the public and the private (albeit in quite different legal contexts), a strong argument can be made that the Supreme Court has provided an answer in each case that is exactly the reverse of what it should have been. Putting it another way, *Hofer* was a case where the autonomy and deference-based claims of the Hutterite community had considerable force while *Gould* involved a situation where a "private" organisation by reason of its public profile and involvement had in effect lost its entitlement to make such "privacy" claims. Secondly, while McLachlin J.'s analysis should not necessarily lead to the further conclusion that the Yukon Order of Pioneers would also be subject to judicial review,[78] what it does provide is the beginnings of a methodology for analysing autonomy-based claims for the purposes of determining the extent to which (if at all) particular organisations and activities should be subject to the regime of public law, a regime which has various levels of intensity.

In the specific context of the availability of judicial review, the English courts (starting with *Datafin*[79]) have been moving in this direction though my sense of the jurisprudence is that there remains some uncertainty as to the connection between the availability of judicial review under the relevant rules and the applicability of the substantive grounds of review. Thus, as noted already, in *Datafin* itself judicial review was held to be an appropriate way of proceeding but the basis for conducting judicial review was somewhat more constrained than it might otherwise have been. In contrast, there are at least hints in the judgment of Bingham M.R. (as he then was) in *R.* v. *Disciplinary Committee of the Jockey Club, ex parte Aga Khan*,[80] that the Jockey Club, while not subject to judicial review because it was not governmental, was nonetheless a public body which might, in the context of a claim to "private" law remedies, be subjected to the substantive criteria of judicial review.[81] In this, the Master of the Rolls can be seen as standing in rather stark contrast

---

[77] *Gould*, above at n. 70, 658.

[78] Indeed, I do not see the analysis as having the consequence that all service clubs engaged in activities having a public profile or value would be subject to the Act; e.g., a fraternal order distributing food parcels at Christmas.

[79] Above at n. 3.

[80] [1993] 2 All ER 853 (hereafter referred to as *Aga Khan*).

[81] Ibid., 866–7. In this regard, see *Stevenage Borough Football Club Ltd.* v. *The Football League Ltd.*, The Times, 1 Aug. 1996 (Ch D). An action for an injunction restraining the Football League from implementing its criteria for membership, Carnwath J. (in a restraint of trade context) elaborated on the "public" nature of the Football League in the course of asserting the amenability of the League to a challenge to its Rules on the basis that they were "arbitrary or capricious". Ultimately, however, the challenge foundered on the basis of delay and acquiescence.

to another member of the Court, Hoffmann L.J. who regarded the situation of the Jockey Club as one involving the exercise of private power not subject to public law.[82] Indeed, the explanation for this difference between the two judgments may well rest in their disagreement on whether, absent the control over horse racing exercised by the Jockey Club, government would have felt compelled to intervene.

This divergence between the two judges raises a more general question and one that transcends the technical issue of the availability of particular forms of remedy.[83] To what extent is it appropriate in determining the application of administrative law principles, either at all or as a matter of intensity, to be concerned about whether the role being exercised or function being performed is a governmental one? In the introduction to this paper, I suggested that one of the strongest claims that can be made for administrative law standards of review being applied to private prisons stems from a conception that the detection and punishment of criminals is an archetypical state role in our society, a role underscored in Canada by the commitment of the Charter of Rights and Freedoms to the "principles of fundamental justice" when "life, liberty and security of the person" are at stake. However, there is a question as to whether there are all that many inherent state domestic roles beyond this, a question that assumes particular significance in an era of deregulation, privatisation and corporatisation.

Thus, there may well be problems with defining the issue, as in the *Aga Khan*'s case and also in R. v. *Football Association Ltd., ex parte Football League Ltd.*[84] and R. v. *Chief Rabbi of the United Hebrew Congregations of Great Britain and the Commonwealth, ex parte Wachmann*,[85] in terms of whether the state would have become a regulator had it not been for the existence of a regime of private control and regulation conducted by reference in part at least to the concerns of the public interest. Echoing an argument made by Murray Hunt,[86] not only will that be a highly speculative inquiry particularly in these days of government deregulation and downsizing but it is highly dubious whether it provides an adequate touchstone for the identification of public power that should be subjected to some at least of the administrative law standards of review or scrutiny. Indeed, in relation to matters once but no longer subject to governmental control or regulation, there is a converse problem in treating any newly-emerged private sector ordering or

---

[82] Ibid., 873.

[83] Indeed, in my view, there is nothing necessarily wrong or illogical in, on occasion, having limited application of the substantive standards of administrative law within judicial review and full application of those same standards in the context of "private" law remedies.

[84] [1993] 2 All ER 833.

[85] [1993] 2 All ER 249, denying access to judicial review of a decision taken by the Chief Rabbi to remove another rabbi from office. See also *Ex parte Stewart-Brady*, The Times, 22 Nov. 1996 (C.A.), leaving open the question of whether the Press Complaints Council was amenable to an application for judicial review.

[86] In his paper in this volume.

regulation as "a privatisation of the business of government itself"[87] and therefore automatically subject to the substantive and/or remedial principles of administrative law. It is also too confining (at least beyond the remedial domain) to see the appropriate test for the application of administrative law principles in terms of whether (as in *Datafin*) the process of private control or regulation has been "woven" into a broader system of governmental regulation.[88] While all of these factors may be relevant concerns in the conduct of any such inquiry, no one of them has a claim to be necessarily determinative and what is called for is a more expansive inquiry into the nature of the role played by the "private sector" ordering mechanism that is before the Court in any particular case. More specifically, that inquiry should involve the type of historical and sociological perspectives that McLachlin J. brought to bear in her analysis of the problem in *Gould* and should also be firmly rooted in the notion that "public power" and "governmental power" are not coextensive.[89]

While this has, in no sense, been intended as a comprehensive canvassing of the overlaps between the traditional domain of administrative law and that of legal controls on the private sector, my hope is that it has provided an indication of the extent that both historically and today any clear separation of the two is not an integral part of common law tradition. Under the influence of often quite broad conceptions of the nature and extent of the public interest, administrative law and so-called "private" law cross-fertilise one another. Sometimes, as perhaps indicated by *Hofer*, that may produce inappropriate outcomes with principles of autonomy and privacy compromised too much by the intrusion of public law values. However, on other occasions, such as the flirting of the common law with procedural norms in the realm of employment law or the demand that public utilities be available on a non-discriminatory basis, it represents the legitimate triumph of broader conceptions of the public interest and of what constitute public functions over traditional principles of freedom of contract or rights to autonomy and privacy.

The essential thesis that I have been endeavouring to advance to this point (for the most part within the context of procedural fairness jurisprudence) is made somewhat more generally in a recent article by Paul Finn, now a judge of the Federal Court of Australia. The title of his paper is "Controlling the Exercise of Power".[90] Eschewing for the most part administrative law examples, Finn identifies what he regards as the role of the common law in mediating between those possessing power and those affected by its exercise. Drawing upon a much broader range of examples than dealt with in this paper, Finn isolates four principal categories where such control is exercised:

---

[87] A term used by Hoffmann L.J. in *Aga Khan* (above at n. 80, 874) by reference to *R. v. Advertising Standards Authority, ex parte The Insurance Services plc* (1990) 2 Admin LR 77.

[88] An expression used by Bingham M.R. in *Aga Khan*: ibid., 867.

[89] For an insightful elaboration of the intersection of the principles of contract and public law, see Janet McLean, "Contracting in the Corporatised and Privatised Environment" (1996) 7 *PLR* 223.

[90] (1996) 7 *PLR* 86.

restrictions placed on exercise of power "because of the significance attributed to the rights of the individual that would be affected by the exercise of the power claimed";[91] disproportionality and unfairness "which results from its exercise";[92] "preventing exploitative conduct and of protecting the vulnerable";[93] and the protection of "reasonable" or "legitimate expectations".[94]

While now is not the occasion to unpackage the more detailed content of these four categories, what they and the specific examples used by Finn exemplify is yet another way of articulating the breakdown of the barrier between the public and private domains in the workings of the common law. Not only do we see within the four categories traditional concerns of administrative law such as the provision of participatory rights when valued interests and rights are at stake but also Finn uses language reflective of some of the emerging concerns of public law—the protection of legitimate expectations, the need for proportionality in the exercise of public power, substantive unfairness. Indeed, ultimately, what this thesis may involve in terms of common law methodology is that courts should first ask in response to any assertion of a claim against the exercise of a power not whether that power is public or private but rather what is the nature of the wrong that is being asserted and whether in general terms that represents a credible or principled claim. Thereafter and only as a secondary matter does the character of the exerciser of the power become relevant. Only then would the judge inquire whether there are any reasons based on the status of the wielder of power that indicate that the principle being appealed to should or should not be applied and, if so, with what intensity and with what remedial responses.

THE RELEVANCE OF DEREGULATION, PRIVATISATION AND CORPORATISATION

What impact might the previous discussion have on the way in which courts react when confronted with manifestations of the current tendencies of most governments to engage in so-called rationalisation and downsizing of the regulatory state? Because this phenomenon comes in so many different forms, is proceeding with varying levels of intensity, and is the result of often quite distinct political philosophies and hence has divergent objectives, generalisation is not easy. Nevertheless, I would venture to make two broad comments or claims.

First, the evidence suggests that even the most complete government dissociation from previous involvement such as the sell-off of state assets and denial of any continuing participatory interest in a particular field should not

[91] Ibid., 88.
[92] Idem.
[93] Idem.
[94] Ibid., 89.

of necessity mean that the courts will not scrutinise challenged exercises of power in that area by reference to overarching public interest concerns other than autonomy and freedom of contract. The evidence of the extent to which the private domain has become infused with public law values is strong.

Secondly, while aspects of the post-War regulatory state can be attributed to the failures and rigidities of the common law, there is a sense in which the common law has always played a role in the maintenance of an equilibrium. In the recent past, when state power has been exercised too intrusively, the common law has countered that by the use of concepts of individual autonomy and civil liberties. With the partial or complete withdrawal of the state from many areas of previous state monopoly or concern, there is reason to believe that the common law's role in the maintenance of equilibrium will turn to the need to protect broader public interests against the unbridled use of private power. To a degree, we can anticipate that state control, regulation and involvement will be replaced by judicial regulation and policing of the expanded or resurgent private sector. Indeed, as noted earlier, in a Canadian context, the evolving recognition of the impact of the Canadian Charter of Rights and Freedoms on "private" law can be seen, in one sense, as facilitating or emphasising this role of the courts and, in another, as one of the first manifestations of the search for mechanisms to achieve and justify the maintenance of equilibrium.

Let me provide an example which provides a sense of both of the phenomena that I have just described. Let us suppose that governments across Canada withdraw completely from the ownership and regulation of telephones and the telephone industry as part of a conscious decision that free competition will better serve the public interest and that government involvement is counter-productive, hindering technological advances, and perhaps even "illegitimate". At the same time, the Parliament of Canada, in recognition of its numerous failures and flaws, repeals its anti-combines legislation.[95] With the "return" of this domain to the private sector would presumably come a resurgence in the reliance on and evolution of public utility and restraint of trade common law. Already existing, though temporarily quiescent common law would resurface. Courts would also justify this intervention at least in part as a legitimate assertion of regulatory power in a domain no longer occupied by the state and as a counterbalance to what would otherwise be unchecked (save by what may be a flawed market place) private power.

Of course, in the use of this example, I am neither making a plea for nor a prediction of a direct transfer of regulatory responsibilities to the courts with those regulatory responsibilities exercised by reference to the same panoply of public policy considerations that were the underpinnings of the previous ownership or regulatory regime. Aside from the development and effective

---

[95] In the current environment, the first is probably far more likely than the second; indeed it is in large measure happening.

Administrative Law at the Margins 157

operation of such a regime being obviously beyond the courts' capacities,[96] it would also deny any impact to the motivations that prompted the legislative withdrawal; to the parliamentary view that deregulated, private enterprise would work better. On the other hand, the *deregulated* world into which the telephone industry would be released is not an *unregulated* environment but rather one in which there have always been and now are more and more common law constraints on the use of private power, some of which are derived at least in part from the principles of judicial review of administrative action. Absent clear statutory exemption from even those constraints, this is and should be the world in which the privatised and deregulated sectors will participate.

What is also vital to recognise is that the example presented above represents in a sense the most extreme version of government deregulation or withdrawal: total privatisation and an abjuring, at least in the political arena, of any continuing state concern in the interests of the promotion of free markets. At other levels in the current exercise, the overall state interest in the matter is either inherent (as, I would argue, in the privatised prison situation identified in the introduction), implied or express. In those circumstances, even where the power is being exercised by the private sector (private prisons once again and also self-regulation by industries and professions such as second-hand car dealers and powers transferred from the Ontario Securities Commission to the Toronto Stock Exchange in the province of Ontario), the private sector can clearly be seen as acting as the delegate of the state. As such and absent legislative provisions to the contrary, one would expect that delegated power to be performed in large measure, if not totally, by reference to the same standards demanded by the courts in the context of administrative law/judicial review litigation.

In the domain of commercial activities and the provision of services, there is also the phenomenon, as in New Zealand, of the State-Owned Enterprise as a replacement for utilities operated within government departments or as traditional Crown corporations. Here, the motivations for change are undoubtedly ones that are predicated on a policy of wanting to balance continued state involvement in the particular domain with the conduct of operations much more in accordance with a private sector model and, in many instances, in generally even competition with and subject to the market forces that are decisive for "purely private" participants in the same domain. Nonetheless, the state continues to be implicated directly and that implication in the New Zealand context is made express by subsection 4(1)(c) of the State-Owned Enterprises Act 1986. It states that one of the obligations of such

---

[96] This point is made much more strongly by Mark Aronson in his paper in this volume, in the course of which he questions the likelihood of judicial review having any significant impact in a privatised, outsourced world and, in particular, challenges the arguments advanced elsewhere by Michael Taggart that judicial review could accommodate a broader regulatory role by resurrecting its common law policing of discrimination in the operation of public utilities and the pursuit of common callings: above at n. 52, 214.

bodies is the exhibition of "a sense of social responsibility by having regard to the interests of the community in which it operates, and by endeavouring to accommodate or encourage these when able to do so". Much has been written about the phenomenon of State-Owned Enterprises in the New Zealand context[97] and important litigation[98] has ensued both as to their overall character and the nature of the obligation contained in this subsection: Are its directions even legally enforceable? If they are, what are the standards by which adherence to them is to be judged?

In this context, I do not want to dwell on what are the appropriate answers to these questions. Indeed, they are not at all obvious ones in so far as they arise out of what is an uneasy and perhaps ultimately unworkable legislative compromise, one that demands a certain schizophrenia on the part of those responsible for their management.[99] However, the example does provide some flavour of the various permutations and combinations that are possible in an era of downsizing and deregulation. Moreover, what that variety of formats also emphasises is the highly contextual nature of the inquiries that the courts will be called upon to make. However, in all of this, there may be two bedrock values or principles that transcend context: first, that government dissociation or disengagement will seldom, if ever, mean the disappearance of all public law values other than autonomy or privacy but, secondly, that direct government presence even within a largely private sector format is still a highly relevant matter in setting the parameters for the legitimate scope of judicial intervention.

CONCLUSION

This paper has, in one sense, been a summary description in the context of administrative law of the fudging at the margins of the distinction between the public and the private, a fudging that has had an impact on both the grounds on which actions can be challenged and the remedies available when wrongs have occurred. Moreover, it has also been my intention to demonstrate that this blurring has been present in our law for a long time and perhaps could not really have been avoided. More importantly, however, I have tried to make the case that the points at which the blurring occurs do vary over time dependent on changing conceptions of what the respective relations between public interest and private autonomy should be in the nation state.

---

[97] See M. Taggart, "Corporatisation, Privatisation and Public Law" (1991) 2 *PLR* 77; M. Chen, "Judicial Review of State-Owned Enterprises at the Crossroads" (1994) 24 *Victoria University of Wellington Law Review* 51.

[98] See, in particular, *Mercury Energy Ltd.* v. *Electricity Corporation of New Zealand Ltd.* [1994] 1 WLR 521 and the case comment by M. Taggart, "Corporatisation, Contracting and the Courts" [1994] *PL* 351.

[99] See M. Taggart, "State-Owned Enterprises and Social Responsibility: A Contradiction in Terms?" [1993] *NZ Recent Law Review* 343.

At the level of the common law, the parameters within which the phenomenon is now pertinent have clearly been affected by the extent to which there has been a growth in what Finn describes as the common law's essential mission as a controller in the exercise of power in its various manifestations.[100] It is also one that has been influenced by increasing levels of interdependencies within nation states and now, perhaps even more dramatically, by globalisation.[101]

All this has meant a much closer identity of the principles informing the conduct of judicial review of administrative action and those regulating the use of private power with the level of judicial activism clearly increasing in the private domain. This has led to my final argument which is to the effect that, given both the historical artifacts and the current practices of the courts, the common law will at least in some measure provide checking and accountability mechanisms in those areas where the state in accordance with current trends goes about deregulating, privatising and corporatising. Increased common law policing and regulation of private power, identification of transcendent public policy concerns even in the most completely privatised domain, the common law's role as the preserver of equilibrium, the emerging values of the Charter, as well as the inevitability in a shrinking world of interdependence will coalesce to provide a powerful antidote to the extreme versions of or aspirations for privatisation, deregulation and corporatisation.

[100] Above at n. 90.
[101] See the paper by Alfred Aman in this volume.

8
Intermediate Associations and the State

JANET McLEAN

INTRODUCTION

A number of papers in this volume have questioned whether the "source of power" test is adequate to determine who should be subject to judicial review or whether a more functional test would better respond to the mixed regulatory framework of contemporary government. I wish to take these broad themes and to explore them in relation to "private" associations not for profit.[1] In so doing I wish to raise the claims of cultural pluralism alongside the claims made on behalf of market pluralism discussed elsewhere in this volume.

The church and trade union cases at the turn of this century, and the academic writings which attended them, suggest that a source of power test in this context served the state's desire to assert itself against perceived rivals to its power. When read against this historical account it is not surprising that the theory fits uneasily at a time of corporatisation and privatisation when states do not merely tolerate but actively promote such rivals. The proffered alternative "public function" approach requires careful refinement if it is to be applied to these associations on the margins, which often wield substantial power over individuals. I suggest that the democratic functions of such associations should be considered when determining the extent (if any) of judicial intervention. Recognising that the state has no monopoly on power is not by itself justification for intervention by the courts (another branch of the "state" broadly conceived). I shall attempt to illustrate these comments by reference to a Supreme Court of Canada case involving the expulsion of a member of a Hutterite Brethren colony. I argue that the Court's intervention was inappropriate on those particular facts and had the effect of undermining rather than enhancing democratic values.

---

[1] This paper began as a commentary to David Mullan's paper, "Administrative Law at the Margins", in this volume.

SOURCE OF POWER

John Allison describes the "thinness" of the common law's account of the state as an abstract concept and suggests that our difficulties in identifying the province of administrative law are a direct consequence.[2] Another way of exploring these issues is to consider how the common law has characterised other forms of corporate life, groups which mediate between the state (however defined) and the individual. The intense academic debate about the legal and moral personality of the group at the turn of the twentieth century paralleled and sometimes intersected with the debate about who is the state.[3] A critical question which arose in relation to groups was what is the source of group power. At the end of the twentieth century, legal thinking is dominated by a view that public power is delegated from above and private power is consensual. An examination of group or corporate life over this century shows that that distinction has never been particularly clear nor compelling. At the turn of the twentieth century, one view was that all forms of corporate life depended on a state grant of power. It was not always uncontroversial to regard groups as the product of consensual arrangements between individuals.

These issues were thrown into focus by a number of church and union cases at the turn of the twentieth century. I do not have the space to go into them in detail here except to make some general observations about the way the judges approached these controversies and the explanations which were offered by the academic commentators for that intervention. In one important decision the majority of the House of Lords characterised trade unions as wholly created and limited by statute rather than merely recognised by such legislation and otherwise free to develop their purposes according to the wishes of their membership.[4] In the other major decision the House of Lords assumed jurisdiction to determine the true objects and purposes of the Free Church of Scotland—including theological questions such as the essentiality

---

[2] See his paper in this volume.

[3] In relation to the intersecting debates see especially H.A.L. Fisher (ed.), *The Collected Papers of Frederic William Maitland* (Cambridge University Press, Cambridge, 1911) and J. Dewey, "The Historic Background of Corporate Legal Personality" (1926) 35 *Yale LJ* 655. See also O.F. Gierke, *Political Theories of the Middle Age* (trans. and preface by F.W. Maitland) (Cambridge University Press, Cambridge, 1900); A.V. Dicey, "The Combination Laws as Illustrating the Relation between Law and Opinion in England During the Nineteenth Century" (1904) 17 *Harv LR* 511; A.W. Machen, "Corporate Personality" (1911) 25 *Harv LR* 253, 347 (2 pts); W.M. Geldart, "Legal Personality" (1911) 27 *LQR* 90; F. Pollock, "Theory of Corporations in the Common Law" (1911) 27 *LQR* 219; H. Laski, "The Personality of Associations" (1915–16) 29 *Harv LR* 404; W.S. Holdsworth, "English Corporation Law in the 16th and 17th Centuries" (1922) 31 *Yale LJ* 382; W.A. Sturges, "Unincorporated Associations as Parties to Actions" (1924) 33 *Yale LJ* 383; E.M. Dodd, "Dogma and Practice in the Law of Associations" (1928–29) 42 *Harv LR* 977; H.K.C. Wang, "The Corporate Entity Concept (or Fiction Theory) in the Year Book Period [:II]" (1943) 59 *LQR* 72.

[4] *Osborne v. Amalgamated Society of Railway Servants* [1910] AC 107.

of the establishment doctrine and predetermination.[5] The result was to vest all the church property in the 24 congregations which their Lordships judged to be the "true believers" and to leave the remaining 1100 with none.[6]

These cases represent a bold assertion by the courts of centralised authority over the democratic processes of groups at the margins. The groups' dependence on the state for the grant of power was justification for all later intervention. That the instrument of such state grant could be legislation in one case and trust deed in the other was of no consequence to the intervention which followed. Disposition of property by trust deed was treated by nineteenth century lawyers as if it were the legislative disposition of property.[7]

Attempts to rationalise this approach saw the resuscitation of medieval law which was to the effect that only the state can create an artificial person. There were two related theories governing legal identity—the fiction and concession theories. It is the latter which is the more important to our discussion. The medieval controversies which had spawned those theories themselves reflected the struggles between church and empire, and between dynastic and popular forms of government.[8] It is notable that they were recalled at a time when there was again a perceived threat to the state. The concession theory was to the effect that the state alone could create and legitimate such bodies. It treated all associations (profit making or otherwise) as "conjurations" and "conspiracies" except as far as they derived their powers from the state. On this view everything was delegated from above and was the subject of royal licenses and charters (including the power to create trusts). Arguably, the doctrine served the claims of an emerging nation state against rivals such as religious congregations, guilds, communes and the like. This fear of "partial institutions" and their description as "worms in the entrails of natural man" is attributed to Hobbes, as is the view that citizens entering upon civil society relinquish all rights and possess only those granted from above.[9] There are clear echoes of such a view in Holdsworth. Writing in 1922, and making direct reference to the state's tolerance of trade union activities he says:[10]

> "[F]or the abandonment of the state of its sovereignty has in effect set up a new feudalism which is every bit as regressive in its ideas and as mischievous as the feudalism of the Middle Ages. Our modern experience is a striking illustration of the political wisdom of the Roman lawyers when they taught the expediency of 'keeping the corporate form under lock and key'. In fact creation by and subordination

---

[5] *Free Church of Scotland v. Overtoun* [1904] AC 515.

[6] As David Mullan notes in his paper this decision was reversed by legislation.

[7] For example, nineteenth century lawyers conflated the distinction between state-imposed restrictions on alienation and privately-imposed restraints, and treated the policy underlying rules proscribing the latter as continuous with the policy opposed to the old feudal restraints. See G.S. Alexander, "The Dead Hand and the Law of Trusts in the Nineteenth Century" (1985) 37 *Stan LR* 1189, 1191.

[8] Dewey, above at n. 3, 664.

[9] Laski, above at n. 3, 425.

[10] Holdsworth, above at n. 3, 383.

to the state are the only terms upon which the existence of large associations of men can be safely allowed to lead an active life."

Even as late as 1929 Warren suggested that courts should allow no exceptions to the rule forbidding legally cognisable private associations in the absence of legislative authorisation: "[I]t is only for the King or the King in Parliament or, in America, for the legislature to create legal units".[11]

The concession theory would have treated the municipal corporation the same as the charitable trust. Not only is the power regarded as delegated from the state but the bodies to whom it is delegated are seen as themselves part of the state. Challenges to the concession theory and its continued application came from different sources such as the pluralists represented by Laski[12] and the realists. Geldart provides an example of the latter; while the charitable trust may in theory be enforced by the Attorney-General, he bridles:[13]

> "But that is a long way from seeing in every charitable trust and every corporation a set of officers of the state. We shall find it hard, for instance, to reconcile the facts of our corporate University and College life with such a view. We shall think it strange that every private person who makes a charitable disposition, which he can do without needing to ask any one's leave, should be held to create a new office of state."

He suggests the state is rather a *parens patriae* "who may punish, correct, regulate and protect, not an all absorbing State of which all smaller bodies are mere departments".[14]

Dicey's contribution to this particular debate was to recognise the power of trade unions as based on the consent of the individual members rather than dependent on state grant.[15] In his view individuals could do anything which was not in itself illegal, including the surrender of their rights to the group. He discussed the right to associate with reference to all the legislation over the nineteenth century which had forbidden combinations of workers (and at one time employers).[16] In the absence of such legislation, he suggested, the ability to associate is an extension of an individual's freedom and part of one's contractual capacity. He acknowledged that sometimes the effect may be to limit a member's freedom and even the freedom of those who stand outside the group. Strictly speaking then, the intellectual origins of the source of power test are not found in the work of Dicey but in much earlier civil law writings. While Dicey is usually cited as fostering a view of the state as the

---

[11] Quoted by Dodd, above at n. 3, 977–8.
[12] Above at n. 9.
[13] Geldart, above at n. 3, 100.
[14] Idem.
[15] Dicey, above at n. 3.
[16] See the Combination Act 1800, 37 Geo 3 c. 123 (1797), 39 Geo 3 c. 69 (1799), 57 Geo 3 c. 19 (1817) (also concerning potentially treasonable or seditious societies).

source of all public power,[17] his unitary model (so called) acknowledges the significant power derived from the individual in the surrender of individual rights. His contribution here is to the consent/coercion dichotomy. Unlike Hobbes and Bentham, he accepts that the state is the font of all power in relation to public forms of power but he does not regard the state as the creator of private forms of power, such as the right to contract, own property or to join associations. Indeed, he emphasises that the state itself is subject to the same law as between itself and citizens as governs the relationships between citizen and citizen. To him we can trace the view that, if it is not delegated from the state, it is not public power: it may nevertheless be considerable power, and more than a mere aggregation of the power of individuals.

The academic discussions at the turn of the century tended to concentrate on these general theories about the legal personality of associations and its source. That is, they directly confronted the role of the state *vis-à-vis* the group, whether for profit or not for profit. A distinct shift can be detected in the writing after 1930 to focus on questions about whether the technical bases of jurisdiction and intervention properly fitted the facts and character of individuals' relationships to groups. Judicial characterisation of groups as formed around property interests (trusts) or based on a consensual submission to rules allowed judges to protect individuals from group power while remaining ambiguous as to the source and nature of that power. Even within the contractual and property explanations for intervention, group power could be regarded as delegated from the state if one considers property and contractual rights the product of civil society rather than pre-social. In any event, these questions ceased to be the focus of academic concern which had shifted to considering the fictional nature of this account of group life.[18] Examples of the fiction under strain include the fact that it is always the executive committee who is sued for damages for a wrongful expulsion. On a pure view of contract every member of a group who voted for a wrongful expulsion could be sued. Traditional contract norms would not have allowed a dismissal in bad faith to have been actionable on that ground alone (motivation for breach being irrelevant). And a mere "scintilla" of property was sufficient basis on which the courts could intervene.[19]

A possible explanation of the shift in focus is that the threat to the group was perceived to be greater from within than from without.[20] And it coincides with a more explicit recognition of the natural rights of the individual, includ-

---

[17] In his *An Introduction to the Study of the Law of the Constitution* (Macmillan, London, 10th ed. 1959), 92 Dicey characterises everything from a non-sovereign legislature to a school board, or a railway company with the capacity to make by-laws, as a subordinate law making authority.

[18] See, e.g., Z. Chafee, "The Internal Affairs of Associations Not For Profit" (1930) 43 *Harv LR* 993, 1003.

[19] R. Pound, "Equitable Relief Against Defamation and Injuries to Personality" (1916) 29 *Harv LR* 640, 678.

[20] Remarked upon by Geldart, above at n. 3, 106.

ing the socialisation of property rights. What is particularly interesting during that later period, is the general lack of interest in the relationship between the state and the group and the sometimes unexamined elevation of the individual over the group. It is only at the point at which the state redefines itself through processes of corporatisation and privatisation that questions about the role of the group *vis-à-vis* the state have arisen again in the literature, this time focussing on the "public function" elements of association life.

THE PUBLIC FUNCTIONS OF PRIVATE ASSOCIATIONS

If the source of power test is so problematic, how might a public function test apply to associations not for profit to determine their susceptibility to judicial review? Whatever their legal form, associations range from gentlemen's clubs, churches, political parties, trade unions, professional associations, sporting clubs, Inns of Court, to the Selden Society. These associations at certain times have substantial powers over their members and sometimes affect the wider public. They serve very different functions in a democracy at different times. On one view of the state, such associations mediate between central authority and individuals. This mediation takes both positive and negative forms. Associations may provide the spiritual and moral sustenance which allows individuals to flourish. The concept of "flourishing" not being neutral, this may entail enhancing individual's abilities to pursue their own self interest or to deliberate, exercise citizenship, and pursue goals higher than self interest. Alternatively groups may act as partial shelters or buffers from the state's power and as focal points for resistance (e.g., shielding dissident expression from the majority).

While private associations may be the matrix in which private preferences are formed and aggregated with others, they may also serve as instruments of public policy inducing believers to act in ways consistent with their policies, and as vehicles of alliance which help to influence the development of public policy.[21] That is they may themselves form loose coalitions with other collectivities which make up the state. Unions sometimes explicitly seek to influence the public sphere and may enlist the state on their side of an otherwise private struggle or in another mode may contribute to forming public goals. Political parties explicitly work to harness public power.

Some associations can be described in terms of intimacy, privacy, and home relationships. The group may be bound together by shared commitments and philosophy rather than by adherence to formal rules. Or, by contrast, the group may be large and relatively unselective. The categories are not

---

[21] M. Tushnet, "The Constitution of Religion" (1985–86) 18 *Conn LR* 701, 732. See also M. Dan-Cohen, "Between Selves and Collectivities" (1994) 61 *U Chi LR* 1213; J.R. Macey, "Packaged Preferences and the Institutional Transformation of Interests" (1994) 61 *U Chi LR* 1443.

necessarily fixed: a religious association may sometimes seek to influence the broader public arena; some sporting clubs (such as football and gun clubs) may serve to mobilise the deepest passions of adherents. Whether they are characterised as part of the state, as buffers against the state, as intimate and familial type enterprises, or as intermediary bodies between the state and individuals, the legal characterisations of associations do not necessarily take account of the democratic functions which they perform. I suggest that the democratic function of an association may help to inform the proper level of intervention, if any, by the courts.

THE HUTTERITES

Let us take as an example an association whose function in a democracy is as a buffer between the majority and the individual. There is no doubt that the Hutterite Church exercises substantial power over its members. *Lakeside Colony of Hutterian Brethren* v. *Hofer*[22] sharply raises issues about how far Western democracies are willing to tolerate different legal systems and cultural pluralism. The more independent the association is, the more it may need protection from a tyrannious majority: but equally it is more likely that the majority will regard the association as itself tyrannous and as conflicting with core public values. While the Hutterite community may seem a strange and unique case, similar issues arise when groups attempt self-government in other contexts (aboriginal peoples, for example). This is also a case where freedom of religion is at stake. Different common law jurisdictions have displayed varying commitments to this value but all tend to categorise the activities of the church into the religious which is to be left alone and the secular where the court may enter. Some churches would accept that divide. Indeed many churches, especially those which have their origins in the established religions, share or are the source of many of the so-called universal values of the nation state.[23]

The Hutterites are not one of these.[24] Hutterites reject the idea of private property, live together on communal land holdings and dedicate all their labours to the group.[25] They have separate schools, have only paid taxes since 1968 and do not accept old age pensions, family allowances, or other forms

---

[22] [1992] 3 SCR 165 (hereafter referred to as *Hofer*).

[23] For example, protestantism brought with it an enhanced status for the individual.

[24] Although they pride themselves on their democratic processes according to M.H. Ogilvie, "Ecclesiastical Law—Jurisprudence of Civil Courts—Governing Documents of Religious Organizations—Natural Justice: *Lakeside Colony of Hutterian Brethren v. Hofer*" (1993) 72 *Can Bar Rev* 238, 242.

[25] The government had evinced its objection to the communal nature of their communities by legislation such as the Albertan Land Sales Prohibition Act 1944 and the Communal Property Act 1947. For a good recent account, see W. Janzen, *Limits of Liberty: The Experience of Mennonite, Hutterite, and Doukhobor Communities in Canada* (University of Toronto Press, Toronto, 1990).

of government social assistance in return. The Church allows only adult, baptised males as members. Families of members are allowed to live on the land, have no personal property, devote their labours to the group and submit themselves to its rules. The Church has enormous power over the spiritual, physical, economic and social lives of its members and their families.

The Church operates by processes of consensus and submission. A central tenet of the Hutterite belief, according to its founder, is "the peaceful submission to God and the believing group".[26] This is reflected in its decision-making and disciplinary processes. There is a cultural and religious imperative to achieve absolute harmony and community of interest between all the members in all things. Disobedience is punished by shunning the offender who must then eat and worship separately from the group. The offender is accepted back into the group when he or she submits to or accepts the punishment. If the punishment is not accepted then the offender is excommunicated. Offering the punishment is effectively an offer of a means of reconciliation. The distinction between expulsion or voluntary departure may not exist in Hutterite culture because there is always an element of self-expulsion. Failure to accept an expulsion (valid or not, if indeed those concepts apply) amounts to the commission of a new offence.

On one point of view, the Hutterite Church operates as a mini-state. It has its own system of law. In order to conduct limited transactions with the outside world (such as the purchase of land and the sale of produce) it adopts some of the legal instruments of the nation state in which it has established its territory. These include a private Act of Incorporation and articles of association. But the Church regards its jurisdiction as the primary one and the intervention of Canadian law as the wrongful coercion of a foreign power (if negative) or wrongful delegation of the Church's responsibility (if benevolent, such as the Canadian Pension Plan scheme).[27] Church and state are not separated under this view: the church is the state. No part of life is unsanctified.

The facts of *Hofer* are relatively few. Mr. Hofer dissented in a dispute over communal property and whether the Church should apply for patents. He was subjected to the shaming ritual but refused reconciliation, and was expelled. He stayed on the property, taking some of the believers and livestock with him. The Church, which eschews all violence, sought the intervention of the Court in order to get its property back. The Church may have thought it had a good chance of achieving its desired result because in an earlier case the Supreme Court had enforced the Church's rule that expelled members had no rights to Church property, such property being held on trust for the whole.[28]

---

[26] Jacob Hutter (from whom the group took its name), quoted in Janzen, ibid., 60.
[27] Janzen, ibid., 248.
[28] *Hofer* v. *Hofer* [1970] SCR 958. This was touted as a great success for religious freedom but was met by unsuccessful pleas for legislative reform. In 1947 the Manitoba government received submissions about whether a person leaving the colony could be given an equitable share of the assets. A committee was set up to consider the issue. It reported that the complete renunciation of personal property was a central part of the religious vows and said that to allow people

However, in this case the Court avoided comment on the validity of the property rules themselves[29] although implicitly it gave them recognition. A majority of the Supreme Court of Canada decided that Hofer had not been given proper notice of expulsion; with the consequence that if the Colony wanted to expel him validly it had to repeat the process in a fair manner.

How would such facts be considered under a source of power test? The power of the Hutterite Church could be regarded as delegated from the nation state. On this view, the use by an association of the legal instruments of the nation state such as a private act of incorporation or articles of association is evidence of a delegation of power from the nation state to the association or at least may be regarded as a waiver of autonomy implying acceptance of the nation state's values as they affect property in particular. (The Hutterites always maintained, and the facts would seem to confirm, that these instruments were strictly to regulate their relationships with the outside rather than their internal arrangements). On this view the courts should be able to intervene to protect civil and property rights. The commitments of the nation state to religious freedom and freedom of association (values not necessarily shared by the association itself) require a certain deference to the activities of the group but only until the nation state is compelled to intervene by reason of its other commitments such as to the protection of property, individual rights and fair processes. Implicit is a secular view which regards matters of faith and doctrine as outside the proper realm for state intervention, and civil rights and property as matters within it.

If one approaches the jurisdiction of the Canadian courts as based on a rule of recognition, the first and fundamental question is whether the court should recognise the rules of the Church and thereby lend its coercive power to the enforcement of such rules. That is, the group's power is the product of consent between its members rather than the product of delegated power. If the court were to find the particular rules repugnant then it should not intervene to enforce them. Having recognised the rules, the courts may consider whether the Hutterites followed them but no more than that. If the leaving were voluntary then only the rights attaching under Hutterite law to voluntary departures would apply (in this case none; property is abandoned forever). If it were involuntary the question is whether the Church followed its own processes. But even this limited intervention may be problematic given that in the mini-

property on dissolution would be like saying "in spite of your solemn undertaking upon joining your church, and in spite of your contract under seal, you can leave your community and gain compensation for work done while a member of the community". For an account see Janzen, ibid., 69. In 1971 the issue was raised again when a Bill was introduced into the Manitoba legislature which would have required a colony to take money from its communal assets and to pay it to any Hutterite who left the colony. The Bill failed.

[29] In the Manitoba Court of Appeal below, where the majority held that Hofer had been treated fairly and was bound to leave the Colony, the dissentient expressed repugnance at the scheme of ownership and suggested it might be void as contrary to public policy: *Lakeside Colony of Hutterian Brethren* v. *Hofer* (1991) 77 DLR (4th) 202, 210–11, per O'Sullivan J.A.

state, as in the larger one, law and rules are as often discovered as made. Great deference to the Church's own evaluation may be required especially given the often complex layers of law and custom.

Taking a more functional approach yields a different analysis. If one regards the Hutterites as a place of shelter for dissidents against the majority then one must allow the possibility that even values to do with property and process may differ in the Hutterite state. Process itself is not necessarily neutral or universal; neither is property (property in this case having distinctly metaphysical overtones). But the focus should be on process writ large. What cause was served by the Court's requiring the process of expulsion to be undertaken again—without the involvement of the women and unbaptised men? That is scarcely using judicial power to enhance democratic participation. More than that, if the Court had not intervened, the Hutterites could not have forced an expulsion because they reject the use of all forms of violence. Mr. Hofer would have continued to attempt to attract followers to his particular version of the faith. The group would have been forced to make some kind of accommodation. Having said that, I should add that the Court's role may have been different if the women, who could not be members or participate in decision-making processes but who gave their labour in exchange for a right to live on the commune, had brought an action. It is difficult to imagine how such a claim would be brought, how it might be framed, and indeed what kind of remedy a court could offer. It may still be that the claims on the state by individuals who are excluded from participation or who are themselves minorities in an association may sometimes be higher than the claims of an association to independence from the state. (We would need to know more about the dynamics of participation in Hutterite culture.) But Mr. Hofer's case is not of that kind. The underlying cause of his dispute with the church was his wish for more strict separation from the state. He always accepted the property rules of the group and indeed wished for more strict adherence to them. A more functional approach to judicial intervention in these associations on the margins should take account of factors such as the capacity for exit and voice, and the question of how best to reinforce participatory values. Such factors do not by themselves always mandate intervention.

Finally the Hutterite example raises more subtle questions about the content of public and private law values and the extent to which judicial review is about vindicating the private rights of individuals against the state and other powerful bodies. The most basic of these is whether the issue in the Hutterite case is susceptible to a hearing process. The Church is based on a principle of shared commitment, that is who you are (and what you believe) is more important than what you do.[30] Indeed it may be that the disciplinary

---

[30] See L.L. Fuller, "Two Principles of Human Association", in K.I. Winston (ed.), *The Principles of Social Order: Selected Essays of Lon L. Fuller* (Duke University Press, Durham, 1981), 67.

action arose out of Mr. Hofer's general demeanour of disobedience rather than the breaking of a specific rule. He was disciplined not so much for his acts but for the state of mind his actions betrayed.

CONCLUSION

As we come to the end of the twentieth century it may still be the case that associations not for profit pose a greater threat to the state (and the individual) than associations for profit. In this brief account I have attempted to illustrate that the source of power test was a response to the threat to the state posed by the trade unions at the turn of this century. Of recent times the courts have been much more concerned with the threat such groups pose to individuals. I do not mean to suggest that that concern is misplaced but merely that the democratic function of an association may help to inform the proper level of intervention by the courts.

9

The Reach of Administrative Law in the United States

JACK M. BEERMANN*

INTRODUCTION

Political and economic institutions in the United States have developed under a strong presumption against government intervention both as a regulator and as a provider of goods and services. Industries that in much of the industrialised world have traditionally been publicly owned have largely been held in private hands in the United States, including broadcasting, telephony, electricity, and long distance transportation and shipping by rail and air. These industries have been subject to heavy government regulation, including rate and service regulation, legal barriers to entry, and in some cases have been subsidised directly or indirectly through the grant of monopoly status and guaranteed return on investment, but they have been carried out largely under non-governmental ownership.

The privatisation movement that is sweeping the industrialised world has also had effects in the United States. In a sense, it was started here in the last century, where, perhaps out of a greater distrust of government power than exists in other areas of the world, regulation and not government ownership has been the norm. In the United States, in areas like telecommunications, cable television and electricity, privatisation was always the reality, so movement has been directly toward competition in these industries.

However, the boundaries between the public and the private are not so clear. On one side, questions are raised by the phenomenon of the government corporation which, unlike the typical corporation formed by an attorney under state incorporation practices, is chartered by the legislature to perform a particular purpose or set of purposes. Some such corporations are explicitly placed in a department of government, some are separate from the government but completely or largely under government control while still others are under little or no government control and have issued shares to the public.

---

* Thanks to Ron Cass, Steve Marks, Larry Sager, Mike Taggart and the participants in the Boston University School of Law Faculty Workshop for comments on an earlier draft and to Shirin Everett and Diego Rotsztain for research assistance.

Here, questions often arise concerning the reach of administrative law and constitutional law into the workings of these corporations.

On the other side are private associations. Some private associations are social clubs with little in the way of government regulation or effect on the public interest. Others, however, perform important regulatory functions such as certifying physicians to practice specialties or accrediting institutions of higher learning. While it is rare that a private association would be subjected to administrative law or constitutional constraints, there are often powerful reasons for subjecting their actions to judicial scrutiny to ensure both procedural and substantive fairness.

This essay examines disparate doctrines of administrative law, corporate law, constitutional law and common law with an eye toward revealing ways that norms of procedural and substantive fairness are felt within and beyond the normal scope of administrative law.[1] While this is not an exhaustive look at the issues, it is hoped that a framework for analysis can be detected and that ideas for further examination are inspired. A strong message is that scrutiny of private decision-making has been much lower than public decision-making, perhaps because of the greater distrust and fear of government power in the United States.

THE FORMAL REACH OF STATUTORY ADMINISTRATIVE LAW: THE ADMINISTRATIVE PROCEDURE ACT

The APA's Application to Agencies

Although administrative law in the United States has its roots in the common law, its reach and substance today are governed largely by legislative enactment in a very positivist fashion. The Administrative Procedure Act (APA) is a procedural code for agency action, and it also contains a chapter governing judicial review of agency action. Although there are independent constitutional constraints on government action (discussed below), the APA itself contains provisions that govern its reach and thus mark out the domain of administrative law.

The provisions of the APA apply to all "agencies" of the United States government. An agency is defined by the APA as "each authority of the Government of the United States, whether or not it is within or subject to review by another agency, but does not include" Congress, the courts and other exceptions.[2] This definition is very broad, although courts limited it by interpreting it to apply only to establishments that have the power to take

---

[1] For an interesting look at the legal justifications of bureaucratic power in the United States, see G.E. Frug, "The Ideology of Bureaucracy in American Law" (1984) 97 *Harv LR* 1276.

[2] Title 5 U.S.C. § 551(1).

action that, if left undisturbed by a higher authority, would have actual legal effect.[3] The paradigm cases are rulemaking and adjudication.

Although one might think otherwise by negative implication based upon the exclusion of the courts and Congress from the definition of agency, the Supreme Court has held that the President is not an agency and thus not subject to judicial review under the APA.[4] However, other high level officials in the executive branch, such as Heads of Departments (Cabinet Secretaries) are subject to the APA when making decisions of potential legal effect. Establishments within the executive branch whose primary function is to advise the President have not been held to be agencies since their actions have no external effects.

There is no basis in law for subjecting entities other than agencies as defined by the APA to the requirements of the APA and since the passage of the APA there is no federal administrative common law governing the conduct of entities not considered federal agencies. In other words, the APA does not govern the activities of non-agencies.

The APA and Government Corporations

In many cases a simple inquiry will determine whether a government corporation[5] is an agency for the purposes of the APA. Congress, when it creates government corporations, often specifies that the corporation is not an agency or is not part of the government of the United States. In such cases, the APA will not apply even if the corporation is wholly owned and controlled by the federal government, simply because Congress has made the statutory decision not to subject the entity to the APA.

A more difficult question may arise when Congress creates a government corporation without specifying whether it is an agency of the United States. Sometimes Congress specifies that the corporation is part of a particular Department or existing agency, and in such cases, if the corporation functions as an authority of the government, it should be treated as an agency for APA purposes. The corporate form in such cases may be desirable because of the function involved. If the government function involves participation in private transactions in the market, the corporate form may be more convenient than a traditional agency that is not separately incorporated. Theoretically, the corporate form should not affect the status of the corporation as an agency of the United States for purposes of the applicability of the APA—it would still be an "authority" of the federal government.

---

[3] See *Soucie* v. *David*, 448 F. 2d 1067 (D.C. Cir. 1971).
[4] See *Franklin* v. *Massachusetts*, 505 U.S. 788.
[5] For a detailed examination of government corporations in the United States, see A.M. Froomkin, "Reinventing the Government Corporation" [1995] *U Ill LR* 543.

If, however, it is unclear whether the corporation is functioning as an authority of the United States, some examination of the the relationship between the agency and the government and the agency's function may be necessary to determine whether the corporation should be treated as an APA agency. It is impossible to offer hard and fast answers to the questions likely to arise in such cases, which hopefully will be rare since Congress appears to be attentive to the question when it creates government corporations.

For the purposes of applying the APA, then, in most cases there is no need to investigate whether the government corporation is carrying out government functions or is acting more as a market participant. Regardless of function, if the creating legislation or charter granted by Congress specifies that the corporation is not an agency, that governs for the purposes of applying the APA,[6] and when Congress states that the corporation is located within an existing agency or department, the corporation should be treated as an agency.

This heavily statutory method of determining whether an entity is an APA agency is consistent with the Supreme Court's treatment of most questions arising under the APA. In most situations, the Court has been relatively strict, declining to add procedural requirements beyond those specifically called for in the APA. In the *Vermont Yankee* case,[7] the Court held that courts may not impose upon rulemaking agencies procedures in addition to those specified in the APA. *Vermont Yankee* rejected a line of lower court decisions that had fine-tuned rulemaking procedures according to the nature of the issues presented in the rulemaking and had often increased procedural requirements beyond those in the APA. The Court stated very clearly that absent unconstitutionality, the courts lack the authority to impose procedural requirements beyond those specified in the APA.

The Court has also stuck closely to the APA and other statutes in deciding which agency actions are subject to judicial review. The APA establishes a right of review of final agency action[8] on behalf of a party adversely affected or aggrieved by agency action.[9] Further, the APA governs the standards courts are to apply in conducting judicial review, with the arbitrary and capricious test the governing standard for review of most rulemaking and the substantial evidence test the standard for review of adjudication.[10] The APA also contains exceptions to the entitlement to judicial review—agency action is unreviewable if a statute precludes judicial review or if agency action is "committed to agency discretion by law".[11]

[6] See *Lebron v. National Rail Passenger Corporation*, 115 S. Ct. 961, 970–71 (1995) (citing Corporation for Public Broadcasting and Legal Services Corporation as well as Amtrak as examples of government corporations designated in their charters not to be government agencies).
[7] *Vermont Yankee Nuclear Power Corporation v. Natural Resources Defense Council Inc.*, 435 U.S. 519 (1978).
[8] Title 5 U.S.C. § 704.
[9] Title 5 U.S.C. § 702.
[10] Title 5 U.S.C § 706.
[11] Title 5 U.S.C. § 701(a). In defining "committed to agency discretion by law" the Supreme Court has looked to pre-APA common law and has expanded the exception beyond what

The President's lack of agency status has had an interesting effect on the availability of review over certain administrative decision-making. There are some administrative mechanisms over which the President has final authority. For example, while the Department of Commerce conducts the census of the population of the United States every ten years, the results of the census are sent to the President for transmission to Congress. Similarly, when the Defense Base Closure and Realignment Commission decides that a base should be closed, it makes a recommendation to the President who then transmits the final list to Congress. The President's actions are not reviewable because they are not "agency" actions. The Supreme Court has held that the agency action prior to the President's involvement is also not reviewable because it is not final since nothing can actually happen without Presidential approval.[12] Thus, by sticking closely to the APA's finality requirement, the Court has shielded agency action from judicial scrutiny.

The conclusion that the Court's methodology leads to is that the applicability of the APA to action of any entity will be determined by whether that entity is an "agency" within the APA's definition. There is no set of federal common law principles that would impose APA-like procedural requirements on entities not considered agencies under the statute. Further, the legislative declaration that an entity is not an agency or authority of the United States government, in a statute creating an entity such as a government corporation, should be dispositive. Therefore, no administrative law duties will be imposed on government corporations declared by Congress not to be agencies.

The absence of specification in the corporate charter regarding whether a government corporation is to be considered a government entity complicates matters, but not much. In my view, the choice of the corporate form should be strong evidence that Congress did not intend agency status unless Congress locates the corporation within an agency or department. Otherwise, the APA will add a significant extra layer of procedure to those presumably specified in the corporate charter and the judicial review provisions will add substantive restrictions beyond those contained in the charter and in corporate law. If there is a need to determine whether a government corporation is an agency, the federal courts are likely to analogise to cases involving whether government corporations are state actors for constitutional purposes and focus primarily on the issue of government control and secondarily on whether the corporation appears to be performing a function assigned by Congress.

Congress probably meant by the phrase. In this case, then, the Court has limited judicial review for reasons not embodied in the APA itself.

[12] See *Dalton* v. *Specter*, 511 U.S. 462 (1994); *Franklin* v. *Massachusetts*, above at n. 4.

Government Corporations and Freedom of Information

There is one non-constitutional area of administrative law which has a somewhat broader reach than the APA. Congress has enlarged the coverage of the Freedom of Information Act (FOIA), which establishes rights and procedures for obtaining information from government agencies, beyond the definition of "agency" in § 551(1) of the APA to include "any executive department, military department, Government Corporation, Government controlled corporation; or other establishment in the executive branch of government (including the Executive Office of the President), or any independent regulatory agency".[13]

The reason for the amendment is that, as stated above, courts had construed the APA's definition of agency to include only those establishments that had power to make decisions with legal affect. This makes sense since it would be anomalous to impose APA-type procedural requirements on entities that do not produce rules or orders but only reports, recommendations and the like. There are many establishments within the executive branch that function as advisory or research bodies and do not take action that directly affects the public. It is not anomalous to impose on such entities the open records requirements contained in the FOIA and related provisions. Thus, when Congress amended the definition of "agency", it did so in a way that was specific to FOIA and the like so that the non-action agencies were not burdened with APA procedural requirements.

There is a separation of powers problem lurking here. From the President's perspective, Congress is up to no good when it forces executive branch advisory entities to open their records to public scrutiny. Congress does not function under similar burdens. Courts have been sensitive to this and have held that even under FOIA's expanded definition of agency, entities whose primary role is to advise the President are not FOIA agencies and thus need not open their records to the public.[14]

Constitutional Law and Government Corporations

While a congressional declaration of non-agency status should be dispositive for the purposes of applicability of the APA, it does not answer the question whether the entity's actions are government action for the purposes of the Constitution. In other words, entities without administrative law obligations

---

[13] 5 U.S.C. § 552(e). For an example of a FOIA agency that might not be an APA agency, see *Energy Research Foundation v. Defense Nuclear Facilities Safety Board*, 917 F. 2d 581 (D.C. Cir. 1990).

[14] See *Meyer v. Bush*, 981 F. 2d 1288 (D.C. Cir. 1993) (President's Task Force on Regulatory Relief is not an agency subject to FOIA); *Rushworth v. Council of Economic Advisors*, 762 F. 2d 1038 (D.C. Cir. 1985) (Council of Economic Advisors is not an agency subject to FOIA).

may nonetheless be required to respect constitutional limits on government action and recognise individual constitutional rights.

The leading case in the United States on this issue is *Lebron v. National Railroad Passenger Corporation*.[15] In that case, the National Railroad Passenger Corporation (known as Amtrak) rejected Lebron's proposed political advertisement for a billboard in New York City's Pennsylvania Station known as "the Spectacular". The rejected advertisement satirised Coors beer as the "Right's Beer" and included an image of a can of Coors beer heading like a missile toward a group of Nicaraguan peasants. Amtrak relied on a policy of not allowing political advertising on the Spectacular to reject the proposed display.

Amtrak was created by an Act of Congress and was incorporated under the District of Columbia Business Corporation Act. Many of Amtrak's powers and duties, however, are established by federal statute.[16] Its main function involves operating inter-city and commuter rail services, which previously had been largely privately operated but were failing. It was established as a "for profit" corporation. The statute also provides that Amtrak is not an agency or establishment of the United States government.

The key factor that led the Supreme Court to hold that Amtrak was a government actor for constitutional purposes despite Congress's provision that Amtrak was private was that it was controlled by the Federal government. By statute, the President appoints six of the nine members of Amtrak's Board of Directors. Further, the government's ownership of all of Amtrak's preferred stock (in return for government subsidies) entitles the Secretary of Transportation, a presidential appointee, to appoint the seventh and eighth members of the nine person board. The ninth member is then chosen by the other eight. In addition to the government's power over the Board, the Court also noted Congress's power to amend the statutes that govern Amtrak's operations.

It seems relatively simple to conclude that the government's power to control Amtrak makes it a government actor for constitutional purposes. However, another aspect of the Court's analysis raises some interesting questions regarding the status of government corporations. In addition to government control, the Court also relied heavily on the fact that Amtrak was created to advance the important government policy of continuing and improving railroad passenger service.[17] The Court coupled this with a characterisation of the choice of the corporate form for government corporations generally as a convenience to allow them to behave like commercial, rather than governmental, entities while acknowledging that they were still government agencies, albeit in the corporate form.[18]

---

[15] Above at n. 6 (hereafter referred to as *Lebron*).
[16] The Rail Passenger Service Act of 1970, codified, in current form, at 49 U.S.C. 501 ff.
[17] *Lebron*, above at n. 6, 967.
[18] Ibid., 972.

The problem with the reliance in *Lebron* on the governmental policy aspects of Amtrak's mission is that this element will be present with regard to nearly all government corporations. It is difficult to imagine a government corporation that is not formed to advance a governmental policy. While some policies might seem somewhat peripheral, such as the United States Olympic Committee's function of administering the United States' entries in the Olympic Games, it would seem difficult for courts to distinguish between government corporations that advance government policies and those that do not.[19]

For example, in a post-*Lebron* case, the United States Court of Appeals for the Ninth Circuit was called upon to decide whether the Federal Home Loan Mortgage Corporation (Freddie Mac) is part of the government for the purpose of applying the Constitution.[20] Freddie Mac is a federally chartered corporation that purchases home mortgages, securitises them and sells shares on the open market. Freddie Mac decided that the American Bankers Mortgage Corporation (ABM) was ineligible to sell or service qualified mortgages because of problems with delinquencies and reporting. ABM sued Freddie Mac for violating its fifth amendment due process rights in the termination decision. Unless Freddie Mac is a government actor, fifth amendment due process constraints do not apply, although the contractual relationship between Freddie Mac and ABM contained some procedural constraints that would presumably be judicially enforceable.

The ninth circuit held, in agreement with other courts, that Freddie Mac clearly furthers important government objectives. Those objectives include improving the nationwide availability of mortgages, increasing access to mortgages for low and moderate income persons and creating a stable secondary market for mortgages. These purposes are recited in the statute under which the corporation was created.[21]

Despite these clear governmental objectives, the court held that the lack of government control over Freddie Mac was dispositive and required a negative answer to the argument that Freddie Mac was a government actor for constitutional purposes. The court pointed out that stock in Freddie Mac is publicly traded with 13 of 18 directors appointed by voting shareholders. Five directors are appointed by the President. The court held that presidential power to appoint a minority of the directors did not give the government enough control over the corporation to make it a government actor for constitutional purposes.

---

[19] Cf. *Garcia* v. *San Antonio Metropolitan Transit Authority*, 469 U.S. 528 (1985) (characterising distinction between traditional government functions and non-traditional government functions as unworkable for purposes of tenth amendment analysis).

[20] See *American Bankers Mortgage Corporation* v. *Federal Home Loan Mortgage Corporation*, 75 F. 3d 1401 (9th Cir. 1996), cert. denied, 117 S. Ct. 58 (1996) (hereafter referred to as *ABM*). See also *Liberty Mortgage Corporation Ltd.* v. *Federal Home Loan Mortgage Corporation*, 822 F. Supp. 956 (E.D.N.Y. 1993) (holding also that Freddie Mac is not a part of the government despite its function and establishment as a federally-chartered corporation).

[21] See Title 12 U.S.C. § 1451 note, cited in *ABM*, ibid., 1406 n. 1.

In addition to the government control argument, the plaintiffs also argued that the particular corporate activity challenged (determining eligibility to sell and service mortgages) is by nature a government function and is carried out under such close government regulation that Freddie Mac should be deemed a government actor when performing the particular function. This appears to be a fairly strong argument. Government should not be able to avoid constitutional scrutiny of its activities merely by performing those functions through a profit-making stock corporation. The government is keenly interested in Freddie Mac's administration of standards of eligibility for participation in the programme. In a sense, heavy government regulation of Freddie Mac gives the government an effective majority on the board of directors on those subjects within the scope of government regulation.

Nonetheless, the court rejected the argument that heavy government regulation created a sufficient nexus between government and the corporation to make the corporation a government actor. The court recited a legal maxim that " 'extensive regulation does not transform the actions of the regulated entity into those of the government' ".[22] This maxim arose in a case in which the Supreme Court held that a privately owned electric utility was not a government actor when it terminated service to one of its customers even though it was heavily regulated by the state and may have been granted a monopoly over electric service in its area.[23] The court of appeals in *ABM* also rejected the argument that Freddie Mac was performing a purely governmental function when it determined who was eligible to participate in its mortgage activities. The court held that both the government and private parties performed functions like those performed by Freddie Mac.

The major problem with the court's analysis of the various factors urged by the plaintiffs to find that Freddie Mac was a government actor in the particular situation is that each factor was viewed in isolation. A more holistic approach might lead to the opposite conclusion, that when a government corporation acts in a closely regulated area in one of the more public-regarding parts of its mission, it is in effect the government for the purposes of the Constitution. Thus, Freddie Mac might be the government when it decides whether to terminate a mortgage company's participation in the programme, but might not be the government when it hires and fires employees for the food service in its office building. Perhaps this dividing line would be unclear and thus lead to too much litigation over the boundary between private and government action, but that is not so obvious that some consideration of the possibility would not be worthwhile. In any case, the courts appear willing to hold that a government chartered corporation is a state actor only where the

[22] Ibid., 1409, quoting *San Francisco Arts & Athletics Inc.* v. *United States Olympic Committee*, 483 U.S. 522, 544 (1987). See also *Lewis* v. *United States*, 680 F. 2d 1239, 1241 (9th Cir. 1982) (Federal Reserve Bank is not federal agency for the purpose of government's tort liability; "fact that the Federal Reserve Board [a federal agency] regulates the Reserve Banks does not make them federal agencies").

[23] See *Jackson* v. *Metropolitan Edison Co.*, 419 U.S. 345 (1974).

government controls the corporation through corporate law mechanisms as opposed to government control through regulatory action which can be exercised on all members of society, not just government corporations.

Corporate Law Constraints on Government Corporations

When Congress states that a government corporation is not an agency or instrumentality of the United States government, that immunises the corporation's actions from APA and other administrative law-type review. That raises the question of whether corporate law provides a tenable substitute. For the reasons that follow, the answer is probably no. It should be noted, however, that I have not undertaken an exhaustive review of the corporate law and charter-based restraints on government corporations. Rather, this section focuses on the traditional corporate law doctrines that might apply to government corporations that have issued shares to the public.

If a government corporation's actions are evaluated under corporate law, in most cases the standard of judicial review will be much more lenient than the standards of judicial review that govern in federal and state administrative law. Further, in corporate law, judicial scrutiny is focused on the effects of corporate action on the corporation itself rather than effects on the public.[24] This last point means that if a government corporation is acting on behalf of the government so that administrative law-type scrutiny might be appropriate, corporate law standards do not provided an avenue for administrative law-type scrutiny. There is no general corporate law standard for evaluating whether corporate action is in the public interest the way that agency action is tested under the arbitrary and capricious standard. Some standard would need to be adapted from administrative law if the government corporation's actions are to be evaluated for their effects on the public.[25]

A digression into administrative law standards of review is appropriate here to provide a basis for comparison with the standards that govern in the corporate law area. The dominant standard of review of agency policy decisions is the APA's arbitrary and capricious test.[26] Under that test, agency action will be set aside if:[27]

> "the agency has relied on factors that Congress has not intended it to consider, entirely failed to consider an important aspect of the problem, offered an explanation of its decision that runs counter to the evidence before the agency, or is so

---

[24] Most corporate law in the United States is state law, and thus varies among jurisdictions. The brief comments that follow are a non-expert's view of general principles that tend to be very similar from state to state, with examples drawn from Delaware corporate law because Delaware is the dominant corporate law jurisdiction in the United States.

[25] If the government corporation is a non-profit corporation or has for some other reason issued no stock, then it is even more difficult to imagine how corporate law could provide an effective check on corporate conduct.

[26] See Title 5 U.S.C. § 706(2).

implausible that it could not be ascribed to a difference in view or the product of agency expertise".

While in some cases the Supreme Court has applied this test in a manner that makes it appear fairly demanding,[28] in other cases in which it appears that the agency considered alternatives and applied its expertise in a fair manner, the Court's scrutiny of the substance of the agency decision has appeared fairly light.[29] The contentious issues here, as in the corporate law area, have concerned how much deference courts should give to administrators, but it appears that the level of deference in administrative law does not approach the level of deference afforded directors' decisions in corporate law.

The usual case in which corporate action is reviewed in court involves a decision by the corporation's board of directors that is alleged to be contrary to the corporation's interests. This generally provokes a suit against the directors (or a sub-group of the board) sometimes by the corporation directly but more typically through a derivative suit in which shareholders assert a claim in the name of the corporation which the directors have elected not to assert. In some cases, the directors' actions are judged under the business judgment rule while in others, usually raising issues of divided loyalty, they are examined more closely.

The business judgment rule comprises two inquiries which may be characterised as a procedural component and a substantive component. The procedural component asks whether the board of directors' decision was made by a reasonable process—mainly whether the directors were informed of the proposed action and had an opportunity to independently evaluate the issues. In a case where a reasonable procedure was followed, the substantive component asks whether there was a rational basis for the board's decision. This scrutiny is normally very lenient although it becomes more demanding when adequate procedures were not followed and when there is a suggestion that the directors were not independent or were operating with divided loyalty or out of self-interest. In such cases, the court may substitute its judgment for that of the board under a more substantial standard of review.

Most shareholder litigation involves derivative suits in which the shareholders allege that the corporation should sue a third party or a sub-group of its directors or other officials. In cases against third parties, the board of directors have the final decision whether the corporation's claim should be pursued, and a refusal to bring suit, if challenged by the shareholders in court, is evaluated under the business judgment rule. Scrutiny is likely to be very lenient. If the suit is against a sub-group of directors, the directors whose actions are not in question form a Special Litigation Committee to decide

---

[27] *Motor Vehicle Manufacturers Association* v. *State Farm Mutual Automobile Insurance Co.*, 463 U.S. 29, 43 (1983).
[28] Idem.
[29] See, e.g., *Baltimore Gas and Elec. Co.* v. *Natural Resources Defence Council Inc.*, 462 U.S. 87 (1983).

whether pursuing the claim would be in the best interests of the corporation. If the Special Litigation Committee recommends that the claim not be pursued then the derivative suit will be terminated unless the court concludes that the Special Litigation Committee's recommendation violates the business judgment rule.[30]

In some cases, shareholders will sue the entire board over a decision that is alleged to have been not in the best interests of the corporation but which does not involve allegations of divided loyalty of directors. The business judgment rule has been thought in such cases to be very lenient, with minimal scrutiny requiring a reasonable procedure and a rational basis for the board to believe that the transaction was in the best interests of the corporation. However, in a leading case in this area, the standard appeared somewhat more stringent in the sense that where before scrutiny of the procedures had appeared perfunctory, the court in *Smith* v. *Van Gorkom*[31] engaged in a serious examination of the procedures leading to the acceptance of a merger proposal and found them wanting. In *Van Gorkom*, shareholders alleged that the board made a mistake in accepting a cash merger because a higher price might have been received from another buyer. The Delaware Court held, under the business judgment rule, that the directors were liable for the losses suffered by the shareholders because the procedures were inadequate to fully inform the directors of the situation. The Court held that the directors were "grossly negligent" for failing to adequately inform themselves of the total situation before agreeing to the merger.

This decision appeared in the corporate world to be a substantial tightening of standards of care for directors. It is almost unheard of for directors to be held liable to a corporation under the business judgment rule. This decision was probably of greatest concern to insurance companies that issue liability policies to directors. In Delaware, and apparently in other jurisdictions as well, the decision provoked an amendment to the corporate law statutes allowing corporate charters to provide that directors cannot be held liable to the corporation for good faith errors.[32] This eliminates even business judgment rule scrutiny in cases of good faith errors by directors.

There is somewhat greater scrutiny of corporate decisions when the interests of the shareholders and managers are clearly at odds. For example, takeovers that would be profitable to shareholders might be rejected if they would result in the loss of jobs for management. In such cases, the business judgment rule allows for somewhat heightened scrutiny of corporate decisions. Here the standard, even in the substantive prong, is more reasonable-

---

[30] See *Zapata Corporation* v. *Maldonado*, 430 A. 2d 779 (Del. 1981). Although the standard under *Zapata* appears to be lenient, it has been criticised as too harsh because it allows the court to scrutinise carefully the independence of the committee and the merits of the committee's decision. See R. Clark, *Corporate Law* (Little, Brown & Co., Boston, 1986), 646–47.

[31] 488 A. 2d 858 (Del. 1985).

[32] Delaware General Corporations Law § 102(b)(7) (1993).

ness than rational basis and involves greater substantive and procedural scrutiny.[33] In even clearer cases of self-dealing, for example if the board approves a transaction in which a director has a personal interest, then the standard is heightened even further to allow judicial scrutiny of the fairness of the transaction to the corporation.[34]

There are some similarities between the standards of judicial review of agency action and the standards under which corporate decisions are reviewed. The procedural element of the business judgment rule is similar to the procedural focus often present in administrative law, when courts demand that agencies in rulemakings evaluate alternatives and explain themselves on major issues raised by the record. However, by and large, corporate law's focus on the welfare of the corporation does not translate easily into administrative law's focus on the welfare of society. Thus, if a government corporation's actions are immune from administrative law scrutiny, corporate law does not provide a tenable substitute.

FAIRNESS, PROCEDURAL DUE PROCESS IN ADMINISTRATIVE LAW IN THE UNITED STATES AND PRIVATE ASSOCIATIONS

The right to fair procedure in adjudicatory hearings in federal government agencies is established by the APA and at the state level is controlled by state administrative procedure acts. Sections 556 and 557 of the APA, which govern formal adjudication in federal agencies, contain procedural safeguards akin to those found in courts of law. Because the APA meets or exceeds the requirements of the due process clause of the Constitution, resort to constitutional law in agency adjudication is rarely necessary.

As a preliminary matter, it must be noted that the agency's choice about whether to employ adjudicatory procedures is constrained by constitutional due process doctrine. In a pair of cases familiar to students of the administrative law of the United States, the Supreme Court mapped out a rough line between those cases in which an agency must use adjudicatory procedures and those cases in which an agency is free to employ a legislative-type procedure. In the first case, *Londoner v. Denver*,[35] the city of Denver's Board of Public Works decided to assess the cost of street paving against each abutting property owner based on the benefit conferred on the owner's property. The Court held that due process required that each owner receive an adjudicatory hearing on the benefit conferred to the particular piece of property. The Court held that when individuals are affected by decisions made on the basis of individualised determinations, due process requires a hearing for each affected

---

[33] See *Unocal Corporation v. Mesa Petroleum Co.*, 493 A. 2d 946 (Del. 1985).
[34] See Delaware General Corporations Law § 144 (1993) (in transaction with director, director's interest must be disclosed and transaction must be fair to corporation).
[35] 210 U.S. 373 (1908).

person. In the second case, *Bi-Metallic Investment Co. v. State Board of Equalization*,[36] the Court held that a legislative process was sufficient for the Board to increase the value of all taxable property in the city of Denver by 40 percent. The Court held that due process does not require individual hearings for across the board decisions affecting numerous individuals.

Due Process Rights of Recipients of Government Benefits and Government Employees

Protected Interests

There is a great deal of constitutional law concerning the due process rights of individuals injured by government action when the state or federal agency failed to employ APA or other statutorily prescribed adjudicatory procedures or when established procedures are alleged to be constitutionally inadequate. These cases arise largely in the areas of government benefits and government employment, and involve claims that benefits or employment were denied, terminated or modified without procedures sufficient to meet the requirements of due process. There is also some state law involving the procedures that private voluntary associations, including labour unions, must use when dealing with their members. Not being a comparativist, I will not draw any comparisons to doctrines styled as "natural justice" or "procedureal fairness" in the jurisprudence of Commonwealth countries, but the comparisons should be obvious.[37]

In all cases raising a due process claim that the government has not employed fair procedures, there is a threshold requirement that the plaintiff establish that he or she has a protected interest, usually either property or liberty, at stake. The existence of a protected interest, except when constitutionally-defined liberty is involved, is determined by looking to an external source of law, such as the statute governing the benefits programme or regulating the government employment. The existence of a protected interest in such cases involves the purely positive law question of whether governing law creates an entitlement to the benefit or employment. If the benefit is purely a gratuity, or if the employment is governed by the at-will rule under which an employee may be discharged without cause, then there is no protected interest and no procedural rights attach.

A pair of examples should help to illuminate this area. In *Board of Regents v. Roth*[38] a state university professor sued after his one-year contract was not renewed, claiming he was entitled to a hearing on whether his performance

---

[36] 293 U.S. 441 (1915).
[37] See generally H. Rigney, "On Reviewing the Right to Fair Procedure" (1981) 5 *Hastings Int'l and Comparative LR* 73.
[38] 408 U.S. 564 (1972).

was satisfactory. The Court held that he had no procedural rights since neither his contract nor the state law governing his employment created an entitlement to employment beyond the one-year term of his contract because there was no standard in either the contract or state law under which the plaintiff was entitled to be evaluated for renewal. An entitlement would be created if the contract of state law provided that the plaintiff was entitled to be rehired if his performance met a certain standard. Since there was no such standard, the Court held that the plaintiff had no constitutional right to a hearing either before or after the decision not to rehire him was made.

By contrast, in *Perry* v. *Sindermann*,[39] another college teacher whose contract was not renewed was given an opportunity to prove that state law and practices created an entitlement to continued employment. If she could prove such an entitlement, either through a formal contract or an unwritten understanding that might give rise to an implied contract, the Court held that she would have an entitlement and thus would be constitutionally entitled to procedures consistent with due process.

The Supreme Court has made it very clear that it looks only to substantive law to determine whether a property interest exists. In some cases, the statute or regulation creating the entitlement also contains procedures that the agency is supposed to follow in deciding questions under the programme. Defendants have argued that the entitlement should be limited by the procedures contained in the provision creating the entitlement on the theory that to add procedures would add to the entitlement itself.[40] The Court has rejected this argument and held that while the state substantive law determines whether there is an entitlement in a case involving state employment, once an entitlement is found, procedural minima are determined by federal constitutional law, and procedural provisions in the statute creating the entitlement are not relevant.[41]

In the liberty area, the existence of a protected interest is determined by a mixture of constitutional law and non-constitutional entitlement analysis. There is an area of constitutionally protected liberty, such as freedom from imprisonment and freedom of bodily integrity, that exist independent of statute or common law. Other liberty interests are created under entitlement theory. For example, the Court has held that once a criminal is convicted and sentenced, absent a statute creating an entitlement, there is no right to early release on parole and thus due process is not implicated in parole board proceedings. However, if a statute creates an entitlement to parole, then the due process norms must be followed by the parole board in deciding whether to grant parole.[42]

---

[39] 408 U.S. 593 (1972).
[40] See, e.g., *Cleveland Board of Education* v. *Loudermill*, 470 U.S. 532, 541–42 (1985).
[41] See also *Arnett* v. *Kennedy*, 416 U.S. 134 (1974), in which a majority of the Court agreed on the same analysis applied later in *Loudermill*, ibid.
[42] See *Board of Pardons* v. *Allen*, 482 U.S. 369 (1987).

The Requirements of Due Process

The basics of due process involve a meaningful opportunity to present one's case to the decision-maker. Normally, this requires notice of the issues, an opportunity to present evidence and argument at a hearing, the opportunity to confront and cross-examine opposing witnesses, the right to address opposing evidence, the right to an impartial decision-maker and an explanation of the decision.

These due process basics are not very precise, and the Court has held that the actual procedures required vary depending on the particulars of the situation. An issue that often arises is whether the hearing must come before the adverse government action or whether a post-deprivation hearing is sufficient. The Court established in *Mathews* v. *Eldridge*[43] a three-factor balancing test for determining what due process requires in any particular case. Under the balancing test, a court evaluates the procedures employed by balancing (1) the importance of the protected interest to the claimant; (2) the fairness and reliability of existing procedures and the value of additional procedures sought; and (3) the public interest in confining the procedures to those already recognised. Under this balancing test, the Supreme Court has held that welfare recipients and government employees with entitlements must be given a hearing pre-deprivation while disability benefits may be terminated without a pre-termination hearing as long as a meaningful post-termination hearing is available. If a property or liberty interest is held to exist, each claim of entitlement to additional procedures is evaluated under the three part balancing test.

Fairness, Fair Procedure and Private Associations

In most situations, private economic or social conduct is not subject to procedural or substantive constraint akin to the procedural due process norms and the arbitrary and capricious standards that apply to government action. Corporate law and corporate charters govern the relationship between corporations and their shareholders and impose procedural and substantive constraints on that relationship.[44] In most private areas, however, there is nothing approaching the intrusiveness of administrative law and constitutional due process. For example, the dominant law of employment in the United States

---

[43] 424 U.S. 319 (1976).

[44] It should also be noted that if a voluntary association is incorporated, its policies regarding membership criteria and the like may be judged under the business judgment rule. See *NAACP v. Golding*, 342 Md. 663, 679 A. 2d 554 (1996). But see *Original Lawrence County Farm Organization Inc. v. Tennessee Farm Bureau Federation*, 907 S.W. 2d 419 (Ct. App. Tenn. 1995) (holding that an incorporated voluntary association is treated exactly the same as an unincorporated association with regard to membership decisions).

is the at-will employment doctrine under which employees may be fired for no reason and without any procedural protections.

This is not to say, however, that private associations are completely free from judicial scrutiny. In some circumstances, common law and statutory doctrines have developed to regulate the conduct of private associations in ways that resemble a weak form of administrative and due process law.[45]

There have been a substantial number of judicial decisions regarding the relationship between private associations and their members or persons applying for membership. The private groups here include professional and trade associations, condominium and neighborhood associations and labour unions. Some of these areas, such as condominium associations, are closely regulated by charter and statute while in other areas, such as professional and trade associations, common law doctrines have developed.

Contract law is an important source of legal supervision of the conduct of private associations.[46] These associations often have detailed by-laws governing membership criteria and discipline of members and the by-laws often contain both substantive and procedural provisions. State law has developed to enforce the by-laws under the theory that they are contracts among the members of the associations.[47] The weakness here is that contract-based enforcement may not be available to a non-member seeking to join since a non-member is not party to the contract embodied in the by-laws.[48] Further, these by-laws often contain provisions requiring that all disputes be settled through internal processes such as arbitration, and when courts enforce these, judicial scrutiny is minimal.[49]

---

[45] Antitrust issues have also arisen with regard to the activities of private associations. Trade and professional associations provide a forum for collusion among competitors. However, other competitors seeking membership in such associations, and thus hoping to share in the benefits of the collusion, are not attractive antitrust plaintiffs because they do not suffer the sort of injury that the courts have held are addressed by antitrust laws. See *Sanjuan* v. *The American Board of Psychiatry and Neurology Inc.*, 40 F. 3d 247 (7th Cir. 1994), cert. denied, 116 S. Ct. 1044 (1996) (rejected applicant for board certification does not suffer antitrust injury) (hereafter referred to as *Sanjuan*).

[46] Interestingly, in the period before courts were willing to intervene in the affairs of private associations, the common law's "hands-off" approach may have made judicial enforcement of association rules at the instance of the association unavailable. See *Charles O. Finley & Co. Inc.* v. *Kuhn*, 569 F. 2d 527 (7th Cir. 1978), cert. denied, 439 U.S. 876 (1978), citing *American Federation of Technical Engineers* v. *La Jeunesse*, 63 Ill. 2d 263, 347 N.E. 2d 712, 715 (1976) (private association may not sue to enforce fine imposed on member; courts are unavailable to association or member to intervene in internal association matters). The classic scholarly discussion regarding legal controls on the affairs of private associations is Z. Chafee, "The Internal Affairs of Associations Not for Profit" (1930) 43 *Harv LR* 993. See also Note, "Judicial Control of Actions of Private Associations" (1967) 76 *Harv LR* 1011.

[47] See *National Association of Sporting Goods Wholesalers Inc.* v. *F.T.L. Marketing Corporation*, 779 F. 2d 1281, 1285 (7th Cir. 1985) (applying Illinois law and holding that by-laws of association are contractual in nature).

[48] See *Triester* v. *American Academy of Orthopaedic Surgeons*, 78 Ill. App. 3d 746, 756, 396 N.E. 2d 1225, 1232 (1979) (court stated that it could find no Illinois case that allows a non-member to enforce membership criteria).

[49] See *Sanjuan*, above at n. 45. The seventh circuit, acting under Illinois law, has also enforced an agreement among major league baseball owners not to sue over league matters. See *Charles*

Courts have also developed non-contract based principles for requiring voluntary associations to treat members and applicants fairly both substantively and procedurally. While courts often cite as an important principle that courts should not intervene in the affairs of a private association, courts have sometimes been willing to act when membership in an association is important for earning a living in a trade or profession.[50] In such cases, courts have required that policies be reasonable and that fair procedures be used for determining who can be a member and whether a member should be disciplined. However, courts have insisted that even in cases in which review is available, the scope of judicial review is quite narrow.[51]

The basic requirements imposed by courts reviewing decisions of voluntary associations are that the associations follow their own rules and "afford members rudimentary 'due process' ".[52] Where important economic interests are implicated, the voluntary association must employ fair procedures.[53] The "fair procedure" standard has not been extensively spelled out, but it appears to demand more elaborate procedures than the "rudimentary due process" required when the economic power of the association is not great.[54] The review of association action for consistency with its own rules may also involve some attention to whether the association's actions were arbitrary or fraudulent.

Courts have also reviewed the disciplinary decisions of labour unions, in a style very similar to judicial review of agency action. In one such case, the court stated that there are two primary requirements that the union must

O. *Finley Inc.* v. *Kuhn*, above at n. 46. Illinois appears to be a leading state in the law regulating voluntary associations, perhaps because many such associations that are important to professions and trades, especially in the medical area, are headquartered there.

[50] See *Sanjuan*, above at n. 45; *Jacobson* v. *New York Racing Association Inc.*, 33 N.Y. 2d 144, 149–50, 305 N.E. 2d 765, 768 (1973). See also *Marjorie Webster Junior College Inc.* v. *Middle States Association of Colleges and Secondary Schools Inc.*, 432 F .2d 650 (D.C. Cir. 1970), cert. denied, 400 U.S. 965 (1970).

[51] See *National Association of Sporting Goods Wholesalers Inc.* v. *F.T.L. Marketing Corporation*, above at n. 47.

[52] Ibid., 1285. See also *Original Lawrence County Farm Organization, Inc.* v. *Tennessee Farm Bureau Federation*, above at n. 44. In what may be a somewhat more stringent, or at least more comprehensive, standard, the Missouri Court of Appeals has stated that in reviewing an association's censuring of a member (here the National Association of Social Workers) it looks to four factors: (1) whether the rules or charter have been followed; (2) whether fair procedures have been followed; (3) whether the association acted with fraud, malice or collusion; and (4) whether the rules or charter violate law or public policy. See *Shapiro* v. *Butterfield*, 921 S.W. 2d 649, 652 (Mo. Ct. App. 1996).

[53] See *National Association of Sporting Goods Wholesalers Inc.* v. *F.T.L. Marketing Corporation*, above at n. 47. See also *Falcone* v. *Middlesex County Medical Society*, 34 N.J. 582, 170 A. 2d 791 (1961) (holding that courts will scrutinise decision of Medical Society where membership is an economic necessity for physicians who wish to practice in area). The *Falcone* opinion includes an extensive history of the legal treatment of private associations in the United States. *Falcone* itself is widely cited and is a leading case on judicial scrutiny of the membership practices of medical associations and other private associations.

[54] See *National Association of Sporting Goods Wholesalers Inc.* v. *F.T.L. Marketing Corporation*, idem.

meet, first that the disciplinary action be heard before a "fair and impartial tribunal" and second that there be "some evidence" to support the union's decision.[55] The decision must also be consistent with the union's stated disciplinary criteria. The court made it clear that its procedural requirement was meant to be much more lenient than due process might require for action taken by a government agency. The substantive standard of review, namely "some evidence", also appears very lenient, while the requirement that the union observe its own rules can be explained as part of the contract governing the relationship between the union and its members. However, while the court's authority to review the union's decision appears to be based in common law, there is also a federal statute requiring labour unions to treat their members fairly.[56]

Thus, while its scope is not very great, there is a small area of law in the United States under which common law has developed with a strong resemblance to administrative law, albeit in substantially weakened form.[57]

In some situations, plaintiffs have attempted to bring their cases even closer to the administrative law model by alleging that the voluntary association is a state actor or is engaged in a public function so that heightened scrutiny of association actions is justified.[58] There are two bases for the argument that a private association is a state actor, first that the association is performing a government function and second that membership in the association may determine whether a private party is eligible for some government benefit or license. (I am not considering here arguments that the association actually is a government entity, as is the case with some government corporations.) These arguments, when the association is privately owned and managed, have not been very successful.

In *National College Athletic Association* v. *Tarkanian*,[59] the plaintiff was suspended from his position as basketball coach for a state university because the university was placed on probation by the NCAA for rules violations and told that during its probation it must sever its ties with Tarkanian because of his role in the violations. The NCAA is a private association of colleges and universities that governs intercollegiate athletics. In addition to more traditional state action arguments based on joint action between the NCAA and

---

[55] See *Sheet Metal Workers Local No. 218* v. *Massie*, 255 Ill. App. 3d 697, 627 N.E. 2d 1154 (1993).

[56] See Title 29 U.S.C. § 411(a)(5).

[57] This common law also includes a doctrine familiar to administrative law, that internal association remedies must be exhausted before judicial relief may be sought. This is a very strong principle in these cases. See, e.g., *NAACP* v. *Golding*, above at n. 44, 679–80; 562.

[58] There is, of course, a wealth of case-law and scholarship regarding state action, but here I look only at the narrower set of issues when private associations perform functions that resemble professional licensing in form and effect.

[59] 488 U.S. 179 (1988). In *Saumell* v. *New York Racing Association Inc.*, 58 N.Y. 2d 231, 447 N.E. 2d 706 (1983), amended by 69 N.Y. 2d 805 (1984), a private owner of race tracks conceded that it was a state actor because it had a state-granted franchise and worked with the state to enforce state racing rules.

the state university, Tarkanian argued that the NCAA performed a government function and was thus a state actor. Tarkanian argued that through its rules and enforcement procedures, the NCAA was engaged in discipline of state employees, a government function.[60] The Court rejected this argument, noting that while the NCAA might have required the suspension for the university to retain its status in that organisation, it was the university's decision whether to actually suspend Tarkanian.

One reason for the Court's skepticism in *Tarkanian* was the sense that the supervision of college athletics was not really a governmental function. That may be contrasted with the operation and maintenance of public beaches, which has been viewed as a government function. A New Jersey court has ruled, apparently under New Jersey law, that a private association that manages such beaches is a public actor and thus must open its membership to the public at large, and not only to the residents of the town in which the beach is located.[61] The court noted that the association's activities "paralleled those of a municipality in its operation of the beachfront".[62]

Although the involvement of public trust beaches distinguishes this case from others involving private associations, in its opinion holding that the association was engaged in state action, the court relied upon cases involving doctors seeking staff privileges at a private hospital or membership in a local medical society. The court characterised those cases as establishing a principle that:[63]

> "a nonprofit association that is authorized and endeavors to carry out a purpose serving the general welfare of the community and is a quasi-public institution holds in trust its powers of exclusive control in the areas of vital public concern. . . . When a nonprofit association rejects a membership application for reasons unrelated to its purposes and contrary to the general welfare, courts have 'broad judicial authority to insure that exclusionary policies are lawful and are not applied arbitrarily or discriminately'."

This is very broad language and parallels the common law regulating innkeepers and common carriers, but should not be read as a broad state action holding.

Thus, courts may be more receptive to performing judicial review of the actions of private associations when their actions mirror public functions or where they are engaged in functions that are designed to advance the welfare of the public.

---

[60] 488 U.S. 179.

[61] See *Matthews* v. *Bay Head Improvement Association*, 95 N.J. 306, 471 A. 2d 355, cert. denied, 469 U.S. 821 (1984). For an interesting exposition on the law regulating beach access, see M. Poirier, "Environmental Justice and the Beach Access Movements in the 1970s in Connecticut and New Jersey: Stories of Property and Civil Rights" (1996) 28 *Conn LR* 719.

[62] Ibid., 330; 371.

[63] Ibid., 328–29; 367, quoting *Greisman* v. *Newcomb Hospital*, 40 N.J. 389, 192 A. 2d 817 (1963). See also *Jacobson* v. *New York Racing Association Inc.*, above at n. 50 (approving *Greisman* and other cases placing duties on private associations but questioning conclusion that state action is involved).

A more traditional state action analysis is employed when the claim is that membership in the private association is necessary to be eligible for a public benefit, position or license. For example, in a case involving the suspension of a jockey from working at privately owned race tracks, the association that owned the race tracks conceded it was a state actor since it had a franchise to operate race tracks in the area and its actions had the same effect as an official suspension of the jockey's license.[64] However, it is unclear whether this reasoning would hold if the state and the association were not closely related through the grant of the franchise and general cooperation in regulating the business of horse racing.[65]

CONCLUSION: WHY ADMINISTRATIVE LAW?

Administrative law is that branch of the law regulating administrative bodies operating under statutory authority. While there are some tricky boundary issues, by and large administrative law, properly so called, applies only to actions attributable to governmental entities serving regulatory functions under law. In the American experience, this understanding of the scope of administrative law is informed by a great deal more suspicion and fear of governmental power than private power, even when a private entity performs a function with close parallels to traditional governmental functions.

The non-constitutional aspects of administrative law in the United States, on the federal level, are contained primarily in the Administrative Procedure Act. Most important is the APA's definition of agency, which determines which federal entities are subject to the dictates of the APA. Further, because the reach of the APA is determined with reference only to positive, statutory law, legislative declaration of agency status, or of non-agency status, is determinative and thus if Congress declares that an entity such as a government corporation is not an agency, the APA will not apply to that entity regardless of whether the entity is controlled by the government and exercises a regulatory function.

---

[64] *Saumell* v. *New York Racing Association Inc.*, above at n. 59. Interestingly, the court held that the association retained its common law right to exclude others from its premises, but it nonetheless held that the jockey was entitled to due process protections before being suspended. The court also rejected application of the state APA, concluding that even if the association was a state actor, it was not an agency subject to the state APA, which might be more protective than due process. See ibid., 240; 710.

[65] See *Sanjuan*, above at n. 45 (fact that board certification is necessary to be eligible for some public position does not make board state actor any more than requirement of advanced degree for some state jobs makes all colleges and universities state actors). See also *Johnson* v. *Educational Testing Service*, 754 F. 2d 20 (1st Cir. 1985), cert. denied, 472 U.S. 1029 (1985), in which the court held that the Educational Testing Service, which administers college and graduate school entrance exams, is not a state actor even though some state schools rely on the test scores in making admissions decisions.

The reach of constitutionally-based administrative law doctrines, such as procedural due process, is limited by the state action doctrine which holds that, except in very narrow circumstances, the Constitution of the United States applies only to state action, i.e. action undertaken by an arm of the government. Here, legislative intent is a factor in determining whether an entity is governmental, but legislative intent is not determinative, because otherwise the government could avoid constitutional restrictions by declaring an entity it controls to be non-governmental.

The difficult boundary question here is how to identify entities that, while nominally separate from government, should nonetheless be considered for constitutional purposes as part of the government. While different tests have been used at different times and under different circumstances, the only methodology that appears to withstand analysis within the framework of contemporary state action doctrine is one that treats as government actors those entities that are controlled by government through mechanisms akin to ownership, rather than regulatory means of control. In the case of the government corporations, this means that such corporations are state actors only if the government has the power to appoint a majority of the directors, either because the statute creating the corporation specifies governmental appointment or because the government has the power of appointment through ownership of the corporation's shares.

The ownership test for state action should be contrasted with a test that looks more simply to whether the erstwhile private entity's actions are controlled by government without regard to the mechanism of control. While a pure control test may be appealing, when the government's control is achieved through the mechanism of government regulation, there is no good reason to treat the private entity as a government actor when the private entity may actually be the unwilling subject of regulation rather than a voluntary participant in a plan to exercise government's coercive power on others.

The strongest argument for treating regulated entities as government actors when they act under government control derives from a public choice analysis under which the "subjects" of regulation actually band together to procure favourable regulation so they can enlist the coercive power of government to accomplish aims that they could not achieve in the unregulated market. Much regulation is explained by public choice analysis as procurement by private entities, through the political process, of artificially high prices or barriers to competition or both. Since such entities have used governmental power for their own gains, it is arguable that they should be subjected to the legal controls on such power.

It would be very difficult to apply such an analysis to actual legal disputes. For example, automobile companies have by and large fought government safety regulation on the grounds that it is too expensive or unnecessary. In some cases, however, individual automakers may favour particular safety regulations when they believe that they have the ability to comply more cheaply than competitors. It would be almost impossible to treat the private implementation of a government safety standard as state action when done by one automaker and private action when done by another, unwilling, automaker. More generally, it would be difficult, if not impossible, to distinguish "procured" regulation from regulation imposed by government against the private entities' wishes. Only "true believers" in public choice theory, who view all legislation as having been procured by a powerful interest group, might feel comfortable employing this analysis because they would not suffer from the uncertainty others experience concerning the reasons behind regulation.

Other possible tests for state action suffer from similar difficulties. As discussed above, some courts, in determining whether a government corporation is a state actor, have looked to whether the corporation is fulfilling a government purpose or a regulatory function. But it is very difficult to distinguish government functions from private functions. There are private analogues to almost everything government does. Government and private entities operate schools and hospitals, they provide emergency and non-emergency medical care, they operate bus and other transportation lines, they create securities markets and issue securities and they determine and apply standards of conduct for participation in such markets, they provide police protection, they predict the weather, they adjudicate disputes between private parties, they create and apply standards for product safety and they create and apply standards for fair business practices, to name a few of the activities performed both by government and private entities.

There is perhaps one area in which the governmental nature of the function points strongly to a finding of state action even when the fuction is performed by a private actor, and that is the fulfillment of the government's responsibilities to those in its custody, such as prisoners. One form of privatisation that has occurred in the United States is the practice of contracting out by government for services that might otherwise have been performed by government employees. There are private companies that operate prisons under government contract, and such companies should be considered state actors in their dealings with prisoners so that privatisation does not lead to diminution of government's responsibilities to the prisoners. For example, the Supreme Court has held that a private physician, under contract to provide medical services to prisoners in state custody, is a state actor when treating prisoners and is thus constitutionally liable if his services fall below those mandated under the state's constitutional duty to provide medical care to prisoners.[66] It may be that the governmental nature of the function of operating prisons compels the conclusion that any entity doing so is engaged in state action.

In the case of privatised industries, it may be difficult both conceptually and politically to shed the urge to subject private entities exercising what looks

---

[66] See *West* v. *Atkins*, 487 U.S. 42 (1988).

like regulatory authority over others in the industry to non-constitutional and constitutional administrative law controls. As a normative matter, such treatment may actually be preferable to the American positivist view on the reach of the APA and the relatively narrow view of what constitutes state action for constitutional purposes, but it is at least worthwhile to consider whether another form of regulation would be more suited to the situation than traditional administrative law controls. Traditional regulation of utilities and other private businesses with monopoly power or "affected with the public interest" (in common law terms) may be more attuned to the regulatory needs here than administrative law.

The administrative law and state action issues discussed above should be held distinct from the narrow judicial scrutiny that is sometimes available over the membership and other decisions of private entities such as professional societies and trade organisations. While there is obviously a resemblance to judicial review of agency action, the resemblance does not actually run very deep, and the review is much closer in kind and effect to corporate law (or the law of business associations as it is sometimes called) than to administrative law. In American law, the distrust of government power makes administrative law different in kind from the law regulating private centres of power, even when there is good reason to be suspicious or fearful of private power.

The law regulating private associations has developed in recent years with an eye toward judicial scrutiny over the membership decisions of private associations where membership affects important economic interests. This review occurs largely under common law, and that fact is important in the United States since this common law is state law and thus cannot be subsumed under federal administrative law. That power is involved does not provide a convincing argument that this branch of law is administrative law, since a great deal of the common law regards the use and potential abuse of private power. Private groups, such as professional organisations, do not exercise government power any more than a private landowner exercises government power when she excludes others from her land under property law. There are theories that would subject the landowner's actions to constitutional scrutiny, but that would require a radical reorientation of state action doctrine.

There are also other developing areas of scrutiny of private decision-making that, while they might be of interest to administrative lawyers, are far removed from administrative law. For example, the rise of anti-discrimination norms, largely through legislation, in employment law and even in the conduct of social clubs such as dining clubs and country clubs has placed employment and membership decisions of private organisations under greater scrutiny than ever before. Interestingly, the reasons for such scrutiny may be similar to those relied upon to subject private organisations to judicial review, namely that important business interests are at stake, and thus decisions affecting membership in social clubs, as well as basic employment opportunities, should not be made in a discriminatory fashion. For example, male-only and racially discriminatory dining clubs and country clubs are viewed as devices that exclude women and minorities from important business contacts.

The law that subjects the decisions of private economic organisations to review for procedural fairness and adherence to organisational rules, seems at first glance more closely related to anti-discrimination law than administrative law. A comparative analysis of administrative law norms and the norms underlying these developments might prove fruitful. Given administrative law's traditional focus on control of government power, the burden ought to be on those attempting to expand administrative law beyond the public/private divide to establish the need and the conceptual soundness of their effort.

10

Public Law and Control over Private Power

PAUL CRAIG*

For the sake of clarity it should be made clear at the outset that the object of this paper is not to consider all the controls over private power which exist within any legal system. This would require an in-depth analysis of contract, tort, trust, restitution, corporate law and so on. While this might be interesting in and of itself it would be impossible within the limits of the available space.

The focus of this paper will rather be upon the extent to which public law does, and should, exert control over private power. Any discussion of this topic is dependent upon some vision of the divide between the public and private spheres. To attempt an analysis without addressing this issue will invite critical comment to the effect that one has assumed that a body is purely private when others would contend that it is, in reality, exercising a species of public power. This is particularly so, given that the very nature of the divide between "public power" and "private power" has become more blurred as of late, as a result of changes in the pattern of government. How should we address this issue? It can be approached in a variety of ways.

The traditional way of tackling it may be termed the *institutional* approach. This entails an analysis of those types of institutions which are felt to wield public power. Analyses of this nature normally build out from the paradigm of a body which unequivocally has public power, such as a department of government. The formal authority of the state is coupled with real substantive power over the area in question, and normally bodies of this nature will have a monopoly over the subject matter in question. Institutional analyses then proceed to consider whether other bodies should also be held to be public for these purposes even if they are not formally part of government *stricto sensu*.

In most legal systems there will be a plethora of bodies which might well be characterised as public in this sense. These include bodies which are *de facto* private, but which are nonetheless clothed with some indirect state

---

* An earlier and shorter version of this paper was presented at a Workshop on "Controlling Public Power in Southern Africa", held at the University of Cape Town, South Africa, on 8–11 March 1996.

authority, and where the bodies in question exercise regulatory authority over a particular area. We can move further out along our institutional spectrum and find other institutions which are also *de facto* private, which have no measure of indirect state support, but which nevertheless wield monopoly power over the relevant area. Sporting regulatory bodies provide apt examples of this type of institution. The light of institutional analysis then normally shifts to bodies of a corporate nature which some would claim should be subject to public law controls by virtue of the very monopoly power which they exert, especially where this power is buttressed by statutory provisions which protect this monopolistic position. Institutional analyses of this nature are important. An examination of the nature of public power from this perspective will be included within the ensuing discussion. This aspect of the analysis will also examine the extent to which answers to such institutional questions are facilitated by the degree of utilisation, or non-utilisation, of the concept of the state by a given legal system.

It should not, however, be thought that the institutional approach is the only method through which to investigate the question at hand. Such analyses must be complemented by those of a more *functional* nature. The essence of the functional approach is to ask why one is seeking to ascribe the label public or private to a particular institution? What are the *consequences* of deciding that a particular body has public power even if it is nominally private? The normal response to inquiries of this nature is that it leads to the application of public law principles to such a body, even if it is formally private. In a general sense this response is incontrovertible. The very generality of this response does, however, conceal a host of more specific questions, the answers to which are by no means obvious. For the sake of clarity we can divide these more specific inquiries into two kinds. There are, on the one hand, "macro" questions, the principal example of which is whether the ascription of the label public should lead to the application of a completely different system from that which governs private forms of ordering. But different in what sense? Legal systems may distinguish between public and private law in any one of three possible ways: there may be different jurisdictions, different rules of procedure, or different bodies of law. There are, on the other hand, also more particular "micro" questions. For example, assuming that a legal system does apply different rules to bodies which are deemed to have public power, does it follow that all such rules are equally applicable to all such bodies? Might we not decide that a body does exercise public power to some degree which warrants the application of certain rules of public law, but that not all of these rules are equally suitable?

There is a third facet to this inquiry which is *structural* in nature. How far does the overall structure of the legal system within a particular state have implications for the question at hand? How far does this dictate and indeed constrain the manner in which public law controls over private power are thought about and analysed?

THE INSTITUTIONAL APPROACH

The question as to whether a body exercises public power can arise in a number of differing contexts. In the United Kingdom system the question has arisen most recently in judicial decisions as to whether an institution is sufficiently public to have the public law procedures which are contained in section 31 of the Supreme Court Act 1981 applied to it. The assumption is then made that bodies which are felt suited to these procedures for seeking judicial review should also be subject to the procedural and substantive norms which comprise public law. Whether this latter assumption should so readily be made will be examined in due course. Our initial focus will, however, be on the tests which the courts have applied to determine whether an institution is indeed sufficiently public to warrant the application of the procedures for judicial review which apply to public bodies *stricto sensu*.

Public Power: Possible Tests[1]

The most obvious test is to consider the *source of the authority's power*: if that power is derived from statute then the body is presumptively public. There are two fundamental difficulties with this test. First, applied literally it would bring within public law the activities of any body regulated by statute, even if that body generally operated within the private commercial sphere. The second problem is a converse of the first. A body may owe the source of its public authority to statute, but not all of its operations should nonetheless be regarded as raising public law issues. Local authorities and other public bodies operate in an ordinary commercial capacity on many occasions.[2]

Closely related to the preceding criterion is that of the *scope of the prerogative orders*. If we are to have a separate set of remedies for public law, then to regard the scope of the prerogative orders as *prima facie* evidence of the scope of public law might be reasonable, particularly given the centrality of position accorded to such orders within the scheme of section 31.

The objection to this criterion is that there is a tendency to see the ambit of such orders as fixed. There is little justification for this. Historically those orders were used flexibly to provide a remedy against institutions not covered by existing forms of redress.[3] There are indications that they could be used to

---

[1] See generally J. Beatson, " 'Public' and 'Private' in English Administrative Law" (1987) 103 LQR 34; P. Cane, "Public Law and Private Law: A Study of the Analysis of and Use of a Legal Concept", in J. Eekelaar and J. Bell (eds), *Oxford Essays in Jurisprudence, third Series* (Clarendon Press, Oxford, 1987), ch. 3.

[2] Lloyd L.J. in *R. v. Panel on Take-overs and Mergers, ex parte Datafin plc* [1987] QB 815, 847 implied that if the source of the power was statutory then the body would be subject to judicial review. For the reasons given in the text I doubt, with respect, whether the source test can be taken so generally.

[3] *Groenvelt v. Burwell* (1700) 1 Ld Raym 454 is particularly instructive.

cover any duty of a public nature, whether it be derived from statute, custom, prerogative or contract, a view echoed by Lord Diplock himself.[4] The tendency to ossify them, to regard their boundaries as immutable, is a more recent phenomenon. There is no reason why a duty may not be of a public law nature, whatever its derivation.

To focus upon the scope of the prerogative orders as the criterion for the meaning of public law does however lead to the following conundrum. On the one hand, if their scope is interpreted flexibly in the above manner they cease to furnish a ready criterion, or certainly not one which is distinguishable from the third test to be considered below. The nature of a "public" as opposed to a "private" duty still has to be determined, and if the ambit of the prerogative orders simply covers any "public law" obligation we are no further forward in our determination of whether such an obligation is present in any particular case.[5] On the other hand, if a narrow definition of the prerogative orders is adopted, so that they apply only to bodies created by statute, or pursuant to the prerogative, then we are faced with a formalistic criterion. This test renders the applicability of different procedures turn upon the often fortuitous incident of whether a particular authority's powers were derived from a particular source, irrespective of the real power wielded by such a body.[6]

The difficulties of a formalistic test have inclined the courts towards a more open-textured criterion which requires them to consider the *nature of the power* wielded by the particular body. The formulation of this criterion has varied. For example, in *R. v. Panel on Take-overs and Mergers, ex parte Datafin plc*[7] Lloyd L.J. stated that if the source of the power was statutory then the body would be subject to judicial review, but would not if the source of power was contractual. However in between these "extremes" one would have to look at the nature of the power. Thus if the body was exercising public law functions, or such functions had public law consequences then section 31 would be applicable. This formulation appears to beg the question,[8] as do such statements that if a duty is a public duty then the body is subject to public law. Lord Donaldson M.R., by way of contrast, seemed only to be concerned with the source of a body's power in order to exclude those institutions whose power was based upon contract or consent.[9] Any other body could be subject to review if there was a sufficiently public element. How far power which is based upon contract or consent is subject to judicial review will be considered more fully below.

The uncertainty which this third test generates is to be expected. It is the price to be paid for moving away from formalistic tests based upon the source

---

[4] *O'Reilly v. Mackman* [1983] 2 AC 237, 279.
[5] See the observations of Lord Donaldson M.R. in *R. v. East Berkshire Health Authority, ex parte Walsh* [1985] QB 152, 162.
[6] See also H.W.R. Wade, "Procedure and Prerogative in Public Law" (1985) 101 *LQR* 180.
[7] [1987] QB 815, 846–9 (hereafter referred to as *Datafin*).
[8] As admitted by Lloyd L.J., ibid., 847, who nonetheless denied the circularity.
[9] Ibid., 838–9.

of power or upon the narrow definition of the prerogative orders given above. Statements that a body must have a sufficiently "public element" or must be exercising a public duty cannot function as anything other than conclusory labels for whatever we choose to put them on. They cannot guide our reasoning in advance. In *Datafin* itself the court was, as will be seen, influenced by a number of such factors including: the undoubted power wielded by the Panel, the statutory cognisance given to its existence, the penalties, direct and indirect, which could follow from non-compliance with its rules, and the absence of any other redress available to the applicants.

Public Power: The Institutional Spectrum

It is clear that traditional public bodies will be able to use the application for judicial review, and that they can be subjected to such actions. What concerns us now are "other" types of case in which applicants have sought to bring their claims within section 31. The object of the discussion within this section is not to provide an exhaustive account of all the instances along the institutional spectrum in which the courts have had to decide whether a body is sufficiently public to be subjected to public law principles. Limits of space preclude such an undertaking. It is rather to give a sense of the types of institutions in relation to which the question of whether they exercise public power is of relevance within the modern state. For the purposes of this analysis we can usefully juxtapose the three types of case considered within the following sections. These categories of case reveal the difficulties of deciding which species of power should be deemed to be public power.

Regulatory Bodies: The "Privatisation of the Business of Government"

Hoffmann L.J. coined this phrase in *R. v. Disciplinary Committee of the Jockey Club, ex parte Aga Khan*,[10] and it provides an apt description of one important category of case which has been admitted into the public law procedures. These cases concern regulatory bodies which are private, but which have been integrated, directly or indirectly, into a system of statutory regulation. *Datafin* is the outstanding decision in this category.[11]

In that case the applicants complained that the Panel on Take-overs and Mergers (the Panel) had incorrectly applied their takeover rules, and had thereby allowed an advantage to be gained by the applicant's rivals who were bidding for the same company as the applicants. The Panel was a self-regulating body which had no direct statutory, prerogative or common law powers, but it was supported by certain statutory powers which presupposed its existence, and its decisions could result in the imposition of penalties. The

---

[10] [1993] 2 All ER 853, 874.
[11] Above at n. 7.

Panel opposed judicial review, arguing that it was not amenable to the prerogative orders which had been restricted to bodies exercising powers derived from the prerogative or statute. The court rejected this view. The "source" of a body's powers was not the only criterion for judging whether a body was amenable to public law. The absence of a statutory or prerogative base for such powers did not exclude section 31 if the "nature" of the power being exercised rendered the body suitable for judicial review. The nature of the Panel's powers was held to satisfy this alternative criterion for a number of reasons.

First, the Panel although self-regulating did not operate consensually or voluntarily, but rather imposed a collective code on those within its ambit.[12] Secondly, the Panel was performing a public duty as manifested by the government's willingness to limit legislation in this area, and to use the Panel as part of its regulatory machinery.[13] There had been an "implied devolution of power"[14] by the government to the Panel, and certain legislation presupposed its existence. Thirdly, its source of power was only partly moral persuasion, this being reinforced by statutory powers exercisable by the government and the Bank of England.[15] Finally, the applicants did not appear to have any cause of action in contract or tort against the Panel.[16]

Similar reasoning can be found in other cases, such as *R. v. Advertising Standards Authority, ex parte The Insurance Services plc*.[17] The applicant complained that an adverse report on it made by the Advertising Standards Authority (ASA) was procedurally irregular. The initial question was whether the ASA was susceptible to judicial review. The court held that it was, following the *Datafin* case. The ASA had no powers granted to it by statute, and had no contractual relationship with the advertisers whom it controlled. It was, however, part of a scheme of government regulation of the industry in the following sense. A Community directive required member states to make provision for the control of misleading advertising. This was implemented in the United Kingdom by regulations which gave the Director General of Fair Trading powers to investigate complaints of misleading advertising. The essence of this regulatory scheme was that the Director General would only take legal proceedings against a firm if the matter had not been satisfactorily

---

[12] Ibid., 825–6 and 845–6.
[13] Ibid., 838–9, 848–9 and 850–1.
[14] Ibid., 849.
[15] Ibid., 838–9 and 851–2.
[16] Ibid., 838–9. See also *R. v. Panel on Take-overs and Mergers, ex parte Guinness plc* [1990] 1 QB 146; *R. v. Civil Service Appeal Board, ex parte Bruce* [1988] ICR 649, [1989] ICR 171.
[17] [1990] COD 42. See also *Bank of Scotland v. Investment Management Regulatory Organisation Ltd.* [1989] SLT 432; *R. v. Financial Intermediaries Managers and Brokers Regulatory Association, ex parte Cochrane* [1990] COD 33; *R. v. Code of Practice Committee of the Association of the British Pharmaceutical Industry, ex parte Professional Counselling Aids Ltd.* [1991] COD 228; *R. v. Visitors to the Inns of Court, ex parte Calder* [1993] 2 All ER 876. Compare *R. v. Fernhill Manor School, ex parte Brown* [1992] COD 446.

resolved through the ASA. The court held that in these circumstances the ASA was susceptible to control through judicial review.

Regulatory Bodies: Contract, Power and Control

The courts have experienced rather more difficulty in determining the boundaries of judicial review in a group of cases which are not far removed from those in the preceding section. These cases also concern regulatory bodies which have control over a particular industry, and in that sense exercise a degree of real power over those who are subject to their remit. However, what serves to distinguish these cases from those considered above is that there is no governmental involvement in these areas as such. These regulatory institutions are not part of a schema of statutory regulation. Whether this should make a difference will be considered in due course. The courts have on the whole been unwilling to extend judicial review to cover such instances.

The story begins with the decision in *Law* v. *National Greyhound Racing Club Ltd*.[18] In that case the plaintiff, a trainer whose licence was suspended, sought a declaration outside section 31 that the decision was *ultra vires*. The National Greyhound Racing Club (NGRC) argued that the case should have been brought within section 31. This was rejected by the court. It held that the power which the NGRC exercised over those engaged in greyhound racing was derived from contract, and was of concern only to those who took part in this sport. While the exercise of this power could have benefits for the public (by, for example, stamping out malpractices), this was true for many other domestic tribunals which were also not subject to judicial review.

The force of the ruling in *Law* was felt in relation to other such regulatory authorities. A number of actions arose concerning the Jockey Club in which the court reluctantly declined to admit the case into the section 31 jurisdiction because of the holding in the *Law* case.[19]

An opportunity to reconsider the point arose in yet another Jockey Club case. In *Aga Khan*[20] the applicant was an owner of racehorses and was therefore bound to register with the Jockey Club and to enter a contractual relationship whereby he adhered to the rules of racing established by it. One of the applicant's horses was disqualified after winning a major race, and he sought judicial review of this decision. The Court of Appeal found that in general the Club was not susceptible to judicial review, and it did not accept the argument that the decision in *Law* had been overtaken by that in *Datafin*. The court acknowledged that the Club regulated a national activity and Bingham M.R. accepted that if it did not regulate the sport then the government would

[18] [1983] 1 WLR 1302.
[19] Both of these cases were decided in 1989, but were only fully reported later: *R.* v. *Disciplinary Committee of the Jockey Club, ex parte Massingberd-Mundy* [1993] 2 All ER 207; *R.* v. *Jockey Club, ex parte RAM Racecourses Ltd.* [1993] 2 All ER 225.
[20] Above at n. 10.

in all probability be bound to do so. Notwithstanding this, the court reached its conclusion because the Club was not in its origin, constitution, membership or history a public body, and its powers were not governmental. Moreover, the applicant in this particular case would have a remedy outside section 31 because he had a contract with the Jockey Club. The court did, however, leave open the possibility that some cases concerning bodies like the Jockey Club might be brought within the public law procedures, particularly where the applicant or plaintiff had no contractual relationship with the Club, or where the Club made rules which were discriminatory in nature.[21]

A similar reluctance to subject the governing authorities of sporting associations to judicial review is also apparent in R. v. *Football Association Ltd., ex parte Football League Ltd.*[22] The Football Association (FA) was the governing authority for football and all clubs who wished to play had to be affiliated to it. The FA sanctioned various competitions, the most important of which was the Football League (FL). The FL ran the four divisions comprising the league and had a contractual relationship with the FA. The dispute arose from the decision by the FA to establish the Premier League which would be run by it and not by the FL. In order to facilitate the top clubs breaking away from the FL and forming the Premier League, the FA declared void certain rules of the FL which rendered it difficult for clubs to terminate their relationship with the FL. The FL then sought judicial review of this decision, arguing that the FA had a monopoly control over the game, and that although there was a contract between the FA and the FL the rules of the FA were, in reality, a legislative code which regulated an important aspect of national life in the absence of which there would have to be a public body to perform the same function. Rose J. rejected the application for judicial review. He held that the FA was not susceptible to judicial review, notwithstanding its monopolistic powers. It was not underpinned in any way by any state agency, nor was there any real governmental interest in its functions, nor was there any evidence that if the FA did not exist a public body would have to be created in its place.

The disinclination to intervene via judicial review with such bodies is not restricted to those which operate in the sporting arena. In R. v. *Lloyd's of London, ex parte Briggs*[23] it was held that Lloyds of London was not amenable to judicial review in an action brought by "names" who had lost money in insurance syndicates which had covered asbestosis and pollution claims. The court held that Lloyds was not a public body regulating the insurance market, but rather a body which ran one part of the market pursuant to a private Act of Parliament. The case was concerned solely with the contracts between the names and their managing agents.

---

[21] Ibid., 867 and 873. In both the *RAM* and *Massingberd-Mundy* cases, above at n. 14, the applicant did not have a contractual relationship with the Club.
[22] [1993] 2 All ER 833 (hereafter referred to as *Football Association*). See also R. v. *Football Association of Wales, ex parte Flint Town United Football Club* [1991] COD 44.
[23] [1993] 1 Lloyd's Rep 176.

It is interesting to reflect a little further on the cases discussed within this section precisely because they do raise in stark form the question as to the boundary of public law. If one stands back from the individual decisions one can perceive three principal strands in the courts' reasoning.

The first is that *not all power is public power*. The courts undoubtedly recognise that these regulatory authorities exercise power over their area, but they do not necessarily accept that this should be characterised as a species of public power. Thus in the *Aga Khan* case Hoffmann L.J. had this to say about the Jockey Club:[24]

> "But the mere fact of power, even over a substantial area of economic activity, is not enough. In a mixed economy, power may be private as well as public. Private power may affect the public interest and the livelihoods of many individuals. But that does not subject it to the rules of public law. If control is needed it must be found in the law of contract, the doctrine of restraint of trade, the Restrictive Trade Practices Act 1976, arts 85 and 86 of the EEC Treaty and all the other instruments available for curbing the excesses of private power."

A second related strand in the courts' reasoning concerns the *suitability of the public law controls* for the types of body under discussion. This is an important point. The volume of case-law which is concerned with the public/private divide can all too easily lead us to forget that there are *consequences*, in terms of the procedural and substantive norms which are held to be applicable to such bodies, as a result of ascribing the label "public" to them. The concern as to whether such norms are always well suited to the bodies considered within this section finds expression in the judgment of Rose J. in the *Football Association* case:[25]

> "for my part, to apply to the governing body of football, on the basis that it is a public body, principles honed for the control of the abuse of power by government and its creatures would involve what, in today's fashionable parlance, would be called a quantum leap."

A third factor which has clearly influenced the court is more pragmatic in nature: if these bodies are deemed to fall within public law then *where should we stop*? Rose J. had this in mind when reflecting that if the FA is sufficiently public for the purposes of section 31 then presumably the governing authorities of virtually all other sports, from tennis to motor racing and from golf to cricket, would be too.[26] And if this is so then why should not the exercise of power by private corporate undertakings which have a monopolistic position be subject to the strictures of public law?[27] This then raises consequential practical concerns about the capacity of the courts to deal with this breadth

---

[24] Above at n. 10, 875.
[25] Above at n. 22, 849.
[26] Ibid., 849.
[27] Sir Gordon Borrie, "The Regulation of Public and Private Power" [1989] *PL* 552.

and volume of material without becoming "even more swamped with applications than they are already".[28]

There is no doubt that people will differ as to the cogency of these reasons. For some all species of power are "public", and nominally private exercises of power *should* be subject to equally rigorous controls as when such power is exercised by a public body *stricto sensu*. We will return to these issues later. For the present it will suffice to say that these are endemic problems about the scope of public law which would be present even if the whole section 31 procedure had never been invented.

Activities which are "Inherently Private"

Some activities are regarded as inherently private, or not public, and in that sense unsuited to the judicial review procedure. The *Wachmann*[29] case provides an example of this. The applicant sought judicial review of a disciplinary decision which removed him as a Rabbi because of conduct which rendered him morally unfit to continue in the position. Simon Brown J. refused the application, holding that the jurisdiction of the Chief Rabbi was not susceptible to judicial review. He held that the section 31 procedure could only be used when there was not merely a public, but a governmental interest in the decision-making power in question. The Chief Rabbi's functions were said to be essentially intimate, spiritual and religious, and the government could not and would not seek to discharge them if he were to abdicate his regulatory responsibility, nor would Parliament contemplate legislating to regulate the discharge of these functions. Moreover, the reviewing court was not in a position to regulate what was essentially a religious function, i.e. whether a person was morally fit to carry out their spiritual responsibilities.

Future prospects

It remains to be seen how far the courts will be willing to take the scope of judicial review. The reservations of many among the judiciary at the prospect of extending review to the exercise of private power have been noted above. Some advocate a broader approach. Thus Lord Woolf would, it seems, be in favour of extending review to cover all bodies which exercise authority over another person or body in such a manner as to cause material prejudice to that person or body. These controls could, on principle, apply to bodies exercising power over sport and religion.[30]

---

[28] *Football Association*, above at n. 22, 849.
[29] R. v. *Chief Rabbi of the United Hebrew Congregations of Great Britain and the Commonwealth, ex parte Wachmann* [1993] 2 All ER 249; R. v. *Iman of Bury Park James Masjid Luton, ex parte Sulaiman Ali* [1992] COD 132.
[30] "Judicial Review: A Possible Programme for Reform" [1992] *PL* 221, 235.

This view, the effect of which is to bring a wide range of bodies along our institutional spectrum within the sphere of public law controls, provides an apt link between the first and second parts of this paper. The implications of moving this far will be considered within the section which follows.

Vertical v. Horizontal Application of Constitutional Provisions

It may be helpful at this juncture to make reference to an issue which may have some indirect impact on the topic discussed thus far. This is the question of whether relevant constitutional provisions have an horizontal as well as a vertical impact: can these constitutional provisions be used against private parties or only against the government itself? The key question is then as follows: if the courts decide that such provisions should have an horizontal as well as a vertical dimension what will be the impact of such a decision on the institutional perspective considered above?

The answer in principle must be that even if the courts do take this step, all of the institutional issues considered above will still remain "live questions". The reason is as follows. For a court to decide that provisions of a Constitution are capable of having an horizontal impact cannot literally mean that all such provisions will always be of relevance in relation to any kind of defendant in any kind of situation. If this were to be so then it would literally mean that should a Constitution contain, for example, an administrative justice provision, then it could be invoked in domestic disputes, ordinary contractual problems and the like. Although this would be logically possible, it is very unlikely that any legal system would wish to go this far. Nor does such a conclusion follow necessarily or logically from the decision that the Constitution *can* have an horizontal impact. There are two reasons why this is so.

On the one hand, experience attests to the fact that it is perfectly possible for a legal system to decide that, for example, certain rights apply in relations between private parties, without thereby concluding that the general principles of administrative law can or should be applied in these circumstances.[31] On the other hand, it would still be necessary for a court to decide whether the factual and legal situation presented before it should be characterised as one involving issues of, for example, administrative justice at all. This question of prior characterisation will necessarily take us back to the institutional discussion considered above.[32]

---

[31] See, e.g., experience within the European Community, P.P. Craig and G. de Burca, *EC Law: Text, Cases and Materials* (Oxford University Press, Oxford, 1995), chs 4, 7 and 8.

[32] The decision to accord horizontal impact to provisions of a Constitution may have some influence on how a legal system chooses to deal with these institutional issues. It may, for example, render it easier for a court to reach the conclusion, if it is so minded, that the principles of public law should apply to bodies which are nominally private, but which are felt to exercise a species of public power. This does not, however, affect the general line of argument advanced in the text.

The Institutional Spectrum and a Conception of the State

Public law within the United Kingdom has not traditionally employed a conception of the state. The reasons why this is so are complex, as is revealed by Allison's scholarly analysis.[33] Whether the division between public and private would be rendered any easier if a conception of the state were to assume a more formal part in the reasoning of United Kingdom courts is, however, more questionable.

Allison argues that the very distinction between public and private law is dependent upon "a prevailing and well-developed theory of the state, which appreciates the distinctness of the state administration and ascribes to it qualities which can be used to justify special legal consequences".[34] Commenting on the relatively recent introduction of the public/private divide demanded by the remedial reforms in the United Kingdom, he states that, "in England, neither party politics nor political theory is, at present, likely to produce the theory of a distinct state administration required for a working distinction between public and private law".[35] Allison concludes his discussion of this issue by pointing to the irony that lawyers in the United Kingdom have begun to take account of the state and to transplant continental ideas at the very time at which the state was becoming "increasingly indistinct and administrative disputes difficult to identify".[36]

Whether explicit utilisation of the state within public law discourse has the centrality which Allison accords to it is, however, questionable.

The fact that a legal system such as the French employs a conception of the state does not, as Allison's own analysis clearly demonstrates, necessarily render it any easier for that system to decide which bodies fall within the ambit of public as opposed to private law. The French legal system's employment of the state, with the attendant idea of *service publique*, has not rendered it markedly easier for that legal system to decide which bodies along the institutional spectrum should be held to fall within the regime of public law.[37]

This is surely because the nature of the state itself, and the special qualities which are felt to distinguish the state from other legal actors, are contestable. Every legal system will have to address this issue directly or indirectly, but it is not self-evident that formal usage of the idea of the state markedly affects the matter. The fact that a particular legal regime builds its jurisprudence explicitly around the concept of the state and *service publique* will not, in and of itself, provide any automatic answer as to which types of hybrid bodies

---

[33] See J.W.F. Allison, *A Continental Distinction in the Common Law: A Historical and Comparative Perspective on English Public Law* (Clarendon Press, Oxford, 1996) and his paper in this volume.
[34] Ibid., 37.
[35] Ibid., 104.
[36] Ibid., 108.
[37] Ibid., 58–71.

should be subject to a regime of public law. The *answers* to such inquiries can be formally expressed by declaring that a certain body partakes sufficiently of the qualities of the state itself to be considered part thereof for the purpose of the application of public law norms. This conclusion will, however, be reached by considering, expressly or impliedly, the types of formal and substantive factors which are used by our own courts, even if a different legal system might well apply those criteria differently to the facts of a specific case. Utilisation of a concept of the state will not, therefore, provide an answer *ex ante* or *a priori* to these difficult questions.

An apt example of the preceding points can be taken from the jurisprudence of the European Court of Justice (ECJ). The Court has held that directives can only be binding upon the state, as opposed to a private party, because Article 189 of the EC Treaty provides that directives are binding on the state to whom they are addressed. The correctness of this reasoning is not of immediate concern to us here. As a consequence of this ruling the ECJ has had to decide which bodies constitute the state. The closest that the Court has come to a definition is in the *Foster* case where it held that the state could include: any body, whatever its legal form, which has been made responsible, pursuant to a measure adopted by the state for providing a public service under the control of the state and has for that purpose special powers beyond those which result from the normal rules applicable to relations between individuals.[38] This may seem to be an admirable definition of the state for modern purposes. Two points are, however, of relevance for the present analysis.

On the one hand, utilisation of a conception of the state as such has not itself facilitated the decision as to which bodies should be subject to the relevant rule of public law. It has not short circuited the analysis of "special powers", etc, which will of necessity be central to any such discussion.

On the other hand, the ECJ's jurisprudence on this point serves as a classic warning that we should take care when defining the state to bear in mind the purposes for which the definition is of relevance. Note in this respect, that directives were said not to be binding on individuals because the wording of Article 189 was held to preclude this: directives are, by this Article, only binding on the state to whom they are addressed. The crucial issue is then the ambit of the state, given this premise. It can be strongly argued that the broad test articulated by the ECJ in *Foster* is inappropriate for the following reason. The only body within the "state" which will normally have power to implement a directive will be a central department of government. Certainly not a body such as British Gas, the defendant in the *Foster* case. In this respect British Gas is no different from any private individual.

---

[38] Case C-188/89, *Foster v. British Gas plc* [1990] ECR I-3313, para. 20. For general discussion, see P.P. Craig and de Burca, above at n. 31, 184–6.

THE FUNCTIONAL APPROACH

"Macro Considerations": General Implications Flowing from the Ascription of the Label "Public"

When public lawyers consider the issue of public power they normally do so because, as noted in the introduction to this paper, they believe that certain consequences should follow from the ascription of this label. It is felt that "public law principles" or a "regime of public law" should be applied to undertakings which are characterised in this manner. It must, however, be recognised that there is an ambiguity in such formulations. They could, as noted earlier, be indicative of a separate jurisdiction to determine public law cases; separate procedures for public and private law disputes; or a distinct body of procedural and substantive principles, different from those which apply to private undertakings and private species of power.

Separate jurisdictions, combined with a *distinct corpus of procedural and substantive principles for public law,* are the norm in most civil law countries. The advantages and disadvantages of this approach are well known.[39] The former include: the development of greater expertise in matters of a public law nature; the fashioning of principles which are suited to the particular needs of public bodies; and the facilitation of the kind of interchange between courts and administration which is a feature of, for example, the *Conseil d'Etat*. The disadvantages are equally well documented. Such a regime requires the allocation of disputes to the appropriate section of the judicial system, which can be especially problematic in relation to many of the recent changes in the pattern of government, whereby governmental functions have been privatised or contracted out to private undertakings.[40] The existence of a formal jurisdictional divide between public and private law cases can also generate complex case-law designed to resolve those types of case in which there is felt to be both a public and a private law component to the dispute. French law once again exemplifies this in the jurisprudence which has evolved to determine when a plaintiff in a damages action caused by the servant of a public body is enabled to proceed against the public body itself in the administrative law courts, and when the only action is held to lie against the servant in the private law courts.[41]

Common law systems have, on the whole, eschewed a formal jurisdictional divide of the kind which is commonly to be found within civil law countries.

---

[39] L.N. Brown and J. Bell, *French Administrative Law* (Clarendon Press, Oxford, 4th ed. 1993); R. Chapus, *Droit du Contentieux Administratif* (Montchestien, Paris, 1991); G. Braibant, *Le Droit Administratif Francais* (Reison de la Fondation Nationales des Jacuves Politiques and Dalloz, Paris, 3rd ed. 1992).

[40] See, e.g., the collection of essays in the Special Issue of the *European Review of Public Law* (1994) on this topic.

[41] Brown and Bell, above at n. 39, 174–83.

The ascription of the label "public" to a certain type of body may nonetheless have one of the other consequences outlined above.

Thus a legal system may decide that bodies which are deemed to be public should have certain *distinct procedures* applied to them, in the sense that the manner of seeking relief is different in cases which are of a public law nature. The existence of such procedures for seeking relief may well be coupled with the creation of a separate division within the judicial system, to which cases of a public law nature are assigned. The United Kingdom currently has a system of this kind.[42] The special procedures for bringing an action against public bodies, in particular the obligation to secure leave before the action can proceed and the existence of short time limits, are said to be justified by the position of such bodies and the functions which they perform. The experience in the United Kingdom amply demonstrates the difficulties which are attendant upon this approach: cases arise in which the applicants have sought relief outside the strict time limits laid down for public law cases, and the courts, in their desire not to bar an action which they believe to have merit, have fashioned exceptions to the procedural rules to enable such applicants to proceed by way of the ordinary procedures which govern private law actions, even though the core of the dispute may indisputably have been of a public law nature.[43]

The difficulties which flow from the existence of separate jurisdictions, or even from separate procedures for seeking relief, have meant that certain countries have declined to build distinctions of these kinds into their legal systems. Or to put the same point in a different way, the recognition that a body exercises public power has not been held to lead to consequences of this kind.

However, all legal systems do draw certain consequences, of the third kind outlined above, from the ascription of the label "public": the characterisation of the institution as public, or the recognition that it wields public power, will lead to the application of *procedural and substantive norms* which differ in certain respects from those which apply to private undertakings. Yet here too the picture is more complex than it might appear at first sight. There are two reasons why this is so.

On the one hand, although we might now characterise certain norms as being "public law" in nature, it is by no means certain that they have always been regarded in this manner. It is clear that some of these principles have been applied to a range of institutions which are not public bodies *stricto sensu*. One only has to think of the basic norms of procedural justice, such as the right to a fair hearing and the like, to realise that the courts have long applied such principles to bodies such as unions, trade associations and the like.[44] Now this might be seen as a prime example of the legal system's ability to recognise that institutions other than public bodies *stricto sensu* can

---

[42] P.P. Craig, *Administrative Law* (Sweet and Maxwell, London, 3rd ed. 1994), ch. 15.
[43] Idem.
[44] Ibid., ch. 8.

wield public power, with the consequence that these other bodies should also be subject to public law species of control. It is, however, by no means certain that this is how the courts which decided these cases viewed the matter. Procedural rights of this kind may well have been perceived as a facet of certain kinds of private ordering. The same point can be made concerning some of the substantive principles which are said to be part of the corpus of public law jurisprudence. If such principles are felt to be exclusively those of public law, how then does one explain the fact that, for example, the rules relating to the duties of trustees/fiduciaries have a similar origin and content? Historically, the explanation resides partly in the fact that there were proximate connections between the ideas of private and public trust, and hence also in the substantive rules pertaining in both areas. Yet in the modern day, the law of trusts is generally regarded as falling within private law, notwithstanding the continued similarity in the substantive principles which are applied to this type of case and the paradigmatic public law dispute.

On the other hand, the idea that the ascription of the label "public power" leads to the application of a distinct corpus of procedural and substantive norms has come under strain as a result of changes in the way in which even classic forms of private ordering are perceived. Contract and corporate law now contain many common law and statutory constraints of a kind which did not exist in a previous age. In this sense there is little doubt that private law has become subject to a greater degree of public control than has hitherto been the case. Moreover, there is equally little doubt that public law doctrines might be made greater use of within contract law than has hitherto been the case.[45]

"Micro Considerations": Do All Public Law Norms Apply to All Bodies which Wield Public Power?

The essence of the argument within this section can be presented quite simply: the fact that a particular institution is felt to possess public power should not lead inexorably to the conclusion that all principles of a public law nature should be equally applicable to such bodies; the more broad ranging is our definition of public power, the more we require a nuanced approach in order to determine which of the public law principles should be held to apply to a body which appears somewhere along the line of the institutional spectrum of public power. This point has not been lost on the courts in the United Kingdom. They have been concerned about the suitability of public law principles to certain types of bodies which applicants have sought to label public for the purposes of the rules for seeking relief. Thus we have already seen that

---

[45] J. Beatson, "Public Law Influences in Contract Law", in J. Beatson and D. Friedmann (eds), *Good Faith and Fault in Contract Law* (Clarendon Press, Oxford, 1995), ch. 10.

Rose J. was reluctant to apply principles which had been honed to the position of governmental departments and the like, to bodies such as the Football Association. The remainder of the discussion within this section will seek to exemplify the basic proposition outlined above.

We may take as a first example, the possible application to sporting regulatory bodies and the like of *the procedural rules for the seeking of relief* which presently exist in the United Kingdom. We have already seen from the preceding discussion that the courts have, thus far, decided that these bodies are not sufficiently public for the purposes of these procedures. The House of Lords has, however, not yet pronounced upon this category of case, and Lord Woolf, writing extra-judicially has made it clear that he does not necessarily share the views of the Court of Appeal.[46] Let us then imagine that the House of Lords does take a different view on this issue. Does it automatically follow that the key elements of the rules for seeking relief are equally applicable to such institutions?

The requirements of leave and short time limits have been justified on the grounds that they serve to protect public bodies from applications which have little chance of success, and also because they enhance legal certainty. These considerations are said to be of importance for bodies which are discharging public functions. It is clear that these reasons were framed very much with the idea of a public body *stricto sensu* in mind. It is by no means self-evident that they are equally relevant when we come to consider the position of institutions such as the Jockey Club, the Football Association, Lloyd's of London and the like. If we do decide to deem these bodies public for the purposes of the application for judicial review, we do so principally because of the degree of regulatory power which they wield within a particular area of life. This is not, however, equivalent to saying that they exercise public responsibility of the kind which is the justification for the requirements of leave and short time limits for public bodies *stricto sensu*. This follows *a fortiori* if we choose to bring within the remit of the United Kingdom rules certain types of corporations.

A second example which illustrates the same point concerns the *application of the procedural and substantive norms* which comprise the core of judicial review. Let us once again focus upon the types of bodies considered in the preceding paragraph. Is it self-evident that we would wish to apply all of the procedural and substantive norms of public law to such bodies; or that we would wish to utilise them in the same manner as when they are applied to traditional governmental institutions? The answer to this question may well vary depending upon the particular type of procedural or substantive norm which arises for consideration, as the following contrast indicates.

We may well have little difficulty in deciding that basic principles of procedural fairness should be applied to such regulatory institutions. Indeed, as we have already seen from the preceding discussion, the courts have through

---

[46] Lord Woolf's ability to change the law in this respect may be somewhat diminished given that he has now become the Master of the Rolls within the Court of Appeal.

various legal devices reached the conclusion that these principles should be applied to at least some bodies of this nature, such as trade associations, trade unions and the like. Even the application of such procedural norms can be problematic if we decide to extend the label "public" to certain species of corporate power.

It is, however, when we come to consider the application of substantive public principles to bodies of this kind that more problems can arise. A plethora of more particular questions arise for consideration. Would we, for example, wish to apply the full rigours of jurisdictional review as developed in cases such as *Anisminic*, *Racal* and *Page*[47] to such regulatory bodies or to certain kinds of corporation? Do we think that the principles concerning the control of discretion (such as impropriety of purpose, relevancy, reasonableness, proportionality, legitimate expectations, and rights-based arguments) can or should be imposed upon institutions of this nature? Should we apply them at all, or with modifications which are suited to the nature of the body under scrutiny?[48] Would, for example, a corporation which is deemed to wield public power have to comply with emerging principles such as proportionality when deciding upon managerial choices, and how would controls of this nature fit with existing norms of corporate law?

Difficult questions of this nature are bound to arise the further we move along the institutional spectrum from the paradigm of a governmental body. Having said this it should also be acknowledged that legal systems have in the past tackled questions of this kind, and, moreover, that changes in the pattern of government mean that they will have to do so again in the modern day.

One of the principal historical examples of the courts fashioning particular norms of a public law nature to deal with aggregations of power which are nominally private is to be found in the jurisprudence concerning the pricing policies of certain corporate bodies. Case-law and doctrinal writing of considerable lineage has established the proposition, both in the United Kingdom and in the USA, that some private bodies which wield *de jure* or *de facto* monopoly power as a result of governmental grant, or flowing from the nature of the activity in question, may not have the normal contractual freedom over pricing policy. The courts, reasoning from first principle, imposed an obligation to charge no more than reasonable prices for the services or goods which were being provided.[49]

---

[47] *Anisminic Ltd. v. Foreign Compensation Commission* [1969] 2 AC 147; *In re Racal Communications Ltd.* [1981] AC 374; *R. v. Lord President of the Privy Council, ex parte Page* [1993] AC 682.

[48] There is some indication that regulatory bodies, even if they are not deemed to be sufficiently public for the purposes of the rules relating to the seeking of public law relief, will be subject to constraints in the way which they exercise their discretion which are not markedly different from those which do apply to public bodies. See in this respect, *Shearson Lehmann Hutton Inc. v. Maclaine Watson & Co. Ltd.* [1989] 2 Lloyds Rep 570.

[49] P.P. Craig, "Constitutions, Property and Regulation" [1991] *PL* 438; M. Taggart, "Public Utilities and Public Law", in P.A. Joseph (ed.), *Essays on the Constitution* (Brooker's Wellington, 1995), 214.

Changes in the pattern of government in the modern day have, in many respects, raised the problem in a more acute and general manner than hitherto. One of the features of the changing pattern of government has been the contracting out of activities to private undertakings of functions which had been previously performed by government itself.[50] This increasingly widespread practice will necessarily raise questions as to the nature of the governing principles which should apply to such undertakings. Space precludes any extensive analysis of this problem. Suffice it to say here that the courts will, in such circumstances, have to decide selectively which of the principles of public law should apply to such bodies, and whether they have to be modified by way of comparison to the application of the same generic principle to public bodies *stricto sensu*. Moreover, it should also be acknowledged that statutory intervention, which has taken the form of increased procedural and substantive control over the activities of privatised utilities, is implicitly premised on the assumption that such bodies do not fit within the normal paradigms of private corporate power.[51]

STRUCTURAL CONSIDERATIONS

In answering any of the more particular issues posed in the preceding pages we should also bear in mind the structural considerations, flowing from the nature of any particular legal system, which will influence and constrain these responses. The United States system may be taken by way of example.

As might be expected, there is a considerable body of material from the USA concerning the "private exercise of governmental power". Such exercises of power can assume varying forms, including contracting out of governmental functions to private undertakings, the use of private parties as agents for the application of government policy, and the delegation of standard setting or licensing to what are, in essence, private parties. There are, in addition, private regulatory bodies which possess monopoly power within their assigned area. As might be also expected, there is a growing body of academic literature analysing the legality of power being accorded to this "fifth branch of government".[52] No attempt will be made to summarise the details of this literature, nor is it of immediate concern to the present inquiry. What is of interest is the way in which United States' constitutional and adminis-

---

[50] Craig, above at n. 42, ch. 3; M. Freedland, "Government by Contract and Public Law" [1994] *PL* 86.

[51] See, e.g., Competition and Service (Utilities) Act 1992 (U.K.).

[52] See, e.g., L.L. Jaffee, "Lawmaking by Private Groups" (1937) 51 *Harv LR* 201; D.M. Lawrence, "Private Exercise of Governmental Power" (1986) 61 *Ind LJ* 647; H.I. Abramson, "A Fifth Branch of Government: The Private Regulators and their Constitutionality" (1989) 16 *Hastings Const LQ* 165; R. Cass, "Privatization: Politics, Law and Theory" (1988) 71 *Marq LR* 449; H.J. Krent, "Fragmenting the Unitary Executive: Congressional Delegations of Administrative Authority Outside the Federal Government" (1990) 85 *NwULR* 62.

trative law doctrine structures and constrains the academic arguments in this area.[53]

The lines of inquiry pursued in this literature focus primarily, albeit not exclusively, upon the constitutionality of any delegation of power to the private actor, and the issue of whether action by a private regulator constitutes "state action". The former inquiry may lead to the conclusion that there has been an unconstitutional delegation of power. Assuming that this is not so, the existence of state action will be a prerequisite for the the possible application of constitutional due process. On the assumption that there is state action, the actual determination of whether the due process clause applies to the instant case will depend upon whether the applicant can show that he or she has a life, liberty or property interest of the kind which is protected by the Constitution. This inquiry will be followed by a determination of how much process is due in the circumstances of the case, judged by the *Mathews v. Eldridge* calculus,[54] as well as a determination of whether there is any substantive due process claim.

There are two reasons for the emphasis placed upon constitutional doctrine. One is that it is obviously important in its own terms. It is clearly correct to focus upon the issue of whether the relevant power should be capable of being delegated to a private actor at all, and equally correct to place emphasis upon the possible application of procedural rights derived from the due process clause of the Constitution. The other, less obvious, reason for this focus is that it is difficult to apply traditional administrative law doctrine to these situations, given the framework of American administrative law.

Leaving aside the application of constitutional rights, many administrative law challenges in the United States will be based upon the Administrative Procedure Act (APA). The APA regulates both adjudication and rulemaking, albeit to varying degrees. Process rights relating to formal adjudication are governed by section 554 of the APA, in conjunction with sections 556 and 557. Substantive challenges to formal adjudication are based on section 706. Process rights in relation to informal agency action are to be found in the *Overton Park* doctrine,[55] while substantive challenges will, once again, be based upon section 706. Formal and informal rulemaking are regulated by sections 553 of the APA, together with sections 556 and 557 in the context of formal rulemaking. Once again substantive review will be founded upon section 706. This is rightly praised as an impressive general statute, providing the bedrock upon which modern American administrative law has developed.

The problem in the present context is quite simple: all the key sections of the legislation are explicitly premised upon the existence of an agency adjudication, agency rule, or agency action. The definition of agency is provided in section 551, which states that the term covers "each authority of the

---

[53] See Jack Beermann's paper in this volume.
[54] 424 U.S. 319 (1976).
[55] *Citizens to Preserve Overton Park v. Volpe*, 401 U.S. 402 (1971).

Government of the United States", subject to certain listed exceptions. While it is possible that some private exercises of governmental power could come within this definition, it is also clear that many others could not.

What this means therefore is that the structure of United States' constitutional and administrative law doctrine directly shapes the nature of the possible responses to the problems created by nominally private bodies exercising a degree of public power. A claimant can seek to use constitutional doctrine in order to invalidate the legislative grant of power as an illegal delegation, and can attempt to found rights upon the Constitution. The exclusion of such private bodies from the purview of the APA means that the process rights contained therein are inapplicable, and perhaps even more importantly, there is no conceptual basis for substantive challenge.

It is interesting to compare, in structural terms, the situation in the United States with that in the United Kingdom. What we find in the United Kingdom is, in essence, the converse of the position in the United States. The absence of a written constitution in the United Kingdom has meant that there is no meaningful jurisprudence concerning the types of power which can be delegated by government to private actors. This is not to say that it would be logically impossible for the courts to develop legal principles on this issue, but rather that they have not done so, and that there would be significant obstacles in their way. The absence of constitutional grounds for challenge has meant that the courts in the United Kingdom have increasingly made use of administrative law doctrine to exert control where they believe that this is warranted. What this means, more specifically, is that in the United Kingdom there is nothing to confine judicial review in this area akin to the definitional limit which exists within the APA. If the courts feel that private bodies exercising monopoly power over a particular area should be subject to the procedural and substantive principles of judicial review, they can so find. So far they have not done so but, as we have seen above, a case on this topic is yet to go to the House of Lords.

CONCLUSION

No attempt will be made to summarise the preceding arguments. One final point should, however, be made. The principles of judicial review do not exist in a vacuum. They, explicitly and implicitly, mesh with other political mechanisms designed to ensure the accountability of public power. These political mechanisms have themselves largely been fashioned against the backdrop of traditional public bodies. The implications for these broader notions of accountability, of extending the definition of public power, and public law, to other kinds of institutions must not be excluded from our consideration.

11

The Underlying Values of Public and Private Law

DAWN OLIVER*

In this paper I am seeking to identify common underlying values in public and private law. My search has been in both case-law and statutes as the two interact very closely with one another. In a sense it may be said that the courts and parliament distill or pull values out of the air or atmosphere in which they have formed, when they need them.

My quest for common values has the advantage that I do not need to define public or private law, as I am in search of pervasive values in the legal system. But I acknowledge that the values I have identified are not the only ones underlying the system, and that public law has additional uniquely "public" values—and so no doubt has private law. I do not have the time to seek to identify those specifically public or private values here, but I suggest that a place to start to find high level values in public law might be the "Seven Principles of Public Life" recently identified by Lord Nolan's Committee on Standards in Public Life, namely duties of selflessness, integrity, objectivity, accountability, openness, honesty and leadership.[1] It may be that these are among the "transcendent values" to which Murray Hunt refers in his paper in this volume. Other possible public law values might include the protection of national security, and efficiency and effectiveness in government, which (in the guise of the interests of good administration) are protected by the special procedural privileges afforded to respondents in applications for judicial review by our Supreme Court Act 1981—short time limits, the need for the applicant to obtain leave to apply, discretion to refuse a remedy, and so on. This kind of value, it seems to me, does not have general parallels in purely private law—though public and private law are not easily separable[2] and we

---

* I am grateful to colleagues who have commented on earlier drafts of this paper, especially Nick Bamforth, Eric Barendt, Stephen Guest, Jeffrey Jowell, Andrew Le Sueur and William Twining. I am also grateful for points made by participants at the conference on "The Province of Administrative Law" at which this paper was delivered, and in the light of which I have revised it. The many defects are entirely my own responsibility.

[1] *First Report of the Committee on Standards in Public Life*, Cm 2850 (1995), 14.
[2] See Paul Craig's discussion of the continuum or spectrum between public and private law and Mark Aronson's discussion of "mixed" power, and a trichotomy in place of the dichotomy between public and private law, in their papers in this volume.

find traces of these public law values at some of the margins.[3] Also, many of these values do not operate at as high a level of generality as the values to which I shall devote the rest of this paper.

My search for common underlying values is, I know, an ambitious one. One problem is that values exist at varying levels of generality in the legal system and in various sectors within it, and it would clearly not be possible to draw parallels across all the subdivisions of law at all levels. For instance, the values implicit in the maxim that "he who comes to equity must come with clean hands" have little in common with the concept that I owe a duty of care to my neighbour or with the rules of natural justice in administrative law. Each of these tenets expresses a value, but each value is of limited and rather local applicability in the legal system. However, my general argument in this paper will be that important common key values—dignity, autonomy, respect, status and security[4]—are being developed at a high level of abstraction in public and private law. Together these support what I shall refer to as paramount values of democracy, citizenship and participation. A metaphor for this would envisage the key values as keystones in a series of arches in a building on which rests a roof, representing the paramount values in the structure.

THE GCHQ CASE

I shall start with one of the leading public law cases decided by the House of Lords in recent years, R. v. *Minister for the Civil Service, ex parte Council of Civil Service Unions*.[5] In looking at this case I shall try to lay the foundations for my argument that key values can be found across public and private law. The case concerned the employment of civil servants at General Communications Headquarters (GCHQ), whose main functions were to ensure the security of the United Kingdom's military and official communications and to provide signals intelligence for the government. In 1983 the Prime Minister, Mrs. Thatcher, in her capacity as Minister for the Civil Service, issued an oral instruction under the Civil Service Order in Council (which was promulgated under the royal prerogative) to the effect that the terms and conditions of service of civil servants employed at GCHQ would be revised so as to exclude them from membership of any trade union other than a departmental staff association approved by the director of GCHQ. This instruction was given because of concern about damage to national security that could be caused by industrial action at GCHQ, where there had been a history of industrial action between 1979 and 1981. Civil servants were offered a payment of £1,000 as compensation for the loss of their trade union membership,

---

[3] See further the papers by Murray Hunt, Alison Harvison Young, David Mullan and Paul Craig in this volume.

[4] I discuss the meanings of these terms below.

[5] [1985] AC 374 (hereafter referred to as *GCHQ*).

Underlying Values of Public Law 219

and those who were not willing to accept the change of terms would either be transferred to another part of the civil service or be dismissed.

Previous practice by the government had been to consult the unions forming the Council of Civil Service Unions before altering terms and conditions of service, but in this case there had been no consultation because the Prime Minister feared that such consultation might itself precipitate the industrial action, and thus damage to national security, which the instruction was designed to prevent.

If this case had arisen in a jurisdiction with a Bill or Charter of Rights the problem would have been conceived of as raising issues to do with the right of free association, rights to belong to a trade union and so on. The question would have been whether the interference by government with such rights was justified under one of the exceptions spelt out in the Bill or Charter of Rights. In the United Kingdom, however, we have no Bill of Rights, and so the problem was tackled in another way.

The government's case was, first, that powers exercised under the royal prerogative were not reviewable. It was claiming for itself an area of autonomy or freedom of action. There was support in the case-law for this view at the time. Secondly, the government claimed that the requirements of national security overrode any duty which the minister may have had to consult before making a decision.

The applicants claimed that the fact that a power derived from the royal prerogative no longer precluded judicial review, and that the previous practice of the government had given rise to a legitimate expectation of prior consultation with the unions before conditions of service were changed. In other words, they challenged the autonomy of the government in this area.

So the focus was on the source of the government's power and its decision-making process rather than on whether removal of trade union membership rights was lawful from a substantive point of view, and given its impact on affected individuals, which would have been the approach under a Bill of Rights.

The House of Lords found that the test for whether a power exercised by government was reviewable or not was the nature of the power being exercised, not the legal source of the power—a functional approach. So the simple fact that a power derived from the royal prerogative did not of itself mean that the courts had no jurisdiction to review its exercise. In principle some powers, whether they derive from the prerogative or not, are of their nature not justiciable (treaty making, defence, mercy, the grant of honours, the dissolution of parliament and the appointment of ministers were given as examples). Other prerogative powers however are, in principle, subject to review. The problem of the control of power is one to which I shall return, but we focus next on the grounds for judicial review.

Having decided that, in principle, decisions about the terms and conditions of employment in the civil service were justiciable, the House of Lords found that the past practice of consultation of civil service unions before terms and conditions were altered had created a legitimate expectation on the part of civil servants and their unions that the unions would be consulted when such decisions were being made. It had therefore been unfair of the government not to consult them here.

Lord Diplock took the opportunity in this case to try to enumerate the grounds for judicial review. He drew from the case-law three grounds for review: illegality, irrationality and procedural impropriety. The failure to consult the unions in this case was an example of procedural impropriety. And a possible fourth ground for review was lack of proportionality.

However, in this case the House of Lords found that there would have been a real risk to the interests of national security if notice had been given to the unions of the proposed change, and on that basis their Lordships decided that procedural propriety must give way to the interests of national security. The unions lost their case.

The question I want to address is whether there are any values underlying this decision and judicial review in general that might be of universal or at least very wide relevance in public law, and whether the same values have relevance in private law. To do so, we need here to consider, albeit briefly, the grounds for judicial review in England, remembering that these operate without a Bill or Charter of Rights, and to seek the high level values those grounds embody. I shall suggest that we can find values in these grounds for review by focusing not on the process and procedures of decision-making, which is the normal perspective of public lawyers, but on the significance of the action or decision for the individuals affected by it. In other words, we focus on the outcomes of decisions that are subject to review rather than the decision-making inputs.[6]

PROCEDURAL IMPROPRIETY

Broadly stated, procedural propriety requires that, where there is statutory power to interfere with individual liberties or where a person's living or other existing or possible future social status or security are at stake in a dispute having a public law element, then in principle the person whose rights or interests are to be interfered with should be given the benefit of a fair decision-making procedure.[7] This entails that the person whose rights or interests are at stake is entitled to know the case against him and to have an opportunity

---

[6] A similar shift of focus is taking place in public service law, where the Weberian concentration on process and procedures is being supplanted by focuses on outputs and outcomes—or performance. See the paper by Wade MacLauchlan in this volume.

[7] For full accounts of this ground see H.W.R. Wade and C.F. Forsyth, *Administrative Law* (Clarendon Press, Oxford, 7th ed. 1994), Part V; P.P. Craig, *Administrative Law* (Sweet and Maxwell, London, 3rd ed. 1994), chs 8–9; S.A. de Smith, Lord Woolf and J. Jowell, *Judicial Review of Administrative Action* (Sweet and Maxwell, London, 5th ed. 1995), chs 7–12.

to put his own case. In some circumstances, but not yet as a general rule, reasons must be given for a decision adverse to a person's interests.[8] This head of review also includes, as in the *GCHQ* case, rights to the satisfaction of legitimate expectations that a fair procedure will be followed when a decision is made. Thus, where a body has been led to believe that it can rely on the continued following of past procedural practice in its relations with state bodies, in principle it should continue to be able to do so.[9] Legitimate expectations are also spreading into substantive areas, thus breaking down distinctions between the three grounds of review.[10] Procedural propriety also requires absence of bias on the part of the decision maker.

Why is procedural propriety a requirement of decision-making—what values does it entail? The requirement for procedural propriety should make it more likely that a decision of this kind will be taken in the light of relevant information and after due consideration of the interests of the individual affected. This requirement provides protection for individuals' interests, for instance in their job, their security, their property, status and so on. Additionally, where reasons are given the decision maker is accountable in that the reasons open up possibilities for challenges to be made to the decision which may be determined either through internal complaints procedures, or independently by the courts or a tribunal, or by parliament, or, indirectly and through the ballot box, the public. This in turn opens up the possibility of a second look at the decision, again with a view to affording protection to the individual.

These, then, are instrumental grounds for review and not ends in themselves. Applying this point to the *GCHQ* case, as we have seen, a number of vital interests were at stake for the members of the civil service unions. First, their freedom—autonomy—to choose to belong or not to belong to a lawful association. Secondly, the fact that the unions' functions included the protection of their members' job security and conditions of employment—and thereby their status in the wider community, their security, income and career prospects—meant that withdrawal of membership put these interests at risk. Also at stake in the *GCHQ* case were the respect, even the dignity of the union members deriving from their membership of an independent professional trade union.

---

[8] See Wade and Forsyth, ibid., 541–5, 942–5, 981–2; De Smith, Woolf and Jowell, ibid., paras 8-014, 9–049 to 9.053; Craig, ibid., 310–16; *R. v. Civil Service Appeal Board, ex parte Cunningham* [1991] 4 All ER 310; *R. v. Secretary of State for the Home Department, ex parte Doody* [1994] AC 531. Cf. *R. v. Universities Funding Council, ex parte Institute of Dental Surgery* [1994] 1 WLR 242.
[9] *GCHQ*, above at n. 5.
[10] De Smith, Woolf and Jowell, above at n. 7, paras 13.026 to 13.035; Craig, above at n. 7, 672–5; Wade and Forsyth, above at n. 7, 418–20. See, e.g., *R. v. Commissioners of Inland Revenue, ex parte Unilever plc* [1996] STC 681; *R. v. Inland Revenue Commissioners, ex parte Preston* [1985] AC 835; *R. v. Inland Revenue Commissioners, ex parte MFK Underwriting Services Ltd.* [1990] 1 All ER 91.

IRRATIONALITY

The second ground for the review of discretion listed by Lord Diplock in the *GCHQ* case was irrationality, which derives from the doctrine of "*Wednesbury* unreasonableness".[11] The doctrine requires that in taking decisions regard must be had to relevant considerations, irrelevant considerations must be ignored, and a decision maker must not act so unreasonably that no reasonable authority would have so decided. It accords a wide area of discretion—autonomy—to public bodies, as long as they remain within the four corners of their powers, while seeking also to secure that the interests of private individuals are not unnecessarily interfered with. This irrationality doctrine protects individuals against the improper exercise of power by public bodies to their detriment.

ILLEGALITY

Last, but by no means least, illegality as a ground for review: this is an element in some of the most fundamental principles of English constitutional law, many of which are now taken for granted. The state may not change the law in a way that interferes with the liberties of individuals without the consent of parliament:[12] thus a democratic procedure is imposed on law making of this kind, which should provide protection for the autonomy, status and security of individuals. The government, being in a position of power over individuals and in particular being entitled to enforce its orders coercively, may not itself determine legal disputes, and hence there should be a separation between the personnel of the judiciary and the executive and legislature:[13] thus individuals are to be protected against decisions being taken by public bodies that are in their own rather than the public interest, that are unlawful, ill-informed, influenced by irrelevant considerations and so on.

Thirdly, even though a state body is entitled when applying a policy to adopt and apply guidelines for reasons of consistency and convenience, nevertheless that state body should always be willing to listen to someone who has

---

[11] For full accounts of this ground see Wade and Forsyth, above at n. 7, ch. 12; Craig, above at n. 7, ch. 12; De Smith, Woolf and Jowell, above at n. 7, ch. 11. See also J. Jowell and A. Lester, "Beyond *Wednesbury*: Substantive Principles of Administrative Law" [1987] *PL* 368; P. Walker "What's Wrong with Irrationality?" [1995] *PL* 556; Sir Robert Carnwath, "The Reasonable Limits of Local Authority Powers" [1996] *PL* 244.

[12] *Proclamations' Case* (1611) 12 Co Rep 74, 76: "Also it was resolved that the King hath no prerogative, but that which the law of the land allows him". This principle explains the need to pass legislation on matters such as compulsory purchase and planning permission, for without such legislation the executive would be breaching this principle.

[13] *Prohibitions Del Roy* (1607) 12 Co Rep 63 (the monarch may not sit as a judge in the royal courts). See also *Brownlow* v. *Cox and Michil* (1615) 3 Bulst 32 (the monarch may not withdraw matters of state from the cognisance of the courts).

something new to say as to why the policy does not or should not apply to them:[14] thus in general individuals will be treated equally and not in a discriminatory way, but their special needs will be taken into account: this provides protection for their dignity, status and security.

Fourthly, powers granted by parliament which affect individuals should be used for the purpose for which they were granted and not for some ulterior purpose, and in particular not so as to further the political interests of the party in power to the detriment of individuals:[15] this protects the interests of individuals against the partisan use of power by public bodies.

Lastly, people should be treated equally by the state unless there is a relevant difference between them or their circumstances and those of others in similar situations.[16] This protects the dignity and respect of individuals.

THE UNDERLYING VALUES OF PUBLIC LAW

I hope that I have already indicated, in my brief summary of the grounds for judicial review and my account of the *GCHQ* case, that by implication they embody certain key underlying values which can be summarised as autonomy, dignity, respect, status and security. I shall explain these shortly, but first a word of explanation of what I mean by values.

The *Shorter Oxford English Dictionary* definition of value is helpful here: "That which is worthy of esteem for its own sake; that which has intrinsic worth". There are of course many things that could be regarded as values—respect for life, concern for others, courage, truth, beauty, health—but I am trying to identify the ultimate and most pervasive underlying values in public—and private—law, of which in my view there are very few.[17]

The values I have in mind are close to the "background rights" Ronald Dworkin refers to, "rights that provide a justification for political decisions by society in the abstract".[18] But values, as I conceive them, are not themselves rights, though rights are expressions of, or means to protect, values.[19]

---

[14] *British Oxygen Co. Ltd.* v. *Board of Trade* [1971] AC 610. And see Wade and Forsyth, above at n. 7, 364–5 and 537; De Smith, Woolf and Jowell, above at n. 7, ch. 11; Craig, above at n. 7, 391–6.
[15] *Padfield* v. *Minister of Agriculture* [1968] AC 997. And see further below at n. 43.
[16] De Smith, Woolf and Jowell, above at n. 7, paras. 13–036 to 13–045; *Vestey* v. *Inland Revenue Commissioners (No. 2)* [1980] AC 1148 (Inland Revenue has no power to dispense with the duty to pay tax). See also Bill of Rights of 1689, Arts. 1 and 2, prohibiting the use of suspending and dispensing powers.
[17] For a very lucid discussion of the meanings of values see W.L. Twining and D. Miers, *How to do Things with Rules: A Primer of Interpretation* (Weidenfeld and Nicolson, London, 3rd ed. 1991), 138–40. And see L.L. Fuller, *The Morality of Law* (Yale University Press, New Haven, 1969).
[18] R. Dworkin, *Taking Rights Seriously* (Harvard University Press, Cambridge, 1978), 93.
[19] However Dworkin argues that the most fundamental of rights is the right to equal concern and respect in ch. 6 of *Taking Rights Seriously*, ibid. Here is the concept of a right to the benefit of one of the ultimate and pervasive values which I consider to underlie public—and private—law.

For instance, the right to due process—in English terms the rules of procedural propriety and natural justice—provides protection for values, but it does not of itself treat those values as rights.

Nor are values the same as principles.[20] Dworkin in *Taking Rights Seriously*[21] uses "principle" to mean "a standard that is to be observed, not because it will advance or secure an economic, political, or social situation deemed desirable, but because it is a requirement of justice or fairness or some other dimension of morality. Thus, ... the standard that no man may profit by his own wrong [is] a principle".[22] I believe that Dworkin's principles are *applications* of what I mean by values, but at a lower level on the ladder of abstraction[23] than the levels I am aiming at. They are also often instrumental, or extrinsic, rather than intrinsic. For instance, Dworkin refers to the case of *Riggs v. Palmer*[24] in which a man named in the will of his grandfather was held not entitled to inherit, because he had murdered the testator. On one level, as Dworkin states, the case illustrates the maxim or principle that a man may not profit from his own wrong; on another, more abstract, level, I suggest, it may be taken to illustrate the operation of high level values, for example autonomy and respect, which the heir had denied his grandfather.

Values have to contend with other considerations in the law and legal policy, and this is one of the reasons why I do not regard them as rights. For instance, upholding the autonomy, dignity, respect, security and status of individuals may involve weighing up the competing claims to these values of other individuals. It also involves consideration of the wider implications of giving precedence to such values. For instance, upholding the security and status of all employees could have detrimental effects on the management of an enterprise, which could in turn undermine the viability of the enterprise and thus threaten the well-being of the workforce and others with interests in the enterprise.

Values, then, are part of the climate, the "background" in which judges operate. Perhaps Neil McCormick's "background moral view of how life in an organised society ought to be for individuals" is the nearest to my concept of underlying values.[25] Raz uses the term "value" at one point to mean something that constitutes or implies the existence of reasons for action.[26] This is a helpful contribution to what I am getting at, but of course some reasons for action are bad, and would not merit being given the name "value".

---

[20] For a discussion of the different meanings of "principle" and related terms, see A.W.B. Simpson, "The Common Law and Legal Theory", in W.L. Twining (ed.), *Legal Theory and Common Law* (Basil Blackwell, Oxford, 1986).

[21] *Taking Rights Seriously*, above at n. 18, esp. chs 2 and 4.

[22] Ibid., 22.

[23] A ladder of abstraction is "a continuing sequence of categorisations from a low level of generality up to a high level of generality": Twining and Miers, above at n. 17, 56.

[24] 115 N.Y. 506, 22 N.E. 188 (1889).

[25] N. McCormick, "Jurisprudence and the Constitution" [1983] *Current Legal Problems* 13, 22.

[26] J. Raz, *The Morality of Freedom* (Clarendon Press, Oxford, 1986), 397.

THE FIVE KEY VALUES

I have suggested that we can identify five key values—autonomy, dignity, respect, status and security—in public law. These are terms of art and do not have a fixed or very concrete meaning. Also, as we shall see, they mesh together. But some words of explanation may help.

Autonomy means, strictly, living under one's own laws, or self-government. Raz defines autonomy as the idea that people should make their own lives.[27] Often autonomy is assumed to mean, and mean only, freedom to operate in the market, but such a narrow view would miss the point I am trying to make, for it does not link with our other key values. It does not, for instance, take account of the issues raised in the law of relationships—marriage, parents and children—where developments over the last century have increased the autonomy of the more vulnerable parties to those relationships, but not to any great degree by reference to market activity.

Dignity (the Latin "dignus" means worthy), for me, means honour, reputableness.[28] The meanings, among many, of respect in the *Shorter Oxford English Dictionary*, which I attach to respect in this context are "regard, consideration".[29] Respect affects the nature of a person's relations with others. I agree with Birks that respect requires that "[a] society which holds out to its members the promise that they do all have equal worth must allow them to vindicate that interest against those who treat them as having little worth and flout the restraints which allow each life an equal chance to fulfil itself".[30]

By status I mean a person's position or standing in society—membership of a profession and the like.[31] A person may have many statuses. His or her position in society may depend on reputation, professional qualifications, membership of social organisations[32] such as trade unions, clubs, churches and so on.

---

[27] Raz, ibid., 369. Raz argues that "[u]ltimately those who live in an autonomy-enhancing culture can prosper only by being autonomous" (p. 394); and see generally Raz, ibid., 14 and 15. A new term for autonomy is "self-ownership" but I do not propose to use it here: see A. Reeve, "The Theory of Property: Beyond Private versus Common Property", in D. Held (ed.), *Political Theory Today* (Stanford University Press, Stanford, 1991). See also D. Held, *Models of Democracy* (Stanford University Press, Stanford, 1987), ch. 9.

[28] I note in passing that s. 10 of the Constitution of the Republic of South Africa Act 1993 provides for a right to respect for and protection of dignity.

[29] I do not accept for these purposes the *Shorter Oxford English Dictionary* meaning "*deferential* regard or esteem felt or shown towards a person . . ." (emphasis added).

[30] P. Birks, *Harassment and Hubris: The Right to an Equality of Respect* (the John Maurice Kelly Memorial Lecture at University College Dublin, 1995), 54. For the case for respect as a right—or more accurately a right to equal concern and respect—see Dworkin, above at n. 18, 182. He suggests that this right operates in the sphere of the design of political institutions.

[31] See *Shorter Oxford English Dictionary*. I do not use the term status as Maine did to indicate the Law of Persons: Sir Henry Maine, *Ancient Law: its connection with the early history of society, and its relation to modern ideas* (1861, reprinted 1959), 149. See Alison Harvison Young's paper in this volume for a discussion of the dissents in *Gould* v. *Yukon Order of Pioneers* [1996] 1 SCR 571 in which the status issues were, unusually, articulated.

[32] Such as the Yukon Order of Pioneers, considered in *Gould* v. *Yukon Order of Pioneers*, ibid.

And finally, security, by which I mean the condition of being protected from or not exposed to danger.[33] This involves protection against unwanted and damaging change—loss of income, livelihood or home, for instance.[34] This point illustrates well my point that these values are not rights. Most new policies that governments adopt involve elements of unwanted change for many citizens and it is certainly not the case that the law gives—or could give—each individual a right not to have their lives changed. But it does, I suggest, provide some protection, whether through procedural devices or rights to compensation, against such changes being imposed where the impact on particular individuals is specially adverse.

The *GCHQ* case illustrates these values well: the trade union members' autonomy was reduced by the ban on their freedom to join trade unions of their choosing. Their dignity and respect were damaged by withdrawal of membership of professional bodies and the implication, which they found grossly offensive, that they would be willing to damage the national interest for their own ends by industrial action. Both their security and their status—their job protection, their professional status through membership of independent professional bodies, ultimately, if they lost their jobs, their income and their participation in the civil service within which they had important roles to play—were at stake in their loss of membership of trade unions. Unemployment resulting from dismissal would have reduced their standard of living and thus the ways in which they could participate in society.

We can see from this case how these five values cannot always be disentangled from one another. Dignity and respect, in particular, are close relations. Security, status and respect are linked to dignity and autonomy in many ways, but they are, in my view, different to the extent that they are principally about a person's place in, and opportunities to participate in, social organisations—they are essentially social rather than individualistic values.

There is not the space here to consider further cases on judicial review, but I hope that I have indicated sufficiently in my earlier discussion of the grounds for judicial review (procedural impropriety, irrationality and illegality) how they reflect the influence of these five key values.

THE STATE AND THE FIVE KEY VALUES

So far we have been concentrating on the ways in which judicial review protects the five key values for the benefit of individuals. But the *GCHQ* case was

---

[33] See *Shorter Oxford English Dictionary*.

[34] T.H. Marshall, *Citizenship and Social Class, and other essays* (Cambridge University Press, Cambridge, 1950) considered that the introduction of social rights protected by statute in the twentieth century enabled individuals to participate in society as citizens. Marshall meant by this "social element" of citizenship "the whole range from the right to a modicum of economic welfare and *security* to the right to share to the full in the social heritage and to live the life of a civilised being according to the standards prevailing in society": ibid., 11 (emphasis added).

decided in favour of the government. The grounds for giving priority to the government over the union members, and thus for subordinating the five key values as they related to individuals to other considerations in that case, were that the removal of union membership rights from civil servants was justified by national security (note the use of the term security) considerations. This brings me to the next point in my argument—that state bodies too commonly claim to be entitled to the benefit of the five key values. I shall suggest that this sort of claim is misconceived and abuses the concepts embodied in the five key values.

The analogy between national security and individual security cannot of course be pushed too far—national security and individual security are not the same—but the parallels between the positions of individuals and public bodies are useful, though currently they are causing considerable confusion in English law. In the nature of things public bodies will from time to time seek protection of their own freedom of action (autonomy), their dignity and the respect to which they consider themselves entitled. All too often they will be concerned to protect their own status and security against pressures of public opinion[35] and accountability.

Often, in claiming the benefit of the five key values for themselves, state bodies' motives will be altruistic ones—efficient, effective public administration requires freedom of action, accountability is expensive and impedes administrative efficiency, state security benefits the whole community . . . and so on. I concede that, if this is how the key values are interpreted in relation to bodies exercising public functions, there must be situations when they prevail over the interests of individuals, though there is not the time here to explore what those situations might be. But it is my case that many of the problem areas in public law arise from clashes and confusions between the claims of individuals and of public bodies to the benefit of the key values. In effect the key values are conceptually different when claimed by public as opposed to private bodies. I shall also suggest that there are some parallels in private law, where there are conflicting interests between relatively powerless individuals and relatively more powerful bodies and organisations.

There are two inconsistent strands in the developing case-law in England about the area of state autonomy. Lord Woolf has expressed the view that public bodies, like private bodies, are entitled to a private life—meaning that some of their activities are rightly governed by private law.[36] The *Malone* case of 1979 assumed that state bodies with legal personality that was not explicitly limited in its scope had the same freedom of action as individuals,[37] and

---

[35] This was formerly protected by the law of sedition, now more or less obsolete. See *Entick v. Carrington* (1765) 19 St Tr 1030 for an example of government concerns about the effect on social order of the existence of seditious material, even in private hands and not circulated.
[36] "Public law—Private law: Why the divide? A Personal View" [1986] *PL* 220, 223.
[37] *Malone* v. *Metropolitan Police Commissioner* [1979] Ch 344. See also John Allison's discussion of the law relating to "the state" as being part of the law of persons in his paper in this volume.

thus that they did not have to justify their actions in terms of the public interest—or against any other criteria. That was a case about telephone tapping and the assumption was that, as there was nothing intrinsically unlawful (and in particular nothing tortious) about a telephone tap, a decision to do such a thing could not be subjected to judicial review. In 1993 in the *Hibbit & Saunders* case[38] the court decided that judicial review of the tendering process in contract was not available, even though the tenderer in that case had been treated unfairly by the government department, thus lending support to the principle that public bodies have the same freedom of action and autonomy as private bodies in that area of activity.[39] The whole idea of jurisdiction—the *ultra vires* rule—which has, until recently,[40] been said to lie at the heart of judicial review in England, rests on the view that, within the four corners of its powers,[41] a public body has freedom of action which the courts should not interfere with.

However, the law on the question of the autonomy of public bodies in England is changing. There is now authority for the view that public bodies must justify their actions against recognised criteria, and cannot simply rely on the same freedom of action as individuals can. Laws J. in *R. v. Somerset County Council, ex parte Fewings* in 1995 maintained that:[42]

> "[f]or private persons, the rule is that you may do anything you choose which the law does not prohibit. It means that the freedoms of the private citizen are not conditional upon some distinct and affirmative justification for which he must burrow in the law books. Such a notion would be anathema to our English legal traditions. But for public bodies the rule is opposite, and so of another character altogether. It is that any action to be taken must be justified by positive law. A public body has no heritage of legal rights which it enjoys for its own sake. . . . The rule is necessary in order to protect the people from arbitrary interference by those set in power over them."

It will be noted that this broad statement is not consistent with the decisions in *Malone* and *Hibbit & Saunders*, noted above, but it encapsulates a movement in the law towards the position that public bodies do not have interests of their own or residual, unreviewable freedoms and must justify their actions

---

[38] R. v. *The Lord Chancellor, ex parte Hibbit & Saunders (A firm)* [1993] COD 326; The Times, 12 Mar. 1993.

[39] See also T.C. Daintith, "Regulation by Contract: The New Prerogative" [1979] *Current Legal Problems* 41 and "The Executive Power Today", in J. Jowell and D. Oliver (eds), *The Changing Constitution* (Clarendon Press, Oxford, 3rd ed. 1995); B. V. Harris, "The 'Third Source' of Authority for Government Action" (1992) 108 *LQR* 626.

[40] See De Smith, Woolf and Jowell, above at n. 7, paras 5-041 to 5-043; D. Oliver, "Is the *Ultra Vires* Rule the Basis of Judicial Review?" [1987] *PL* 543; Harris, ibid. Cf. C. Forsyth, "Of Fig Leaves and Fairy Tales: The *Ultra Vires* Doctrine, the Sovereignty of Parliament and Judicial Review" [1996] *CLJ* 122, arguing that the *ultra vires* doctrine remains one of a number of bases for judicial review.

[41] *Associated Provincial Picture Houses Ltd.* v. *Wednesbury Corporation* [1948] 1 KB 223.

[42] [1995] 1 All ER 513, 524. See G. Nardell, "The Quantock Hounds and the Trojan Horse" [1995] *PL* 27.

in terms of the public interest, not their own interests.[43] They are not, in other words, entitled to the benefit of our five key values in their own right.[44]

This is currently the approach in relation to the activities of local authorities, which are normally statutory bodies with explicitly limited powers. Here the courts have been willing to limit their freedom of action by restricting their powers to those expressly granted in enabling legislation, and imposing higher order standards of conduct than they would on ordinary private bodies[45] (though as we shall see private bodies in positions of power are also

[43] On the impropriety of public bodies acting in their own interests see for instance *Padfield v. Minister of Agriculture*, above at n. 15, 1061, per Lord Upjohn (a decision or policy must not be based on political considerations). Cf. *R. v. Waltham Forest London Borough Council, ex parte Baxter* [1987] 3 All ER 671 where a local councillor had voted in accordance with the party line notwithstanding his view that the decision was unreasonable, because he believed that party unity was of great importance in the run up to the general election and he felt that his party's policies were very much in the public interest, even though in this particular respect he thought they were mistaken. Sir John Donaldson M.R. held that it could be proper for a local councillor to take the view that it was in the interests of a local government area that his own party should be returned to office and to vote with that outcome in mind.

The Committee on Standards in Public Life formulated Seven Principles of Public Life, which include duties of selflessness, integrity, objectivity, accountability, openness and honesty which deny the right of public bodies to act in their own interests: above at n. 1, 14. The House of Commons Code of Conduct and Guidelines (H.C. 604, 1995–96), approved by the House of Commons (H.C. Deb., Vol. 282, col. 392, July 24, 1996), endorse these principles. The following documents also reject the idea that public officers or public bodies are entitled to act in their own private interests: the Civil Service Management Code issued under the Civil Service Order in Council 1995, ch. 4, section 4.1, Annex A; the revised *Questions of Procedure for Ministers*, para. 1, published in the Public Service Committee First Special Report: the Government Response to the Second Report from the Committee (Session 1995–96) on Ministerial Accountability and Responsibility, 1996–97 H.C. No. 67, which emphasises the importance of ensuring that there is no conflict between a minister's public duties and private interests; *Guidance to Officials on Drafting Answers to Parliamentary Questions* (see H.L. Deb., 13 Nov. 1996, WA 105).

The Government's position is that "possible embarrassment of Ministers has never been a factor in considering whether information should be made available under the [Code of Practice on Access to Government Information]": H.L. Deb., 13 Nov. 1996, *WA 106*.

[44] See also Wade and Forsyth, above at n. 7, 391–3: "The powers of public authorities are . . . essentially different from those of private persons. A man making his will may, subject to any rights of his dependants, dispose of his property just as he may wish. He may act out of malice or a spirit of revenge, but in law this does not affect his exercise of his power. In the same way, a private person has an absolute power to allow whom he likes to use his land, to release a debtor, or, where the law permits, to evict a tenant, regardless of his motives. This is unfettered discretion. But a public authority may do none of these things unless it acts reasonably and in good faith and upon lawful and relevant grounds of public interest. . . . The whole conception of unfettered discretion is inappropriate to a public authority, which possesses powers solely in order that it may use them for the public good. . . . It is only where powers are given for the personal benefit of the person empowered that the discretion is absolute. Plainly this can have no application in public law". And see M. Taggart, "Corporatisation, Privatisation and Public Law" (1991) 2 PLR 77, 83.

[45] See for instance *R. v. London Borough of Ealing, ex parte Times Newspapers* (1987) 85 LGR 316 (boycotting of newspapers by local authority libraries for political reasons held unlawful); *R. v. Lewisham London Borough Council, ex parte Shell UK Ltd.* [1988] 1 All ER 938 (boycotting of a company's products by a local authority for political reasons held unlawful); *R. v. Brent London Borough Council, ex parte Assegai* (1987) 151 L.G. Review 891 (restriction of access to public areas of local authority buildings held unlawful); *Wheeler v. Leicester City Council* [1985] AC 1054 (withdrawal of licence to use local authority sports field for political reasons held unlawful); *West Glamorgan County Council v. Rafferty* [1987] 1 All ER 1005 (local authority's claim

increasingly subjected to higher duties). This, I suggest, is the better approach. Any freedom of action accorded to public bodies is different in kind—a different concept[46]—from the value of individual autonomy that we are considering in this paper.

The most striking recent example of the courts deciding that public bodies do not have the same rights and freedoms in law as individuals is *Derbyshire County Council* v. *Times Newspapers Ltd.* in which the House of Lords opined that "a democratically elected body should be open to uninhibited criticism. The threat of a civil action for defamation must inevitably have an inhibiting effect on free speech"[47] and held that at common law a local authority did not have the right to maintain an action in defamation to protect its governing reputation, as it would be contrary to the public interest for the organs of government to have that right. Hence the authority in question could not bring an action in defamation—a civil action whose purpose is to protect a person's dignity, respect, status and security in society. The decision applies generally to public bodies—not only elected bodies—exercising governmental and administrative functions, and possibly where a public body is exercising broader functions.[48] It is not clear to what extent the principle may extend to private—or privatised—bodies exercising public functions.[49]

THE PROBLEM OF PUBLIC AND PRIVATE POWER

Although it may be obvious that the state should not benefit from the key values and that it should be placed under higher order duties of good administration,[50]

---

for possession of its land defeated by the failure of the authority to fulfil its statutory duty to provide legitimate sites); *R.* v. *Wear Valley District Council, ex parte Binks* [1985] 2 All ER 699 (local authority's withdrawal of an informal licence to a stall holder to set up on the authority's land was subject to review). And see S. Arrowsmith, "Judicial Review and the Contractual Powers of Local Authorities" (1990) 106 *LQR* 277.

[46] Using "concept" as distinct from "conception", as Dworkin does in *Taking Rights Seriously*, above at n. 18, 134–7. Dworkin illustrates this distinction as follows: (i) there is a difference between a general concept of fairness, and a particular conception of fairness; (ii) the equal protection clause in the United States constitution makes the concept of equality a test of legislation, but it does not stipulate any particular conception of that concept (ibid., 236).

[47] [1993] AC 534, 547, per Lord Keith.

[48] See E. Barendt, "Libel and Freedom of Speech in English Law" [1993] *PL* 449.

[49] In *British Coal* v. *National Union of Mineworkers* (unreported but noted in R. Lewis, "A Sticky Wicket for Fair Comment", The Times, 13 Aug. 1996) French J. halted a defamation action brought by British Coal (formerly the publicly owned National Coal Board) against the National Union of Mineworkers in June 1996 on the ground that the Government exercises close ministerial control over the coal industry and it had operated under a statutory framework since 1946. Together these factors rendered British Coal a public authority of the type Lord Keith had in mind in the *Derbyshire* case.

[50] This expression was used by D.J. Galligan, "Judicial Review and the Textbook Writers" (1982) 2 *OxJLS* 257.

high principles[51] or institutional morality,[52] I suggest that exploring the reasons for confining the benefit of these values to individuals provides some insights into the nature and worth of these values.

Public bodies and private bodies exercising public or governmental functions[53] possess many kinds of power,[54] which do not have direct parallels normally in purely private relationships (but see later discussion on this point). For instance, they have the power to distribute largesse in the form of cash benefits, licences and so on (much of this would fall within Reich's "new property"[55]); they have *de facto* or *de jure* power to punish, either through the criminal justice system or other means—the withdrawal of benefits, for instance;[56] and they have power to win cooperation through persuasion and the authority and legitimacy that they derive from their elected or public status.

The importance of power for public law and constitutional theory is highlighted by McCormick, for instance: "a constitutional theory which focuses exclusively on rights and which ignores the principles and rules regulating powers is a partial and one sided theory". Thus "[i]t is an important task for public lawyers and legal theorists to explicate and elaborate principles of

---

[51] The higher order duties of public bodies were neatly expressed by Simon Brown L.J. in *R. v. Inland Revenue Commissioners, ex parte Unilever plc*, above at n. 10, 695: "It may no doubt be helpful to consider whether a person could in private law act with impunity in the manner complained of as unfair in public law proceedings; people's conduct and relationships are, after all, generally regulated in private law according to accepted tenets of fairness. But one must beware of placing too great reliance upon any suggested parallels: they may mislead more than assist. . . . Public authorities in general . . . are required to act in a high-principled way, on occasions being subject to a stricter duty of fairness than would apply as between private citizens". Simon Brown L.J. went on to refer to Lord Mustill's reference in *R. v. Inland Revenue Commissioners, ex parte Matrix-Securities Ltd.* [1994] 1 WLR 334, 358 to "the spirit of fair dealing which should inspire the whole of public life".

[52] The phrase used by J.L. Jowell in "The Rule of Law Today", in Jowell and Oliver, above at n. 39.

[53] Judicial review extends to such bodies and functions: *R. v. Panel on Take-overs and Mergers, ex parte Datafin plc* [1987] QB 815 (hereafter referred to as *Datafin*); *R. v. Disciplinary Committee of the Jockey Club, ex parte Aga Khan* [1993] 2 All ER 853 (hereafter referred to as *Aga Khan*). See Wade and Forsyth, above at n. 7, 659–67; De Smith, Woolf and Jowell, above at n. 7, paras. 3-023 to 3.054; Craig op. cit., 562–77.

[54] J.K. Galbraith's *Anatomy of Power* (Houghton Mifflin, Boston, 1983) analyses state and private power very illuminatingly. The sources of power that he lists are property, personality and organisation. The state generally has access to these more than private bodies. The instruments of power are compensatory (i.e. the ability to secure compliance through the use of rewards or the allocation of benefits, which the state employs in many ways), condign (the use of punishment, again more at the disposal of the state than of private organisations) and conditioned power (the power that derives from public attitudes and acceptance that certain bodies ought to be obeyed).

[55] C.A. Reich, "The New Property" (1964) 73 *Yale LJ* 733.

[56] See, e.g., *Wheeler v. Leicester City Council*, above at n. 45, in which the council withdrew access to a sports practice ground from a rugby club to punish it for not endorsing the council's policy on apartheid. Lord Roskill held the decision to be unlawful because it punished the club when it had done nothing wrong. See also *R. v. Lewisham London Borough Council, ex parte Shell UK Ltd.*, above at n. 45; *R. v. London Borough Council, ex parte Times Newspapers*, above at n. 45; De Smith, Woolf and Jowell, above at n. 7, para. 3-042.

reasonableness governing the pursuit of public policy".[57] Their power and the imbalance between such bodies and private individuals justifies in large part the imposition of higher order duties on public bodies and other organisations exercising public functions. It also, I suggests, leads to the imposition of restrictions and higher order duties on powerful private bodies or parties to relationships.

For the most part the higher order duties of procedural propriety, illegality (in its special public law sense) and rationality that are imposed on state bodies and those exercising public functions do not have a *direct* parallel in duties imposed on private bodies. But it would be wrong to suppose that there are no parallels.[58] In the case of privately-owned utilities and their provision of services to the public there is often a public law or public policy element in the legal regime. The common law has recognised in the past the special duties that should be imposed on "common callings" and owners of monopolies whose modern equivalent may be the, now privatised, utilities.[59] These doctrines are, I understand, alive and thriving in some common law jurisdictions. The problems posed by monopolistic utilities are met to some extent by provision for statutory regulation and other forms of control and accountability. There is, in sum, a body of law that imposes higher order duties on powerful monopolistic or public service providing private bodies.

However, the common law, as it evolves in England,[60] is encountering problems in the relationship between judicial review and contract. English courts have adopted the default position that judicial review is not generally the appropriate procedure or remedy where the relationship between the parties is contractual or precontractual.[61] However, this does not seem to preclude judicial review where the respondent body's contracting powers derive directly or indirectly[62] from statute.

---

[57] McCormick, above at n. 25, 20.

[58] See Sir Gordon Borrie, "The Regulation of Public and Private Power" [1989] *PL* 552 and P. Finn, "Controlling the Exercise of Power" (1996) 7 *PLR* 86.

[59] See P. Craig, "Constitutions, Property and Regulation" [1991] *PL* 538; M. Taggart, "Public Utilities and Public Law", in P.A. Joseph (ed.), *Essays on the Constitution* (Brooker's, Wellington, 1995), 214; Forsyth, above at n. 40; De Smith, Woolf and Jowell, above at n. 7, paras. 3–11 and 3–1; A.W.B. Simpson, *A History of the Common Law of Contract: The Rise of the Action of Assumpsit* (Clarendon Press, Oxford, 1975); *Harris* v. *Dackwood* (1810) 3 Taunt 264; B. McAllister, "Lord [sic] Hale and Business Affected with a Public Interest" (1929–30) 43 *Harv LR* 759.

[60] The problems in Scotland are less serious, as the availability of a supervisory jurisdiction does not depend on whether a question is a matter of public or private law: see *West* v. *Secretary of State for Scotland* 1992 SLT 636 (which decided that the supervisory jurisdiction in Scotland is not available in respect of contractual relations); W.J. Wolffe, "The Scope of Judicial Review in Scots Law" [1992] *PL* 625; Lord Clyde, "The Nature of the Supervisory Jurisdiction and the Public/Private Distinction in Scots Administrative Law", in W. Finnie, C.M.G. Himsworth and N. Walker (eds), *Edinburgh Essays in Public Law* (Edinburgh University Press, Edinburgh, 1991); see De Smith, Woolf and Jowell, above at n. 7, para. 3–011; Wade and Forsyth, above at n. 7, 666–7.

[61] See for instance *GCHQ*, above at n. 5.

[62] See the position in relation to local government, text accompanying n. 45 above. See also Murray Hunt's paper in this volume.

The courts are getting round the exclusion of contractual relations from the supervisory jurisdiction by imposing similar duties, enforceable in contract instead of through the application for judicial review, on contractual relationships[63] or by focusing on the public or governmental functions that may underpin a private body's activities,[64] or by invoking common law doctrines such as restraint of trade.[65] These matters are considered at length in other papers in this volume.[66]

Where there is an imbalance of power in relationships, and especially where the more powerful party can act in ways that reduce the dignity, autonomy, respect, security and status of the less powerful party, then the law (usually statute rather than the common law) does commonly impose higher order duties on the superior. Tony Honoré explored the statutory trends in the fields of landlord and tenant, employment and marriage in his Hamlyn lectures of 1982, and brings out the common thread of a desire to provide security for weaker parties in these relationships.[67]

UNDERLYING VALUES IN PRIVATE LAW: FROM THE LAW OF PERSONS TO THE LAW OF RELATIONSHIPS

There are strong similarities between the development of judicial review and the law of relationships. They have in common *de facto* and, to a much reduced extent, *de jure* imbalances of power. We can draw some parallels in this context with Sir Henry Maine's discussion of the move from status (or "the Law of Persons"[68]) to contract. Between status and contract lies autonomy.

In employment law, for instance, there are elaborate statutory requirements of procedural propriety before an employee can be dismissed, involving the giving of warnings and reasons, and possible appeal against dismissal to an

---

[63] See Oliver, above at n. 40. For cases see *Herring* v. *Templeman* [1973] 3 All ER 569; *Glynn* v. *Keele University* [1971] 1 WLR 487; *Edwards* v. *SOGAT* [1971] Ch 354; *Breen* v. *AEU* [1971] 2 QB 175; *Lapointe* v. *L'Association de Bienfaisance et de Retraite de la Police de Montreal* [1906] AC 535; *Pharmaceutical Society of Great Britain* v. *Dickson* [1970] AC 403. See also the papers by David Mullan and Janet McLean in this volume, and *Lakeside Colony of Hutterian Brethren* v. *Hofer* [1992] 3 SCR 165. For the parallels in the position in the United States see the paper by Jack Beermann in this volume: broadly the requirements are that the body should follow a fair procedure, comply with its own rules and show a plausible basis for its decision.

[64] *Datafin*, above at n. 53; *Aga Khan*, above at n. 53.

[65] See *Nagle* v. *Feilden* [1966] 2 QB 633. For the imposition of other higher duties outside contract in private relationships, see *Edwards* v. *SOGAT*, above at n. 63. See also De Smith, Woolf and Jowell, above at n. 7, para. 13-040.

[66] See the papers by David Mullan, Janet McLean and Alison Harvison Young.

[67] T. Honoré, *The Quest for Security: Employees, Tenants, Wives* (Stevens & Sons, London, 1982). He focuses on the vulnerability of the dependant parties to these relationships and explores the extent to which society gives them greater security.

[68] On the importance of the law of persons in the English legal system's failure to develop a concept of the state see John Allison's paper in this volume.

Industrial Tribunal. We can see here, I think, a mechanism to protect the five key values for the benefit of employees, which stems partly from the importance of a person's job to that person and their place and status in society, and partly from the fact of a hierarchical relationship in which there is an imbalance of power between employer and employee.

Where disputes about children and their upbringing arise, children are now in principle entitled to make their own decisions once they have achieved a sufficient degree of maturity and intelligence to do so.[69] If such decisions are taken to the courts, children now have rights to have their ascertainable wishes and feelings taken into account.[70] Parents are no longer regarded as simply having rights arising out of their relationship with their children, but parental responsibilities too.[71]

In marriage, wives have obtained autonomy in relations with their husbands through the rejection of the doctrine of unity (at common law husband and wife were one and the one they were was the husband[72]), the criminalisation of marital rape,[73] the introduction of separate property and equal rights—now responsibilities—for parents in respect of their children.

The transformation of these relationships,[74] once carrying duties of allegiance (in the case of husbands and wives and employers and employees[75]) and obedience on one side and rights of control (almost ownership) on the other, has been obtained through concepts such as the right not to be subjected to physical violence (including marital rape and chastisement), the right to be treated reasonably, the right to assert autonomy within the relationship, the control of the exercise of power by the more powerful party in a hierarchical relationship and the right of exit from the relationship. So the law now generally imposes, by a combination of statute and case-law, duties on the stronger party to consult the weaker party and listen to their views, and duties of reasonableness, so that the less powerful party is not arbitrarily deprived

---

[69] *Gillick* v. *West Norfolk Area Health Authority and the Department of Social Security* [1986] AC 112.

[70] Children Act 1989, s. 1(3)(a) and (4).

[71] Children Act 1989, s. 2. By s. 3 of the Act "parental responsibility" means "all the rights, duties, powers, responsibility and authority which by law a parent of a child has in relation to the child and his property".

[72] 2 *Blackstone's Commentaries on the Laws of England* (1765–69), ch. 15, 441: "By marriage the husband and wife are one person in law: that is the very being and legal existence of the woman is suspended during the marriage, or at least is incorporated and consolidated into that of the husband".

[73] *R.* v. *R.* [1991] 4 All ER 481.

[74] I have discussed this set of similarities in D. Oliver, "What is Happening to Relations between the Individual and the State?", in Jowell and Oliver, above at n. 59. See also D. Oliver and D. Heater, *The Foundations of Citizenship* (Harvester Wheatsheaf, London, 1994).

[75] See 4 *Blackstone's Commentaries*, above at n. 72, ch. 14, 203: ". . . the breach of civil or ecclesiastical connections, when coupled with murder, denominates it a new offence, no less than a species of treason, called *parva proditio*, or *petit treason*: which however is nothing else but an aggravated degree of murder; although on account of the violation of private allegiance, it is stigmatised as an inferior species of treason. . . . Petit treason . . . may happen three ways; by a servant killing his master, a wife her husband, or an ecclesiastical person his superior".

of the social status and security derived from the relationship and, at the same time, can retain their dignity, autonomy and respect within the relationship.

I think we can detect a similar historical trend where there is an imbalance of power in relations between the state and individuals. The move from parental rights to parental responsibility is mirrored in public law: it is now a matter of responsibility for the state to take the interests of individuals into account when making decisions, where once decisions were a matter of right deriving from sovereignty and authority. At common law the relationships between master and servant, parent and child, husband and wife were microcosms, in some respects, of that between the King and the subject: obedience—allegiance—was owed by the person in subjection to the superior or sovereign in each of these relationships.[76] The legal progression from that position in private relationships has been through emancipation of the "subject" to, now, the imposition of higher duties of consideration and respect—responsibilities—on the superior, and recognition that the former "subject" or weaker party to the relationship has a rightful place in society at large.[77]

The weaker party is thus no longer solely dependent for his or her status and security on the personal relationship with employer, spouse, parent, even, on this set of analogies, with the state. Each person is entitled to rely to a considerable extent on the legal and social recognition of their worth as individuals. This is reflected, for instance, in the rules of natural justice—whether at common law or imposed by statute (as in the employment protection field)—especially the rule against bias, which depersonalises the relationship between the individual and the superior party in the relationship.

Instead of the former hierarchical relationships between superiors at various levels and their "subjects", all individuals are now recognised as sovereigns without subjects, and responsibilities are imposed at large and between equals, taking due account of imbalances of power. This change in the legal basis of relationships is brought about and sustained by rights to participate in decision-making for the weaker or inferior party.

Thus what were once relationships of subjection at common law have moved to emancipation. In practice duties of procedural propriety, legality and rationality are imposed through the jurisdiction of the courts to deal with disputes between husbands and wives, employers and employees, parents and children, and, where necessary, to terminate or adjust relationships.

---

[76] Blackstone describes the relationship between King and subject as follows: ". . . allegiance, . . . the tie or *ligamen* which binds every subject to be true and faithful to his sovereign *liege* lord the king, in return for that protection which is afforded him". The duties of allegiance to the sovereign were protected by the criminal law of treason: 4 *Blackstone's Commentaries*, ibid., ch. 6, 74. For the position in relation to private relationships see previous note.

[77] Note, for instance, the former legal position of women as summarised in *Beresford-Hope* v. *Lady Sandhurst* (1889) 23 QB 79, 95, per Lord Esher M.R.: "I take it that by neither the common law nor the constitution of this country from the beginning of the common law until now can a woman be entitled to exercise any public function". The Sex Disqualification (Removal) Act 1919 removed most of the disabilities, and anti-discrimination legislation prohibits most forms of sex discrimination.

In other relationships, when undue influence exists between a stronger and a weaker party, the trend is for the law to impose a duty on the superior to take "reasonable steps" to ensure that the potentially improperly pressured party is properly advised.[78]

These are examples, I suggest, not just of emancipation but of the democratisation of relationships and of decision-making and dispute resolution. Hence in these areas of private law we can detect, I suggest, the growth of acceptance of the five key values to the benefit of the former "subjects" and the imposition of some higher duties on the superior party in the relationship which resemble those that are placed on public bodies, and which are designed to promote the key values.

It would be misleading to exaggerate the extent of the law's recognition of a person's autonomy in family-type situations. Although husbands and parents have lost much of their power over their families, the courts have been willing to interfere with the autonomy of minors and wives in various ways. Courts have ordered that a sixteen year old anorexic girl be subjected to treatment she did not wish to have[79] and that a pregnant woman in labour should have her baby delivered by Caesarian section against her will to save her and the child.[80] Such examples could be multiplied. What is happening, though, is that the courts are feeling their way towards a balance in favour of autonomy, dignity and respect on a case by case basis, often having difficulties resolving very hard choices between paternalism and autonomy on the way.

UNDERLYING VALUES IN PRIVATE LAW: PROPERTY LAW

In property law, as in public law, imbalances of power can pose threats to the five key values for the less powerful parties in property relationships.[81] I would say a strong underlying value in land law is that the security and status of individuals in society that flows from their property-related rights, ought to be protected by the law. This has led to the development of a number of protective doctrines. Property law is not, or not only, concerned with Hayekian freedom and the market. It is also commonly concerned about the intrinsic worth of individuals—hence the development of legal protection of new, unorthodox, rights of occupation of land, especially the matrimonial or other home, via equitable doctrines, constructive trusts, licences and so on (as well as through statutory measures such as the Family Law Act 1996 Part IV protection against violence, and Rent Act security of tenure). These may be

---

[78] *Barclays Bank* v. *O'Brien* [1994] AC 180.
[79] *In re W (A minor) (Medical treatment: court's jurisdiction)* [1992] 3 WLR 758.
[80] *In re S (Adult: refusal of treatment)* [1992] 3 WLR 806.
[81] R. Cotterrell, "The Law of Property and Legal Theory", in Twining, above at n. 20, 94.

seen to afford security to those whose occupation of the home is at risk. This security has been granted either by developing the common law of property rights for the benefit of the person whose security is threatened,[82] or by limiting what were believed to be the property rights of those in a position to damage that security.[83] These devices are not generally concerned to give the occupier the benefit of the exchange value of the property in question,[84] but to protect his or her security. In many respects they resemble the administrative law doctrine of legitimate expectation.

Here, as in many areas of the law, lessons are to be learned about weighing up the positive and negative implications of giving security to some at the expense of the interests of others. For many years the statutory security of tenure offered to tenants under the Rent Acts led to a shortage of rented property, possibly to the disadvantage of many in the class of people for whose benefit it was introduced.[85] This point illustrates how the key values are only part of the backdrop against which legal policy is developed and have to be weighed against other considerations.

By way of further example of the importance of property law for individuals, the underlying value of trust law, I suggest, is concern for the status and security of the beneficiaries: it extends protection to legitimate expectations of status and security that arise when property is settled on beneficiaries. To the extent that trust law also binds settlors and trustees it involves the idea that if, by their actions, they create legitimate expectations, then generally they ought not to disappoint them. In this field some duties akin to those imposed on public decision makers may be imposed on trustees—for instance the duty to avoid conflicts of interest and to weigh up the interests of beneficiaries, in effect to take relevant considerations into account and to disregard irrelevant considerations: these are very close to the *Wednesbury* reasonableness duties imposed in public law.

The significance of concepts of property for security and status is acknowledged in Reich's adoption of the term "property" in his essay on "The New Property", in which the term is applied to state benefits on which individuals rely for their security—licences, cash payments, government contracts and so on.[86]

---

[82] For example, the constructive trust interest in the home of spouses and cohabitants who are not on the legal title.
[83] See, for instance, the development of the doctrine of detrimental reliance in constructive trusts and proprietary estoppel: *Lloyds Bank plc* v. *Rosset* [1991] 1 AC 107; and see A. Lawson, "Detrimental Reliance in the Family Home" (1996) 16 *Legal Studies* 218.
[84] See Cotterrell, above at n. 81, 81–98.
[85] This is one of the issues considered by Honoré, above at n. 67.
[86] Reich, above at n. 55.

UNDERLYING VALUES IN PRIVATE LAW: THE LAW OF OBLIGATIONS

The law of tort is also concerned with protecting[87] the plaintiff's autonomy, status and security against interference and restoring the status quo ante so far as possible if damage has been suffered. Specific torts very obviously protect social status (defamation[88]), security (interference with contract, negligence resulting in financial loss) and autonomy and dignity in privacy (nuisance and trespass to land). Autonomy and dignity are also protected by the torts of false imprisonment, assault and battery, and negligence resulting in personal injury. It is significant in my view that the protection of the law of nuisance has recently been extended to enable those who occupy property as their home to sue,[89] so that the tort now protects security and respect for the home life of others, in a wider way than when the tort was linked to ownership and other formal interests in land.

It is also significant that injunctions have been granted in nuisance actions to protect privacy-type rights, even though as yet an explicit right to privacy has not been acknowledged. Birks suggests that a tort of contemptuous harassment (having many of the elements of privacy) is currently developing in the case law. Using as his starting points the cases of *Khorasandjian* v. *Bush*[90] (in which a person who had been the victim of harassment was held entitled to an injunction) and *Kaye* v. *Robertson*[91] (in which an actor who had been photographed while in intensive care was held entitled to an injunction against publication of the photos and story) Birks suggests that the common law as it has developed in England recognises the equivalent of the Roman law delict *iniuria*, a tort of "contemptuous harassment" which protects an individual's right to equality of respect. He adopts Hobbes' comment[92] that "[c]ontempt is when a man thinks another of little worth in comparison to himself".[93] This, Birks suggests, is the essence of the lack of respect that is protected by the evolving tort.

---

[87] Tony Weir has commented that "tort law is protective" (comparing tort with contract, which is "productive"): T. Weir, "Complex Liabilities", in A. Tunc (ed.), *International Encyclopedia of Comparative Law: Volume XI; Torts* (J.C.B. Mohr, Tübingen, 1983), para. 12–6.

[88] A statement is defamatory if it lowers a person "in the estimation of right-thinking members of society generally": *Sim* v. *Stretch* (1936) 52 TLR 669.

[89] *Hunter* v. *Canary Wharf Ltd.* [1996] 2 WLR 348, 365, per Pill L.J. (a substantial link between the person enjoying the use and the land on which he or she is enjoying it is essential but occupation of property as a home does confer on the occupant a capacity to sue in private nuisance). This approach has the merit of avoiding inconsistencies, e.g., between members of a family as occupiers.

[90] [1993] QB 727.

[91] [1991] FSR 62.

[92] The Whole Art of Rhetoric, II.2 (Sir William Molesworth, ed. *The English Works of Thomas Hobbes*, London 1840, vol. 6, 452).

[93] Birks, above at n. 30, 54.

Underlying Values of Public Law 239

In contract, as in trusts, the concern is often to fulfil legitimate expectations or reliance interests created in the plaintiff by the defendant:[94] in different ways both of these protect security. This is particularly clear in the field of promissory and proprietary estoppel, for instance. Here there is a strong parallel with the development of legitimate expectations as a ground for review in judicial review.

In the field of company law, the concern again is, through the contract in the articles of association, to fulfil the expectations of shareholders and to protect third parties in relationships with the company whose interests are affected by its activities. Clearly security is an underlying value here. These values are protected by the contract-based participation rights of shareholders and the rights to information about the company of third parties. Of course the legal position here is far from perfect, but I would say nonetheless that these are important values underlying the legal regime in company law.

We see these recurring values of autonomy, protection of status and security and fulfilment of legitimate expectations reflected not only in the causes of action in each of these areas of law but also in the defences available. Defences of undue influence and duress protect autonomy and the status, security, respect and dignity of the weaker party to a relationship. Self-defence protects the defendant's autonomy, status and security. Both prevent abuses of power.

It would of course be wrong to overstate the case that the five key values underlie private law—just as it would be wrong to exaggerate the pervasiveness of these values in public law. In private law privacy, the most obvious way in which rights to dignity, autonomy and respect could be protected, is undeveloped, but developing.[95] Duress, undue influence, promissory estoppel are also in a relatively raw state of development. Marital rape became a crime only in 1991.[96] My argument is, however, that the common law—and to an extent statute law[97]—is moving fairly steadily in the direction of our five key values in both public and private law.

CONCLUSIONS: TOWARDS DEMOCRACY, PARTICIPATION AND CITIZENSHIP

Having established, I hope, that there is this set of common underlying values in public and private law, and having established also that they help to protect individuals against imbalances of public and private power—and to that

---

[94] See L.L. Fuller and W.R. Perdue, "The Reliance Interest in Contract Damages" (1936) 46 *Yale LJ* 52 and 373; H. Collins, "Contract and Legal Theory", in Twining, above at n. 20, 136; B.S. Markesinis and S. F. Deakin, *Tort Law* (Clarendon Press, Oxford, 3rd ed. 1994), 10.

[95] See Birks, above at n. 30, 54.

[96] R. v. R. [1991] 4 All ER 481.

[97] For instance, the reform of divorce law; and the law relating to relations between parents and children has been radically reformed by statute in recent years and the trend has been strongly in favour of the five key values.

limited extent promote equality[98]—I want to suggest that the five underlying key values we have identified together contribute to, even to a large extent constitute, important *paramount* values, namely democracy, participation and citizenship.

It is my view that a very important development has been the grafting of principles[99] that protect the status and security of individuals in society on to the old case-law and common law principles that protect individuals' rights as autonomous, emancipated individuals. In the field of public law this is especially obvious in the rules of procedural propriety—fairness, natural justice and, of vital importance, procedural legitimate expectations. These principles associated with procedural propriety enable individuals to participate in decisions that are made about their own interests, and they impose accountability on the decision-maker, especially where reasons have to be given for decisions. In private law relationships too, participatory devices protect security—for instance in the statutory requirements for due process to be followed before an employee is dismissed.

These participatory devices protect individuals from having their jobs, their right to earn a living, their family, their privacy, their use of their income, their membership of organisations of civil society and so on, taken from them arbitrarily. This protection implies respect for individuals and for their status and security in society. With security and status go a stake in society. Hence, the development of administrative law (and some private law) requirements that enable people to protect their own status and security protects, among other things, their ability to be participating citizens.

The judicial review cases on illegality and irrationality, including substantive legitimate expectations, also protect the position of the individual in the community, by preventing arbitrary interference with the status quo, discrimination and so on. The protection of expectations in certain parts of private law, for instance contract and trusts, also protects the position of individuals.

In private law, especially tort, but in family, discrimination and employment law too, the increasing protection of the dignity, autonomy and respect of individuals in ways referred to earlier, especially those in weak positions, promotes social solidarity by making it illegitimate to treat sections of the community as inferior.

I suggest that we can detect a movement in the common law (and to an extent in statute law) in these developments towards a notion of citizenship, not only in a political sense but also in a civic and social sense, operating on private relationships and private social organisations through the parallel private law doctrines.

In other areas too public law is developing a concept of participating citizenship. The relaxation of the rules on standing to apply for judicial review

---

[98] See Murray Hunt's paper in this volume.
[99] On the meaning of principles and their relationship with values see text accompanying note 20 above.

enables organisations of civil society such as trade unions, charities and campaigning organisations to challenge the legality of government action.[100] This, I suggest, is a new frontier, a new value that public law is developing. My own sense is that the courts are taking on a role as a forum for political debate and settlement of disputes with a political dimension—a Grand Inquest of the Nation forum—in response to the increasingly obvious inability and unwillingness of the House of Commons to do so.

But participation at a more abstract level—not participation in particular decisions that affect the participating individual, but participation (if it wishes) by the populus generally, in the political process and the "public culture"[101]—is facilitated by some of the five key values and their expression in law, especially in the exercise of freedoms of association and speech.

This extension of recognition of the importance of participation beyond politics and into public culture is, I suggest, part of citizenship in the sense of participation in civil society. Here the comments by Marshall,[102] that citizenship involves "the right to share to the full in the social heritage and to live the life of a civilised being according to the standards prevailing in society" emphasise the breadth of citizenship. Recognition of the importance of this element of the place of the individual in society establishes the links between citizenship and the values of autonomy, dignity and respect. These values are not simply about the importance of the individual qua atomistic person, but are very much associated with the importance of the individual's place in society generally. This, I suggest, is acknowledged in rights to free speech and association in public and private life, which are justified partly by the interests of the individual,[103] but rest also on the public interest in participatory citizenship.[104]

---

[100] R. v. *Inland Revenue Commissioners, ex parte National Federation of Self-Employed and Small Businesses* [1982] AC 617; R. v. *Social Services Secretary, ex parte Child Poverty Action Group* [1990] 1 QB 540; R. v. *Secretary of State for Employment, ex parte Equal Opportunities Commission* [1993] 1 All ER 1022; R. v. *Inspectorate of Pollution, ex parte Greenpeace Ltd. (No. 2)* [1994] 4 All ER 329; R. v. *Secretary of State for the Home Department, ex parte Fire Brigades Union* [1995] 2 WLR 464; R. v. *Secretary of State for Foreign Affairs, ex parte World Development Movement Ltd.* [1995] 1 All ER 611; and see De Smith, Woolf and Jowell, above at n. 7, ch. 2, esp. para. 2–119; Craig, above at n. 7., 489–98; P. Cane, "Standing Up for the Public" [1995] *PL* 276.

[101] To borrow a phrase used by Raz in "Free Expression and Personal Identification" (1991) 11 *OxJLS* 301, 302, in the context of free speech: "[Free speech] is essentially a right actively to participate in and contribute to the public culture".

[102] Marshall, above at n. 34.

[103] For instance, the interests of individuals in having the opportunity, by expressing their views, of having their ways of life validated, thus giving them what Raz calls "the stamp of public acceptability" (above at n. 101, 311) and what I would call dignity and respect. Public acceptability also allows the individuals whose way of life is accepted to feel part of society and thus to feel that they are citizens. "People's relations to the society in which they live is a major component in their personal well-being. It is normally vital for personal prosperity that one will be able to identify with one's society, will not be alienated from it, will feel a full member of it" (Raz, ibid., 313).

[104] See E. Barendt, *Freedom of Speech* (Clarendon Press, Oxford, 1985); Raz, ibid., 309; and J.H. Ely, *Democracy and Distrust: A Theory of Judicial Review* (Harvard University Press, Cambridge, 1980).

So, to summarise, it is my case that the five key values operate increasingly in both public and private law, and that they underpin three paramount values of democracy, participation and citizenship which operate widely, but not as yet universally, across large tracts of the common law. They are also reflected in much of the statutory overlay of case-law. They have to contend with other considerations in the development of the law, but they are an important frontier and driving force or motor for the development of the law.

12

Criminal Justice from the Bottom-up: Some Thoughts on Police Rulemaking Processes

HUDSON JANISCH AND RON LEVI*

"The role of racial minorities in the development of justice policy will continue to be *ad hoc* until a strategy is developed that teaches the government and the public the differences between provision of information, consultation and collaboration with stakeholders in developing justice reforms.

There is no one correct method of consulting with the public in the development of justice policy. The sheer variety of policies and circumstances calls for a more sophisticated approach to this area. . . . With the limited resources and support that many community groups have, consultation with them must be efficient and effective, if they are not to be exhausted through perpetual consultation with government."[1]

INTRODUCTION

This paper grapples with a potential interface between administrative and criminal law. In the Canadian context, cross-pollination between the two areas has been limited. It is our belief, however, that the time has come to straddle the divide, and to engage teachers, students and practitioners of criminal and administrative law in thinking about traditional areas from new perspectives. While there are many potential interfaces between administrative and criminal law, we have chosen to consider the application of rulemaking in the context of policing. It is the police who, on a daily basis, administer criminal justice systems; police officers' roles in crime control and law enforcement symbolise social control and legal accountability. We believe that the key to reform in this area lies in the rulemaking process, itself a

---

* We are grateful for the insightful and constructive comments of Mr. Justice David Doherty of the Court of Appeal of Ontario, and for Philip Stenning's thoughtful comments on this topic.

[1] Commission on Systemic Racism in the Ontario Criminal Justice System, "Participation by Racial Community Groups in Criminal Justice Policy Development" (Draft Working Paper) by Scott & Aylen, Barristers and Solicitors (21 Dec. 1993), 102.

burgeoning concept in contemporary Canadian administrative law.[2] The express goal of this paper is to rekindle debates surrounding police rulemaking. At the same time, it represents an initial foray for us into this area. This project is intended to draw from, and build upon, fundamental values of administrative law, in an effort to integrate various groups in criminal justice policy-making. Our proposals closely mirror Dawn Oliver's synthesis of paramount legal values, notably "democracy, citizenship and participation".[3]

THE NATURE OF THE PROBLEMATIC: PERCEPTIONS OF CRIMINAL JUSTICE

At a fundamental level, accountability in the criminal justice system speaks to the limits of the rule of law, the institutional relationships between courts and administrators of the criminal process, and the interaction between democratic accountability, public confidence and legitimacy. As Stuart has observed, "[i]t is the very essence of democracy and the rule of law that state power not be autocratic".[4] Recently, Canadian public consciousness has shifted toward an analysis of the latent dynamics of this interaction. The widely publicised trial of Paul Bernardo in Toronto, along with the controversial plea agreement entered into by Karla Homolka, have engendered public cynicism about the discretion afforded to those engaged in crime control. This "profound and widely felt sense of public disquiet",[5] leading to the Report of Mr. Justice Galligan on plea bargaining, that of Mr. Justice Campbell on the conduct of the police forces involved in the investigation, as well a legislative attempt to rescind the controversial plea agreement itself, evidences the public's desire for controls and information regarding the extensive discretion of these state agents. The wrongful convictions of Guy Paul Morin and Donald Marshall Jr., the Manitoba Aboriginal Justice Inquiry and the conclusions of the Ontario Task Force on systemic racism in the justice system, have reinforced underlying apprehension regarding the lack of control and review of police and prosecutors.[6] These are

---

[2] See generally J.M. Evans, H.N. Janisch, David J. Mullan and R.C.B. Risk, *Administrative Law: Cases, Text, and Materials*, (Emond Montgomery Publishing Ltd., Toronto, 4th ed. 1995) ch. 4 (hereafter referred to as Evans *et al.*).

[3] See Dawn Oliver's paper in this volume.

[4] D. Stuart, "Policing Under the Charter", in R.C. Macleod and D. Schneiderman (eds), *Police Powers in Canada: The Evolution and Practice of Authority* (University of Toronto Press, Toronto, 1994), 75, 78.

[5] *Report of the Honourable Patrick T. Galligan Appointed to Inquire Into and Report on Certain Matters Relating to Two Decisions Respecting Karla Homolka Made by Officials in the Ministry of the Attorney-General* (Ministry of the Attorney-General, Toronto, 1996), 7.

[6] For more information see ibid.; *Bernardo Investigation Review: Report of Mr. Justice Archie Campbell* (Ministry of the Solicitor-General and Correctional Services, Toronto, 1996); Bill S-11, An Act Concerning one Karla Homolka, 1st Sess., 35th Parl., 1995 (1st reading 17 Oct. 1995, died on the order paper 2 Feb. 1996); *R. v. Morin* (1995) 37 C.R. (4th) 395 (Ont. C.A.); Nova Scotia,

"old",[7] yet recurring, problems, which tend only to be thought about when "the wheel comes off".[8]

Heightened public consciousness regarding criminal justice often leads to a (mis)perception that criminal justice administrators rule by fiat; the exercise of discretion, and the inevitable implementation of discretionary law and institutions, is commonly perceived as a shift away from a legal regime based upon certainty and predictability. In such cases, the reality that "ours is a government of [individuals] . . . who use laws"[9] becomes harshly evident. In the context of policing specifically, the public, the courts and the police must all determine the ambit of shifting police powers:[10]

> "The steady rise in crime rates, combined with dramatic media spectacles at home (Oka) and elsewhere (the Rodney King episode), have eroded public confidence in the police to a degree unprecedented in this century. At the same time the Canadian Charter of Rights and Freedoms has raised new questions about police powers, casting doubts on practices of long standing. . . . *[Canadians] are unaccustomed to thinking about what our police should or should not do in very precise terms.*"

Changes in the policing environment—including population, demographic, technological and fiscal changes—have prompted the Ontario Ministry of the Solicitor-General to host a recent session regarding the review of police services in an attempt to achieve a new structure and organisation of policing.[11] Despite strides being made toward implementing various conceptions of "community policing",[12] relations between police and citizens continue to be strained:[13]

> "[Preliminary consultations of the Ontario Task Force on Systemic Racism showed] that concerns about systemic racism in police practices remain widespread and are deeply felt. . . . [The Task Force] also found considerable suspicion of community policing, especially among black and other racial youths. Many feel excluded from

---

Royal Commission on the Donald Marshall, Jr, Prosecution, *Commissioners' Report: Findings and Recommendations* (Nova Scotia Government Printer, Halifax, 1989) (Chair: T.A. Hickman; Commissioners: L.A. Poitras and G.T. Evans); Manitoba, *Public Inquiry into the Administration of Justice and Aboriginal People* (Queen's Printer, Winnipeg, 1991) (Commissioners: A.C. Hamilton and C.M. Sinclair); *Commission on Systemic Racism in the Ontario Criminal Justice System* (Queen's Printer, Toronto, 1995) (Co-chairs: D.P. Cole and M. Gittens) (hereafter referred to as *Commission on Systemic Racism*).

[7] This refers to G.H. Williams, "Police Rulemaking Revisited: Some New Thoughts on an Old Problem" (1984) 47(4) *Law & Contemp Probs* 123.

[8] R. Reiner, *The Politics of the Police* (University of Toronto Press, Toronto, 2nd ed. 1992), 4.

[9] R.V. Ericson, "Rules For Police Deviance", in C.D. Shearing (ed.), *Organizational Police Deviance: Its Structure and Control* (Butterworths, Toronto, 1981), 83, 85.

[10] "Introduction" in Macleod and Schneiderman, above at n. 4, xi (emphasis added).

[11] Ontario, Ministry of the Solicitor-General and Correctional Services, *Review of Police Services in Ontario: A Framework for Discussion* (May 1996), 20–21.

[12] The notion of "community policing" is quite vague. It "is a plastic concept, meaning different things to different people": see J.E. Eck and D.P. Rosenbaum, "The New Police Order: Effectiveness, Equity and Efficiency in Community Policing", in D.P. Rosenbaum (ed.), *The Challenge of Community Policing: Testing the Promises* (Sage, California, 1994), 3.

[13] *Commission on Systemic Racism*, above at n. 6.

the co-operative partnerships with the police that community policing envisages; they fear that racial equality is not on the community policing agenda."

At its root, this paper addresses accountability. Yet, while much reform has been focussed upon *ex post* mechanisms, this paper argues for a proactive understanding through "rulemaking". Rulemaking's essence is in "lay[ing] down a norm of conduct of general application", unlimited to an adjudicative-style concern "with the immediate parties to a particular dispute".[14] The benefits of rulemaking are both the enactment of the rule and the consultative element in the rule's formulation. In the policing context, where a plethora of top-down standards, guidelines and policies are already in place, the innovation may be more procedural than substantive; as noted by Max Radin, procedure may well be the essence of law.[15] In realising democratic norms, the procedural is an archway to the substantive. The complexity of discretion and enforcement of criminal justice requires a multi-faceted, interdisciplinary approach. This paper is intended to provoke further research in this area by surveying major elements to consider in the policing context, even if at times briefly. It is hoped that academics, judges, and policy-makers will continue to explore this nexus of criminal and administrative law, and devise mechanisms for community partnership in the elaboration of policing policy.

DEMOCRACY AND THE IDEA OF POLICING: ON MUTUALLY DEPENDENT YET ANTAGONISTIC CONCERNS

Even if one can remedy specific tensions or clarify particular misconceptions, it is arguable that the symbiotic antagonisms between policing and democracy are simply intractable. While interdependent, the relationship between the two tends to turn adversarial, since police carry both the responsibility to protect fundamental rights and freedoms as well as the power to abuse them.[16] At the very least, public perception of police can be difficult to improve, especially "while handling traffic enforcement or interpersonal disputes where one side must be taken to accomplish a resolution".[17] Furthermore, the very nature of criminal justice triggers questions of accountability; since the goal of crime control is to ensure accountability of law-breakers, those implementing the system occupy a particular societal status.[18] A recent article in the *British*

---

[14] See Evans *et al.*, above at n. 2, 359–60.
[15] M. Radin, "The Achievements of the American Bar Association: A Sixty Year Record" (1940) 26 *ABAJ* 19, 23.
[16] See T.J. Jones, T. Newburn and D.J. Smith, "Policing and the Idea of Democracy" (1996) 36 *Brit J Criminology* 182, 187.
[17] R.V. Ericson, *Reproducing Order: A Study of Police Patrol Work* (University of Toronto Press, Toronto, 1982), 62.
[18] A similar point is made by Stenning in discussing "accountability *for* criminal justice": P.C. Stenning, "Introduction", in P.C. Stenning (ed.), *Accountability for Criminal Justice: Selected Essays* (University of Toronto Press, Toronto, 1995), 3.

Journal of Criminology, entitled "Policing and the Idea of Democracy", endeavours to distill fundamental notions of democracy so as to apply them to the elaboration and delivery of police services. The nub of the problem, for the authors, appears to be that "virtually all proposals for police reform can be theoretically justified by reference to one 'democratic' principle or another".[19] The elaboration of a new rulemaking process, however, may lead to a paradigm shift in policing itself. In other words, 'policing' may well be affected by the understanding of democracy which underlies this proposal. The title of this section, "Democracy and the Idea of Policing", emphasises the discursive relationship between democracy and policing, with each necessarily influencing the other.

Policing is often considered a primary reason for maintaining a state in the first place. Often understood as policing "by consent",[20] the legitimacy of policing is deeply rooted in traditional democratic theory, "wherein democratic regimes are conceived as those which rule *by consent* of the governed".[21] Yet, this justification of policing may require critical reexamination in the shadow of negative public opinion.[22] More dramatically, the premises of such a doctrine are contestable in light of racially motivated conduct by police officers, often with fatal consequences.[23] Exacerbating the inherent struggles of the democratic relationship is the traditional separation of police and politics, the perception being that "policing and politics don't mix".[24] Reform becomes more difficult to achieve, since "as part of the legal doctrine of independence, methods of controlling police discretion are more difficult to implement".[25] The balance to be reached is a delicate one:[26]

> "The problem is that we do not want a police force that is under the direct control and direction of the government of the day, yet we also do not want a force which is not accountable and responsive to the general will of the citizens it serves. While various methods and schemes of accountability have been attempted over the years, the police today remain relatively free of outside interference."

And yet, that police remain truly above (endemic) politics is an illusory goal; rather, the rhetoric only entails that those who make policing decisions and

---

[19] Jones, Newburn and Smith, above at n. 16, 182.

[20] For an excellent discussion see R. Morgan, " 'Policing by Consent': Legitimating the Doctrine", in R. Morgan and D.J. Smith (eds), *Coming to Terms With Policing: Perspectives on Policy* (Routledge, London, 1989), 217.

[21] Jones, Newburn and Smith, above at n. 16, 187.

[22] On the "rise and fall of police legitimacy," see generally Reiner, above at n. 8, 57–104.

[23] See, e.g., *Commission on Systemic Racism*, above at n. 6.

[24] Reiner, above at n. 8, 1. For more detail, including a historical review, see P.C. Stenning, "Police and Politics: There and Back and There Again?", in Macleod and Schneiderman, above at n. 4, 209ff.

[25] J.C. Robb, "The Police and Politics: The Politics of Independence" in Macleod and Schneiderman, ibid., 178.

[26] C. Mitchell, "Regulating Professional Police", in R.P. Saunders and J. McMunagle (eds), *Saunders & Mitchell: An Introduction to Criminal Law in Context: Cases, Notes and Materials* (Carswell, Toronto, 3rd ed. 1996), 179, 182.

how they make them "becomes opaque and obscured".[27] The relationship between police decisions and democratic governing is apparent, given that "[p]olicing decisions are not matters of neutral professional expertise, as the case law suggests . . . . [p]olicing decisions are questions of political choice and value".[28] In Britain, Robert Reiner has forcefully argued that the policing function is, in fact, highly politicised, refraining from referring to it as "political football" only "because the ball seems to be so consistently hogged by one side".[29]

Lack of accountability becomes less palatable when one appreciates that a chief role of the North American policing function is the restriction of liberty, which seemingly entails confrontation and subterfuge.[30] Furthermore, traditional structures of police organisations tie in neatly to this paradigm of law enforcement. Centralisation of command, increased impersonality between citizens and police,[31] and the internal handling of most instances of police discipline[32] lead to the estrangement of police from the citizenry, which practically speaking calls into question the relationship between police forces, the societies they serve, and democracy. Unfortunately, "opportunities to 'consult' with the police are not regarded with confidence".[33] Policing by consent needs to be "restored":[34]

> "The crisis in policing derives from the unsuccessful attempt by the police to deal with rising crime by increasingly sophisticated internal organisation and reliance on complex technical hardware. This has led to an evaluation of efficiency in terms of reaction times to public calls for assistance, so-called fire brigade policing, which has in turn led to an experience of the police by the public as a crisis intervention force. The outcome has been a continuing alienation of the public from the police, accompanied by a growing police autonomy buttressed by a sense of professionalism. . . . [The consequences include] a trend towards the militarisation of the police into a repressive force. . . ."

Yet, much recent debate has ceased to focus upon democratic processes, mainly concerning itself with simple "managerialism".[35] Quality of service

---

[27] R. Reiner, "Police Research in the United Kingdom: A Critical Review", in M. Tonry and N. Morris (eds), *Modern Policing* (University of Chicago Press, Chicago, 1992), 435, 483.

[28] R. Reiner, "Counting the Coppers: Antinomies of Accountability in Policing", in Stenning, above at n. 18, 78.

[29] R. Reiner, "In the Office of the Chief Constable" (1988) 41 *Curr Legal Probs* 135.

[30] See e.g., R.A. Leo, "*Miranda*'s revenge: Police Interrogation as a Confidence Game" (1996) 30 *Law & Soc Rev* 259, 266.

[31] See A.J. Reiss Jr, "Police Organization in the Twentieth Century", in Tonry and Morris, above at n. 27, 91–2.

[32] For a general discussion of the potential role of public complaints in this context, see A.J. Goldsmith, "Public Complaints Procedures in Police Accountability" in Stenning, above at n. 18, 110–134.

[33] Commission on Systemic Racism in the Ontario Criminal Justice System, "Police Services Boards and Police Governance in Ontario" (Draft Working Paper) by K. Liao (April 1994), 16 (hereafter referred to as *Police Services Boards*).

[34] M.J. Clarke, "Citizenship, Community and the Management of Crime" (1987) 27 *Brit J Criminology* 384, 384.

[35] I. Loader, "Democracy, Justice and the Limits of Policing: Rethinking Police Accountability" (1994) 3 *Social & Legal Stud* 521, 522.

and questions of efficiency, the hallmark of the "new penology",³⁶ have begun to replace debates surrounding the legitimacy of police powers,³⁷ isolating police from the judgements of the communities they serve. While perhaps more true in some jurisdictions than in others, police have "gradually [become] cut off from the aspirations, desires, and concerns of citizens".³⁸ In the Canadian context, police are still "held in high regard";³⁹ yet, a growing number of controversies (such as those identified earlier) can only tarnish their reputation. That there is less call for police reform in Canada than other countries more likely reflects differing research structures and agendas⁴⁰ than a societal consensus.

Tensions between democracy and policing are compounded by the inevitability of discretion in the enforcement of criminal justice. While twentieth century police forces have taken on attributes of "centralized public bureaucracies",⁴¹ North American structures of police work entail a discretionary component foreign to most bureaucratic forms of organisation:⁴²

> "The exercise of discretion is highly institutionalised in the American system of criminal justice in a way that is inconsistent with the bureaucratisation of decision making. Bureaucracies preclude officials from making decisions under conditions of low visibility and without systematic hierarchical review and limit individual discretion in the selection and application of rules. Yet none of these constraints is institutionalized in contemporary police bureaucracies in America. What is particularly striking is that the greatest discretionary powers are lodged with the lowest-ranking officials in the system and that most discretionary decisions are not made a matter of record. The retention of these discretionary powers of law enforcement by patrol officers is an effective limit on bureaucratic police power."

Even Kenneth Culp Davis, an ardent believer in the need for rules to confine and structure discretion of state officials, baldly asserted that efforts to eliminate police discretion "would be ridiculous", remarking that "[d]iscretion is the essence of police work".⁴³ Discretion is the grey zone, the inevitable gap between rule and practice, fact and appearance, objectivity and subjectivity.⁴⁴ As such, it is the police officers with the most contact with citizens which inevitably retain the greatest scope of discretionary authority. This results in

---

³⁶ M.M. Feeley and J. Simon, "The New Penology: Notes on the Emerging Strategy of Corrections and its Implications" (1992) 30 *Criminology* 449.
³⁷ Loader, above at n. 35, 522.
³⁸ M.H. Moore, "Problem-Solving and Community Policing", in Tonry and Morris, above at n. 27, 117.
³⁹ B.N. Leighton, "Visions of Community Policing: Rhetoric and Reality in Canada" (1991) 33 *Can J Criminology* 485, 513.
⁴⁰ Ibid., 513–4.
⁴¹ Reiss, above at n. 31, 69.
⁴² Ibid., 74–5.
⁴³ K.C. Davis, *Police Discretion* (West Publishing, St. Paul, 1975), 140.
⁴⁴ See generally K. Hawkins (ed.), *The Uses of Discretion* (Clarendon Press, Oxford, 1992).

a pyramid-like structure of discretion,[45] elegantly exposed in James Q. Wilson's study of police behaviour:[46]

> "[A]s all police officers and many citizens recognize, discretion is inevitable—partly because it is impossible to observe every public infraction, partly because many laws require interpretation before they can be applied at all, partly because the police can sometimes get information about serious crimes by overlooking minor crimes, and partly because the police believe that public opinion would not tolerate a policy of full enforcement of all laws all the time.
>
> In almost every public organization, discretion is exercised—indeed, from the client's viewpoint, the problem arises out of how and whether it is exercised—but the police department has the special property (shared with a few other organizations) that within it discretion increases as one moves *down* the hierarchy. . . ."

Legal doctrine tends to justify the divide between police and others, with theories of independence "permeat[ing] the whole of the criminal-justice system in Canada".[47] Canadian courts have adopted British understandings of constabulary independence, subject to statutorily-created police boards.[48] The police hold an independent "civil office of trust",[49] a doctrine which has taken root in the "ideological armoury of both senior police officers and judges, as well as many politicians".[50] While the traditional common law cases establishing the "original" authority of police officers have been criticised on many grounds,[51] Croom-Johnson L.J. of the English Court of Appeal has well articulated the black-letter law, holding that "[t]he independence of a constable, and a fortiori a chief constable, from outside control, whether by a local authority or the executive, has been repeatedly upheld".[52] In Canada, much of the case-law has surrounded the issue of employment relations, a central concern having been whether a master/servant relationship exists between police boards and the police.[53]

Historically, police discretion has been shielded from judicial scrutiny, courts maintaining that a police officer must "do what is necessary to dis-

---

[45] T.K. Moran and J.L. Cooper, *Discretion and the Criminal Justice Process* (Associated Faculty Press, Port Washington, New York, 1983), 46.

[46] J.Q. Wilson, *Varieties of Police Behavior: The Management of Law and Order in Eight Communities* (Harvard University Press, Cambridge, 1968), 7.

[47] Robb, above at n. 25, 177.

[48] See generally P. Ceyssens, *Legal Aspects of Policing* (Carswell, Toronto, 1994), 1–12 to 1–13.

[49] Idem. See also P.C. Stenning, "Trusting the Chief: Legal Aspects of the Status and Political Accountability of the Police in Canada" (SJD Dissertation, University of Toronto, 1983) and A.J. Goldsmith, "The Impact of Police Collective Bargaining Upon Municipal Police Management in Ontario, 1973–1984: A Socio-Legal Analysis" (SJD Dissertation, University of Toronto, 1986).

[50] Stenning, above at n. 24, 217.

[51] Reiner has noted that the central British decisions were simply "*obiter* on *obiter*": above at n. 29, 145. See also general discussion by Ceyssens, above at n. 48, 1–6 to 1–12.

[52] *R. v. Secretary of State for the Home Department, ex parte Northumbria Police Authority* [1989] QB 35, 39.

[53] See, e.g., *Reference Re Constitutional Questions Act (Ontario)* [1957] 7 DLR (2d) 222 (Ont. C.A.) and *Pembroke (City) Police Services Board v. Kidder* (1995) 123 DLR (4th) 596, 604–5 (Ont. Gen. Div.).

charge his duties in the administration or enforcement of the law so long as he acts on reasonable and probable grounds".[54] In a case involving the Canadian Charter of Rights and Freedoms, the Supreme Court in *Beare* unanimously said this about police discretion:[55]

> "The existence of the discretion conferred by the statutory provisions [permitting fingerprinting prior to conviction] does not, in my view, offend principles of fundamental justice. Discretion is an essential feature of the criminal justice system. A system that attempted to eliminate discretion would be unworkably complex and rigid. Police necessarily exercise discretion in deciding when to lay charges, to arrest and to conduct incidental searches. . . . The *Criminal Code* provides no guidelines in any of these areas. The day-to-day operation of law enforcement and the criminal justice system none the less depends upon the exercise of that discretion."

The Court further rejected a structuring of police discretion, holding that imposing additional standards, regardless of whether they "would constitute some improvement to the present unstructured system",[56] is not mandated by the Charter. Rather, the Court appears to rely implicitly upon the exclusionary remedy of section 24 of the Charter, should the discretion be exercised improperly or arbitrarily.[57] Instead of encouraging the formulation of prospective rules, the Court prefers to remain in the domain of the *ex post*. This is likely related to police officers' traditional independence at common law,[58] dictating that a constable's "authority is original, not delegated, and is exercised at his own discretion by virtue of his office".[59] A separation of powers between the investigation and resolution of criminal activity is maintained.[60] Prospective rules and standards are explicitly discouraged by the courts, as is evident in the following passage referred to approvingly by the Supreme Court:[61]

> "It is not only impossible but inadvisable to frame a definition which will set definite limits to the powers and duties of police officers appointed to carry out the powers of the state in relation to individuals who come within its jurisdiction and protection . . . *It is infinitely better that the courts should decide as each case arises whether, having regard to the necessities of the case and the safeguards required in the public interest, the police are under a legal duty in the particular circumstances.*"

---

[54] *286880 Ontario Ltd.* v. *Parke* (1974) 52 DLR (3d) 535, 541 (Ont. H.C.).
[55] *R.* v. *Beare* [1988] 2 SCR 387, 410–11 (hereafter referred to as *Beare*).
[56] Ibid., 411–12.
[57] Ibid., 411.
[58] In Ontario, this understanding of the police has been reaffirmed by statute. Section 42(3) of the Police Services Act, R.S.O. 1990, c. P.15 states that "[a] police officer has the powers and duties ascribed to a constable at common law".
[59] *New South Wales (Attorney General)* v. *Perpetual Trustee Co* [1955] AC 457, 489.
[60] Ontario Attorney-General's Advisory Committee on Charge Screening, Disclosure and Resolution Discussions, *Report of the Attorney-General's Advisory Committee on Charge Screening, Disclosure, and Resolution Discussions*, by G.A. Martin (Queen's Printer, Toronto, 1993), 37ff.
[61] *R.* v. *Schacht* (1973) 30 DLR (3d) 641, 646 (Ont. C.A.) (emphasis added); *var'd* [1976] 1 SCR 53. A majority of the Supreme Court of Canada referred to this passage as "forthright and enlightening": [1976] 1 SCR 53, 65.

This, to put it bluntly, encourages the administering of justice without trial.[62] Furthermore, while Charter protections have undoubtedly limited the scope of police powers, such as in the area of search and seizure,[63] the whole of criminal procedure has witnessed an expansion of traditional notions of waiver. Canadian courts often find defendants to have waived their constitutional protections, even if a waiver was clearly not intended. Comparing cases in which defendants are found to have waived or forfeited their rights evidences a clear differentiation in the Court's attitude toward waiver in the police station and waivers effected in the courtroom.[64] Police stations remain the gatehouses of criminal procedure, courts the mansions.[65]

In elaborating the parameters of criminal procedure, Canadian courts remain acutely aware of the needs of law enforcement and tend to resist changes that would have an impact upon the efficient exercise of police powers. Investigatory necessity is not the only factor which influences the Supreme Court of Canada's tempering of Charter rights. Rather, for a majority of the Court, investigatory expedience also appears to tip the crime control/due process balance:[66]

> "We must not, as a Court, lose sight of the realities of crime investigation and the functioning of modern police forces of varying sizes, with shifts, labour agreements and limitations put on overtime for financial considerations of course, but also, if not more important because police officers have a right to a personal and family life."

Court review of prosecutorial discretion has followed a similar path. While it is now clear that trial courts can impose a stay of proceedings where they find an abuse of process,[67] such instances are necessarily limited to the "clearest of cases" where there is "overwhelming evidence that the proceedings under scrutiny are unfair to the point that they are contrary to the interest of justice".[68] As Stuart has pointed out, "[b]eing too wedded to the dramatic remedy of stay may have made the courts too cautious in assessing claims of abuse".[69] In *R. v. Scott* the Supreme Court did not find an abuse of process where the Crown entered a stay of proceedings to avoid an evidentiary ruling, even though the Crown then recommenced the proceedings in another

---

[62] J. Skolnick, *Justice Without Trial: Law Enforcement in Democratic Society* (Wiley & Sons, New York, 1969).

[63] For a brief exposition see Stuart, above at n. 4.

[64] See R. Levi, "Toward a General Standard of Waiver in the Criminal Process" (LLM Thesis, University of Toronto, 1996).

[65] Y. Kamisar, "Equal Justice in the Gatehouses and Mansions of American Criminal Procedure: From *Powell* to *Gideon*, From *Escobedo* to . . .", in A.E.D. Howard (ed.), *Criminal Justice in Our Time* (University Press of Virginia, Charlottesville, 1965), 1.

[66] R. v. *Brydges* [1990] 1 SCR 190, 216 (hereafter referred to as *Brydges*).

[67] Stuart, above at n. 4, 89–90.

[68] See, e.g., the decision of a majority of the Supreme Court in R. v. *Power* [1994] 1 SCR 601, 616 (hereafter referred to as *Power*).

[69] D. Stuart, "Prosecutorial Accountability in Canada", in Stenning, above at n. 18, 344.

court.⁷⁰ In *R. v. Power*⁷¹ a majority of the Court laid down that courts should be reluctant to review prosecutorial discretion out of concern for efficiency, the doctrine of separation of powers, the Rule of Law, and differences in institutional competence and roles. At the end of the day, L'Heureux-Dubé J., for the majority, determined that prosecutorial discretion "is especially ill-suited to judicial review".⁷²

While the Court's reluctance to subject the actions of prosecutors to judicial review has been sharply criticised,⁷³ we argue that the Court is somewhat justified in doing so. Reviewing discretionary conduct in an *ex post*, adjudicative forum, is an ineffective means of structuring discretion and providing guidelines for future conduct. Rather, particular cases tend to raise particular facts; policy-making by induction must be limited by sensitivity to the individual case before the court. Where the Court impedes the development of structural frameworks to govern prosecutorial discretion, however, is in *encouraging secrecy and "confidentiality" by Crown prosecutors*. In the face of a publicly available Crown policy manual, the majority asserts that there is benefit in keeping enforcement policies confidential to allow flexibility, with disclosure promoting "inflexible and static policies which are not necessarily desirable".⁷⁴ Openness is one of the main benefits of rulemaking, a process which need not confine the discretion of those engaged in it. As the Crown policy manual itself points out:⁷⁵

> "Notwithstanding the broad discretion that must necessarily be accorded to prosecutors, and upon which the sound administration of justice greatly depends, it is also necessary in the public interest to have some uniform prosecution policies and standards applicable across the province. They are found in this manual and are intended to assist and guide individual prosecutors in exercising their prosecutorial discretion. They set out appropriate considerations for prosecutorial decision-making, while maintaining and supporting flexibility and Crown discretion."

The Canadian courts' stance of "conservative deference"⁷⁶ toward police and prosecutors demonstrates an intransigent unwillingness to intervene in the delivery of crime control services. This, we maintain, is the beginning of a workable approach to the issue of discretion in the criminal justice system. Court remedies, imposed *ex post*, are often unnecessarily harsh and blunt instruments in guiding future conduct, a reality which potentially has an impact on the effectiveness of structuring discretion in that context:⁷⁷

⁷⁰ *R. v. Scott* [1990] 3 SCR 979.
⁷¹ *Power*, above at n. 68, 620–26.
⁷² Ibid., 623.
⁷³ See, e.g., K. Roach, "Developments in Criminal Procedure: The 1993–94 Term" (1995) 6 *Supreme Court LR (2d)* 281, 337–42.
⁷⁴ *Power*, above at n. 68, 626.
⁷⁵ Ontario, Ministry of the Attorney-General, *Crown Policy Manual*, Introduction: Statement from the Attorney-General and Deputy Attorney-General (16 Dec. 1993).
⁷⁶ Stuart, above at n. 69, 353.
⁷⁷ M.L. Friedland, "Controlling the Administrators of Criminal Justice" (1989) 31 *Crim LQ* 280, 281.

"[T]he remedy available affects the rule itself. If the only available remedy for a violation of a rule is that the proceedings will be terminated, the judges interpreting the rule will be inclined to make the rule less onerous for the prosecutor than they might if other remedies were available."

Instead of the present system of court review, the Canadian criminal justice system is well situated to take advantage of rulemaking, and thus enhance the values of openness, democratic accountability, participation and legitimacy. Such an approach would integrate the regulators (i.e. police and prosecutors) and the regulated (i.e. citizens' groups) in the formulation of norms of conduct. At its root, the process is bottom-up rather than imposed from above.

The courts, however, should not be entirely passive in this regard. The judges must encourage the development of consultation-based "prospective statements of policies and principles intended to guide the conduct of those subject to regulation".[78] Rulemaking must not relieve courts of their role in structuring discretion in the criminal justice system. Canadian courts can and should encourage the structuring of police discretion.[79] For example, when presented with cases involving the exercise of police discretion, courts should acknowledge the value of consultative rulemaking in the structuring and guiding of that discretion.

However, this cannot be undertaken in isolation from social context. Grounded in legal notions of independence, police culture produces and reproduces attitudes of internal solidarity, loyalty and secrecy. As Goldsmith observes, "[t]hese cultural attributes pose obvious problems for legality and formal accountability in policing".[80] Focus is often upon obedience and hierarchy,[81] with the preeminent value being an officer's ability to 'handle situations'.[82] In shifting the paradigm toward enhancing democracy and participation, inevitable clashes with culture arise. Rules inherent in police officers' "occupational culture"[83] strongly motivate the exercise of discretion. As Mark Moore points out, "[p]robably the biggest obstacle facing anyone who would implement a new strategy of policing is the difficulty of changing the ongoing culture of policing",[84] since police work tends to produce "cognitive lenses through which to see situations and events".[85] In the context of police discretion and rulemaking, Andrew Goldsmith has emphasised the

---

[78] *Ainsley Financial Corp.* v. *Ontario Securities Commission* (1994) 121 DLR (4th) 79, 83 (Ont. C.A.). This point ties in rather nicely: prospective rules can be helpful not only in guiding police conduct, but in clarifying and articulating the scope of criminal conduct for all concerned.

[79] M.L. Friedland, "Reforming Police Powers: Who's in Charge?", in Macleod and Schneiderman, above at n. 4, 113.

[80] A.J. Goldsmith, "Taking Police Culture Seriously: Police Discretion and the Limits of Law" (1990) 1 *Policing & Soc* 91, 94.

[81] Moore, above at n. 38, 107–8.

[82] Wilson, above at n. 46, 31.

[83] Ericson, above at n. 17, 14.

[84] Moore, above at n. 38, 150.

[85] Skolnick, above at n. 62, ch. 3.

centrality of police culture, criticising legal scholars for ignoring this constraint:[86]

> "[N]one of the scholars interested in the phenomenon of police rulemaking confronts sufficiently realistically either the potential resistance of the police culture to the *results* of police rulemaking, nor the potential benefits of involving street-level police officers in the *process* of rulemaking."

Proposed reforms to policing, however, abound. While Goldsmith speaks of integrating existing police culture, others construe the culture of policing as an obstacle to effective reform. Commentators refer to "changing the organisational structure" so as to allow openness to be embraced as a value; others stress the importance of specifically articulating the dominant values of police forces, so as to enhance both internal and external accountability.[87]

Properly conceived and implemented, police rulemaking can be understood as part and parcel of trends toward "community policing". These movements are identifiable as a reevaluation of the interplay between democracy and policing generally, including themes such as input, accountability to citizens, empowerment, proactive social and economic programmes, and the reduction of barriers between police and citizen.[88] While such enterprises vary in their content and efficacy, one commentator has broadly defined community policing arrangements as "new organisational strategies that seek to redefine the mission, the principal operating methods, and the key administrative arrangements of police departments".[89] Reliance upon "effective working partnerships"[90] between citizens and police are considered integral to this process. Rulemaking mechanisms in which both the regulators (police) and the regulated (citizens and community groups) can structure the exercise of discretionary authority fits well with the understanding that "the gist of virtually all community-based policing proposals involves a greater involvement of the community, both directly and indirectly (through elected politicians) in the determination of the objectives, priorities, and policies that will guide the police force in performing its role".[91] This has been specifically noted in a brief to the Canadian Solicitor-General:[92]

> "With the idea that members of the community should have an *agenda-setting role* as well as a *say in operational matters* (e.g., problem-solving), it becomes obvious

---

[86] Goldsmith, above at n. 80, 102 (emphasis in original).
[87] Moore, above at n. 38, 150–51.
[88] This necessarily incomplete list is generated from lists of what community policing "is" and what it "is not" in *Symposium on Community-Based Policing: Report to Prairie Region Solicitor-General of Canada* (Prairie Justice Research, School of Human Justice, University of Regina, Saskatchewan, 1991), 8 and the *Commission on Systemic Racism*, above at n. 6.
[89] Moore, above at n. 38, 103.
[90] Ibid., 123.
[91] Stenning, above at n. 24, 229.
[92] A. Normandeau and B. Leighton, *A Vision of the Future of Policing in Canada: Police-Challenge 2000* (Background Document) (Solicitor-General, Ottawa, 1990), 73, as cited in Stenning, above at n. 24, 229–30.

that *ongoing consultations need to take place* between the police and the public. . . . Individuals may bring relatively limited matters or concerns to the attention of the police. Neighbourhood groups and associations may make representations to the police or even constitute a form of town council that has a continuing role in setting police policies. The business community, too, will want input into the activities of the police. Finally, the media, with the ability it has to shape public opinion about crime and the efficacy of police efforts, needs to be dealt with. . . ."

The notion of partnership with the community, and having communities participate in the development of policy and practice, lies at the heart of community policing. Unfortunately, present community policing reforms do little to achieve any significant changes in the structure of policy formation; "[i]nstead, the police refer to community/police 'partnership' and 'consultation' that results in police 'management' of racialised communities and a continuation of conventional policing strategies".[93] As a result, neither rulemaking nor community policing writ large are panaceas for the problems of police discretion.[94] It is hoped that the rulemaking *process* can help attain some of the goals of community policing proposals, with the resultant structured police discretion an added benefit. Furthermore, as Goldsmith points out, rulemaking would then have the distinct potential to "become a highly fruitful police accountability mechanism".[95] The rulemaking we envision integrates and extends Goldsmith's proposal. While integrating police culture into the rulemaking process, thereby including voices that have not traditionally been heard in policy formation, the rulemaking we envisage also integrates communities in a similar effort. It is through rulemaking that democratic reforms to police practices may be realised, and aspirations of participatory administrative law mechanisms can be achieved.[96]

At this juncture, however, it is important to distinguish the types of reform we are advancing from the community consultation requirements in Britain, established by section 106 of the Police and Criminal Evidence Act.[97] This provision, which calls upon police forces to obtain the views and cooperation of the public through consultation, does not engage the community in a rulemaking process. While constituting "an exercise in public participation",[98] such an approach tends not to incorporate the public as a partner in crime control, but focuses solely on the assistance of the public in policing the neighbourhood. In such a context, it is not altogether surprising that the implementation of section 106, often through the establishment of police-community consultative committees, "function[s] more as a means of com-

[93] *Police Services Boards*, above at n. 33, 15.
[94] See e.g. *Commission on Systemic Racism*, above at n. 6, 336 and Goldsmith, above at n. 80, 112.
[95] Goldsmith, ibid., 112.
[96] The importance of the presence of different voices at the table is emphasised in Alison Harvison Young's paper in this volume.
[97] Police and Criminal Evidence Act 1984 (U.K.), s. 106.
[98] Morgan, above at n. 20, 221.

municating police perspectives to the public than the reverse, and that their political effect is to legitimate the myth of policing by consent".[99] While much fanfare surrounded the recommendations of Lord Scarman regarding the implementation of such local consultative committees,[100] such attempts to involve communities have often "had little substantive input into local policing policy".[101]

In contrast, key democratic principles which should influence policing reform have been enumerated as equity, delivery of service, responsiveness, distribution of power, information, redress, and participation.[102] Rulemaking has the potential to help meet many of these democratic issues of police governance and delivery of services. Similarly, the stated goals of community policing structures are also achievable under this system, the community being able to engage, with police officers and personnel, in the structuring of discretionary police practices. At the very least, rulemaking provides the opportunity for *dialogue*, which may often make the resulting rule more palatable for all concerned, thereby enhancing legitimacy and ideally producing rules which accommodate the often competing interests at stake. The influence of the public, those on the receiving end of criminal justice enforcement, is central in this regard:[103]

> "Public participation in the police rulemaking process has received wide endorsement among police legal scholars as well as from some US governmental and semi-official commissions of inquiry. To allow public involvement offers several attractive benefits: it is patently democratic, it opens up a world to scrutiny which has arguably been too isolated, and it exposes police thinking to new ideas. It also provides an opportunity for the police to explain their perspective on law enforcement to members of the public, not unlike the way in which neighbourhood watch arrangements currently operate."

Finally, such a project is clearly in the interest of any forward-looking police force. The investigation of crime tends to be a reactive activity, with police relying heavily on support from, and communication with, the communities they serve. Fostering stronger relationships with community members by engaging in policy-oriented rulemaking not only eases the tensions between police and citizens, but also provides valuable information to police regarding the nature and prevalence of crime in the community. Public cooperation is necessary for the police to realize their "*own*" objectives".[104] This dependence of police forces on the community structure is reflected in the Solicitor-General's 1990 Discussion Paper, *A Vision of the Future of Policing in Canada*,

---

[99] Reiner, above at n. 27, 484.
[100] See especially Reiner, above at n. 8, 250–270.
[101] T. Jones, T. Newburn and D.J. Smith, *Democracy & Policing* (Policy Studies Institute, London, 1994), 277.
[102] Jones, Newburn and Smith, above at n. 16, 190ff.
[103] Goldsmith, above at n. 80, 108, but see problems with public participation at 108–9.
[104] S.P. Savage, "The Police: Political Control or Community Liaison?" (1984) 55 *Political Q* 48, 58 (emphasis in original).

which emphasises the re-emergence of community policing in North America. The partnership envisaged clearly contemplates the exchange of information regarding crime between communities and police officers, an exchange which allows for a focus upon a proactive approach to policing.[105] This proposal differs from traditional Canadian community policing efforts, including citizens' advisory councils and consultative committees. While focussing on problem-solving and community involvement, such programmes shy away from engagement in formal rulemaking activity and dialogue regarding the very bases of the rules being implemented. Consultative rulemaking should be seen as not simply a reinforcement of underlying values; rather, the process can result in concrete and pragmatic improvements in crime control.

THE PRESENT STRUCTURE IN ONTARIO: THE DIFFERENCE RULEMAKING COULD MAKE

The current legal regime in the Province of Ontario appears ideally situated to benefit from a participatory rulemaking approach. Many mechanisms, already in place, act to oversee police activity. Citizen participation in processes of police accountability, severely rejected by the police when initially proposed, is now institutionalised. Furthermore, the Ontario Police Services Board, a "municipal-police governing authority"[106] which oversees all police forces in the province, has the statutory authority to establish police policies. Yet, for all of this institutional structure, little has truly changed in the realm of democratic accountability of the police. The exercise of police discretionary power continues to be a "police matter", with little focus on discourse between police forces and the communities they police and serve. This has been the historical reality:[107]

> "Legal precedent dating back centuries concerning the common law Office of Constable has tended to safeguard independence and discretion in the exercise of these powers and authority from outside influence or control. The advent of organized, professional policing in the last 150 years has produced para-military, internal-control models of maintaining discipline and managing police performance. Hallmarks of this heritage remain very much in evidence under the current Police Services Act."

And yet, there is a recognition today that "the ability of the police to protect the community and to apprehend those who break the law relies, in large measure, on the trust and co-operation of the public. The police would be

---

[105] Solicitor-General of Canada, *A Vision of the Future of Policing in Canada: Police-Challenge 2000* (Discussion Paper) (Supply & Services Canada, Ottawa, 1990), 18–30.
[106] Stenning, above at n. 24, 230.
[107] Above at n. 11, 56.

profoundly hindered in the performance of their duties without the willing support of the public".[108]

At this juncture, it is necessary to briefly outline the oversight bodies currently in place in Ontario. This discloses an interesting interplay between power vested in municipal police forces, and the powers of the provincial government and civilian review bodies. Present mechanisms tend to focus on the adjudication of individual cases of complaints rather than a concerted, formalised effort to engage in prospective community consultation. This adjudicative-style methodology, focussing on the resolution of individual cases, does little to engage the relevant parties' attention toward the formulation of prospective standards.[109] While it is clear that adjudication cannot be ignored, this exposition will demonstrate that consultative rulemaking remains the most viable and attractive route to achieve democratic accountability and formal structuring of necessary discretionary practices.

Police forces in Ontario are guided in their behaviour by various documents. Various legislative enactments, including the Criminal Code, prescribe standards for police officers, outlining duties and proscribing certain conduct. Much of the general rules of criminal procedure can be found by reference to specific statutory provisions. The provincial Police Services Act, and its attendant regulations, outline the duties of police officers and detail the responsibilities of the various monitoring bodies.[110] The regulations under the Act, along with other *guidelines*, which are not necessarily binding on individual forces, are published in the *Police Standards Manual*.[111] Finally, each municipal force maintains its own internal *Policy and Procedures Manual*, a document which is unavailable for public inspection. Again, the importance of police culture in interpreting and following the prescriptions of these documents can be determinative. Policing often sacrifices "legality" for "efficiency," and the internal rules produced by the culture of policing "provide sufficient pretexts and intra organisational power to subvert, distort or deflect the pristine intents behind external rules".[112]

The guiding document for all forces in Ontario is the Police Services Act. The Act begins with a declaration of principles, which clearly reinforces the importance of community policing. Section 1 of the Act mandates a need for co-operation between police and the community, sensitivity to the diversity of Ontario society, the need for police forces to be representative of their communities, and the importance of respect for the victims of crime. Responsibility for the administration of the Act (and, hence, of police services

---

[108] Idem.
[109] For a recent overview, see H.N. Janisch, "Further Developments With Respect to Rulemaking by Administrative Agencies" (1995) 9 *Can J Admin L & Prac* 1.
[110] Above at n. 59.
[111] Ontario, Ministry of the Solicitor-General and Correctional Services, *Policing Standards Manual for the Province of Ontario* (Ministry of the Solicitor-General and Correctional Services, Toronto, 31 Mar. 1992).
[112] Goldsmith, above at n. 80, 95.

in the province) is vested in the Solicitor-General, whose duties and powers are sweeping.[113] While the majority of the statutory duties are carried out by provincial Police Service Advisors, the strong-arm of the Solicitor-General is the Ontario Civilian Commission on Police Services. This statutorily-created Commission, whose proceedings are generally held in public,[114] has the mandate and power to direct municipal police services boards and/or police forces to comply with prescribed provincial standards, investigate municipal police matters, inquire into crime and law enforcement generally (if so directed by the Lieutenant-Governor), and act as an appellate body for police disciplinary proceedings. It does not appear that the Commission's enforcement powers are limited to enforcing those standards which have been enacted as binding regulations. It appears that standards which are 'mere guidelines' may also be enforced by the Commission, which retains a great deal of enforcement power. Following a hearing, where the Commission determines that prescribed standards are repeatedly or flagrantly not being met, it may take the following measures:[115]

1. Suspending the chief of police, one or more members of the board, or the whole board, for a specified period.
2. Removing the chief of police, one or more members of the board, or the whole board from office.
3. Disbanding the police force and requiring the Ontario Provincial Police to provide police services for the municipality.
4. Appointing an administrator to perform specified functions with respect to police matters in the municipality for a specified period.

---

[113] Section 3(2) of the Police Services Act provides:

"The Solicitor-General shall,
(a) monitor police forces to ensure that adequate and effective police services are provided at the municipal and provincial levels;
(b) monitor boards and police forces to ensure that they comply with prescribed standards of service;
(c) monitor the establishment and implementation of employment equity plans;
(d) develop and promote programs to enhance professional police practices, standards and training;
(e) conduct a system of inspection and review of police forces across Ontario;
(f) assist in the co-ordination of police services;
(g) consult with and advise boards, municipal chiefs of police, employers or special constables and associations on matters relating to police and police services;
(h) develop, maintain and manage programs and statistical records and conduct research studies in respect of police services and related matters;
(i) provide to boards and municipal chiefs of police information and advice respecting the management and operation of police forces, techniques in handling special problems and other information calculated to assist;
(j) issue directives and guidelines respecting policy matters;
(k) develop and promote programs for community-oriented police services;
(l) operate the Ontario Police College".

[114] See s. 21(6) of the Police Services Act, which is subject to the exceptions in s. 21(7).
[115] See s. 23 of the Police Services Act. On the duty of fairness in such situations, see Ceyssens, above at n. 48, 4–6 to 4–7.

The provincial commission, then, has direct control over the municipal police services boards, which are mandated for every municipality which maintains a police force.[116] All members of the police force are under the jurisdiction of a municipal board, which is directly "responsible for the provision of police services and for law enforcement in the municipality".[117] For our purposes, the most interesting responsibilities of a municipal police services board concerns its relationship with the police force, notably with the Chief of Police and with individual officers. Strong board powers may be perceived as running contrary to established notions of police independence, especially since the composition of a majority of the municipal boards and the full provincial commission is determined by the province,[118] and the appointment process is notably lacking in standards, criteria and democratic accountability.[119] This focus on the provincial level, rather than a more community-specific one, "raises the question of whether provincial standardisation and centralisation of control over policing brings about structural accountability. . . . There is quiet recognition that the board members who are supposedly 'the community' have largely failed to represent the full spectrum of community interests (which are sometimes in conflict with each other), and at the same time, look after the interests of police services personnel".[120]

Among other things, the Police Services Act provides that municipal boards shall: "generally determine, after consultation with the chief of police, objectives and priorities with respect to police services in the municipality", including the establishment of "policies for the effective management of the police force".[121] In 1992 the Toronto Board adopted a community consultation approach, which looks to integrate, on an on going basis, community groups in the consultation process, with the resulting considerations and resolution being made publicly available. While informal consultation is widespread even among more traditional administrative agencies, the Toronto Board's consultation structure is rather progressive in this regard. The following resolution of the Board approaches notions of rulemaking:[122]

1. THAT the board adopt the following objectives of community consultation:
   – Ensure equal and effective access from a broad range of community groups (whether ethno-specific or formed around specific issues).

---

[116] See s. 27 of the Police Services Act.
[117] See s. 31(1) and (2) of the Police Services Act.
[118] See ss. 21 and 27 of the Police Services Act. See *Police Services Boards*, above at n. 33, 42.
[119] P.C. Stenning, "Providing for Democratic Control and Accountability of Municipal Policing in Ontario" (Brief Presented to the Standing Committee on the Administration of Justice of the Legislature of Ontario, 11 June 1990), 6.
[120] *Police Services Boards*, above at n. 33, 13–14.
[121] See s. 31 of the Police Services Act.
[122] *Minutes of the Meeting of the Metropolitan Toronto Police Services Board*, No. 356 "Community Consultation" (25 June 1992).

- There must be a permanent or ongoing consultation process.
- The Board has a responsibility to account as to how the community input has been factored into its decision-making.
- The Board must keep the communities advised of policing issues and seek input into its decision-making process in a timely and effective manner.
- The consultation process must be structured to ensure that those who participate in the process properly inform the constituencies they represent and solicit input from them.
- The considerations and resolutions arising from the consultation process must be broadly and regularly disseminated to the public to ensure that the process remains open and accessible.

2. THAT the Board adopt a multi-faceted and flexible consultation process that builds upon the current consultation as well as integrate community-specific advisory groups, community-based organisations and ad-hoc problem solving/prevention meetings.
3. THAT the Police Services Boards create a newsletter to be distributed on a regular basis.

Care must be taken, however, not to place undue faith in such a process. In the past, it has been said that "[t]he police-community consultation process is not one of true consultation because the agenda is set by the police or by racial community groups chosen by the police".[123]

A further barrier to community participation remains the legislatively enshrined doctrine of police independence.[124] This operational independence remains regardless of the consultations undertaken by police services boards. While the original Police Services Bill provided that the board could give orders and directions to the police chief, Philip Stenning notes that this was the "subject of considerable disagreement" in legislative committee, with substantial division over the power relationships between the board and the police chief.[125] This dynamic is all the more interesting when one considers the potentially political nature of both provincial commissions and municipal boards:[126]

"[An] explanation for the creation of police boards would seem to be the desire of the central (provincial) authorities to remove the municipal police forces out of the control of local political interests and back into the sphere of their own political influence. In this context, the creation of police boards as institutions of government of municipal police forces may be seen not so much as a measure to 'remove the

---

[123] *Police Services Boards*, above at n. 33, 15.
[124] See s. 31(4) of the Police Services Act: "[t]he board shall not direct the chief of police with respect to specific operational decisions or with respect to the day-to-day operations of the police force".
[125] Stenning, above at n. 24, 221.
[126] P.C. Stenning, "The Role of Police Boards and Commissions as Institutions of Municipal Police Governance", in Shearing, above at n. 9, 172.

police from politics', as an attempt to move the control over municipal police forces from one sphere of political interests toward another. Clearly, it would always be very much in the interests of the proponents of such a change to create the impression that the new governing authority is in some way demonstrably less 'political' than its predecessor."

With respect to police independence, tension implicitly exists between the duty of the Police Services Board to determine policing objectives, priorities, and policies (with or without consultation) on the one hand, and statutorily enshrined independence over daily operation and specific operational decisions on the other.[127] This independence is vested in the chief of police, who administers and oversees the force in accordance with the board's policies, as well as having authority over disciplinary matters. Furthermore, this (con)fusion of responsibility tends to obfuscate the ultimate decision-maker, "blurring who takes responsibility for what".[128]

It is in the context of disciplinary hearings that the public complaints system in place in Toronto has garnered considerable attention worldwide. After much police resistance and a tumultuous birth,[129] the Police Complaints Commissioner now deals with complaints from members of the public. Briefly, this system is designed to deal with the lack of legitimacy often accorded to internal disciplinary proceedings. Goldsmith has noted that "[t]he widely attributed failure of internal complaints mechanisms reflects a loss of public confidence in the way in which the police have responded previously (or more to the point, not responded) to expressions of citizen dissatisfaction and to evidence of misconduct more generally within their own ranks".[130] In stark contrast, the Toronto Police Association at one time stated that it "fervently believes that the only good external complaints system is a dead complaints system".[131] While many advantages have been associated with the complaints system in place (as well as some drawbacks),[132] it remains essentially a limited adjudicative mechanism. Consultative rulemaking could raise broader issues and focus attention more firmly on major policy considerations:[133]

> (a) Lawmaking by rule is more efficient than lawmaking by adjudication because it allows agencies to focus upon a few proceedings raising only the major policy issues;

[127] See s. 31 of the Police Services Act.
[128] *Police Services Boards*, above at n. 33, 51, citing a Municipal Councillor who referred to this as an "escape accountability clause".
[129] See C.E. Lewis, "Police Complaints in Metropolitan Toronto: Perspectives of the Public Complaints Commissioner", in A.J. Goldsmith (ed.), *Complaints Against the Police: The Trend to External Review* (Clarendon Press, Oxford, 1991), 153.
[130] A.J. Goldsmith, "External Review and Self-Regulation: Police Accountability and the Dialectic of Complaints Procedures", in Goldsmith, ibid., 19.
[131] P. Walter, "President's Message" (5 Nov. 1987) *News and Views*, as cited in Lewis, above at n. 129, 167.
[132] An excellent overview of complaints mechanisms is provided in Goldsmith, above at n. 129.
[133] See Janisch, above at n. 109, 7.

(b) Rulemaking requires focussing on the questions of law and policy, attention not being diverted to the facts of individual cases;
(c) Rulemaking allows agencies to initiate own changes.

Involving the public as complainants in the process, while certainly an improvement over previous systems of self-regulation, does not view the public as an advisor, nor a participant, nor a partner in the delivery of police services.[134] However structured, the handling of individual complaints necessarily creates an adversarial setting; the problem is handled on an individual basis, if at all, and no mechanism is put in place for ensuring a broader institutional response to the issue. Goldsmith, for one, has argued that such complaints mechanisms should not be understood as "supplanting internal accountability mechanisms", but rather as sources of information which can "contribute to the development of responsive police forces".[135] While the Ontario public complaints commissioner can make recommendations which must be commented upon,[136] it is clear that a more direct, and effective, mechanism of integrating community understandings into police practices and the structuring of discretionary authority would be to engage in some form of rulemaking. In a rulemaking process lies the opportunity to satisfy the "broader question [of] whether community and police expectations are being reconciled and met".[137] Hastings and Saunders have said:[138]

> "The focus of accountability here shifts from the individual officer to the police service. The concern is to develop structures and processes for addressing and redefining the problem of the redistribution of power and control in what are supposed to be partnerships between the police and the community in the co-production of social order. At this level, accountability involves giving mobilised community groups and their representatives a real and significant role within these partnerships. It also places a responsibility on either the police or other levels of government to assist in the mobilisation of disadvantaged groups. Current accountability mechanisms fail this test: they not only are unable to address the larger notions of police accountability and responsiveness but, more importantly, in appropriating the discourses of accountability they mask the real challenge which remains to be faced in the next few years."

To recap: There are a variety of control mechanisms in place, each with its own rules, standards and guidelines. There is little shortage of rules to guide conduct. It is the efficacy of existing rules, the process by which they were derived, and their general legitimacy which needs to be questioned.

---

[134] R. Hastings and R.P. Saunders, "Strategies for Police Accountability and Community Empowerment" (excerpts from "Strategies for Police Accountability and Community Empowerment" (Prepared for the CROP-IISL Seminar on *Law, Power and Poverty* (Onati, Spain: May 1995))), in Saunders and McMunagle, above at n. 26, 192.

[135] Goldsmith, above at n. 130, 15.

[136] See s. 101 of the Police Services Act.

[137] Above at n. 11, 61.

[138] Hastings and Saunders, above at n. 134, 192–3.

Community consultation does take place, as it does in most aspects of governing. Rulemaking's formalised structure, and the integration of groups which may not otherwise be heard (including, as we will argue, 'beat' officers themselves), can help allay some of the difficulties in the present system. Trends toward community policing are evident in the Toronto Board's consultation policy. Unfortunately, it is unclear what actual impact the Board's (mostly) part-time members have on police policy formulation. Furthermore, Boards themselves are not necessarily representative of community concerns, especially given their composition. Indeed it is even possible that the very existence of such institutions may shield policy development from further scrutiny, since those involved can point to the imprimatur of civilian representation within the existing structure. Accountability, in this sense, may be very different from the simple ability to provide an account,[139] which the current structure provides to its members.

TO FILL A VACUUM

To this point we have sought to show that neither courts nor legislatures adequately address the issue of discretion in criminal law enforcement. Indeed, virtually all commentators (particularly in the United States) have noted the inherent limitations of both judicial and legislative approaches to police accountability and have viewed some form of administrative control as the optimal long-term solution. Even the strongest supporters of the exclusionary rule concede that the judiciary possess extremely limited capacity to supervise the full range of police activities on a day-to-day basis and that the most effective controls would be those developed and administered by the police authorities themselves. By the mid–1970s, experts on the police had reached a consensus that administrative rulemaking was the best hope for police accountability.[140]

In moving from criticism towards prescription we need to explore briefly what is meant by rulemaking before considering its appropriateness in the police context. Thereafter, we will need to contrast earlier American enthusiasm for rulemaking with Canadian reticence, as well as more recent reassessment in the United States, just as rulemaking has come into vogue in Canada. It will then be necessary to assess particular problems with rulemaking in the police context. Finally, we conclude by asking what role should be envisaged for the courts.

---

[139] See R.V. Ericson, "The News Media and Account Ability in Criminal Justice", in Stenning, above at n. 18, 137, describing this as "account ability", which he defined as "the capacity to provide a record of activities that explains them in a credible manner so that they appear to satisfy the rights and obligations of *accountability*" (emphasis in original).

[140] S. Walker, "Controlling the Cops: A Legislative Approach to Police Rulemaking" (1986) 63 U Det LR 361, 362.

WHAT IS RULEMAKING?

Rulemaking is in its essence an administrative procedure designed to facilitate the formulation and implementation of norms of conduct of general and prospective application. A distinct process has been developed for rulemaking which allows for extensive and broad-based consultation and participation. Goldstein well described administrative rulemaking as:[141]

> "A procedure by which an administrative agency undertakes to confine and structure its discretion by articulating its operating policies in the form of rules. The first steps usually consist of an extensive study in order to produce a proposal for consideration. The study is made in consultation with various interested parties, which, in the case of the police, might be the prosecutor, the judges, city agencies, local community groups, and the special interests that may be involved. The proposed rules are then published, and reactions to them are solicited. The agency then revises its proposal in the light of the criticism received. Implicit in the procedure is a process of drafting, redrafting and redrafting again in an effort to best meet the situation to which the rules are intended to apply. Once a start is made on the process, it calls for building upon precedent."

Yet, rulemaking need not be confined to its traditional structure. Developing structures include "negotiated rulemaking", which proposes that, in the elaboration of rules to guide and structure future conduct (e.g. of police officers), the full range of interested parties be invited to participate in a consultative process of negotiation. In the United States for instance, the Higher Education Act stipulates that the Department of Education must elicit public input into the drafting of regulations, which are then submitted to a committee including students, schools, financial institutions, guarantors and lenders.[142] In criminal law, one can envisage systematic and on-going involvement of a wide range of community representatives and others, including commercial institutions, landlords, community members, youth groups and homeowners. In encouraging the participation of such groups in the (re)fashioning of policy, the process takes on a "collective bargaining" approach,[143] leading to greater representation of social concerns and realities. Pelesh has pointed out the potential substantial advantages of negotiated rulemaking:[144]

> "The potential advantages of negotiated rulemaking are substantial. It engages interested parties, who usually can be readily identified in advance, directly and

---

[141] H. Goldstein, *Policing a Free Society* (Bollinger, Cambridge, Mass., 1977), 115.

[142] See P.J. Harter, "First Judicial Review of Reg Neg a Disappointment" (1996) 22 *Admin & Reg L News* 1.

[143] See Goldsmith, above at n. 80, 104–6.

[144] M.L. Pelesh, "Regulations Under the Higher Education Amendments of 1992: A Case Study in Negotiated Rulemaking" (1994) 57(4) *Law & Contemp Probs* 151, 156. For an excellent analysis, see L. Susskind and G. McMahon, "The Theory and Practice of Negotiated Rulemaking" (1985) 3 *Yale J on Reg* 133, and see the influential article by P.J. Harter, "Negotiating Regulations: A Cure for Malaise" (1981) 71 *Geo LJ* 1.

immediately in the process. It allows these parties to focus on their interests, rather than their positions, which in turn encourages trade-offs. By involving them in the details of the development of regulations, the process wins their support for the regulatory product because it is *their* product. Negotiated rulemaking diminishes the likelihood of adversarial conduct and later legal challenges, and it builds legitimacy for the results. By 'frontloading' dispute into the negotiating committee, the process also reduces the time and cost of promulgating final rules."

While this model may help crack a policy loop which has done little to build consent for criminal law enforcement policy, there are clearly difficulties in integrating widespread community consultation with such an approach. It may be that these logistic difficulties led Goldsmith to limit his vision of public participation in police rulemaking to a narrower set of issues, choosing instead to stress public involvement by other means.[145] While the purpose of this paper is not to offer specific methods of implementation, the thrust of our proposal is to fully integrate public involvement, in a process akin to a "community engagement dialogic model" recently proposed with respect to education reform in the United States.[146] With these general descriptions in mind, we need to turn to consider the suitability of procedures of this nature to policing.

APPROPRIATENESS IN POLICE CONTEXT

By the mid-1970s there was widespread agreement amongst American experts that administrative rulemaking had many benefits to offer in a policing context. These included:

(a) Provision of an appropriate level of check on the broad discretion routinely exercised by the police in all aspects of their work;
(b) Response to the concern that when exercising discretion officers made substantive law enforcement policy without the benefit of planning, coordination and open discussion of agency and community priorities;
(c) Recognition that internally-developed rules are preferable and more effective than those imposed by external authorities;
(d) Opportunity for the police department to formulate positive, proactive policies rather than simply being reactive to community and political pressure;
(e) Acknowledgement that detailed rules for the treatment of suspects could provide what the courts have never been able to supply:

---

[145] Goldsmith, above at n. 80, 108–9.
[146] See M.A. Rebell and R.L. Hughes, "Schools, Communities, and the Courts: A Dialogic Approach to Education Reform" (1996) 14 *Yale L & Pol Rev* 99, promoting reliance on community dialogue.

comprehensive and coherent definition of the rights of suspects together with procedures for assuring that they are respected; and

(f) Progress towards uniformity of law enforcement with any divergences from this objective incorporated in rules which render them visible and requiring explanation.[147]

Most importantly, it was argued that rulemaking was not inconsistent with needed discretion. Indeed, it was recognised that discretion had many positive virtues and that rules could be deployed to guide and control rather than eliminate it. As K.C. Davis put it with customary vigour: "A rule does not necessarily eliminate discretion. The choice is seldom between no discretion and unlimited discretion. Almost all choices involve one mix of rule and discretion and another mix of rule and discretion".[148]

The process side of rulemaking would seem to make it particularly appropriate in light of the current shift toward "community policing". Not only will this development bring the police closer to the citizens they serve by, for example, reinstituting the foot patrol and neighbourhood police station, but it requires that they develop new policing strategies through citizen participation. As Albert Reiss noted in 1992, "[t]he dilemma of modern policing seems to lie in determining whether to continue opting for rational, bureaucratic administration centering on crime events and their control or, rather, to transform policing into a community and social problem-centred bureaucracy that is accountable to localized groups".[149]

While, as we have seen, major pioneering steps have been taken in Ontario with respect to civilian review, it has to be recognised that any complaints-driven review mechanism is inherently incapable of responding to broader concerns for police accountability and community empowerment. After surveying civilian review of police misconduct in Ontario and other North American jurisdictions, Hastings and Saunders found:[150]

> "there is little in either current legislation or practices which broadens the notion of police accountability beyond the assessment of the performance of individual officers and its fit with either the criminal law or other policy and procedural regulations.
>
> There is little indication that the popular notion of police service and accountability to client communities has been translated into operational structures and processes which give these same communities a partnership role in decisions relating to the definition of problems and priorities within a community, nor in the design, implementation or evaluation of the programs or initiatives which constitute the service to these clients."

---

[147] See Walker, above at n. 140, 366; Goldsmith, above at n. 80, 101–2.
[148] K.C. Davis, "An Approach to Legal Control of the Police" (1974) 52 *Tex L Rev* 703, 706.
[149] Reiss, above at n. 31, 93–4.
[150] Hastings and Saunders, above at n. 134, 191–2.

Rulemaking would be a very useful inclusive procedure should we wish to go beyond only involving the public as *complainants*, and include them as *participants* in the delivery of policing services. However, a more profound shift to *partnership* in the design and delivery of policing services, involving as it does the redistribution of power and control between the police and community in the co-production of social order, would outstrip the relatively modest participatory aspirations of notice and comment rulemaking. Nevertheless, should we aspire to get beyond complaints-driven civilian review, citizen involvement through rulemaking will likely have a role to play. Indeed, what is striking about the contemporary debate is not that it is not deeply committed to public consultation, but that effective administrative means have yet to be developed to channel this commitment in a meaningful way.

What prevails here is not the total absence of rules, but the relative unimportance of the matters with which they deal. Thus conventional police manuals overemphasise trivial matters of internal discipline and ignore most of the critical issues related to the exercise of police authority. As the President's Crime Commission pointed out in 1968, "such manuals almost never discuss ... the hard choices policemen must make everyday: whether or not to break up a sidewalk gathering, whether or not to silence a street corner speaker, whether or not to intervene in a domestic dispute, whether or not to stop and frisk, whether or not to arrest".[151]

Andrew Goldsmith, to whose work we will return in a moment, has drawn up a challenging compilation of critical issues going to the heart of police discretionary authority which are seldom covered by comprehensive rules:[152]

"These more important issues such as how to deal with public gatherings, whether or not to get involved in domestic disputes, whether or not to stop and search or to arrest, tend to get ignored. These are issues of obvious importance in police work and in which guidelines would seem not only proper but desirable. Other areas of importance can be suggested on the same basis: carrying and use of firearms; proper responses to intoxicated persons; use of paid informants; procedure for investigation of complaints against police officers; cautioning of juveniles and minor traffic offenders; prosecution policies in cases of uncooperative victims and rights and procedures associated with internal discipline."

For Davis the question was not one of whether, but how much. As he put it, "[t]he surprising fact is that police activities are so little controlled by rules".[153] This perception, of course, is deeply rooted in a broader understanding of administrative law. It is to this we must now turn.

---

[151] United States, President's Commission on Law Enforcement and the Administration of Justice, *The Challenge of Crime in a Free Society: A Report* (Dutton, New York, 1968), 103.
[152] Goldsmith, above at n. 80, 107–8.
[153] Davis, above at n. 148, 705.

RULEMAKING: AMERICAN ENTHUSIASM, CANADIAN RETICENCE

In 1976 K.C. Davis proclaimed, "[t]he United States is entering the age of rulemaking, and the rest of the world in governments of all kinds, is likely to follow. The main tool of getting governmental jobs done will be rulemaking authorised by legislative bodies and checked by courts".[154] He was adamant that the police and prosecutors should all be subject to established principles of administrative law:[155]

> "The governmental know-how that has developed around our most advanced administrative agencies should be applied to both police and prosecutors, who are among our most backward agencies. We should fully exploit all the promising potentialities of the simple idea that administrative law thinking can be profitably applied in criminal administration.
>
> The police are among our most important policymaking administrative agencies. They make policy for peacekeeping and service activities that consume most of their time, and they make policy for law enforcement that takes less than half of their time. One may wonder whether any other agencies—federal, state, or local—make so much policy that so directly and vitally affects so many people."

Davis's enthusiasm to colonise criminal law and administration by administrative law principles was so great that at one point it threatened to collapse in on itself when he was challenged by Ronald Allen. In quoting one of Davis's most famous aphorisms about the striking breadth of responsibility given to administrative agencies back at him, Allen contended: "We do not say to the police: 'Here is the problem. Deal with it'. We say, 'Here is a detailed code. Enforce it'. In short, the police perform a very different function from that of a regulatory agency".[156] Indeed, should Davis's enthusiasm with respect to policymaking be taken completely literally, a very real question could arise as to whether he was advocating an unconstitutional usurpation as it might amend or repeal the criminal law, a task reserved for the legislature.

Whatever the attractiveness of Allen's concern from a theoretical point of view, as a practical matter Davis's enthusiasm for rulemaking carried the day. It was endorsed with ever greater urgency by all three of the "blue-ribbon" commissions on criminal justice in the late 1960s and early 1970s. Consider the language of the American Bar Association's report, *Standards Relating to the Urban Police Function*, in 1973:[157]

---

[154] K.C. Davis, *Administrative Law of the Seventies* (Lawyers' Co-operative Press, New York, 1973), 168.
[155] Davis, above at n. 148, 703.
[156] R. Allen, "The Police and Substantive Rulemaking: Reconciling Principles and Expediency" (1976) 125 *U Pa LR* 62, 97.
[157] American Bar Association, Advisory Committee on the Police Function, *Standards Relating to the Urban Police Function* (Institute of Judicial Administration, New York, 1973), 116.

"Police discretion can best be structured and controlled through the process of administrative rulemaking by police agencies. Police administrators should, therefore, give the highest priority to the formulation of administrative rules governing the exercise of discretion, particularly in the areas of selective enforcement, investigative techniques, and enforcement methods."

At this juncture, we need to notice a somewhat ironic development in which American ardour for rulemaking has cooled significantly just as Canada begins to display a new interest in administrative legislation and not merely adjudication. Twenty years after Davis's confident prediction, there is now widespread disillusionment in the United States with the whole idea of trying to regulate everything by way of ever more detailed rules.[158] Nowhere has this been better captured than in Philip Howard's 1995 best-seller, *The Death of Common Sense: How Law is Suffocating America*. While recognising that governments today are called on to provide more extended social programmes, provide greater oversight in areas such as worker safety and control over common resources such as the environment, Howard argues most persuasively that the cause of stupefying prolixity lies not in role, but technique:[159]

"Much of the growth in law, however, was due not to government's expanded role but to its techniques. We changed our attitude toward legal detail: The words of law expanded far faster than the new areas of law. The Federal Register, a daily report of new and proposed regulations, increased from 15,000 pages in the final year of John F. Kennedy's presidency to over 70,000 pages in the last year of George Bush's. The Interstate Highway System, still the country's largest postwar public works program, was authorized by a 1956 statute that ran 28 pages. A transportation act passed by Congress in 1991, which almost none of you probably noticed, was ten times longer. Today's local fire and building codes have roughly the same purposes as those of forty years ago, but are much longer.

. . . .

While lawmakers and bureaucrats demonstrated their energy in making laws, they showed no facility for paring them back. Most of these new legal dictates were stacked on top of the prior year's laws and rules. The agencies created by Congress have multiplied these statutory dictates, like fishes and loaves, into many more thousands of rules and regulations. EPA alone has over 10,000 pages of regulations. The result, after several decades of unrestrained growth, is a mammoth legal edifice unparalleled in history: Federal statutes and formal rules now total about 100 million words.

. . . .

Once the idea is to cover every situation explicitly, the words of law expand like floodwaters that have broken through a dike. Rules elaborate on prior rules; detail breeds greater detail. There is no logical stopping point in the quest for certainty."

---

[158] See, e.g., M. Asimow, "California Underground Regulations" (1992) 44 *Admin LR* 43; T.O. McGarity, "Some Thoughts on 'Deossifying' the Rulemaking Process" (1992) 41 *Duke LJ* 1385; J.L. Mashaw, "Improving the Environment of Agency Rulemaking: An Essay on Management, Games and Accountability" (1994) 57(2) *Law & Contemp Probs* 185.

[159] P.K. Howard, *The Death of Common Sense: How Law is Suffocating America* (Random House, New York, 1994), 25–7.

Objections to rulemaking are widespread in the United States. By way of contrast, in Canada we seem, somewhat belatedly, to be moving into the age of rulemaking with a very extensive system of notice and comment rulemaking at the federal level, a general Quebec statute and a very demanding new Securities Act in Ontario which goes well beyond what is normally required in the United States to render public participation meaningful.[160] As Cass Sunstein has recently asserted, arguments against rulemaking may be "chastening", yet "do not defeat the project of those who are enthusiastic about rules".[161] It is against this background that we should move on to consider several somewhat more specific concerns about police rulemaking.

PARTICULAR PROBLEMS WITH RULEMAKING IN THE POLICING CONTEXT

We need to consider here first, the limits of volunteerism in rulemaking; second, the role of police culture and mediated rulemaking; third, the nature of police culture and the extent to which it would be appropriate to incorporate it in rulemaking, and fourth, the overall desirability and feasibility of public participation in police rulemaking.

Research reveals a particularly wide gap between aspiration and implementation when it comes to police rulemaking. Despite overwhelming support for such an undertaking in all the many studies, and a clear consensus among all the academic commentators (itself no mean achievement) very little has actually been achieved. "The central defect with the administrative rulemaking concept as generally proposed", Samuel Walker observed some ten years ago, "is its voluntaristic approach. Experience has demonstrated that law enforcement agencies will not undertake rulemaking voluntarily".[162] Indeed, where rules have been developed, such as ones dealing with the use of deadly force, domestic violence and intelligence gathering (spying), they have almost all been developed through a process of crisis management, often in response to a lawsuit, political pressure or other emergency. In the absence of any effective incentives (other than intermittent crises), Walker proposed that state legislatures or local city councils should enact legislation or city ordinances *requiring* law enforcement agencies to undertake *systematic* rulemaking.

The question then arises as to whether such external stimulation will undermine what, as we have seen, has always been a central claim of proponents of rulemaking—internally developed rules are preferable and more effective than those imposed by external authorities. This external-internal dilemma may be most usefully explored by way of a return to the work of Andrew

---

[160] See Evans *et al.*, above at n. 2, 359–79.
[161] C.R. Sunstein, "Problems with Rules" (1995) 83 *Cal LR* 953, 1022.
[162] Walker, above at n. 140, 382.

Goldsmith, who in a particularly stimulating article entitled "Taking Police Culture Seriously: Police Discretion and the Limits of Law", contends that there is not a policy vacuum after all.[163] While formal law does not permeate fully to street level and formal administrative control is at best contingent, internal rules operate to guide and regulate police officers' response to external rules such as departmental regulations. These internal rules are pervasive and fill in apparent policy vacuums in police work such as responses to domestic violence and mentally disturbed persons in which substantial normative guidance has traditionally come from the police culture, rather than from external norms.

Why, Goldsmith then asks, should not these norms of police culture be recognised and assimilated into formal rules?[164]

> "One can therefore speak of the failure of external legal regulation in two senses. First, there is the demonstrated inability of external rules to influence and control certain aspects of police work, especially where competing internal rules and standards can be seen to exist. Then there is the failure of external rules to even address some aspects of police work. In contrast, it would seem that internal rules play an active and significant role in many spheres of police operations. Therefore it can be argued that the informal 'rule-world' of the police culture should be recognized for its *potential* as well as actual role in regulating police conduct. It would seem possible to foresee an official recognition of the police culture's contribution to normative regulation of police work in both 'policy filled' and 'policy vacuum' areas, as much because of the desirability of structuring police discretion as because of its inevitable ability to deflect and distort external rules."

This more positive and realistic assessment of the role of police culture is seen as being best implemented by way of negotiated rulemaking, rather than by notice and comment. Such negotiated rulemaking would seek, through an informal process of bargaining among groups, to avoid traditional regulatory processes which are all too often slow, cumbersome and overly adversarial. "The collective bargaining or negotiated rulemaking approach arguably comes closest to realizing the goal of responding empathetically and constructively to the concerns of the police culture and to the demands of street-level police work".[165]

But can this recognition of a police culture capable of autonomous behaviour be reconciled with the broader public interest? Goldsmith's impression of the constituent elements of police culture is that it is to a considerable extent benign—a bond of solidarity between officers, and membership in a craft in which learning is by apprenticeship on the job, not at police college, and respect is won from colleagues on the job, not from attentive supervisors. At the same time, he also acknowledges that in many respects the values internalised by street-level police officers do not accord with the rule of law ideal

---

[163] Goldsmith, above at n. 80, 93.
[164] Ibid., 96 (emphasis in original).
[165] Ibid., 106.

of law enforcement; as where the action perspective of the police "crime-fighter" is frustrated by externally imposed rules and procedures, which are seen as unwarranted impediments to effective law enforcement.

Goldsmith does not fully explain how "Dirty Harry's" views are going to be filtered out in a negotiation process which is empathetic and constructive in its response to police culture. At the same time, respect for police culture may have to be bought at considerable cost to more general public involvement in police rulemaking.

"The assumption", Goldsmith asks most provocatively, "that public participation in police rulemaking is an unqualified human good is open to question".[166] He goes on to suggest that "because the average citizen is hardly a stakeholder of any real consequence with respect to a range of issues pertaining to operational police work, it is scarcely an affront to democracy if no explicit role for public participation is provided in police rulemaking *for those issues*".[167] While his emphasis is not to be ignored, drawing a line at what is, or is not, "operational police work" will no doubt prove to be very problematic, an issue we have already noted in discussing the present structure in Ontario. One has only to consider, for example, the difficulties involved in distinguishing between "policy" and "operational" decisions for the purposes of government tort liability.[168]

There is also concern, at least in the United States, that the "public" does not speak with anything approaching one voice on matters of law enforcement policy:[169]

> "Whether public involvement in rulemaking would help resolve these conflicts, if only by making the debate public, or aggravate them by polarizing the community through a process that may encourage public posturing by the advocates of different positions, is not clear."

While we return to this deeply troubling question in our conclusion, our contention is that rulemaking processes allow for the integration and flourishing of pluralistic communities. While it may be more difficult to reach palatable rules in heterogenous communities, the resulting rules as well as the process of reaching those rules allow pluralistic societies to thrive.[170] That a consensus needs to be *reached* should not discourage us from engaging in dialogic processes and reaping rulemaking's potential benefits. As Alison Harvison Young elaborates, pluralist approaches to administrative law share commonalities with recent legal focus on processes of "contextualisation".[171] The integration of different voices leads to broader, and more functional, understandings of law and decision-making.

---

[166] Goldsmith, above at n. 80, 108.
[167] Ibid., 109 (emphasis in original).
[168] For a review of the law governing liability for the negligent exercise of statutory powers see Evans *et al.*, above at n. 2, 1447–84.
[169] Walker, above at n. 140, 389.
[170] Sunstein, above at n. 161, 969.
[171] See Alison Harvison Young's paper in this volume.

A ROLE FOR THE COURTS?

We noted earlier the courts' unwillingness to review the discretionary activity of criminal justice officials. We have also asserted that *ex post* review may be inappropriate in most cases, preferring instead a proactive approach to discretionary authority. Courts, however, should encourage such rulemaking, and not maintain an entirely passive stance when faced with cases involving the exercise of discretion. The adoption of rulemaking processes should be explicitly encouraged by courts while deciding cases on a daily basis. While there has, as yet, been little judicial support for any notion that the courts should require the structuring of overly-broad grants of discretion by administrative agencies, two interesting cases on the volatile border between criminal, administrative and constitutional law should be noted. They may well be an indication of things to come.

In *Gallant's* case,[172] a prisoner at a maximum security penitentiary was ordered to be transferred to a "high maximum" facility. The basis of his transfer was his suspected involvement in extortion, drugs and threats of violence. The authorities refused to identify those who had informed against him on the grounds that to do so would be to place their lives at risk. Mr. Justice Pratte concluded that the principles of "fundamental justice" did not have the same flexibility as "natural justice" and that the respondent had not been given a real opportunity to answer the allegations made against him. However, he then held that the complete discretion granted the authorities by statute to transfer prisoners met the requirements of section 1 of the Canadian Charter of Rights and Freedoms.[173]

By contrast Madam Justice Desjardins, in a spirited dissent, pointed to American cases in which courts had not been willing to simply accept the conclusion of the authorities as to the danger in which informants might be placed if their identities were revealed. "In many of these cases, there are indications that administrative rules have been designed to assist and guide prison authorities in accommodating the need for fairness in disciplinary proceedings with prison security. None are present in this case".[174]

A similar concern was carried over into the *Gough* case.[175] Here there had been a revocation of parole without revealing to the parolee the identities of the victims of alleged sexual assaults. The Parole Board relied on regulation 17(5) of the Parole Regulations which allowed for non-disclosure where, in

---

[172] *Gallant v. Trono, Deputy Commissioner, Correctional Services Canada* (1989) 36 Admin LR 261 (Fed. C.A.) (hereafter referred to as *Gallant*).

[173] Canadian Charter of Rights and Freedoms, Part I of the Constitution Act, 1982, being Schedule B to the Canada Act 1982 (U.K.), c. 11 (hereafter referred to as Charter of Rights and Freedoms). See *Gallant*, ibid., 272.

[174] *Gallant*, ibid., 281.

[175] *Gough v. Canada (National Parole Board)* (1990) 45 Admin LR 304 (F.C., T.D.) (hereafter referred to as *Gough*).

the Board's opinion, disclosure could reasonably be expected to threaten the safety of individuals. After reviewing regulation 17(5), Madam Justice Reed concluded:[176]

> "These are disturbingly broad provisions. While I do not find it necessary to decide whether Reg. 17(5) is *ultra vires* (perhaps it can operate in certain circumstances), it suffices to say that when that regulation is used to deny a paroled inmate the kind of information which was denied in this case, it is inapplicable for that purpose."

While there may be some concern here that this sort of approach involves the court inappropriately in the design of institutional procedures, it is evident that persistent unwillingness to confine discretion may well deprive it of the essential predictive qualities of "law" for the purposes of section 1 of the Charter of Rights and Freedoms. Continued judicial reliance on such approaches will encourage criminal justice officials to consider rulemaking to guide their discretion. Once this attitude is prevalent, community involvement can be encouraged as the most effective approach.

CONCLUSION

In advancing police rulemaking as an example of what should fall comfortably within the province of modern administrative law, one will undoubtedly encounter conventional criticism about the efficacy of rules, their relevance, and the pitfalls of rulemaking generally. At this stage, however, it is important to return to first principles. At times, one must return to basics in order to re-discover old ideas in a new setting. To believe that discretion could be eliminated would be exceptionally naive; rather, what is required is an increase in mutual confidence and respect between police and the communities they serve. Mr. Justice Doherty elegantly articulates the contemporary problem in discussing the concept of "reasonable cause":[177]

> "The requirement that the facts must meet an objectively discernible standard is recognized in connection with the arrest power, and serves to avoid indiscriminate and discriminatory exercises of the police power. A 'hunch' based entirely on intuition gained by experience cannot suffice, *no matter how accurate that 'hunch' might prove to be*. Such subjectively based assessments can too easily mask discriminatory conduct based on such irrelevant factors as the detainee's sex, colour, age, ethnic origin or sexual orientation. Equally, without objective criteria detentions could be based on mere speculation. A guess which proves accurate becomes in hindsight a 'hunch'."

In a heterogeneous society, defining "community" becomes a difficult task; a difficulty with which all policing reform must grapple. "Like the concept of 'community', the concept of 'community policing' is in the eye of the

---

[176] *Gough v. Canada (National Parole Board)* (1990) 45 Admin LR 304, 324.
[177] *R. v. Simpson* (1993) 12 OR (3d) 182, 202 (Ont. C.A.) (emphasis added).

beholder".[178] Critics notwithstanding, people generally aspire to excel in their work. Both police forces and the public have a strong interest in developing rulemaking processes that, in aspiring toward the structuring of police discretion, engage participants in an on-going process of policy formulation. It is the estrangement of the policing function that has led, in part, to the need to develop "community policing" programmes. By positing a continuing process, rulemaking does not suffer from the one-shot nature of other programmes.

Police officers are not strangers to rules and guidelines. Existing policies and procedures are rather elaborate, focussing on a variety of issues, from the mundane (e.g., how to dress for court appearances) to the more controversial (e.g., high-speed chases). While there may be elements of police culture which focus on how officers 'handle situations' rather than how closely they follow manuals, there is little reason to believe that the introduction of a rulemaking process would be met with police resistance. Furthermore, it may well be that, if they were to have a hand in the elaboration of policy and procedures, individual officers (and, as a result, perhaps police culture generally) could change their perspectives. Similarly, public cooperation with the police could be enhanced, with parties legitimately feeling that they had contributed to implemented policy, and can continue to do so. Through this mechanism, police and citizens are less likely "to then reject the terms of such rules or to frustrate the realisation of the purposes behind the rules".[179] In Ontario, consultation mechanisms are already in place. The development of community-centric policing models has begun to set the stage for the implementation of a full-blown rulemaking process. Once largely foreign to Canadian law, rulemaking is inching its way toward greater acceptance. Evidence of this "brave new world" is readily found in the ways the Ontario Securities Commission is now required to operate.[180]

The infrastructure for police complaints in Toronto has deservedly received wide recognition. Attempts to integrate the public into the sanctuaries of police discipline, while initially met with opposition by members of the force, can now be treated as significant building blocks. The time has come, however, to slowly move away from an excessive emphasis on the adjudicative. Certainly, some of the more general issues dealt with at the level of complaints can be dealt with in a more satisfactory, and likely less adversarial, policy-making forum. It is not that the individual case is unimportant; rather, the reality is that for every individual complaint there are likely others who choose not to complain, and that no effective machinery is in place to generalise the lessons which could be learned from individual complaints.[181]

---

[178] Leighton, above at n. 39, 487.

[179] Goldsmith, above at n. 80, 105.

[180] See Janisch, above at n. 109 and P. Anisman, "Authorizing Regulation: The Securities Amendment Act 1994", in P. Anisman and R.F. Reid (eds), *Administrative Law: Issues and Practice* (Carswell, Toronto, 1995), 49.

[181] For a thorough discussion, see Goldsmith, above at n. 130. It is interesting to note that, in Ontario, the Police Complaints Commissioner may make recommendations regarding the practices or procedures of a police force: see s. 101 of the Police Services Act.

Davis's insistence on the benefits of rulemaking should not be ignored. Yet, his understanding of rulemaking as a top-down imposition, namely the transfer of "most of the policy-making power from patrolmen to the better qualified heads of departments, acting on the advice of appropriate specialists",[182] must be adapted to changing needs. It is at the level of policy formation that a wide range of concerns can be dealt with effectively and efficiently. As Dawn Oliver notes, citizenship encompasses extended participation in both politics and public culture.[183] While existing legal structures support this key value of participation, our project is concerned with the formation of criminal justice policy, which remains particularly one-sided. Innovative solutions must be found; for as Mark Aronson emphasises, adaptable methods of achieving accountability and legitimacy are necessary.[184] While various forms of rulemaking exist, we would urge that future reform look to a host of actors participating in the process, even with radically divergent views, so that criminal justice policy may begin to be understood as the product of a "bottom-up" process of deliberation.

---

[182] This is the view espoused in K.C. Davis, *Discretionary Justice: A Preliminary Inquiry* (Louisiana State University Press, Baton Rouge, 1969), 90–1.

[183] See Dawn Oliver's paper in this volume.

[184] See Mark Aronson's paper in this volume.

13

The Politics of Deference: Judicial Review and Democracy

DAVID DYZENHAUS*

INTRODUCTION

How should judges in common law jurisdictions respond to administrative determinations of the law? Should they defer to such determinations or evaluate them in accordance with their sense of what the right determination should have been? Buried in these often highly technical questions of administrative law are important issues in political and legal theory. Hence, to answer the questions one has to engage in a full discussion of the politics of judicial deference. I will start with a sketch of why these administrative law questions are so freighted with politics before examining the politics of judicial deference.

The role of judges in the legal order has always been controversial, though there was a time when at least the terms of the controversy were quite clear. At a time when legal order could be conceived as made up of a division of powers between the legislature, the judiciary, and the executive, one could agree that it was the task of the legislature to make law, of the executive to implement the law, and of judges to ensure that the executive stayed within the bounds of the law. Opinion divided on the question whether the legislature was the sole source of law or whether it was answerable to principles of a higher law, instantiated in the common law.

---

* This article is dedicated to the memory of my friend, teacher, and former colleague, Etienne Mureinik, whose tragic death in July 1996 deprived South Africa, the common law world, and the conference for which this paper was written of one of the most acute minds working in administrative law. In particular, his death leaves unworked out his idea of a legal culture of justification, a topic which, as will become clear below, is of crucial importance to my own work.

Sujit Choudhry's superb research assistance, especially two memoranda he put together on English case law and on English public law theory, made writing this article a far less onerous task. His research was funded by a grant from the Cecil J. Wright Foundation of the Faculty of Law at the University of Toronto. I also thank Kent Roach and Terry Hancock for comments on a draft of this paper, and, most of all, Mike Taggart, to whose 45 editorial suggestions I have tried my best to respond.

The Canadian material is in part adapted from my earlier articles, "Developments in Administrative Law: The 1991–92 Term" (1993) 4 *Supreme Court LR (2d)* 177 and "Developments in Administrative Law: The 1992–93 Term" (1994) 5 *Supreme Court LR (2d)* 189.

The camps which divided on this question were, roughly speaking, democratic positivists and liberal antipositivists. Democratic positivists, following the tradition established by Jeremy Bentham, argued that the legislature is the sole source of law and that its legitimacy derived from its accountability to the people. For judges to claim that the law was anything but the law enacted by the legislature was, therefore, for them to act undemocratically. In order for judges to fulfil their role in the legal order of enforcing the will of the people, that will had to be expressed in legislation which made it as clear as possible what that will is. Put differently, lack of ambiguity is what made judicial deference to the will of the legislature possible. Conversely, ambiguity or alleged ambiguity in the law gave judges the occasion for judicial legislation, and thus was best avoided. Positive law is, then, the law of the legislature which has the attributes which enable judicial deference to legislative will.

Bentham was a great opponent of the common law, even advocating its abolition. His opposition was driven by more than his sense that the common law was too messy to ever have the attributes of positivity. He was also concerned about what he saw as the judicial device in a common law system of alleging that ambiguity existed in legislation in order to superimpose the judges' sense of right and wrong on the legislation. In other words, the common law provided a resource to judges which they could use to bootstrap themselves to the apex of the legal order.

Antipositivists, following a tradition most famously articulated by Sir William Blackstone, argued that the common law was not a mess but the legal repository of the moral values of the people. Judges, in enforcing common law values, were, on this view, giving effect to the will of the people. In using the common law as the value-laden background against which legislation was to be interpreted, judges were not setting themselves against the people's will because that background, no less than legislation, was the product of the people. Since proponents of this view identified common law values with the rights and liberties of the individual, we can therefore refer to them as liberal antipositivists.

The division into democratic positivists and liberal antipositivists is rough because the former set great store by the rights and liberties of the individual while the latter generally acknowledge that where a statute speaks clearly it legitimately overrides the common law. Nevertheless, the camps represent the poles on a continuum between which debate still moves today.

Albert Venn Dicey notoriously made both of its poles the supports of his model of the rule of law, and administrative law theory has yet to move out of his shadow.[1] This is the case despite the fact that Dicey wrote at the end of the era when legal order could be conceived in the simple way sketched

[1] A.V. Dicey, *Lectures Introductory to the Study of the Law of the Constitution* (Macmillan, London, 1st ed. 1885). For an instructive account of Dicey, see P.P. Craig, *Public Law and Democracy in the United Kingdom and the United States of America* (Clarendon Press, Oxford, 1990), ch. 2.

above. Dicey wrote, that is, at a time when the administrative state was on the cards. He could see the potential growth of administrative agencies which had power delegated to them by the legislature to develop the legal regimes governing the particular social programmes given to their charge.

Dicey's understanding of the rule of law not only made no place for such agencies; it was deliberately constructed as an ideological obstacle in the way of their growth. The major component of the obstacle is the assumption that law of the land to which public officials are to be held accountable is a unitary set of legal rules, maintained as such by judges of the superior courts who have ultimate interpretative authority over the law. Dicey reconciled that interpretative authority with the sovereignty of the legislature by adverting to the fact that the English Parliament did not generally use legislation as a blunt instrument to overrule judges' interpretation of statutes in the light of the common law. From this practice of non-intervention he inferred tacit approval by Parliament of the rule of law, a doctrine which, in his view, united parliamentary sovereignty with the "supremacy of law", meaning the supremacy of judicial interpretation.[2] In summary his argument is: the rule of law is an essential moral good; administrative agencies with power to make and interpret their own law do not fit within the model of the rule of law; therefore, allegiance to the rule of law entails opposing the administrative state.

Dicey's model could not, however, provide more than an intermittent obstacle to the administrative state for two reasons. First, the growth of the administrative state was driven by the popular demand for redistributive and welfare programmes, a demand which was expressed in the statutes that laid the basis of that state. Second, the democratic pole of Dicey's model required judicial deference to clear expressions of legislative intent, and so required deference to the intent to delegate law-making power to administrative agencies. It seemed to follow that even judges who were determined to assert their place as guardians of the rule of law against a looming administrative "despotism" could be brought into line by statutory command. Indeed, legislatures discovered a more sophisticated device than the threat of statutory reaction to judicial intransigence. They began to resort to the preemptive device of the privative or ouster clause, the statutory provision which tells judges that the decisions of the agency constituted by a statute are immune to judicial supervision.[3] In short, the practice of legislative non-intervention on which Dicey's model of the rule of law depended seemed to have died.

[2] See Dicey, *An Introduction to the Study of the Law of the Constitution* (Macmillan, London, 8th ed. 1924), ch. XIII.

[3] I shall in what follows adopt the term "privative clause" since it is far more indicative of a particular judicial attitude than the bland "ouster (or preclusive) clause". For the idea of privation suggests both a depriving and a privatisation. It thus conveys much more than the thought that something has been expressly removed or ousted from the court's purview that would otherwise lie therein. First, it conveys the thought that what has been removed is what should properly have been left to the court. Second, it conveys the thought that something that would otherwise have been public has been improperly made a private matter—one for decision outside the supposedly open public realm in which courts operate.

But, as I have already suggested, administrative law theory has not yet moved out of Dicey's shadow. One reason for this is that, as Sir William Wade has pointed out, the use of privative clauses has the paradoxical effect of appearing to increase judicial power.[4] The device of the privative clause, far from performing its intended preemptive role, perversely perpetuates what it seeks to avoid. It requires judges to provide an interpretation of legislative intention faithful to a more general legislative intention which has it that judges should have no role in providing such an interpretation. Since the effect would be to give agencies protected by a strong privative clause an unlimited jurisdiction, judges are forced to find some way of reconciling the privative clause with the incontestable idea that the legislature must have intended some legal limits to the agency's jurisdiction. The logic of the doctrine of *ultra vires*, that there are legal limits to any statutory delegation of law-making power to an agency, is one to which the legislatures of common law legal orders are as committed as their judiciaries. And if that logic is tied to alleged facts about legislative intent, it requires judges facing a privative clause to make some distinction of the kind between jurisdictional and non-jurisdictional errors of law. The former are mistakes made by an agency about the scope of its power and which it is not therefore entitled to make, while the latter are mistakes which are made within the scope of its power and which it therefore may be entitled to make.

Such distinctions cannot, however, be implemented in a satisfactory fashion because there is no practical way of determining what is jurisdictional and what is non-jurisdictional error of law. This is a fact more or less frankly recognised in the United Kingdom in the wake of the leading House of Lords decision in *Anisminic Ltd. v. Foreign Compensation Commission*.[5] In the result, the United Kingdom position seems to be that, whether or not there is a privative clause, there is no principled reason for a court to refrain from correcting what it perceives to be errors in an agency's determination of the law.

The Canadian Supreme Court, in contrast, is still wrestling with the task of elaborating a test which could make the distinction work, a commitment dating from its firm entrenchment of the distinction in its leading decision, *Canadian Union of Public Employees Local 963 v. New Brunswick Liquor Corporation*.[6] But, as we will see more clearly below, the (inevitably) unsatisfactory nature of its test, as well as a recent move to deprivatise privative

---

[4] H.W.R. Wade, *Constitutional Fundamentals* (Stevens & Sons, London, rev. ed. 1980), 88–9.
[5] [1969] 2 AC 147 (hereafter referred to as *Anisminic*).
[6] [1979] 2 SCR 227 (hereafter referred to as *CUPE*). In *CUPE* the issue before the Court was an interpretation by the Public Service Labour Relations Board of New Brunswick of a statutory provision in the Public Service Relations Act, RSNB 1973, c.P-25, s.102(3)(a). The Board, whose determinations were protected by a privative clause, held that the provision excluded the employer, the New Brunswick Liquor Corporation, from replacing striking employees with management personnel.

clauses, make its position in substance little different from that in the United Kingdom.[7]

In sum, privative clauses amount to a clear statutory command which judges find themselves compelled either to ignore or radically to rewrite. The result is an apparent increase in judicial power because judges are no longer without exception bound by the clear statutory command of the legislature. But the compulsion is not one whose force is limited to judges wishing to preserve a role for themselves at the apex of the legal order. Legislatures must also acknowledge that the power they delegate is inherently limited by law. It follows that judges when they read down privative clauses are at one level respecting the intention of the legislature (a more abstract and long term intention) that there are inherent legal limits to official power.

The force of the compulsion is perhaps best illustrated by the fact that, at least in Canada, the judges who have felt it most recently have not been motivated by a Diceyan fear of the administrative state. Since they are for the most part either quite well disposed or at least not outright hostile to the administrative state, their common motivation has had much more to do with worries about the rule of law, with concerns about maintaining legal standards to which public officials are accountable.

The irony is that this saga is being played out at a time when the opponents of the administrative state are to be found within the apparatus of the state, as governments get themselves elected on the basis of their determination to do away with state delivery and regulation of public programmes. The pressing problems of administrative law are going to be problems to do with the reach of public power. They will be problems to do with whether public legally enforceable standards of accountability apply to the bewildering range of quasi-public and allegedly private institutions and bodies which are competing to take over the tasks of the administrative state. Governments, as well as removing standard mechanisms of public law accountability, may well resort to privative clauses to protect the process of privatisation from the reach of standards developed during the heyday of the state. Hence, while the political context of administrative law is in a process of radical change, the issue of the judicial role in upholding the rule of law remains a relative constant. Indeed, if the current debate in the United Kingdom is anything to go by, the change in political context has reignited that issue.[8]

At present, that debate is for the most part firmly bound by the terms sketched at the outset of this article. The central question remains whether

---

[7] That is the position which obtains as a result of *R. v. Lord President of the Privy Council, ex parte Page* [1993] AC 682 (hereafter referred to as *Page*), where it was held, *inter alia*, that the common law, no less than a statute, can confer final and conclusive jurisdiction . See, e.g., the discussion in P.P. Craig, "Jurisdiction, Judicial Control, and Agency Autonomy", in I. Loveland (ed.), *A Special Relationship? American Influences on Public Law in the UK* (Clarendon Press, Oxford, 1995), 173, 173–5.

[8] That debate is of course also fuelled by questions about the relationship between the law of the United Kingdom and its obligations under the law of the European Community.

the legal limits of an agency's power are just those limits the legislature intended to set, or whether the common law sets limits as well.

Liberal antipositivists argue that the story of *ultra vires* in the United Kingdom shows that the doctrine of *ultra vires* should itself be discarded along with the idea of legislative intention with which it is usually linked. Judges, they say, have a basis in the legal order for enforcing the law which is not dependent on any facts about legislative intent. The common law is the obvious alternative in a legal order where there is no written constitution, and the question then becomes how far different members of this camp are prepared to go. Do they rest content with the weak claim that the common law provides merely the basis for judicial evasion of privative clauses and for resolving "ambiguities" in statutes? Or do they make stronger claims about the common law protecting the rights and liberties of the individual to the extent that judges can legitimately (are *legally* entitled to) resist clear legislative encroachments on certain rights and liberties? Sir John Laws has opened up this particular issue with (given the general make-up of the Bench) an unfortunately phallic metaphor for the judicial role, saying that it is time to strip away the *ultra vires* "figleaf" from the fact of a judicial power autonomous of any statutory base.[9]

The other camp, the heirs of democratic positivism, are reluctant to concede that judges have a basis of legitimacy independent of statute.[10] They argue that the weak claims made within the antipositivist camp are easy to meet. In regard to the issue of the basis for the judicial creation of the doctrine of *ultra vires*, they respond by saying that that creation can itself be regarded as based on legislative intent. In regard to the issue of the justice of the common law filling gaps or resolving ambiguities in legislative intent, they respond by saying that such a practice is dependent on there not being clear indications of legislative intent to the contrary. To be sure, both responses turn out to be in substance identical, since the idea of legislative intent invoked in the first is one which, as in the second, is about legislative legitimation inferred from a lack of explicit legislative contradiction.

The real fear of the democratic positivists is the slippery slope that leads to the stronger claims about the priority of certain common law values over statute. In their view, it is for politicians and not judges to decide whether certain political and moral values are going to be made the criteria of valid law. However, as the most elaborate presentation of their views illustrates, their own version of the story of *ultra vires* belies their confidence in their position. For they do not argue that the figleaf metaphor is wrong—that judges were

---

[9] Sir John Laws, "Illegality: The Problem of Jurisdiction", in M. Supperstone and J. Goudie (eds), *Judicial Review* (Butterworths, London, 1992), 51, 67.
[10] Sir William Wade is the leading exponent of this view. See H.W.R. Wade and C.F. Forsyth, *Administrative Law* (Clarendon Press, Oxford, 7th ed. 1995), esp. 735–9 and C. Forsyth, "Of Fig Leaves and Fairy Tales: The *Ultra Vires* Doctrine, the Sovereignty of Parliament, and Judicial Review" [1996] *CLJ* 122.

in fact just giving effect to legislative intent. Rather, they argue that one has to keep the figleaf in place in order to "preserve the decencies".[11] One must, in other words, pretend that the judges were giving effect to legislative intent because, if we strip away the pretence, we are visibly on the slippery slope.

Now there are different versions of this position. One is that the judges wrested power away from the legislature; however, it is best to ignore this fact, remaining content with apparent legislative acquiescence and hence tacit legitimation of this state of affairs. The other is that judges were acting in accordance with fundamental constitutional/legal responsibilities in bringing the legislature to heel and that legislative acquiescence is best seen as evidence of legislative ackowledgement of the same set of constitutional fundamentals.[12] However, it is best not to acknowledge that judges have this basis in constitutional fundamentals for acting because it might go to their heads.

No-one in the democratic camp finds the first version adequate by itself, and so it is always offered together with the second version. But the trouble with the second version is that there is no real difference between it and the antipositivist position, except for the claim that the figleaf has to be kept in place both for decency's sake and to avoid judges' extending their power base. If that claim is to be understood as one based in principle—the idea that the figleaf must remain in place for democracy's sake—then it is question-begging. For its proponents have not yet begun to supply the theory of democracy in which such a claim must be situated.

In addition, the compromise democratic positivists make in balancing their view of democratic principle with the rule of law idea that there are legal limits to any political power is a bad one. As already suggested, the pressing problems of administrative law are going to be about the reach of public power. One of the factors that makes the new political context of administrative law so problematic is that new power holders will often not get their power directly from any statutory instrument, but, much more likely, through a contract with some branch of government. Hence, a doctrine of *ultra vires* tied to facts about legislative intent will not be of any help since there is no statutory instrument on which to hang the claim of inherent legal limits on power. However, if there is a basis independent of legislative intent for judicial enforcement of the rule of law, then there is the potential for judges to continue to play a role in maintaining the rule of law in the new political context.

It may well be the case that the democratic positivists are untroubled by this scenario if it is also the case that they are, by and large, in agreement with the political programmes that drive privatisation. It would follow that, strange as this may seem, the true heirs to Dicey's concerns about the erosion of the rule of law may be those who would resist government attempts to bring about an era of unrestrained "private" power. They have to cope with

[11] Forsyth, ibid., 136.
[12] Wade and Forsyth, above at n. 10, 737–8.

a much more complex legal order, one in which it is assumed that administrative agencies legitimately have power to make and interpret law at the same time as administrative power is increasingly devolved on quasi-public and private entities. The task that faces them is no less than providing a theory of democratic legal order, one which justifies a workable account of the role for judicial review in the new political context.

In this task, liberal antipositivists have the advantage over democratic positivists of frankly confronting the fact that judges have a crucial role to play in upholding the values of the legal order. But they persist both in maintaining judges at the apex of the legal order and in equating the values of the legal order with common law values understood in the individualistic way which implies hostility to the administrative state.[13]

In this paper, I hope to show that a close examination of some leading Canadian decisions, mainly on the topic of judicial deference to administrative decisions, can assist us in this task. I will argue that Dicey's model requires judges to adopt a principle of deference which has to be rejected. This is the principle I will call submissive deference, since what it requires of judges is that they submit to the intention of the legislature, on a positivist understanding of intention.

The alternative principle is the principle of deference as respect. Deference as respect requires not submission but a respectful attention to the reasons offered or which could be offered in support of a decision, whether that decision be the statutory decision of the legislature, a judgment of another court, or the decision of an administrative agency. I will argue that only this principle can rearticulate the proper relationship between the legislature, administrative agencies and the courts. I will argue further that the sense it makes requires the courts to reject the Diceyan model of law in which the idea of submissive deference is an essential component. I also suggest that the model of the rule of law to which the principle of deference as respect is committed might well prove fruitful in the new political context of administrative law, in particular because of its explicit commitment to the value of equality.

THE PARADOX OF THE RECOGNITION OF RATIONALITY

The most astonishing fact about the Supreme Court of Canada's role in administrative law is that two of the Court's most important decisions in this domain were not only decided in the same year, but are so in tension with

---

[13] T.R.S. Allan has done the pioneering work in constructing a liberal antipositivist basis for administrative law. See T.R.S Allan, *Law, Liberty, and Justice: The Legal Foundations of British Constitutionalism* (Clarendon Press, Oxford, 1993). I explore the problematic tendencies in his work in a book review in (1995) 45 *UTLJ* 205. For a powerful account of why Ronald Dworkin's legal theory, the principal inspiration of contemporary liberal antipositivism, is unlikely to prove helpful in this task, see M. Allars, "On Deference to Tribunals, With Deference to Dworkin" (1994) 20 *Queen's LJ* 163.

each other that they have created a central paradox for Canadian administrative law. That is, taken together, these decisions make a statement about Canadian administrative law which is contradictory but also true. The two decisions are *CUPE* and *Nicholson* v. *Haldimand-Norfolk Regional Board of Commissioners of Police*.[14]

CUPE's contribution to the paradox is the following proposition. The courts should take a hands-off approach when an administrative body interprets ambiguous language in a statute, when that ambiguity pertains to matters within the body's particular expertise. This contribution can be summed up in a deference principle, one which requires courts to defer, other things being equal, to administrative determinations of the law.

Nicholson held that the courts, in deciding whether the procedures by which such determinations are made are valid (meaning in this context "fair"), should look to criteria other than whether the courts regard the agency's function as more judicial or more administrative in nature. Since this distinction had largely sealed off the so called "administrative area" from judicial scrutiny, *Nicholson* proposed that the courts should thenceforth take a hands-on approach to administrative action. *Nicholson* is thus an interventionist decision.

So, crudely speaking, we have a contradiction in what the Court was prescribing for the future: the Court in the same year made two landmark decisions which, taken together, tell courts to adopt a non-interventionist and an interventionist stance.

Just how crude one thinks this description is will depend largely on how firmly one holds to the substance/procedure distinction. If one thinks, as the Court doubtless did in 1979, that the decisions were given in two more or less discreet worlds within the administrative system, there might appear to be no tension at all. Courts should generally defer on matters of substance, but be ready to intervene when the fairness of the procedures by which substantive matters are decided is in issue.

It is worth noting here that the Court itself has no longer been able to function in terms of the distinction. It was only a matter of time before it had to decide whether the deference principle required judicial deference to the questions of law involved in determining what procedures an agency should follow in deciding substantive issues. And it in effect decided that deference on this issue may be required in *International Woodworkers of America Local 2–69* v. *Consolidated Bathurst Packaging Ltd*.[15]

---

[14] [1979] 1 SCR 311 (hereafter referred to as *Nicholson*). *Nicholson* by and large followed the reasoning of Lord Reid in *Ridge* v. *Baldwin* [1964] AC 40.

[15] [1990] 1 SCR 282. Here the issue was whether the Ontario Labour Relations Board violated procedural fairness when it permitted the policy implications of certain matters before tripartite panels to be discussed by a full board meeting in the period between the conclusion of the hearing before the panel and the panel's final decision on the matter. The parties to the matter were not informed of the meeting nor given access to it. Gonthier J., for the majority of the Court, held that this was a legitimate process as long as it was subject to various qualifications

Such a decision was more or less inevitable because in *Nicholson* the Court was adamant that the appropriateness of rules of fairness or natural justice could not be properly evaluated outside of the particular administrative law context in which they were to be applied. And since *CUPE* required deference to an agency's more expert sense of what was best in its own context, it should also require deference to an agency's sense of what was fair in such a context.

But what made the breakdown of the process/substance distinction inevitable is something deeper than any particular piece of judicial reasoning. It is the result of the judges' (belated) acceptance of the welfare state and their consequent willingness to permit some measure of autonomy for administrative decision-making. And in order to avoid making that acceptance toothless, the autonomy of the administrative process had to be taken to include both the procedures by which decisions are made and the substance of the decisions which issue from that process.

Until this time, three basic attitudes to administrative tribunals had prevailed among judges. Some thought the administrative process was somehow outside the law because it was so irrational—the realm of political arbitrariness and caprice. Others thought the process was necessarily subject to the law, which meant subject to the Diceyan hierarchical arrangement where judges police the administrative process in a way which leaves no room for judicial deference to tribunals. The last, and perhaps biggest group, adopted some combination of the first two attitudes.

CUPE and *Nicholson* together made it very difficult for judges publicly to adopt these attitudes. But the contradiction that leads to paradox is implicit in either of the two landmark decisions taken by itself. All the other decision does is bring the contradiction to the surface.

CUPE tells judges that because administrative tribunals can make rational decisions about the law, judges must not assume that the courts should have the last word about what the law is. But *CUPE* also thereby invites judges to intervene when administrative tribunals in fact fail to live up to the standards which in principle make their decisions rational. *Nicholson* tells judges that processes of administrative decision-making are rational, and thus amenable

necessary to maintain the independence of the members of the panel. *CUPE* played a very different role in the majority judgment, where it seemed to indicate judicial deference to the administrative sense of procedural fairness, than it did in Sopinka J.'s dissent, a judgment which nicely illustrates the paradox sketched below. For Sopinka J. used *CUPE* together with *Nicholson* as authority for the following proposition. *CUPE* holds that boards may legitimately make policy, while *Nicholson* holds that there is nothing inherently unreviewable about policy-making. Because the board meeting exercised a policy-making function, it is therefore in principle subject to the rules of procedural fairness. In a subsequent decision, *Tremblay* v. *Québec (Commission des affaires sociales)* [1992] 1 SCR 952, Gonthier J. appears to have moved the Court closer to Sopinka J.'s position. See my discussion in "Developments in Administrative Law: The 1991–92 Term" (1993) 4 *Supreme Court LR (2d)* 177, 200–205. In *CAIMAW* v. *Paccar of Canada Ltd.* [1989] 2 SCR 983 (hereafter refered to as *Paccar*) La Forest J. for the majority of the Court said, *obiter*, that deference to procedural determinations is due only when these are protected by a privative clause.

to judicial scrutiny, even where the agency making the decision is not like a court. But, as already suggested, *Nicholson* also contains an implicit limitation on judicial review by requiring judicial attention to the particular administrative context.

The impulse behind both judgments is, I suggest, the same—the judicial sense of the need for a positive response to the fact that the administrative state is here to stay (even if has recently come under the most sustained political attack since its entrenchment). The impulse leads to an attempt to put into effect a judicial recognition of the inherent or at least potential rationality of the administrative process. And the recognition, in order to be positive, had also to take into account that the criteria for rationality of the administrative process often are and should be different from the criteria for rationality of the judicial process. In other words, judges had to recognise that tribunals have a deserved claim to at least some autonomy in the legal order.

But for the courts to recognise the administrative process as inherently or at least potentially rational, is also precisely what creates the paradox of the recognition of rationality. To recognise rationality is at the same time to claim a judicial role in supervising the administrative process to ensure that it meets standards of rationality, even if a sincere attempt is made to conceive these differently.

We have then the idea that administration is at least in principle and often in practice rational. Taking this to be true leads to paradox because to recognise rationality in practice is always at the same time to begin to measure a practice against standards of rationality. To date the only model of rationality with which the courts have generally been comfortable is one which approximates the way in which judges think decisions should be made. The recognition of the rationality of administration thus seems to carry with it the risk of the imposition of judicial standards of rationality. And that means that a return to Diceyan type judicial review is an ever present danger.

It should be no surprise then that the Court has been far from successful in elaborating the deference principle articulated in *CUPE* in a way that looks markedly different from interventionist periods in the past.[16] That is to say, appearances to the contrary, *CUPE* by itself contained the seeds for an expansion of judicial review. In the next section, I discuss several examples of the way in which the paradox has played itself out in practice.

---

[16] Beetz J.'s judgments for the Supreme Court in two cases—*Syndicat des employés de production du Québec et de l'Acadie* v. *Canada Labour Relations Board* [1984] 2 SCR 412 (hereafter referred to as *Syndicat des employés*) and *U.E.S., Local 298* v. *Bibeault* [1988] 2 SCR 1048 (hereafter referred to as *Bibeault*)—are considered the main culprits here.

THE PARADOX IN PRACTICE

In *CUPE* Dickson J. for the Court did not say that judges should defer to privative clauses merely because the legislature has deemed it fit to include such a clause in the statute in issue. Rather he said, in the passage most often quoted from his judgment, that courts should defer when there is good reason to defer, the expertise of the tribunal being the major factor to be taken into account. As a result the deference principle for which CUPE stands is fundamentally ambiguous. On the one hand, it offers a formal reason for deference—courts should defer to administrative determinations of the law when the legislature requires them to do so. On the other hand, it articulates a substantive rationale for deference, one which says that courts must defer when there are reasons, such as superior agency expertise, for deference.[17]

This ambiguity left Canadian courts in a dilemma. Should they defer merely because the legislature has said so despite the fact that the substantive rationale for deference is not in place? And should they defer when there is a substantive rationale for deference despite the fact that the legislature has not included a privative clause in the relevant statute, perhaps even has expressly allowed for appeals on questions of law?

This dilemma surfaced clearly only in the very recent jurisprudence of the Court, although it played a crucial subterranean role from the start. Its late arrival on the surface is explained wholly by the fact that *CUPE* superimposed another layer of conundrum on top of the dilemma because of its formal reason for deference—obedience to legislative command. In the nature of things, the Court did not follow the logic of that formal reason which requires a court's self-exclusion from supervising agencies protected by a privative clause. Rather, it said, first, that within an agency's area of expertise or jurisdiction, its determinations of the law should be set aside only if patently unreasonable. Second, it said that the courts should not be alert to brand an agency's determination of the law jurisdictional for the purposes of judicial review, thus clearly implying that the standard for review on jurisdictional questions is correctness.[18] The conundrum of how to distinguish between which determinations of law are jurisdictional and which are not and how to

---

[17] He said in *CUPE*, above at n. 6, 235–6:

> "Section 101 [the privative clause] constitutes a clear statutory direction on the part of the Legislature that public sector labour matters be promptly and finally decided by the Board. Privative clauses of this type are usually found in labour relations legislation. The rationale for protection of a labour board's decisions within jurisdiction is straightforward and compelling. The labour board is a specialised tribunal which administers a comprehensive statute regulating labour relations. In the administration of that regime, a board is called upon not only to find facts and decide questions of law, but also to exercise its understanding of the body of jurisprudence that has developed around the collective bargaining system, as understood in Canada, and its labour relations sense acquired from accumulated experience in the area."

[18] *CUPE*, ibid., 233 and 237.

distinguish a test for patent unreasonableness from one for correctness then occupied the Court for over a decade.

By and large the Court adhered loyally to the idea that there is a real distinction between jurisdictional questions of law and others, and that it should adopt different standards of review depending on the nature of the question answered by the agency. Never did any Canadian judge approach Lord Denning's cynical dictum after *Anisminic* that the distinction between jurisdictional and other questions is so malleable that the courts can always characterise a question as jurisdictional, should they want to review on a standard of correctness.[19]

At times, however, the Court's assertive declarations in a Diceyan tone of its duty to uphold the rule of law over agencies led commentators as well as members of the Court to worry that it was straying from *CUPE*'s spirit. One judge especially, Beetz J., who had a strong record of judgments for employers in review of labour board decisions, was thought to have subverted that spirit.[20] But his judgments were for unanimous courts. And even those among its members who would be most easily categorised as friendly to *CUPE*'s deference principle did not on occasion escape a temptation to make Diceyan pronouncements about the Court's role as guardian of the rule of law.[21]

Indeed, whatever Beetz J.'s intentions in the most notorious of his judgments,[22] it is difficult to fault him jurisprudentially. As long as the Court conceived its role in terms of a duty to police the limits of jurisdiction by enforcing a correctness standard in regard to such limits, but could not design a bright line test between jurisdictional and other issues, it was doomed to be mired in a conceptual bog of its own making.

In the second of his major judgments, Beetz J. even did his best to reconcile the formal reasons for deference with the substantive rationale. He did so by suggesting that courts should rely on the kinds of reasons that make up a substantive rationale for deference in determining whether a question is jurisdictional. Courts should apply, he said, a "pragmatic and functional approach". This would be an approach sensitive to "the purpose of the statute creating the tribunal, the reason for its existence, the area of expertise of its members and the nature of the problem before the tribunal".[23]

This dictum soon became as canonical for the Court as Dickson J.'s articulation in *CUPE* of both formal and substantive reasons for deference. But the apparent pragmatism of the approach was undermined by three

---

[19] *Pearlman* v. *Keepers and Governors of Harrow School* [1979] QB 56, 70. This view now seems the dominant one in the United Kingdom, following the decisions by the House of Lords in *Re Racal Communications Ltd.* [1981] AC 374, 382–3, per Lord Diplock, and in *Page*, above at n. 7, 701, per Lord Browne-Wilkinson.

[20] Above at n. 16.

[21] For example, Dickson J. in *Jacmain* v. *Attorney-General of Canada* [1978] 2 SCR 15, 29, and Laskin C.J. in *Crevier* v. *Attorney-General of Québec* [1981] 2 SCR 220.

[22] *Syndicat des employés*, above at n. 16.

[23] *Bibeault*, above at n. 16, 1088.

considerations. First, the distinction between jurisdictional and other questions is an unworkable formal one and so its preservation is at odds with a pragmatic approach. Second, Beetz J. still found it appropriate to pronounce in formalistic language on the importance of the Court's role in maintaining the rule of law. Third, he declared the intention of the legislature to be the single most important factor in determining whether a question is jurisdictional.[24] It was thus left completely unclear whether courts were to treat the idea of legislative intent as a fiction constructed on the basis of substantive considerations or whether legislative intent should play an independent formal role.

These problems, none of which can be blamed on Beetz J. given that each is present in the structure of *CUPE*, made it very difficult to give a coherent account of the politics of deference. Prior to *CUPE*, formalistic approaches usually travelled with a judicial conservatism—one which tried to preserve at all costs a rationale for ultimate judicial power over the determination of all questions of law. But the move to recognition of substantive reasons for judicial deference to administrative determinations of the law opens up inevitable problems about the judicial evaluation of substance.

Such problems manifested themselves both when, in the face of a privative clause, judges had to decide on the jurisdictional/other issues of law distinction and when, having decided that the issue was not a jurisdictional one, the question was whether the agency's determination of the issue met the test of patent unreasonableness. When there was judicial consensus both that the issue was not jurisdictional and that it had not been unreasonably determined, it often seemed to be the case that judges were using the language of reasonableness to describe what they clearly thought to be a correct, and therefore, *a fortiori* reasonable, agency determination. Dickson J.'s reasoning in *CUPE* on the topic of the agency's interpretation of the terms of its governing statute is one of the best examples here.[25] And as Sopinka J. frankly pointed out in *Paccar*,[26] the issue of reasonableness might only properly arise once a judge had come to the conclusion that the administrative determination was not in fact correct. I am unaware of any judgment of the Court in which a judge has stated that an administrative determination, though incorrect, had to be upheld because it was not patently unreasonable.

When a judge disagreed with an administrative determination of the law, she had, therefore, one of two options open to her. She could categorise the determination as jurisdictional in nature, thus permitting review on a standard of correctness. Or she could try to articulate why the determination, though within jurisdiction, was patently unreasonable. When judges engaged in the former exercise, one could charge them with departing from the spirit

---

[24] Bibeault, above at n. 16, 1088.
[25] *CUPE*, above at n. 6, 235–7.
[26] Above at n. 15, 1018.

of *CUPE*.²⁷ But it was very difficult to make that charge stick given the problems inherent in the structure of *CUPE* itself. And when a judge had no option but to find that the agency's determination was within jurisdiction, it usually seemed that a finding that that determination was patently unreasonable was driven by the judge's sense that it was incorrect.

One fine example of this is the dissenting judgments of two of the standard bearers of *CUPE*, Wilson and L'Heureux-Dubé JJ., in *Paccar*.²⁸ Here the British Columbia Labour Relations Board, under the protection of a privative clause, decided that an employer could unilaterally impose new and detrimental terms on its employees after a collective agreement had terminated. The question before the Court was whether this decision was a patently unreasonable interpretation of section 27 of the British Columbia Labour Code, which enjoined the Board to secure industrial peace, improve the practices and procedures of collective bargaining, and promote conditions favourable to the orderly and constructive settlement of disputes.

The dissenting judges shared the premise that the interpretation was inconsistent with the objective of Labour Codes to promote equality of bargaining power between employers and employees. In her judgment, Wilson J. dealt with the point that the privative clause clearly remitted to the Board the question of how to translate that objective into practical policy in the following passage:²⁹

> "[D]oes describing a Board's decision as a 'policy choice' insulate it from review if the policy on which the choice is based is inconsistent with the policy of the legislation under which it purports to be made? I do not believe so. A policy choice is only truly a policy choice if the choice is made between policies which are equally consistent with and supportable by the legislation."

In other words, even within its area of specialisation, a Board has to be true to the basic objective of its governing statute, on the judge's understanding of what is consistent with implementing that objective. *CUPE* is then implicitly relied on as authority for the proposition that administrative determinations of law/policy must be held to standards of rationality whose content judges have a legitimate role in deciding.

L'Heureux-Dubé J.'s basic premise was different. She started by arguing, not that the policy content of the decision was inherently irrational, but that the Board had not explicitly justified its decision in terms of whether it met the statute's objective of securing industrial peace, etc. The implication might seem to be that the Board might have been able to offer an adequate justification, one that could meet the reasonableness standard, so that the problem is one of failure to provide reasons on crucial issues. However, the judge then had to explain why there was this particular onus on the Board to provide

---

[27] Beetz J.'s judgment in *Syndicat des employés*, above at n. 16, is a good example.
[28] *Paccar*, above at n. 15, 1020 and 1026.
[29] Ibid., 1022–3.

such reasons. And her explanation here is that its interpretation was fundamentally inconsistent with the objective of the statute. In other words, the Board would have found it next to impossible to supply reasons that could justify its departure from her understanding of the policy requirements of the statutory scheme.[30]

The only way to explain these two dissents is that both judges thought that the Board had lost jurisdiction when it ceased to operate in accordance with a particular understanding of the value of equality of bargaining power which they attributed to the legislature.[31] And then the judges might seem to be superimposing substantive moral limits as jurisdictional limits on a clear statutory delegation of power to an administrative agency.

My point is not that they were wrong to do so, for I will argue later they were right. Nor is my point that any of the judges could somehow avoid getting engaged in an interpretative, value-laden choice as to the legal limits of the tribunal's powers. Rather, if judges were to take seriously the formal reason for deference articulated in *CUPE*—the legislative command to judges to adopt a hands-off approach—their value choice should have been to let the tribunal make the value choice. To do otherwise, was to enter into an evaluative contest within the tribunal's area of specialisation, an area protected by legislative command. (It is worth noting in this regard that Dickson C.J. concurred in one of the majority judgments in *Paccar*.) Nor, finally, is my point that the minority judgments were irreconciliable or even difficult to reconcile with *CUPE*, taken as a whole. After all, the judges had to draw a line somewhere, and *CUPE* said that tribunals could not be patently unreasonable within jurisdiction. Rather, my point is that *CUPE* taken as a whole is riddled with tension since the formal and the substantive rationales for deference are in conflict. To anticipate a bit, I do not think that it is possible for judges to avoid interpretation and interpretation requires substantive evaluation. In short, the formal rationale for deference cannot be taken seriously.

Paccar can be usefully contrasted with the Court's decision in *Lester (W.W.) (1978) Ltd.* v. *United Association of Journeymen and Apprentices of the Plumbing and Pipefitting Industry, Local 740*.[32] The Newfoundland Labour Relations Board had to deal with a situation of "double breasting", one in which a company creates a parallel company in order to employ non-union labour, thus evading the scope of a collective agreement binding on the first company. It did so by declaring the parallel company bound by the collective agreement because it was a "successor" to the first. The statutory provision it relied on referred explicitly to the situation where one enterprise "sells, leases, transfers or otherwise disposes of" the business.

The majority of the Court held that the Board's determination was non-jurisdictional but patently unreasonable because there was no evidence that a

[30] *Paccar*, above at n. 15, 1043–6.
[31] For a very illuminating analysis along these lines, see Allars, above at n. 13, 189–90.
[32] [1990] 3 SCR 644 (hereafter referred to as *Lester*).

transfer or other disposition of a business had taken place. In effect, the majority held that the Board had by its decision enacted an anti-"double breasting" provision into the statute under the guise of interpreting the successorship provision.

Wilson J., in a dissent concurred in by Cory J. and Dickson C.J., repeated an earlier warning that the Court was straying from the spirit of *CUPE*:[33]

> "[T]here has been a tendency in the post-*C.U.P.E.* era to return to a less stringent test for judical review than the one established in *C.U.P.E.* This backsliding has been largely predicated upon a rather Dicean [sic] view of the rule of law and the role that the courts should play in the administration of government. That approach to curial review in the administrative context is, in my opinion, no longer appropriate given the sophisticated role that administrative tribunals play in the modern Canadian state. I think we need to return to *C.U.P.E.* and the spirit which *C.U.P.E.* embodies."

But she went on to hold that the Board was entitled to deference not simply because its decision were protected by a privative clause, but because it was "clearly arguable" that the Board's "liberal" interpretation of the successorship provision was "consonant with the purpose and intent of the overall legislative scheme, i.e., to facilitate and preserve collective bargaining regimes between unions and employers".[34] That is, she found here both that the Board had not lost jurisdiction and that its interpretation was not patently unreasonable. And both findings, I suggest, are driven by her sense that the Board's decision did accord with the value of equality from which the Board in *Paccar* had strayed.

Such descents into substance by judges who agree that the issue is one within the jurisdiction of the tribunal but who are at odds over how to deal with the substantive merits of the tribunal's actual decision were both inevitable after *CUPE* and signalled *CUPE*'s demise. They were inevitable because of the mixed message which *CUPE* sent and, even more important, because if the spirit of *CUPE* was to be more than a will-o'-the-wisp, it was the substantive part of the message that had to be heeded. If it were not, then even when there were good substantive reasons for deference but no formal command to do so, courts would be entitled to review on a standard of correctness.

The Court has now held that when such reasons exist, courts must defer on a spectrum ranging from correctness to patent unreasonableness.[35] While this holding whittles away at the distinction beteeen form and substance and is for that reason welcome, the idea of a spectrum is inherently confusing—a clear product of *CUPE*'s mixed message.

[33] Ibid., 651.
[34] Ibid., 653.
[35] *Pezim* v. *British Columbia (Superintendent of Brokers)* [1994] 2 SCR 557, following the implied rationale of *Bell Canada* v. *Canada (Canadian Radio-Television and Telecommunications Commission)* [1989] 1 SCR 1722 (hereafter referred to as *Bell Canada*).

In addition, by making a distinction between "true" or "strong" and other privative clauses, the Court has started on the slippery slope to holding that, when there are not very weighty substantive reasons to defer, courts should reinterpret the legislative command to defer.[36] I would again venture that the Court is here whittling away at the form/substance distinction while remaining trapped by it.

Now if one can rely on judges to deal properly with substantive reasons for deference, the descent into substance might seem welcome. Deference would not then depend on whether or not the legislature had commanded such an attitude but on whether judges should have such an attitude.

The problem, as I will argue more fully later, is not so much that judges will not agree on what kind of reason is a substantive one, and when and how it should count, but that the question of reasons for deference can never be wholly or even mostly kept apart from the judge's evaluation of the merits of the agency's determination. It is no accident that Beetz J.'s articulation of the substantive rationale for deference in the pragmatic functional approach was, as he said, to be deployed to determine the administrative decision's unreasonableness once it had been used to determine that the decision was within the agency's jurisdiction.[37]

It is, perhaps, awareness of this fact that has led the standard bearers of *CUPE* to retreat on occasion to the formalist element of that judgment, or, at least, to back off substance because of their sense that the descent into substance involves a battle of judicial views about correctness.

An example of retreat to formalism is Cory J.'s dissent in the first of the decisions which made the distinction between true and other privative clauses. He dissented mainly because of his sense that it would proliferate review if one allowed the question of deference to be settled by the judicial evaluation of substance rather than by a formal legislative command.[38]

An example of retreat from substance is Wilson J.'s judgment in *National Corn Growers Association v. Canada (Import Tribunal)*.[39] She gave a separate judgment, in which Dickson C.J. concurred, warning for the first time that the Court was beginning to stray from the spirit of *CUPE*; and she backed this warning with a sophisticated theoretical discussion of the rule of law. While

---

[36] *Dayco (Canada) Ltd.* v. *CAW-Canada* [1993] 2 SCR 230 (hereafter referred to as *Dayco*) and *United Brotherhood of Carpenters and Joiners of America, Local 579* v. *Bradco Construction Ltd.* [1993] 2 SCR 316 (hereafter referred to as *Bradco*).

[37] *Bibeault*, above at n. 16, 1088.

[38] "To open the way to many and varied judicial interpretations of the words of any privative clause as to whether it was more or less privative in nature can do little but encourage a proliferation of litigation and interminably delay a final resolution. It would defeat the aim of legislators who no matter what the words chosen . . . were seeking to have the courts refrain from interfering with the decisions of the statutory labour boards or tribunals": *Dayco*, above at n. 36, 311. In the subsequent decision, *Bradco*, above at n. 36, 350 Cory J. repeated his concern that the Court's approach was undermining *CUPE*, but said he would thenceforth "loyally follow the reasoning of the majority".

[39] [1990] 2 SCR 1324 (hereafter referred to as *Corn Growers*).

her concerns were directed mainly at Beetz J.'s perceived misdemeanours, she was clear that the majority's approach to the matter before the Court triggered the same concerns about the erosion of the deference principle, even though the majority had found, with her, that the tribunal's determination met the reasonableness standard. The majority erred, she said, in determining the issue of patent unreasonableness by engaging in "the kind of detailed review of a tribunal's findings that this Court's jurisprudence makes clear is inappropriate".[40] That is, courts should avoid the descent into substance by remaining at a more abstract level because—the implicit reason—such a detailed review must engage with judicial views about correctness.[41]

It is significant that L'Heureux-Dubé J., who with Cory J. is the remaining *CUPE* standard bearer on the present Court, concurred in the majority judgment in *Corn Growers*. As her dissent in *Paccar* shows, the main feature which distinguishes it from Wilson J.'s dissent in that case is that L'Heureux-Dubé J. takes the tack of going into detail in order to defend or attack a tribunal's determination within jurisdiction.

This willingness to go to bat for tribunals has served her well in her dissents to two decisions by the Court on the standard of review to be applied to human rights tribunals adjudicating matters arising out of complaints in terms of federal and provincial codes of rights.[42] In both of these cases, the majority of the Court, noting that the legislature had not seen fit to shield such tribunals with a privative clause, insisted that the standard of review had to be correctness. Their reasons pertained to the legal nature and far-reaching implications of the issues at stake in human rights adjudication. They also held that the tribunals failed to meet this standard. Both of these decisions are setbacks to the constitutional commitment to equality between Canadians and one can confidently predict that Wilson J. would have spoken strongly in dissent.

But she would not have been able to do so on the basis adopted by L'Heureux-Dubé J.—that there can be reasons to defer even when there is no privative clause—for those reasons involve the kind of descent into substance which Wilson J. wanted courts to avoid. She could, of course, have defended the tribunals' determinations on the basis that they were correct. And so detailed is L'Heureux-Dubé J.'s defence allegedly using the standard of reasonableness that in a separate dissent in the first of these decisions, two of the judges held with the majority that the standard for review in such cases is correctness but that L'Heureux-Dubé J. had shown that the tribunal was correct.[43] But that defence would have required Wilson J. to reduce the spirit of

---

[40] Ibid., 1347–8.
[41] Hence Wilson J. is in a sense in agreement with Sopinka J. in *Paccar*; see text accompanying note 26 above.
[42] *Canada (Attorney-General) v. Mossop* [1993] 1 SCR 554 (hereafter referred to as *Mossop*) and *Gould v. Yukon Order of Pioneers* [1996] 1 SCR 571 (hereafter referred to as *Gould*).
[43] Cory and McLachlin JJ.

CUPE to its formal part, which she would surely have been loath to do. For if judges regard deference as a purely formal matter detached from any substantive rationale for deference, deference jurisprudence becomes a matter of judicial accounting. And, as the English as well as the Canadian experience shows, creative accounting permits review on substance or correctness when judges are so disposed.

In short, formalism without substance is futile. But the relationship between formalism and substance is such that the latter inevitably undermines the former.

However, not even L'Heureux-Dubé J. has been able to resist the retreat to formalism in her judgments for the Court in two decisions where the logic of the situation seemed to demand that the court descend into substance. In both the situation was one in which the issue fell within the jurisdiction of at least one tribunal protected by a privative clause and so would normally have been subject to reasonableness review. But the issue came to court because of conflicting decisions so that it appeared that the reviewing court would, for the sake of coherence in the legal order, have to choose between the decisions. If it was then the case that both decisions met the reasonableness standard, it appeared further that the only way to adjudicate between them would be on a standard of correctness.

In the first of these decisions, *Domtar Inc. v. Québec (Commission d'Appel en Matière de Lésions Professionnelles)*,[44] L'Heureux-Dubé J. held that the commitment to the formal element of the deference principle is of such great importance that it outweighs the disadvantage of living with the incoherence created by what she called a "jurisprudential conflict", one in which two different administrative tribunals give conflicting interpretations of the same statute in cases involving different parties. She said:[45]

> "The advisability of judicial intervention in the event of conflicting decisions among administrative tribunals, even when serious and unquestionable, cannot, in these circumstances, be determined solely by the 'triumph' of the rule of law. Where decisions made within jurisdiction are not patently unreasonable, the issue instead turns on whether the principles underlying curial deference should give way to other imperatives. In my opinion, the answer is no."

To hold otherwise would, she said, alter "the already delicate institutional relationship between administrative tribunals and courts with reference to the impugned decision" and this risked that the "arbitrariness which the judicial sanction is designed to remedy may . . . become the result".[46]

In the subsequent decision, *British Columbia Telephone Co. v. Shaw Cable Systems (BC) Ltd.*,[47] the Court was faced with a situation in which the con-

---

[44] [1993] 2 SCR 756 (hereafter referred to as *Domtar*).
[45] Ibid., 795.
[46] Ibid., 795–6.
[47] [1995] 2 SCR 738 (hereafter referred to as *BC Tel*).

flict was even starker.⁴⁸ A British Columbia labour arbitration board held that a company—BC Tel—violated an exclusive-work provision in a collective agreement when it contracted out cable installation work to a company whose workforce did not belong to the union. However BC Tel, in contracting out, was falling into line with a ruling made after the labour arbitration board's ruling by a federal agency, the Canadian Radio-Television and Telecommunications Commission (CRTC).

The case came to the Supreme Court by way of an appeal against a decision by the Federal Court of Canada, where Mahoney J. had held that that the CRTC's decision was patently unreasonable because it did not take into account the labour arbitration board's decision. In doing so, it had exceeded its extensive powers by requiring BC Tel to violate its collective agreement with the union.⁴⁹

L'Heureux-Dubé J. recognised that here there were two genuinely conflicting decisions, although she held that the conflict was short of what she termed an "operational conflict"; one in which the individual is forced to ignore one of two orders, because these require contradictory courses of action. She was prepared to assume that the conflict was operational but she held that this did not require the Court to go into the merits of the decisions. She relied here on an analogy with the constitutional doctrine of paramountcy, whereby a court is able to declare inoperative provincial legislation to the extent that it is in conflict with federal legislation.⁵⁰

She then said that the courts could apply the paramountcy doctrine in the administrative context by using a pragmatic and functional approach to decisions in operational conflict. The approach would determine which tribunal the legislature intended to be paramount. The criteria she identified as playing a role in such an approach are all in a sense structural, that is, they pertain to the tribunal's place in the legal order and so allow a court to avoid considering the merits of the actual decisions.⁵¹

First, the courts should consider the "legislative purpose behind the establishment of each administrative tribunal", the idea being that the "more important the tribunal, the more likely the government would have intended that tribunal's purpose to take precedence over that of another tribunal".⁵² Second, the more central a decision is to the purpose of a tribunal, the more likely it is that that tribunal should take precedence over a tribunal whose decisions are less central to its purpose. Third, a tribunal whose decisions

---

⁴⁸ Indeed, L'Heureux-Dubé J. held in *Domtar*, above at n. 44, that the situation was not even one of true jurisprudential conflict, but she was prepared to treat it as such for the sake of resolving the issue of the appropriate judicial attitude in such cases.

⁴⁹ (1993) 13 Admin LR (2d) 250, 260–65. Strictly speaking, the test need not have been the unreasonableness test, since the CRTC's decisions, by contrast with the labour arbitration board's, were not protected by a privative clause and were subject to appeal.

⁵⁰ *BC Tel*, above at n. 47, 768–70.

⁵¹ Ibid., 770–3.

⁵² Ibid., 771–2.

fulfil a policy-making or policy-implementation role to a greater degree than another tribunal's will take precedence over it.

On these criteria, she said, the answer to the question of precedence in the case was clear. The CRTC was fulfilling "Parliament's intention of regulating monopoly service providers in the public interest" while the labour arbitration board was "merely interpreting a private contract relating to the internal arrangements made by BC Tel to carry out the activities assigned to it".[53]

While the rest of the Court agreed with L'Heureux-Dubé J.'s disposition of the matter as well as with her reason for doing so, the other judges were concerned that her test for true conflict was too strict. In addition, Cory J. expressed a concern to do with her view that the CRTC's decision was public in nature by contrast with the private nature of a decision interpreting a collective agreement, so that the former in virtue of that fact had to take precedence.[54] He said:[55]

> "A collective agreement is much more than a private arrangement. It provides the foundation for labour relations. It exists so that peace in labour relations can be achieved and maintained. This goal which is so important for our society is the aim of all labour legislation."

I quote this extract in order to suggest a general problem with the retreat to formalism, in this case a retreat to what may appear to be structural factors from the substantive issues involved in evaluating the tribunals' decisions.

Recall that in *Paccar* Wilson and L'Heureux-Dubé JJ. dissented because of their sense that the tribunal's decision undermined the value of equality which a statute governing employment relations was meant to serve. Put differently, they understood the decision as placing employment relations on a slippery slope to pre-collective bargaining standards, to a world which Wilson J. said had "ceased to exist".[56] And in *Lester* she upheld the Board's decision to extend a successorship provision to the practice of double breasting because that extension increased the reach of the same value.

It is, of course, an excess of wishful thinking to suppose that Wilson J. was right in her claim in *Paccar* that the world had ceased to exist in which private power, in the form of the economic power of the 'haves', dominated employment and other relations. The realm of the public which was carved out in the creation of the administrative state, a realm premised on rich understandings of the equality of all citizens, is being privatised with increasing rapidity and vehemence. Cory J.'s reminder to the Court in *BC Tel* that the

---

[53] *BC Tel*, above at n. 47, 772–3.

[54] Several judges expressed their general concurrence with Cory J., as well as with McLachlin J., who confined her concerns to the issue of whether there was a true operational conflict. It is unclear whether (and I suspect unlikely that) this concurrence extended to Cory J.'s worry about the diminution in status of labour arbitration boards.

[55] *BC Tel*, above at 47, 776.

[56] See *Paccar*, above at n. 15, 1025–6. She was quoting here from the majority reasons of Professor Bora Laskin (as he then was) in *Re Peterboro Lock Mfg. Co.* (1954) 4 LAC 1499, 1502.

control of labour relations serves a *public* value, one of crucial importance to "our society", is a salutary warning to judges. It warns them of the need for judicial sensitivity to the forces of political change increasingly behind the legal issues before the courts.[57] In contrast, the retreat from substance in which L'Heureux-Dubé J. has at times engaged obscures such issues.

Now it may seem that the thesis for which I am arguing is the absurd one that judges must defend social democracy at all costs, that administrative decisions that uphold equality must be upheld while those that detract from it must be struck down. However, I have in mind something which I hope is more subtle.

First, my thesis is not that equality is a central concern in all or even many cases of judical review. However, equality is implicated in a lot of the decisions regarded as landmarks in Canadian administrative law, as a read through the leading casebook will attest.[58] For example, if one reads through the passages in *CUPE* where Dickson J. in effect vindicated the decision of the New Brunswick Labour Relations Board, it is clear that his support for the Board's determination is driven by his sense that it preserved equality of bargaining power as between employer and employee.[59]

Nor are such examples confined to review for error of law. Review for procedural error may implicate the value of equality even more often. Thus, *Nicholson* and its most important successor, *Knight* v. *Indian Head School Division No. 19 of Saskatchewan*,[60] were both about equality in the following sense. Both concerned the issue whether a category of public employees hitherto considered not entitled to a hearing before dismissal were so entitled. The extension of the right to procedural fairness in these contexts is premised on the view that the state and public actors are rightly held to higher moral standards than are "private" individuals. And that must be because the state is obligated to exemplify what it is to treat all citizens as equals.[61]

---

[57] Cory J.'s acute sense of such issues is reflected in his important lone dissent in *Canada (Attorney-General)* v. *Public Service Alliance of Canada* [1991] 1 SCR 614. The Public Staff Relations Board had decided that teachers working for a private company to which a penitentiary had contracted out teaching services for inmates were "employees in Public Service" and therefore were to be included in the teaching group bargaining unit. Sopinka J. for the majority of the Court (L'Heureux-Dubé J. concurring) held that this decision was patently unreasonable.

[58] J.M. Evans, H. N. Janisch, David J. Mullan and R.C.B. Risk (eds), *Administrative Law: Cases, Text, and Materials* (Emond Montgomery Publications Ltd., Toronto, 4th ed. 1995).

[59] As he put it, if, in the context of a public sector strike, the employer were permitted to replace striking workers with management, the "right to strike would be sterilised and the supposed choice of settlement techniques . . . would become illusory": see *CUPE*, above at n. 6, 242.

[60] [1990] 1 SCR 653 (hereafter referred to as *Knight*).

[61] See L'Heureux-Dubé J. for the majority in *Knight*, ibid., 668–9. As she put it : "The duty to act fairly does not depend on doctrines of employment law, but stems from the fact that the employer is a public body whose powers are derived from statute, powers that must be exercised according to the rules of administrative law". Note that, later in her judgment, L'Heureux-Dubé J. qualified the point about statutory basis in ways that might have important implications for requiring procedural fairness of employers where the basis is not strictly a statute but rather a statutory delegation of power to a public official to enter into a contract with a private individual or entity to perform public services. She said that there need only be a "strong 'statutory

The second reason why my thesis about the role of equality in judicial review is not too simple-minded is that it does not hold that the issue is one about whether the judge agrees with the agency about the interpretation of equality. I have tried to show that even judges who seek to be loyal followers of *CUPE* have trouble working out its mixed message and are tempted on occasion to embrace its formalist part in order to avoid descending into substance. However, I want now to argue that one can reject formalism, or, perhaps better put, any strict dichotomy between form and substance, without reviving the kinds of judicial activism which Dickson J. in *CUPE* sought to put to rest.

My thesis depends on a theory which connects the value of equality with the rule of law through the idea of a legal culture of justification.[62] And that idea, as I will now argue, gives a role to the agency's reasoning which offers judges a new understanding of the deference principle.

EQUALITY AND THE RULE OF LAW

Recall that in *BC Tel* Mahoney J. for the Federal Court of Appeal found the CRTC's decision to be patently unreasonable because it had failed to take into account the labour arbitration board's decision. In so doing, he was, in my view, relying on an implicit theory about the role of the rule of law in the administrative context. Much the same theory is implicit in L'Heureux-Dubé J.'s judgment in *Paccar* when she started by arguing, not that the policy content of the decision was inherently irrational, but that the Board had not explicitly justified its decision in terms of whether it met the statute's objective of securing industrial peace, etc.

While L'Heureux-Dubé J. then seemed to offer little hope that such a justification could be made, the fact that she left open the space for such a justification is significant. For in leaving open that space she, in contrast with Wilson J., acknowledged the independent weight that judges should give to the tribunal's reasoning. And it is a curious feature of such an acknowledgement that it requires the close judicial scrutiny of the tribunal's reasoning that Wilson J. generally sought to avoid. That is, L'Heureux-Dubé J.'s approach raises starkly the paradox of the recognition of rationality—that to recognise rationality in practice is always at the same time to begin to measure a practice against standards of rationality. How then is such a recognition consistent with a deference principle? It is consistent, I will argue, if we understand

flavour'" to the office (quoting from H.W.R. Wade, *Administrative Law* (Clarendon Press, Oxford, 5th ed. 1982), 498–99): *Knight*, ibid., 672. And she affirmed a non-statutory basis for review on procedural grounds, claiming that "[l]ike the principles of fundamental justice in s. 7 of the *Canadian Charter of Rights and Freedoms*, the concept of fairness is entrenched in the principles governing our legal system": ibid., 683.

[62] I owe this term and the idea to Etienne Mureinik; see, e.g., his "Emerging from Emergency: Human Rights in South Africa" (1994) 92 *Mich LR* 1977.

deference in terms of its secondary dictionary meaning—deference as respect —and not in terms of its primary dictionary meaning—deference as submission.

It is Dicey's model which adopts the deference principle according to its primary meaning of submission to authority. It is only if law can be construed positivistically that deference of this kind can work. However, it is crucial to see that deference of this kind need not involve a humble renunciation of judicial power. Far from it. Since it presumes that there will be a fact of the matter as to legislative intent which judges are uniquely equipped to discover, its consequence is that, absent other factors, judges owe no deference to administrative determinations of the law.

When other factors are present, most notably, when there is a privative clause, Diceyan judges will try to reach an accommodation between such factors and their model. All the twists and turns in the Court's jurisprudence on the issue of substantive review for error of law and jurisdiction are explicable in terms of different *ad hoc* attempts to reach such an accommodation.

Deference as respect, by contrast, provides an ideal which can inform an attempt to rearticulate the relationship between the legislature, the courts and the administration in such a way that the courts retain a legitimate role as the ultimate authority on the interpretation of the law.

In statutory interpretation, this ideal requires of judges that they determine the intention of the statute, not in accordance with the idea that there is some prior (positivistic) fact of the matter, but in terms of the reasons that best justify having that statute. Since a statute states a series of conclusions to deliberations rather than the reasoning that led to these conclusions, judges have here to reconstruct the reasoning that justifies those conclusions. And since in issue is what those conclusions are, this reconstructive project is one which at the same time plays a role in determining their content.

When the statute is one that sets up a regulatory regime and a tribunal to decide disputes that may arise out of the regime, this interpretative approach requires judges to take the tribunal's decision seriously. More precisely, they have to take the tribunal's reasoning seriously because what they are primarily concerned to do is to find the reasons that best justify any decision, whether legislative, administrative or judicial. And, if the court has before it not only a statute to interpret, but also a tribunal's interpretation of that statute, then the tribunal's interpretation makes a difference to the structure of the interpretative context.

One should not underestimate this difference. It might well be true that a court would come to a different conclusion as to statutory meaning than the one the tribunal reached had the tribunal not given a reasoned decision, but the context is different just by virtue of that decision. The issue for the court is not then what decision it might have reached had the tribunal not pronounced, but whether the reasons offered by the tribunal justify its decision.

There are what one can think of as both formal and substantive reasons for this attitude of judicial deference. Formally speaking, whether or not there is a privative clause, the legislature has chosen the tribunal and not the court as its front line adjudicative body. More substantively, because the tribunal is closest to the problems out of which the issue arises, can deal with them relatively quickly and cheaply, and may have in addition developed a considerable expertise, the court should take the tribunal's reasoning seriously. That is to say, it must treat the reasoning with respect by asking whether that reasoning did in fact and also could in principle justify the conclusion reached.[63]

Moreover, the court must adopt that attitude whatever the subject matter of the tribunal's reasoning—whether the issue is fact or law (including the tribunal's powers, other statutes, the common law, and constitutional law). The court should therefore intervene only if it is prepared to discharge the onus of showing, not that it would have reached a different decision, but that the decision reached is not reasonably supportable.

"Reasonable" means here that the reasons do in fact or in principle support the conclusion reached. That is, even if the reasons in fact given do not seem wholly adequate to support the decision, the court must first seek to supplement them before it seeks to subvert them. For if it is right that among the reasons for deference are the appointment of the tribunal and not the court as the front line adjudicator, the tribunal's proximity to the dispute, its expertise, etc, then it is also the case that its decision should be presumed to be correct even if its reasons are in some respects defective.

"Reasonable" should not therefore be taken to mean that there could reasonably have been another resolution of that issue. If one understands reasonableness in such a way, one is willy-nilly operating within Dicey's shadow. When Diceyan judges have to interpret a privative clause they are faced with a legislative command to which their doctrine of deference requires submission. But that requirement is at odds with their understanding of their role at the apex of the intepretative hierarchy. Their "solution" is to adopt a "two or more right answer" thesis when, and only when, the issue is one apparently within a tribunal's jurisdiction and that jurisdiction is protected by a privative clause.

While this thesis contradicts the idea of submissive deference to one correct answer as to what the law is, it permits Diceyan judges, albeit in an *ad hoc* way, to live with privative clauses. First, it permits them to adjudicate in the old way when there is no privative clause. Second, it permits them to retain

---

[63] I remain undecided on the important topic of whether my argument entails the claim that there is a common law duty on tribunals to give reasons. As has often been pointed out, a reason-giving requirement invites both judicial activism and distortion of the administrative process. See, e.g., M. Shapiro, "The Giving Reasons Requirement" [1992] *Univ. of Chicago Legal Forum* 179 and R.A. Macdonald and D. Lametti, "Reasons for Decision in Administrative Law" (1989–90) 3 *Can J of Admin L & Prac* 123. A most promising basis for a reason-giving requirement in particular classes of cases is laid out by Sedley J. in R. v. *Higher Education Funding Council, ex parte Institute of Dental Surgery* [1994] 1 WLR 242.

the standard of correctness for determining the scope of jurisdiction. Finally, the *ad hoc* nature of their methodology permits them, when there is a privative clause, to reason that the tribunal's decision was not in fact one among the range of reasonable decisions.

In sum, the idea that there are two reasonable answers is one which implements a positivist solution to the problems Dicey's model has in compromising with the administrative state. It seeks to preserve judges in their place at the apex of the interpretative hierarchy by adopting a "solution" which treats privative clauses as a legislative tie-breaker on certain issues. However, as we have seen, that solution is completely *ad hoc* and thus no solution at all.

This brings me to the last and most substantive reason for adopting the principle of deference as respect. The principle is inherently democratic. It adopts the assumption that what justifies all public power is the ability of its incumbents to offer adequate reasons for the decisions which affect those subject to them. The difference between mere legal subjects and citizens is the democratic right of the latter to require an accounting for acts of public power.

The legislature, the administration and the courts are then just strands in a web of public justification. The courts' special role is as an ultimate enforcement mechanism for such justification. When administrative tribunals make decisions on points of law, those subject to the decision are entitled to require that the tribunal should offer reasons that in fact justify the decision. Should they not be satisfied, recourse to the courts should be available. But that recourse must be on the basis of the question whether the tribunal's decision was supportable by the reasons it in fact and could in principle have offered.

Deference as respect thus seems to avoid the dangers of judicial activism, even though it invites judges closely to scrutinise tribunal determinations of the law. It may however be thought that it risks a judicial quietism which comes about when the judicial stamp of approval is required merely because a tribunal has offered a full set of reasons for its decision. But judicial quietism is avoided just because the ideal which guides deference as respect is a democratic one which links form to substance—to the value of equality.[64]

In review for procedural error, the principle of equality is more formal, requiring as it does that a court attend to considerations to do with the provision of fair opportunities to participate in the administrative process. That is, to be treated as an equal one must be given the right to be heard by an impartial tribunal, with both the content of the right and of the kind of impartiality due to one varying according to the context. However, as cases like *Knight* illustrate, form easily shades into substance since to require a hearing for employees prior to dismissal requires giving reasons for the dismissal, a factor which changes the status of the employee.

---

[64] My project is thus on all fours with that proposed by Sir Stephen Sedley; see, e.g., his "Human Rights: A Twenty-First Century Agenda" [1995] *PL* 386, esp. 399.

In review for error of law where the value of equality is implicated because the legislative regime in question is an equality-promoting one, that value plays a rather different role. Although the administrative state has become much more than the welfare state, it was put in place in order to follow through on the promise of substantive equality before the law, once formal equality had been by and large achieved by legal subjects.

Now that state is under attack on at least three fronts. It is argued, first, that its delivery of services to the public is inefficient; second, that public resources can no longer support the levels of delivery which had come to be taken for granted; third, that it is morally wrong for the state to be committed to the substantive value of equality.

Part of the problem with addressing the first two issues is that they are often confused with the third. Attacks on the very existence of the administrative state are often disguised as arguments about ineffeciency and lack of resources. The need to disguise is significant—it tells us that, despite popular misgivings about inefficiency and lack of resources, there is still a popular commitment to equality.

Administrative agencies are going to play a crucial role in determining how, in an era of fiscal restraint, the administrative state can best be reconfigured. But it makes a great deal of difference whether one regards that process as genuinely one of reconfiguration or as one whose aim is to destroy the institutional and legislative expressions of a political commitment to equality. When judges find themselves confronted with administrative determinations of the law that flow from this changing political situation, they should not be embarrassed to ask how those determinations advance the cause of equality. For the administrative state has entrenched equality as one of the values of the rule of law.[65]

However, the attitude of deference as respect requires that judges defer to such an agency determination not on the basis of whether they agree with it, but, rather, on the basis whether the agency has justified its determination in terms of its commitment to the value that provides the rationale for the administrative state. Sometimes, as in *Paccar*, the agency determination will be so out of kilter with any understanding of a commitment to equality that it may seem that such a justification is not available. But generally matters will not be so clear and the issue will be one of whether the agency provided a reasonable justification.

I also want to suggest that the attitude of deference as respect may be helpful in another regard. Recall that the paradox of the recognition of rationality arises because one process of reasoning and decision-making—the administrative process—is recognised by another—the judicial process—as

---

[65] I mean here to imply that this was a process of recognition through entrenchment; that is, the value was one to which the rule of law has always been committed. I argue for this position in *Legality and Legitimacy: Carl Schmitt, Hans Kelsen, and Hermann Heller in Weimar* (Clarendon Press, Oxford, forthcoming).

both autonomous and subject to judicial supervision. The danger, then, is that judges, whether consciously or unconsciously, will impose their own standards of rationality on the administrative process. Deference as respect, however, seems to me to open up space for judicial sensitivity to particular tribunals' own sense of how best they can respond to their mandates.

In an era where agencies are going to face complex questions about the relationship between private and public power, and may increasingly differ among themselves about how to resolve such questions, judges will have to be alert to both the substance and the form of the rule of law. My thesis is that the substance of the rule of law is the equality of all citizens before the law and that the form of the rule of law is the procedures whereby public officials demonstrate that they have lived up to—are accountable to—that substance.[66]

It is an anti-positivist thesis in that it claims a distinct moral content to the rule of law. But it is also a democratic thesis, in that it requires that the content be developed through the institutions of government and not determined by abstract philosophising. And until political leaders are prepared frankly to declare in their legislation that the institutions of state should serve the cause of inequality, I suggest that it is the thesis which judges should adopt.[67]

---

[66] My account of interpretation is clearly indebted to Ronald Dworkin. See, e.g., R. Dworkin, *Law's Empire* (Fontana Press, London, 1986). But there are some differences. Like Dworkin, I do not think that judges deciding questions of law should decide those questions on policy grounds; rather they should decide the questions on the basis of which decision as to the law is best justified by the principles immanent within the law. However, in my view, Dworkin's understanding of principles immanent in the law makes no room for a space accorded by judges as a matter of legal principle to tribunals autonomously to develop the law. In other words, Dworkin accepts the Diceyan picture of judges at the apex of the interpretative legal hierarchy. I lay the groundwork for a different, more democratic account of interpretation in *Legality and Legitimacy: Carl Schmitt, Hans Kelsen, and Hermann Heller in Weimar*, ibid.

[67] I leave dangling the question whether judges and tribunals should obey the legislature's commands when these are inequitable. My own view is that when such commands reach a certain pitch of inequity, they offend against the ideals of the rule of law even when these ideals are largely implicit because there is no written constitution. See my *Hard Cases in Wicked Legal Systems: South African Law in the Perspective of Legal Philosophy* (Clarendon Press, Oxford, 1991), esp. ch. 10.

14

The "Ebb" and "Flow" of Administrative Law on the "General Question of Law"

MADAME JUSTICE CLAIRE L'HEUREUX-DUBÉ*

The term administrative law refers to the delegation of powers by the legislative branch to administrative bodies in order to carry out state policies. These bodies are entrusted with the task of regulating society's economic and social pursuits in the public interest. This kind of delegation of powers, unknown to our forbears, came into existence out of an increasingly complex society and the inability of legislators to achieve the degree of expertise required to deal with increasingly diversified and specialised areas of human activity. It was thought then that courts should be confined to their customary areas of expertise in civil and criminal law and were not the appropriate forum to take a leadership role in the economic and particularly social spheres implicating the mass of citizens. In the wake of these developments the central question has become defining the appropriate relationship between administrative bodies and the judiciary.

For the purposes of this paper, I will concentrate on the judicial review aspect of administrative law, an area which exemplifies changing views regarding this relationship between administrative bodies and the courts. In judicial review Cardozo's admonition that "the law has its epochs of ebb and flow"[1] is apposite.

Rendered seventeen years ago, the Supreme Court of Canada's judgment in *Canadian Union of Public Employees Local 963* v. *New Brunswick Liquor Corporation*,[2] has been described as "one of the most influential judgments in modern Canadian administrative law".[3] In the wake of *CUPE*, it could no

---

* I wish to thank my law clerks, Ian Lee and Sarah Lugtig, for their invaluable assistance in the research for and preparation of this paper.

[1] Benjamin N. Cardozo, "A Ministry of Justice" (1921) 35 *Harv LR* 113, 126.

[2] [1979] 2 SCR 227 (hereafter referred to as *CUPE*).

[3] J.M. Evans, H.N. Janisch, David J. Mullan and R.C.B. Risk, *Administrative Law: Cases, Text and Materials*, (Emond Montgomery Publications Ltd., Toronto, 3rd ed., 1989), 414 (hereafter referred to as Evans *et al.*), quoted in *Corn Growers Association* v. *Canada (Import Tribunal)* [1990] 2 SCR 1324, 1331, per Wilson J (hereafter referred to as *Corn Growers*).

longer be assumed that an administrative tribunal's interpretation of its statute would be subject to correction on judicial review simply because the reviewing judge disagreed with the board's interpretation. The Supreme Court, it seemed, had sent a message to lower courts to show some deference to specialised bodies charged with administering legislation. Dickson C.J. had admonished courts "not [to] be alert to brand as jurisdictional . . . that which may be doubtfully so".[4] Having decided that the Board in that case had been given jurisdiction to interpret its enabling statute, his review of the Board's interpretation was limited to asking whether it "was so patently unreasonable that its construction cannot be rationally supported by the relevant legislation and demands intervention by the court upon review".[5]

With *CUPE* and subsequent cases, a new course was charted for administrative tribunals. However, it has become apparent that some tribunals have been "left behind". Human rights tribunals, in particular, have repeatedly been denied deference on questions of law over the past three years on the ground that the interpretation of human rights legislation raises a "general question of law".[6] The courts consider themselves well equipped to deal with such questions without the need to defer to any administrative expertise. In several of these cases, I have found myself in disagreement with my colleagues on the Supreme Court of Canada over this issue, but I do not intend to address this conflict here. In this paper I propose to look at the notion of the "general question of law" and its implications for human rights tribunals through the "ebb and flow" of the recent Supreme Court of Canada jurisprudence.

To understand where we are now, it is useful to look at where we have been.

The contrast between the approach taken by the Supreme Court in *CUPE*, and the approach it had taken previously, could scarcely have been more dramatic. Less than a decade earlier, the Supreme Court of Canada had adopted a definition of jurisdictional error so broad that it encompassed virtually all questions of statutory interpretation. The decisions reflecting this trend are well known: *Port Arthur Shipbuilding* and *Metropolitan Life*, labour relations cases decided in 1969 and 1970, respectively, and *Bell*, a human rights case decided in 1971.[7] The Supreme Court appears to have been influenced by

---

[4] *CUPE*, above at n. 2, 233.

[5] Ibid., 237.

[6] See *Zurich Insurance Co.* v. *Ontario (Human Rights Commission)* [1992] 2 SCR 321 (hereafter referred to as *Zurich Insurance*); *Dickason* v. *University of Alberta* [1992] 2 SCR 1103; *Canada (Attorney-General)* v. *Mossop* [1993] 1 SCR 554 (hereafter referred to as *Mossop*); *University of British Columbia* v. *Berg* [1993] 2 SCR 353 (hereafter referred to as *Berg*); *Gould* v. *Yukon Order of Pioneers* [1996] 1 SCR 571 (hereafter referred to as *Gould*). Contra, *Ross* v. *New Brunswick School District No. 15* [1996] 1 SCR 825 (hereafter referred to as *Ross*).

[7] *Port Arthur Shipbuilding Company* v. *Arthurs et al.*, [1969] SCR 85; *Metropolitan Life Insurance Co.* v. *International Union of Operating Engineers, Local 796* [1970] SCR 425(hereafter referred to as *Metropolitan Life*); *Bell* v. *Ontario Human Rights Commission* [1971] SCR 756 (hereafter referred to as *Bell*).

developments in England, where the House of Lords in the *Anisminic* case[8] had confirmed the same interventionist approach to judicial review.

Although these cases do not refer explicitly to Dicey, it is nevertheless clear that Dicey's theory of the rule of law commanded unquestioning loyalty in Canadian courts. According to Dicey, it was the role of the courts to ensure that any official or agency exercising delegated authority abided by the terms on which the legislature granted such power.[9] There was no suggestion that the ordinary courts might be compelled or even inclined to accept the views of the delegate on questions of law: indeed, deference of this kind was antithetical to the idea that the ordinary law, as externally determined by the ordinary courts, should be supreme. Moreover, as Paul Craig observed, no consideration was given to the "efficacious discharge of regulatory legislation . . . except in so far as it was viewed as a natural correlative of the proper maintenance of external judicial supervision delimiting the boundaries of the legislative will".[10]

The law reports of the 1960s and early 1970s are replete with instances of courts quashing decisions of administrative tribunals where the reviewing court did not agree with the tribunal's interpretation of its statute. In *Metropolitan Life*,[11] for example, the Supreme Court disagreed with a labour relations board about who the "members" of a union were, for the purposes of determining whether fifty-five per cent of the employees in the bargaining unit were "members" of the union. The Court declared the decision a nullity, saying that the Board had exceeded its authority by asking a question other than that which the statute had remitted to it.

In *Bell*,[12] the Supreme Court of Canada's first ever judicial review case involving human rights legislation, the Court was even more interventionist. It restrained a board of inquiry appointed under the Ontario Human Rights Code from even inquiring into a complaint of discrimination, because it disagreed with the Human Rights Commission's view that certain premises constituted a "self-contained dwelling unit" within the meaning of the prohibition against rental housing discrimination.

The *Bell* decision caught the attention of the media because of its broad social implications.[13] It was also the subject of considerable academic com-

---

[8] *Anisminic Ltd.* v. *Foreign Compensation Commission* [1969] 2 AC 147 (hereafter referred to as *Anisminic*). See C. L'Heureux-Dubé, "L'arrêt *Bibeault*: une ancre dans une mer agitée" (1994) 28 *La Revue Juridique Thémis* 731, 736.

[9] A.V. Dicey, *An Introduction to the Study of the Law of the Constitution* (Macmillan, London, 10th ed. 1959), ch. 4.

[10] P.P. Craig, "Dicey: Unitary, Self-Correcting Democracy and Public Law" (1990) 106 *LQR* 105, 118–9, quoted in *Corn Growers*, above at n. 3, 1334, per Wilson J.

[11] Above at n. 7.

[12] Above at n. 7.

[13] See, e.g., "Justice Prevailed—At Last", *The Globe and Mail*, 4 Feb., 1971, 7; "Government to Plug Loophole in Rights Code", *The Globe and Mail*, 16 June, 1971, 5.

mentary, almost all of it negative.[14] Professor Paul Weiler, for example, argued that the phrase "self-contained dwelling unit" was ambiguous, and that the Court had offered no reason consistent with the policy of the statute for restricting the application of the Human Rights Code in the way it did. According to Weiler, "[the] case [was] only too typical of situations where the courts reverse the interpretation of a statute given by the tribunal charged with its immediate administration".[15]

Several other commentators criticised the Supreme Court's reliance on the statement by an English judge who suggested that judicial review by way of an application for an order of prohibition is available "where one gets a perfectly simple, short and neat question of law as we have in the present case".[16] Professors Evans, Janisch, Mullan and Risk, for example, wrote:[17]

> "The decision in *Bell* can also be considered as an example of the shortcomings of the courts in the interpretation of statutes, especially those that embody programmes of social reform or economic regulation. . . . Wide slices of public policy, and the competing claims of interest groups that government exists to adjust, cannot, without severe distortion, be fragmented into a series of 'perfectly simple, short and neat' questions of law."

Concerns such as these led to a reconsideration by the courts of the traditional approach followed in *Metropolitan Life* and *Bell*. Evans *et al.* observed, in a passage adopted by Justice Wilson in *Corn Growers*, that the courts' change of heart required them to accept two ideas. First, "statutory provisions often do not yield a single, uniquely correct interpretation, but can be ambiguous or silent on a particular question, or couched in language that obviously invites the exercise of discretion".[18] And second:[19]

> "the specialist tribunal to which the legislature entrusted primary responsibility for the administration of a particular programme is often better equipped than a reviewing court to resolve the ambiguities and fill the voids in the statutory language. Interpreting a statute in a way that promotes effective public policy and administration may depend more upon the understanding and insights of the front-line agency than the limited knowledge, detachment, and modes of reasoning typically associated with courts of law."

---

[14] P.W. Hogg, "The Jurisdictional Fact Doctrine in the Supreme Court of Canada: *Bell* v. *Ontario Human Rights Commission*" (1971) 9 *Osgoode Hall LJ* 203; I.A. Hunter, "Judicial Review of Human Rights Legislation: *McKay* v. *Bell*" (1972) 7 *UBC LR* 17; P. Weiler, *In the Last Resort: A Critical Study of the Supreme Court of Canada* (Carswell, Toronto, 1974), 139–43; Evans *et al.*, above at n. 3, 544.

[15] Weiler, ibid., 142.

[16] R. v. *Tottenham and District Rent Tribunal, ex parte Northfield (Highgate) Ltd.* [1957] 1 QB 103, 108, per Lord Goddard C.J., quoted in *Bell*, above at n. 7, 772.

[17] Evans *et al.*, above at n. 3, 544.

[18] Ibid., 414, quoted in *Corn Growers*, above at n. 3, 1336.

[19] *Corn Growers*, ibid., 1336.

An early reconsideration came just four years after *Bell*, in a case known as *Nipawin*.[20] Chief Justice Dickson, then a puisne judge, wrote:[21]

> "if the Board acts in good faith and its decision can be rationally supported on a construction which the relevant legislation may reasonably be considered to bear, then the Court will not intervene."

However, it was in *CUPE* that the Court set out fully both the reasons for deference and the appropriate standard of review. Dickson C.J., acknowledging the vague nature of the text of section 102(3)(a) of the Public Service Labour Relations Act, wrote that "[o]n one point there can be little doubt—section 102(3)(a) is very badly drafted. It bristles with ambiguities".[22]

Where the legislation contained a privative clause, according to Dickson C.J., there was a compelling rationale for not interfering with such decisions and for leaving the choice of an interpretation to the Board whose role it was to implement the statute and further the legislative policy embodied in it:[23]

> "The labour board is a specialized tribunal which administers a comprehensive statute regulating labour relations. In the administration of that regime, a board is called upon not only to find facts and decide questions of law, but also to exercise its understanding of the body of jurisprudence that has developed around the collective bargaining system, as understood in Canada, and its labour relations sense acquired from accumulated experience in the area. . . . The Act calls for a delicate balance between the need to maintain public services, and the need to maintain collective bargaining. Considerable sensitivity and unique expertise on the part of Board members is all the more required if the twin purposes of the legislation are to be met."

In his view, the decisions of the Board, in the exercise of its jurisdiction, should not be interfered with unless "the Board's interpretation [of the law is] so patently unreasonable that its construction cannot be rationally supported by the relevant legislation and demands intervention by the court upon review".[24]

One might have expected that this impressive shift in judicial attitudes towards administrative agencies would have applied equally to human rights tribunals. The Supreme Court had recognised that statutory interpretation is not an exact science, and that administrative tribunals have a role to play in interpreting their legislation so as to advance the legislature's policies. The Court appeared to have abandoned, once and for all, the theory that "perfectly short, simple and neat" questions of law were the province of the judiciary.

---

[20] *Service Employees' International Union, Local No. 333* v. *Nipawin District Staff Nurses Association* [1975] 1 SCR 382.
[21] Ibid., 388–9.
[22] *CUPE*, above at n. 2, 230.
[23] Ibid., 235–6.
[24] Ibid., 237.

Indeed, in the 1980s, it was thought by some observers that the courts treated human rights agencies *more* deferentially than they had historically treated labour relations tribunals! In 1987 Mary Eberts wrote that:[25]

> "Although human rights commissions seem to be underfunded by the governments that created them, they nonetheless enjoy a considerable amount of deference from the courts. *Human rights commissions have not had the same struggle to establish their legitimacy and expertise in the area confided to them by Legislatures as did the labour relations boards established in the thirties and forties.*"

This belief was not without basis in authority. In *Bhadauria*,[26] the Supreme Court had held that the Ontario Human Rights Code created a comprehensive scheme for the enforcement of the rights protected in the Code, to the exclusion of a common law action in the ordinary courts. In his reasons on behalf of the Court, Laskin C.J. specifically mentioned the "wide range of remedial authority" with which boards of inquiry were vested under the Code.[27] Commenting on *Bhadauria*, Professor Alison Harvison Young wrote:[28]

> "This case has quite rightly been heralded for its vision of human rights commissions as central, legitimate, and integral elements in a social and political framework that seeks to eliminate discrimination, rather than as annoying, 'inferior' bodies in competition with ordinary courts that are seen to make the work of ordinary courts more cumbersome."

Later, in a case commonly known as *Action Travail des Femmes*,[29] the Court seemed to confirm the broad remedial powers of human rights boards, when it held that a federal human rights tribunal had the jurisdiction to order an innovative, systemic employment programme against the Canadian National Railway as a remedy for pervasive discrimination.

However, as Professor Harvison Young noticed also, in this decision and others, the Supreme Court's confirmation of the findings of a human rights tribunal may have constituted a "happy coincidence of opinion" rather than deference to acknowledged expertise.[30] As she points out, in *Action Travail des Femmes* no reference was made to the fact that a panel of experts had

---

[25] M. Eberts, "Ontario Human Rights Commission", in N. Finkelstein and B. Rogers (eds), *Recent Developments in Administrative Law* (Carswell, Toronto, 1987), 265 (emphasis added). See also A. Harvison Young and R.A. Macdonald, "Canadian Administrative Law on the Threshold of the 1990s" (1991) 16 *Queen's LJ* 31, 42–3.

[26] *The Board of Governors of the Seneca College of Applied Arts and Technology v. Bhadauria* [1981] 2 SCR 181.

[27] Ibid., 194. To be fair, Laskin C.J. also mentioned the "wide rights of appeal" which were provided under the Code.

[28] A. Harvison Young, "Keeping the Courts at Bay: The Canadian Human Rights Commission and its Counterparts in Britain and Northern Ireland: Some Comparative Lessons" (1993) 43 *UTLJ* 65, 90.

[29] *Canadian National Railway Co. v. Canada (Canadian Human Rights Commission)* [1987] 1 SCR 1114.

[30] Harvison Young, above at n. 28, 92.

made the order in question. In fact, Dickson C.J. had relied on the principle of the *courts* as the guardians of the quasi-constitutional rights embodied in human rights legislation.[31] She does, however, acknowledge that such decisions were positive for human rights tribunals, given the court's application of a purposive approach similar to that employed by the tribunals. Moreover, other decisions evidenced a reluctance on the part of the courts to intervene prematurely in the inquiry process undertaken by human rights commissions.[32]

When the time actually came for the Court to decide upon the standard of review for human rights tribunals' interpretations of their legislation, the proponents of deference were to be disappointed. The old theory of "perfectly simple, short and neat" questions of law, supposedly dead and buried, had been quietly resurrected under a different name: the *"general"* question of law.

The occasion for this resurrection was the case of *Mossop*.[33] The complainant there was denied bereavement leave to attend the funeral of his partner's father, as the collective agreement provided for such leave on the death of the parents of a common law spouse only if the spouse was of the opposite sex. The Canadian Human Rights Tribunal concluded that this limitation constituted discrimination on the basis of "family status", within the meaning of the Canadian Human Rights Act. The majority of the Court agreed with La Forest J. that the Tribunal's interpretation of "family status" should be reviewed according to a standard of correctness.

Noting the absence of a privative clause, from which he concluded that "the normal supervisory role of the courts remains",[34] La Forest J. then stated that, as an *ad hoc* board, the Human Rights Tribunal lacks the specialised expertise and continuous existence of a labour relations board. Moreover, even compared to an *ad hoc* labour arbitrator, the Human Rights Tribunal lacked the arbitrator's consensual and specialised jurisdiction.[35] In his opinion, the situation of an arbitrator "is entirely different from the situation of a human rights tribunal, whose decision is imposed on the parties and *has direct influence on society at large in relation to basic social values*".[36] Finally, in a passage reminiscent of the *Bell* decision, La Forest J. concluded:[37]

> "The superior expertise of a human rights tribunal relates to fact-finding and adjudication in a human rights context. It does not extend to *general questions of law* such as the one at issue in this case. These are ultimately matters within the province of the judiciary, and *involve concepts of statutory interpretation and general legal reasoning* which the courts must be supposed competent to perform."

---

[31] Harvison Young, above at n. 28, 71.
[32] Ibid., 89–92.
[33] Above at n. 6. See also *Berg, Gould, Ross*; above at n. 6.
[34] *Mossop*, ibid., 584.
[35] Ibid., 585.
[36] Idem (emphasis added).
[37] Idem (emphasis added).

The majority may not have referred explicitly to the definition of "family status" as a "perfectly simple, short and neat question of law", but one could be forgiven for harbouring the suspicion that the majority's concept of "general questions of law" amounts to much the same thing.

Up to this point, the Supreme Court had developed a jurisprudence of deference with respect to a tribunal's interpretation of provisions in its enabling statute provided these fell within its jurisdiction. While the construction of provisions which limited jurisdiction remained subject to a correctness standard, the majority judgment in *U.E.S. Local 298* v. *Bibeault*[38] had established a pragmatic and functional approach for ascertaining into which category a particular question of law might fall. I will be discussing the methodology embodied in *Bibeault* in more detail later. Suffice it to say here, that a myriad of factors relating to the policy objectives, institutional structure, and relevant roles within the legislative scheme are considered in determining whether the legislature intended that the interpretation of a statutory provision falls within a tribunal's jurisdiction and thus merits deference.

In *Mossop* the majority qualified this deferential stance on questions of law within jurisdiction, as being applicable only in the presence of a privative clause, or, in its absence, a level of expertise on the part of the tribunal which made it a more competent interpreter than the courts. It therefore established as the general or background principle that the interpretation of questions of law within jurisdiction which did not require specialised expertise would be reviewed on a correctness standard. A further factor which was considered particularly relevant in the case of human rights tribunals was the social impact of the tribunal's interpretation of its enabling statute. While little direct reference is made to the nature of the social implications of the tribunal's interpretation, one might glean from both Chief Justice Lamer's and Justice La Forest's analyses that it is the change from traditional understandings of social institutions, the family in this case, which warrants concern on the part of the courts.

It bears mentioning that the majority decision in the case of *Zurich Insurance*,[39] which preceded *Mossop*, was its natural precedent. At issue in this case was whether differentiation in automobile insurance rates on the basis of age, sex or marital status constituted the reasonable and *bona fide* grounds which were exempt under Ontario's human rights legislation. Sopinka J., writing for the majority, found the appropriate standard of review to be one of correctness, relying largely on the existence of a statutory right of appeal in the enabling legislation, and a lack of expertise on the part of the tribunal. He concluded: "while curial deference will apply to findings of fact, which the Board of Inquiry may have been in a better position to determine, such deference will not apply to findings of law in which the Board has no particular expertise".[40]

---

[38] [1988] 2 SCR 1048 (hereafter referred to as *Bibeault*).
[39] Above at n. 6, cited in *Mossop*, above at n. 6, 578, per Lamer C.J.
[40] *Zurich Insurance*, ibid, 338.

Following *Mossop,* a number of decisions delivered by the Supreme Court enunciated or referred to the notion of the "general question of law", always in relation to human rights tribunals. In *United Brotherhood* v. *Bradco* Sopinka J., writing for seven judges on this issue, held expertise to be the determinative factor as to whether deference may be shown by the courts on questions of law, even in the absence of a privative clause, or the presence of a statutory right of appeal. He stated that "a lack of relative expertise on the part of the tribunal *vis-à-vis* the particular issue before it as compared with the reviewing court is a ground for a refusal of deference".[41] Citing *Zurich Insurance* and *Mossop*, Sopinka J. observed that: "[a] similar conclusion has been reached with respect to deference to human rights tribunals on questions of law. . .".[42]

The direct question of the appropriate standard for human rights tribunals arose again in 1993 in *Berg*.[43] The question at issue here was the Human Rights Tribunal's interpretation of services offered to University students by faculty members in the context of on-going studies as being "customarily available to the public". To determine the appropriate standard of review in this case, Lamer C.J. referred to the above-quoted passages from Justice La Forest's judgment in *Mossop,* as well as to the dictum in *Zurich Insurance* regarding the lack of expertise of a human rights tribunal. Writing for the majority in this case Lamer C.J. arrived at the following result, this time with a qualifier:[44]

> "[I]t is clear that the question of what constitutes a service customarily available to the public *is a general question of law with wide social implications*, in which the Council has no expertise. There being no reason why deference should be given to the Council in question, the appropriate standard of review is one of correctness."

Of note, however, is the accompanying emphasis on a greater degree of deference with respect to factual findings of the tribunal. Also noteworthy is that in neither this case, nor *Mossop,* did the human rights legislation in question contain a statutory right of appeal; this represents a significant difference from the circumstances involved in *Zurich Insurance.*

Although the language of *Mossop* and the judgments closely succeeding it seem to establish a general principle of review on a correctness standard for questions of law, one might conclude that, in practice, this principle essentially created an exception to deference as regards human rights tribunals on the basis of their perceived lack of relevant expertise. Moreover, in directly following *Zurich Insurance* on this point, the majority decisions in the cases following *Mossop* have given little additional consideration to the intention

---

[41] *United Brotherhood of Carpenters and Joiners of America, Local 579 v. Bradco Construction Ltd.* [1993] 2 SCR 316, 335.
[42] Idem.
[43] Above at n. 6.
[44] Ibid., 369 (emphasis added).

of the legislature with respect to human rights tribunals where no statutory right of appeal exists in the human rights legislation. Indeed, it seemed as if the absence of such a provision made very little difference to the Court's analysis.

However, in the Supreme Court's decision in *Pezim v. British Columbia (Superintendent of Brokers)*,[45] a case concerning statutory interpretation by a securities commission, Iacobucci J. held that the central question facing the courts was the search for the legislative intent regarding the appropriate point at which a tribunal would fall on a continuum of standards of review. He then described the standard for human rights tribunals not as an exception but as an example at the extreme end of a spectrum of standards of review, ranging from reasonableness to correctness:[46]

> "At the correctness end of the spectrum, where deference in terms of legal questions is at its lowest, are those cases where the issues concern the interpretation of a provision limiting the tribunal's jurisdiction (jurisdictional error) or where there is a statutory right of appeal which allows the reviewing court to substitute its opinion for that of the tribunal and *where the tribunal has no greater expertise than the court on the issue in question, as for example in the area of human rights*."

Indeed, recently in *Ross*,[47] the Court relied upon *Pezim* as authority for applying a correctness standard in reviewing both the finding of discrimination and the consequent remedial order by a human rights tribunal. These had been entered against a school board whose teacher had publicly expressed "invidiously discriminatory" views. While noting that the majority judgment in *Pezim* had stated that "the central question to be asked in ascertaining the appropriate standard of review is 'to determine the legislative intent conferring jurisdiction on the administrative tribunal' ",[48] La Forest J. found the case also to establish that decisions of human rights tribunals necessarily fell at the correctness end of the spectrum. In a conclusion strongly reminiscent of his opinion in *Mossop*, he states:[49]

> "On the basis of this difference between human rights tribunals and labour tribunals, the Court confined the superior expertise of a human rights tribunal to fact-finding and adjudication in a human rights context. The standard of review on the basis of reasonableness is applicable to these matters. *In relation to general questions of law, courts must be supposed to be competent, and a standard of correctness is appropriate*."

Nonetheless, deference was shown to the findings of fact by the tribunal, which in turn had a strong influence on the Court's own interpretation of the statutory provision at issue.

---

[45] [1994] 2 SCR 557 (hereafter referred to as *Pezim*).
[46] Ibid., 590 (emphasis added).
[47] Above at n. 6.
[48] *Pezim*, above at n. 45, 589–90, quoted in *Ross*, ibid., 845.
[49] *Ross*, ibid., 847 (emphasis added).

The most recent statement of the "general question of law" doctrine as applied to a human rights tribunal can be found in the majority decision in *Gould*.[50] Here a human rights tribunal had found that limiting membership in a fraternal order to men constituted sex discrimination in the provision of services to the public. The tribunal based its decision primarily on the organisation's role in compiling a historical record for the Territory. A gender restriction on membership was held to have the effect of excluding women's perspectives from historical materials made available to the public. The tribunal decision had been successfully appealed. In the majority judgment of the Supreme Court, after citing both *Mossop* and *Berg*, La Forest J. concluded:[51]

> "I note that we are here once again involved in an issue of statutory interpretation and *general legal reasoning*. . . . On the basis of the foregoing, it is quite clear that the question of what constitutes 'services to the public' for the purposes of s. 8(a) of the Yukon Act is *a general question of law*, one which an appellate court must review on the basis of correctness."

Also noteworthy is Iacobucci J.'s statement, in a separate concurring opinion, concerning the level of deference owed to the factual findings in the case:[52]

> "In these circumstances, where the issue is not the facts themselves but rather the inferences to be drawn from agreed facts, the policy considerations which ordinarily militate in favour of deference are significantly attenuated. . . ."

This was in response to my dissenting observation that the board's inquiry and decision involved determinations which were primarily factual in nature, which the legislation largely protected from curial review, and which thus did not constitute general questions of law.[53]

This short jurisprudential history of judicial review relating to the concept of the "general question of law" reveals the term to encompass potentially any interpretation by a human rights tribunal of its enabling statute in deciding whether a specific set of circumstances may constitute discrimination. The reasons of the Supreme Court for restricting such tribunals' jurisdiction in these matters appear to be as follows: first, and foremost, the principle that statutory interpretation is normally the province of the judiciary; second, the lack of specific expertise in statutory interpretation in this context on the part of the tribunal when compared to that of the courts; and third, the broad social implications of decision-making in the human rights domain.

These reasons appear to draw upon the general constitutional principle of the supervisory role of the courts with respect to administrative action, the very principle upon which the supposedly repudiated theory of "perfectly simple, short, and neat" questions of law was based. However, what may

---

[50] Above at n. 6.
[51] Ibid., 600–1 (emphasis added).
[52] Ibid., 585.
[53] Ibid., 631–5.

have been termed once an exception to the *CUPE*-inspired stance of deference to administrative decision-making based on constitutional principles is now described as an expression of the general legislative intent to place these bodies' statutory interpretation at the extreme "correctness" end of a spectrum of standards of review, even absent a statutory right of appeal.

Before I explore these points further in an attempt to address the tensions they create, it may be helpful first to compare the road our Court has taken to that followed by the United States Supreme Court. The American jurisprudence, under the *Chevron*[54] doctrine of curial deference, has witnessed a similar "ebb and flow" in the development of standards of judicial review. The *Chevron* case established a two-stage inquiry for courts in addressing the issue of judicial deference to agency interpretations of law. The first stage involves determining if Congress has spoken clearly to the specific question at issue. If the statute is clear, the inquiry stops there and the court applies what courts in Canada would term a correctness standard to statutory interpretation, thereby substituting its construction of the provision in question if it differs from that given by the agency. However, if the statute is ambiguous or silent on the issue, the court will not apply its own interpretation but rather must ask itself whether the agency's interpretation is permissible. This is akin to the reasonableness standard used in Canadian administrative law.

Not surprisingly the United States courts have also been faced with the question of how to treat questions of law. As Justice Scalia indicated in a well-known law review article on the *Chevron* decision, the doctrine spurred a "lively debate" in his own court with respect to whether the standard of deference could apply equally to "pure questions of statutory interpretation".[55]

The debate is strongly evident in the 1987 decision of *Immigration and Naturalization Service* v. *Cardoza-Fonseca*,[56] where an Immigration Judge had equated standards of proof articulated in two different sections of the enabling statute. Justice Stevens, also the author of the *Chevron* opinion, held that "the question whether Congress intended the two standards to be identical is a pure question of statutory construction for the courts to decide".[57] He interpreted the requirement in *Chevron* of assessing the clarity of the statute with respect to the precise question at issue, as being limited to ambiguities in the *application* of the provision. In his view, if the question is a legal one, it "is well within the province of the Judiciary".[58]

Justice Scalia, while concurring in the result reached by the Court, entered separate reasons on this issue, referring to his colleague's interpretation as an

---

[54] *Chevron USA Ltd.* v. *Natural Resources Defence Council*, 467 U.S. 837 (1984) (hereafter referred to as *Chevron*).
[55] A. Scalia, "Judicial Deference to Administrative Interpretations of Law" [1989] *Duke LJ* 511, 512.
[56] 480 U.S. 421 (1987).
[57] Ibid., 448.
[58] Idem.

"evisceration" of the doctrine or a "doctrine of desperation".[59] He observed that such an application would result in curial deference only when the court was unable to construe the statute in question. In his view the Supreme Court "has consistently interpreted *Chevron* . . . as holding that courts must give effect to a reasonable agency interpretation of a statute unless that interpretation is inconsistent with a clearly expressed congressional intent".[60]

Shortly thereafter the Supreme Court heard the case of *National Labour Relations Board* v. *United Food and Commercial Workers Union, Local 23*,[61] where again the precise issue involved a "pure question of statutory construction". In this case, the eight sitting members of the Court were evenly divided between the majority's approach in *Cardoza* and Justice Scalia's previously lone view. In the same year, Judge Bork, writing an opinion for the District of Columbia Circuit Court of Appeals, held that the Supreme Court's decision in *Chevron* rejected the view that "a court may freely review an agency on pure questions of law".[62]

By 1992, with the decision in *National Railroad Passenger Corporation* v. *Boston and Maine Corporation*,[63] there could be no doubt that the approach advocated by Justice Scalia had been adopted unanimously by the Supreme Court. This case involved the construction of a provision of the Rail Passenger Act by the Interstate Communications Commission which all members of the court agreed was a "straightforward matter of statutory interpretation". Justice Kennedy, writing for the majority, asserted that where the statute is silent or ambiguous with respect to a particular issue, the agency interpretation will be granted deference provided it is not "in conflict with the plain language of the statute".[64] The court must determine whether the interpretation in question is reasonable in terms of the structure and text of the enactment in question. Justice White, while dissenting in part, concurred with this application of the *Chevron* doctrine in cases of statutory interpretation.[65] Moreover, the District of Columbia Circuit Court of Appeals has continued to apply such an approach.[66]

Some authors have concluded that the doctrine still affords an "escape hatch" for judges who do not agree with an agency's interpretation of its enabling statute.[67] These writers have noted that the judiciary may simply find

---

[59] 480 U.S. 421, 454 (1987).
[60] Idem.
[61] 484 U.S. 112 (1988).
[62] *National Fuel Gas Corporation* v. *Federal Energy Regulatory Commission*, 811 F. 2d 1563, 1569 (D.C. Cir. 1987).
[63] 503 U.S. 407 (1992).
[64] Ibid., 417.
[65] Ibid., 425.
[66] See *Airline Pilots Association* v. *Federal Aviation Administration*, 3 F. 3d. 449 (D.C. Cir. 1993).
[67] D.A. Dripps, "A Shade of Deference (courts' treatment of administrative agencies' statutory interpretation)"(1996) 32 *Trial* 70. See also B. Schwartz, "Administrative Law Cases During 1992" (1993) 45 *Admin LR* 261, 278.

that Congress is clear with respect to its intent at the first stage of the *Chevron* test through reliance on traditional canons of statutory construction. One author has even faulted Justice Scalia for relying on this outlet in his dissenting opinion in *Babbitt*,[68] the case more commonly known as the "Spotted Owl" decision.

What I most wish to emphasise in concluding this brief description of the American experience is that the *Chevron* doctrine of curial deference applies equally to what the Supreme Court of Canada has termed "general questions of law". In fact, the American doctrine has been extended to questions going to the jurisdiction of the Board or agency in question, both in *obiter dicta* of the Supreme Court and in Circuit Court decisions.[69] After much deliberation as to the appropriate boundaries in the relationship between the courts and administrative tribunals with respect to statutory interpretation, the United States judiciary appears to be headed in a different direction from the Canadian courts.

In the article by Justice Scalia mentioned earlier, he asserts that the *Chevron* doctrine is consonant with the constitutional role of the judicial arm of the American government. In his view, the only theoretical basis upon which one could apply such a doctrine within their constitutional structure, can be its congruence with legislative intent. Indeed, Justice Scalia believes that the doctrine establishes a *presumption* in favour of Congress' intent to accord the jurisdiction to administrative bodies to interpret ambiguous or open-ended statutory provisions.[70] His rejection of the exception for "pure questions of statutory interpretation" is now well understood.

While the Supreme Court of Canada could not be said to have established a *presumption* of a legislative intention of deference in *CUPE* and the cases following it, this jurisprudence has concluded that the search for legislative intent is the primary concern in determining the appropriate standard of review. For all its great significance, however, *CUPE* did not give any specific guidance as to how to determine whether an administrative tribunal has authority over a particular decision, so as to trigger curial deference in respect of the decision. Dickson C.J. simply said that the courts should "not be alert to brand as jurisdictional that which may doubtfully be so",[71] and mentioned a number of characteristics which had led him to show deference in that case.[72] However, ten years later the Supreme Court, in an opinion penned by Beetz J., articulated a more fully developed methodology. Of course I am referring to the "pragmatic and functional approach" described in *Bibeault*.[73]

---

[68] *Babbitt* v. *Sweet Home Chapter of Communities for a Great Oregon*, 115 S. Ct. 2407 (1995). See Dripps, ibid., 71.

[69] See *Dole* v. *United Steelmates of America*, 494 U.S. 26 (1990); *Oklahoma Natural Gas Company* v. *Federal Energy Regulatory Commission*, 28 F. 3d 1281 (D.C. Cir. 1994).

[70] Scalia, above at n. 55, 516.

[71] *CUPE*, above at n. 2, 233.

[72] Ibid., 236.

[73] Above at n. 38.

Justice Beetz's pragmatic and functional approach seeks to ascertain the intention of the legislature in conferring jurisdiction on the particular administrative tribunal, by considering factors such as the wording of the statute, the purpose of the statute and the role of the tribunal in carrying out this purpose, and the nature of the problem before the tribunal. The Supreme Court of Canada has applied this approach several times.[74]

I expanded on this approach in *Mossop* in arriving at my conclusion that the tribunal was exercising a decision-making power which Parliament intended to entrust exclusively to it, and that its decision was therefore entitled to curial deference. A deeper elaboration of the pragmatic and functional approach was, in my view, necessary in order to prevent the courts from granting themselves jurisdiction in policy-related questions where the board played a significant role in policy development. As I said in *Mossop*, "[w]here the answer depends upon a policy choice, the question is simply who is best placed to make these choices".[75] Inherent in such an approach may be the view that the legislature is not always clear as to its intent in such questions, and that the Court may be required to play a slightly more normative role in making such determinations, all the while remaining grounded in a consideration of the institutional structure and purposes of the enabling statute.

How then have we moved away from the search for legislative intent only for administrative bodies charged with protecting human rights? The Court has yet to elaborate a specific rationale for the principle of the "general question of law" as regards human rights tribunals, other than that such a question engages social implications. In trying to imagine what the justification might be, I have arrived at five possible explanations, all of which merit close scrutiny.

First and foremost, perhaps, is the fact that courts have long regarded their power of control and surveillance of inferior tribunals as their most important power. Professor Dyzenhaus explores this phenomenon in his paper. He illustrates how elements of the debate between those who saw this role as paramount, the "liberal antipositivists", and those who were more concerned with the legislature's clear intent, the "democratic positivists", continue to inform the doctrine of courts today. As he explains, even in the modern administrative state, "administrative law theory has not moved out of Dicey's shadow".[76]

Albeit reluctantly, through the years the judiciary has come to accept their inability to handle the flow of cases coming before these tribunals and the consequent necessity for a middle ground. This is where *CUPE* comes in. However, it was not really until *Bibeault* that courts found the proper ratio-

---

[74] *ILWU* v. *Prince Rupert Grain Ltd.* [1996] 2 SCR 432, 448. See also *CAIMAW* v. *Paccar of Canada Ltd.* [1989] 2 SCR 983, 1000; *Canada (Attorney-General)* v. *Public Service Alliance of Canada* [1991] 1 SCR 614.

[75] *Mossop*, above at n. 6, 599.

[76] See David Dyzenhaus's paper in this volume.

nale to ground the non-interventionist stance they have since taken. This, of course, leaves unanswered the question of why this stance has not been taken as regards human rights tribunals.

A second possible explanation may be that, in the search for legislative intent, the availability of a broad right of appeal in some human rights statutes was interpreted as an indication for the courts to be involved in the process of enforcing and adjudicating the rights created in human rights legislation. This was the case in *Zurich Insurance*.[77]

A third reason for treating human rights tribunals differently may find its origin in the fact that these are generally *ad hoc* boards set up to hear a particular case. Such tribunals are usually headed by a law professor. This could account for the perception that the tribunals lack the specialised expertise and continuous existence, whereas other boards, such as a labour board, may develop a capacity for consistency and accuracy in statutory interpretation which is greater than that afforded to the ordinary courts.

The fourth rationale which may be underlying differential treatment of human rights tribunals is the "quasi-constitutional" nature of the rights that they enforce. In their role as final arbitrators on constitutional issues, courts have developed an approach which can ensure the strong enforcement of rights and the balancing of state, individual and societal interests which are required. As the entitlements created in human rights legislation are seen as having greater importance than others created by statute, their interpretation may warrant the principled, purposive and vigilant reasoning which the courts can provide.

A fifth and related justification for departing from a stance of judicial deference as regards human rights bodies may be based in the social implications of their decisions. It might be thought that if human rights bodies had an unfettered power to interpret their broadly worded and purposive statutes they would be able to depart much too drastically from the basic social norms and values accepted by the government officials who are the source of the delegated power, and, indeed, by the electorate, who are the original source of this political power. This concern is reminiscent of the role which the "legal antipositivists", as described by Professor Dyzenhaus, believed the courts to have.[78]

Considered collectively, these five rationales appear to present a comprehensive justification for taking a less deferential stance with respect to human rights tribunals. However, if we examine each explanation separately, it becomes perhaps less evident that the courts need to depart from the *Bibeault*-inspired search for legislative intent in relation to judicial review of human rights tribunals.

As I have indicated already, the first concern, the maintenance of the supervisory role of the courts, could be conceived as lying at the base of a

---

[77] Above at n. 6.
[78] See David Dyzenhaus's paper in this volume.

pragmatic and functional approach. As I stated in developing my adaptation of the *Bibeault* test in *Mossop,* the concept of jurisdiction continues to play a significant role in defining the relationship between administrative tribunals and the ordinary courts through the mechanism of judicial review.[79] Granted this model represents a shift from the Diceyan reliance on traditional canons of statutory construction to a more systemic understanding of the legislation; however, as reflected in the judgments of *CUPE* and the cases which have followed it, such a move may have become necessary if courts are to continue their role of ensuring the legitimacy of the delegation of political power in a modern administrative state. In essence, the development of administrative bodies concerned with flexibility, expertise-based policy development, accessibility, and efficiency has not eliminated the need for the courts' supervision, but rather necessitated a fundamental shift in their approach to jurisdictional matters.

Given that a supervisory role for the court has been maintained in the functional approach, we are then faced with the four further concerns which may dictate greater intervention on the part of the courts in the decisions of tribunals involved in the domain of human rights.

The second reason, that is, the statutory right of appeal as indicator of a legislative intent of full review, is compelling. We may indeed wish to create an exception for human rights tribunals operating under such a regime. However, absent a statutory right of appeal, as was the case in *Mossop* and *Berg,* there may be other indications of legislative intent which merit our attention. It is well accepted that contemporary human rights regimes were developed in response to the inadequacy of more traditional, court-like schemes to combat discrimination in Canadian society.[80] While the reforms of the 1960s and 1970s may have had their critics, particularly those who protested against this "legislating of morality", Evelyn Kallen explains that this is not the primary objective of such legislation. In her view, the primary goal of human rights legislation is to eliminate discriminatory acts and their effects, not to change the attitudes of the object of a particular complaint. However, as she states also: "while the legislation may not change attitudes, it can introduce a climate in which the possibility of attitudinal change is maximised".[81]

The legislation also recognises that discrimination is wide-spread and may be unintentional, in the sense that it grows not from racist or otherwise directly prejudiced convictions, but rather from the fear on the part of "average" Canadians of losing accustomed comforts, conveniences or financial resources. Given this reality, the "community vindication" of the victims of discrimination is seen in such schemes as essential.[82] In order to discharge this unique, effect-based task, contemporary human rights models rely on a

---

[79] *Mossop*, above at n. 6, 595 and 600.
[80] E. Kallen, *Ethnicity and Human Rights in Canada* (Oxford University Press, Toronto, 2nd ed. 1995), 229.
[81] Ibid., 228.
[82] Ibid., 232.

specialised blend of educational and legal techniques. These are generally undertaken by both full-time trained staff and citizen commissioners, who are expected to advise government and community groups, as well as to develop policy. In addressing complaints, commissioners are dedicated to the possible settlement of the issue, through a wide and flexible range of remedies.

If settlement is not achieved, the Commission may refer a complaint to a tribunal, which will be appointed from a pre-established panel of members who sit for a specified period of time.[83] Kallen further asserts that the work of the commissions and tribunals in receiving and adjudicating complaints plays an important role in the public education process[84] and thus in the on-going shaping of a more tolerant, less discriminatory society. It is important to remember that this source of redress is generally provided without cost, as is the case with many schemes involving complainants who are unlikely to have the same financial resources as the objects of their complaints.

The history and contemporary reality of today's human rights legislation and institutions indicate a legislative intent to create a unique system, which could develop the sensitivity and expertise needed to apply broad principles in a flexible and accessible manner in an ever changing social context. The goal of this unique system is the elimination of discrimination both by remedying its effects at the community level and by preventing future discriminative acts through changing the public's attitudes. Inherent in this scheme appears to be the understanding that the courts do not provide an adequate forum to address these issues. Given the institutional context in which we find ourselves in this discussion, it seems that human rights schemes which include a statutory right of appeal may be an exception to this legislative intent as opposed to the primary indication thereof.

If we accept this as an accurate description of human rights bodies, our perception that such bodies do not have sufficient expertise to undertake statutory interpretation may then also change. The Supreme Court has repeatedly acknowledged that these bodies have superior expertise with respect to fact finding and adjudication in the human rights context, even in the presence of a statutory right of appeal.[85] However, in considering the policy objectives and structure of human rights legislation and the institutions it creates, the distinction between such determinations and the tribunal's interpretation of its enabling statute becomes somewhat blurred.

The difficulty posed by the fact/law distinction in the human rights domain has been explored not only by me, in my opinions in cases such as *Mossop*, *Berg*, and *Gould*, but also by authors who have commented on certain of these cases.[86] In fulfilling the general policy objectives of human rights legislation,

---

[83] Idem.
[84] Ibid., 233.
[85] See *Zurich Insurance*, *Mossop*, *Berg*, and *Ross*; above at n. 6.
[86] See A. Harvison Young, "Human Rights Tribunals and the Supreme Court of Canada: Reformulating Deference" (1993) 13 Admin LR (2d) 206, 212–3.

the Commission and Tribunal members are required to be equipped to apply the broad principles and provisions enumerated in its statute to new circumstances in a changing social environment. This requires not only factual findings, but also statutory interpretation in a very specialised context. For these reasons, as I said in *Mossop*, "[t]he work of the Commission and its tribunals involves the consideration and balancing of a variety of social needs and goals, and requires sensitivity, understanding, and expertise".[87]

What may be somewhat unique about this expertise, at least from a judge's point of view, is that it requires broadly worded, principled statutory provisions to ensure its exercise as opposed to the more technical or term-laden legislation which guides tribunals in other domains, such as the securities commission or the labour board. Hence, perhaps, the term, "general" questions of law. Nonetheless, when a court intervenes in such a tribunal's application of its statute to a particular set of facts on the basis that it is misconstruing a general question of law, it may act to negate the tribunal's expertise and powers in a way which contradicts the goals of the legislation.

The fourth concern, regarding the quasi-constitutional nature of human rights, may also explain why the courts see themselves as equally or indeed more competent to interpret such statutes. Given their jurisdiction to interpret constitutional provisions, particularly as regards the Charter of Rights and Freedoms, it may seem logical that the courts are best placed to protect similar entitlements in human rights legislation. However, the task of applying constitutional provisions is in reality quite different from that of applying those we have come to understand as "quasi-constitutional". Constitutional interpretation is truly a question of statutory construction, albeit through a purposive and principled approach. The goal is to ensure that state laws and action satisfy the principles enshrined in the constitution, the very principles upon which our "free and democratic society" is based.

The rights enshrined in human rights legislation are not enforceable against the state in its legislative and executive roles, but rather against the actions of individuals, organisations, or the government in its relationship to the complainants. The goal of human rights legislation is thus different from that of the Charter of Rights and Freedoms. It is to give the individual back a sense of dignity and self-worth, to compensate the person for the wrong done him or her, and to stop the discrimination. Such objectives require a consideration of a much broader set of factors and a greater sensitivity to the context of the individuals concerned than does statutory interpretation under the Charter of Rights and Freedoms.[88]

Moreover, the limits to the scope of the prohibitions against discrimination will necessarily be different. For example, whereas the state may, under section 1 of the Charter of Rights and Freedoms, be considered justified in

---

[87] *Mossop*, above at n. 6, 609.
[88] For a full discussion of the distinction between constitutional issues and those decided in the "quasi-constitutional" human rights domain, see Harvison Young, above at n. 28, 70–92.

violating an individual's constitutional right in the pursuit of another socially important goal, an individual who discriminates cannot balance his or her priorities in the same way. While he or she may be exonerated by showing that the distinction is a legitimate one in the circumstances, this is equivalent to finding that no discrimination has taken place, not that it is reasonably justified.

While the courts have developed a purposive and principled approach to interpreting human rights legislation, if they do so without the benefit of the expertise and reasoning of the human rights commission or tribunal, and without an appreciation of the institutional and social context in which the individuals find themselves, they may too easily reach a result which frustrates the intention of the legislature in creating these protections and the human rights scheme. Moreover, the notion of "general questions of law" seems less concerned with too restrictive an interpretation of human rights legislation, and more with too liberal a construction.

The final rationale is perhaps the one most clearly stated by the Supreme Court in *Mossop* and the cases which follow it, that being the need to control the social implications of the decisions of human rights tribunals. Controlling the social impact of such decisions seems to remain a central element to the supervisory role which the Court has maintained for itself. In *Mossop*,[89] for example, the Court was concerned about departing too drastically from the traditional sense of the concept of family. In *Berg*[90] the issue was the extent of the reach of the prohibition against discrimination to the various relationships which may arise between individuals and organisations in a particular community.

A rationale for intervention in human rights deliberations and decisions based on the social implications of these outcomes sits somewhat uncomfortably with legislative intent. Human rights schemes are set up to counteract the effects of discrimination. This is accomplished through an efficient, flexible and accessible system, made up of bodies with considerable expertise in both recognising and remedying inequality in its infinite variety of forms. The provisions of the statute are necessarily broad and the mandated approach is a principled one, based on the on-going policy objectives which guide the interpretation of the particular enactment. One might well say that social impact and change are the *raison d'être* of human rights legislation and institutions.

To find that the social implications, *per se*, of the tribunal's interpretation will trigger the substitution of a judicial construction of the statute may too easily frustrate the objectives of the legislation in question. Certainly, to avoid this unfortunate result, this rationale may require further exploration and elaboration to articulate the scope of the social implications which will merit the courts' attention. The judiciary may also need to consider the serious social implications of the decisions of other tribunals; for example, those of a

---

[89] Above at n. 6.
[90] Above at n. 6.

board enforcing environmental legislation. Furthermore, it may remain desirable in any event to consider the tribunal's reasons in the institutional context to ensure that the social impact meant to be addressed under the human rights legislation is not unnecessarily restricted upon review.

Having explored these possible rationales for not applying the search for legislative intent embodied in *Bibeault* to human rights tribunals, the next logical step is to ascertain whether a pragmatic and functional approach could indeed meet the various concerns. As I have explained, the supervisory role of the courts is not being eliminated in this approach, but rather modified. The question is whether these modifications are appropriate.

In its primary emphasis on seeking the intent of the legislature, the pragmatic and functional model necessarily takes into account important factors such as a statutory right of appeal. However, it does so with an understanding of what role such a provision plays in the institutional context of human rights legislation. In the absence of such an indication on the part of the legislature, this approach may be desirable as it prevents us from too easily overlooking the primary intent of the legislature in creating such schemes, and the somewhat unique nature of the expertise which commission and tribunal members are expected to develop.

The functional approach also provides a mechanism to ensure that the special importance these quasi-constitutional rights are given is respected, for this is a primary principle underlying both the legislation and jurisprudence in the human rights domain. Were a board to ignore this principle, and thereby place the right on an even par with another purely statutory entitlement, this could potentially be found to be unreasonable and therefore reviewable.

The issue of social implications perhaps provides the greatest challenge for a pragmatic and functional test. However, in the absence of a clear rationale which can differentiate these from the social impact the legislature has clearly intended, it seems necessary to at least hear the tribunal's views on the matter and to judge their reasonableness in consideration of the purposes and institutional structure of the statute. As the pragmatic and functional test recognises a role for the court with respect to jurisdiction, these concerns could potentially be taken into account in answering the question which I posed in *Mossop*: "Who should answer this question, the board or the court?"[91] This approach recognises that the court maintains an important role, yet ensures that the human rights board will not be prevented unnecessarily from undertaking its mandate of social change.

Professor Dyzenhaus may well challenge my approach. He has outlined the conceptual difficulties with maintaining an emphasis on legislative intent and jurisdiction, while at the same time attempting to enunciate deferential principles. In the place of such a model he advocates a shift to "deference as respect" to replace the traditional "deference as submission" of the Diceyan

---

[91] Above at n. 6, 604.

model. He describes a spirit of mutual regard and consideration between the courts and the administrative bodies where each recognises the role of the other in our modern state. The tribunals maintain the role of hearing and deciding the issue before it, while the courts must ensure that the reasons given by such bodies are rationally justified in the context of their administrative domain. For many tribunals, in order for their decisions to be considered justified, the value of equality must be furthered by their interpretation as this is seen as a central principle underlying the creation of administrative bodies.[92]

In a sense, Professor Dyzenhaus may be saying that what I have termed a pragmatic and functional approach need be applied to the decisions of *all* tribunals. Certainly, one could argue the value of this conclusion in the case of human rights tribunals as it may be only through such an approach, with the added normative consideration as regards policy questions, that their expertise and policy objectives can be taken into account. However, at the very least, the pragmatic and functional model as it stands now, has the potential to be similarly grounded in respect on the part of the courts for the reasons of those bodies which were created to carry out the social, economic, and other policies embodied in their enabling legislation. It remains to be seen how this doctrine will develop and upon what principles.

My purposes in writing this paper have been to explore the concept of the "general question of law" and its implications for human rights tribunals through an examination of the "ebb and flow" of the Supreme Court's jurisprudence in this area. In exploring this issue, I have hopefully contributed to the all-important discussion of what constitutes the best rationale for judicial review of statutory interpretation of these bodies, and, consequently, the most appropriate relationship between them and the ordinary courts. This will not be an easy task given the complex and dynamic nature of the modern administrative state.

A few years ago, one of my counterparts on the Supreme Court of the United States began an address to law students at Duke University with a solemn admonition. "Administrative law is not for sissies", he said.[93] Scholars of administrative law know that this warning applies with equal, if not greater, force to the brand of administrative law which has been developed in Canada. With relatively little guidance from Parliament or the legislatures, the Canadian courts have dramatically reformed the law of judicial review over the last twenty-five years, in recognition of the fact that administrative agencies have an important role to play in the advancement of legislative policies through the interpretation of statutory standards and the exercise of discretion.

At the same time, however, the Supreme Court of Canada has carved out a "general questions of law" exception which it applies only to the decisions of human rights tribunals, and this sits uncomfortably with the reforms of the

---

[92] See David Dyzenhaus's paper in this volume.
[93] Scalia, above at n. 55, 511.

past quarter-century. As the rationale for judicial deference is further refined, this exception may, eventually, prove unnecessary to the task of defining the appropriate relationship between the courts and human rights tribunals. While we may currently be at an "ebb" stage in the development of this relationship, perhaps the "flow" is forthcoming.

15

Feminism, Pluralism and Administrative Law

ALISON HARVISON YOUNG*

INTRODUCTION

Observers interested in both administrative law and feminist theory have noted, in recent years, parallel strains in both fields. In Canada, for example, the suggestion has been made that in the Canadian Supreme Court's administrative law judgments sometimes can be heard echoes of "feminist methodologies or approaches". This common ground has, to date, not been explored by either feminists or administrative lawyers.

In this paper I consider the links between functionalist and pluralist approaches to administrative law and certain strains of feminist thought. Although I am locating this mostly within the framework of the Canadian Supreme Court, my primary interest is to consider the relationship between these approaches. The Supreme Court is an ideal context for this for a few reasons. First, it is readily possible to identify strains of the various approaches and methodologies in certain opinions. Second, an examination of the various judgments emanating from the Court reveals some deep tensions and divisions on fundamental matters of approach and methodology. For example, while some judges tend to continue to embrace a strongly Diceyan, unitary vision of judicial review and administrative law, others tend to favour a more pluralistic, functional and principle-based or value-based approach. The latter approach is most compatible with feminist theory and methodologies, and as my later discussion of *Gould* v. *Yukon Order of Pioneers*[1] will indicate, the Court's opinions sometimes run along gender lines.

The first part of this paper will consider the parallels between elements of functionalist and pluralist approaches to administrative law and feminist methodology and approaches. The second part will consider selected issues which manifestly illustrate the parallel strains and also document the tensions

---

* I am indebted to the following people for their input and comments: Paul Craig, John Dawson, David Dyzenhaus, Claire L'Heureux-Dubé, Murray Hunt, and Rod Macdonald, and of course to Michael Taggart for his unflagging efforts and enthusiasm as well as his editorial comments. I am also very grateful to Agnieszka Charys, whose research assistance proved invaluable.

[1] [1996] 1 SCR 571 (hereafter referred to as *Gould*).

which they underline. These will include: (i) deference and the standard of review debate; (ii) bias; (iii) the influence of women judges and the "reach" of public law; and (iv) in conclusion, an assessment of the effect of both the influence of feminist thought as well as the influence of female judges on the Supreme Court of Canada to date. My conclusion is that the neither the presence of female judges nor the influence of feminist thought has "revolutionised" the Court or the law of the land.[2] These views continue, more often than not, to be present as dissenting opinions. On the other hand, these views are exercising significant influence in the sense that they are broadening the discourse on a number of issues to include new perspectives, considerations and possible answers.

FEMINISM, FUNCTIONALISM AND ADMINISTRATIVE LAW

An attempt to define feminism is fraught with difficulty, as many definitions are not entirely compatible. It is safe to say, however, that a recurrent preoccupation of feminist thought has been to identify, articulate and expose the senses in which society, including law and legal institutions, have in the past discriminated, and continue to discriminate against and subordinate women. Central to recent debate within feminist thought has been the role played by gender difference. Carol Gilligan, in her book *In a Different Voice*,[3] articulated gender differences and greatly contributed to the "difference" limb of feminism which has emphasised placing value on attributes like caring, a more female attribute, instead of trying to force women to abandon these qualities and conform to male norms. Gilligan's view has been strongly criticised by some (such as Catharine MacKinnon), who argue primarily that relying on a theory of difference is doomed to reinforce the powerlessness of women, because it masks the reality of power and oppression which remains, according to this view, the central injustice.[4] Gilligan's work has, however, been tremendously influential and has spawned an enormous body of literature addressing the implications of gender difference for ways of approaching—and re-approaching—our institutions. For example, men are said to tend to think of themselves as being in a rather atomistic relationship with the world around them; women are said to tend to think of themselves as much more

---

[2] There are a number of studies which have attempted to measure the extent to which having women judges on Canadian courts has affected the outcome of decisions: see P. McCormick and T. Job, "Do Women Judges Make a Difference: An Analysis by Appeal Court Data" (1993) 8 *Canadian Journal of Law & Society* 135. See also P. McCormick, "Judicial Career Patterns and the Delivery of Reasons for Judgment in the Supreme Court of Canada, 1949–1993" (1994) 5 *Supreme Court LR (2d)* 499 and P.H. Russell, "The Supreme Court in the 1980s: A Commentary on the S.C.R. Statistics" (1992) 30 *Osgoode Hall LJ* 771.

[3] Harvard University Press, Cambridge, 1982.

[4] C.A. MacKinnon, *Feminism Unmodified* (Harvard University Press, Cambridge, 1987), 32 ff.

"connected" to the world around them.⁵ A great deal of literature has also looked at "feminist methodologies" or approaches, meaning the ways in which women are inclined to approach and solve problems. This paper draws from these ideas. For example, a common observation, related to the notion that women are more concerned with "connection" than "autonomy", is that women are attentive to context in the course of making decisions, although different feminists may disagree about the implications of those differences.⁶ Another theme, also related to the "connection" point, is that women tend to value the sustenance of relationships more than winning in particular cases and that this also involves a greater degree of tolerance for difference. This will be discussed below.

At the outset, it will be useful to identify the factors which may contribute to the initial perception that the judgments of the Supreme Court of Canada tend to reflect feminist strains.

First of all, a first blush with Canadian administrative law reveals a great deal of language such as "contextualisation".⁷ In addition, doctrines such as the "patent unreasonableness" standard of review, which signals deference to other decision-makers, can be readily associated with a feminist emphasis on openness to different perspectives. This is also true of the famous *dicta* in *U.E.S., Local 298* v. *Bibeault*⁸ about taking a "pragmatic and functional" approach to the determination of a tribunal's jurisdiction. And one of the most enthusiastic applications of the patent unreasonableness standard of review was by Wilson J. in the *Corn Growers* case.⁹ In addition, there have

---

⁵ R. West, "Gender and Jurisprudence" (1988) 55 *U Chic LR* 1 is a superb example of feminist scholarship which explores the implications of a feminist analysis of the liberal and critical legal studies schools of theory.

⁶ For example, Gilligan's implication is that we all stand to gain from celebrating the constructive qualities that women have, such as a tendency to prefer conciliation to confrontation. Others seem to see them simply as differences which exist, will continue to exist, and which should be celebrated by women.

⁷ See, e.g., *Ross* v. *New Brunswick School District No. 15* [1996] 1 SCR 825, 870, 872 and 875, per La Forest J.; *Phillips* v. *Nova Scotia (Commission of Inquiry into the Westray Mine Tragedy)* [1995] 2 SCR 97, 159, per Cory J.; *Canadian Pacific Ltd.* v. *Matsqui Indian Band* [1995] 1 SCR 3, 65–6 and 68–72, per Sopinka J. (dissenting); *IWA* v. *Consolidated Bathurst Packaging Ltd.* [1990] 1 SCR 282, 301, per Sopinka J. (dissenting); *Syndicat des employés de production du Quebec et de l'Acadie* v. *Canada (Human Rights Commission)* [1989] 2 SCR 879, 890 and 896–7, per Sopinka J. (quoting Lord Denning M.R. in *Selvarajan* v. *Race Relations Board* [1976] 1 All ER 12, 19).

⁸ [1988] 2 SCR 1048, 1088.

⁹ *National Corn Growers Assn.* v. *Canada (Import Tribunal)* [1990] 2 SCR 1324 (hereafter referred to as *Corn Growers*). In this case, the Court was unanimous in upholding the Tribunal's decision, and unanimous in applying the "patent unreasonableness" standard. But Wilson J. wrote concurring reasons (joined in by Dickson C.J. and Lamer C.J.) in which she expressed disagreement with the approach taken by the plurality. Wilson J. said (ibid., 1347–8):

"One must, in my view, not begin with the question whether the tribunal's *conclusions* are patently unreasonable; rather; one must begin with the question whether the tribunal's interpretation of the provisions in its constitutive legislation that define the way it is to set about answering questions is patently unreasonable. If the tribunal has not interpreted its constitutive statute in a patently unreasonable fashion, the courts must not then proceed to a wide ranging review of whether the tribunal's conclusions are unreasonable. It seems to me,

been some landmark cases involving women: *Action Travail des Femmes*[10] in which the Supreme Court of Canada upheld the tribunal finding of systemic discrimination against women as well as the forward looking affirmative action remedy it imposed; and *R. v. Lavallée*[11] which extended the possibility of raising the plea of self-defence to cover a woman who had shot her abusive partner in the back of his head as he left the room, having just told her he would return to kill her later. Of course, the final contributing factor to this "feminist" perception is the fact that there have been three female judges appointed to the Supreme Court since 1979.[12]

But this first impression does not last. What is behind this perception? The core of this perception lies, I believe, in the "functionalist" approach to review which in the administrative context flows from a principle-based or value-based,[13] pluralist model, as opposed to a Diceyan model of review, and which is one strain present in Canadian judgments.[14] By functionalist I mean an approach which takes the purpose and nature of the administrative body in question seriously, and which recognises that the particular context is relevant to the interpretive process.[15] I do not mean "functionalist" in the sense

however, that this is what my colleague has done. And in the process he has engaged in the kind of detailed review of a tribunal's findings that this Court's jurisprudence makes clear is inappropriate' (emphasis in original).

This version of deference, however, differs significantly from the more engaged version of "deference as respect" employed by Madame Justice L'Heureux-Dubé in her dissent in *Canada (Attorney-General) v. Mossop* [1993] 1 SCR 227 (hereafter referred to as *Mossop*) and propounded by David Dyzenhaus in "Developments in Administrative Law: The 1992–93 Term" (1994) 5 *Supreme Court LR (2d)* 189 and developed further in his paper in this volume.

[10] *Canadian National Railway Co. v. Canada (Canadian Human Rights Commission)* [1987] 1 SCR 1114 (hereafter referred to as *Action Travail des Femmes*). This decision was written by Dickson J. The issue had to do with the interpretation given by the Canadian Human Rights Tribunal to the remedial provisions of the Canadian Human Rights Act. It was not a case decided under the Charter of Rights and Freedoms, but it was decided in the early days of the Charter at a time when the Court seemed to be enthusiastic about the values it reflected. It is interesting to note that, in marked contrast to the *Mossop* case, which arose through the same process from the same statute, there was no discussion whatsoever of the standard of review in *Action Travail des Femmes*, something which I understood (before *Mossop*) not as a matter of judicial deference but as a "happy coincidence of opinion on the merits": see A. Harvison Young, "Keeping the Courts at Bay: The Canadian Human Rights Commission and its Counterparts in Britain and Northern Ireland: Some Comparative Lessons"(1993) 43 *UTLJ* 65, 92.

[11] [1990] 1 SCR 852 (hereafter referred to as *Lavallée*). This decision, which was unanimous, was authored by Wilson J.

[12] Wilson J., who was appointed to the Supreme Court on 30 March 1982, retired on 4 Jan. 1991. The two other female judges, L'Heureux-Dubé and McLachlin JJ., were respectively appointed on 15 April 1987 and 30 March 1989.

[13] The term most frequently used to describe principle or value-driven review is "rights-based". The problem with that term is that it may be understood as coterminous with individual rights which have often been somewhat antithetical to the goals of regulation. In fact, it is often used to include democratic and pluralist values such as accountability, participation, etc. When I use the term "rights-based" I am simply denoting those theories of review that recognise that certain values, principles or rights should guide the exercise of judicial review.

[14] For a useful discussion of modern theories of judicial review, see P.P. Craig, *Administrative Law*, (Sweet and Maxwell, London, 3rd ed. 1994).

[15] For a discussion of the notion and importance of institutional competence, see R.A. Macdonald, "On the Administration of Statutes" (1987) 12 *Queen's LJ* 488.

that Evans *et al.* describe the anti-Diceyan movement. They rightly criticise functionalism for its failure to attach sufficient weight "to considerations of democratic accountability and to fundamental rights, and to the positive contributions that the courts can make to realising these goals".[16] Functionalism, on its own, does not propound any theory of review beyond the message that the administrators should be left alone to implement their socially progressive programmes. Of course, this becomes problematic when, as in the present era, dynamics change and government initiatives are inclined to cut down or eliminate various programmes. Functionalism does not present a basis for discriminating as between the conservative and social welfare initiatives. Although I am using the language of functionalism in this paper to refer to the approach or methodology of review, I am assuming an underlying principle-based, pluralist model. Functionalism, in other words, describes the orientation that interpreters should have, whereas the principle or value-based, pluralist model supplies the more substantive values. For the purposes of this paper, it is not necessary to fill in the content of principle-based theories of review. This will vary a great deal. David Dyzenhaus has recently propounded equality as the foundation of rights-based review.[17] Dawn Oliver has articulated a number of principles that may be seen in similar terms.[18] The term "rights-based pluralist" model refers to a model within which respect for a variety of groups and normative orders is central.[19] A vision that places equality at the centre, such as that propounded by Dyzenhaus,[20] is a very good example of a rights-based, pluralist approach. The point is, for present purposes, that such an approach presupposes positive value in protecting the integrity of different normative orders; it does not purport to simply apply all norms as though universal without regard for differences in context, or without regard for the possibility that various groups or orders generate their own

[16] J.M. Evans, H.N. Janisch, David J. Mullan, R.C.B. Risk, *Administrative Law: Cases, Text and Materials*, (Emond Montgomery Publishing Ltd., Toronto, 4th ed. 1994), 31 (hereafter referred to as Evans *et al.*).

[17] See David Dyzenhaus's paper in this volume where he explicitly articulates a rights-based theory, with equality as the core value. See also C. Sunstein, *After the Rights Revolution* (Harvard University Press, Cambridge, 1990) and *The Partial Constitution* (Harvard University Press, Cambridge, 1993).

[18] See Dawn Oliver's paper in this volume.

[19] This is to be contrasted with "interest-group pluralism" as discussed by Sunstein, *The Partial Constitution*, above at n. 17, 25:

"There are many different forms of pluralism, but the unifying pluralist claim is that laws should be understood not as a product of deliberation, but on the contrary as a kind of commodity, subject to the usual forces of supply and demand. Various groups in society compete for loyalty and support from the citizenry. Once groups are organized and aligned, they exert pressure on political representatives, also self-interested, who respond to the pressures thus imposed. This process of aggregating and trading off interests ultimately produces law, or political equilibrium."

The purpose of pluralism as advocated in this paper is consistent with the principle of "deliberative democracy" as articulated by Sunstein. This vision is premised on the idea of deliberative relationships among often heterogeneous individuals, groups and institutions.

[20] See his paper in this volume.

norms to begin with. In Canada, pluralism is understood as an aspect of a multicultural society, and the fostering and tolerance of diversity are strongly held values.

The parallels between pluralism and the discourse of an influential strain of feminism or feminist methodology are striking, and I will consider elements of these parallels more closely below. It will be useful here, however, to set out a "broad brush" picture of this parallel.

In the following passage, Paul Craig sets out the link between a pluralist model of administrative law and a functionalist approach to judicial review:[21]

> "The idea that the meaning of legal terms should reflect and be shaped by the distinctive needs of power structures within particular areas of society fits comfortably within pluralist thought; and the assumption that the interpretation of any of these terms by the ordinary courts should necessarily be preferred to that of the agency is thought to be unwarranted."

There is a considerable body of feminist literature that addresses the "gendered" aspects of judging and ways of countering these historical tendencies, and much has been written on the "standpoint" that judges should take.[22] The following passage from an article by Martha Minow, while quintessentially feminist, also reflects a pluralist approach:[23]

> "Two exercises can help those who judge to glimpse the perspectives of others and to avoid a false impartiality. The first is to explore our own stereotypes, our own attitudes toward people we treat as different—and, indeed, our own categories for organizing the world. . . . The second exercise is to search out differences and celebrate them, constructing new bases for connection. *A third approach is to cherish difference and welcome anomaly. Still another is to understand that which initially seems strange and to learn about sense and reason from this exercise—just as philosophers, anthropologists, and psychologists have urged us to take seriously the self-conceptions and perceptions of others.* . . . These exercises in taking the perspective of the other will deepen and broaden anyone's perspective. For judges, who debate the use of the coercive forces of the law in relation to issues of difference, these exercises are critical. . . . One judge explained that law's coercive power must be applied to assure 'the viability of a pluralistic democracy', which depends upon the willingness to accept all of the 'thems' as 'us'."

It is clear from these passages that the central concerns are rather different, but the common ground is also striking. This common ground lies largely in the notion that legal meanings are shaped by their contexts, and that the views

---

[21] Craig, above at n. 14, 32. See Macdonald, above at n. 15.

[22] See, e.g., K. O'Donovan, "Engendering Justice: Women's Perspectives and the Rule of Law" (1989) 39 *UTLJ* 127; M-J. Mossman, "Feminism and Legal Method: The Difference It Makes" (1986, unpublished paper), 4–5.

[23] M. Minow, "Foreword: Justice Engendered" (1987) 101 *Harv LR* 10, 79–81 (emphasis added). For a more recent application of some of these points by the same author in relation to the Clarence Thomas Senate Judiciary Committee hearings in the United States, see "Stripped Down Like a Runner or Enriched by Experience: Bias and Impartiality of Judges and Jurors" (1992) 33 *Wm & Mary LR* 1201.

of "ordinary" judges, external to (or above) these other orders, should not simply be imposed but must, to some extent, take account of the "other" views and realities.[24] There is one focal point which brings out the relationship between functionalism, pluralism and feminism most clearly. This is a rejection of Dicey's version of the rule of law, and in particular of the idea that Parliament has a monopoly on law-making, and of the notion that the "ordinary" courts are "superior". The second is a consideration of some of the implications of both approaches, as reflected in notions of standing or, in Canadian law, the "patent unreasonableness" standard of review for error.

Rejecting Dicey

The criticisms of the Diceyan vision of the rule of law and its implications for administrative law are well known.[25] Two criticisms in particular point to common ground between functional and feminist approaches: the rejection of the "ordinary" courts as superior, neutral and objective arbiters of the will of the legislator and the recognition that Parliament does not have a monopoly on law-making.[26] The emphasis, however, differs. In the case of the "superiority" of the ordinary courts, Harry Arthurs put the point for the functionalists:[27]

> "There is no reason to believe that a legally-trained judge is better qualified to determine the existence or sufficiency or appropriateness of evidence on a given point than a trained economist or engineer, an arbitrator selected by the parties, or simply an experienced tribunal member who decides such cases day in and day out. There is no reason to believe that a judge whose entire professional life has been spent dealing with disputes one by one should possess an aptitude for issues which arise often because an administrative system dealing with cases in volume has been designed to strike an appropriate balance between efficiency and effective rights of participation."

Arthurs' point is one of relative expertise, and it is key to the arguments of functionalists.[28] But a related concern was that apart from the question of expertise, "ordinary" judges were likely to be hostile to the usual goals of modern public administration. As Evans *et al.* put the point:[29]

---

[24] It is interesting to observe that, of the two passages, the one by Minow seems to presuppose a more authoritative role for the judge: while the judge must take account of these other realities, it is still the judge's opinion that will prevail. Of course, this may be an unfair observation given that Minow is talking about judging in general and not specifically about administrative law.

[25] See the paper by Murray Hunt in this volume.

[26] This tradition in Canada has been most strongly associated with John Willis, "Three Approaches to Administrative Law: The Judicial, the Conceptual and the Functional" (1935) 1 *UTLJ* 53; see also "The McRuer Report: Lawyers' Values and Civil Servants' Values" (1968) 18 *UTLJ* 351. For a summary of the functionalist critique, see Evans *et al.*, above at n. 16, 29–31.

[27] H.W. Arthurs, "Protection against Judicial Review" (1983) 43 *La Revue du Barreau* 277, 289.

[28] See Macdonald, above at n. 15.

[29] Above at n. 16, 30.

"far from being a 'neutral' prescription for the protection of liberty, Dicey's version of the rule of law was designed to put public administration into a straitjacket. For example, the judicial model of procedural fairness was likely to hamper an agency's capacity for effective decision-making, and to benefit only those with the means to hire a lawyer. In addition, the courts' approach to the interpretation of legislation was driven by an ideology that generally deplored government intrusion in the operation of the market, and the limitation of common law rights of individuals to pursue their own economic interests."

Feminist critiques of the Diceyan model are familiar. First of all, the critique insists that the so-called neutral or objective perspective is actually a *male* perspective, and thus objects to treating this point of view as a *universal* point of view.[30] This perspective has structured legal method which has offered, in the words of one, "little opportunity for fundamental questioning about the *process* of defining the issues, selecting relevant principles, and excluding irrelevant details".[31] The "selective choice of facts and principles identified as 'relevant' enables the preservation of the status quo under the guise of 'neutral' legal method". In this way, legal method is, according to some feminists, "'structured in such a way that it is impervious to a feminist perspective'".[32]

The Diceyan version of the rule of law has analogous implications for administrative law to the feminist critique just outlined. The placement of the ordinary courts at the top of the pyramid focuses on the control of agencies (which are distrusted to begin with) and fosters a generalist or universalist approach to administrative law. The structure itself is hostile to (or impervious to) specialist regimes, or to what one might call, legal pluralism.

A corollary to both a feminist and a pluralist critique of Dicey is the recognition that power can come from a number of sources. In pluralist terms, this recognition fuels a vision of review which may be wider than Dicey's, and for feminists, it has led to a sustained critique of the public/private distinction in law generally. But for pluralist administrative lawyers and feminists alike, what counts as public is no longer (if it ever was) a simple matter of tracing the statutory pedigree. This raises another shared implication: the need to conceive of appropriate controls, which may sometimes mean (*inter alia*) broadening the scope of judicial review. In short, both the functionalist and the feminist critiques complain of certain entrenched values or perspectives excluding or resisting other legitimate perspectives.

This discussion brings us to another aspect of the parallel between feminist and functionalist methodologies. Both approaches beg the question as to what political theory underlies them. Just as there is a tension in administrative law between liberal and pluralist ideals, there is a tension between liberal and

---

[30] O'Donovan, above at n. 22, 131, citing K. Lahey, "Until Women Themselves Have Told All That They Have to Tell"(1985) 23 *Osgoode Hall LJ* 519, 526.

[31] Mossman, above at n. 22, 4–5, cited in O'Donovan, above at n. 20, 129 (emphasis in original).

[32] O'Donovan, ibid., 130.

(some) feminist ideals. For example, some feminist approaches are liberal in nature and some explicitly reject liberalism (e.g., equality of result versus equality of opportunity).[33] Similarly, rights-based theories of review vary as to what rights come into play and how they are construed. In Canada this is further complicated by the Charter of Rights and Freedoms. Of course, in Canada, it is clear that we do have rights-based review, though what the rights mean is less clear. It is also far from clear what role functionalism/pluralism will continue to play. It is arguable that the Charter will push the courts back in the direction of Dicey by entrenching them as the gate-keepers of rights and reinforcing their role at the top of the pyramid.

The Values of Pluralism

There are some interesting resonances between the implications of a pluralist model of administrative law and some feminist methodologies. A basic and important implication of a pluralist model is the emphasis placed on rights of participation. This arises out of the recognition that Parliament does not have a monopoly over public power, and from the concern that a failure to address issues of citizen input and participation directly will reinforce the influence of the most powerful groups in the public arena.[34]

Feminist approaches or methodologies also place great value on participation. Perhaps a difference in orientation between feminism and pluralism is that the former arises out of past experience while the latter seems more prophylactic. A current example in the Canadian context is the response from women's groups to the federal government's announcement of plans to set up a regulatory agency to deal with new reproductive technologies.[35] A virtually unanimous response focuses on the membership in the agency itself and a concern that the rules of the game not be simply set by the "experts". One way of reading this is to say simply that the feminist position is just one more lobby with an axe to grind. But some versions of feminism place a strong value on pluralist values. In discussing Carol Gilligan's work, Katherine O'Donovan states that the "prevailing model [of justice] is based on notions of abstraction, logic, objectivity, and neutrality. Women's views of the importance of connection and a morality of relationships are largely excluded."[36] The substance of the concern with "connection" and the

---

[33] A number of feminist writers have recently attempted to address directly the ideal role of the state from a feminist perspective. See, e.g., C.A. MacKinnon, *Toward a Feminist Theory of the State* (Harvard University Press, Cambridge, 1989) and D. Rhode, "Feminism and the State" (1994) 107 *Harv LR* 1181.

[34] J.L. Mashaw, R.A. Merrill and P.M. Shane, *Administrative Law: The American Public Law System* (West Publishing, St Paul, 1992), 35: "a pluralist vision of administrative process sees both procedural design and judicial policing of those designs primarily as devices for providing access to policymakers for all relevant interests". See generally Craig, above at n. 14, 31.

[35] Bill C-47.

[36] O'Donovan, above at n. 22, 134.

morality of relationships may also suggest an affinity for the values of pluralism in a larger sense, meaning a sense of complexity and the existence of different "normative orders" which gives rise, in turn, to a new set of concerns about the (in feminist terms) "morality of relationships". This focuses attention on the particular normative sphere in its own terms, locating the "reviewer" in a place which one might conceptualise as further away from the court and closer to the agency itself. This of course stands in contrast to the traditional Diceyan model which places the court itself at centre stage, leaving very little space for the body under scrutiny. This point is reinforced by the emphasis feminists often place on "a recognition of a multiplicity of standpoints, of different versions and visions".[37] Martha Minow emphasises a vision of justice that asks judges to adopt other perspectives:[38]

> "The process of looking through other perspectives does not itself yield an answer, but it may lead to an answer different from the one that the judge would otherwise have reached. Seen this way, the difference dilemma is hard, but not impossible."

Minow is not talking about administrative law, but her comments have clear applicability to pluralist models of administrative law and judicial review. One can, for example, understand the "patent unreasonableness" standard of review for error in just these terms, as a device that calls upon the reviewing court to place itself within the agency or tribunal in question and take that context or perspective into account. Minow also quotes Drucilla Cornell's statement that "[t]he danger of certainty is that it turns against the generous impulse to open oneself up to the other, and to truly listen, to risk the chance that we might be wrong".[39] There are other examples of the implications of Minow's visions on other aspects of administrative law; an obvious one would be the law of standing, which Minow would understand quite broadly.

The point then is that one can trace a convergence of views in some respects at least between pluralist and feminist models. This convergence is at least partly responsible for the "feminist impression" which some have gleaned from the administrative law output of the Canadian Supreme Court.

PERCEPTION MEETS REALITY

To what extent is this feminist model reflected in the administrative law doctrine? The answer, these days, is rather complex. While it is not difficult to identify the echoes, they tend to be controversial and are frequently heard in

---

[37] O'Donovan, above at n. 22, 134.

[38] Above at n. 23, 60. In *Plessy* v. *Ferguson*, 163 U.S. 537 (1896) Mr Plessy's attorney had implored the justices to put themselves in the position of a black person restricted to certain railway coaches reserved for non-whites. This seems to have influenced Harlan J.'s dissent: see Minow, ibid., 59.

[39] D. Cornell, "The Poststructuralist Challenge to the Ideal of Community" (1987) 8 *Cardozo LR* 989, 1018, cited in Minow, above at n. 23, 57.

dissenting judgments. Three issues will be considered in this section. The first is the notion of deference as reflected by the standard of review applied by the courts. The second issue concerns bias, a subject which is currently being rethought both at the level of the ordinary courts as well as within the province of administrative law. The final issue which will be considered is in many respects the most fundamental; the public/private divide and the reach of "public" law itself.

Deference and the standard of review

The most obvious indicator of the relatively weak influence of feminist thought on current administrative law doctrine is the resurrection with a vengeance of the "correctness" standard of review, and with it, the decline of "deference as respect".[40] There are a number of recent decisions that track this development (going back to CUPE[41]) but one of the most vivid is Mossop.[42] In that case the Tribunal established by the Canadian Human Rights Commission had reached the conclusion that Mossop had been the victim of unlawful discrimination on the grounds of "family status" when he had been refused bereavement leave to attend the funeral of his male partner's father. In reaching this decision, the Tribunal found that Mossop and his partner constituted a family within the meaning of the Canadian Human Rights Act.[43] Mossop provides a useful case study because the reasoning of the majority in favour of the correctness standard stands in such contrast to the reasoning of L'Heureux-Dubé J., who would have applied a standard of patent unreasonableness.[44] The correctness standard applied by the majority in Mossop is, as Dyzenhaus has noted, vintage Dicey. First, as the Chief Justice's opinion indicates, the reasoning reflects what Dyzenhaus labels

---

[40] David Dyzenhaus uses this term. See above at n. 9 and in his paper in this volume.
[41] *Canadian Union of Public Employees Local 963* v. *New Brunswick Liquor Corporation* [1979] 2 SCR 227 (hereafter referred to as *CUPE*). As Dyzenhaus observes, this was the first time the Supreme Court "clearly announced the principle of judicial deference to tribunals' decisions on points of law" : above at n. 9, 190.
[42] Above at n. 9. Other cases that confirm the trend include *United Brotherhood of Carpenters and Joiners of America, Local 579* v. *Bradco Construction Ltd* [1993] 2 SCR 316 and *Dayco (Canada)* v. *CAW-Canada* [1993] 2 SCR 230 (hereafter referred to as *Dayco*). Another case decided that year which applied a correctness standard and upheld the British Columbia Council of Human Rights tribunal decision was *University of British Columbia* v. *Berg* [1993] 2 SCR 353. For a comment on the decline of deference, see A. Harvison Young, "Human Rights Tribunals and the Supreme Court of Canada: Reformulating Deference" (1993) 13 Admin LR (2d) 206.
[43] RSC 1985, c. H-6.
[44] Dyzenhaus argues that the "patent unreasonableness" standard of review is itself a product of the Diceyan model, which prefers to presume that the legislator may have had more than one possible interpretation in mind rather than submit to administrative authority; above at n. 9, 208ff. On this reasoning, the judge embarks on "a sympathetic analysis of the reviewed decision. The inquiry proceeds by asking whether the body in question succeeded in justifying its decision. . . . If . . [the judge] cannot go all the way, then it finds not that the body made a patently unreasonable decision but that it made an incorrect one": ibid., 211.

"submissive deference"—deference to the legislator. Second, La Forest J. was also of the view that "[t]he normal approach to interpreting a tribunal's enabling statute should be that the courts retain their general supervisory jurisdiction".[45] Absent from the majority approach in *Mossop* was any suggestion that the Court should approach the project of review with any sort of "sympathy" for the perspective taken by the tribunal. The framing of the issue as a question of law for determination by the "ordinary" courts insulates the judges from any obligation to engage with the tribunal and instead legitimates the inclination to disregard the justifications of the tribunal in the name of legislative intent.[46]

In dissent, L'Heureux-Dubé J. took a very different approach, characterised by what Dyzenhaus calls "deference as respect":[47]

> "Deference as respect requires an inquiry into reasonableness in that it requires a judge to embark on a sympathetic analysis of the reviewed decision. The inquiry proceeds by asking whether the body succeeded in justifying its decision. It thus requires that there be a genuine attempt at justification and it then revisits the issue of justification in every respect."

This notion of deference is not blind or submissive, but rather a principle which advocates engaging with the justifications employed by the tribunal or body in question. It presupposes a level of openness to the tribunal which is consistent with the models of judging outlined by Minow and other feminists: it is inclusive, presupposes certain substantive values[48] and, in Drucilla Cornell's terms, is willing to risk being wrong.[49] It flows from a principle or value-based model of review which also broadens in some ways the scope of review for error by augmenting the list of considerations to be taken into account by the tribunal and the reviewing court.[50] As the notion of engagement inherent in the principle of "deference as respect" indicates, a pluralist model requires judges to come down from their pedestals and consider the issues in all their particular complexities. In a well known lecture Madam Justice Bertha Wilson quoted these words from Patricia Cain: "what we want from our judges is a special ability to listen with connection before engaging

---

[45] *Mossop*, above at n. 9, 198.

[46] See, e.g., the reasons of Lamer C.J. in *Mossop*, ibid., 580–82.

[47] Dyzenhaus, above at n. 9, 211. Dyzenhaus argues that, at the end of the exercise, if the result has been justified, the conclusion is that it is correct, not that it is reasonable.

[48] Though precisely what they are or how they are to be interpreted is not pre-ordained. In L'Heureux-Dubé J.'s dissent in *Mossop*, above at n. 9, 611–15, she placed weight on the "quasi-constitutional" status of the legislation.

[49] See text accompanying n. 39 above.

[50] Dyzenhaus suggests that L'Heureux-Dubé J.'s claim that she was applying a standard of patent unreasonableness is "almost wholly undercut by her deployment, independent of the Tribunal's own reasons for judgment, of a sophisticated rights-based model of adjudication which relied strongly on a wealth of literature advocating recognition of the legitimacy of same-sex relationships. It was therefore warranted for the other two dissenters to adopt her arguments wholesale in support of their conclusion that the Tribunal's decision was correct" above at n. 9, 211, citing from *Mossop*, above at n. 42, 623–34.

in the separation that accompanies judgement".[51] This feminist account adds force to the pluralist case for sympathetic review.

There are other indicators of the decline of pluralist/functionalist values. The same arguments that support the principle of deference as respect on matters of law can also be marshalled to support the procedural rulings of a board or tribunal.[52] Nevertheless, the Supreme Court "has reasserted the preeminence of the regular courts on procedural questions and relegated deference to procedural rulings to a very limited domain".[53]

It is perhaps even less surprising that when Charter rights are in issue, the Court refuses to accord any respect to tribunal expertise on procedural questions.[54] This is obviously out-of-step with a functionalist/pluralist approach to administrative law in that it accords insufficient weight to the various normative orders that exist in the administrative universe and presupposes an unwarranted level of superiority on the part of the courts. In terms of feminist values expressed by authors such as Minow and O'Donovan, it is a structure that will not encourage dialogue or openness to the body's procedural environment, but rather legitimates the raw imposition of the reviewing judge's view of the matter. In the speech mentioned earlier, Wilson J. referred to Carol Gilligan's work[55] at length, and considered the extent to which it may be understood as explaining the male affinity for the adversarial process as one which results in winners and losers.[56] She said:[57]

> "I think it may in part explain the traditional reluctance of the courts to get too deeply into the circumstances of a case, their anxiety to reduce the context of a dispute to its bare bones through a complex system of exclusionary evidentiary rules. . . . It is so much easier to come up with a black and white answer if you are unencumbered by a broader context which might prompt you, in Lord MacMillan's words, to temper the cold light of reason with the warmer tints of imagination and sympathy."

This comment could just as easily refer to the Diceyan model of review on the one hand and a pluralist model on the other. A principle-based pluralist model

---

[51] Patricia Cain, "Good and Bad Bias: A Comment on Feminist Theory and Judging" (1988) 61 *S Cal LR* 1945, 1954, quoted in B. Wilson, "Will Women Judges Really Make a Difference?" (1990) 28 *Osgoode Hall LJ* 507, 521.

[52] M. Loughlin, "Procedural Fairness: A Study of the Crisis in Administrative Law Theory" (1978) 28 *UTLJ* 215. See also D. Mullan, "Judicial Deference to Administrative Decision-Making" (1985–6) 50 *Sask LR* 503. For a nuanced treatment of the concept of fairness from a pluralist perspective, see R.A. Macdonald, "Judicial Review and Procedural Fairness in Administrative Law:I" (1980) 25 *McGill LJ* 520.

[53] Evans *et al.*, above at n. 16, 200.

[54] There is some basis for arguing that the Charter came at a bad time for administrative law (or at least "post-Diceyan" administrative law) as it reinforced and broadened the supremacy of the judiciary and crystallised its position as society's gatekeeper of human rights: see Harvison Young, above at n. 10, 73.

[55] *In a Different Voice—Psychological Theory and Women's Development* (Harvard University Press, Cambridge, 1982).

[56] Wilson, above at n. 51, 519–21.

[57] Ibid., 520–1.

of review does not start with a distrust of the agency, and arguably places value on the notion that one purpose of review is to encourage agencies to pay attention to their systems and procedures.

The standpoint taken by the courts with respect to error of law and natural justice/fairness are merely two examples among a number which could be similarly considered.[58] The point is that, in the sphere of administrative law, the Supreme Court as a whole appears to be moving away from the functionalist/pluralist values that have been associated with feminist values. It is somewhat ironic that this development has been taking place over the very period during which there have been, for the first time, female judges on the Court. In fact, the "high-water mark" of the functionalist/pluralist model of review is said to be Dickson J.'s (as he then was) judgment in *CUPE*.[59] That decision was rendered in 1979—the year in which Madam Justice Bertha Wilson became the first woman to be appointed to the Supreme Court. This does not mean, of course, that the female judges have not made their marks in many respects, or, for that matter, that male judges have not adopted "feminist approaches" in some cases. But it does seem that the overall influence of pluralist/feminist values is relatively weak these days.

Bias

One of the most interesting and immediately pertinent elements of the relationship between feminism and administrative law has to do with the feminist critique of impartiality. There has been a great deal of scholarship recently which has asserted the gendered nature of judging norms, as has been discussed already in this paper.[60] It is not coincidental that at a time when the number of women in the profession and on the bench has been growing, the concept of bias has begun to show signs of strain, both in its application to judges and to administrative decision-makers. Traditional notions of impartiality as objective and neutral have always been problematic in certain administrative law contexts, such as labour relations, where expertise is valued. But the signs of strain became evident a few years ago as a flurry of bias cases

---

[58] The law of standing is another one which can be seen as rather gendered. In her speech, Wilson J., having set out the affinity between the male affinity for the adversarial process and reducing a case to its "bare bones", she continued (ibid., 521):

"[I]t may also explain the hostility of some male judges to permitting intervenors in human rights cases. The main purpose of having intervenors is to broaden the context of the dispute, to show the issue in a larger perspective or as impacting on other groups not directly involved in the litigation at all. But it certainly does complicate the issues to have them presented in polycentric terms."

[59] Above at n. 41.

[60] See, e.g., R. Graycar, "The Gender of Judgments: An Introduction", in M. Thornton (ed.), *Public and Private: Feminist Legal Debates* (Clarendon Press, Melbourne, 1995). See also Minow, above at n. 23.

went to the Supreme Court of Canada.[61] One of those cases was *Newfoundland Telephone Co. v. Newfoundland (Board of Commissioners) of Public Utilities*.[62]

There, Andy Wells, an outspoken consumer advocate, had been appointed to the Public Utility Board. The Newfoundland Telephone Co. raised the issue of reasonable apprehension of bias on the basis of Well's comments to the press that the company executives were "fat-cats" who were making their salaries off the backs of the average rate-payers and did not deserve those salaries. Wells had made these or similar comments both before and after the beginning of the hearings. In upholding the allegation of bias, the Supreme Court was clearly uncomfortable about applying the "reasonable apprehension of bias" test to the various stages of the regulatory process. In the end, it drew the distinction between the "open mind" test, which permits the decision-maker to have and express views as long as he or she is open to contrary views, and the usual "reasonable apprehension of bias" test which applies once the hearing commences. One problem with this is that, as commentators have observed, the distinction between stages may be quite arbitrary. But the more fundamental problem is that it does not grapple with the concept of bias itself. It is interesting to note, nevertheless, that the "open mind" test is strongly reminiscent of the feminist standpoint advocated by Drucilla Cornell's endorsement of the notion that we should "truly listen, to risk the chance that we might be wrong".[63] As the ideal of nineteenth century notions of objectivity and neutrality have crumbled under the pressure of the principled recognition that all judges bring some baggage to the bench and the more practical recognition that differences between the baggage may often be gendered, the pressure increases to reconsider the notions of bias, and with it the enterprise of judging.

In Canada, two recent cases are striking illustrations of the issue; one is a criminal case and the other arose in an administrative law setting. In *R.D.S. v. The Queen*[64] the Court of Appeal upheld the Nova Scotia Supreme Court's decision which had overturned an acquittal and ordered a new trial on the basis of the Crown's argument that the judge's comments had given rise to a reasonable apprehension of bias. The case had involved a charge of assault brought against a Black youth. The police officer claimed that the youth had deliberately run into him with his bicycle while he was in the process of arresting another youth. The police officer and the youth were the only witnesses and gave very different accounts of what had happened that evening. In

---

[61] See *Save Richmond Farmland Society v. Richmond* [1990] 3 SCR 1213; *Old St. Boniface Residents Assn. Inc. v. Winnipeg* [1990] 3 SCR 1170.
[62] [1992] 1 SCR 623 (hereafter referred to as *Newfoundland Telephone*).
[63] Above at n. 39.
[64] (1995) 145 NSR (2d) 284. This case is currently on appeal to the Supreme Court of Canada. For a useful and stimulating discussion of this case, see R.F. Devlin, "We Can't Go On Together With Suspicious Minds: Judicial Bias and Racialized Perspective in R. v. R.D.S." (1995) 18 *Dal LJ* 408.

deciding that the Crown had not proved its case beyond a reasonable doubt, Judge Sparks, a woman of colour, made the following comments:[65]

> "The Crown says, well, why would the officer say that events occurred the way in which he has relayed them to the Court this morning. I'm not saying that the constable has misled the Court, although police officers have been known to do that in the past. And I'm not saying that the officer overreacted, but certainly police officers do overreact, particularly when they're dealing with non-white groups. That, to me, indicates a state of mind right there that is questionable. I believe that probably the situation in this particular case is the case of a young police officer who overreacted. And I do accept the evidence of Mr. S. that he was told to shut up or he would be under arrest. That seems to be in keeping with the prevalent attitude of the day."

This case is now on appeal before the Supreme Court of Canada. It is of particular importance on the subject of bias because it underlines the inescapable fact that Judge Sparks' "baggage" is clearly not the same "baggage" as that carried by the predominantly white male judges of the past who have developed the standards of impartiality and objectivity. But this is not new. As Lord MacMillan once remarked:[66]

> "[I]mpartiality is not easy of attainment. For a judge does not shed the attributes of common humanity when he assumes the ermine. The ordinary human mind is a mass of prepossessions inherited and acquired, often none the less dangerous because unrecognized by their possessor."

The reality and the ideal of increased diversity among judges and within our society in general has forced this recognition, which flies in the face of the "tabula rasa" model of impartiality.

The next, and more interesting question, is what to do about it. Does this mean that all decisions are necessarily "biased" and that our judiciary should be socially representative in the hope of spreading the negative effects of the bias around? This is a very sceptical view and I mention it only in passing.[67] The solution is, I will suggest, to focus our attention on the process of judging rather than the attainment of impartiality in the sense usually reflected by our approaches to the notion of bias in the law. Before discussing this further however, I will turn briefly to the second case.

Gale v. *Miracle Food Mart*[68] concerned the appointment of Professor Constance Backhouse as the Board of Inquiry to adjudicate a group of complaints by a number of grocery store employees alleging systemic discrimination. The respondent challenged her appointment on the basis that it gave rise

---

[65] *R.* v. *R.D.S.*, Y093–168 (2 Dec. 1994), 68–9.

[66] Quoted by Wilson, above at n. 51, 508.

[67] For a discussion of this position, see David Wood, "Judicial Fairness and Systemic Bias", in S. Parker and C. Sampford (eds), *Legal Ethics and Legal Practice: Contemporary Issues* (Clarendon Press, Oxford, 1995), 197.

[68] (1993) 12 Admin LR (2d) 267 (Ont. Ct., Gen. Div.).

to a reasonable apprehension of bias. Professor Backhouse is well known as a feminist and legal historian who teaches law at the University of Western Ontario and had published in the area. In addition, she had been one (of one hundred and twenty) complainants in a complaint against Osgoode Hall Law School alleging systemic discrimination in a number of respects. The respondent claimed that her prior involvement with these issues gave rise to a reasonable apprehension of bias. The Court refrained from making a determination as to whether her general advocacy or background with respect to systemic discrimination raised, in itself, a reasonable apprehension of bias. It held, however, that she had gone "beyond the position of advocate and descended personally, as a party, into the very arena over which she has been appointed to preside in relation to the very same issues she has to decide".[69] In doing so, the Divisional Court applied the well-worn test for reasonable apprehension of bias: would the situation give rise to such an apprehension on the part of a reasonable and right-minded person who was well informed as to the issues.[70]

Gale raises some similar issues to those in *Sparks*. Like *Sparks* it forces a confrontation with the impossibility of the "tabula rasa" model of impartiality. In the administrative law context, however, this is complicated by the issue of expertise. Although the Divisional Court did not rule on the point, one senses from the reasons given that it would have been uncomfortable treating Professor Backhouse's background as "expertise", though very little elaboration is given. But the real problem is that the issue of what counts as bias once the veil of the impartial judge has been lifted remains as intractable as ever. It seems as though we are between the proverbial rock and hard place. Either we perpetuate the myth of tabula rasa impartiality, which is increasingly difficult in an era of greater diversity, or we succumb to the arbitrariness of whatever "baggage" the particular decision-maker carries. This, I would suggest, is a false dichotomy and can be resolved to some degree by focusing on approaches suggested above in relation to pluralism and feminism. A respect for diversity or pluralism, and the inclination to pay close attention to context is shared by many feminist scholars and pluralists. The focus should shift from the "baggage" that we all have to the enterprise of making judgements.

Building on the work of Hannah Arendt, Jennifer Nedelsky has developed a compelling picture of both the process of judging and a reconception of the notion of impartiality. The process of judgement is discursive:[71]

---

[69] Ibid., 278. Of course, an obvious question raised by this is whether, for example, a judge who has been a party to a divorce can hear a divorce case.

[70] The authority cited for this test is *Committee for Justice and Liberty* v. *National Energy Board* [1978] 1 SCR 369.

[71] Jennifer Nedelsky, Faculty of Law and Department of Political Studies, University of Toronto, "Judgement, Diversity and Relational Autonomy", unpublished paper presented at the Annual Meeting of the Political Science Association, San Francisco, 1996.

> "As we form our judgement, we imagine trying to persuade others. We test our judgement against what others would say. So to return to the contrast with mere liking or preference, when we say I like that picture, we have no need to wonder whether others would agree, what it is we would say to them to persuade them of the validity of our assessment. Validity cannot be ascribed to preference. But when we say the painting is beautiful, we know we are making a judgement, which appeals to, demands the agreement of others. So we try to imagine what others would say, we enter into an imaginary dialogue with them, we try to woo their consent."

This model shifts the focus from the pre-existing "baggage" of the judge, to the community of those with whom the judge enters into the imaginary dialogue. Nedelsky explains this as follows:[72]

> "Arendt says that when we take the standpoint of others into account to achieve an enlarged mentality, we do not want to know how they actually judge, for that would be simply to replace our idiosyncrasies with theirs. We should ask how we would judge in their position. The reference to the judgement of others is necessary to make a truly free, that is genuine, judgement possible. The ability to think in the place of others makes it possible for us to liberate ourselves from the 'subjective private conditions', that is, as Arendt says, from the 'idiosyncrasies which naturally determine the outlook of each individual in his privacy and are legitimate as long as they are only privately held opinions, but which . . . lack all validity in the public realm and this enlarged way of thinking, which as judgement knows how to transcend its own individual limitations, on the other hand cannot function in strict isolation or solitude; it needs the presence of others "in whose place" it must think, whose perspectives it must take into consideration, and without whom it never has the opportunity to operate at all'."

It is interesting to consider how this model might change the way we look at cases such as *Sparks* and *Gale*. As far as *Sparks* is concerned, one might begin by being less concerned about the possibility that Judge Sparks was "biased" at the outset, and more concerned with her reasons in themselves. Her reasons do suggest that she had engaged in a discursive analysis. She had heard the police officer's evidence. It is clear that she did not believe him, but her explanation might be seen as attempt to persuade the broader audience why. While it might well have been prudent for Judge Sparks to simply state that she accepted the evidence of Mr S over that of the police officer, that sort of "prudence" is less conducive to the sort of discursive judging advocated by Nedelsky. It makes it easy for judges to avoid confronting their subjective preferences and subjecting them to the light of reason through the (at least imagined) dialogue with others. One suspects that if the community of "others" is even reasonably diverse, her reasoning is likely to survive scrutiny, particularly considering the difficult history of race relations in the Halifax area where the case arose.

[72] Unpublished paper presented at the Annual Meeting of the Political Science Association, San Francisco, 1996, 13–4. The quotations are from Hannah Arendt, *Crisis in Culture*, 220–21.

The problem with *Gale* is that Professor Backhouse was never given a chance to enter into the process, as she was prevented from adjudicating to begin with. The application of the "reasonable apprehension of bias" test by the Divisional Court assumed that her "baggage", at least in terms of her previous status as a party in the Osgoode Hall Law School case, rendered her too partial to judge such issues. This approach undervalues the significance of her expertise in the area, which is so important in administrative law in particular. It fails to recognise that in developing her expertise, she would also necessarily have become very familiar with arguments against, for example, a broad understanding of systemic discrimination or of the potential remedies. Nedelsky's model would focus some attention on this as a positive factor, as it would increase the range of perspectives to be taken into account in making a judgement.[73] But, it seems to me, it requires that we have a chance to assess the reasoning before condemning the judge for lack of impartiality. It is also worth noting that the Ontario Human Rights Code provides for an appeal on the merits from the Board's decision in any event.[74]

In summary, the law on bias is another area which reflects the commonalities between feminist and pluralist approaches to law. The current difficulty, or, as I would suggest, impossibility, of applying the traditional "reasonable apprehension of bias" test as a way of ensuring impartiality can only be resolved by reconceiving the models of judging and impartiality themselves. Nedelsky's model is very useful in this regard, and has particular relevance in administrative law because the emphasis on "community" is very compatible with the conception of different regulatory bodies as constituting different (though possibly overlapping) communities.

THE INFLUENCE OF WOMEN JUDGES AND THE REACH OF PUBLIC LAW

My comments on this subject will be restricted for the most part to the laboratory of the Supreme Court of Canada. An evaluation of the influence of women Supreme Court judges on the reach of public law depends, to some extent, on what sort of influence one has in mind.

To begin with, as outlined above, it is hard to argue that women have advanced the pluralist agenda given current trends as measured by the

---

[73] This approach might also cast some light on *Newfoundland Telephone*, above at n. 62. First of all, the emphasis on the perspective of others is particularly apt in a Public Utility Board setting where the Board members are appointed because they represent certain constituencies. Wells was appointed as a consumer advocate. The point is that such a Board setting may be understood to require that the members engage in debate with one another (as well as with those appearing before it) in reaching a decision. Second, Nedelsky's model might make an outright refusal to engage in such debate a problem in and of itself, whatever the content of the actual opinion expressed.

[74] R.S.O. 1990, c. H-19, s. 42(1).

outcomes of appeals. In this sense, then, one might argue that they have not made a difference.[75] On the other hand, a review of the cases does suggest that the female judges have tended to be sympathetic to the notion that agencies' interpretations of their legislation deserve some presumptive level of deference, if only weak deference. Put another way, the women on the court have been much less likely to frame the starting point in terms of the supervisory jurisdiction of the "superior" courts as, for example, La Forest J. tends to do.[76] They have also been particularly likely to employ, at least implicitly, rights-based or principle-based notions of review, as did L'Heureux-Dubé J. in *Mossop*. This is not meant to imply that the women generally vote the same way[77] or that when they do the split is along gender lines. Apart from the *Lavallée* case,[78] it is difficult to point to particular cases in which the women seem clearly to have driven the result or the reasoning.[79] In fact, it is also worth noting that some of the most "progressive" judgments on gender issues were authored by judges such as Dickson C.J., and the fact that he was on the Court and was Chief Justice at the time of cases such as *Lavallée* may well have contributed to the climate that made Wilson J.'s positions in those cases more acceptable.

Having made these points, it is tempting to conclude that, but for a fleeting period of some influence, women have not been making much difference on the Court. This, however, understates the case. Women are making a difference—they are staking some positions that have not generally been taken. They are, to use feminist terms, expanding the discourse. One of the symptoms of this is the somewhat greater propensity for women to write or join dissenting opinions.[80] In 1992 Peter Russell observed that:[81]

[75] Recent studies have examined the decisions of women judges to see if differences are apparent. In general, these studies are not showing differences based on the gender of the judges. For example, women judges seem neither less nor more likely to acquit (or convict) accuseds in criminal matters than are their male counterparts: see McCormick and Job, above at n. 2.

[76] See *Mossop*, above at n. 9.

[77] A good example of a case in which the two women on the court took divergent positions was the criminal case of *R v. Seaboyer* [1991] 2 SCR 577, also known as the "rape shield" case. At issue was the constitutionality of the recent "rape shield" legislation which precluded almost all uses of the victim's sexual history by the defence. While McLachlin J. sided with the majority in striking down the provision, L'Heureux-Dubé J. would have upheld it. Gonthier J. joined her dissent.

[78] Above at n. 11. This landmark decision held that a battered woman who killed her abuser was entitled to raise the plea of self-defence, in spite of the fact that she had not been in "imminent danger" at the very moment she shot him, as the test previously had required. Wilson J. reasoned that the traditional test did not take the reality of women into account, and particularly the fact that, due to disparity of size with men, requiring them to be in arm-to-arm combat (as in a bar-room brawl) would amount to a death sentence for most women. Perhaps the most remarkable aspect of this decision is that it was unanimous.

[79] Another example is *R. v. Morgentaler* [1988] 1 SCR 30, in which the Supreme Court struck down the abortion provision in the Criminal Code. Dickson C.J. and Wilson J. wrote separate reasons but both agreed that the legislation should be struck down.

[80] McCormick, above at n. 2. One of the surprising findings of this study is that there has been a *decrease* in the number of dissenting and separate concurring opinions since the beginning of Mr. Justice Cartwright's Chief Justiceship in 1967 (ibid., 509). McCormick notes that "[t]here is

"an interesting feature of the data on judgment writing is that the three women members of the Court wrote frequently in dissent. This indicates, perhaps, not so much a common ideological disposition as a remarkable independence of mind."

The negative interpretation of this would be that women are, and continue to be, powerless. But within the feminist approach taken by Minow, Nedelsky and others, the dissents may be seen as contributions to the widening of various debates and discourses. Nedelsky advocates diversity in the judiciary as a means of widening the standpoints that judges can take into account:[82]

"My model of the community of diverse judges, lawyers, and academics is that the ongoing norms of exchange and 'testing' would be such that in a judge's training and 'on-the-job' learning, she would have encountered, and learned to take into account a wide variety of standpoints. If the faculty and student body of law schools, the practising bar, as well as the judiciary reflected the full diversity of society, every judge would have had long experience in exercising her judgement through the process of trying to persuade (in imagination and in dialogue) people with a wide variety of backgrounds, experiences and perspectives."

Dissents such as those written by L'Heureux-Dubé and McLachlin JJ. in *Gould* now form part of the other judges' tapestries of experience, and serve functions similar to the training and other means to which Nedelsky refers.

The very presence of "different voices" at the judgment table is an important component of a vision of justice that places high value on the wide participation of members of society and a continuous wrestling with different perspectives, even if they do not prevail in particular circumstances.[83] Minow sees the judicial arena as "a forum for contests over competing realities", and continued: "[w]e need settings in which to engage in the clash of realities that breaks us out of settled and complacent meanings and creates opportunities for insight and growth".[84]

The "clash of realities"—in gendered terms—has presented itself in a number of recent administrative law cases in Canada. The most potent symbol of

---

some suggestion that women judges are more likely than men judges to write or join minority opinions, a tendency that is all the more striking given that women judges have served during a recent period characterised by a reduced plurality in Supreme Court decision-making": ibid., 517.

[81] Above at n. 2, 791. Russell also comments that "[o]f the more recently appointed justices who have written a substantial number of judgments in *Charter* cases, Madame Justice McLachlin has been the marked dissenter with over half of her judgments in dissent": idem. In administrative law at least, one has the impression that Madame Justice L'Heureux-Dubé has been mounting a strong challenge to McLachlin J.'s earlier distinction in this regard.

[82] Above at n. 71, 27.

[83] This is a point that Minow makes in relation to the fundamentalist Christians in Louisiana who supported the Balanced Treatment Act in light of their concern about the curriculum in public schools. Minow clearly is of the view that their position in that case deserved to lose, but she goes on to say "[i]f the fundamentalists lose in this case, they can continue to struggle to challenge the meaning of the commitment to separate church and state, and they may convince the rest of us in the next round": above at n. 23, 93.

[84] Ibid., 95.

this is the case of *Gould*.[85] The issue in this case was whether the Yukon Order of Pioneers, in denying membership to Ms Gould on the basis of her sex, had committed an act of prohibited discrimination under the Yukon Human Rights Act, section 8 of which provides that "[n]o person shall discriminate when offering or providing services, goods, or facilities to the public. . . ."[86] The core issue revolved around the conception of "service to the public", which forms the threshold between permissible and prohibited discrimination. In other words, it draws the boundary between public and private law. The fact that the Supreme Court divided along gender lines on such a basic issue is accordingly of some significance.

Before looking at the difference between the majority and dissenting opinions on this issue, it should be noted that this is one subject where some gender schisms have recurred. In *Dickason* v. *University of Alberta*,[87] the majority of the Court held that the University's mandatory retirement policy did not constitute prohibited discrimination within the meaning of the Act, with the reach of anti-discrimination legislation forming a constant refrain. L'Heureux-Dubé and Wilson JJ. (joined by Sopinka J.) held that the policy was not justified. Similarly, the Court in *McKinney* v. *University of Guelph*[88] divided along analogous lines, with Wilson J. in particular adopting a broad understanding of the notion of "government action" for the purpose of the applicability of the Charter.

[85] Above at n. 1. The case also served as another episode in the continuing "error of law" and standard of review saga. The Board upheld Ms Gould's complaint, and one of the questions the Supreme Court had to determine was the standard of review to be applied. My comments in the text are confined to the issue of whether the issue of membership was a "public" service, but it is worth noting here that part of the difficulty of the case lay in the fact that the Board had focused on the collection and preservation of Yukon history as the "public" service, rather than membership itself. La Forest J. summarised the Board's reasoning as follows (ibid., 98):

"The public service of collecting and preserving the Yukon's history could not be performed properly without the active input, through membership in the Order, of female members of the population. From a 'common sense standpoint' the Board accepted that history will be distorted in favour of the male role if it is recorded exclusively by men."

Writing for the majority, La Forest J. dismissed Gould's appeal from the Yukon Court of Appeal and the Yukon Supreme Court which had both allowed the Order's appeal against the Board's decision. The majority held that the appropriate standard was one of correctness as this was a question of law. It went on to hold that neither the collection and distribution of historical information nor membership could be seen as a service offered to the public as no "public relationship" was created.(Iacobucci J. wrote concurring reasons.) L'Heureux-Dubé and McLachlin JJ. wrote separate dissenting opinions. L'Heureux-Dubé J. argued that the issue was really one of fact rather than law and that therefore the standard was one of patent unreasonableness and that the Court should defer to the Board. McLachlin J. did not discuss the standard of review at all, but did rule that membership itself constituted a service to the public, and that refusal of membership to Ms Gould on the basis of sex constituted prohibited discrimination.

[86] R.S.Y. 1986 (Supp.), c. 11, s. 8(a).

[87] [1992] 2 SCR 1103.

[88] [1993] 3 SCR 718 (hereafter referred to as *McKinney*). The case dealt with whether university mandatory retirement policies violated s. 15 of the Charter. The answer given was no, but Wilson and L'Heureux-Dubé JJ. dissented. Four of the seven judges (La Forest, Dickson, Gonthier and Sopinka JJ.) held that universities are not "government" for the purpose of attracting Charter protection.

There are a number of common threads that run through these dissenting judgments. First, they all favour broad interpretations of human rights legislation. L'Heureux-Dubé J. in particular refers to McIntyre J.'s dicta in *Ontario Human Rights Commission and O'Malley* v. *Simpson-Sears Ltd.*[89] and Dickson C.J. in *Action Travail des Femmes*[90] in support of the principle that such legislation is not to be narrowly interpreted but is rather "quasi-constitutional" in nature and is to be broadly and purposively interpreted.[91] Second, they tend to favour stronger substantive protection against discrimination.

I wish, however, to focus on a more fundamental thread connecting these dissents which brings us more directly back to *Gould*. That is the threshold question of where the protection of public law begins.[92] The lines drawn on this issue replicate the feminist critique of the public/private distinction in general.[93]

The core disagreement in *Gould* was over the question whether the Order had discriminated in "offering or providing services . . . to the public". A complicating factor was the fact that the Board had concentrated not on *membership itself* as such a service, but on some of the activities carried on by the Order such as the collection and distribution of historical material about its members and the Yukon. The Board had then concluded that, because the exclusion of women as members "tainted" the historical product that was offered to the public, the Order could be said to have discriminated in providing services to the public. It is not surprising that the Yukon Status of Women Council intervened to argue instead that membership itself was a service offered to the public.

---

[89] [1985] 2 SCR 536 (hereafter referred to as *Simpson-Sears*).
[90] Above at n. 10.
[91] See *Gould*, above at n. 1, 636–8.
[92] I am not, of course, suggesting that women have any monopoly on these opinions. Any doubt on that score is resolved by a review of decisions such as *Simpson-Sears*, above at n. 89 (which was unanimous) and *Action Travail des Femmes*, above at n. 10, 1132–46. But it is another matter to suggest that the public/private distinction might have particular resonance for women.
[93] For a discussion of this, see D. Rhode, *Justice and Gender* (Harvard University Press, Cambridge, 1989). Under the subject-heading "False Dichotomies and the Public Private Distinction", she writes (ibid., 125–6):

> "A defining feature of liberal political theory has been its commitment to spheres of individual autonomy free from state intrusion. . . . The boundaries between these 'separate spheres' has always been murkier than much liberal jurisprudence acknowledges. The state is inevitably implicated in defining whose rights will be enforced and on what terms, and in contributing to patterns of individual wealth and power that are backed by government authority."

But, Rhode notes, the traditional dichotomous treatment neglects the connection between the two; individual achievements in the marketplace are highly dependent on family resources and socialisation patterns (ibid., 126):

> "A society truly committed to liberal ideals of equal opportunity in the public sphere could not tolerate the kind of unequal opportunites in the private sphere that characterise contemporary American life."

When the question of whether the service was "public" or not is finally considered, the difference in approach between La Forest J.'s test and that propounded by McLachlin and L'Heureux-Dubé JJ. is reminiscent of ships passing in the night.

I will begin with the judgment of La Forest J. First, he held that in determining what constituted a service to the public, it is necessary to ask whether a public relationship is created between the service provider and the service user.[94] In relying on this as the test, he manifests an inclination to narrow it, as L'Heureux-Dubé J.'s response on this point indicates:[95]

> "We held in *Berg* that it is not necessary for a service to be available to the public 'at large' in order for it to create a public relationship between the provider and users of the service. I hasten to add, however, that if a service is provided to members of the public at large, the relationship between the provider and the users is necessarily public."

Second, in rejecting the argument that membership itself is a service offered to the public, La Forest J. held that it did not give rise to a "public relationship". He reached this conclusion by considering the purposes of membership in terms of the Order's descriptions such as "Klondike Brotherhood" and "male camaraderie", bringing it within the protected sphere of "intimate association".[96] In reviewing the considerations applied by American authorities in analogous situations, he summarised them approvingly:[97]

> "Essentially, the more intimate and personal the nature of the relationship among the members, the more likely it is that the organization will be characterized as 'private'."

In considering whether the collection and preservation of the historical records (as opposed to making the product available to the public) creates a public relationship, La Forest J. emphasised that the historical work was done out of interest by members for other members and was purely private. A strong implication of his approach is one of self-definition: a service is private if its members wish it to be. In essence, La Forest J. drew a narrow picture of the "public" notion, one which tracks his opinion in *McKinney* that a university was not "government" and therefore did not attract the Charter.[98]

---

[94] In referring to the "public relationship" test, he cited in support *University of British Columbia v. Berg*, above at n. 42.

[95] *Gould*, above at n. 1, 641.

[96] La Forest J. reviewed the American case-law and cited in support *Roberts v. United States Jaycees*, 468 U.S. 609 (1984).

[97] *Gould*, above at n. 1, 611. La Forest J. also states that "[a] public relationship is to be determined by examining the relevant factors in a contextual manner": ibid., 612.

[98] *McKinney*, above at n. 88. His opinion (shared by three of the six other judges who sat on the case) was that the Charter was not intended to cover activities by non-governmental entities created by government for legally facilitating private individuals to do things of their own choosing. The opinion also emphasised the legal autonomy of universities.

Both McLachlin and L'Heureux-Dubé JJ. saw the matter very differently from their colleagues in the majority.[99]

McLachlin J. concentrated on the question of whether membership was a service offered to the public and disagreed sharply with La Forest J. on this point. But the difference is one of the basic factors that come into play, as the following extract from her reasons indicates:[100]

> "The question, as I see it, is whether the club or association offers its members benefits of such public nature and importance that women as well as men should be able to enjoy them. . . . In my view, membership in the Yukon Order of Pioneers provides. . . [such] benefits. . . . It collects and preserves the history of the Yukon Territory and its pioneers. It honours those pioneers, in various ways. It endows its members with a special status—status as themselves being a 'modern' pioneer, part of the select society of past pioneers. As Justice L'Heureux-Dubé J. puts it, 'the Lodge has a public image and importance which is inconsistent with a seclusive group'."

McLachlin J. continued:[101]

> "To be a member of the Order is to seek and to gain a respect in the community as a person who may, someday, be counted among the pioneers qualified not only for immediate benefits like participation in documenting pioneer history and public parades, but the ultimate benefit of a special resting place amongst other 'pioneers' in the Yukon's public cemeteries. Membership in the Order confers all these public benefits and more. Can it be right that it is denied to one-half the Yukon population, its women?"

L'Heureux-Dubé J. also took these factors into account. In considering the benefits of membership, she noted:[102]

> "Prestige and opportunities to socialize are intrinsic advantages to membership in an association and, depending on the characteristics of the association, may be far more valuable than the extrinsic privileges conferred on members."

There are two aspects of these reasons which point to the central difference from the reasons of the majority. First, both dissenters looked well beyond the formal structure of the Order to the community context in which it is situated, with a view to understanding the social dynamics. Although La Forest J. referred to the need to consider the factors "in a contextual manner",[103] he does not really consider the social influence of the Order within the community. Second, unlike the majority, both judges saw the public/private question here as a normative one: should this be treated as a private association

---

[99] The two dissenters wrote separate reasons for judgment. L'Heureux-Dubé J. devoted a considerable amount of attention to the standard of review issue. McLauchlin J. concentrated on the issue of membership as a service offered to the public.
[100] *Gould*, above at n. 1, 656.
[101] Ibid, 656–7.
[102] Ibid., 648.
[103] Ibid., 612.

or not? On the other hand, La Forest J. treated the issue as a descriptive matter: does it have the qualities of a public service, not *should* it.

In the final analysis, this difference of opinion in the Supreme Court is a microcosm both of "gendered judging" and of the gender critiques of the public/private distinction. La Forest J.'s approach to the issue brings to mind Wilson J.'s comments about some of the implications of Carol Gilligan's work on the different ethical senses of men and women:[104]

> "It is not difficult to see how this contrast in thinking might form the basis of different conceptions of justice. . . . I think it may in part explain the traditional reluctance of courts to get too deeply into the circumstances of a case, their anxiety to reduce the context of the dispute to its bare bones through exclusionary evidentiary rules. This is, it seems to me, one of the characteristics of the adversarial process. . . . It is so much easier to come up with a black and white answer if you are unencumbered by a broader context which might prompt you, in Lord MacMillan's words, to temper the cold light of reason with the warmer tints of imagination and sympathy."

Gould, then, may be understood as a case that does remind us that justice and judging may well continue to be gendered phenomena. But the fact that these dissents now form part of the discourse is itself something that feminists such as Minow see as the essence of "justice engendered"—it adds to the perspectives and makes complacency about the status quo less comfortable, forcing us to engage in sustained reflection and, hopefully, encouraging us to be more willing to take the chance of being wrong. This is where women judges have made, and are making, a difference in administrative law, as well as in other areas of the law.

[104] Above at n. 51, 520–1.

Bibliography

ABRAMSON, H.I. (1989) "A Fifth Branch of Government: The Private Regulators and their Constitutionality", 16 *Hastings Constitutional Law Quarterly* 165.
ALEXANDER, G.S. (1985) "The Dead Hand and the Law of Trusts in the Nineteenth Century", 37 *Stanford Law Review* 1189.
—— (1987) "The Transformation of Trusts as a Legal Category, 1800–1914", 5 *Law and History Review* 303.
ALLAN, T.R.S. (1988) "Pragmatism and Theory in Public Law", 104 *Law Quarterly Review* 422.
—— (1993) *Law, Liberty, and Justice: The Legal Foundations of British Constitutionalism*.
ALLARS, M. (1994) "On Deference to Tribunals, With Deference to Dworkin", 20 *Queen's Law Journal* 163.
—— (1995) "Private Law but Public Power: Removing Administrative Law Review from Government Business Enterprises", 6 *Public Law Review* 44.
ALLEN, R. (1976) "The Police and Substantive Rulemaking: Reconciling Principles and Expediency", 125 *University of Pennsylvania Law Review* 62.
ALLISON, J.W.F. (1996) *A Continental Distinction in the Common Law: A Historical and Comparative Perspective on English Public Law*.
ALLOTT, P. (1992) "The Theory of the British Constitution", in H. Gross and R. Harrison (eds), *Jurisprudence: Cambridge Essays*.
AMAN, A.C. (1980) "Institutionalizing the Energy Crisis: Some Structural and Procedural Lessons", 65 *Cornell Law Review* 491.
—— (1992) *Administrative Law in a Global Era*.
—— (1993) "The Earth as Eggshell Victim: A Global Perspective on Domestic Regulation", 102 *Yale Law Journal* 2107.
—— (1995) "A Global Perspective on Current Regulatory Reform: Rejection, Relocation or Reinvention?", 2 *Indiana Journal of Global Legal Studies* 429.
—— (forthcoming) "Federalism, Fragmentation and the Global Economy".
ANDREWS, D.M. (1994) "Capital Mobility and State Autonomy: Toward a Structural Theory of International Monetary Relations", 38 *International Studies Quarterly* 193.
ANGUS, W.H. (1974) "Judicial Review: Do We Need It?" 26 *Administrative Law Review* 301.
ANISMAN, P. (1995) "Authorizing Regulation: The Securities Amendment Act 1994", in P. Anisman and R.F. Reid (eds), *Administrative Law: Issues and Practice*.
ARMIT, A., and BOURGAULT, J. (1996) *Hard Choices or No Choices*.
ARMSTRONG, M. (ed.) (loose-leaf, undated) *Communications Law and Policy in Australia*.
ARNOLD, T.W. (1935) *The Symbols of Government*.
ARONSON, M. (1995) "Ministerial Directions: The Battle of the Prerogatives", 6 *Public Law Review* 77.

ARONSON, M. and DYER, B. (1996) *Judicial Review of Administrative Action* (3rd ed.).
ARROWSMITH, S. (1985) *Government Procurement and Judicial Review*.
—— (1990) "Judicial Review and the Contractual Powers of Local Authorities", 106 *Law Quarterly Review* 277.
—— (1994) "Protecting the Interests of Bidders for Public Contracts; The Role of the Common Law", *Cambridge Law Journal* 104.
ARTHURS, H.W. (1980) "Jonah and the Whale: The Appearance, Disappearance and Reappearance of Administrative Law", 30 *University of Toronto Law Journal* 225.
—— (1983) "Protection against Judicial Review", 43 *La Revue du Barreau* 277.
ASIMOW, M. (1992) "California Underground Regulations", 44 *Administrative Law Review* 43.
ATIYAH, P.S. (1995) *An Introduction to the Law of Contract* (5th ed.).
AUSTIN, J. (1885) *Lectures on Jurisprudence, or, The Philosophy of Positive Law*.
BALDWIN, R. (1995) *Rules and Government*.
—— and MCCRUDDEN, C. (eds) (1987) *Regulation and Public Law*.
BACKHOUSE, C. (1994) "Racial Segregation in Canadian Legal History: Viola Desmond's Challenge, Nova Scotia, 1946", 17 *Dalhousie Law Journal*, 299.
BAMFORTH, N. (1993) "The Scope of Judicial Review: Still Uncertain", *Public Law* 239.
BARAK-EREZ, D. (1994–5) "A State Action Doctrine for An Age of Privatization", 45 *Syracuse Law Review* 1169.
BARENDT, E. (1985) *Free Speech*.
—— (1993) "Libel and Freedom of Speech in English Law", *Public Law* 449.
BARKER, A. (ed.) (1982) *Quangos in Britain: Government and the Networks of Public Policy-Making*.
BAXTER, R. (1978) *Political Ideas in Modern Britain*.
BAYNE, P. (1991) "The Court, the Parliament and the Government—Reflections on the Scope of Judicial Review" 20 *Federal Law Review* 1.
BEATSON, J. (1987) "'Public' and 'Private' in English Administrative Law", 103 *Law Quarterly Review* 34.
—— (1995) "Public Law Influences in Contract Law", in J. Beatson and D. Friedmann (eds), *Good Faith and Fault in Contract Law*.
BEESLEY, M. (ed.) (1994) *Regulating Utilities: The Way Forward*.
BELOFF, M. (1989) "Pitch, Pool, Rink . . . Court? Judicial Review in the Sporting World", *Public Law* 95.
BENN, S.I., and GAUS, G.F. (1983) "The Public and the Private: Concepts and Action", in S.I. Benn and G.F. Gaus (eds), *Public and Private in Social Life*.
BERLIN, I. (1967) "Two Concepts of Liberty", in A. Quinton (ed.), *Political Philosophy*.
BERNS, S.; BARON, P.; and NEAVE, M. (1996) *Gender and Citizenship: Materials for Australian Law Schools*.
BIRKINSHAW, P.; HARDEN, I.; and LEWIS, N. (1990) *Government by Moonlight: The Hybrid Parts of the State*.
BIRKS, P. (1995) *Harassment and Hubris: The Right to an Equality of Respect*.
BLACKSTONE, W. (1765–69) *Commentaries on the Laws of England*.
BORINS, S. (1995) "The new public management is here to stay", 38 *Canadian Public Administration* 122.
—— (1995) "A last word", 38 *Canadian Public Administration* 137.
BORRIE, G. (1989) "The Regulation of Public and Private Power", *Public Law* 552.

BOYER, B. (1972) "Alternatives to Administrative Trial-Type Hearings for Resolving Complex Scientific, Economic and Social Issues", 71 *Michigan Law Review* 111.
BRADLEY, A.W. (1994) "The Sovereignty of Parliament—In Perpetuity?", in J. Jowell and D. Oliver (eds), *The Changing Constitution* (3rd ed.).
BRAIBANT, G. (1992) *Le Droit Administratif Francais*.
BRENNER, M.A. (1988) "Airline Deregulation—A Case Study in Public Policy Failure", 16 *Transportation Law Journal* 179.
BROWN, L.N., and BELL, J.S. (1993) *French Administrative Law* (4th ed.).
BROWNE-WILKINSON, N.C.H. (1992) "The Infiltration of a Bill of Rights", *Public Law* 397.
BUTLER, A.S. (1993) "Constitutional Rights in Private Litigation: A Critique and Comparative Analysis", 22 *Anglo-American Law Review* 1.
CAIN, P. (1988) "Good and Bad Bias: A Comment on Feminist Theory and Judging", 61 *Southern California Law Review* 1945.
CANE, P. (1987) "Public Law and Private Law: A Study of the Analysis and Use of a Legal Concept", in J. Eekelaar and J. Bell (eds), *Oxford Essays in Jurisprudence, third series*.
—— (1994) "Mapping the Frontiers", in P. Birks (ed.), *The Frontiers of Liability*.
—— (1995) "Standing Up for the Public", *Public Law* 276.
—— (1996) *An Introduction to Administrative Law* (3rd ed.).
CARDOZO, B.N. (1921) "A Ministry of Justice", 35 *Harvard Law Review* 113.
CASS, R.A. (1988) "Privatization: Politics, Law and Theory", 71 *Marquette Law Review* 449.
CAWSON, A. (1986) *Corporatism and Political Theory*.
CEYSSENS, P. (1994) *Legal Aspects of Policing*.
CHAFEE, Z. (1930) "The Internal Affairs of Associations Not for Profit", 43 *Harvard Law Review* 993.
CHAPUS, R. (1991) *Droit du Contentieux Administratif* (3rd ed.).
CHAYES, A. (1976) "The Role of the Judge in Public Law Litigation", 89 *Harvard Law Review* 1281.
CHEN, M. (1994) "Judicial Review of State-Owned Enterprises at the Crossroads", 24 *Victoria University of Wellington Law Review* 51.
CHEVALLIER, J. (1996) "Public Administration in Statist France", 56 *Public Administration Review* 67.
CLAPHAM, A. (1993) *Human Rights in the Private Sphere*.
—— (1996) "The Privatisation of Human Rights", *European Human Rights Law Review* 20.
CLARK, R. (1986) *Corporate Law*.
CLARKE, M.J. (1987) "Citizenship, Community and the Management of Crime", 27 *British Journal of Criminology* 384.
COLLINS, H. (1986) "Contract and Legal Theory", in W.L. Twining (ed.), *Legal Theory and Common Law*.
—— (1992) *Justice in Dismissal: The Law of Termination of Employment*.
COLSON, J-P. (1970) *L'Office du juge et la preue dans le contentieux administratif*.
CONARD, A.F. (1942) "The Privilege of Forcibly Ejecting an Amusement Patron", 90 *University of Pennsylvania Law Review* 809.
CORNELL, D. (1987) "The Poststructuralist Challenge to the Ideal of Community", 8 *Cardozo Law Review* 989.

CORRY, J.A. (1933) "Administrative Law in Canada", 5 *Proceedings: Canadian Political Science Association* 196.
—— (1935) "Administrative Law and the Interpretation of Statutes", 1 *University of Toronto Law Journal* 286.
COSGROVE, R.A. (1980) *The Rule of Law: Albert Venn Dicey, Victorian Jurist.*
COTTERRELL, R. (1986) "The Law of Property and Legal Theory", in W.L. Twining (ed.), *Legal Theory and Common Law.*
CRAIG, P.P. (1990) "Dicey: Unitary, Self-Correcting Democracy and Public Law", 106 *Law Quarterly Review* 105.
—— (1990) *Public Law and Democracy in the United Kingdom and the United States of America.*
—— (1991) "Constitutions, Property and Regulation", *Public Law* 538.
—— (1994) *Administrative Law* (3rd ed.).
—— (1995) "Jurisdiction, Judicial Control, and Agency Autonomy", in I. Loveland (ed.), *A Special Relationship? American Influences on Public Law in the U.K.*
—— and DE BURCA, G. (1995) *EC Law: Text, Cases and Materials.*
CRANSTON, R. (1994) "Reviewing Judicial Review", in G. Richardson and H. Genn (eds), *Administrative Law and Government Action: The Courts and Alternative Mechanisms of Review.*
CARNWATH, R.J.A. (1996) "The Reasonable Limits of Local Authority Powers", *Public Law* 244.
CRONKITE, F.C. (1935) "Legal Education—Which Trend?", 13 *Canadian Bar Review* 375.
DAINTITH, T.C. (1979) "Regulation by contract: The New Prerogative", *Current Legal Problems* 41.
—— (1994) "The Executive Power Today", in J. Jowell and D. Oliver (eds), *The Changing Constitution* (3rd ed.).
—— (1994) "The Techniques of Government", in J. Jowell and D. Oliver (eds), *The Changing Constitution* (3rd ed.).
DAN-COHEN, M. (1994) "Between Selves and Collectivities", 61 *University of Chicago Law Review* 1213.
DAVIS, K.C. (1969) *Discretionary Justice: A Preliminary Inquiry.*
—— (1973) *Administrative Law in the Seventies.*
—— (1974) "An Approach to Legal Control of the Police", 52 *Texas Law Review* 703.
—— (1975) *Police Discretion.*
—— and PIERCE, R.J. (1994) *Administrative Law Treatise* (3rd ed.).
DEANE, H.A. (1955) *The Political Ideas of Harold J. Laski.*
DEDDASCH, C. (1962) *Procedure administrative contentieuse et procedure civile.*
DELBRÜCK, J. (1993) "Globalization of Law, Politics and Markets—Implications for Domestic Law—A European Perspective", 1 *Indiana Journal of Global Legal Studies* 9.
DEMPSEY, P.S. (1992) "The State of the Airline, Airport and Aviation Industries", 21 *Transportation Law Journal* 129.
DE SMITH (1960) *The Lawyers and the Constitution.*
DE SMITH, S.A.; WOOLF, H.; and JOWELL, J. (1995) *Judicial Review of Administrative Action* (5th ed.).
DEVLIN, R.F. (1995) "We Can't Go On Together With Suspicious Minds: Judicial Bias and Racialized Perspective in R. v. R.D.S.", 18 *Dalhousie Law Journal* 408.

DEWEY, J. (1926) "The Historic Background of Corporate Legal Personality", 35 *Yale Law Journal* 655.
DICEY, A.V. (1885) *An Introduction to the Study of the Law of the Constitution* (1st ed.).
—— (1904) "The Combination Laws as Illustrating the Relation between Law and Opinion in England During the Nineteenth Century", 17 *Harvard Law Review* 511.
—— (1915) "The Development of Administrative Law in England", 31 *Law Quarterly Review* 148.
DICKEN, P. (1992) *Global Shift: The Internalization of Economic Activity* (2nd ed.).
DIVER, C.S. (1981) "Policymaking Paradigms in Administrative Law", 95 *Harvard Law Review* 393.
DIXON, N. (1996) "Should Government Business Enterprises be Subject to Judicial Review?", 4 *Australian Journal of Administrative Law* 198.
DODD, E.M. (1928) "Dogma and Practice in the Law of Associations", 42 *Harvard Law Review* 97.
DOERN, B., and PHIDD, R. (1992) *Canadian Public Policy: Ideas, Structure and Process* (2nd ed.).
DREWRY, G. (1986) "Public Lawyers and Public Administrators: Prospects for an Alliance?", 64 *Public Administration* 173.
—— (1994) "Revolution in Whitehall: The Next Steps and Beyond", in J. Jowell and D. Oliver (eds), *The Changing Constitution* (3rd ed.).
DRIPPS, D.A. (1996) "A Shade of Deference (courts' treatment of administrative agencies' statutory interpretation)", 32 *Trial* 70.
DRUCKER, P.F. (1969) *The Age of Discontinuity: Guidelines for a Changing Society*.
DUGUIT, L. (1970) *Law in the Modern State*.
DURKHEIM, E. (1964) *The Division of Labour in Society*.
DUSSAULT, R., and BORGEAT, L. (1985) *Administrative Law: A Treatise* (2nd ed.).
DUXBURY, N. (1990) "Some Radicalism about Realism? Thurman Arnold and the Politics of Modern Jurisprudence", 10 *Oxford Journal of Legal Studies* 11.
DWORKIN, R. (1978) *Taking Rights Seriously*.
—— (1986) *Law's Empire*.
DYSON, K.H.F. (1980) *The State Tradition in Western Europe: A Study of an Idea and Institution*.
DYZENHAUS, D. (1991) *Hard Cases in Wicked Legal Systems: South African Law in the Perspective of Legal Philosophy*.
—— (1993) "Developments in Administrative Law: The 1991–92 Term", 4 *Supreme Court Law Review (2d)* 177.
—— (1994) "Developments in Administrative Law: The 1992–93 Term", 5 *Supreme Court Law Review (2d)* 189.
—— (1995) Book review, 45 *University of Toronto Law Journal* 205.
—— (forthcoming) *Legality and Legitimacy: Carl Schmidt, Hans Kelsen, and Hermann Heller in Weimar*.
EBERTS, M. (1987) "Ontario Human Rights Commission", in N. Finkelstein and B. Rogers (eds), *Recent Developments in Administrative Law*.
ECK, J.E., and ROSENBAUM, D.P. (1994) "The New Police Order: Effectiveness, Equity and Efficiency in Community Policing", in D.P. Rosenbaum (ed.), *The Challenge of Community Policing: Testing the Promises*.
EDWARDS, J.Ll. J. (1964) *The Law Officers of the Crown*.

ENGLAND, G. (1995) "Recent Developments in the Law of the Employment Contract: Continuing Tension Between the Rights Paradigm and the Efficiency Paradigm", 20 *Queen's Law Journal* 557.

EPSTEIN, R. (1987) "The Public Trust Doctrine", 7 *Cato Journal* 411.

ERICSON, R.V. (1981) "Rules For Police Deviance", in C.D. Shearing (ed.), *Organizational Police Deviance: Its Structure and Control*.

—— (1982) *Reproducing Order: A Study of Police Patrol Work*.

—— (1995) "The News Media and Accountability in Criminal Justice", in P.C. Stenning (ed.), *Accountability for Criminal Justice: Selected Essays*.

ERNST, J. (1994) *Whose Utility? The Social Impact of Public Utility Privatization and Regulation in Britain*.

ERRERA, R. (1986) "Changes in Judicial Review: An Outsider's Reflections", 64 *Public Administration* 189.

EVANS, B.B. (1987) "Private Prisons", 36 *Emory Law Journal* 253.

EVANS, J.M.; JANISCH, H.N.; MULLAN, D.J.; and RISK, R.C.B. (eds) (1995) *Administrative Law: Cases, Text and Materials* (4th ed.).

FARRAR, J., and MCCABE, B. (1995) "Corporatisation, Corporate Governance and the Deregulation of the Public Sector Economy", 6 *Public Law Review* 24.

FEELEY, M.M., and SIMON, J. (1992) "The New Penology: Notes on the Emerging Strategy of Corrections and its Implications", 30 *Criminology* 449.

FELDMAN, D. (1993) "Courts, Constitutions and Commentators: Interpreting the Invisible", 16 *Holdsworth Law Review* 37.

FIELD, J. (1987) "Making Prisons Private: An Improper Delegation of a Government Power", 15 *Hofstra Law Review* 649.

FINKELMAN, J. (1935) "Separation of Powers: A Study in Administrative Law", 1 *University of Toronto Law Journal* 313.

—— (1939) "Government by Civil Servants", 17 *Canadian Bar Review* 166.

FINN, P. (1994) "Public Trust and Public Accountability", 3 *Griffith Law Review* 224.

—— (1996) "Controlling the Exercise of Power", 7 *Public Law Review* 86.

FISHER, H.A.L. (ed.) (1911) *The Collected Papers of Frederic William Maitland*.

FISHER, W. W. III; HORWITZ, M.J.; and REED, T.A. (eds) (1993) *American Legal Realism*.

FLOGAITIS, S. (1986) *Administrative Law et droit administratif*.

FORBES, R.E. (1976) "Judicial Review of the Private Decision Maker: The Domestic Tribunal", 15 *University of Western Ontario Law Review* 123.

FORSYTH, C.F. (1987) "The Scope of Judicial Review: 'Public Duty' not 'Source of Power'", *Public Law* 356.

—— (1996) "Of Fig Leaves and Fairy Tales: The *Ultra Vires* Doctrine, the Sovereignty of Parliament, and Judicial Review", *Cambridge Law Journal* 122.

FOSTER, C.D. (1992) *Public Ownership and the Regulation of Natural Monopoly*.

FOUCAULT, M. (1979) "Governmentability", 6 *Ideology & Consciousness* 5.

—— (1980) *Power/Knowledge: Selected Interviews and Other Writings 1972–1977*.

FRANKFURTER, F. (1933) "Introduction", to "A Symposium on Administrative Law Based upon Legal Writings 1931–33", 18 *Iowa Law Review* 129.

—— (1941) "The Final Report of the Attorney-General's Committee on Administrative Procedure", 41 *Columbia Law Review* 585.

FREEDLAND, M. (1994) "Government by Contract and Public Law", *Public Law* 86.

FRIEDLAND, M.L. (1989) "Controlling the Administrators of Criminal Justice", 31 *Criminal Law Quarterly* 280.

—— (1994) "Reforming Police Powers: Who's in Charge?", in R.C. MacLeod and D. Schneiderman (eds), *Police Powers in Canada: The Evolution and Practice of Authority*.
FRIEDMANN, W. (1954) "The Public Corporation in Great Britain", in W. Friedmann (ed.), *The Public Corporation: A Comparative Study*.
—— (ed.) (1954) *The Public Corporation: A Comparative Study*.
—— (1959) "Public and Private Law Thinking: The Need for Synthesis", 5 *Wayne Law Review* 291.
—— (1972) *Law in a Changing Society* (2nd ed.).
—— and GARNER, J.F. (eds) (1970) *Government Enterprises: A Comparative Study*.
FROOMKIN, A.M. (1995) "Reinventing the Government Corporation", *University of Illinois Law Review* 543.
FRUG, G.E. (1984) "The Ideology of Bureaucracy in American Law", 97 *Harvard Law Review* 1276.
FULLER, L.L. (1969) *The Morality of Law*.
—— (1981) "Two Principles of Human Association", in K.I. Winston (ed.), *The Principles of Social Order: Selected Essays of Lon L. Fuller*.
—— and PERDUE, W.R. (1936) "The Reliance Interest in Contract Law", 46 *Yale Law Journal* 52 and 373.
GALBRAITH, J.K. (1972) *The New Industrial State*.
—— (1984) *The Anatomy of Power*.
GALLIGAN, D.J. (1982) "Judicial Review and the Textbook Writers", 2 *Oxford Journal of Legal Studies* 257.
—— (1992) *Administrative Law*.
GARANT, P. (1966) "Les fins au droit public moderne au Québec", 8 *Les Cahiers de Droit* 251.
GELDART, W.M. (1911) "Legal Personality" 27 *Law Quarterly Review* 90.
GIERKE, O.F. (1902) *Political Theories of the Middle Ages*.
GILLIGAN, C. (1982) *In a Different Voice—Psychological Theory and Women's Development*.
GOLDSMITH, A.J. (1986) "The Impact of Police Collective Bargaining Upon Municipal Police Management in Ontario, 1973–1984: A Socio-Legal Analysis", SJD Dissertation, University of Toronto.
—— (1990) "Taking Police Culture Seriously: Police Discretion and the Limits of Law", 1 *Policing and Society* 91.
—— (1991) "External Review and Self-Regulation: Police Accountability and the Dialectic of Complaints Procedures", in A.J. Goldsmith (ed.), *Complaints Against the Police: The Trend to External Review*.
—— (1995) "Public Complaints Procedures in Police Accountability", in P.C. Stenning (ed.), *Accountability for Criminal Justice: Selected Essays*.
GOLDSTEIN, H. (1977) *Policing in a Free Society*.
GOW, J.I. (1994) *Learning from Others: Administrative Innovations Among Canadian Governments*.
GRAHAM, C., and PROSSER, T. (1991) *Privatizing Public Enterprises: Constitutions, the State and Regulation in Comparative Perspective*.
GRAYCAR, R. (1995) "The Gender of Judgments: An Introduction", in M. Thornton (ed.), *Public and Private: Feminist Legal Debates*.
HAAR, C.M. and FESSLER, D.W. (1986) *The Wrong Side of the Tracks: A Revolutionary Rediscovery of the Common Law Tradition of Fairness in the Struggle Against Inequality*.

HALE, M. (1787) "De Portibus Maris", in F. Hargrave (ed.), *Collection of Tracts relative to the Law of England*.
HALLIGAN, J. (1994) "Political and Managerial Reform in a Small State: The Relevance of the 1980s", in A. Farazmand (ed.), *Handbook of Bureaucracy*.
HARDEN, I. (1992) *The Contracting State*.
—— and LEWIS, N. (1986) *The Noble Lie: The British Constitution and the Rule of Law*.
HARLOW, C. (1980) " 'Public' and 'Private' Law: Definition Without Distinction", 43 *Modern Law Review* 241.
—— (1994) "Changing the Mindset: The Place of Theory in English Administrative Law", 14 *Oxford Journal of Legal Studies* 419.
—— and RAWLINGS, R. (1984) *Law and Administration*.
—— and RAWLINGS, R. (1992) *Pressure Through Law*.
HARRIS, B.V. (1992) "The 'Third Source' of Authority for Government Action", 108 *Law Quarterly Review* 626.
HARTER, P.J. (1981) "Negotiating Regulations: A Cure for Malaise", 71 *Georgetown Law Journal* 1.
—— (1996) "First Judicial Review of Reg Neg a Disappointment", 22 *Administrative and Regulatory Law News* 1.
HARVISON YOUNG, A. (1993) "Keeping the Courts at Bay: The Canadian Human Rights Commission and its Counterparts in Britain and Northern Ireland: Some Comparative Lessons", 43 *University of Toronto Law Journal* 65.
—— (1993) "Human Rights Tribunals and the Supreme Court of Canada: Reformulating Deference", 13 *Administrative Law Reports* (2d series) 206.
—— and MACDONALD, R.A. (1991) "Canadian Administrative Law on the Threshold of the 1990s", 16 *Queen's Law Journal* 31.
HASTINGS, R., and SAUNDERS, R.P. (1996) "Strategies for Police Accountability and Community Empowerment", in R.P. Saunders and J. McMunagle (eds), *Saunders & Mitchell: An Introduction to Criminal Law in Context: Cases, Notes and Materials*.
HAWKINS, K. (ed.) (1992) *The Uses of Discretion*.
HAY, G.A. (1996) "Reflections on *Clear*", 3 *Competition and Consumer Law Journal* 231.
—— and MCMAHON, K. (1994) "The Duty to Deal under Section 46: Panacea or Pandora's Box?", 17 *University of New South Wales Law Journal* 54.
HELD, D. (1987) *Models of Democracy*.
HENDERSON, E.G. (1963) *Foundations of English Administrative Law: Certiorari and Mandamus in the Seventeenth Century*.
HIBBITTS, B. (1994) "The Politics of Principle: Albert Venn Dicey and the Rule of Law", 23 *Anglo-American Law Review* 1.
HILL, M. (1976) *The State, Administration and the Individual*.
HOBBES, T. (1668) *Leviathan*.
HODGE, G. (1996) *Contracting Out Government Services: A Review of International Evidence*.
HOGG, P.W. (1971) "The Jurisdictional Fact Doctrine in the Supreme Court of Canada: *Bell v. Ontario Human Rights Commission*", 9 *Osgoode Hall Law Journal* 203.
HOLDSWORTH, W.S. (1922) "English Corporation Law in the 16th and 17th centuries", 31 *Yale Law Journal* 382.
HOLLAND, T.E. (1924) *The Elements of Jurisprudence* (13th ed.).
HONORÉ, T. (1982) *The Quest for Security: Employees, Tenants, Wives*.

HOOD, C. (1989) "Rolling Back the State or Moving to a Contract or Subsidiarity State", in O.P. Coaldrake and J.R. Nethercote (eds), *What Should Government Do?*
HOPKINS, E.R. (1939) "Administrative Justice in Canada", 17 *Canadian Bar Review* 619.
HORWITZ, M. (1980) "Law and Economics: Science or Politics?", 8 *Hofstra Law Review* 905.
HOWARD, P.K. (1994) *The Death of Common Sense: How Law is Suffocating America*.
HOWE, R.B. and ANDRADE, M.J. (1994–5) "The Reputations of Human Rights Commissions in Canada", 9(2) *Canadian Journal of Law and Society* 1.
HUNTER, I.A. (1972) "Judicial Review of Human Rights Legislation: *McKay v. Bell*", 7 *University of British Columbia Law Review* 17.
—— (1977) "Civil Actions for Discrimination", 55 *Canadian Bar Review* 106.
JAFFE, L.L. (1937) "Lawmaking by Private Groups", 51 *Harvard Law Review* 201.
JANISCH, H.N. (1985) "Bora Laskin and Administrative Law: An Unfinished Journey", 35 *University of Toronto Law Journal* 557.
—— (1977) Review Essay, 4 Dalhousie Law Review 824.
—— (1995) "Further Developments with Respect to Rulemaking by Administrative Agencies", 9 *Canadian Journal of Administrative Law and Practice* 1.
JANSEN, W. (1990) *Limits of Liberty: The Experience of Mennonite, Hutterite, and Doukhobor communities in Canada*.
JOHNSON, A.W. (1992) *Reflections on Administrative Reform in the Government of Canada 1962–1991*.
JONES, T.J.; NEWBURN, T.; and SMITH, D.J. (1994) *Democracy and Policing*.
—— (1996) "Policing and the Idea of Democracy", 36 *British Journal of Criminology* 182.
JOWELL, J. (1994) "The Rule of Law Today", in J. Jowell and D. Oliver (eds), *The Changing Constitution* (3rd ed.).
—— and LESTER, A. (1987) "Beyond *Wednesbury*: Substantive Principles of Administrative Law", *Public Law* 368.
KALLEN, E. (1995) *Ethnicity and Human Rights in Canada* (2nd ed.).
KAMISAR, Y. (1965) "Equal Justice in the Gatehouses and Mansions of American Criminal Procedure: From *Powell* to *Gideon*, From *Escobedo* to . . .", in A.E.D. Howard (ed.), *Criminal Justice in Our Time*.
KANTOROWICZ, E.H. (1957) *The King's Two Bodies: A Study in Medieval Political Theology*.
KELSEY, J. (1995) *Economic Fundamentalism*.
KENNEDY, D. (1982) "The Stages of the Decline of the Public/Private Distinction", 130 *University of Pennsylvania Law Review*, 1349.
KENNEDY, W.P.M. (1934) "Aspects of Administrative Law in Canada", 46 *Judicial Review* 203.
KERNAGHAN, K. (1996) *The Ethics Era in Canadian Public Administration*.
KERNAGHAN, D.K. (1970) "Civil Liberties in the Canadian Community", in C. Beck (ed.), *Law and Justice: Essays in Honour of Robert S. Rankin*.
KRENT, H.J. (1990) "Fragmenting the Unitary Executive: Congressional Delegations of Administrative Authority Outside the Federal Government", 85 *Northwestern University Law Review* 62.
KROTOSZYNSKI, R. (1995) "Back to the Briarpatch: An Argument In Favor of Constitutional Meto-Analysis in State Action Determinations", 94 *Michigan Law Review* 302.

LACEY, N. (1992) "The Jurisprudence of Discretion: Escaping the Legal Paradigm", in K. Hawkins (ed.), *The Uses of Discretion*.
LACEY, N. (1995) "Feminist Legal Theory Beyond Neutrality", *Current Legal Problems* 1.
LAHEY, K. (1985) "Until Women Themselves Have Told All That They Have To Tell", 23 *Osgoode Hall Law Journal* 519.
LASKI, H.J. (1915) "The Personality of Associations", 29 *Harvard Law Review* 404.
—— (1933) "Duguit's Conception of the State", in W.I. Jennings *et al.* (eds), *Modern Theories in Law*.
LASKIN, B. (1940) "Tavern Refusing to Serve Negro—Discrimination", 18 *Canadian Bar Review* 314.
LAWRENCE, D.M. (1986) "Private Exercise of Governmental Power", 61 *Indiana Law Journal* 647.
LAW COMMISSION (U.K.) (1994) *Administrative Law: Judicial Review and Statutory Appeals*.
LAWS, J. (1989) "The Ghost in the Machine: Principle in Public Law", *Public Law* 27.
—— (1992), "Illegality: The Problem of Jurisdiction", in M. Supperstone and J. Goudie (eds), *Judicial Review*.
—— (1993) "Is the High Court the Guardian of Fundamental Constitutional Rights?", *Public Law* 59.
—— (1995) "Law and Democracy", *Public Law* 72.
LEIGHTON, B.N. (1991) "Visions of Community Policing: Rhetoric and Reality in Canada", 33 *Canadian Journal of Criminology* 485.
LEO, R.A. (1996) "*Miranda*'s revenge: Police Interrogation as a Confidence Game", 30 *Law and Society Review* 259.
LESSARD, H.; RYDER, B.; SCHNEIDERMAN, D.; and YOUNG, M. (1996) "Developments in Constitutional Law: The 1994-95 Term", 7 *Supreme Court Law Review (2d)* 81.
LEVI, R. (1996) "Toward a General Standard of Waiver in the Criminal Process", LL.M. thesis, University of Toronto.
LEVINSON, H. (1970) "Towards Principles of Public Law", *Journal of Public Law* 326.
LEWIS, C.E. (1991) "Police Complaints in Metropolitan Toronto: Perspective of the Public Complaints Commissioner", in A.J. Goldsmith (ed.), *Complaints Against the Police: The Trend to External Review*.
LEWIS, N. (1996) *Choice and the Legal Order: Rising Above Politics*.
L'HEUREUX-DUBÉ, C. (1994) "L'arrêt *Bibeault*: une ance dans une mer agitée", 28 *La Revue Juridique Thémis* 731.
LOADER, I. (1994) "Democracy, Justice and the Limits of Policing: Rethinking Police Accountability", 3 *Social and Legal Studies* 521.
LOUGHLIN, M. (1978) "Procedural Fairness: A Study of the Crisis in Administrative Law", 28 *University of Toronto Law Journal* 215.
—— (1991) "Sitting on a fence at Carter Bar: In praise of J.D.B. Mitchell", *Juridical Review* 135.
—— (1995) "The Pathways of Public Law Scholarship", in G.P. Wilson (ed.), *Frontiers of Legal Scholarship: Twenty-five Years of Warwick Law School*.
MACDONALD, R.A. (1980) "Judicial Review and Procedural Fairness in Administrative Law: I", 25 *McGill Law Journal* 520.
—— (1987) "On the Administration of Statutes", 12 *Queen's Law Journal* 488.
—— and LAMETTI, D. (1989) "Reasons for Decision in Administrative Law", 3 *Canadian Journal of Administrative Law and Practice* 123.

MACEY, J.R. (1994) "Packaged Preferences and the Institutional Transformation of Interests", 61 *University of Chicago Law Review* 1443.
MACHEN, A.W. (1911) "Corporate Personality", 25 *Harvard Law Review* 253, 347.
MACKINNON, C.A. (1987) *Feminism Unmodified*.
—— (1989) *Toward a Feminist Theory of the State*.
MACLAUCHLAN, H.W. (1991) "Developments in Administrative Law: The 1989–90 Term", 2 *Supreme Court Law Review (2d)* 1.
MAINE, H. (1861) *Ancient Law: its connection with the early history of society, and its relation to modern ideas*.
MAITLAND, F.W. (1900) "The Corporation Sole", 16 *Law Quarterly Review* 335.
—— (1900) "Introduction", in O. Gierke, *Political Theories of the Middle Ages*.
—— (1901) "The Crown as Corporation", 17 *Law Quarterly Review* 131.
—— (1908) *The Constitutional History of England: A Course of Lectures*.
MARKESINIS, B.S., and DEAKIN, S.F. (1994) *Tort Law* (3rd ed.).
MARSHALL, T.H. (1950) *Citizenship and Social Class, and other essays*.
MARTIN, B. (1993) *In the Public Interest: Privatization and Public Sector Reform*.
MASHAW, J.L. (1994) "Improving the Environment of Agency Rulemaking: An Essay on Management, Games and Accountability", 57(2) *Law and Contemporary Problems* 185.
—— MERRILL, R.A.; and SHANE, P.M. (1992) *Administrative Law: The American Public Law System* (3rd ed.).
MCALLISTER, B. (1930) "Lord [sic] Hale and Business Affected with a Public Interest", 43 *Harvard Law Review* 759.
MCAUSLAN, P. (1983) "Administrative Law, Collective Consumption and Judicial Policy", 46 *Modern Law Review* 1.
—— (1988) "Public Choice and Public Law", 51 *Modern Law Review* 687.
—— and MCELDOWNEY, J. (eds) (1985) *Law, Legitimacy and the Constitution: Essays marking the Centenary of Dicey's Law of the Constitution*.
MCCORMICK, N. (1983) "Jurisprudence and the Constitution", *Current Legal Problems* 13.
MCCORMICK, P. (1994) "Judicial Career Patterns and the Delivery of Reasons for Judgment in the Supreme Court of Canada, 1949–1993", 5 *Supreme Court Law Review (2d)* 499.
—— and JOB, T. (1993) "Do Women Judges Make A Difference: An Analysis by Appeal Court Data", 8 *Canadian Journal of Law and Society* 135.
MCCOY, E., and MCCOY, C.A. (1990) "Privatisation and State Activity: The 'Privatisation' of Public Service Culture and the Privatisation of Tradeable Enterprise as Contradictory Elements within an Analysis of New State Reform", *Policy, Organization and Society* 32.
MCCRUDDEN, C. (1994) "Racial Discrimination", in C. McCrudden and G. Chambers (eds), *Individual Rights and the Law in Britain*.
MCGARITY, T.O. (1994) "Some Thoughts on 'Deossifying' the Rulemaking Process", 41 *Duke Law Journal* 1385.
MCKENNA, I.B. (1982) "A Common Law Action for Discrimination in Job Applications", 60 *Canadian Bar Review*, 122.
MCCLEAN, J. (1996) "Contracting in the Corporatised and Privatised Environment", 7 *Public Law Review* 223.
MINOW, M. (1987) "Foreword: Justice Engendered", 101 *Harvard Law Review* 10.

MINOW, M. (1992) "Stripped Down Like a Runner or Enriched by Experience: Bias and Impartiality of Judges and Jurors", 33 *William and Mary Law Review* 1201.
MISRAHI, J.J. (1996) "Factories with Fences: An Analysis of the Prison Industry Enhancement Certification Program in Historical Perspective", 33 *American Criminal Law Review* 411.
MITCHELL, C.N. (1996) "Regulating Professional Police", in R.P. Saunders and J. McMunagle (eds), *Saunders & Mitchell: An Introduction to Criminal Law in Context: Cases, Notes and Materials* (3rd ed.).
MITCHELL, J.D.B. (1965) "The Causes and Effects of the Absence of a System of Public Law in the United Kingdom", *Public Law* 95.
MOLOT, H. (1968) "The Duty of Business to Serve the Public: Analogy to the Innkeeper's Obligation", 46 *Canadian Bar Review* 612.
MOORE, M.H. (1992) "Problem-Solving and Community Policing", in M. Tonry and N. Morris (eds), *Modern Policing*.
MORAN, M., and PROSSER, T. (eds) (1994) *Privatization and Regulatory Change in Europe*.
MORAN, T.K., and COOPER, J.L. (1983) *Discretion and the Criminal Justice Process*.
MORGAN, R. (1989) "'Policing by Consent': Legitimating the Doctrine", in R. Morgan and D.J. Smith (eds), *Coming to Terms with Policing: Perspectives on Policy*.
MOSSMAN, M-J. (1986) "Feminism and Legal Method: The Difference It Makes", unpublished paper.
MULLAN, D. (1986) "Judicial Deference to Administrative Decision-Making", 50 *Saskatchewan Law Review* 503.
MULLINS, J. (1996) "Handling Complaints Related to Government Services Delivered by Contractors", in K. Cole (ed.), *Administrative Law and Public Administration: Form vs. Substance*.
MUREINIK, E. (1994) "Emerging from Emergency", 92 *Michigan Law Review* 1977.
NARDELL, G. (1995) "The Quantock Hounds and the Trojan Horse", *Public Law* 27.
NEDELSKY, J. (1996) "Judgement, Diversity and Relational Autonomy", unpublished paper.
NORMAN, K. (1987) "Problems in Human Rights Legislation and Administration", in S.L. Martin and K.E. Mahoney (eds), *Equality and Judicial Neutrality*.
NORMANDEAU, A., and LEIGHTON, B. (1990) *A Vision of the Future of Policing in Canada: Police-Challenge 2000*.
NOTE (1967) "Judicial Control of Actions of Private Associations", 76 *Harvard Law Review* 1011.
NOTE (1983) "Arbitrary Exclusion of "Undesirable" Racetrack and Casino Patrons: The Courts' Illusory Perception of Common Law Public/Private Distinctions", 32 *Buffalo Law Review* 699.
NOTE (1989) "The Anti-discrimination Principle in the Common Law", 102 *Harvard Law Review* 1193.
ODENT, R. (1981) *Cours de contentieux administratif*.
O'DONOVAN, K. (1989) "Engendering Justice: Women's Perspectives and the Rule of Law", 39 *University of Toronto Law Journal* 127.
OECD (1995) *Governance in Transition: Public Management Reforms in OECD Countries*.
OGLIVIE, M.H. (1992) "Ecclesiastical Law—Jurisprudence of Civil Courts—Status of Clergy: *McCaw v. United Church of Canada*", 71 *Canadian Bar Review* 597.

—— (1993) "Ecclesiastical Law—Jurisdiction of Civil Courts—Governing Documents of Religious Organizations—Natural Justice: *Lakeside Colony of Hutterian Brethren v. Hofer*", 72 *Canadian Bar Review* 238.
OLIVER, D. (1987) "Is the *Ultra Vires* Rule the Basis of Judicial Review?", *Public Law* 543.
—— (1993) "Judicial Review and the Shorthand Writers", *Public Law* 214.
—— (1994) "What is Happening to Relations Between the Individual and the State?", in J. Jowell and D. Oliver (eds), *The Changing Constitution* (3rd ed.).
—— and HEATER, D. (1994) *The Foundations of Citizenship*.
OSBORNE, D., and GAEBLER, T. (1993) *Reinventing Government: How the Entrepreneurial Spirit is Transforming the Public Sector*.
PANNICK, D. (1992) "Who is Subject to Judicial Review and in Respect of What?", *Public Law* 1.
PATEMAN, C. (1983) "Feminist Critiques of the Public/Private Divide", in S.I. Benn and G.F. Gaus (eds), *Public and Private in Social Life*.
PATON, G. (1972) *A Textbook of Jurisprudence* (4th ed.).
PECK, C.J. (1979) "Some Kind of Hearing for Persons Discharged from Private Employment", 16 *San Diego Law Review* 313.
PEDERSON, W.F. (1978) "The Decline of Separation of Functions in Regulatory Agencies", 64 *Virginia Law Review* 991.
PELESH, M.L. (1994) "Regulations Under the Higher Education Amendments of 1992: A Case Study in Negotiated Rulemaking", 57(4) *Law and Contemporary Problems* 51.
PERILLO, J.M. (1995) "Abuse of Rights: A Pervasive Legal Concept", 27 *Pacific Law Review* 37.
PERRUCCI, R. (1994) *Japanese Auto Transplants in the Heartland*.
PETERS, B.G., and SAVOIE, D.J. (eds) (1994) *Governance in a Changing Environment*.
POIRIER, M. (1996) "Environmental Justice and the Beach Access Movements in the 1970s in Connecticut and New Jersey: Stories of Property and Civil Rights", 28 *Connecticut Law Review* 719.
POLLOCK, F. (1911) "Theory of Corporations in the Common Law", 27 *Law Quarterly Review* 219.
—— (1929) *A First Book of Jurisprudence for Students of the Common Law* (6th ed.).
—— and MAITLAND, F.W. (1898) *The History of English Law before the Time of Edward I* (2nd ed.).
POUND, R. (1916) "Equitable Relief Against Defamation and Injuries to Personality", 29 *Harvard Law Review* 640.
PROBERT, B. (1994) "Globalisation, Economic Restructuring and the State", in S. Bell and B. Head (eds), *State, Economy and Public Policy in Australia*.
PROSSER, T. (1994) "Regulation, Markets and Legitimacy", in J. Jowell and D. Oliver (eds), *The Changing Constitution* (3rd ed.).
—— (1995) "Bringing Constitutional Principles Back In", in R. Bellamy, V. Bufacchi and D. Castiglione (eds), *Democracy and Constitutional Culture in the Union of Europe*.
PUSEY, M. (1991) *Economic Rationalism in Canberra: A Nation-Building State Changes its Mind*.
RADIN, M. (1940) "The Achievements of the American Bar Association: A Sixty Year Record", 26 *American Bar Association Journal* 19.

RAWLINGS, R. (1995) "Courts and Interests", in I. Loveland (ed.), *A Special Relationship? American Influences on Public Law in the UK.*
RAZ, J. (1986) *The Morality of Freedom.*
—— (1991) "Free Expression and Personal Identification", 11 *Oxford Journal of Legal Studies* 303.
REBELL, M.A., and HUGHES, R.L. (1996) "Schools, Communities and the Courts: A Dialogic Approach to Education Reform", 14 *Yale Law and Politics Review* 99.
REEVE, A. (1991) "The Theory of Property: Beyond Private versus Common Property", in D. Held (ed.), *Political Theory Today.*
REICH, C.A. (1964) "The New Property", 73 *Yale Law Journal* 733.
REINER, R. (1988) "In the Office of the Chief Constable", *Current Legal Problems* 135.
REINER, R. (1992) *The Politics of the Police* (2nd ed.).
—— (1992) "Police Research in the United Kingdom: A Critical Review", in M. Tonry and N. Morris (eds), *Modern Policing.*
—— (1995) "Counting the Coppers: Antinomies of Accountability in Policing", in P.C. Stenning (ed.), *Accountability for Criminal Justice: Selected Essays.*
REISS, A.J. (1992) "Police Organization in the Twentieth Century", in M. Tonry and N. Morris (eds), *Modern Policing.*
RHODE, D. (1989) *Justice and Gender.*
—— (1994) "Feminism and the State", 107 *Harvard Law Review* 1181.
RIDEOUT, R. (1996) "Implied Terms in the Employment Contract", in R. Halson (ed.), *Exploring the Boundaries of Contract.*
RIGNEY, H. (1981) "On Reviewing the Right to Fair Procedure", 5 *Hastings International and Comparative Law Review* 73.
ROACH, K. (1995) "Developments in Criminal Procedure: The 1993–94 Term", 6 *Supreme Court Law Review (2d)* 281.
ROBSON, W.A. (1959) "Administrative Law", in M. Ginsberg (ed.), *Law and Opinion in England in the 20th Century.*
RODD, J.C. (1994) "The Police and Politics: The Politics of Independence", in R.C. Macleod and D. Schneiderman (eds), *Police Powers in Canada: The Evolution and Practice of Authority.*
ROGAT, Y. (1962–3) "Mr Justice Holmes: A Dissenting Opinion", 15 *Stanford Law Review* 3 and 254.
ROLLAND, L. (1947) *Précis de droit administratif* (9th ed.).
ROSE, N. (1987) "Beyond the Public/Private Division: Law, Power and the Family", 14 *Journal of Law and Society* 61.
ROSENBLOOM, D.H. (1994) "The Evolution of the Administrative State and Transformation of Administrative Law", in D.H. Rosenbloom and R.D. Schwartz (eds), *Handbook of Regulation and Administrative Law.*
RUSSELL, P.H. (1992) "The Supreme Court in the 1980s: A Commentary on the S.C.R. Statistics", 30 *Osgoode Hall Law Journal* 771.
SALMOND, J.W. (1902) *Jurisprudence, or, The Theory of Law.*
SAMPFORD, C. (1991) "Law, Institutions and the Public/Private Divide", 20 *Federal Law Review*, 185.
SAMUELS, G. (1983) "Public Law and Private Law: A Private Lawyer's Response", 46 *Modern Law Review* 558.
SASSEN, S. (1988) *The Mobility of Labor and Capital.*
—— (1991) *The Global City: New York, London, Tokyo.*

—— (1994) *Cities In A World Economy*.
—— (1997) "Towards A Feminist Analytics of the Global Economy", 4 *Indiana Journal of Global Legal Issues* 55.
SAUNDERS, P., and HARRIS, C. (1994) *Privatization and Popular Capitalism*.
SAVAGE, S.P. (1984) "The Police: Political Control or Community Liaison?", 55 *Political Quarterly* 48.
SAVOIE, D. (1995) "What is wrong with the new public management?", 38 *Canadian Public Administration* 112.
—— (1995) "Just another voice from the pulpit", 38 *Canadian Public Administration* 133.
SCALIA, A. (1989) "Judicial Deference to Administrative Interpretations of Law", *Duke Law Journal* 511.
SCHWARTZ, B. (1993) "Administrative Law Cases During 1992", 45 *Administrative Law Review* 261.
SEDLEY, S. (1994) "Governments, Constitutions, and Judges", in G. Richardson and H. Genn (eds), *Administrative Law and Government Action: The Courts and Alternative Mechanisms of Review*.
—— (1994) "The Sound of Silence: Constitutional Law Without a Constitution", 110 *Law Quarterly Review* 270.
—— (1995) "Human Rights: A Twenty-First Century Agenda", *Public Law* 386.
SHAPIRO, M. (1986) "APA: Past, Present, Future", 72 *Virginia Law Review* 447.
—— (1992) "The Giving Reasons Requirement", *University of Chicago Legal Forum* 179.
SHARPE, R.J. (1985) "Bora Laskin and Civil Liberties", 35 *University of Toronto Law Journal* 632.
SHONFIELD, A. (1965) *Modern Capitalism: The Changing Balance of Public and Private Power*.
SIMMONDS, N.E. (1984) *The Decline of Juridical Reason: Doctrine and Theory in the Legal Order*.
SIMPSON, A.W.B. (1975) *A History of the Common Law of Contract: The Rise of the Action of Assumpsit*.
SINCLAIR, M. (1993) "Judicial Review of the Exercise of Public Power", *Denning Law Journal* 193.
SINGER, J.W. (1996) "No Right to Exclude: Public Accomodations and Private Property", 90 *Northwestern University Law Review* 1283.
SKINNER, Q. (1966) "Thomas Hobbes and his Disciples in France and England", 8 *Comparative Studies in Society and History* 153.
—— (1989) "The State", in T. Ball, J. Farr and R.L. Hanson (eds), *Political Innovation and Conceptual Change*.
SKOLNICK, J. (1969) *Justice Without Trial: Law Enforcement in Democratic Society*.
SMITH, S. (1932) Book review, 10 *Canadian Bar Review* 612.
STENNING, P.C. (1981) "The Role of Police Boards and Commissions as Institutions of Municipal Police Governance", in C.D. Shearing (ed.), *Organizational Police Deviance: Its Structure and Control*.
—— (1983) "Trusting the Chief: Legal Aspects of the Status and Political Accountability of the Police in Canada", SJD Dissertation, University of Toronto.
—— (1994) "Police and Politics: There and Back and There Again?", in R.C. Macleod and D. Schneiderman (eds), *Police Powers in Canada: The Evolution and Practice of Authority*.

STENNING, P.C. (ed.) (1995) *Accountability for Criminal Justice: Selected Essays.*
STEWART, R.B. (1975) "The Reformation of American Administrative Law", 88 *Harvard Law Review* 1667.
STRANGE, S. (1986) *Casino Capitalism.*
STUART, D. (1994) "Policing Under the Charter", in R.C. Macleod and D. Schneiderman (eds), *Police Powers in Canada: The Evolution and Practice of Authority.*
—— (1995) "Prosecutorial Accountability in Canada", in P.C. Stenning (ed.), *Accountability for Criminal Justice: Selected Essays.*
STURGES, W.A. (1923), "Unincorporated Associations as Parties to Actions", 33 *Yale Law Journal* 383.
SUGARMAN, D. (1983) "The Legal Boundaries of Liberty: Dicey, Liberalism and Legal Science", 46 *Modern Law Review* 102.
SUNSTEIN, C. (1990) *After the Rights Revolution.*
—— (1993) *The Partial Constitution.*
—— (1995) "Problems with Rules", 83 *California Law Review* 953.
SUSSKIND, L., and MCMAHON, G. (1985) "The Theory and Practice of Negotiated Rulemaking", 3 *Yale Journal on Regulation* 133.
SWIMMER, G. (ed.) (1996) *How Ottawa Spends 1996–97: Life Under the Knife.*
TAGGART, M. (1991) "Corporatisation, Privatisation and Public Law", 2 *Public Law Review* 77.
—— (1993) "State-Owned Enterprises and Social Responsibility: A contradiction in terms?", *New Zealand Recent Law Review* 343.
—— (1993) Book review, 4 *Public Law Review* 271.
—— (1994) "Corporatisation, Contracting and the Courts", *Public Law* 351.
—— (1995) "Public Utilities and Public Law", in P.A. Joseph (ed.), *Essays on the Constitution.*
—— (1996) "Outside Canadian Administrative Law", 46 *University of Toronto Law Journal* 649.
TAYLOR, A.J. (1972) *Laissez-faire and State Intervention in Nineteenth-Century Britain.*
TAYLOR, G.D.S. (1986) "The Limits of Judicial Review", 12 *New Zealand Universities Law Review* 178.
TOUSTER (1982) "Holmes A Hundred Years Ago: *The Common Law* and Legal Theory", 10 *Hofstra Law Review* 673.
TURPIN, C. (1972) *Government Contracts.*
—— (1989) *Government Procurement and Contracts.*
TUSHNET, M. (1985) "The Constitution of Religion", 18 *Connecticut Law Review* 701.
TWINING, W.L. (ed.) (1986) *Legal Theory and Common Law.*
—— and MIERS, D. (1991) *How to do Things with Rules: A Primer of Interpretation* (3rd ed.).
VAN CAENEGEM, R.C. (1987) *Judges, Legislators and Professors: Chapters in European Legal History.*
—— (1988) *The Birth of the English Common Law.*
—— (1991) *Legal History: A European Perspective.*
—— (1995) *An Historical Introduction to Western Constitutional Law.*
VERKUIL, P. (1978) "The Emerging Concept of Administrative Procedure", 78 *Columbia Law Review* 258.
VINCENT, A. (1987) *Theories of the State.*

VINING, J. (1978) *Legal Identity: The Coming of Age of Public Law*.
VIZKELETY, B. (1992) "Discrimination, the Right to Seek Redress and the Common Law: A Century-Old Debate", 15 *Dalhousie Law Journal* 304.
WADE, E.C.S., and BRADLEY, A.W. (1985) *Constitutional and Administrative Law* (10th ed.).
WADE, H.W.R. (1961) *Administrative Law* (1st ed.).
—— (1980) *Constitutional Fundamentals*.
—— (1985) "Procedure and Prerogative in Public Law", 101 *Law Quarterly Review* 180.
—— (1991) "Beyond the Law: A British Innovation in Judicial Review", 43 *Administrative Law Review* 559.
—— (1992) "The Crown—Old Platitudes and New Heresies", 142 *New Law Journal* 1275 and 1315.
—— and FORSYTH, C.F. (1994) *Administrative Law* (7th ed.).
WALKER, P. "What's wrong with irrationality", *Public Law* 556.
WALKER, S. (1986) "Controlling the Cops: A Legislative Approach to Police Rulemaking", 63 *University of Detroit Law Review* 361.
WANG, H.K.C. (1943) "The Corporate Entity Concept (or Fiction Theory) in the Year Book Period [:II]", 59 *Law Quarterly Review* 72.
WEILER, P. (1974) *In the Last Resort: A Critical Study of the Supreme Court of Canada*.
WEIR, T. (1976) "Complex Liabilities", in *International Encyclopedia of Comparative Law; Volume XI; Torts*.
WEST, R. (1988) "Gender and Jurisprudence", 55 *University of Chicago Law Review* 1.
WILBERFORCE, R. (1986) "Foreword", in M. Taggart (ed.), *Judicial Review of Administrative Action in the 1980s: Problems and Prospects*.
WILLIAMS, G.H. (1984) "Police Rulemaking Revisited: Some New Thoughts on an Old Problem", 47(4) *Law and Contemporary Problems* 123.
WILLIAMS, S.L. (1993) "Political and Other Risk Insurance: OPIC, MIGA, EXIMBANK and Other Providers", 5 *Pace International Law Review* 59.
WILLIS, J. (1935) "Three Approaches to Administrative Law: The Judicial, the Conceptual and the Functional", 1 *University of Toronto Law Journal* 53.
—— (1938) "Statutory Interpretation in a Nutshell", 16 *Canadian Bar Review* 1.
—— (1961) "Canadian Administrative Law", 6 *Journal of the Society of Public Teachers of Law* 53.
—— (1968) "The McRuer Report: Lawyers' Values and Civil Servants' Values", 18 *University of Toronto Law Journal* 351.
—— (1974) "Canadian Administrative Law in Retrospect", 24 *University of Toronto Law Journal* 225.
WILSON, B. (1990) "Will Women Judges Really Make A Difference?", 28 *Osgoode Hall Law Journal* 508.
WILSON, J.Q. (1968) *Varieties of Police Behaviour: The Management of Law and Order in Eight Communities*.
WILSON, W. (1887) "The Study of Administration", 2 *Political Science Quarterly* 481.
WOOD, D. (1995) "Judicial Fairness and Systemic Bias", in S. Parker and C. Sampford (eds), *Legal Ethics and Legal Practice: Contemporary Issues*.
WOOLF, H. (1986) "Public Law-Private Law: Why the Divide? A Personal View", *Public Law* 220.
—— (1990) *Protection of the Public—A New Challenge*.

WOOLF, H. (1992) "Judicial Review: A Possible Programme for Reform", *Public Law* 221.
—— (1995) "Droit Public—English Style", *Public Law* 57.
WRIGHT, C.A. (1946) "Discrimination—Licensed Beer Parlour Refusing to Serve Negro", 18 *Canadian Bar Review* 730.

Index

Abuse of rights doctrine, 16–17
Administrative law
   assimilation of norms within private domain, 146–8
   assimilative tendency, 135
   breakdown of barrier between public and private domains, 155
   core set of principles, 134
   dominant theory of state, and, 92–3
   financial pressure, and, 96
   goals of accountability and participation, 70
   identification of public power, and, 153–4
   legal controls on private sector, and, 154
   legitimacy of state power, and, 43
   meaning, 1–20
   mixed governmental methods, and, 69–70
   new century, for, 90–117
   nineteenth century, 92–5
   past approaches, 92–6
   privatisation, and, 2–6
   regulatory reforms, and, 96
   state, and
      current approaches, 96–108
   US Administrative Procedure Act, 93
Administrative law at margins, 134–59
Amtrak
   government actor, as, 177–8
   nature of, 103–4
Anti-discrimination principle, 6
Australia
   Freedom of Information Acts, 58–9
   outsourcing, 40–70
   privatisation, 40–70

Boundaries of administrative law, 20
Business affected with public interest, 7

Canada, 18–19
   anti-discrimination legislation, 150–1
   Judicial Review Procedure Acts, 146–8
   new public management, and, 129
Casino
   exclusion of successful gamblers, 11–12
   revocable licence, 12
Chief Rabbi
   judicial review, and, 31
Church
   procedural norms, 149–50

City Technology College
   judicial review, and, 35–7
Civil law
   state in, 72–74
Common callings doctrine, 7–8
Common law
   state, and, 74–9
Community service obligation (CSO), 66–9
   forms, 66–7
   functions, 67
   identification, 66
   Ministerial regulation, 69
   qualification, 66
   sources, 67–8
Concession theory, 162–3
Constitutionalisation
   judicial review, and, 33–8
Constitutionalism, 21–39
   academic response to, 22–3
   amenability to review, and, 33–8
   contractualisation, and, 21–39
   Diceyan model, 24–5
   meaning, 21–2
   modern administrative state, 25
   modern, doctrinal manifestations, 26
   normative foundation, 25–6
   public law jurisdiction, and, 26–7
   role of courts, and, 23–4
   two versions, 23–7
Contracting out, 21
Contractual power
   judicial review, 46

Contractualisation
   constitutionalism, and, 21–39
Corporatising government, 112–14
   "economic growth model", 112
   increased bargaining on part of state, 113
   market approach, 113–14
Corporatisation
   relevance of, 155–8
Courts
   constitutionalism, and, 23–4
Crown, 77–8
   conceptual confusion, 78–9
   evolution of concept, 77

Democracy
   judicial review, and, 279–307

Deregulation
  relevance of, 155–8
Developmental individualism, 71
Diceyan integrationism, 71
Discrimination
  tort of, 14–15
Dismissal
  natural justice, and, 139–40, 141, 142
Due process, 137–41

Equality principle, 6
European Court of Justice
  effect of directives, on, 74
European law
  influence in UK, 19–20

Federal corporations
  United States, 103–5
Feminism, 331–56
  contextualisation, and, 333–34
  decline of pluralist/functionalist values, 342–4
  deference as respect, and, 342–3
  functionalism, and, 332–49
  impartiality, and, 346–7
  meaning, 332
  pluralism, and, 331–56
  reasonable apprehension of bias, 349
  women judges, 349–56
    "clash of realities", 351–2
    dissents, 350–1, 353
    gender schisms, 352
    "gendered judging", 356
    public/private distruction, and, 353–5
    Supreme Court of Canada, 349–56
Football Association
  judicial review, and, 32
France
  decentralisation, 79–80
  distinction between public and private law, 72–3
Freddie Mac
  part of government, whether, 178–80

Free Church of Scotland
  objects and purposes, 161–2
Free market
  regulatory reforms, and, 110–11
Freedom of contract
  natural justice, and, 139
Functionalism
  feminism, and, 332–49

GCHQ case, 218–220
General question of law, 308–30. *See also* Judicial review
  Chevron doctrine, 320–1
  discrimination, and, 324–5
  ebb and flow of administrative law, 308–30
  human rights tribunal, 318
    control over social implications, 327–8
    expertise, 325–6
    social implications of decisions, 322–3
  meaning, 318
  "pragmatic and functional approach", 321–2
  "quasi-constitutional" nature of human rights, and, 323, 325
  search for legislative intent, 322–3
  statutory construction, 320
  statutory rights of appeal, and, 324
  supervising role of courts, and, 323–4
  US Supreme Court, 319–20
Globalisation, 90–1
  regulatory reform, and, 109
Good faith doctrine
  contract, and, 145–6
Government procurement, 143–5
  common law, 143
  "preferred" bidders, 144
  private and public sectors, 145
  private contracting, and, 143–4

Human rights tribunals
  general question of law, 318
  judicial review, 312–14, 316–17
Hutterites, 166–70
  expulsion from, 148–9, 167
  hearing process, and, 169–70
  jurisdiction of Canadian courts, and, 168–9
  mini-state, as, 167
  nature of association, 166–7
  power of, 166
  source of power test, and, 168
  values as to property and process, 169

Imam
  judicial review, and, 32
Impartiality
  feminism, and, 346–7
Intermediate associations
  functions, 165
  legal personality, 164–5
  powers, 165
  public functions, 165–6
  state, and, 160–70

Jockey Club
  judicial review, and, 33
Judicial review, 27–33
  amenability to, 27–33
  anti-social effects of privatisation and outsourcing, 50–1

assumption of jurisdiction over non-statutory powers, 28
attitude of deference as respect, 306–7
Bentham, and, 280
Blackstone, and, 280
British Columbia Labour Relations Board, 293–4, 295
changing political situation, and, 306
Chief Rabbi, 31
City Technology College, 35–7
constitutionalisation, and, 33–8
contractual power, 46
correctness standard, 315, 316–17
creation of administrative state, and, 300–1
deference as respect, 286
deference on spectrum ranging from correctness to patent unreasonableness, 295–6
deference to privative clauses, 290–1
democracy, and, 279–307
democratic positivists, 280, 284
Dicey, and, 280–1
disenchantment with, 44–5
equality, and, 301–2
equality and rule of law, 302–7
expansion of coverage, 27–8
Football Association, 32
general question of law, 308–330
human rights legislation, 310–11
human rights tribunals, 297, 312–13, 314, 416–317
influence of Diceyan model on, 30
"innominate" ground, 47
interpretative approach, 303
Jockey Club, 33
judicial attitudes to tribunals, 288–9
jurisdictional determination, 292–3
lack of legal support, and, 45–6
law, question of, 311–12
liberal antipositivists, 280, 284
limits, 45–51
Lord Chancellor, 34–5
monopolistic power, concept of, 88
"nature of the function" test, 29
New Zealand, 48
obedience to legislative command, 290
"operational conflict", and, 299
paradox of recognition of rationality, 286–90
paramountcy doctrine, 299
parliamentary intention, and, 30–1
patent unreasonableness test, 292
politics of deference, 292
price regulation of utilities, 50
price setting, and, 49
privatisation, and, 285–6
privative clauses, and, 282–3, 312

procedural error, 301, 305–6
provision prohibiting anti-competitive conduct, and, 49–50
reach of public power, and, 283–5
"reasonable", meaning, 304–5
retreat from substance, 296–7
retreat to formalism, 296–8
role of judges, 279
rule of law, 291
social democracy, and, 301
"source of power" test, 29, 160–5. *See also* Source of power test
submissive deference, 304–5
substance/procedure distinction, 287–8
substantive merits of impugned decision, and, 47–8
Supreme Court of Canada, 286–9
Take-over Panel, 28
Training and Enterprise Council, 37–8
web of public justification, and, 305
Jurisdictional error
broad definition, 309–10

Legal profession
concept of state, and, 77
Lord Chancellor
judicial review, and, 34–5

Market cooptation, 114–17
formulation and carrying out of governmental rules, and, 116
public uses of private interest, 114–15
role of state, and, 115–16
Mixed economy
public/private dichotomy, and, 52–3

Natural justice
dismissal, and, 139–40, 141, 142
and expulsion from Hutterite Colony, 148–9
freedom of contract, and, 139
property interest, and, 138–41
Negative freedom
state, and, 80
Negotiated rulemaking, 105–8
advantages, 106
convener, 106–7
litigation costs, and, 105–6
multiple perspectives, 108
US Department of Education, and, 107–8
New Zealand
deregulation of utilities environment, 48
State-Owned Enterprise, 157–8

Ontario
tort of discrimination, 14–15
Outsourcing, 40–70. *See also* Privatisation
contract documentation, 68

Outsourcing (*cont.*):
  information, pivotal role, 58–66
    consumer, and, 60
    corruption, and, 60–1
    service providers, 64
    third party enforcement, 65
  informal regulation, 66–9
  meaning, 41
  restructuring, and, 41–2

Passive individualism, 71
Pluralism
  feminism, and, 331–56
Police rulemaking processes, 243–78
  accountability, and, 244–5
  administrative law, and, 270–1
  American enthusiasm, 270–2
  appropriateness in police context, 267–9
  benefits, 278
  Canada, 243–78
  Canadian reticence, 270–2
  civilian review, 268–9
  community policing, 245–6, 255
  consent, and, 247
  control mechanisms, 264–265
  courts, role of, 275–276
  criminal justice, and, 243–278
  critical issues, 269
  democracy, and, 246–258
  discretion in enforcement, and, 249–54
    independence, and, 251
    judicial scrutiny, 250–1, 253
  efficacy, 276
  formality, 273
  function of policing, 248
  gap between aspiration and implementation, 272–3
  guidance documents, 259–60
  investigatory expedience, and, 252
  "managerialism", 248–9
  meaning, 265–7
  municipal boards, 261
  negotiated, 266–7
  oversight bodies, 259
  perceptions of criminal justice, 244–6
  police complaints, and, 277
  Police Services Act, 259–64
  politics, and, 247–8
  present structure in Ontario, 258–65
  problems, 272–4
  process, 268
  provincial commission, 261
  public interest, and, 273–4
  public participation, 274
  reasonable cause, and, 276–7
  "rulemaking", 246
  social context, 254–5
  technique, 271–2

Policy making/service delivery dichotomy, 56–8
  justification of outsourcing, and, 56–7
  outsourcing, and, 56–8
Price regulation of utilities
  judicial review, and, 50
Prime necessity doctrine, 7
Prisons
  privatisation, 98–102. *See also* Private prisons
Private associations
  public functions. *See also* Intermediate associations
Private prisons, 98–102
  judicial scrutiny, and, 137
  public law procedures, and, 99
Privatisation, 206, 40–70. *See also* Outsourcing
  bad debtors, and, 65
  effect on state administration, 83
  informal regulation, 66–9
  information, pivotal role, 58–66
    consumers, and, 60
    corruption, and, 60–1
    service providers, 64
    third party enforcement, 65
  meaning, 41
  relevance of, 155–8
  restructuring, and, 41–2
  welfare services, 102
Procedural decency, 137–41. *See also* Natural justice
Property rights
  natural justice, and, 138–41
Public and private law
  context, regard for, 85–8
  developing distinguishing criteria, 84–5
  state, and, 84–8
Public corporations, 81
Public function
  meaning, 84–5
Public law
  academic debates as to scope, 120–1
  "amber" approach, 121–2
  arguments for expansion, 38–9
  government, and, 120–2
  "green light" theory, 121
  meaning, 1
  opportunity for expansion, 38–9
  "red light" theory, 121
  scope, 27–33
  values, 3–4
Public law control over private power, 196–216
  activities "inherently private", 205
  application of procedural and substantive norms comprising
  core of judicial review, 212–13

application of public law norms, 211–14
basic norms of procedural justice, 210–11
common law systems, 209–10
contexts, 198
de facto private institutions, 197
distinct procedures applied to public
  bodies, 210
European Court of Justice, 208
functional analyses, 197
functional approach, 209–14
future prospects, 205–6
implications of ascription of label
  "public", 209–11
institutional approach, 196
institutional spectrum, 200–6, 207–8
"macro considerations", 209–11
micro considerations, 211–14
nature of power, 199–200
possible tests, 198–200
pricing policies of corporate bodies, 213
procedural rules for seeking relief, 212
regulatory bodies, 200–5
  Advertising Standards Authority, 201
  contract, 202–5
  control, 202–5
  Football Association, 203, 204
  Jockey Club, 202–3, 204
  Lloyds of London, 203–4
  National Greyhound Racing Club, 202
  Panel on Take-overs and Mergers,
    200–1
  power, 202–5
  privatisation of business of government,
    200–2
scope of prerogative orders, 198
separate jurisdictions, 209
service publique, concept of, 207–8
source of power, 198
state, conception of, 207–8
structural analysis, 197
structural considerations, 214–16
  Administrative Procedure Act (APA),
    215–16
  "private exercise of governmental
    power", 214
  "state action", 215
  United Kingdom, 216
  US example, 214–16
vertical v horizontal application of
  constitutional provisions, 206
Public law/private law dichotomy, 53–6
  contractual arrangements, and, 54–5
  outsourcing, and, 55–6
  "single package", conception of administrative law, 53–4
Public management, 118–33
  Canada, 129
  cost of government, and, 127–8

law, role of, 118
new, 118–33
OECD study of reforms, 128
questioning of command culture, 132–3
reduction of costs of government services,
  130
"traditional public service delivery",
  128–9
Public/private dichotomy, 52–3
  mixed economy, and, 52–3
Public/private divide, 4–5
Public service law, 118–33
  adaptability to culture of new public
    management, 130
  balance between central government and
    client-identified orientation, 123–4
  client control, 131
  clients, emphasis on, 119
  discipline-building practices, 126
  educational initiatives, 126–7
  elements of discipline of, 122–7
  identification of client, 123
  independence, 131–2
  options for lawyers, 130–1
  policy component, 123
  professional integrity, 131–2
  professional motivation, 131–2
  relevance, 119
  rule of law functional as infrastructure for
    government, 133
Public utilities, 7

QUANGOS, 81

Racecourse
  procedural fairness, 10–11
  revocable licence, 8–9

Regulatory reform, 109–17
  "Contract with America", 111
  free market, and, 110–11
  globalisation, and, 109
  public/private dichotomy, and, 116
  state action or inaction, 109
Regulatory trends, 90
Revocable licence, 8–9, 11–12
Rule of law
  Diceyan model, 24–5
  equality, and, 302–7
  state, and, 75

Source of power test, 160–5
  concession theory, 162–3
State
  accepting significance of, 88–9
  administrative law, and
    current approaches, 96–108
    arbitrary power, 40

State (cont.):
  civil law, in, 72–4
  common law tradition, 74–9
    centralisation, 76–7
    Crown, concept of, 77–8
    legal profession, 77
    rule of law, 75
    seventeenth century revolutionary settlement, 76
  creation of agencies to regulate privatised industries, 82–3
  demarcation of public law, and, 89
  discretionary power, 40
  distinction between public and private law, and, 72
  governmental expansion, and, 79
  hybrid institutional forms, 81
  increased powers, development of, 81–2
  intermediate associations, and, 160–70
  meaning, 75–6, 79
  modern, taking account of, 79–83
    identification, 80–1
  negative freedom, and, 80
  public and private law distinction, and, 84–8
  relationship with industry, 83
  role as regulator, 91–2
State-Owned Enterprise
  New Zealand, 157–8

Take-over Panel
  judicial review, 28
Tendering law
  private and public sectors, 145
Theoretical and institutional underpinnings, 71–89
Trade unions
  nature of, 161
  right to associate, and, 163–4
Training and Enterprise Council
  judicial review, and, 37–8

Underlying values of public and private law, 217–42
  autonomy, 225
    English case law, 227–30
  citizenship, 239–40
  contractual relations, 232–3
  democracy, 239–40
  democratisation of relationships, 236
  dignity, 225
  employment law, 233–4
  family law, 234–5
  five key values, 225–6
    state, and, 226–30
  GCHQ case, 218–20
  illegality, 222–3
  irrationality, 222
  national and individual security, 227
  obligations, law of, 238–9
  participation, 239–40
  private law, 233–9
  problem of public and private power, 230–3
  procedural impropriety, 220–1
  property law, 236–7
  public power, and, 230–3
  relations between state and individuals, 235
  relationship between judicial review and contract, 232
  security, 226
  status, 225
  tort, law of, 238–9
  value, meaning, 223–4
United States, 171–95
  administrative law
    government functions, 193
    non-constitutional aspects, 191
    prisoners, 193
    private functions, 193
    privatised industries, 193–4
    public choice analysis, 192
    reach of doctrines, 192
    rights of recipients of government benefits, 184–6
    scope, 191
    scrutiny of private decision-making, 194–5
    tests for state action, 192
  Administrative Procedure Act, 172–83
    agency actions subject to judicial review, 174–5
    agencies, application to, 172–3
    government corporations, 173–5
    President, 175
  boundaries between public and private, 171–2
  constitutional law
    government corporations, and, 176–80
  delegating public responsibilities to private sector, 98–102
  due process, 183–191
    government employees, 184–186
    property interest, 185
    protected interests, 184–5
    requirements, 186
  federal corporations, 103–5
    forms, 103–4
  formal reach of statutory administration law, 172–83
  freedom of information
    government corporations, 176
  government corporations, 173–5
    Amtrak, 177–8
    arbitrary and capricious test, 180–1
    business judgment rule, 181

comparison of judicial review and corporate law, 183
constitutional law, and, 176–80
corporate law constraints, 180–3
creation by Congress, 173–4
derivative suits, 181–2
directors, and, 181–2
Freddie Mac, 178–80
freedom of information, 176
holistic approach, effect of, 179
shareholders, and, 181–2
National Performance Review, 97
President
lack of agency status, 175
private associations, 172
privatisation, 171
procedural fairness, 183–91
contract law, and, 187–8
disciplinary decisions of labor unions, 188–9
exclusionary policies of private associations, 190
National College Athletic Association, 189–90
private association as state actor, 189
private associations, 186–91
public trust, and, 190
public law
veneration of, 17–18
reach of administrative law, 171–95

Welfare services
privatisation, 102
Women judges
influence of, 349–56
Wrongful dismissal
procedural fairness, and, 140–2

Yukon Order of Pioneers
membership restricted to males, 151–2